D0438176

AMERICAN LIVES

AMERICAN LIVES

Looking Back at the
Children of the Great Depression

John A. Clausen

*With a Foreword
by Glen H. Elder, Jr.*

THE FREE PRESS
A Division of Macmillan, Inc.
New York

Maxwell Macmillan Canada
Toronto

Maxwell Macmillan International
New York   Oxford   Singapore   Sydney

3 1336 04104 0941

Copyright © 1993 by John A. Clausen

All rights reserved. No part of this book may be reproduced or transmitted in any form or by any means, electronic or mechanical, including photocopying, recording, or by any information storage and retrieval system, without permission in writing from the Publisher.

The Free Press
A Division of Macmillan, Inc.
866 Third Avenue, New York, N.Y. 10022

Maxwell Macmillan Canada, Inc.
1200 Eglinton Avenue East
Suite 200
Don Mills, Ontario M3C 3N1

Macmillan, Inc. is part of the Maxwell Communication Group of Companies.

Printed in the United States of America

printing number
1   2   3   4   5   6   7   8   9   10

Library of Congress Cataloging-in-Publication Data

Clausen, John A.
     American lives: looking back at the children of the Great Depression: John A. Clausen.
         p.   cm.
     Includes bibliographical references and index.
     ISBN 0-02-905535-0
     1. Success—United States—Psychological aspects—Longitudinal studies.
     2. Performance—United States—Longitudinal studies. 3. Success—United States—Psychological aspects—Case studies. 4. Performance—United States—Case studies. I. Title.
     BF637.S8C522   1993
     305.2'0973'0904—dc20   93-12171
                                                               CIP

A somewhat expanded version of Chapter 7 appeared as "The Life and Family of Karl Schulz" in *Family, Self and Society: Toward a New Agenda for Family Research*, published and copyrighted by Lawrence Erlbaum Associates in 1992.

In memory of Peter Anthony Clausen, 1944–1991
A strong, sound voice for arms control,
Though cut short, a life to celebrate

CONTENTS

Foreword by Glen H. Elder, Jr.   vii

Preface   xiii

Acknowledgments   xvii

1   Introduction: Adolescent Planful Competence
    and the Shaping of the Life Course   1

2   The Studies, Their Context, and the Data   26

3   Introduction to the Life Histories   61

4   A Finder of Resources: Stuart Campbell   70

5   Still Learning at Seventy: Mary Wylie   113

6   Antecedents of Planful Competence   144

7   Uphill All the Way: Karl Schultz   175

8   Destined for the Law: Henry Barr   210

9   Competence in Men's Lives and Careers   242

10 Men's Lives: Beyond the Job   281

11 Programmed for Marriage: Alice Neal   315

12 Against All Adversity: Beth Green   349

13 Planful Competence in Women's Lives   387

14 Women's Lives: Marriage and Changing Roles   420

15 Family Relationships   454

16   The Later Years: Looking Forward and Back   487

17   Epilogue   517

Appendix A: Supplementary Tables   531

Appendix B: Major Sources of Data and Measures   545

Notes   559

References   577

Index of Names   585

Index of Subjects   588

FOREWORD

During the last half of the twentieth century, human lives have become a vibrant field of study in the social and behavioral sciences. A general shift in attention from age-specific domains to the full life-course of human careers and development reflects the emergence of contextual life-span questions, the growth of longitudinal studies and their data archives, and the evolution of life-course theory. Indeed, greater understanding of the life course is becoming a requirement of the scientific study of human development and aging.

No volume represents this paradigm change more than John Clausen's *American Lives,* an extraordinary book that applies a professional lifetime of wisdom on human careers and development to an account of lives from childhood through the later years. All of the Study members come from the pioneering Berkeley longitudinal studies which were launched in 1928–31 at the Institute of Child Welfare (now Human Development), University of California, Berkeley. They were all born in the 1920s and studied through periodic and annual follow-ups across the 1930s. Most have been followed up to the 1990s.

Within the changing times of the century, the book views the individual as actor and employs a constructionist perspective on human lives. The study is concerned with the process by which people shape their lives through the choices they make. Hence the central question is not how social systems or history shaped human lives, the objective of my earlier work on children of the Great Depression (1974–1986), but why these Americans made certain choices within particular situations (such as class, gender, and so forth) and thereby constructed their lives. Compared to most passive, oversocialized concepts of the human organism that prevailed

vii

up to the 1960s, the present study exemplifies the expanding prominence of constructionist perspectives on lives.

To appreciate the distinctive qualities of Clausen's approach, it is important to note that it does not merely focus on personality in developmental perspective or on social pathways and careers, or even mainly on the influence of these pathways on personality—research foci that are common in the literature today. Indeed, most life studies examine either the social or developmental trajectories of people's lives. By contrast, this study assumes that competence and social influence at the end of adolescence give shape to the evolving life course.

Nearly 50 years of the study members' lives provide abundant evidence for this premise. Life course and personality stability as well as indications of successful aging are concentrated among men and women who entered adulthood with qualities such as intellectual curiosity and reliability. Men with these qualities in adolescence were more accomplished in both work and family by the later years. Of course not all such men did well, nor were the less competent always destined for failure. But measurements of specific attributes in late adolescence were predictive of later experiences.

What are these personal qualities? The operational definition of Clausen's term for competence, "planful competence," comprises three primary dimensions: *self-confidence, dependability,* and *intellectual investment.* According to these dimensions, the planfully competent adolescent is equipped with an ability to evaluate accurately personal efforts as well as the intentions and responses of others, with an informed knowledge of self, others, and options, and with the self-discipline to pursue chosen goals.

It is one thing to show that planful competence in adolescence has much to do with occupational and family success during the early years of adulthood, and quite another to demonstrate, as Clausen does, that how one starts out in adult life has much to do with the experience of old age more than a half century later. The search for connections across the two halves of life is one of the most distinctive features of the life course paradigm on human development. By seeing human lives as a whole, we seek pathways of exploration across the entire life span.

The answer as to why some people with advantages in life come to old age embittered and preoccupied with self, while others who are less privileged feel grateful for the life they have led, cannot be found merely in the last years of life. The life course is a whole, and early competencies and experiences often find expression across the entire span. As John Clausen shows, the planfully competent in adolescence are more likely than other age-mates to find life satisfaction and fulfillment during their last years.

This approach to the whole life course is one of the most rewarding features of the book as it breaks through the myopic barriers of age-specific analyses, generates provocative questions about unknown territories, and calls for renewed efforts toward the explanation of life-span continuity, stability, and diversity. To be sure, the approach is extraordinarily demanding of appropriate data and resourceful investigators, and is filled with uncertainties that are never part of experimental studies. Long-term studies must make the best of the data at hand and efforts to do so are not always successful. Nevertheless, from any angle, one must be impressed with the new perceptions, problems, and understandings that arise from such work. After reading this book, child developmentalists and gerontologists will certainly be less able to claim that they have no issues of mutual concern.

Fresh questions and explanatory puzzles also arise from the study's constructionist perspective on individuals since a focus on choice necessarily increases an awareness of differences in life course. How did some adolescents with minimal competence manage to rise above such limitations by the later years of life? Or why did other people tend to remain incompetent across the years? A constructionist perspective on the life course underscores the variability of lives, facilitating the discovery of complexity. Variability may seem to be a commonplace discovery, but it represents a much neglected topic. Earlier life studies sought to discover the average ages of marriage, child-bearing, et cetera, but Clausen seeks to understand the opposite—why do some people marry early and others marry later? We are indebted to this book for giving due appreciation to this question.

Variation of this kind presents a major challenge for explanatory research, and Clausen skillfully pursues this objective through both quantitative and qualitative analyses. The quantitative analyses employ familiar techniques, such as multiple regression and subgroup comparisons, in charting patterns of continuity and change across the life course. The most common subgroup comparison across time compares people who ranked high and low on planful competence during adolescence. The subgroups were also used to select study members for an intensive qualitative study of biographical patterns. A total of 60 men and women were selected for in-depth life history interviews. Six of the study members are each the focal point of a chapter-length narrative of their lives, ranging from accomplishments and setbacks or disappointments to important turning points.

These biographical chapters stand on their own as life history specimens and are also used to establish life themes across the volume's chapters. The life histories, nested within the larger sample, provide a vital sense of the individual as actor and choice-maker across the evolving life course as well as rich insights for understanding paths taken and paths foregone. Individual life histories can, of course, be misleading without statistical evidence from the core sample. Clausen is well aware of such limitations and explicitly warns the reader about them. With these cautions in mind, he has developed a uniquely valuable interplay between the two sets of data, as well as seminal analyses for new points of departure.

This observation brings me to my final point. In theory and especially in methodology the study can be said to represent a genuine intellectual recombination of two major eras of life study: the phase before 1940, which is most closely identified with the early Chicago school of sociology, and the decades since 1960, which have witnessed something of a renaissance in life studies. William I. Thomas, a leading figure in the first era and in the Chicago school of sociology, valued both quantitative and qualitative analyses of data on human lives, but he regarded the narrative life record as most valuable for the development of sociological understanding. He urged that priority be given to the "longitudinal approach to life history."[*] Studies, he argued, should investigate "many types of individuals with regard to their experiences and various past periods of life in different situations" and follow "groups of individuals into the future, getting a continuous record of experiences as they occur." Thomas never managed to carry out such a study in his lifetime or to relate case and quantitative analyses.

*Edmund H. Volkart, ed., *Social Behavior and Personality; Contributions of W. I. Thomas to Theory and Research* (New York: Social Science Research Council, 1951).

To a remarkable extent, John Clausen has carried out the study prescribed more than 60 years ago by W. I. Thomas, but he has achieved more than that. Unlike any study in the first or second era, this major work enables us to appreciate the complementary value of qualitative and quantitative data and analyses in the study of lives, helping to quash the misguided belief that studies can be only one or the other. As a doctoral student of the postwar Chicago school of sociology and a distinguished scholar of the life course in his own right, John Clausen seems uniquely suited for this intellectual role. With the wisdom of a lifetime, he has brought these historical eras of study together in a pioneering study for our age.

GLEN H. ELDER, JR.

PREFACE

Thirty-three years ago I came to the University of California at Berkeley as the third Director of its Institute of Human Development. Trained as a social psychologist, I had been directing social research on the antecedents and consequences of mental illness at the National Institute of Mental Health for the previous twelve years. I had long been interested in the process by which the helpless infant becomes a competent person, and it was becoming increasingly apparent that we needed to know much more about the process of normal development in order to identify the antecedents of pathology. The Berkeley longitudinal studies had followed infants and children through their adolescent years and a follow-up of study members in their 30s had just been completed. Here was an opportunity to relate the early social settings, parental behaviors, and attributes of young children to their characteristics as adults, their achievements and their problems. The alternative approach, using unreliable retrospective reports of what children had been like and what their parents had done ten or twenty years earlier, made the Berkeley longitudinal data almost irresistible.

An enduring objective over the past three decades has been to describe the lifelong development of our study members and to tell their stories not merely in terms of statistical trends but as flesh and blood persons, capable, fallible, and very often fascinating. This book is the culmination of my thirty-two years of work with the longitudinal studies. To a considerable extent it is a collaborative effort: collaborative with the men and women whose dedicated participation over the past sixty years has made it possible to delineate almost the whole of their lives, and collaborative with my many colleagues.

I have tried to interweave the life stories of individuals with an analysis of the major events and themes manifest in the lives of the whole study group. Born in the 1920s, they were children of the Great Depression and parents of the baby boom generation. Some lives are depicted in detail; the subjects are not only aware that their lives have been selected but have reviewed and commented on their histories. Other lives are briefly described, usually substantially disguised, in order to avoid identifying individuals. Where only snippets of a somewhat problematic life are presented, the negative side of the life is likely to be unduly highlighted. Some of the descriptions of individuals are not flattering, but I hope they are not demeaning. Staff members have tried to reflect their impressions of study members without being judgmental, though sometimes a judgmental note creeps in. In general, persons who are perceived to have problematic relationships have had to face much greater difficulties in their early years than have their more successful peers. When one knows the full circumstances of their early lives, one can not only better understand them but respect and admire them for their perseverance. I hope that no one will feel that he or she has been depicted unfairly. Indeed, I hope that the brief descriptions of persons whose lives have been most problematic have been so well disguised that they will be unable to recognize themselves, and certainly that no one else will be able to recognize them.

I have tried to illuminate the developmental process and the influences upon it without making deep inferences about peoples' motivations. I am not a clinician, nor is clinical assessment the objective of the book. I have tried to relate what we knew about the study members and their upbringing in childhood and adolescence to what happened when they made the transition to full adulthood and subsequently over the decades to the threshold of old age. Clear patterns are discernible.

In any research on human behavior, the life experiences and orientations of the researcher are bound to have an influence on what is examined and what is stressed. My own life has been relatively orderly and stable. My parents, children of working-class immigrants, were good students but both were required to leave school and go to work at the age of 12; their preeminent goal was for their two sons to become college graduates, and they gave us every encouragement. My parents were loving and supportive but there was much stress on conformity and less on intellectual curiosity. College was in many ways a revelation. Then I met Suzanne, my wife, whose own experiences had been as broadly diverse as mine had been constricted. Temperamentally quite different, we have nevertheless each learned from the other and our lives together over the past fifty-three years have been rich and exciting. Our four sons have contributed to our understanding of human development and of ourselves. They have made me more aware of genetic differences; although they share the same basic values, each is unique in ways that we cannot explain in terms of what we ourselves have done. Our sons have helped teach us about changes in social norms. These lives and a few others intertwined with mine are implicated in how I have focused on the life course. Alternative perspectives would, I am sure, yield other insights, and I have tried to present enough detail so that other assessments are possible.

ACKNOWLEDGMENTS

When a researcher draws upon studies designed by others more than sixty years ago, staffed by hundreds of professionals and graduate students over the decades, and supported by a number of foundations and federal agencies, it is all but impossible to acknowledge all those who deserve thanks. Under the general guidance of the first Director of the Institute of Child Welfare, Dr. Herbert Stolz, three studies of child development, all with somewhat different emphases, were designed and directed for thirty years or more by Jean Macfarlane, Nancy Bayley, and Harold E. Jones. Their foresight, professional skills, and dedication created a legacy for my generation and others to come. The originators of the research were backed by many staff members, some of whom oriented me to the studies and became my co-workers after the retirement of the original study directors. My colleagues and successors as Institute Director, M. Brewster Smith, Paul Mussen, Guy Swanson, and Joseph Campos have participated in various supportive ways and have continued to make Institute facilities available to sustain the research.

The research has received financial support from many different sources. The Institute itself was established with the help of a grant from the Laura Spellman Rockefeller Fund. The Rockefeller Foundation funded the Guidance Study for twenty years, at which point federal funding began to become available. Over the years and often on repeated occasions, data collection and analysis have been supported by the Ford Foundation, the National Institute of Mental Health, the National Institute of Child Health and Human Development, the National Institute of Aging, the National Science Foundation, the MacArthur Foundation, the William T. Grant Foundation, and the Spencer Foundation. When critical needs arose, there was always someone to help out. Without all of this assistance along the way, the analyses herein reported would have been impossible. The preparation of this book has been made possible by grant AG4178 from the National Institute of Aging (1982–1989) and assistance from the William T. Grant Foundation (1990–1992).

Over the years, many research assistants have coded interview and questionnaire responses, compiled data, and (until I learned how to communicate with the mainframe computer) carried out computer analyses for me. For the research here reported, I have been assisted primarily by Davida Weinberg, Martin Gilens, Kurt Thompson, and currently, Dr. Constance Jones, who talks to the computer for me when the language needed passes my level of discourse. Betty Webster contributed her superb interviewing skills to the life history interviews and her sprightly writing style to initial drafts of three of the life histories. Throughout the book I have drawn on the work of a number of my colleagues, and I am especially indebted to Jack Block, Diana Baumrind, Wanda Bronson, Dorothy Eichorn, Glen H. Elder, Jr., Carol Huffine, Norman Livson, Harvey Peskin, and Arlene Skolnick, and to the late Mary Cover Jones and Norma Haan.

When this book began to take shape, six or seven years ago, Jane Rateaver typed the initial life history. Since then Stacy Furukawa and Helen Cline have gradually put my fragments together on the word processor. Helen Cline has patiently entered my revisions, prepared the tables, and assisted with the index, all with such speed and accuracy that we have somehow made our deadlines. A number of friends and colleagues have read and given me thoughtful comments on early or late drafts of many of the chapters of this book. My particular thanks to Diana Baumrind, Carol Huffine, Connie Jones, and Bill Sadler. Suzanne and Christopher Clausen have made many helpful suggestions.

My original editor at The Free Press, Peter Dougherty, offered early guidance and gave me detailed comments on the first two-thirds of the chapters. Peter's successor, Bruce Nichols, went over the whole text and made helpful comments on the last third. Once the comments of my editors and colleagues had been taken into account, Kenneth Craik and Paul Bohannan read the entire manuscript and indicated how it could be improved. The staff of The Free Press has been uniformly helpful in speeding along the production of the book. Loretta Denner oversaw copyediting, instructed me in the tasks to be accomplished, and kept me informed of progress toward the final goal.

Finally, I want to express my thanks to and admiration for the study members who agreed to let me tell their stories and to all those who have participated in the research over the decades. For roughly sixty years they have been subjected to interviews, questionnaires, tests, and measurements. Most have stayed with us through thick and thin. They must often have wondered what would come from all this and whether the process would ever end. This is but one more of a long series of products of the research; I hope that it is by no means the last and that it will bring some measure of satisfaction to those have so faithfully participated in the venture.

AMERICAN LIVES

CHAPTER 1

INTRODUCTION

ADOLESCENT PLANFUL COMPETENCE AND THE SHAPING OF THE LIFE COURSE

The study on which this book is based is, I believe, without parallel in any society. For more than sixty years, two generations of behavioral scientists have followed most members of an initial group of 500 infants and children into their 60s and 70s. Nearly 300 have been carried through a full half-century at a cost of millions of research dollars as a result of the perseverance of a large research staff and the dedication of study members to continued participation.

The study members were a reasonably representative sample of children of the residents of Berkeley and parts of Oakland, California, in the 1920s and early 1930s. They were predominantly, but not exclusively, native born and Caucasian. They came from both middle-class and working-class families. Almost all the women became wives and mothers, but many also became businesswomen, teachers, and community leaders. The men became doctors, engineers, and lawyers but also carpenters, mechanics, and salesmen. Among them were a millionaire who died young, an ambassador who appears on national television broadcasts with some frequency, and a dealer in illicit drugs. There are numerous alcoholics as well as teetotalers, men and women who became addicted to tobacco, and men and women who were able to stop smoking. We know a good deal about the "whys" of the behaviors and the attainments of our study members.

Almost all of us would like to understand ourselves better and to change ourselves in some respects, to come closer to an ideal that we hold. Many recent books deal with this theme. Some are by therapists, some by social critics, and some by persons whose own

1

dissatisfactions have led them to look more closely at their own development and what they regard as the reasons for their problems. Some deal with the problem of low self-esteem—either their own or the self-esteem of large segments of the population that are denied access to opportunity. Others deal with the problems of attaining a sense of true manhood or autonomous womanhood in contemporary society. Some feel the need for initiation ceremonies, for male bonding, and for giving rein to the wild man within us. Others seek more soberly to find answers in self-analysis or psychotherapy.

Self-esteem has become the subject of national attention. The California State legislature appointed a task force to look into ways of raising the self-esteem of those children who are most deprived and particularly those who experience the insults attendant on minority status and poverty. The task force report, *Toward a State of Self-Esteem,* acknowledged that we know too little of how self-esteem is developed, but it rightly emphasized the primary role of the family. The aims of the California program are praiseworthy, but there are few specifics. That is inevitable. Too often, the precepts that are bandied about for raising self-esteem are simplistic, suggesting that if we only tell ourselves we are great, we shall feel great. Such precepts may have been the basis for a *New Yorker* cartoon showing a marionette stretching aloft the cross pieces that hold the strings controlling his own body and legs. It cannot be done.

To a considerable degree, we do shape our own lives, but whether we achieve effective, satisfying shapes or distorted, miserable ones depends on many factors, biological, psychological, and social. To understand how these factors interact in influencing our lives, we need to know about the whole course of development, from early childhood to later life. That is the subject of this book.

The tremendous body of data accumulated over the last sixty years of our longitudinal study provides a basis for looking at the origins of successful lives, lives well lived, and lives that have been crisis ridden and often visited by misery. My objective is to show how lives are shaped by the combination of constitutional attributes, parental guidance, social contacts, and the ability of men and women to make wise choices relatively early in their adult lives. I found that we could distinguish clear signs of that ability in the adolescent years in a combination of attributes that I have called *adolescent planful competence.* In part, then, this book is the story of how personality constellations and behavioral tendencies observable in adolescence (and their origins) influenced the later lives of men and women born in the 1920s. But it is more than that. It presents the narrative detailed life histories of men and women from diverse backgrounds who illustrate particular developmental courses and were willing to have their lives and families examined and described.

Perhaps you ask, "Are these lives from a previous generation relevant to us today? Ours is a totally different society from the one in which the study members, born in the 1920s, lived. They experienced the Great Depression of the 1930s, World War II, and then a period of prosperity. The family still had some stability in those days. Drug abuse and sexual license had not become widespread among teenagers."

True. The society of the 1990s is vastly different from that of the 1930s, 1940s, and 1950s, when study members were coming to adulthood and parenting the baby boom generation. Nevertheless, I believe that adolescent planful competence will have the same origins and will still have payoff, and I shall explain why later in this chapter. Moreover, the study members' own children, some of whom we have studied in both adolescence and their adult years, attest to the power of the concept of adolescent planful competence for a generation that has known drugs and easy sex, as well as greater uncertainty in the economic sphere. For many readers, they are your generation.

Consider the situation of youngsters born in the decade prior to the Great Depression. They were observed, interviewed, and tested through their junior and senior high school years. How well could one predict what would happen to them in the next fifty years? Could one guess who would have the most successful careers, whose marriages and family relationships would be most stable and satisfying, and who would experience turmoil and crises along the way? No one could have foreseen the historical events that they experienced or the specific courses that their lives would have taken, but given the slice of history in which they participated and the outcomes they achieved, we can see now what attributes and experiences had the greatest effects on them. We can make after-the-fact predictions, or postdictions, if you will, that are quite impressive, and we can make them just from what we knew when our study members were adolescents in the 1930s and early 1940s. We can pick out some who had the high probability of being winners and some who were much more likely to be losers, or at least to encounter more disappointment in their adult lives. We shall not always be on target with our predictions—predictions are for categories of persons, not individuals—but even where individuals diverge from peers in the same category, we can often say how this came about.

The data available from the Berkeley longitudinal studies permit us to answer questions about individual development that cannot be derived from short-term or cross-sectional studies. We know what the study members were like in late childhood, adolescence, early adulthood, their middle years, and at the edge of old age. We know when they married and divorced, we have seen many of their children, we know how they see themselves, and, for the most part, how they were and are seen by their husbands and wives and by their children. This knowledge permits us not only to say that some lives have a good deal of coherence and others seem chaotic but to identify in adolescence, with a high degree of confidence, major antecedents of later outcomes.

Societies and their cultures provide rough scripts and casts of characters whose interactions tend to shape individual lives. Physical and psychological attributes that reflect the interaction of genes and environment influence both the roles selected and the performances of individuals. To a significant degree, a person's life course is his or her personal creation. This is the basic premise that guided my analysis of the lives of nearly 300 men and women who have been studied at the Institute of Human Development over the past sixty years. In the childhood and early adolescent years, general abilities, goals, values, and typical ways of relating to others take form to a greater or lesser degree, influenced by parental care and guidance, by schooling, and by the scripts of behavior expected in any given social setting. The dependent child becomes an active self, negotiating a way aided or buffeted by interacting and often conflicting influences. The script demands choices, and the choices men and women make early in adult life have consequences for success or failure, stability or change over the rest of their lives.

DEFINING "LIVES WELL LIVED"

How shall lives be described and compared? A life is a progression through time, so we must be interested in both the process itself and in outcomes along the way. Ultimately, we want to characterize lives well lived.

When we think of assessing lives, the word *successful* immediately comes to mind. What do we mean by successful? And successful in whose eyes? Every culture, every era, has its own criteria. In the United States, we tend to think of occupational success, where men, and increasingly women, are concerned, but in Eastern cultures, wisdom, understanding, and "following the Way" are far more highly valued.[1] Where women are concerned, often we think first of maternal virtues and personal warmth, particularly if they were born early in the century. Younger Americans are likely to put a higher valuation on a woman's personal effectiveness in a variety of roles, building a career as well as a family.

A second criterion of a life well lived is happiness. Its pursuit is certainly a major end in Western culture. Every life should have its share of happiness. Indeed, the moral life was seen by the Utilitarians as consisting of "actions that are right in proportion as they tend to promote happiness, wrong as they tend to produce the reverse of happiness."[2] Happiness meant pleasure and the absence of pain. John Stuart Mill went beyond this to examine different varieties of pleasure, stressing the greater value of pleasures derived from "the higher faculties—individual spontaneity, mental cultivation, and self-development."[3]

For many Americans, however, happiness is a rather ephemeral concept. We want to "feel good," but what makes us feel good seems to vary enormously. "Pleasurable satisfaction" is one way the dictionary defines happiness. We all want our children to be happy. The problem is that happiness is not a reproducible quality, readily available to all. Still, we certainly hope that most of the time we and our loved ones will feel happy, not sad or depressed.

"Life satisfaction" has a more enduring ring to it. It connotes a sense of accomplishment, a sense that one is content with what one has done and with one's lot at the time. Many behavioral scientists have focused on life satisfaction as an important outcome to be measured.[4] Measurement is difficult, but the ability to see the positive aspects of one's lot and to accept what one cannot change ultimately becomes a major key to enjoyment in later life. We shall certainly want to look at what our study members say about their satisfactions and dissatisfactions.

A third criterion of a life well lived is good health, especially

mental health. Many persons plagued with chronic illness and physical handicap still live effective happy lives. Anxiety, guilt, and other
manifestations of mental or emotional turmoil, however, can
greatly impair personal effectiveness and preclude a sense of happiness and life satisfaction. Mental health entails a good deal more
than freedom from gross pathology. It entails an internal psychic
system able to maintain its equilibrium by virtue of a good measure
of self-understanding and a flexible organization of defense and
coping mechanisms. The internal system must be coupled with a
behavioral repertoire that incorporates the knowledge and abilities
needed to cope effectively with the demands of the external world
in ways that are not harmful to others.

Several decades ago, Marie Jahoda and a group of consultants attempted to specify some of the ingredients of positive mental
health. The most critical of these entailed the ability to (1) establish and maintain intimate relationships with others, (2) mobilize
their personal resources to meet unexpected demands, (3) achieve
a substantial degree of autonomy or ability to regulate their own
lives, and (4) perceive self and others in realistic terms, free from
distortion arising from psychological vulnerabilities.[5] This is not to
say that such people will be free from all psychopathology. As
George Vaillant noted in his psychiatric study of a group of successful, Harvard graduates, *Adaptation to Life*, psychopathology can be
found in all lives, but in the last analysis the adaptive processes that
a person employs in dealing with problems are all important.[6]

Early in the twentieth century, there was a sharper differentiation
between the ideals held for men and women than prevails today.
Ideally, men were to be strong, silent, and aggressive; women soft,
expressive, and submissive. Men and women were expected to be
parents, but their roles as parents were well differentiated. A "family man" was not expected to be a father in the way that a woman
was expected to be a mother. Having many children has not been a
major goal for most Americans in the past century, but having several was long considered a virtue. In any event, being a good parent
must be considered one of the potential criteria of a life well lived.

There is yet another conception of the exemplary life that is
more difficult to measure than most of those previously mentioned.
It is perhaps most readily brought to mind by a movie frequently
shown during the Christmas season, *It's a Wonderful Life*. The unlikely hero, George, played by Jimmy Stewart, has spent his adoles-

cent and early adult years as a rather shy but conscientious and friendly person. Instead of going to college, as he had planned when he graduated from high school, he replaced his deceased father in the small-town savings and loan where his father had worked. As bank manager, he was able to help his younger brother go to college and to employ his bumbling uncle. Ultimately he won the girl he loved, and that made him a winner in one sense, but his life was a mixture of mundane concerns and happy family times. When the savings and loan was threatened with bankruptcy because of a misdirected payment, George felt he was a failure and was on the verge of suicide. Miraculously, a guardian angel, Clarence, appeared to show him what might have happened—a tragedy that might have occurred, happy events that would never have materialized—had George not lived. George returns to his family to find the whole community mobilized to rescue the savings and loan and to show their love for him.

It's a Wonderful Life proposes a moral dimension on which human lives may be assessed. It is not one that we normally think of in connection with "success," and it is very hard to measure, though apparently we recognize it when we see it. The Good Samaritan was such a person. Placement along the moral dimension is more complex by far than assessing criteria of occupational success such as prestige, pay, and job satisfaction. Each of us faces different dilemmas. To locate any person's life along the moral dimension, we must know how that person's acts impinge upon others, how others perceive him or her. Is the community a better place, or have some lives been enriched because this person was a friend or neighbor? Often a person may be perceived as praiseworthy by some who know him and as much less admirable by others. Few of us are lacking in human empathy, and few of us are untainted by some instances in which we harmed others. No study can probe deeply enough to know all the intentions or circumstances underlying particular actions or all of the consequences of those actions. What a long-term longitudinal study can do, however, is to give some insight into the processes by which men and women resolve some of the inevitable dilemmas they confront.

The hero of *Wonderful Life* was very much a moral man, but he was almost destroyed by a scoundrel. We must surely be able to distinguish moral men and women from scoundrels. Our study membership included a few who might be seen as scoundrels, but once their developmental histories are known, we see them as victims too. Undoubtedly those who were least moral and law abiding were also least likely to remain a part of the research, yet some continued to participate. The ones who stayed with us have often been surprisingly frank in revealing their true colors, albeit sometimes unwittingly. It is important to know how their lives have been shaped, even if we cannot consider them successful.

There are, thus, many different conceptions of success, some of them mutually congruent and others perhaps somewhat conflicting. Our values and goals are derived from our culture, families, peers, and personal experiences in the course of development. They often vary as we accumulate experience and see where particular priorities are likely to lead. One person may find complete fulfillment in a life dedicated to religious contemplation. A Dr. Schweitzer will find that he needs both to contemplate God and to dedicate himself to promoting the well-being of humans as well. Early in the century, a measure of religious dedication was seen by many persons as essential to living the good life.[7] Ethical considerations are certainly of crucial importance in assessing any life, but formal religion is today perhaps less central for most Americans.

Most of us seem to want to balance work, family, and leisure activities in some fashion, but clearly some persons are satisfied to give top priority to one at the expense of the others. Priorities may shift as a consequence of seeing new possibilities for growth or as a consequence of dissatisfaction with the product of one's earlier priorities. We shall want to note the circumstances and timing of such shifts.

The criteria for assessing lives must themselves be adapted to the circumstances of both the individual's place within the larger society and the era. We have noted some criteria that reflect public assessments of success and others that are more subjective. Any evaluation of lives must consider both subjective and objective assessments, both how people feel about themselves and how others feel about them. Once we examine a few life histories, it becomes apparent that assessments by both self and by others will differ over time. No one manages to reach age 60 without some life crises, some heartaches, some experiences of failure as well as success, or instances in which they have hurt others as well as themselves. The man who did not attend his tenth high school reunion because he had not yet "made it" in his own view of himself goes to his twenty-fifth, when he is now a successful businessman. No marriage, however good, runs a uniformly smooth course. Our fortunes may change, and we ourselves may change. Time—and timing—must be part of our evaluative framework.

Time enters into the picture in another way. What is considered to constitute success in one era may be very different from the view of success in another.[8] Civic virtue and selflessness may seem more important than net worth in one presidential era, while the amassing of wealth may appear to be the ultimate goal in another. The functions served by marriage may change within a generation. Therefore, we need to consider both the historical period and the alternative definitions employed at different points in the half-century covered.

The lives of our study members span a period of enormous change in America. Automobiles were just becoming common on the streets of the United States in the 1920s. Radios began to appear as broadcasting stations were established in the major cities. Women's hair was bobbed and sexual mores flouted in the flapper age as skirts went up and inhibitions went down in the mid- and late 1920s. Then came the stock market crash of 1929 and the most prolonged economic depression the country had ever experienced. In Europe, fascism emerged as a sequel to the social and economic ills left by World War I, and its rise to power was assisted by the depression. The threat of war replaced unemployment as a primary concern in the United States. These changes were experienced, if often only dimly recognized, by the oldest group of our study members, born between 1920 and 1922, and they had powerful effects on their parents and those of the younger group of study members, the latter born in 1928 or 1929.

If depression and wartime characterized their early lives, an aura of prosperity and peace (despite the Korean War and the cold war) endured for more than two decades thereafter. The 1950s were a time of economic growth and a seeming return to "normalcy," and it was not until the mid-1960s that the Vietnam War, student protests, and the rise of a powerful counterculture brought an end to the traditional concept of normalcy in the United States.

Arlene Skolnick, analyzing the impact of social change upon the family, notes that

> between 1965 and 1975, the land of togetherness became the land of swinging singles, open marriages, creative divorce, encounter

groups, communes, alternative life styles, women's liberation, the Woodstock Nation, and "the greening of America." A land where teenage girls wore girdles even to gym class became a land of miniskirts, bralessness, topless bathing suits and nude beaches.[9]

Our study members, like other Americans, were taking a new look at themselves, and some of them approved of the new definitions. Most did not approve, on the whole, but many of their children accepted the new definitions. There followed a period when there was much discussion of the generation gap, and some families were torn apart by the discordant views of parents and their adolescent or young adult offspring.

Now, as they enter old age, economic hardship again grips the nation. The children of our study members and their grandchildren face more acute problems than the members themselves. Adults and their offspring again have to cope with change and uncertainty.

Alternative definitions of the good life in historical perspective become especially necessary when gender is considered. Most of the criteria discussed so far apply equally to men and women. Personal effectiveness, life satisfaction, being a loving parent and a good neighbor are worthy goals for both sexes. Success, however, requires further specification. It also requires that we attend to the era under consideration. For men born in the 1920s, success entailed, above all, occupational success. The middle-class goal was a well-paying job in a prestigious occupation. By the late 1930s, many men would add the qualification that the job should be a secure one, not subject to unemployment in a period of depression. Maturity for a man entailed getting married and, in the middle class at least, being able to buy a house in the early years of marriage.

What were the criteria for a woman born in the 1920s? The overwhelming sentiment was that a woman's success consisted of finding the right man—one who would be congenial, loving, and, above all, occupationally successful. Asked in recent years about their personal aspirations early in life, a number of women used a phrasing that came with the computer age: "I was programmed for marriage." By their middle years, their expectations were changing. It will not be surprising, then, to learn that predicting a woman's life course raises very different issues than predicting a man's does.

In the last quarter of the twentieth century, women are far more often taking charge of their own lives than they were a few decades earlier.

The situations that confronted men and women born in the 1920s called for very different priorities and strategies. Men might be called up for military service; women might be left alone with small children to care for. Men's lives tended to be focused on their jobs, women's on their families. The expectable life course of most men did not change greatly over the middle half of the twentieth century, but that of women changed profoundly. In 1920 women were first allowed to vote in the United States. By 1970 the women's movement had largely redefined women's role in American society. Not only did we then begin to have a few influential women in the Congress and in the corporate world, but women with small children were entering the labor force in ever-increasing numbers.[10] Many older women ultimately did so as well. True, job opportunities were less available to women, and relatively few women were able to rise to high occupational status, but many found a new sense of identity in their jobs. Therefore, we shall have to examine women's lives and men's lives separately if we are to grasp the peculiar circumstances that each sex has had to cope with.

There are, of course, other issues to be considered in discussing the life course in the United States in the latter half of the twentieth century, and one has to do with the increasing incoherence of national culture. America is still seen as the land of opportunity by immigrants from impoverished and oppressed nations in the Third World, but its native-born population is much less of one mind about the country's traditions and its role in the world. Freedom and equality remain dominant values, but both are now seen as more difficult to attain. Some people seem to feel that the costs of equality are too great to bear (at least for those who have previously been favored). The gross inequalities that have always existed but were ignored by most white Americans until the second half of this century have been contested in the courts and by civil disobedience, by the enactment of new laws, and by persistent opposition and the defiance of law and order on the part of those denied a piece of the pie.[11] Even in the dominant white middle class, alternative life-styles, marital instability, and the repudiation of many traditional norms appear to threaten the attainment of a clear sense of purpose.

Robert Bellah and his co-authors of *Habits of the Heart* have examined fragments of the lives of a selected group of American citizens from several areas of the country.[12] In seeking the origins of purpose and meaning in these lives, they raise provocative questions about the current brand of American individualism and the single-minded pursuit of self-interest and self-understanding, without firm anchorage in "the biblical and republican traditions" that so impressed Alexis de Tocqueville a hundred and fifty years ago.[13] They note the great involvement of some segments of the population with increasing self-expression and self-fulfillment through various therapeutic activities because people lack meaning in their day-to-day lives.

My objectives are different from those of Bellah and his associates. Certainly the problems they see are very real ones, and American society does lack coherence. But if we look at lives as wholes, not just at fragments, we shall see more clearly that many persons can and do have deeply satisfying lives despite societal changes.

For the most part, I shall be describing middle-class men and women, yet we shall see contradictions and, for the most part, a lack of deep commitment to civic virtue. Philosophical thinking about ultimate purposes was seldom tapped by the data we secured. Nor was the anguish of the urban underclass revealed. If our data are somewhat deficient in showing the relationship of the individual to the larger society, however, they are much more adequate in depicting relationships among individuals, especially in the family. And here, I think, there is less difference between the first and second halves of the twentieth century. Husbands and wives, parents and children in interaction, each seeking both freedom and attachment, spontaneous expression and responsible control, provide the essence of human development in any period.

Given the varied criteria for defining a life as well lived, it is clear that we shall want to look at occupational careers, family life, evidence of mental health or disability, life satisfaction and its sources, and the kinds of relationships people have with their fellows and with their communities. There can be no single definition. Each of us must seek the goals that seem most important to us if we are to be satisfied, and each must seek some balance in meeting our own needs and the needs of others. The balance may change with the years. In the end, a life may be said to have been well lived if its possessor can accept it fully and if most of those whose lives intersected with it can say, "Well done."

APPLYING THE CRITERIA

In viewing the life histories and the quantitative data, we need to consider performance in each of the major social roles that men and women have occupied as these are defined in the society: occupational roles, marital and parental roles, and civic roles. How did individuals measure up as members of an occupational group, to the extent that work was a major commitment? We need to consider performance over time and transitions from one role to another. How easily did people make the transition from school to work, and how quickly did they find work that was satisfying to them? How smoothly did their occupational careers develop? How successful were or are they in terms of achievement, whether measured in occupational prestige, income, or work satisfaction? Were they valued co-workers and supervisors? How well have they managed to coordinate work and family roles? We know that many successful men tend at times to slight the needs of their families. A twenty-year study of managers in AT&T found that those who advanced the furthest had given higher priority to personal success than to family. They had been more restless and impulsive, more driven by ambition. Less driven men went less far, but their family satisfactions were greater.[14] Does success in one role inevitably mean stress or difficulty in another?

Both occupational careers and marriage entail choices. Some people consider their choices more carefully than others. There is a wealth of evidence that the marital choices of the very young are less likely to result in enduring marriages than are those made by more mature persons. In general, getting divorced is a sign of marital failure, but so is staying for a long period in a marriage that is conflict ridden or unfulfilling. The success of marriages must be considered from the perspectives of both members of the marital pair. A happy husband and a miserable wife do not make an "average" happy family. If there are children, their views of their parents' marriage can provide another valuable basis for evaluation.

How successful are parents in rearing children to be effective members of their society—productive, responsible, reasonably satisfied with their lives? Parents may not be held responsible for their children's problems, but most will still feel responsible. How do the children, when they look back from their own adult years, think about their parents? Some regard their parents as having been ideal role models for their own lives; others look back with anger. The members of our study constituted the parents of the baby boom. Their children were adolescents in a period when values were in transition and tensions between the generations were often acutely strained. Not a few of the children turned to alcohol and other drugs. Some were dropouts who subsequently mobilized themselves and are now doing well. Some continue to be dropouts. What are the consequences for the parents when the lives of one or more children go seriously awry? Do the parents blame themselves? How they explain to themselves what has happened often has a profound effect on how they see their own lives.

As our study members reach retirement age, how content are they to look back over their lives, and with what sentiments do they look ahead to what are euphemistically called their "golden years"? Many are now retired. Some are in good health, active, and still fully engaged at 70. Others are experiencing the physical insults that aging often brings. Making the fullest possible use of the resources one has left can be seen as another positive indication of success. Such individuals still have zest in life, while others with equivalent potentialities despair. One woman sadly reflects, "I hope no one will hold my life against me." That life entailed five disastrous marriages, and now she spends her days in front of her television set. A rejected father asks, "Where did my life go wrong?"

My focus is on how the lives of our study members were shaped. How much is heredity? Genes largely determine appearance, and they influence stature, strength, intelligence, and temperament. Some scientists believe that genes are all important in determining the kind of persons we become.[15] Many psychologists and psychiatrists disagree, holding that the influence of parents in early life is crucial.[16] Other behavioral scientists assert that cultural norms and social opportunities are most important.[17] And others say, "It all depends on who you know." One of the most successful men in our study by almost any criterion attributed his productive and happy life to luck. The study staff, however, felt that he had largely created his "luck." Nevertheless, all of these possibilities exist. All account for something, but some account for more of particular life outcomes than others do.

In a television program on childhood, one psychologist commentator stated unequivocally that the first year of life is the most important; it is then that the foundation is laid upon which the whole life structure will be built. Another equally eminent psychologist agreed that the first year is important, but, he said, "no more important than any other year." In the early years, parents are preeminently the shapers of the child's world. Their behavior toward the child, their comments, and the atmosphere of the home constitute a learning environment that is obviously very important. We know that parental conflict and divorce can be devastating to young children, and even to adolescents and college students.[18] Some children are not devastated by terrible family circumstances, however, and some from loving families later seem to fall apart.[19] We cannot yet discern how genetic and environmental features interact, but we know that both are involved and that they are linked in that genetically determined attributes help to determine environmental circumstances.

I address all of these issues, though some can be answered only inferentially. We cannot, for example, determine definitely the contribution of genetic heritage. Almost immediately, the genetic heritage is embellished by the way that others respond to the child who appears active or lethargic, homely or attractive. What we see is the result of the interaction of genetic heritage and social experience in intelligence, temperament, physical attractiveness, and athletic ability.[20]

My objective is to make the individual life understandable without delving deeply into the realm of unconscious motivations. The most obvious place where we see the workings of unconscious motivation is in the later lives of our less competent adolescents. When an interviewer explained to one such study member, now 61 years old, that our objective was to try to understand him and his life, he objected, "How can you understand me when I can't understand myself?" He was right—we cannot know the motivations for any given act—but we could understand that in adolescence this bright youngster had been seriously let down by the father he had so much admired, and before he graduated from high school he began to engage in self-defeating acts, often with the best of intentions.

PREDICTING OUTCOMES OVER THE LIFE COURSE

Do people change in the course of life or stay pretty much the same? When I started working with these data thirty years ago, I felt that this was the wrong question because I knew some people who seemed to have changed enormously over their adult years and others who seemed to have stayed very much the same. For me, the more interesting question was, "Which people change most and which tend to stay pretty much the same, and why?" As I reviewed the lives of some study members to discern patterns of change, I came to the strong conviction that the amount of change people manifested in their adult years was related to the kinds of choices they had made many years before. Moreover, I came to believe that, to a considerable degree, their ability to make strategic choices could be discerned in the adolescent years. Indeed, the long-term study confirms that *an adolescent's competence by the end of the high school years and the antecedents that gave rise to it strongly influence the direction that the life course will take, the ease of major transitions, and the person's success in performing the major roles that will be enacted over much of the life course.* I define "planful competence" and explain how it was assessed later in this chapter and the next, but for now it will be enough to identify its three components: dependability, intellectual involvement, and self-confidence. Planful competence predicted success in many of the major social roles that were later occupied. For men, it predicted high occupational attainment. More important, perhaps, the personalities of those men and women who were planfully competent adolescents changed much less than those of their less competent peers over the next forty-five to fifty years.

Planful competence in adolescence may seem an unusual basis for prediction. Are not adolescents typically unstable and immature? Adolescence is a time for acting out fantasies and trying out different identities. Especially if we do not go beyond the high school years—to age 18 on the average—how many adolescents really know themselves or know where they want to go? I grant that many do not know where they are going. Nevertheless, some of them are much better equipped to find out than are others, for they are thinking about their options and the transitions that lie ahead, not merely enjoying a period of holiday.

Life is a series of transitions—transitions from one school to another, from school to work, from dependency to economic self-support, from singlehood to marriage and family roles, from active parenthood to empty nest, and so on.[21] From the preadolescent years on, these transitions entail individual choices as well as formal requirements, such as course and grade qualifications for college and graduate school, age specifications for marriage, and work qualifications for particular jobs. The choices may be made after much thought, or one may not even be aware of making a choice. Clearly, the more that people know, in a general way at least, where they want to go next, the more likely they are to prepare for their transitions or at least to envision what they may require in the way of adaptation.

Transitions may be smooth or stressful, especially if they are unanticipated.[22] Some transitions may be turning points, where new possibilities for self-realization are perceived or a new sense of identity begins to be shaped. Some may constitute crises, such as the loss of one's job or of one's spouse.

In summary, the life course entails the negotiation by an active, self-aware person of a set of potentially available roles that are interlinked, many of which are concurrent. Each person makes choices governing the importance of various roles to which he or she commits some level of allegiance for some period of time, accumulating experiences that influence future development and change.

Society's Requirements versus Individual Decisions

Much formal preparation is needed for entering most occupational roles, preparation that entails education and the credentials that go with educational attainment.[23] For career attainment, one can no longer plan to start at the bottom and work one's way to the top in an industrial or business organization; people entering at the bottom have no place to go because jobs much above the bottom require specialized knowledge and skills that are not provided by lower-level jobs.[24] This is especially true in today's computerized, high tech society, but it was largely true even in the late 1930s and the 1940s, when the research subjects were making the transition to adulthood.

To a large degree, rational assessment of opportunities has replaced tradition as the primary basis for choices to be made.

Selection for professional or bureaucratic careers strongly favors those who show high early potential and plan for the development of that potential. Persons with special talents (artistic, athletic, literary) may achieve success through different routes than persons entering most professional and bureaucratic organizations and careers. Such special talents, especially artistic and athletic talents, may lead to high monetary and social rewards, but even here a high degree of training is likely to be required, and success is far less predictable than in professional and bureaucratic careers.

School, work, and retirement may be phases in almost every life course, but they tell us only a small part of the life story. Depending on abilities, interests, and opportunities, individuals opt for different levels and types of education, and they allocate differing priorities to preparation for various adult roles. There exist general expectations as to when it is most appropriate to marry,[25] but these are less clear now than they were a generation ago, and it is individuals themselves who decide if, when, and whom to marry. It is individuals who decide whether and when to have children and how many, though this decision may not be entirely under individual control. These choices may be left to chance. Many adolescents drift through their high school and early adult years riding whatever current there is, but with drifting, the chances of a propitious landfall are diminished. All may not be lost, but those who planned or prepared rather than drifted will tend to have more successful voyages.

To restate the essence of what the research has found, an adolescent's competence by the end of the high school years—planful competence—influences the scheduling of the major social roles later occupied, the stability of role performance, and the person's attainment and life satisfaction over much of the life course. In the next chapter, I describe how competence was assessed and touch on the sources of competence. Here it is essential to explain what I mean by competence and indicate how, through thoughtful preparation by the individual (or the avoidance of reckless acts) and through processes of social selection, competent adolescents are more often than not winners in the game of life. The metaphor is trite, but it serves a useful purpose: Most games entail a substantial element of chance, and life outcomes are very much subject to the influence of chance, as well as competence and other personal attributes.

What Planful Competence Entails

As a first approximation, planful competence entails knowledge, abilities, and controls. It entails knowing: something about one's intellectual abilities, social skills, and emotional responses to others; one's interests and developing them; and about available options and thinking about how to take advantage of or expand them. Planful competence requires the ability to assess accurately the aims and actions of others in order to interact responsibly with them in pursuit of one's objectives. Further, the person must have sufficient self-confidence to pursue his or her goals and desires. In an adolescent, planful competence signifies a substantial level of maturity.

The life course begins to take shape as patterns and habits of intellectual analysis, interpersonal relations, values, and attitudes are developed in childhood and the early adolescent years. By age 18, many young people have developed the capacity to make realistic choices, or at least to inhibit tendencies to make unwise choices. Having parents or other adults who can provide an orientation to potential options and can raise thoughtful questions to help the adolescent identify important issues can make a difference. Having high intelligence and being reasonably self-confident improves both level of aspiration and chances of success. Ellen Langer has used the term *mindful* to characterize much the same orientation as I designate "planfully competent."[26]

In his *Seasons of a Man's Life,* Daniel Levinson suggested that no one life organization can have stability for more than a portion of a decade; a life plan that fits one period will leave some of the individual's needs unfulfilled, so there must be periodic reassessments and transitions.[27] I propose that individuals who by late adolescence have a realistic view of their abilities, know in a general way what they want, and consider the consequences of their choices are more likely to make smooth transitions and adaptations and to remain satisfied with their decisions. If they have considered alternatives and contingencies and have the necessary abilities to do what they want to do, careful choices should produce better outcomes than casual choices or mere drifting.

Life circumstances frequently change, of course. No one can predict accurately what lies ahead. Recessions, corporate reorganizations, disasters, illness, unforeseen opportunities, and a myriad of other unanticipated developments may demand or invite a change in course. The "mindful" and self-confident person assesses risks and benefits, and maintains a high degree of flexibility. He or she may live a more stable life, but stability itself is not an ultimate value. Purposeful change may be necessary to avoid stagnation and permit growth. One does not achieve the success that the most competent men and women have achieved simply by being dependable and predictable. Highly competent adolescents tended to be open to new experiences, but they differed in the degree to which this was the case. Some became much more rigid than others. Competence in adolescence did not predestine men or women to be successful. A few of the least competent adolescents became wonderful human beings, successful by almost all criteria—and a few of the most competent became unhappy, rather hostile persons. But far more often than not, the competent adolescents led successful lives.

Most of us do not at any time try to plan systematically for the distant future, except perhaps to plan for security in old age or to plan a strategy for developing a career. Few make systematic long-range plans in adolescence. The one person I know who had done so—planning first for his M.D. and then his Ph.D. and then for a particular sequence of experience—wound up with a severe neurosis in his 30s. There are limits to the extent to which it is wise to foreclose options. When faced with alternative possibilities requiring an important decision, a planfully competent person is more likely to secure information relevant to that decision and to envision contingencies that may affect outcomes. He or she will be less likely to act impulsively than will a less planfully competent peer. This is not to say that the most competent adolescents will never act impulsively. Perhaps when they do act impulsively, however, it is because they already have a good idea of what they want. They are not tossing a coin to help with the decision. They do not use alcohol to get "smashed" in order to come to a decision about a job, as a few of our less competent men did.

Studies of educational attainment among both men and women attest to the great importance of the family's socioeconomic status, the adolescent's measured intelligence, and parental and peer encouragement of higher education.[28] In turn, educational attainment, coupled with continuing influences of the family's social status and the person's intelligence, predicts later occupational attainment to a high degree.[29] One might—indeed must—therefore look to measures of intelligence in the childhood years and to the family's prior economic status as early indicators of a general orientation toward achievement (whether measured by occupational status or other criteria). Long before the adolescent-to-adult transition, these measures serve as indicators of who is likely to make that transition via the route of longer school attendance and delayed entry into the labor market and, for women born in the 1920s, the marriage market. High intelligence and high family economic status in childhood promote desirable choices and improve the ability to sustain those choices and to achieve desired goals. Conditions that diminish life chances, such as discrimination and economic instability, lessen the predictive power of early planful competence.

When I refer to high planful competence or lack of planful competence, I am referring to a continuum, though more than a single dimension of measurement is entailed and different combinations of dependability, self-confidence, and intellectual involvement can be distinguished. A high IQ tends to go with high planful competence but never ensures it. Sometimes I use total scores on the index of competence and sometimes simply compare persons above and below the mean score in senior high school. This simple dichotomy predicts many quite different outcomes for both men and women.

Timing is critical in the acquisition of competence. Maturity tends to bring increased skills at assessing what one must do to achieve success and smooth relationships with others. As we get older, we are more inclined to think of consequences before acting. Therefore, the attributes that distinguish highly competent adolescents from their peers are less likely to differentiate them in the later years. However, those who have the attributes in adolescence will better prepare themselves for adult roles and will select, and be selected for, opportunities that give them a head start. They get the scholarships in college and the best starting jobs; they choose and are chosen by promising (competent) spouses. Thus, we are dealing not only with the importance of personality attributes but with the strategic importance of an early attainment of competence in processes of social selection. This is the most important point in my argument: the payoff value in contemporary, developed societies of manifest competence by late adolescence.

I do not mean to suggest that adolescent competence ensures success or incorporates all of the elements that contribute to favorable life outcomes. Other facets of personality or personal orientations can make a substantial difference in reported work and life satisfaction. High personal integrity does not require high adolescent competence, nor does high competence ensure integrity in either adolescence or later life.

Unpredictable life experiences—luck, if you will—can have good or bad effects. Beauty and brains both have payoffs, but the brains contribute more to competence, especially for men. Planful competence in adolescence was a less powerful influence in women's lives than in men's, yet one or another of its components strongly affected the choices women made. So did their physical attractiveness, and I shall not neglect its effects.

Predicted Consequences of Adolescent Competence

When I first conceived the idea of trying to predict outcomes from adolescent competence, I formulated a series of hypotheses on the effects of early competence. Not all of them were borne out, but some permitted more powerful prediction than I had imagined possible. I shall state those hypotheses as I did in the early stages of my data analysis and subsequently note where they were off the mark as well as where they were on target.[30]

High competence should tend to lead adolescents to make more realistic choices in education, occupation, and marriage. Such choices should tend to satisfy individual needs over longer periods than would be true of the choices of persons lower in competence. In addition, these competent individuals enjoy the advantage of being seen as desirable mates and employees and as potential leaders. Persons possessing these attributes should tend to lead more stable lives, and the changes that they make in roles and relationships should more often derive from new opportunities that become available or from the effect of external events beyond their control rather than from dissatisfaction or failure in a particular relationship or activity. Further, those who make well-thought-out choices early on will tend to show greater stability in their relationships and their other commitments throughout the life course. They should be less likely to divorce and less likely to shift careers, and their network of significant others should have greater continuity and persistence.

The stability of a marriage depends on the attitudes, temperaments, and ever-changing role relationships between two persons. It may seem unreasonable to expect that the adolescent personality orientations of either spouse will markedly affect the stability of the marriage except in the instance of psychopathology or deviance. We know, however, that very early marriages and marriages made with minimal acquaintance tend to be much more short-lived than those based on longer acquaintance between persons reasonably mature at the time of marriage. Moreover, from early analysis by my colleague, Arlene Skolnick, we know that a person's self-confidence and lack of hostile tendencies are associated with high marital satisfaction.[31] One might anticipate that most planful, competent young men and women will not marry until they feel that they know what they are getting into and are ready to work out their relationships. Obviously, one partner may be much more planful than the other, and either one may change or turn out to have attributes that make a stable marriage unlikely. Nevertheless, adolescent competence should pay off for both men and women. Whether planful competence in adolescence pays off more for one sex than for the other is a matter to be assessed. Dependability and self-confidence will not only influence the choice but should make the chooser a better candidate for a successful marriage. Mutual choice under such circumstances should predict a lasting marriage (or at least longer-lasting marriage in a period when there is much instability in marital ties). Greater maturity will enhance dependability and perhaps the other components of planful competence, so many people who were not highly competent adolescents will have become more competent in their early adult years. We might therefore expect that early adult competence will be an even stronger predictor of marital stability and satisfaction than is adolescent competence.

If competent adolescents do indeed show greater stability in relationships and other commitments, I hypothesized that they should also show less change in personality from one period to another throughout the life course. They should experience more positive feedback from those around them by virtue of their educational and occupational attainment, tending to enhance the attributes they already possess. They should experience fewer sharp disappointments in their early adult years and fewer negative life events. Those low in adolescent competence will less often find satisfying job opportunities; I would expect them more often to shift jobs as well as spouses, and they should experience more pressures to change themselves over the early adult years.

At this point some readers may ask, "Isn't this all quite obvious— just common sense?" Yes and no. It is both common sense and obvious from previous research that high intelligence and high familial socioeconomic status contribute to high occupational achievement. Even in this instance, however, sixty years of research following the same persons has yielded stronger predictions than most behavioral scientists expected.[32] And if my findings are only common sense, it is surprising that so many books and articles on the life course have failed to see what common sense should have revealed. The life course is often described as a series of stages with recurrent discontinuities through which everyone passes.[33] Personality continuity and change have generally been studied as if most of us fit some common pattern. We do not. Some people experience recurrent crises; they often change a great deal over the life course. Others seem to sail smoothly most of the time and to change far less.

Of equal importance to the predictions that can be made from knowing the level of an adolescent's competence is what we have learned as to how competence is engendered—another respect in which the findings of the longitudinal studies go far beyond what is obvious. They demonstrate the importance of firm but understanding and supportive parenting—parenting that challenges the child to do his or her best, regardless of whether the child is raised by two parents, one parent, or even a parent surrogate. The child will not achieve high self-esteem from being told how good he or she is, regardless of performance or effort. Nor will high self-esteem be engendered by mindlessly repeating slogans about self-worth. Self-esteem must be earned. It requires nurture. It cannot be grafted on if it was not earlier nurtured, but it can be acquired through effort. That has not appeared obvious to many people, including some who have written on the topic.

Planful competence does not *ensure* success or afford an overarching theory of the life course. There are a few instances in which very competent adolescents have had dismal later lives, while less competent others, from families in which early experience had seemed devastating, have become effective members of the community. What is perhaps most obvious from our research is that no set of attributes and no one theory of the life course can adequately explain the diversity of individual human lives, not even for a sample of Californians born in the first third of the twentieth century. The task of this book is to illustrate both regularity and diversity and to explain what we can.

THE PLAN OF THE BOOK

The next chapter describes the three originally distinct studies that have been combined in the past thirty years. It sets out information about the backgrounds of the study members' parents, the climate of the time in which the study members grew to adulthood, the schools they attended, and how they were studied.

Chapter 3 briefly explains how the life histories were prepared and offers a perspective for viewing the first two life histories of planfully competent adolescents: a physician, Stuart Campbell, and a homemaking artist, Mary Wylie. Beyond these first two life histories, I take a closer look at the main classes of influence in the shaping of human lives and at some specific antecedents of planful competence, examining how they were relevant in the lives of not only Stuart Campbell and Mary Wylie but of the whole study group. Because the lives of men and women born in the 1920s were based on vastly different scripts, there follow two sequences of four chapters for each sex. They present additional histories and briefer descriptions of less competent adolescents along with statistical data on all the men and women whom we followed into the adult years. These chapters focus especially on their roles as workers and as creators of new families and relationships.

Finally, I examine in greater detail the processes of family interaction and the ways in which our study members are coping as they reach later maturity. A brief Epilogue sums up the most salient findings and the state of our knowledge.

CHAPTER 2

THE STUDIES, THEIR CONTEXT, AND THE DATA

How did it come about that in the late 1920s and early 1930s such long-term studies were begun? Systematic social science research was in its infancy. Sampling surveys such as the Gallup Poll had not been invented. Psychologists gave intelligence tests and constructed "inventories" of beliefs, interests, and attitudes, but these were very crude by current standards. Child development was emerging as a field of study, but at the time there existed only the most rudimentary knowledge of normal growth and development.

When the studies began, the behavioral sciences and the social world in which our study members lived were very different from what they are today. It is important to understand those differences but not to exaggerate their effects on the data collected or on the lives of the three generations (in some cases, four) coexisting today. A broadly eclectic approach to research, coupled with careful, intensive interviewing, observation, inventories, and tests—the approach originally taken—lends itself subsequently to looking at aspects of development not initially envisioned. As new methods and perspectives became available, they could be applied to old data. And as study members were seen repeatedly, new, more sophisticated methods of assessing their personalities, their marriages, and their careers could be brought to bear.

Our study members and their children have had to deal with the social changes of the past half-century. We shall see how the two generations differ, though the focus here is on the original study members. If divorce was less often the cause of family breakup for the parents than for their children, it was nevertheless far more common than in most other developed countries: Nearly a third of our study members divorced. If freer sexuality characterizes the current generation of teenagers, it was nevertheless the case that a number of girls in the study had illegal abortions while still in high school. More important, the family, the school, and the peer group are still the primary agents that socialize the young and prepare them for adulthood. What worked well for one generation may require some modification for another, but the processes of development remain largely the same. Contexts change, but basic principles change far less.

THE INSTITUTE OF CHILD WELFARE

The Institute of Child Welfare, now renamed Human Development, was established at the University of California in 1926 through a grant from the Laura Spellman Rockefeller Foundation. The foundation executive responsible for the grant, Lawrence K. Frank, was not himself trained as a social scientist, yet his fertile imagination made him the initiator of new perspectives and approaches in the behavioral sciences.[1] Together with administrators of the university and members of the state legislature, he worked out an agreement whereby foundation support and state support would create a new organization devoted to the study of the normal development of children. The first director of the institute, Dr. Herbert R. Stolz, a pediatrician, was chief of the Bureau of Child Study and Parent Education of the State of California Department of Education, and its director of research was a young assistant professor of psychology, Dr. Harold E. Jones.

The Berkeley Institute of Child Welfare was not the first of its kind, for similar institutes had been established at a number of eastern and midwestern universities. The institute at the University of California was, however, the only one to undertake long-term longitudinal studies that have been maintained up to the present time, covering essentially the whole life span. Originally there were three studies. Like the study members themselves, the three projects had different objectives and followed different pathways, though now all three have been consolidated.

THE LONGITUDINAL STUDIES

The Berkeley Guidance Study

The Guidance Study (GS) was initiated in 1928 by Jean Walker Macfarlane, a member of the psychology faculty at the University of California in Berkeley and, up to that point, also a member of the Department of Pediatrics at the University of California in San Francisco. She was interested in conducting research on the behavior problems of children, as well as in studying normal personality development. Her plans for research were sufficiently exciting so that the Rockefeller Foundation offered her support to undertake a five-year longitudinal study, support that was subsequently extended for twenty years. Thereafter the newly established National Institute of Mental Health provided periodic support, as did several other agencies and foundations.

In a report on the Guidance Study written ten years after its inception, Jean Walker Macfarlane described her four major objectives:[2]

1. To portray the course of development of numerous specific aspects of personality and to investigate relationships between behavior patterns (adaptive and maladaptive characteristics) and measures of physical status, physical growth patterns, the child's intelligence and rate of intellectual development, socioeconomic measures, and other aspects of the child's social and physical environment.

2. To study in a normal group of children the frequency, persistence, severity, and dynamics of specific maladjustment behavior, by age and by sex, and to discover the relationships of earlier and later manifestations of problems.

3. To add to our knowledge of why some individuals give up or modify early ineffective behavior patterns and develop mature, sturdy, and effective personalities while others rigidly and neurotically cling to immature and ineffectual patterns. (This may be the most important objective.)

4. To compare the persistence of specific maladjustive behavior (stammering, fears, etc.) in a group subjected to guidance procedures and in a group equated but unguided.

It was this last feature that gave the study its name. Professor Macfarlane noted that "in a pioneering stage of a discipline where a small body of ordered facts exists, it is difficult to have neat and clean-cut hypotheses susceptible of final proof, disproof, or explicit modification." She sought rather to draw eclectically on a wide variety of ideas about child development and to collect data that would be sufficiently rich to permit different theoretical schemes to be applied to its analysis.

The study sample contained 252 children and their respective families. Every third birth in Berkeley from January 1928 to July 1, 1929, was enrolled if the parents agreed to participate. Two groups of 126 each were matched on socioeconomic status. The parents in one group would receive guidance in coping with their children's problems, and the other group would remain as a control group. Guidance group mothers and children were studied intensively and cumulatively by a sizable staff through interviews with mothers and, later, with the children, as well as many tests and inventories. The research archive accumulated systematic records of health, regime and physical growth, measurements of mental development, and periodic assessments of the children's behavior, attitudes, and personality as seen through the eyes of parents, siblings, teachers, classmates, and the study staff. Less intensive data were collected on the control subjects, but the mothers were also interviewed periodically, especially up to age 12 or 14. By December 1938, when the children were 9 or 10 years old, 115 families remained in the guidance group and 103 in the control group. The losses of Guidance group members came primarily from the departure of families from the Berkeley area.[3] The GS continued under Professor Macfarlane's directorship until 1965, though she retired from teaching in 1961. Professor Macfarlane continued to be in touch with her study members, whom she knew so well, almost until the time of her death at the age of 95 in 1989.

Jean Walker Macfarlane was not the only long-term member of the staff of the Guidance Study. In 1933 Marjorie Pyles Honzik, a graduate student in psychology, wrote her master's thesis on the attitudes of preschool children toward mental tests, working under Jean Macfarlane's tutelage. Three years later, she received the doctorate and joined the institute's staff. Although she officially retired in 1975, Dr. Honzik still came to her office at the institute several times a week through 1990, fifty-seven years after she started research at the institute.

Over the years, there have been three intensive restudies of Guidance Study subjects: the first in 1958 under Jean Walker Macfarlane's direction, the second in 1970, coordinated with the follow-up of the Oakland Growth Study, and most recently, in 1982, this time coordinated with the restudy of members of both the other groups. I shall say more about the follow-ups later.

The Berkeley Growth Study

The Berkeley Growth Study (BGS) was initially planned by Professor Harold E. Jones, the institute's director of research. Working most closely with him and directing the research for many years was Dr. Nancy Bayley, a developmental psychologist trained at the University of Iowa. The study was on a smaller scale than the Guidance Study, and was apparently intended as a long-term continuing project of the Institute of Child Welfare. Its objective was to study the "mental development and physical growth of normal individuals, observed from birth to maturity."[4]

The Berkeley Growth Study enrolled its members through local obstetricians and pediatricians, in order to have access to the infants at birth. All infants included were born in local hospitals between January 1928 and May 1929, except for a few later-born siblings of these original subjects who were added to the study group. Thus, this group overlapped somewhat with the Guidance Study sample, though most Guidance Study members had been born at home. The Berkeley Growth Study sample was thus not representative of any defined population. The only specification for enrollment beyond being born in a hospital was that the infant be essentially normal, not subject to birth complications.

Nancy Bayley was concerned with the construction of better methods of assessing the developmental status of infants and children too young to be given verbal intelligence tests.[5] Would early competence in handling their bodies and manipulating objects predict later verbal intelligence? The question was simple but very important, and it yielded an indication that different kinds of competence were being tested. The approach was essentially descriptive, portraying the course of development through repeated measures that began at birth and were taken at one-month intervals from birth to 15 months, at three-month intervals from 15 to 36 months, at six-month intervals to age 9 and less frequently in later childhood and adolescence. Although personality measures were less intensive than in the Guidance Study, the emotional reactions of mother and child were observed and rated in the various testing situations, and subsequently a number of inventories that were used in the other studies were also used with Berkeley Growth Study subjects. In 1951, Dr. Dorothy Eichorn joined the staff of the Berkeley Growth Study. After Dr. Bayley's retirement in 1968, until her own retirement in 1990, Dr. Eichorn has taken responsibility for directing the BGS.[6]

The Adolescent (Oakland) Growth Study

Adolescence in America was (and is) clearly a stressful period. The great spurt in growth and the changes in secondary sex characteristics bring both new potentialities and emotional liability. The Adolescent Growth Study was designed to assess how early or late attainment of puberty affected the social and emotional development of boys and girls by studying a sample of youngsters intensively from before the onset of puberty and through the senior high school years (roughly to age 18). Herbert Stolz and Harold Jones began their study in the fall of 1931.[7] Potential enrollees were recruited from five elementary schools in the city of Oakland, bordering on Berkeley. Designated for inclusion were roughly 230 children of white, English-speaking parents who were expected to go to Claremont Junior High School. Home visits were made to explain the purpose of the investigation and to request consent from the parents. Ninety-four percent of the parents consented, giving a potential sample of 215 preadolescents. The youngsters were subsequently brought to the institute for a wide variety of examinations: medical examinations, intelligence tests, anthropometric measurements, photographs, strength tests, tests of eyedness and handedness, tests of reaction time, and others.

Members of the Adolescent Growth Study received several benefits that their classmates outside the study sample did not share. The study maintained a "clubhouse" in a residence next to the junior high school, a place where they could listen to records, dance, hold "bull sessions" (before the days of rap sessions), and otherwise enjoy themselves. In the senior high school years, they were occasionally taken on trips—for example, a ski trip by train to the Sierra—financed through the research budget. The clubhouse and these special excursions gave the staff a chance to observe study members in a wide variety of situations: peer group activities, such as dances and games; conduct in public places; responses to hostility or to frustrations; and so on. Tendencies to show off, to be aggressive toward others, or to withdraw from interaction could be noted and rated, yielding quite different perspectives from those provided by parents, teachers, or the adolescents themselves.

Group tests were given in the classrooms and a wide variety of inventories, opinion tests, interest tests, and projective tests were administered through the high school years. Information was obtained about family composition, socioeconomic status and habits, and regimes in the home, and mothers' personalities were rated along a number of dimensions.

The Adolescent Growth Study involved not only Dr. Stolz and Dr. Harold Jones, but many associates, among them Professor Jones's wife, Mary, who held the doctorate in psychology and was the mother of two children. Mary Jones and Judith Chaffey, who was originally a counselor at the junior high school but then joined the research staff, became major figures in the lives of many of the research subjects. In 1935, Harold Jones became director of the institute, a position that he held until his retirement twenty-five years later. His tenure ensured stability in the longitudinal program.

By the end of the high school years, roughly 160 adolescents remained in the study, the others having for the most part moved away from Oakland and Berkeley with their families. Mary Jones and Judith Chaffey kept in touch with many study members, but it was nearly twenty years before a full-scale follow-up was attempted.

In 1960, Harold Jones retired as director of the institute. I succeeded him and took responsibility for what had come to be called not the Adolescent but the Oakland Growth Study (OGS). Mary Jones continued to spend much time at the institute and to keep in touch with the study members. Unlike members of the other two studies, OGS members had strong ties within the group. On several occasions, we had reunions to celebrate their ties, and many came from long distances to renew acquaintances with old friends. The most recent reunion, held in 1985, was planned as a tribute to Mary Jones, who was then nearly 90 years old and about to leave Berkeley to be with family farther to the south.[8] She died at age 92.

* * *

Each of the studies bore the stamp of its founding father or mother, and, in each instance, one or more women established close ties with the study members and became a very meaningful part of their lives. Perhaps this above all accounts for the success of the institute in securing intimate data from so large a group over so many years.

Subsequent History: The Follow-Up Studies

In 1957, before the first follow-up, the Institute of Child Welfare was renamed the Institute of Human Development. The Ford Foundation had agreed to support independent follow-up studies of the subjects of the Guidance Study and the Oakland Growth Study. There was a certain rivalry between the study directors, and they did not coordinate their efforts in any way. Jean Macfarlane was especially interested in seeing whether the study members, now parents themselves, were replicating the behaviors their parents had exhibited. Study members and their spouses were interviewed and tested, many of them flown to the Bay Area from other parts of the country to spend two or more days. Most, however, still lived within fifty miles of their birthplace.

If families in the control group had encountered problems, it appears that Jean Macfarlane had given them the same kind of guidance that she gave to the so-called guidance group, so she did not attempt to ascertain the long-term effects of guidance. She was much interested in personality change and in life events that might have brought about such change.[9] Dr. Macfarlane herself was involved in a great many of the interviews, even as she had been during the childhood years of her subjects. Study members also received medical examinations and physical, as well as psychological measurements.

In planning the follow-up of the Oakland Growth Study members, Harold Jones was joined by an eminent Austrian psychologist, Dr. Else Frenkel-Brunswik.[10] They sought intensive data on how the 37- to 38-year-old study members viewed their early development and adolescence, their dating and courtship experiences, their marriages, their experiences as parents, their careers, and their social attitudes. On the average, the interviews required eleven hours, stretched over as many as ten different occasions, depending on the amount of time that study members could be available. Those coming from long distances were seen in longer sessions extending over a day or two. Again, there were medical examinations and many other measures. Ninety-nine study members participated, many of them traveling across the country to be interviewed and tested again. Others could not make the trip but were contacted. In 1963 we mailed out a brief questionnaire on smoking practices and received replies from 131 of the original study members. They constituted more than four-fifths of the subjects retained through high school and known to be living.[11]

When I came to the institute in 1960 as its third director, analysis was just beginning on the vast store of data derived from the first follow-up. Professor Frenkel-Brunswik had died before data collection was completed, and Harold Jones had died soon after. It was therefore necessary for me to take hold of analysis plans and to secure additional funding for the work yet to be done. The National Institute of Mental Health provided the funds, and my many colleagues at the institute provided the skills necessary to carry through the analysis and reporting of the data.[12] The delineation of personality change from adolescence to early adulthood was undertaken by Professor Jack Block and Dr. Norma Haan and ultimately reported in their book, *Lives through Time,* which dealt with members of the Oakland Growth Study and the guidance group from the Guidance Study (the control group having data too scanty to permit adequate personality assessments). My colleague Dr. Glen Elder, Jr., focused on the impact of the depression on members of the Oakland Growth Study, reported in *Children of the Great Depression* (1974). Subsequently, Professor Elder, now the Howard W. Odum Distinguished Professor at the University of North Carolina, has published many papers on the study members and their lives, especially as viewed in historical perspective, and I shall at times draw heavily on his published research and that of other colleagues to supplement my own analyses of the data.

In the 1960s, questionnaires were sent to members of all of the studies to ascertain the histories of their tobacco use, if any. A longer questionnaire was sent to OGS members in 1964 to fill in certain data on family relationships, occupational histories, and parenting objectives of the study members, now in their early forties. A full-scale follow-up of members of the BGS was undertaken by Dr. Bayley and me between 1965 and 1968, providing data comparable to those available for members of the other two studies.[13]

Between 1969 and 1971, under the leadership of Dr. Dorothy Eichorn, we undertook a second major follow-up of GS and OGS members, funded by the National Institute of Child Health and Human Development.[14] The Vietnam War was then a major national issue. Our study members were ages 40 to 49, and most had adolescent children. It was the period of the "generation gap," and we planned an intergenerational study (referred to as IGS). Again most study members (and now their spouses) were brought to Berkeley and interviewed, tested, and given medical examinations, though some were seen at home. By 1969 we knew much more clearly what we wanted to learn about the intervening years (though it was soon obvious that we should have inquired much more thoroughly into women's occupational involvements and a number of other topics). We secured a great deal of information about family relationships—relationships with our subjects' parents and their children—and samples of all three generations were interviewed. As many children aged 14 to 18 as could be brought in were seen, and others completed questionnaires. We learned of the aspirations of the offspring, their perceptions of their parents, and their views of the world they inhabited. We learned about the study members' occupational careers, their marital relationships, and their social attitudes. In this follow-up we reached 251 study members, 190 husbands or wives, 171 parents of GS and BGS members, and roughly 240 children of GS and OGS members. The story of the parents was told in *From Thirty to Seventy* (1974) and that of the study members in *Present and Past in Middle Life* (1981).[15]

The cost of bringing study members to Berkeley and mobilizing a staff of highly trained interviewers and tests rose with each successive follow-up. In 1980 we sought to secure funds to see not only study members and their spouses but offspring as well. Our budget request—for roughly $3 million—was too daunting to secure a high enough priority for government funding. Longitudinal studies do not approach the neat precision of a well-conceived research design to test a specific hypothesis. In some ways, they are messy and have loose ends. One can see past mistakes, learn from them but never completely undo them. Human lives are that way too.

Fortunately, there are foundations whose staffs see the value of studying such lives over time. In 1981 the MacArthur Foundation funded our last major follow-up.[16] The budget allocation did not permit us to see the children, but we were able to interview 282 study members and 220 spouses, most of them coming to Berkeley for an intensive day of testing and interviewing. In addition, the great majority of study members filled out a series of questionnaires dealing with occupational careers (including retirement for some), marital relationships, stressful life events, social supports, and health. Many completed life satisfaction charts, graphing their high and low points over the life course.

My colleagues and I concentrated on different facets of the last follow-up, designing sections of the interview protocol and specialized questionnaires. Then several of us secured grants to permit us to analyze the segments for which we were responsible.[17] My own support came from the National Institute of Aging for a study entitled "Occupation and Family in Later Maturity." The grant permitted me to gather more information on a subsample of sixty of the study members living within fifty miles of Berkeley. They constitute the life history sample from which the individual histories included in this book were derived.

A grant from the William T. Grant Foundation made possible the final bit of data collection. Questionnaires were sent to all study members for whom we had current addresses in 1990, asking about their work or retirement status, health, family relationships and activities. Subjects were requested to provide current addresses of their adult children, which most did, and in 1991 we sent out over 500 questionnaires to the offspring, receiving replies from roughly 70 percent.

Table 2.1 summarizes the information on sample sizes and dates of major data collection. As of 1982 we knew of the deaths of 46 study members, most of them from the older, Oakland cohort. At least 20 are known to have died since then and it is likely that a number of those whom we have been unable to trace have also died.

How Representative Is the Current Study Group?

We do not know exactly how many potential study members were lost because their parents did not give permission for their participation. We do know that the great majority did give approval and that most parents thought the benefits of their children's participa-

Table 2.1. **Overview of the Three Longitudinal Studies**

	Berkeley Growth Study	**Berkeley Guidance Study**	**Adolescent (Oakland) Growth Study**
	1928–29	1928–29	1931–32
Recruitment of subjects			
Age of subjects at recruitment	Birth	Birth	10–12
Number of subjects at recruitment[a]	61	252	215
Number of subjects at age 18[b]	39	159	160
Number with adolescent personality data	39	66[c]	94
Intensive Follow-up Studies			
Ford Foundation Follow-up		1958–59	1958–59
Age of subjects		30–31	37–38
Number interviewed		133	99
Berkeley Growth Study (NIMH)	1965		
Age of subjects	37–38		
Number interviewed	50		
Intergenerational Study (NIA)		1969–70	1969–70
Age of subjects		41–42	48–50
Number interviewed		136	97
MacArthur Foundation Study	1982	1982	1982
Age of subjects	53–54	53–54	61–62
Number interviewed	50	142	91
1990 mail survey			
Age of subjects	61–62	61–62	68–70
Number of returns	29	92	67

Notes　a.　In each instance a few subjects were lost very early in data collection. In Berkeley Growth Study, 11 new-born infants were added after 1929.

b.　Subjects for whom some data were available at this age.

c.　Personality data available only for the Guidance Sample.

tion were substantial. This would undoubtedly have been more true in the middle class, where parents valued the expert advice that could be secured from staff, especially in the Guidance Study. On the other hand, the Adolescent Growth Study was able to offer more benefits to the adolescents themselves—first a clubhouse where they could gather, play records, dance, or just "fool around," and later ski trips and other outings not available to nonstudy members. Participation in the study is still prized by many members.

Still, there were mothers who tired of being interviewed every year and who became minimally cooperative. When a staff member of the Guidance Study went to his home to interview Mario Verde, who was about to graduate from high school, the boy's mother reported: "He's not here and he don't want to be pestered all the time. If you want him, go find him at the school ground. We don't want to be bothered no more." Nevertheless, Mario was not only located but was willing to be interviewed. Moreover, he has been a participant in the study to the present. In their adult years, several study members mentioned how tired they had been of being asked about which of their parents they more resembled and similar questions year after year, but they also remembered being able to talk with Jean Macfarlane or Judy Chaffey about areas they could not approach with their parents.

Over the years, about two-fifths of the study members have been lost to us. Some moved away before they finished high school. If the move took them beyond the Bay Area, they disappeared from our studies. By the end of the senior high year, or through age 18, the Berkeley Growth Study retained roughly two-thirds of its original members, the Guidance Study retained roughly three-fourths of the guidance group but fewer of the control group, and the Oakland Growth Study retained approximately three-fourths of its original sample. Retention did not necessarily mean that complete data had been secured in the later adolescent years but at least some data had been secured.

Between high school graduation and the first systematic follow-up, World War II and the Korean War intervened for the OGS members and the Korean War for the Berkeley members. Some could not be traced. A few study members declined to participate or were unable to schedule coming to Berkeley in the first follow-up, and funding did not permit sending teams to interview and test them. Since then, we have tried to keep in touch and have managed to do so with most of the group. Intensive interviews were conducted with 282 study members between 1981 and 1983. By then, death had removed substantial numbers of OGS members, and retirement moves had made others hard to trace.

Whom have we lost apart from those we could not trace or those who have died? Those whose childhood families were most problematic, either in terms of economic well-being or in terms of conflict and divorce, more often dropped out of sight. Yet even among these members most stressed in early life, more than half are still with us if they remained through adolescence. Success breeds a measure of celebration. The highly successful, in work and in family life, enjoy talking about their lives far more than do those whose careers or families have been plagued with problems and disruptions. This means that those who were most competent in their early years were more likely to be with us in their later years.

There is, then, some bias in the attributes of those who remain when compared with the original representative samples. We have somewhat fewer men and women from the working class than we had initially. We have somewhat fewer members from families that disintegrated in their childhood. Nevertheless, we have enough men and women who endured early difficulties and deficits to be able to draw strong conclusions as to how lives are shaped.

THE DATA

The Guidance Study involved the mothers centrally in data collection, and a major focus of that study was the mother-child relationship. The Berkeley Growth Study also involved the mothers when they brought the children in for testing, though there were not intensive interviews as with the Guidance Study. In neither study were the fathers involved to any extent. It now seems amazing that students of child development should have almost totally overlooked the role of the father in the family, but the researchers were creatures of their culture. In the 1920s, it was taken for granted that the American father's role was primarily to earn a living for the family and occasionally to serve as a disciplinarian. In the Oakland Growth Study, even the mothers were only slightly involved as sources of data and the fathers not at all. Mothers were seen at the beginning of the study to approve the child's participation, and they were seen on two later occasions, to learn something about the family composition and material well-being and about the child's habits and the regimes that had been established in the way of child care.

Although there exists a wealth of data on the children's development and behavior, few of the early data on the mother's orientations and child rearing practices of Guidance Study mothers were quantified. The records contain the mother's descriptions of relationships within the family, but they tend to be somewhat fragmentary. Nevertheless, the mother's reports were full enough to give a basis for rating family climate (amount of conflict, centrality of child rearing and so on), as well as specific types of maternal response to the behaviors presented by the child. Some ratings were done early and others recently under a grant to Dr. Marjorie Honzik.[18] Similar ratings were performed for parenting and family climate in the junior and senior high school years for members of the Oakland Growth Study.

In their later childhood and adolescent years, study members were seen by many different staff members, on many different occasions. They were interviewed and observed, they completed many questionnaires and inventories, and parents and teachers also provided their perspectives. No one feels the same every day or presents the same face to the world. When one's face has been seen for dozens of times, however, the image that an observer has formed usually is quite clear and relatively stable. When there are many observations over many occasions, the biases of individual observers and the variations over occasions can be taken into account. That is the great merit of our data on the early and adolescent years: multiple occasions, multiple observers, and varied perspectives. Appendix B contains a summary of the data collection during the childhood and adolescent years and major sources of data and measures for the adult years.

Interviewer Effects

In the adult years, we have fewer observations, and each tends to be more strongly influenced by the personalities of the observers or interviewers who collected the data. One clinical interviewer seemed able to relate closely to almost every respondent she talked with. Others could not conceal their discomfort in certain relationships.

An interviewer who prided herself on her light touch and ability to win praise for her cleverness might be totally put off by a rather sardonic study member who did not wish to be charmed. Thus, the interviewer's personality sometimes intervened to make it difficult to tell just how the study member might have responded if he or she had not been annoyed by the way in which a question was asked. Fortunately, most often there were contacts with several staff members. For the most recent intensive follow-up, in 1981–1982, there were two interviews, one "structured," to yield specific codable information, and one called "clinical," a wide-ranging exploration of the development and relationships of the respondent. Only the clinical interview was used for assessing personality, but in the intensive analysis of life histories, I have drawn on both interviews. Sometimes the two interviewers elicited quite different emotional responses as they focused on various facets of their respondents' lives.

A given study member may be regarded as handsome by one staff member and homely by another. A man characterized as "humorous, who enjoyed bantering with the interviewer" in a morning session was characterized by his afternoon (clinical) interviewer as rather "stern and lacking in social responsiveness." The fact that persons are differently responsive to each other makes precise measurement impossible, but their ways of dealing with particular others often yield valuable insights.

Perhaps this is enough detail to indicate the nature of the tremendous archive of data on which we can draw to document the lives of our study members. Detail on specific instruments is contained in Appendix B.

In the early years of the research, tape recorders had not been invented. Researchers made notes and often tried to get down verbatim statements. More often, they paraphrased what the youngsters and their parents said. From 1970 on, however, we have recordings of the interviews, and they permit us to capture exact quotations and to communicate more fully some feeling of the persons whose life stories are being told.

Current Versus Later Recollections

In the 1930s and 1940s, adolescents were asked about their interests, their attitudes, and many of their activities. Unless they approached the research staff to discuss such matters, they were not asked about the problems of their mothers and fathers or about their own sexual activities. Indeed, even in the early adult years, the original staff members, all born about 1900, hesitated to raise sensitive questions that might offend some study members of their parents and lead to their dropping out of the study. Nevertheless, in many instances, the staff became aware of seething family conflicts and of exhibitions of what used to be called "flaming youth."

At the first intensive follow-up, members of the Oakland Growth Study were asked to report on their experiences with the opposite sex in high school and beyond. They were also asked about relationships in the parental family. In both areas, we learned a good deal we had not known. Sometimes study members were intent on telling us about the torments of living with parental pathologies. In one instance, a man whose case history had been published and only thinly disguised came in to set the record straight. He had been quite maladjusted in high school, lacking in self-confidence, poise, and physical agility. In the publication, his problems were attributed primarily to his having matured physically much later than most of his peers. When he told his story, a totally different perspective on his problems flashed into view. His mother, a self-proclaimed invalid, dominated her husband and her only child from her bed. The boy and his father cooked, washed dishes, and cleaned the house. So far so good. But the boy was also asked to bathe his mother and change her bedclothes into his adolescent years. He described his loathing for aspects of the duties demanded of him. Not surprisingly, he never felt entirely comfortable with the opposite sex. He is a creative and warm human being at 71, and he and I have corresponded, but he has not participated in the study in the past thirty-four years.

Many men and women, however, were quite comfortable in telling us, in the course of the adult follow-up interviews, about events and relationships that were very important to their lives but had been unknown to us. Sexual experiences in adolescence were not as rare as many persons might think today, in the light of the sexual revolution of the 1960s. The sexual revolution of the 1920s perhaps marked a sharper break with the old sexual morality than did that of the 1960s. In any event, roughly a fourth of the men and women in the OGS later mentioned having had intercourse while still in high school. Most often, for the women, at least, it was with the boy or man they later married. Nevertheless, over the years we have learned of far more (illegal) abortions than anyone had suspected. It had been known, particularly by Jean Macfarlane in the Guidance Study, that some girls had gone to another state for a few weeks while still in high school, and the reason must have been discussed, but such information was not in the records.

Suffice it to note that a complete story requires that we draw upon more remote retrospection as well as on reports of relationships and events that immediately preceded our contacts with the study members. Sometimes it was possible to check on how well the later reports jibe with what we knew at the time. Often they permit an, "Ah-ha! Now we understand." Sometimes we can only say, "This is what we now are hearing."

Case histories can give a much better sense of human lives than can statistical tables. We learn how individuals interpreted the situations they encountered, their reasons for the choices they made, or their difficulty in making a choice. We get a sense of the person as actor. Yet case histories can be deceiving. A dramatic instance of a child's overcoming an extremely pathological family setting and becoming a competent, delightful person may almost convince us that early child rearing makes little difference. A systematic testing of that hypothesis, however, requires statistical data. As will be seen, most often a pathological family setting leads to unhappy outcomes in adult life. Of the histories presented in this book, most document that consistent, loving parenting is associated with favorable outcomes. At the same time, it may be useful to see how one person from a pathological family recovered from extreme early misery to become a fairly happy, competent person. Therefore, I report both typical and atypical outcomes. This topic will receive more attention in a later chapter, but it is important to draw on both qualitative and quantitative data if we are to understand the influences upon the lives of persons who have lived through a particular slice of American history.

All three studies began before their subjects had attained puberty. It will be desirable to describe first their family backgrounds and early development. What was the climate of the times, and how did it change over the early years? What schools did study members attend? And how did we assess competence in adolescence?

THE SETTING OF THE STUDIES

No geographical area can be considered "typical" in a country as diverse in population and in regional cultural norms as the United
States. Educational opportunities and occupational potentialities
vary as much as the mix of ethnic groups. It may be presumptuous
to characterize any group as representative of "American lives." In
the study, Afro-Americans, Hispanics, and migrants of Asian origin
are not represented except for a very few blacks. These minority
groups were present in the populations of north Oakland and of
Berkeley to only a limited extent at the time the study started.
While the Guidance Study sample was strictly representative, the
Oakland Growth Study confined participants to Caucasians who
were English speaking. At that time, the population of Oakland
schools was 92 percent Caucasian.[19]

Both Oakland and Berkeley grew rapidly in the early Twentieth
Century. The great San Francisco earthquake of 1906 sent thousands of families across the bay as refugees, and World War I
brought many workers to Oakland's shipyards and railroad termi-
nals. Further migration in the 1920s resulted in a continual over-
crowding of schools and other community facilities. Just before the
Great Depression, a banker's assessment of the local economy observed that "industrially, Oakland has ranked among the three
fastest growing cities of this country."[20] The population of Oakland
was approaching 300,000, while that of Berkeley, just to the north,
was roughly 82,000 in 1930, up from 56,000 in 1920.

In roughly three-fourths of the families of the study members,
both parents were native born and of northern European stock.
Most were nominal Protestants; about a quarter were Catholics.
Many had come to California from midwestern or eastern states in
the decade or so before they started their own families. They
brought with them a wide variety of orientations. Thus, their children represented a broad sampling of American families whose
early lives were spent in the Bay Area of California. We do not know
how many families may have chosen Berkeley or north Oakland because of proximity to the University of California, but it is likely that
at least some did so. Moreover, the importance of the university as
an employer and as a resource undoubtedly tended to raise both
the socioeconomic status of the population and the intellectual climate of the community. The university also afforded adolescents

from less well-to-do families the opportunity to receive a first-rate college education free, while living at home. Many study members availed themselves of that opportunity.

The area was a fortuitous location for a long-term longitudinal study, because a majority of the children of these migrants to the Bay Area have spent the bulk of their lives within fifty miles or so of their early residences. This has greatly facilitated our contacts with them. Nevertheless, study members have moved to all parts of the United States. Geographical dispersion has not prevented the continued participation of most of those who moved outside California, but it has made follow-up studies more expensive.

When the Guidance Study was first conceived, the economic boom of the 1920s was in full swing. The stock market promised fortunes to all who would provide capital for America's further industrial expansion, and margin requirements (permitting one to buy stock with only a partial down payment) were modest. "Two chickens in every pot and two cars in every garage" was the upbeat slogan of the boosters. But when stock prices plummeted and no amount of borrowing would cover the new margin requirements, the banking system went into reverse. Savings were withdrawn from banks, and real estate prices fell, depleting banking assets. By the time the Adolescent Growth Study was underway, the system was nearing a complete collapse. There was no federal deposit insurance, and many families lost all their savings.[21]

As Glen Elder has noted in his book on the Oakland study members, *Children of the Great Depression*, approximately one-third of normally employed persons were out of work in 1932 in the country as a whole.[22] The figure for Oakland was only a shade less—30 percent. Berkeley, with its university and larger proportion of professionals, fared slightly better, but income loss was acute even for those who retained jobs. The employment picture improved a bit in the mid-1930s, but many families struggled along on minimal income, requiring assistance, first from private welfare agencies and finally public relief.

The Parental Families

Between one-fourth and one-third of the study members were the first-born or only children of their parents, while the remainder

Table 2.2. **Educational Attainment of Parents of Subjects of the Three Studies, 1920–1930 (percentages)**

	OGS		GS		BGS	
	Father	Mother	Father	Mother	Father	Mother
Educational Attainment						
Total	101*	100	99	100	100	101
College graduate	17	10	27	17	55	41
Some college	11	15	13	15	17	19
High school graduate	20	23	17	21	7	19
Some high school	20	23	18	25	17	11
Grade school or less	33	29	24	22	4	11

*Percentages may not add to 100 because of rounding.

had older brothers and sisters. The age of the mothers at the time of the birth of the study child ranged from 16 to 45 (averaging 28), while the age of their fathers ranged from 17 to 60 (averaging 31). Almost all of the parents except for a few of the older ones were in their first marriages.

The families were growing, so that the ultimate number of children tended to increase as the child grew older. In all three studies, the most frequent number of children in the family was two. Roughly one child in six was an only child, except in the BGS, where only children were rare. Roughly two-thirds of the families ultimately had two or three children. Perhaps because of the effect of the Great Depression, Guidance Study parents were less likely to have four or more children than the (older) OGS parents and the same-age but more affluent BGS parents.

Roughly three-fourths of the families were intact through the high school years of the study members. Roughly one family in eight was broken by the death of a parent and one in seven by desertion, separation, or divorce by the time the study members were 18 years old. As we shall see, the effects of death or divorce depend to a large extent on the circumstances preceding the event and the resources available to the child thereafter.

Berkeley had a higher proportion of middle-class residents than did Oakland, and this was true of the members of the Berkeley studies as compared with those of the OGS. The greatest difference in status, however, was between the Berkeley Growth Study families and those of the other two studies. The BGS enrolled only hospital-born infants, and as of 1928–1929, most infants were delivered at home unless the family was well off or a serious birthing problem was expected. Because the study was to be limited to normal deliveries, the latter category would have been eliminated. For reasons unknown to the current research generation, a few lower-class families were represented, perhaps because conditions in the home made it an undesirable place for delivering a baby. In any event, the proportion of college graduates among BGS parents was more than twice that in the other two studies.

Table 2.2 shows the educational attainments of fathers and mothers in the three studies. In general, the subjects' fathers were substantially more likely than their mothers to have been college graduates, as was true for the country as a whole. The study group parents somewhat exceeded the educational levels found nationwide but (except for the Berkeley Growth Study, which greatly exceeded national levels) were roughly comparable in educational attainment to their age-mates in other cities with local colleges and universities.

The occupations of the subjects' fathers at the time of the subjects' birth ranged from student and unskilled worker to professional callings, but more than half were in white-collar occupations. Fifty-five percent of the BGS fathers were in professional or higher managerial positions, as against about a third of the GS fathers and a fifth of the OGS fathers. In both the OGS and the GS samples, however, roughly one-third of the fathers were in blue-collar jobs at the time of the subjects' birth. Thus, we shall be examining the lives of men and women drawn more largely from middle-class families than from the working class, and in this respect they were somewhat favored in the opportunities available to them.

The Oakland and Berkeley Schools

The 1930s were not only years of economic depression. They were the years in which "progressive education"—education for social skills, practical skills, and good citizenship rather than purely academic skills—was in the ascendancy. Nowhere was this more true than in Oakland and Berkeley, where many schools had ties to the prestigious School of Education at the University of California. Claremont Junior High and University High School in Oakland were training schools for the university, and their principals were professors of education at the university.[23] Their curricula were developed in accordance with the philosophical views of staff members, some of whom were disciples of John Dewey, the father of the modern progressive education movement. Education through meaningful experience, through doing rather than memorizing, was designed to motivate and generate enthusiasm for learning.

The Adolescent Growth Study was, in fact, regarded by the staffs of the two Oakland schools involved in the research as providing a basis for curriculum planning, for it helped to identify the "needs, interests and abilities" of the youth to be served.[24] The close linkage is reflected in a paper written in 1934 jointly by the vice principal of Claremont Junior High, Helen Hunt, and Judith Chaffey, the institute's liaison with the schools:

> We believe that in the junior high school more than at any other time in school the child is at a point of change in development. . . . We believe that [the three junior high school years] are marked by great emotional instability, by the drive of strong distracting interests, such as, for instance, growing interest in the opposite sex, growing social interests. They are marked, too, by a growing resistance to family authority, and by a most intense drive to conform with the group] and to be established in it. Then, too, we realize . . . that the period is marked by rapid growth. . . . Along with these obvious physical changes come an extreme self-consciousness, an increased consciousness of sex, and interest in personal appearance. The boy is admired for physical prowess, for being a regular fellow; the girls, for being pretty, well-dressed, quiet, ladylike—she becomes outlandishly unreasonable about clothes, make-up, hair styles, and dates.[25]

These concerns were foci of the Adolescent Growth Study, and they seemed to call for major changes in the standard curriculum. The junior high school had originated less than two decades earlier—Berkeley had either the first or second of this new type of school—as a means of easing the transition from the small elementary school, with close personal ties between teacher and pupil, to the large, impersonal high school with specialized teachers in major subjects. Because the junior high years—seventh through ninth grades—were the time of onset of puberty for almost all girls and many boys and because of heightened awareness of sexuality in the 1920s, the consequences of attainment of puberty seemed an important topic for research and for curriculum planning. Throughout the years of the Adolescent Growth Study, its findings were drawn upon by the schools involved, and their implications were discussed in many publications, local and national.

We can say much less about the schools attended by the members of the Guidance Study and the Berkeley Growth Study. We know that Berkeley schools had a good reputation, but there was no official link with the University of California and its School of Education. Nor was there a close link between either study and any of the schools. In the Oakland Growth Study, the students moved together through Clarement and, for the most part, University High, and many knew each other well. In the case of the Guidance Study and the Berkeley Growth Study, the students were scattered in classrooms throughout the city, and few knew which study members, if any, were in the same classes. The fact that they were of the same age meant that they tended to move along together, but it must be remembered that the members of the study constituted only one child in three born in 1928–1929. Moreover, migration into and out of the city would have diluted further the proportion that they constituted within any classroom.

Very few eligible families failed to participate in the Guidance Study, and the randomly selected group thus appears to be truly representative of children born in Berkeley at the time. The Berkeley Growth Study, as we have seen, contained a much larger proportion of children born to families of professionals and the well-to-do, along with a few families requiring welfare assistance.

CONCEPTS AND MEASURES

The central concepts employed in analyzing the lives of the study members are drawn from sociology, psychology, the study of human development, and, to a limited extent, genetics and physiology. The life course is not the exclusive province of any academic discipline.

A human being can survive only as part of a social unit that transforms the helpless organism into a more or less autonomous person having a unique personality—autonomous and unique yet at the same time sharing many behaviors, beliefs, and interdependencies with other members of the societal niche into which the person is born. We must therefore attend to features of the organism itself, the societal niche (family, ethnic group, social class) in which the person is nurtured, and the course of development over the life span. We must attend to the obstacles and opportunities—the sources of stress and of support and aid—that are encountered throughout life. All of these elements enter into the shaping of the individual personality as it exists at any point along the way.

Personality has been defined in many ways. I think of *personality* as a generic term for the relatively enduring set of attributes that a person characteristically exhibits in interactions with others and in self-management at a particular time. In general, we expect these attributes to show a measure of stability and consistency, yet lack of such consistency—unpredictability in certain respects—may itself be an important feature of the personality. Personality incorporates temperament, the level and emotional coloring of responsiveness or disposition, which in part reflects constitutional givens. Personality also reflects learned patterns of behavior in interaction with others in the course of socialization. Such patterns are shaped by cultural norms, moral standards, typical beliefs held within a society at a particular time, and the goals toward which members of that society strive, as well as by the personalities of parents and other agents of socialization.[26]

Psychologists typically seek to encapsulate the most important features of personality in a relatively small number of classifications, such as those relating to extraversion and introversion (being outgoing versus being more reserved and introspective) or aggressiveness versus submissiveness. A number of standardized psychological tests get at the major dimensions that are widely accepted as most important, but most of those tests did not exist when the study started. Moreover, we who inherited the studies faced an additional problem: the original three studies had different objectives and used different methods. In order to arrive at a classification of the personalities of our study members, we had to use some form of ratings that could be applied to the body of data collected for each study at each period.

Fortunately, there exists a standardized language for describing personality, the California Q-set, a set of one hundred items that relate to many of the attributes that I have described as elements of personality.[27] They reflect temperatment, intellectual ability, interpersonal styles, ways of handling anxiety, and, to a limited extent, value orientations. The items were devised primarily for an American population and do not deal specifically with such matters as cultural beliefs. They are used in a technique called a Q-sort to give a description of a person's most and least characteristic traits.

Consider the following sample of items, drawn from the full set:

1.   Is critical, skeptical, not easily impressed
2.   Is a genuinely dependable and responsible person
3.   Has a wide range of interests
4.   Is a talkative individual
5.   Behaves in a giving way toward others

.

.

.

49.   Is basically distrustful of people; questions their motivations
50.   Is unpredictable and changeable in behavior and attitudes
51.   Genuinely values intellectual and cognitive matters

.

.

.

96.   Values own independence and autonomy
97.   Is emotionally bland; has flattened affect
98.   Is verbally fluent; can express ideas well
99.   Is self-dramatizing; histrionic
100.   Does not vary roles; relates to everyone the same way

Some are attributes that almost everyone would consider positive, some are clearly negative, and others may have either positive or negative connotations. All tell us something about typical ways of behaving or presenting oneself.

For any individual, one can ask whether a given item is strongly descriptive or not at all descriptive. The technique of the Q-sort entails having each item on a card and then having sophisticated judges sort these cards into nine piles, putting at the extremes those items that are most strongly descriptive of the individual (scored 9) or least descriptive (scored 1). The judges place toward the middle (5) those that are somewhat descriptive or for which evidence is weak.

Judges (experienced clinical psychologists and social workers) read through materials relating to a particular period in the study member's life and then sorted the items of the Q-sort according to their salience for describing the person at this period. The specifications call for putting a small number of cards at either extreme and the larger number distributed toward the center. Attributes that are less salient are likely to be harder to assign values to, so they tend to pile up toward the middle of the distribution. The distribution resulting from the sorting of the cards provides a characterization of a given individual at a given time— that is, a description of the most salient and least salient attributes of that person at that time, regardless of how that person's characteristics compare with those of other persons. Because of the large number of items, however, this unique characterization correlates substantially with what one would find by rating the individual in terms of his or her standing relative to other persons on the same attribute.[28] Thus a person who receives a 9 rating on the item "Appears to have a high degree of intellectual capacity" almost certainly scores very high on a test of intelligence, while a person who receives a 1 would be found toward the bottom of the distribution of test scores, assuming a valid rating.

At the time of the first adult follow-up, when it was decided to combine the data from the Oakland Growth Study with those from the Guidance Study, three sets of Q-sorts were done: one for the junior high school years, one for the senior high school years, and one for the subject's current personality in early adulthood (centered on 30 and 37 years of age). In general, two or three judges were asked to read over the entire file for a period and then to perform Q-sorts. The judges' scores were then combined to give a best estimate, since judges varied somewhat in their assessment of individuals. The composite scores had an average reliability above .70, which was sufficiently high to permit comparisons over time though lower than the reliability of more segmental measures of personality.[29]

No judge sorted a person at more than a single period. Thus, each set of classifications was based entirely on material from a given period, with no knowledge on the part of any judge of any other period for this person. This provides us, then, with completely independent assessments that can be used to estimate personality resemblance or stability over time, as well as to relate each period's personality to antecedent conditions and experiences.

The process of Q-sorting was both laborious and expensive.

Q-sorts for the junior high and senior high years were performed only for persons who were seen at the time of the first adult follow-up. Moreover, control subjects from the Guidance Study had insufficient data to warrant personality classification. At each subsequent follow-up, Q-sorts for the adult years were performed, but funds were not available to classify the adolescent personalities of those not seen at the first follow-up. Therefore, we lack personality data from adolescence for a significant number of study members. More complete specification of the number of Q-sorts performed and of Q-sort reliabilities is given in Block and Haan (1971).

Q-Sort Components

One hundred items is clearly an impossible number to work with in attempting to classify individuals over time, so at different stages in our work, we used different techniques of factor analysis and component analysis to secure summary measures.[30] Most recently, a new technique of component analysis, developed by Millsap and Meredith, was applied to scores on the Q-sort items from all periods to yield a set of six components of personality that can then be scored for each period.[31] These components, more stable than individual items, provide the primary measure of personality or personal orientations. Each component is the weighted product of a substantial number of individual Q-sort items.

For the most part, the six components have been named by the items that most strongly define the positive and negative extremes, with the first-named attribute having high salience if the component is scored positively and low if scored negatively. The six components are:

1. Self-confident versus victimized
2. Assertive versus submissive
3. Cognitively committed (renamed "intellectually invested")
4. Outgoing versus aloof
5. Dependable (and effective)
6. Warm versus hostile (agreeable, prosocial)

The full set of items included and the weights assigned to each are given in Appendix B. The method that Millsap and Meredith employed allows an item to be included in more than one component. For example, the item "fearful" (full wording: "is vulnerable to real or fancied threat; generally fearful") is included in the list of items defining components 1, 2, and 4; that is, a person who is generally fearful will seldom be self-confident, assertive, or outgoing. In the same way, a highly rebellious person is unlikely to be submissive or dependable in conventional relationships. Nevertheless, people often combine attributes that seem incongruent, and this incongruence can be accommodated by using both the items and the components. For the most part, the components will be my chief descriptors of personality. Occasionally we examine individual items.

The Measure of Planful Competence

In Chapter 1 I described planful competence as entailing knowledge, ability, and controls. To deal competently with a situation or demand, one must be able to assess the situation, identify one's options, and mesh one's acts responsibly with the acts of others. Thoughtfulness and dependability are important. One must be self-confident, at least to the extent of being willing to take on challenges to one's ability. As I searched for a means of indexing early competence, it occurred to me that three of the six components derived by Millsap and Meredith—(1) self-confident versus victimized, (3) cognitively committed (or, as I prefer, intellectually invested), and (5) dependable (which also strongly connotes "effective")— might provide a useful approximation to my concept. The items on which these components are based are given in Table 2.3, along with the weights they receive at each period.

From the items listed in Table 2.3, it will be evident that "self-confident versus victimized" connotes a measure of self-esteem and the ability to interact in a positive way with others and the absence of tendencies that are often labeled neurotic. Self-esteem is not primarily a matter of being self-congratulatory but rather of having confidence in one's ability to cope with whatever comes along. There is a sense of resilience, no suggestion of being fearful, no feeling that one will be victimized, but an ability to maintain control under stress. Self-confidence so defined is certainly a strong element in the definition of competence.

Table 2.3.   **Most Heavily Weighted Items in Personality Components Used for Index of Competence**

Positive Weight		Negative Weight	
Self-confident versus victimized (secure, interpersonally at ease)			
Satisfied with self	1.05	Feels cheated, victimized	.85
Calm, relaxed in manner	1.02	Fearful, vulnerable to threat	.77
Cheerful	.81	Self-defeating	.70
Arouses liking and acceptance	.71	Has preoccupying thoughts	.69
Straightforward, candid	.64	Disorganized under stress	.61
Turned to for advice	.53	Thin-skinned, vulnerable to criticism	.59
Gregarious	.53		
Cognitively committed (Intellectually Invested)			
Values intellectual matters	.81	Uncomfortable w/uncertainty	.63
High intellectual capacity	.65	Conventional	.60
Introspective	.63	Basically submissive	.48
Has high aspirations	.59	Disorganized under stress	.44
Values independence	.59	Gives up when frustrated	.40
Has wide interests	.59		
Thinks unconventionally	.52		
Dependable (and effective)			
Dependable and responsible	.62	Rebellious, nonconforming	.56
Productive, gets things done	.59	Undercontrolled	.52
Overcontrol of impulses	.51	Self-defeating	.47
Satisfied with self	.44	Pushes limits	.44
Calm, relaxed in manner	.43	Unpredictable and changeable	.43
Ambitious	.43		

To make accurate assessments of one's options and build up a store of useful information, high intellectual ability and the effective application of that ability in everyday life—valuing intellectual matters, having wide interests—would seem major desiderata. Component 3, "intellectually invested," combines these attributes with the ability to tolerate ambiguity, to persist in the face of frustration, and (again) to maintain control when under stress. The negative contributions of submissiveness and conventionality connote an openness to new experiences, as does the positive contribution of ability to think unconventionally. High intellectual investment should contribute to consideration of future options, as well as handling existing situations effectively.

Our final component for defining competence is perhaps the most important in the adolescent years, especially for females. "Dependability" (component 5) not only entails responsible, productive behavior but also a strong measure of self-control, regard for the rules of everyday life, and freedom from self-defeating tendencies. As we grow older, most of us learn to inhibit self-defeating tendencies and become more self-controlled; otherwise, we continue to experience rebuff and failure. A reputation for being undependable or unpredictable can make the going tougher at any age, but it can markedly impair an adolescent's chances of positive selection for adult roles.

Behaving irresponsibly in adolescence appears to have more serious consequences for girls because of their more vulnerable social reputations and because pregnancy can so easily be an outcome of such behavior. This occurred for some members of the study and for many of their children. Dependability is related to both productive performance and ability to put the brakes on when there are dangerous curves ahead.

The three components of competence are moderately related, but the pattern of relationships changes over time. In adolescence, dependability and intellectual investment were most highly correlated (at .55 for males and .28 for females), while in the adult years these two components became only slightly related.[32] The intercorrelations of all the components as of the senior high school years and as of later maturity are given in Table A.1 (in Appendix A). Being intellectually invested in the high school years seems to have ensured (or perhaps required) a substantial degree of dependability. Beyond adolescence, most men and women became markedly more dependable, regardless of intellectual ability or the valuing of intellectual matters. As a consequence, this dimension becomes less central to competence, though a marked deficiency prevents effective functioning.

Clearly, adolescent planful competence is not a single dimension but a construct that has somewhat more coherence for males than for females. I consider the combination of the three components to be an index—like an index of economic conditions—whose components do not necessarily move together. It has a special meaning in adolescence, where it connotes getting ready for important decision making. This was and is particularly relevant to career preparation. As we shall see, its relevance for females in the 1930s and 1940s was most apparent in the realm of personal relationships. I believe that it now has equal relevance for men's and women's careers.

The three components that make up the index should contribute to effective functioning throughout life. Beyond adolescence, I refer to this combination as merely an index of competence. A leavening of being outgoing, open to new experience, and warm in interpersonal relations should make the person even more outstanding among peers. I argue that adolescent planful competence has great importance, but it certainly is not the whole story making for a life well lived.

For males, self-confidence retained a modest but consistent relationship with both dependability and intellectual investment from adolescence throughout the life course. For females, self-confidence was only weakly related to the other two components in adolescence but became more strongly related in the adult years. Thus, the meaning of the composite index of competence changes somewhat from adolescence to later maturity as the components shift differentially.

As suggested by the changed relationships among components, the absolute scores received on some components changed markedly over the life course. Males became more self-confident in senior high school than they had been in junior high school, showed little change to early adulthood, but increased in self-confidence at each subsequent assessment. Females, on the other hand, became less self-confident in the senior high school years and dropped a bit further in early adulthood. They showed a substantial increase in the next dozen years but then leveled off. Both sexes became much more intellectually invested into their 40s and then dropped off slightly at the last assessment. Dependability reached a low in senior high school and a high in early adulthood, before slackening slightly. (A detailed analysis of change in the six components over time is given in Haan, Millsap, and Hartke, 1986.)

For combining components in the index of planful competence as here constructed, each component was standardized with a mean of zero and a standard deviation of one, and the scores for the three components were then added to yield a score for each period.[33] Thus, the score at any period reflects the individual's level of measured planful competence in terms of individual saliences relative to the group as a whole at that period. For examining changes over time, raw scores were used.

Planful competence is a multidimensional construct whose components are themselves the resultants or combinations of multiple attributes. I cannot claim that the index used here is in any sense the best that can be devised, but it allows for some flexibility in the mix of attributes that will make for competent performances. A recent book, *Competence Considered,* spells out and documents impressively how the ability to envision "possible selves" and goals and to think through how they might be attained enhances performances relevant to goal attainment.[34] Perceiving oneself as competent is a crucial aspect of consistent, competent performance, and much current research on competence focuses on the subjective perception of it. The importance of the component self-confident versus victimized in relation to the total index of competence and the other components increases over the life course. This is one reason that the term *planful competence* seems more appropriate for the adolescent years than for the later years, though "competence" implies "mindfulness"—using one's intelligence creatively—at all periods.[35]

Measurement of Personality Change

By virtue of giving a profile of the most and least salient descriptions of a person's typical ways of behaving at any given time, the Q-sort lends itself to assessing change over time. One can correlate a person's profile at one period with that at another, comparing the scores on each item over the entire series. For this purpose, I have employed the seventy-three items that have high overall reliability at most periods and for both males and females.[36] The correlation coefficient thus serves as an index of resemblance of the personality at different times. It does not necessarily reflect stability, since everyone shows changes at times, but high resemblance over several periods reflects a substantial measure of stability. As will be seen, some persons change very much, others very little.

Other Measures Employed

Competence is only one of a large number of measures with which we shall be concerned. It encapsulates a great deal of information about individual attributes and life experiences in the preadolescent years, but it does not indicate, for example, whether a person is outgoing or relatively reserved, seen by peers as a warm and sympathetic person or as relatively cool or even hostile, or many other things that we might want to know. The three components of personality that have been combined in the measure of competence deal largely with effectiveness; the other three deal to a greater extent with tendencies in interpersonal relationships. Therefore, we shall want to examine how they influence various facets of the study members' relationships and lives.

Another global characterization of personality is highly relevant to examination of the life course. It is a template for assessing psychological health, again using the Q-sort items. Developed by Norman Livson and Harvey Peskin, it represents the consensus (more accurately, the average item placements) of a group of clinicians as to what the Q-sort profile would be for an ideal, psychologically healthy adult.[37] No distinction was made as to age or gender. An individual's Q-sort profile can therefore be correlated with this ideal sort to determine his or her approximation to psychological health as conceived by this group of psychologists. As we shall see, although the concept of psychological health has a basis totally different from my concept of planful competence and the adolescent classifications of the two have quite different predictive power in adolescence, they tend to converge to a considerable degree in the later years.

Beyond personality, there are many other influences on development and change through the adolescent and adult years. Physical appearance—facial beauty, physique, stature, and so forth—may elicit smiles of approval or frowns of disdain almost from the beginning. Physique influences athletic ability. So does the early attainment of puberty, especially in the high school years. Being endowed with a strong, resilient body and having good health en-

hances self-esteem and self-confidence. So does being endowed
with superior mental ability. These are attributes that can be measured and were measured during the childhood and adolescent
years, and we shall draw upon them. The major measures used are
detailed in Appendix B, and the general nature of each measure
will be described as we go along.

Both the life histories and the statistical analyses lead to the conclusion that no environmental influence in the preadolescent years
compares in importance with parenting. Were the parents attentive
to the child? Did they provide intellectual stimulation? Were they
supportive rather than abusive? Did they involve the child in decisions relating to the child, and were they consistent in the discipline that they imposed upon the child? The measurement of early
parenting and the contribution that parenting practices made to
the child's development of competence will be discussed in
Chapter 6, after the presentation of the initial life histories. Beyond
adolescence, we shall look serially at the occupational careers, marital careers, and parenting by our study members themselves. Each
of the measures will be described in nontechnical terms as we go
along, with the more important ones dealt with in greater detail in
Appendix B.

CHAPTER 3

INTRODUCTION TO THE LIFE HISTORIES

This brief chapter describes how the detailed life histories were prepared and points out in a general way what these histories are designed to do—that is, to show the origins of planful competence in early development and the ways in which adolescent planful competence prepared the person for the transition to the adult years and, indeed, for many transitions in the adult years. Two histories have been selected as basis for fuller discussion of how persons construct their lives. In Chapter 6, I go into much greater detail in presenting the story of how competence is engendered and where it leads; then additional histories will illustrate varied patternings of lives well lived. Beyond the histories will come the systematic analysis of men's and women's experiences—their successes and failures in the major roles they occupied in the six decades during which we have studied them.

The recorded life history of any person must, to a large extent, consist of retrospective reconstructions. Men and women who maintain diaries for long periods of time or exchange correspondence in which they describe in some detail what is happening in their lives provide a record of the more or less current perceptions that individuals have had about themselves and their behavior or the behavior of others in the past. But such evidence is seldom available. Moreover, a person's perceptions of self may have little resemblance to how the person is seen by others. The ideal materials for the construction of a life history combine the individual's own perceptions and attributions of himself or herself with the views of others at the time of given actions or events, thus avoiding retrospective falsification. When we have retrospective reports, our task is to understand not only how the past has influenced the person in the present but how the present has shaped recollections of the past.[1]

Our longitudinal data provide an unexcelled opportunity to delineate life histories in detail from other than purely retrospective accounts, though inevitably retrospective reconstruction of the recent past occurs even in reasonably current reports. Reconstructions of recent events are influenced not only by recall but by emotions and pressures that may still persist. Reconstructions of more remote events are likely to serve the current interests and orientations of the person, whether consciously or unconsciously.

As a number of students of the life course have noted, each of us has a story to tell about our lives, but the story changes over the years.[2] It does not change merely by the addition of new episodes of experience; it changes as our identity itself changes. It remains coherent by transforming past events and experiences. We have all gone through stressful, thoroughly unpleasant episodes that years later we describe as "something I would not have wanted to miss for all the world." Those episodes may have changed our views, but they fit into our life story in a way that makes sense, that says, "Yes, this was the real me in operation." In the histories presented in this book, I draw on records compiled for a variety of sources. The characterizations always entail the perceptions of others—teachers, parents, peers, or research staff—as well as those of the person whose history is presented. Further, we have reports of that person's recollections and interpretations at several times, at least from early adolescence to later maturity, most recently from a life history interview that reviewed many events and issues, past and present.

Finally, the study members whose lives are most completely presented were asked to review the histories we prepared and to give us their reactions to the descriptions and interpretations contained in them. This permitted clarifications and corrections of descriptive accounts, as well as reinterpretations based on the perspective of the person whose life was being described.

HISTORY PREPARATION

Life histories were prepared for a subgroup of members for whom we had intensive data from childhood or early adolescence through at least the mid-50s (through age 63 or 64 for Oakland Growth Study members) and who gave permission to have such histories prepared. Eighty-five percent of study members gave permission. Because I wished to compare their current retrospective accounts with data collected earlier, I limited the sample to a randomly selected subset of those for whom we have adolescent data, at least two instances of lengthy interviews during the adult years, and, with a few exceptions, residence within fifty miles of the University of California, permitting current retrospective interviews on the life course.[3]

As a first step toward the preparation of life histories, research assistants read the early adult interviews and summarized the information from each as well as coding certain facets of the study members' experience during the decade preceding the interview. They were given specifications for the summary of the early adult years, which called for locating the study member in his or her family context and commenting on the stability of the parents' marriage and the social status at home. Educational and occupational attainments, the circumstances and timing of marriage, the birth of children, and participation in other major social roles were to be touched upon. Finally, the summarizer was asked to encapsulate a characterization of the person and his or her sense of identity as of the time of the interview and any marked changes that had occurred in sense of identity since adolescence. Subsequent interviews were examined for indications of continuities or discontinuities, sources of satisfaction and dissatisfaction, and the most salient involvements of the study member.

In addition to coding and summarizing material from the earlier adult interviews, the research assistants were instructed to make notes relating to any major gaps in the developmental record or any seriously ambiguous or discrepant information. An attempt was made in the subsequent life history interview to secure information that would fill in these gaps or clear up the discrepancies.

The life history interview (conducted in 1984 for the most part) was not an attempt to review the whole life course but rather to supplement the clinical and structured interviews that had been conducted two years previously and to elicit the study members' current views on a number of topics that had been coded in the earlier interviews. Thus, we inquired into such matters as adolescent interests and plans, emotional dependency upon parents, the circumstances of marriage and occupational choice, and detailed information about any turning points or major decision points in the life course. In addition, a number of questions were asked to try to get at the study member's current sense of identity and feelings about his or her own life.

Life history summaries were prepared for and life history interviews conducted with sixty study members. From this group I selected a relatively small group for the preparation of more detailed life histories. Each life history has been based on reading and summarizing essentially the entire file for the childhood and adolescent years, reading all of the interview and test materials compiled in the adult years, and drawing on the life history interview and subsequent interviews and conversations relating to early drafts of the history. All of the persons whose lives are most fully depicted have provided data up to at least age 62 and, for the older group, 69 or 70.

How did I decide which lives to select? The first two study members chosen from the subsample of sixty were already somewhat familiar to me. When I first came to the Institute of Human Development, I was almost totally ignorant of the kinds of data that had been gathered. The untimely death of the previous director, Harold Jones, deprived me of the orientation I would normally have had to the Oakland Growth Study that he had planned and directed. I had to assume responsibility for its continuance, and this meant securing grant funds for the analysis of data previously collected. Therefore, I selected a case file to study exhaustively; it was that of the man here called Karl Schulz. By chance he was one of the sixty persons selected for life history interviews, as was Mary Wylie, whose record I subsequently read. Becoming familiar with their lives also helped me to formulate my ideas about competence. Neither was at the top of the list when study members were ranked on adolescent competence, but both were in the top third and remained high in competence in later life. Moreover, both had complete study records, and both were relatively open persons who knew themselves reasonably well.

Beyond these two histories, I wanted to ensure that certain life lines were represented. Mary Wylie was primarily a wife and mother, as were most of the other women in the study, but in their middle years, many women entered the labor force, and I wanted to tell the story of a woman with a strong career. Alice Neal, a member of the Guidance Study, was such a person. She seemed a very unlikely candidate from her high school record, but she was a changer. Rated low on competence in her adolescent years, she became an effective, highly competent manager. She thus serves to illustrate two types of patterning.

Another objective was to represent men and women from families that were well off and those that had to struggle. Henry Barr (a member of the Berkeley Growth Study) was one of the most favored boys in terms of family socioeconomic status, while Stuart Campbell was one of the least favored. Both were near the top in adolescent planful competence.

Finally, after this book was well along, I became aware of the study files of Beth Green, another Oakland Growth Study member. If ever anyone had to cope with adversity, Beth did. I thought her story should be told, and she was willing.

My choice of four subjects from the Oakland study clearly derives from my greater familiarity with the materials of that study plus my interest in viewing the life course to the edge of old age. A crucial consideration in selecting persons for the presentation of such histories was their acceptance of their own lives. Most of us have aspects of our lives that we would rather not review or face up to. It may come as something of a shock even to a secure person to know how he or she was perceived at some earlier period of life or to be reminded that their children have not realized the potential that the parents felt was there. Many of our respondents fended off questions about their feelings or problems at some earlier period, some saying that they did not "relate to" looking at past difficulties. People with significant insecurities and those for whom denial was a major mode of defending against anxiety were eliminated from consideration for the preparation of complete histories (where concealment of identity from the subject would be impossible). Instead we use fragments of their histories or amalgamation of material from several rather similar histories in trying to understand persons who for one reason or another have had problematic lives.

Two of the persons who had interviewed study members—Betty Webster and Hal Gelb—read most of the relevant materials and prepared initial, partial drafts of four of the histories.[4] After discussion with the original analyst-authors, I have recast the histories somewhat, adding data relating to topics not covered in the initial drafts, descriptions of the personality assessments, and modest interpretations. I have reviewed all of the early complete drafts with the study members and revised them somewhat, occasionally removing references that would make the study members readily identifiable by other than themselves and their families. A few details have been altered in each instance, but each of the people who have shared their lives has been willing to risk being identified by my presenting details that seemed crucial to understanding their lives.

The life stories describe how the study member was seen by peers, teachers, the research staff, and occasionally other family members over the years, as well as the member's own view of self. The narrative has been supplemented by some systematic, quantitative data. An invaluable index of personal change is given by the personality Q-sort (described in Chapter 2). This standardized language for describing persons not only allowed us to assess competence but also to assess changes in specific attributes and in overall personality profiles.

We have tried to prepare histories that are accurate and complete without risking an assault on a person's conception of self. We all tend to reconstitute the past in terms of the present. As George Vaillant noted in *Adaptation to Life*, some of his study members, then in their 50s, had completely changed their views from what they were in their student years at Harvard yet they denied that they had changed at all. Direct quotations from an earlier period that contradict one's recollections of that period are rather compelling evidence that those recollections are inaccurate. This will be apparent in several of the histories, and it was disconcerting to the persons involved. I have included their comments when this was the case. If a person is able to examine and accept his or her life (as these persons have been), even if parts of it have been interpreted in ways that seem alien to them, their perspective can greatly improve the understanding to be derived from that life history.

We are doubly indebted to the persons whose histories appear here. We are indebted to them for their willingness to share with us the happy and the painful experiences of life. We are indebted to even more for their willingness to examine the pictures that we have delineated and to tell us in what respects they feel those pictures are accurate or inaccurate. They have in general been basically accepting of the histories as presented.

INFLUENCES ON THE LIFE COURSE

Based on an enormous body of research and theorizing on human development, I have found it useful to distinguish four general classes of influence on the shaping of the life course and on the individual's performance in the various roles that structure that course—son or daughter, student, spouse, parent, worker, friend, citizen, and so on:[5]

1. *The person's own attributes, constitutionally given or developed*—intelligence, appearance, strength, health, temperament.
2. *The sources of socialization, support, and guidance* that initially orient persons to the world in which they will function and subsequently assist them to cope with problems or offer emotional support when effective solutions are limited—parents, schools, peers, husbands or wives, fellow workers, and friends.
3. *The opportunities available to the person or the obstacles that are encountered in the environment,* as influenced by social class, ethnic group, age, sex, and social network, as well as the effects of war, depression, and other major social changes that affect particular birth cohorts differently, and, not the least, the vagaries of chance.
4. *Investments of effort that individuals make in their own behalf*—the drive to achieve, commitments to goals and other persons, and the mobilization of resources to attain desired ends.

These classes of influence are themselves interrelated. For example, parents and peers respond differently (provide different encouragement, control, guidance) to children who are bright, strong, and attractive than to children who are constitutionally less well endowed.[6] Race and sex are both constitutionally given and social definers, enhancing or limiting various options in life. Both their initial temperaments and the encouragement that children receive early in life can influence that fourth, and ultimately crucial, element, the investment of effort and the mobilization of resources to attain one's goals and to cope with inevitable setbacks. We shall see in the lives of Stuart Campbell and Mary Wylie the complexity of development over the life course. There can be no simplistic explanation in terms of one or two aspects of early development, yet we shall often find clear lines of influence when we examine the interactions of these contributing elements.

We shall want to be aware of appearance, intelligence, health, and temperament as they influence the person's social reputation and view of self, as well as his or her ability to excel or at least to perform adequately in various activities. How does the family prepare the child for school, for social interaction with peers, for responsible behavior? What values are imparted? What do the parents teach the child about the good life, and what messages are conveyed to the child by the parents' own behavior, their references to other races, their choices among alternative life-styles and pastimes?

How does the adolescent deal with the onset of puberty and relationships with same- and opposite-sex peers? In adolescence, the person's identity should be firming up; he or she should not only be glimpsing potential futures but should have a reasonably good idea of the kind of person he or she would like to be.

We shall want to see how historical events and social pressures influenced the roles they occupied and the timing of their marriages, their family development, their relationships with their parents and their children. The Great Depression of the 1930s and the world war that immediately followed it had consequences for many of the men and women whom we shall meet. Through the adult years, most repeatedly faced unexpected challenges and occasional setbacks. How did they cope? Did skill at coping in adolescence serve to improve coping ability later on?

These are questions for readers to ponder in relation to the stories of Stuart Campbell and Mary Wylie. I shall try to provide at least partial answers in Chapter 6, following the histories.

THE INITIAL HISTORIES

Every person is unique. No one is typical of a given personality type or social type in all respects. The two persons whose histories are initially presented—Stuart Campbell and Mary Wylie—are typical of competent adolescents in certain respects and differ from many of their competent peers in other respects. Both are, by almost any criterion, competent adults. Stuart Campbell comes close to being an ideal exemplification of the competent male, not only in terms of his extremely high scores on the index of competence at every period of life but his occupational success, his happy marriage and family life, and the extraordinary stability of his personality from adolescence to later maturity. However, the very high degree to which he resembles the "ideal type" of competent male is itself atypical.

Mary Wylie did not score as high on the measure of competence in adolescence, especially in senior high school, but she nevertheless scored in the top third of female study members. She showed somewhat more personality change than many of her peers who were competent in adolescence, but the change occurred in attributes that reflected her attitudes toward others. Mary is quite representative of women who were primarily wives and mothers and never had an occupational career after marriage.

Ultimately, we shall see the diversity that exists within groups classified on the basis of competence as well as the differences between groups.

CHAPTER 4

A FINDER OF RESOURCES

STUART CAMPBELL

In the senior high school years, only one adolescent male scored higher than Stuart Campbell did on the measure of adolescent competence, but that man did not fall into the randomly selected sample of study members whose lives we attempted to summarize after further interviewing. When he entered elementary school, however, Stuart's prospects for becoming an outstanding adolescent did not look bright. Most competent adolescents came from intact families who provided more substantial cultural and economic benefits than were available in Stuart's home. Stuart was raised on the edge of poverty by his grandmother. But Stuart Campbell had an unusual ability to seek and find resources needed both to formulate and to achieve his goals. His life story illustrates both an unusual path through which planful competence was developed and the long-term benefits of that competence.

Stuart Campbell was born in 1920, the oldest of three children, to parents born in Scotland who had come to the United States a year before his birth. Although the parents were not aware of it at the time, apparently Stuart's mother had already contracted tuberculosis. She died when Stuart was 6 years old; his sister Barbara, 4; and his brother James, barely 2. His father abandoned the family following the mother's death and subsequently died in Canada in 1933. The cause of the father's death was said to be pneumonia, but Stuart suspects that a contributory cause was tuberculosis.

Stuart and his siblings were raised by their maternal grandmother, a widow who had come from Scotland for a visit but remained, to the distress of her family in Scotland, to raise the children following the death of her daughter. Throughout her life, she remained a British subject, since she feared she would otherwise lose the income from a small trust fund set up for her in Scotland by her husband. That income, plus a brief period of aid from Associated Charities of the East Bay, supported the family, barely above the subsistence level, until the children were grown.

Although the paternal grandparents also lived in the area, Stuart and his siblings had little contact with them. His maternal grandmother was convinced that her daughter had contracted tuberculosis as a result of caring for the paternal grandparents, one of whom may have had the disease. His grandmother was equally bitter about Stuart's father, who drank heavily. There were quarrels between the grandmother and his father even before the mother's death.

Stuart could recall a time—he was about 6—when his father was jailed for a night in San Francisco for drunken brawling. Highly intelligent but with little education, Mr. Campbell had had a varied career. He had gone to sea and had been in the Yukon before he married and came to the United States, where he became in time a minor administrative staff member with an oil company. After the death of his wife, the father drank more heavily and quarreled steadily with the grandmother, whom Stuart called a "very tough person when she was prejudiced against someone." Stuart's father finally left home, returned to sea, and then went to Canada, where he died. When notified of his father's death, 10-year-old Stuart was quoted as saying, "Well, he was never much of a father to me." His grandmother never let him or his brother forget the image of his father as a drunken, irresponsible man.

Stuart's early memories of his mother are of a very loving, caring person, usually sick, away in a sanitarium near the end of her life. His grandmother became the central adult family figure in his life.

Stuart was 11 when the Oakland Growth Study was organized. Knowledge of his early years comes to us primarily from Stuart himself in later years except for bits of information provided by his grandmother. She was cooperative but not a good informant. In some of the nine interviews with Stuart when he was ages 38 and 39, Stuart described his childhood and his relations with his grandmother and siblings.

Stuart's family moved around a good deal in his childhood years, usually within fifty miles of the bay. He started school (kindergarten) in a small city and went to first grade in Oakland. Although he attended the first grade for only a few weeks before a series of illnesses kept him out of school for the rest of the year, he had learned quite a bit. Moreover, he learned to read when he was ill, and by the next year, when he returned to school and was tested, he read at the fourth-grade level so he was immediately promoted to the second grade.

Because of the children's exposure to tuberculosis, their grandmother was greatly concerned about their health. Stuart was put in a sanitarium for three months, to build him up, and James—considered by his grandmother "a sickly waif"—spent a year in the sanitarium. Despite his absences from school, Stuart was able to stay in grade right along.

Stuart, as the eldest, was expected by the grandmother to take more responsibility than most other children his age. When the children were small, she disciplined them with a belt. Stuart described the way in which she would trap him in a corner. Of course, he added, "It was unthinkable to hit her or shove her out of the way." The belting stopped when she could no longer catch him. Then, he said, her major disciplinary tactic was to threaten to call the police. When the children saw through that, she began to work on their fears and guilt, saying that she would probably die soon—and then where would they be? They pictured themselves in an orphanage. He could remember her saying often, "If you were any kind of a boy you would ... " presumably do whatever she wanted him to do.

On the whole, however, Stuart felt she had been quite indulgent with him rather than restrictive. He felt she set high standards for the children except in the areas of personal hygiene, neatness, and cleanliness, which he had to learn elsewhere. She expected good grades—nothing less than A's—from him. As soon as they could, he and his brother were expected to find jobs, paper routes in both cases, and contribute to the family income.

Stuart and his family lived in a small rental house in a lower-middle-class neighborhood in Oakland, a house a bit shabbier than but not unlike the homes of their neighbors. Although the family was poor, Stuart does not seem to have regarded them as very different from their neighbors except that he and his siblings did not have parents. He was troubled at times, but not excessively, by his grandmother's anxiety about the lack of money. He saw his grandmother as his loyal supporter and said he got along with her much better than his sister (with whom the grandmother did not get along at all) and his brother, despite the grandmother's preference for him.

ADOLESCENCE

Junior High School, 1932–1935

At the initiation of the study in 1932, Stuart was brought to the Institute of Child Welfare by his grandmother, described as "a gaunt, tragic sort of figure, with piercing brilliant blue eyes and a soft Scottish burr." Consistently through the years 1932 to 1938, when Stuart graduated from high school, his grandmother was seen as cooperative, interested in the children, and concerned for their welfare but old fashioned, unhappy, and uncommunicative. Most of our information not colored by retrospection comes from the staff members who observed him and from his responses to the inventories and questionnaires he filled out. His grandmother did report that Stuart was a good boy, helpful and obedient. He had no fears or nervous habits other than chewing his pencil when he studied, but he did get "mad" easily. He found junior high school much more stimulating than grade school.

His grandmother, perhaps not wanting to appear too immodest in her assessment of Stuart, rated him only aevarge in intelligence and alertness but high in talkativeness, cheerfulness, and excitability. The staff members evaluating Stuart over time gave similar assessments except for intelligence, on which he rated very high. It was noted that he showed "an unusual ability to concentrate" and at the same time "a rich and rather mature inner life." At 14 years, 2 months he was described by one evaluator as retaining the air of a mature man with serious problems. At 14 years, 6 months another saw him as dominant in the group, likable, with much prestige. He received straight A's throughout elementary school and most of junior high, not only for academic subjects but for conduct as well.

At the same time, Stuart was not lacking in the capacity to get into mischief with the other boys. When a staff member once found him in the locker room hiding other boys' clothes, his reaction to being caught was good-natured and rather embarrassed. "He seems to have that rather subtle quality of being very much liked, trusted, almost esteemed [by his peers]," the report added.

On a number of occasions, Stuart's behaviors suggested a need to display a strong sense of masculinity. Although he was an excellent debater, he apparently rejected the members of the debating team as "queers." In response to projective tests, he saw father figures as powerful, sadistic, and compelling. The test interpreter wondered whether the boy's lack of contact with his father, coupled with the negative image presented by his grandmother and her warning him not to become like his father, caused him to have some question about his own masculinity. In those same projective techniques, it was the mother figure who urged boys to fame, and in many places Stuart indicated his intention of achieving fame.

When he was about 15, Stuart developed a bad case of acne, which upset him for quite a while. On his own he went to a dermatologist for treatment. While it lasted, the acne contributed to an awkwardness and shyness around adults and, more so, girls, with whom he was not yet comfortable.

In junior high school Stuart was active in sports. Though not outstanding as an athlete, he played some football and basketball, liked horseshoes, and occasionally was reported to have "fooled around on the bars in a noisy fashion." Although he did not know how to dance in the early days of the project, he quickly learned and enjoyed it, participating actively in social events. It was said that he liked the "kissing games," perhaps because he was very shy when it came to kissing.

From his earliest junior high school days, Stuart was perceived by the staff as mature and dependable for his age. He was seen as a leader among the boys. One observer described him as of good intelligence, a leader in classes, an independent thinker who showed much maturity in his judgment. He was tall for his age and serious. In the eighth grade he was vice-president of his class. In low ninth grade Stuart ran for class president but was defeated, perhaps because of his too serious attitude. Active in the Boy Scouts, he early achieved Eagle Scout status. He had a paper route and of necessity learned the value of money from an early age.

There was a high degree of consensus among the psychologists who reviewed Stuart's junior high years. One noted: "Stuart arouses nurturance in others, and the positive responses to him by other adults as well as peers undoubtedly has been extremely important.... He has a desire to achieve in order to make up for his sad, lean days. He is mature, intelligent, dedicated, and realistic about himself. He is not expressive but has deep feelings and emotions. There is a sense of poignancy about the boy that I found appealing."

Well liked as Stuart was by the other project members and by peers during junior high school, he essentially stuck to one friend, a boy from a relatively well-to-do family who lived not far from him and with whom he spent almost all of his time. The two were considered virtually inseparable; what one did, the other joined. Stuart said later that his grandmother disliked his friend and had forbidden him to associate with that boy, but he continued to do so despite her disapproval. Though generally permissive about Stuart's activities, at times she became "almost hysterical" about the association of the two boys and would even telephone that boy's home to insist that Stuart come home. Many years later Stuart explained that his grandmother objected because his friend had enough money to do what he wanted (such as going to the movies) and she felt that he was too much of a distraction to Stuart.

After reviewing all of the materials available for the junior high years, our personality assessors gave Stuart the highest possible ratings on "dependability," "wide interests," "appears intelligent," and "ambitious." Few if any other study members evoked such a consensus among the judges. At the other extreme in ratings—the attributes that were least applicable to Stuart—were "negativistic," "deceitful," "self-indulgent," "withdraws when frustrated," and "brittle ego defenses." The judges found Stuart to be an unusually mature, intellectually invested, and mentally healthy young adolescent. He scored in the upper 5 to 15 percent on each of the components of planful competence, with the highest score on "intellectually invested."

Senior High School, 1936–1938

Surprisingly, Stuart did not go to University High, where most of his friends went from junior high, but rather to a technical high school where most of the students were much less academically oriented. Perhaps some of the staff surmised the reason for this decision on his part, but none put it as succinctly as he did twenty years later when he was bringing his history up to date: "It hurt too much when I wasn't elected" as class president in the ninth grade. This was one of the very few instances in which Stuart's behavior seems to have been self-defeating, but even here there were compensations. Tech had a large representation of Italian-American Catholic working-class youngsters, and Stuart later said this had broadened his perspective by his getting to know a very different set of cultural norms and values from those of his Scottish grandmother and predominantly middle-class peers. At the time of his transfer to Tech, he must have had some qualms about the decision, for he missed his old friends. By his second year at Tech, he was more comfortable with himself and popular with his peers. He had learned that "kids from the other side of the tracks could be smart" even if they were not always neat and clean. He became more comfortable with girls and began to date.

Interviewed in her home in 1936, Stuart's grandmother was again found to be cooperative but too repressed, shy, and uncommunicative to give a satisfactory interview. The interviewer's description of the house and its furnishings was graphic: "The living room was bare, scarcely furnished, ugly; a coal grate occupied the fireplace opening, a few chairs, one an old rocker, others straight chairs, a table and threadbare rug were scattered about. Old-fashioned lace curtains hung at the windows." The grandmother, speaking hesitatingly in a low voice in an apologetic manner, expressed no hopes, desires, or curiosity about Stuart nor was she helpful in giving information. She did show pride that Stuart held the rank of Eagle Scout and thought that other boys liked him—in fact, that he was a favorite. The interviewers wrote: "She said his first night home from senior high school, he put his head down on the table, said he felt just awful, that he was homesick for Claremont (junior high school). However he likes senior high now, his grandmother added."

Stuart regularly attended Sunday school at the Presbyterian church and read the Bible. He read history and newspaper editorials and appeared to have much more interest in national and world affairs than the study group as a whole. Reading was one of his major pleasures. He reported that he also enjoyed studying, listening to the radio, and riding in automobiles. A staff member summed up: "In general his interests seemed quite adult and those an intelligent, maturing, well-adjusted boy would have." He appeared to have an unusual ability to use time productively, in both work and play.

But he could also be a problematic adolescent at times. It appeared that for a period in 1937, Stuart and his best friend acted rather wildly and irresponsibly on a number of occasions. One observer, obviously annoyed with Stuart, described his behavior at the time of physiological testing. She noted that he first appeared very self-conscious and then, with his friend, acted very immaturely:

> He seems to think he is quite the man-about-town. . . . He is quite boisterous in his manners. However, his actions during breakfast were far from those of a man. [He and his friend] began acting like badly trained children. They wanted to tear the place up and walk off with things.

A month or so later, another observer characterized Stuart and his friend as engaging in

> reckless and irresponsible pranks, marking up the walls, trying to spirit away copies of *Life* under their sweaters. Were fairly incorrigible in these tricks, enjoyed being chased out on the front lawn, but good-natured about what they did and amused, that even the pencil marks were not hard to forgive. Spontaneous, humorous happy boys.

The period of acting up seems to have been limited to a matter of a few months, and then the mature, earnest Stuart was back in control. He was already thinking about college, and was concerned to learn the relative merits of Stanford and the University of California (Berkeley) for a medical student and the relative social standing of fraternity and nonorganization men.

Throughout the high school years, as he had done in junior high school, Stuart filled out many psychological inventories and questionnaires. One dealt with wishes, dreams, and fears. The only "wish" Stuart checked was, in 1938, "to get along better with my father and mother." Most often, Stuart seems to have checked questions related to his parents in terms of his grandmother, although at times he included his parents in his thinking. In 1937 he wished his grandmother agreed more with modern children's ideas. He wished she could be happier and have better health in most of those years. Between 1936 and 1938, he wished no one in his family ever quarreled. Only in the early years (never in senior high school) did Stuart say he dreamed about his father and his mother. In the "fears" section, Stuart in 1935, 1936, and 1937 checked a fear that someone in his family might die.

Stuart felt that his grandmother liked him well enough but not better than his siblings. Sometimes, he said, she treated one or both of them better than she treated him. He felt proud of his brother and sister when they were praised; nonetheless, he checked that he fought with them a good deal no matter how hard he tried not to.

The ratings as to whom Stuart loved most in his family are particularly interesting: grandmother 1, mother 2, father 3, brother 4, sister 5, best boy friend 6. He continued to include his parents in his mind as part of the family constellation. One wonders what he thought when he filled out those ratings; although his parents were dead, is this the way he held them in his thoughts?

When asked, "What do you like to do best?" Stuart checked, "Stay and play in the schoolyard and athletics, clubs or games." There were no checks beside "Having friends come to my house." In response to "What would you do if worried about something?" he checked, "Talk to my mother or father about it and ask a friend about it."

Stuart felt he was quite well accepted by others, and indeed he was. He checked that he wished to be like the boys who are most popular in school but not to an extreme degree. He did not want to be like boys who are considered to be queer or different from other boys. He indicated he preferred to do things with one or two others rather than be by himself or with a whole crowd, and he wished there were more kids to play with living near his home.

When asked in another inventory if he liked to have people tell him how to do things, he checked, "I like to do things my own way," each year except 1938, when he checked, " I hate to be told what to do." When asked what he did when he was criticized, he checked each year, "I often feel hurt but don't say anything."

In the section dealing with wishes and aspirations, he wished to live in a nicer home with beautiful furniture. He checked that he was like the "boy who worked after school and on Saturdays" and that he felt good about this.

Responding to the query, "What sort of person would you like to be?" Stuart through 1937 checked, "I want to be a leader in whatever town I live in"; in 1938 he checked, "I want to be a very great person and do great things that people will talk about."

In 1937 and 1938 Stuart reported his vocational aspiration was to be a doctor. Earlier, he had thought he wanted to be an engineer. Stuart moved from an interest in things to an interest in people. He seems to have been reasonably certain of his future vocation as a doctor by the age of 17.

In all six years when he filled out an inventory dealing with "attitudes toward reality," Stuart checked that when he felt lonely, he would "find someone to talk to or be with." He did not wish to be like anyone he had either read about or seen in a show, scoring nearly at the bottom of the group in that category. In an interview years later, he reported that he had much admired the rather macho coaches in high school. Some years Stuart felt he wanted to be grown up, others that he wanted to be grown up not right now but gradually, as he was doing. He did not see himself as much of a worrier in any of the listed categories, nor did he "often feel terribly unhappy," a question to which he checked "no" across the board.

Reviewing Stuart's responses to a series of inventories that asked about his likes, dislikes, political views, social philosophy, and the like, one of the staff psychologists wrote:

This individual's social attitudes appear to be still in a period of formation. Although he is often inconsistent and there are some startling contrasts in the ideas he accepts or rejects, together there seems to be an underlying direction in which his attitudes are going. He becomes more and more consistently liberal in his thinking. He rejects stereotypes which the majority accept. For example, the statement "Everyone should be a booster for his city" is rejected by him every year where 85% to 88% of the boys agree with it. The statement "My country right or wrong" is also rejected by him as compared with only 15% to 24% of the others. One of the traits which seems to characterize the boy's answers on the tests is an idealistic impatience of intolerance and provincial traditions. He believes increasingly in civil liberties. In summary this individual shows no significant change of attitude since 1935 when he first took the test. The main trend has been an increasing consistency in the liberalism of his social outlook.

In early 1938, Stuart was one of four who ran for vice-president of the student body and addressed the high school assembly. A staff observer reported:

While nervous, he was outstanding for his originality and his control of the situation. Was probably the most humorous of the four on the platform. Mentioned as part of his platform the holding of one or two social events to which only boys would be invited. That idea greeted with silence, which would indicate that he lost ground rapidly with his voting public by including such an unwelcome thought. He lost that election but he was undismayed, planned to run for another office he wanted next term.

On the ski trip to Lake Tahoe in Stuart's senior year, an observer noted that he "showed considerable independence of the group though not in any way defiant or defensive. Brought all his own food and ate it at the appropriate meal times instead of having breakfast and lunch in the hotel dining room with the rest." Unable to afford restaurant meals, Stuart had brought sandwiches, which he ate "with almost awesome dignity" in the words of another observer.

In March 1938 Stuart talked with a counselor who seems to have been a favorite of his about a romance that had broken up. When asked whether he thought this girl was all right, he was quoted as saying: "Oh, sure. I have an ideal, you see, and I stuck it on her because she looked sort of like it. Then I realized that she wasn't really that. I'm through with romance. I guess when I'm in college I'll find some girl I like."

Stuart seems to have been quite attached to that particular female counselor; he danced with her at social events and talked with her rather than with girls his own age. He asked again about fraternities and worried about the morals of fraternity houses, asking with little embarrassment about "what they expect me to do, I mean, go the limit? I guess I'm kind of a goody-goody boy. To tell you the truth I haven't gone in for these things much. I never drink—oh, I guess I had a beer at my friend's house once." He did not smoke, either. He was not apologetic, merely expressing serious concern about what conflicts there might be with his code of behavior when he got to college.

On a hiking trip in 1938, Stuart again talked to that counselor very straightforwardly with a minimum of self-consciousness about his romance and asked whether she thought he ought to kiss the girl. "He said he'd had little experience in necking, but he had put his arm around this girl and thought she would like to have him kiss her. He was chiefly worried about what she would think of him. He also talked about his increasingly precarious friendship with his long-time best friend. He'd discovered his friend's inferior intellect, lack of interest in school subjects, different taste in friends."

Summary of Adolescent Material

In the early 1960s, as we prepared to analyze the follow-up data, three psychologists read all of the adolescent material for the high school years and made predictions regarding adult outcomes. None knew anything about Stuart's subsequent history. They came to remarkably similar formulations.

All three thought Stuart would marry somewhere between ages 22 and 29; all three expected him to have two to four children; all three expected him to do four years of graduate work, attaining a professional level of occupation in science (medicine). Each felt remarkably confident about the predictions.

The striking factor about the adolescent material related to Stuart is its remarkable consistency. From his first days with the study at age 11, Stuart was seen as unusually intelligent, mature for his age, and competent. The Q-sort descriptions of Stuart's personality in senior high were remarkably similar to those from the junior high years. Again, he was seen by all raters as absolute tops in dependability and "wide interests" but also now in "values intellectual matters" and "is an interesting, arresting person." Again essentially the same attributes as in junior high were seen as not typical, and again Stuart scored near the top on all three components of planful competence. Stuart Campbell's scores on the Q-sort components are given in Table A3 in Appendix A.

One reviewer of the data on Stuart Campbell at the end of high school, tremendously impressed by this young man from a relatively impoverished background, attributed his superior adaptation to the adverse circumstances of his early years. He had been able to translate those circumstances into challenges that could be met. Like the exiled Duke in Arden Forest in Shakespeare's *As You Like It,* he might have said, "Sweet are the uses of adversity!" Indeed, on at least one occasion he had reported that he thought he had more courage because of the circumstances of his life. He never deplored those circumstances.

STUART AT AGES 37 TO 39

Between March 1958 and January 1960 Stuart was interviewed nine times by a perceptive male psychologist about the same age as

Stuart. He was described as having "close-cropped gray hair, a rather homely but pleasant face, a nice smile which lights up his face.... He's rather witty but deadpans as he goes. He is well-dressed, close-knit, rather slim, moved around in his chair and yet did not seem tense or uncomfortable nor at all involved with the status problems that doctors often get into in similar situations."

Stuart had indeed become a physician, a pediatrician. He now practiced in a small town nestled into the hills in a northwestern state. He had married early, soon after finishing college, had served in the navy toward the end of World War II and again during the Korean War, and was the father of five children. Let us review this transitional period from the time we last had seen Stuart.

In the interviews conducted when he was in his late thirties, Stuart provided many of the details of his childhood that we had lacked. He confirmed almost everything we had learned from him and from observers about him during his adolescence and conveyed a good deal of information about the climate in which he had grown up. The interviewer probed to elicit Stuart's memories of his father. We do not have all of Stuart's exact words, but in summary the interviewer reported: "His memories of his father were meager, but they were nice memories." Stuart had said, "He [father] was good to me all the time.... He was indulgent and he was proud of me.... He would bring me candy, sometimes candy canes so big I couldn't even eat them." But Stuart also remembered his father's coming home in a taxi: "I remember seeing him being unsteady and drunk." It was this side of his father's character, his drunkenness and irresponsibility, that Stuart's grandmother had harped upon, thereby tarnishing but not eradicating the warm memories. Stuart remembered the Scottish phonograph records his father had had, and he kept them and later played them after his father had gone.

Stuart thought he resembled his father in some ways. An uncle had told him he got his intelligence from his father, whom he characterized as "a brilliant man." Stuart thought he also inherited his father's impulsiveness. The father had been a rebel and, as a seaman, a wanderer. Stuart recalled how he had enjoyed that aspect of his navy service.

We learned that his sister had had a much more difficult childhood and adolescence. She had been treated much more harshly by their grandmother than Stuart had, and she rebelled. Conflict was so extreme that she was eventually placed in a foster home. She attended business school rather than college, and she had married young.

Stuart and his younger brother had not gotten along well in the early years. (Stuart had viewed him as a pest.) The younger boy had gone to a tuberculosis sanitarium when he was 4. Stuart reported that he had had "all sorts of good intentions" toward his brother when he returned home, but it was not long before they "clashed pretty steadily." "When I got stuck with him I either ditched him or picked on him." Later, when Stuart was in medical school and his brother in college, they had a couple of fistfights. Nevertheless, the younger boy followed in the older one's footsteps and became a physician (with Stuart's help). The two now had a harmonious relationship.

We learned more about Stuart's boyhood relationship with Bill, his best friend in the high school years, who had lived close by. They shared interests in scouting, but there was another big plus in the relationship. Bill had a father and a mother, too. "That was important," said Stuart. "As a matter of fact, I remember he had a very pretty mother. I was quite stimulated by her when I was 14." Stuart had his first drink, a beer, with her before a scout meeting one night. And Bill taught him to drive a car.

This interviewer explored more thoroughly than most others his respondent's adolescent sexual development, and Stuart was much franker than most other study members. Stuart said that he had just started to go out with girls in high school when the acne began, and he felt unattractive; it bothered him a great deal. For one thing, he had started masturbating when he was about 15, and he remembered reading somewhere that acne was related to masturbation: "I felt that everyone could tell what I was doing just by looking at me. I felt guilty.... I was an Eagle Scout, and I had a lot of fear and a lot of guilt."

Stuart described his adolescent fantasies about sex, so common among middle-class boys of the pre–World War II era, and dealt with in novels like *Catcher in the Rye* but seldom mentioned by our subjects. At a Camporee, Stuart recalled, the boys had sat around talking about girls and reading spicy literature. Once his friend had a car, they followed girls by car and whistled at them. They always hoped they would find a "fast" girl and pick her up, but they never did. While sexual mores were in transition in the 1920s and 1930s,

Stuart and his friends lived in a very different world than would their children.

He had dated rather often in senior high but never even kissed the girls he dated. The interviewer wondered why it never occurred to him to kiss the girls. "Sure, it occurred to me," he said, "but I would never dream of making any advances." He always dreamed of "finding a sexy girl around, like married or something like that," but he never did. He clearly separated in his mind "nice girls," who were as inhibited as he was, from the ones who smoked and petted and "weren't nice girls." He was not attracted to the latter and did not want to go out with them.

Reviewing his adolescent years, Stuart reported satisfaction with his relationships and his good grades, though they were never as good as he, or his grandmother, would have liked. He felt he could have done better but was too easily caught up in other interests, including political and philosophical discussions. He was not a rebel; in fact, he felt he was high on conformity. He would like to have developed more leadership ability, and he was never as good at athletics as he had dreamed he might be.

Before he finished high school, Stuart knew he was going straight on to college. His dream was to go to Stanford, although he knew he did not have the money. Nevertheless, he visited Stanford, where he was entertained overnight. He was eager to know the difference in cost and social standing between members of fraternities and nonmembers. He applied for a scholarship and got one for $200, a significant amount of money in those days, but it would hardly permit enrollment at Stanford. He settled for the University of California, his second choice, and enrolled. He wanted very much to join a fraternity and was rushed by several but lacked the money to join. He had to live at home, of course, so, he said, his social life at Cal was "no joy." A meeting with his favorite member of the study staff revealed that he was quite disgruntled in his first year. The academic work stimulated him and for the first time he began to study hard, but he had no close male friends and felt out of touch. It appears that he experienced a fear of being rebuffed. Although he tried out for various freshman sports, he soon gave those up. He did join the naval Reserve Officers' Training Corps, a source of a uniform as well as training. A commuting student, he was never involved in university life except academically. He felt the same way about medical school. He wanted to go to

Stanford and was accepted there, but again could not afford it, so he went to the University of California Medical School. "It's a really snobbish attitude I guess I still have. If I was given a choice now, I'd still prefer Harvard."

Stuart spoke of his political interests, developed in high school and expanded in college:

> I identified with the New Deal and with Roosevelt—the New Age of Emancipation for the Working Man—that's who I identified with. I was sore for not being in a fraternity and I hated fraternities and sororities with a passion, although I went out with sorority girls. It was a very personal thing with me. This was denied me so I turned against it strongly.

At several points in the interview, this tendency of Stuart to put down what he could not have but really wanted was manifest. At some point he had become aware of this tendency, which, when it operates unconsciously, psychiatrists call a "reaction formation."

Philosophy courses in college led him to question some of his religious beliefs and eventually to dropping out of Sunday school. He was beginning to experience a very different intellectual world from that of his grandmother and of the high school.

From the time he was a college freshman, he went steady for four or five years with the same girl. Other than that girl, he did not make or have many college friends; he was too busy working and studying. "I went steady with this girl for five years and eventually, well, I married her." He said they had kissed and necked and finally had premarital intercourse. They became engaged when he was in medical school and married, reluctantly, he said, when he was 23:

> We married each other just because we had become habituated with each other. I didn't have a lot of enthusiasm really for the marriage. We were married at the time in the war when everyone got married. She felt the same way but we didn't confide in one another. We were really losing interest in one another.

There was a lot of guilt over their sexual behavior. They had had a false pregnancy earlier, at a time when it would have been economically disastrous to get married, and that had contributed to the guilt. He added,

We had a fairly unsatisfactory sexual relationship after we married but it was good before. After eight months she confessed that she was getting no joy out of intercourse. As a matter of fact I had taken out a couple of other girls on the side during that period, too. She asked for a divorce. I tried to get us to a psychiatrist but she told me she really didn't love me anymore and went home to mother. I got the divorce then.

Stuart thought that it might have been a good marriage if they had been more mature. He thought both of them had gotten off easily, the marriage had not produced a child, and neither was badly scarred. He added that he would probably not have gone ahead with the divorce on his own but she had had the courage to say that she did not love him. When she was able to say it, he realized that he really did not love her. It was at this point that his training was completed, and he entered the navy.

Stuart served as a medical officer in both World War II and the Korean War. The early part of World War II was rough because his brother was a pilot. Stuart had wanted to serve in the military but did not want to leave his fiancé. He had gone straight into an internship in the navy following his clinical training. Then he was sent to a receiving hospital in San Francisco and three days later shipped out.

Stuart was the junior medical officer on a ship bound for Eniwetok, a Pacific island under attack, in the later days of the war. Standing off the beachhead, the medical staff had to deal with a wide range of casualties. He was ill prepared for the kinds of surgery he was called upon to perform. He described several aspects of the experience on board that first ship that were traumatic for him, not the least of which was the tiny living space, with three tiers of bunks—his at the bottom—all well below deck, and the small escape hatch. Among other things, he had had night terrors and in fact still had them occasionally. He served under an older physician who put him down because of his limited experience yet never helped him deal with his deficiencies. His shortened medical training had left him without many needed skills. On his next ship, he was senior medical officer, and after that he said he had fun in the navy.

Stuart remarried in 1945 after a short courtship to a young woman, Susan, whom he had met just before he shipped out. He had just completed his internship; she had been a student nurse. They were immediately attracted to each other. She subsequently went to meet Stuart when his ship docked 500 miles to the south, a trip that cost her her place in the nursing school. Immediately after the war ended, they were married, while Stuart was still in the navy. After he left the navy, he set up practice in a small California town outside the Bay Area. Their first child was born at this time. "I wanted to get married badly," Stuart said, and apparently Susan did, too.

Soon they moved back to the Bay Area so Stuart could begin residency training in pediatrics. Two years later, they moved to the area where they now live, and Stuart and Susan put down roots.

Leaving his family had been a traumatic experience during the Korean War, but "once I was in it was all right; everyone was in the same boat. The Korean War was fought by kids just out of high school and men like me who were yanked in.... There was total disorganization." This was undoubtedly a more difficult time for Susan than for Stuart.

When he was asked to describe his wife, he mentioned first that she was an only child, of Scandinavian stock, and "a strong person in her own right." "Also," Stuart added, "there is an identity." By this he meant Susan was, like himself, a first-generation American. His first wife came from a once-wealthy family to whom wealth was very important. Susan came from a hard-working immigrant family like his own. "She isn't religious at all," and there was some conflict over this between them, he said. Stuart stopped attending church for years but has been more interested in religion in recent years. "We have similar political feelings, similar attitudes about life, and success also."

Asked what might irritate him about his wife, he thought she spent money irresponsibly and was not a good money manager. It turned out that no one in the family had an allowance. Everyone had to come to him for money, and that was a bone of contention between his wife and himself. Susan thought she would like to have some money of her own to spend without his review. (When interviewed years later, she mentioned that what was most difficult for her was being dependent.) When he said, "But you can have anything you want," she replied, "No, I can't because I feel like I have to ask you for it." The interviewer noted that Stuart was laughing and said the matter was not settled yet and he could see a lot on her side of the question. The interviewer added, "I think what he hasn't faced is how hard it is for him to give up the control that he exercises this way."

At 38, Stuart and Susan had five children, ranging in age from 3 to 12, the eldest a girl, the rest boys. He had a successful private practice as a pediatrician. Since their marriage, Susan had not worked outside the home. A doctor's hours being erratic at best, the raising of the children was largely in her hands. She had to do most of the disciplining. Stuart said he had been more indulgent with the children than she, but she was the one who was with them all day. He felt that Susan was moodier than he, though she did not seem so outwardly. He reported a lot of shouting and yelling in their home but said they respected each other and their children, wanted them to be individuals and to understand that fighting does not mean lack of love.

Stuart felt that his work had made it impossible for him to spend as much time as he would like with the children. Nevertheless, notwithstanding his erratic hours, the family went on skiing trips and sailing and other excursions together. In another area, Stuart felt he had not been able to do too well as a father: "I think of the masculine role as a craftsman, fixing things, making things.... Kids like to see their father do things around the house. I hate to abdicate as a carpenter.... to see the kids hang around and watch this *real* man make things." On the other hand, he listened to his children and participated with them in athletics. He thought that their home, like many other suburban homes, overemphasized education and books. "We try to give our children every opportunity. Sometimes it is a mistake; I think too often we carry them around too much." He meant literally chauffeuring them. He felt it most important "to give a kid a sense of his own worth."

At 38, Stuart enjoyed his pediatric practice. "I have a pretty heavy practice, I never seem to have any time." He wished the pace were more leisurely but found that hard to control. He had considered working in a group practice or health maintenance organization but said that the best doctors in those groups complained the most, so he stayed where he was. He characterized the practice of medicine as "mostly a muscle activity" and noted that he missed the intellectual stimulation that he had as a student. He thought those who seemed to enjoy medicine most were at the university, but he supposed the other side always looked greener. Stuart was irritated by the dependence of people on their physicians. Clearly he took his responsibility very seriously.

Considering his current situation compared to where he had hoped to be in his teens, Stuart felt that he had done satisfactorily. His goals had become more limited now; his ambition to be a brilliant research man had not been achieved. But "in middle age you begin thinking you do not want to sacrifice as much, you take milder, more obtainable goals. . . . The people I used to think of as being in a rut I now find take on heroic proportions because of the qualities of honesty and steadfastness." He would choose to be a physician again if he had the choice to make but perhaps not a pediatrician. Stuart thought he might have liked dermatology or radiology, with their more regular hours, or perhaps orthopedics or eye work, where there is more surgery. But on the other hand, his greatest satisfaction came from "the sense of achievement when I treat a child, when I do a lot of good for a child. Often you can prevent a parent from doing the wrong thing. . . . a few words will often do a lot of good. [When things go well] it makes the day complete, and when they don't I get irritated and truculent."

While still a "confused registered Democrat" who felt that the Democrats were better leaders, especially in a crisis, at 38 Stuart found himself favoring the Republican position on domestic issues like taxation and the budget. He regarded it very important that the coutnry, which he saw as "the best country possible, the best country that has ever been devised," stay strong militarily to ensure peace and that it should be more vigorous in helping the rest of the world. "The combat is in winning the rest of the world to our way of life." On the one hand he thought that people expected too much of the government; on the other he wanted more federal support for hospitals and education and acknowledged that he was in a "confused state about this."

Stuart described himself as hard-headed about crime, feeling Americans should be tough on law breakers. His attitude toward minorities, particularly blacks, seemed a conscious effort to be fair and equitable in terms of civil rights, flavored with a certain amount of prejudice against blacks. He felt men were much freer and less restricted than women and could not see much advantage to being a woman. After some thought, he considered that the creation of a child and raising a child must be a source of tremendous satisfaction for a woman. In both men and women, he most admired a sense of humor, tenacity, "enjoying even tough going," honesty, and courage. He particularly admired in women femininity, gentleness, and the ability to be pleasant.

Thus far, Stuart felt, he had had a "good life ... I feel sometimes like a lucky guy, that I have not earned a lot of it, that I will someday have to pay for it. Of course I was fortunate to grow up in a community where I had every opportunity." He had had "every opportunity" largely to the extent that he had created his opportunities.

Asked to chart the "best and worst periods" of his life on a form prepared for that purpose, Stuart produced a unique plot. Instead of a smooth or jagged line approximating his ratings over the years, he gave almost every year up to his late 20s an unequivocal rating, discriminating more sharply than any other study member. Moreover, he did it quickly and decisively, to the interviewer's amazement. The chart and some of the labels he placed on the high and low points are given in Figure 4.1.

Figure 4.1. Life Satisfaction Chart for Stuart Campbell

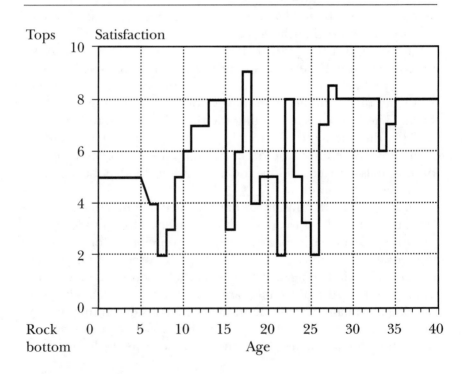

Labeled Points on Stuart Campbell's Life Satisfaction Chart

Age	
1–4	No remembered difficulties
5	Moved to Oakland
6	Death of mother
7	First grade—then out of school
8	Felt like a sissy when back to school
9–11	Much playground activity, adjusting to school
12	Boy Scouts
13–14	Summer camps, happy in junior high, vice-president Claremont, Eagle Scout
15	Acne, defeated as student body president
16	High school at Tech, new school, few friends
17	Acne cleared, popular at Tech, track team, pack trips
18	Into University of California (UC), could not afford fraternity
19–20	Grades at UC adequate, steady girlfriend
22	Working, fear of no money, first year at medical school
22	Steady job for income, medical school much easier
23	Uncertain about marriage but went ahead
24	Marriage ended in divorce
25	Sea duty before World War II ended
26	Remarried, happy in navy
27	Began medical practice, good income, first child
28–29	Residency training at University of California at San Francisco, second child
30–32	Pediatric practice, third and fourth children
33	Recalled to sea duty, worried about money and security
34	Back from navy, hostile about starting again
36–39	Happy marriage, secure practice, good income, fifth child

His "absolute tops" on the life chart completed at age 39 was for his senior year of high school. His acne had cleared, he was popular, he was on the track team, and he was enjoying pack trips and many other activities. Next, just a bit of lower, was the year he and Susan had their first child and he started medical practice. He was

27. Subsequent years were uniformly rated 8 except for the period of his recall into the navy during the Korean War.

Stuart rated three years very low, at 2: the year his mother died, the first year of medical school (with the need to earn money as well as the pressures of a speeded-up program of study), and sea duty the year following his divorce. Age 15, his first year at Tech, overlapping his election loss in junior high, he rated his satisfaction only a little higher, as he did the year of the divorce. The life satisfaction chart presents a graphic illustration of the vicissitudes and turmoil that marked Stuart's transition from adolescence to adulthood.

Summing Up at Age 40

Much had happened to Stuart in the two decades since his adolescence: He had attended college and medical school; seen military service at the end of World War II and during the Korean War; married, divorced, and remarried; served a residency in pediatrics; established his medical practice; fathered five children; and established a home and a reputation in an upper-middle-class community. His one failure, his first marriage, seems to have occurred with remarkably little trauma for either party.

Stuart's political thinking had moved in a conservative direction, not surprisingly given his profession. He had markedly changed his views on patriotism and now was supportive rather than critical of the status quo, in favor of a strong military and tough law enforcement, and ambivalent about the uses of federal money, which he saw as feeding the tendency of people to grow "soft" with too much governmental subsidy. In many respects, then, he had swung widely away from his adolescent views. He was, on the whole, happy with his wife, his children, his profession, his life, and himself. He had achieved many of his youthful goals and had modified those he found unrealistic. The predictions of Stuart's adolescent evaluators had been well borne out.

Despite the turmoil of his early adult years and the changes in his attitudes toward patriotism and the military, Stuart's personality ratings at age 40 were remarkably similar to those made when he was in senior high. No other study member showed such consistency, evidenced by a correlation coefficient of .83 for the two assessments made independently more than twenty years apart. Given the fact that no two raters were ever in perfect agreement, this high a correlation suggests almost no change at all. Again, on every component of competence, Stuart scored near the top.

STUART AT AGE 49

In 1969, when he was age 49, an interviewer described Stuart as "a tall, white-haired handsome man who has a ruddy complexion." She found him

> probably the most interesting, verbally fluent and complex man I have seen. He is very bright . . . and also remarkably sensitive and has put this skill in a pivotal place in his life as a pediatrician and "parent advisor." His masculine identity seems quite complex. He grew up with little contact with men yet he himself is very masculine but his occupation involves using the nurturant aspects of the feminine role. . . . He has great zest for life and little guilt over any past misdeeds except his first marriage. . . . He is an outstanding person.

Stuart now had six children ranging in age from 8 to 23. The oldest and youngest were girls, the other four boys. The first of two interviews focused on Stuart's discussion of his children. His description and discussion of each child was informed by his respect for them as individuals, a good-humored attitude toward each and toward himself as a parent, candor, and understanding, or at the very least the effort to understand. Clearly Stuart not only loved but liked his children. He had observed as well as participated in their growth and development with thoughtful, perceptive interest.

It had not all been easy. Stuart thought that one of his assets as a parent was that he could always communicate with his children. There were lots of arguments and many fights and disagreements, but more pervasive than the disagreements were the agreements, especially those on basic values: honesty, trust, the ability to laugh at oneself, not to deceive oneself, compassion, respect for other people, the desire not to inflict pain—social, physical, or psychological. Stuart felt that his children, whatever their individual differences and their differences with him, all had a strong sense of ethics.

The children, whom Stuart described in some detail, were all very different. Some were much more negative about America's

Vietnam involvement than Stuart was, and he was troubled by the tendency of his children to denigrate the United States and its policies. Like many other adolescents, a couple of the older children had gone through phases of rebellion and had had problems, but good relationships generally prevailed. The younger children were perhaps being raised somewhat more indulgently than the older, but a major difference was that they were receiving a religious orientation (Presbyterian) that the oldest had not been exposed to. Susan, whose lack of religious feeling had at first bothered Stuart, had become much more involved in the church, and Stuart's own involvement had been rekindled through a man whom he admired and who was scoutmaster at the church.

In a discussion of his parents and their backgrounds, Stuart mused about the Scottish culture. He saw it as a "funny mixture of the highlander who is wild, a big drinker and fighter, a great lover, charming and completely irresponsible, and the lowlander who iswho tight-fisted, steady and true, a hard worker and canny and never wastes money." Stuart saw himself as a lowlander: "I'm not a romantic. I'd rather have the security and the money and the reputation of being a good Presbyterian than I would be a gambler."

Stuart's discussion of his wife paralleled his account in earlier interviews. What he liked best about her was that "she is a very honest person and she's very critical of me and I actually like that because she's quite straightforward." They were close, and they communicated freely. As they had grown older, he felt they had also grown more comfortable with one another. Their sexual relationship was better than it was when they were first married. They could laugh at the same things, they could fight, and then they could laugh at themselves.

Stuart noted that he had had no masculine role models and hardly knew any men until about the seventh grade. He thought that as a consequence he was really pretty much female oriented: "I never felt the least bit uncomfortable with women but I would say that I might be still a little bit uncomfortable with men, maybe as a carryover." Here we noted a reversal of what Stuart had told us a decade earlier.

Stuart saw his greatest strengths as a parent in his ability to communicate with his children and in their shared interests and ideals: "I think I'm intelligent to a moderate degree and I'm perceptive and I have, I think, a fair amount of sensitivity to other people. People interest me, I'm people oriented and I can feel people and can also recall how I used to feel and this is a big advantage."

When comparing his own upbringing to that of his children, Stuart had one major regret: He felt that his children, like most other suburban children, had had insufficient life experience. They did not have to struggle for anything, were never deprived of anything, had not had to work for anything. Everything had been handed to them, sometimes whether they wanted it or not. They had been chauffeured around and had fewer needs to pit themselves against the realities of the world. They had been protected and cushioned, he implied, although several of them had traveled extensively. And he felt that, being a physician, he had not had enough time with his children.

Stuart was rarely home at night. He was either on call or attending meetings. He had just finished being chairman of a medical organization, and he was president of a children's hospital, chairman of the medical staff, and on the school board. He had never been busier. Furthermore, he added, now that he was gray-haired, he was considered a "wise man" who is supposed to help people. He just could not say it was time to go home when seven o'clock rolled around if there were important matters to be dealt with.

At 49, Stuart said his goal was "survival," and laughed. To practice good medicine and to keep his sanity was not always an easy task. Looking back, he felt that he had not had any really bad periods in his life except his very early years; overall, his life had been "a soft touch, I haven't had much stress at all. I haven't had any real tragedy in my life." He explained that he was too young to feel much when his mother died, and his grandmother was a vigorous, strong person who took good care of him and his siblings:

There was nothing we needed that she wouldn't give us. During the depression if I went downtown and said I wanted a movie projector, just a cheap toy kind of thing really, but still it was the kind of thing that she really should have said, "No, you can't have it," but she'd say, "Well, I don't know if you can have that or not, it's pretty expensive" but I'd get it. We talked about money and worried about it but we really didn't suffer anything, nor have I really suffered any since then.

Thus, Stuart rejected the idea that he had had a hard or deprived life, even in his early years. He thought that the struggles against economic adversity his family experienced had taught him valuable lessons. He now seemed to have forgotten the period of low morale during college and medical school. Much of his sense of satisfaction and personal worth apparently derived from the feeling that what he had he got on his own. He saw himself as a "kind of chronically optimistic" person. He no longer cared all that much about making a lot of money; it no longer interested him.

It was apparent that Stuart loved his work, both the physical and psychological aspects of his pediatric practice. He gave much extra time to the counseling aspects of his work. It was satisfying to be able to influence family attitudes and relationships in a positive way.

Politically, Stuart had become a Republican, though he admired some Democrats. He and his children had argued violently about the student demonstrations that began in the 1960s and continued to boil up. To Stuart they were a charade, a part of this affluent generation, full of phoniness. He believed in righting injustices, but he thought that a lot of the demonstrators just wanted to destroy "what we've got."

There was more than a suggestion of contradiction in Stuart's interview, with his claim to optimism but strong emphasis on security and caution, a concern for people manifest in his profession but at odds with some of his militaristic, conservative political views. Nonetheless, high self-esteem, good humor, an equable temperament, a generally positive attitude toward life, and strong values continued to characterize Stuart Campbell. He continued to show great continuity in general personality attributes, again scoring very high on each of the components of competence.

A 1969 Interview with Susan Campbell

Susan Campbell, four years younger than her husband, was 45 years old when first interviewed in 1969. The transcript of the interview contains many indications of laughter—sometimes laughter that drowned out what was being said. In summarizing her impression, the interviewer reported: "The whole impression is of a very natural, unaffected, unmade-up person. She has lovely teeth and she smiles a great deal. She moves her hands in a rather graceful way, seems relaxed and at ease while speaking...she looks at you directly and smiles.... She has a sort of starry, wide-eyed look on her face, as if everything was still a perpetual surprise." Throughout the interview, there was spontaneity, mirth, and a very high degree of openness.

Susan's account of the marriage and family life was entirely consonant with that of Stuart, but she naturally emphasized somewhat different aspects. She described the children and their development in some detail, including the aspects that were problematic and those that gave her great pleasure. She noted that there were very few restrictions on the children in the family—no rules telling them when they had to be in or that they had to behave in this or that way.

Postreview comment: Mrs. Campbell said that she had shown the first draft of this excerpt from her interview to one of her daughters, who had disagreed that there were no rules. As she thought more about it, she realized that there had been a few rules, but they were usually quite flexible, and a lot of negotiation went on. Her daughter commented that there might not have been flat rules, but there had been "expectations." Indeed, she commented that she would have liked to have had the rules more clearly spelled out.

Mrs. Campbell then offered to poll the other offspring (now well along in their adult years) as to what they remembered about rules in the family. Each remembered something that he or she had been expected to do: help either before or after dinner, let parents know where they were and when they would be home, practice the piano (each piece five times while mother was preparing dinner), do their homework, and so on. One son thought his parents had been permissive; another said, "Not permissive but liberal." It was clear that the Campbells were flexible. As one son said, "You took care of each situation as it came up so we grew to know what was expected of us." He tries to have the same flexibility with his own youngsters. A humorous note was added by the oldest daughter, who remembered that "you couldn't tell Mom and Dad to shut up." When the youngest son had done that at 2 or 3 years of age, the others were horrified.

In her study of whole families, based on interviews with parents and adolescent children in 1969–1970, Eliane Aerts had seen this family as prototypic of the following description, from the typology developed by Swanson (1974):

> In this family, it is hard to see the existence of standard procedures for the conduct of business. Often things are done, or not done, pretty much as the moment dictates. The parents may or may not consult with each other before coming to a decision or before setting out on some course of action. If either dislikes what the other is doing, his main recourse is to block his partner or to withhold resources (e.g., money, time, encourgement) that are necessary for the support of his partner's activities. Similarly, he will often find that, rather than consultation or discussion, the principal means to get his partner to take some action is to make resources available to the partner, earmarking them specifically for the purpose he intends.

As the older children had gotten into college, at least some of them had been experimenting, in the mode typical of the late 1960s, with drugs and sex. Their mother accepted this as a natural part of growing up and was not judgmental; she knew that her children were basically sound. Still, as she noted, when there were problems, "it hurt." As to how they handled such problems, she reported: "Stuart calls all the shots, because he's far more lenient than I would naturally be, and he respects the kids' individuality far more than I do."

INTERVIEWER: He doesn't discipline them?

SUSAN: He doesn't discipline anybody. (laughs) You know, he will be angry, but if anybody ever wants to do something, I can't remember his ever saying "No." [She went on to describe an instance in which her older daughter wanted to go to a fraternity weekend at Yosemite. Susan had said, "Over my dead body." But Stuart said, "Why not? Yosemite's beautiful this time of year."]

INTERVIEWER: Does that mean that there are relatively few rules and regulations in your home?

SUSAN: I can't think of any, except that when Daddy's tired, everybody has to be quiet! (laughs)

INTERVIEWER: Never things like hours, for example?

SUSAN: Oh, no. [Then she added,] But I always met them at the door when they came in, to see how they were.

On further thought, Susan reported in 1969 that there was one rule: no television on school nights for the youngest daughter. There had been no television set in the house when the others were little. But there was no particular bedtime for the children. Instead, the parents would simply report that they were going to bed at a certain time and then everyone would tend to go. If Stuart had a school board meeting or was kept out late by his medical practice, the boys often waited up so they could talk with him.

The interviewer asked about whether there were discussions in the family about moral questions having to do with the nature of right and wrong.

SUSAN: All the time.

INTERVIEWER: Who starts those?

SUSAN: Well, the kids. Right and wrong on the world political level mostly. This is their favorite pastime. It's been interesting to watch my radical free-wheeling husband. . . . I watch him defend the establishment like a stone wall. He's there and the kids pound on him. And it's incredible. Maybe his feelings have changed a lot since I first met him.

Postreview comment: On reading what she had reported twenty-one years earlier, Mrs. Campbell recalled that when she had questioned Stuart about his change of attitude with reference to "the establishment," he replied, "How can I attack the establishment when I *am* the establishment?"

SUSAN: The kids need to attack him hard. And he stands there, you know, and he says, "I'm not going to apologize for my generation. We've done what we could do." Stuart is the only Republican, you understand. But he's terribly well informed. He reads all the time, and he presents very good arguments. He presents the conservatives' case very well, and also can remind people what happened in the past.

The interviewer then asked about moral issues on a more personal level and Susan replied:

> Daddy calls the shots at our house, and everybody knows what he ex-
> pects, and there's never been any quarrel about that because he's
> uncompromising in insisting on honesty and obeying the law....
> Honesty and not hurting anybody. You know, other people have feel-
> ings and you don't step on anybody just for your own gain.

Susan mentioned some of the sources of disagreements in the
family. She would have liked more help from some of the children
with household tasks, but her husband felt very strongly that "the
kid who is focusing most on helping his mother is focusing in the
wrong way." She would have liked the children to be neater than
they were and at least to pick up their own dirty socks, but they preferred that she not go into their rooms: "And when we had a cleaning lady, I tried to pick up some of the stuff so she could clean. We
don't have a cleaning lady any more. It was too much stress getting
ready for her. All those important piles of papers that, you know,
she just put in one heap."

Susan Campbell described the hassles over the dining room
table, which had been alluded to by her husband:

> If Stuart and I ever get a divorce, it's going to be because of the din-
> ing room table, because everything that he brings home he puts on
> the dining room table—the Monday pile, the Tuesday pile, the
> Wednesday pile, the Thursday pile—there it all is, and he likes it that
> way. Well, it's right in the middle of the house and it distresses me
> because I love flowers and I think that's a good place to put an
> arrangement. It's the only place. It's right in the middle of my life!. . . .
> But this fight is still unresolved. We know how each other feels about
> it and we fight about it, because I pile it all over on the sideboard
> and he unpiles it. (laughs) It's a going fight and I don't know what
> we're going to do about it. But this is my feeling, this is my house to
> live in. It's also Stuart's house to live in. And I don't know how we'll
> ever resolve this conflict.

Susan left no doubt about her tremendous affection for and admiration for her husband:

He's a paradoxical man. I think he's both optimistic and gloomy, and very strong. He has this tremendous sense of responsibility, but he's very playful. He likes to play. He's a delightful companion. He's never boring. He feels very strongly about a lot of things. His scope is huge and he's always ready to try something new, you know. "Let's do it. Let's go. Let's try this." There's not enough time. Nobody has any energy left. (laughs)

Susan pointed out the other side of her husband's concern about her wanting to spend too much money:

We quarrel sometimes about what's important, which is the only thing anyone ever quarrels about, isn't it? Like he will say, "We go on an economy drive. All those kids in college and overhead is high and all this." And we have a big economy drive. But then the next minute he'll say, "I want you to come to Chicago with me because it's lonely in Chicago and I like it when you come." And this is in the same breath that he said, "We've got to stop spending all this money." And when I say, "But it would save $400 if I don't go to Chicago," he says, "But that's important!"

Strong feelings might be expressed in the Campbell household by father, mother, and children, but it was obvious from the responses of all that they enjoyed each other most of the time.

STUART AT AGE 61

An interviewer in 1982 found Stuart

a tall, fit-looking man of 61 with white hair, a ruddy complexion and a rather lined face. He looks his age but at the same time conveys an impression of great vigor. I found Stuart a very attractive man . . . easy to interview, fluent, even eloquent . . . There was a strong flavor of intimacy in the atmosphere of the interview. Stuart has an attractive smile, smiles often, and has considerable ability to laugh at himself . . . his face is mobile and responsive, he is very open, a vibrant, vigorous man.

As usual, Stuart was interestedly cooperative in all the interviews of this period. All of Stuart's children were now grown. Four of the six were or had been married, and there were three grandchildren. Sarah, her architect husband, and their two children lived next door, on Stuart's land. Stuart had built their house and was letting them buy it at a reasonable cost. Sarah had become a nurse. Stuart was very satisfied with her development and glad to have her next door; the relationship was close and mutually beneficial.

The oldest son, now a physician like his father, lived in a small eastern city and was married, with one child. The second son had become an attorney, as had the third, who lived in another northwestern state. He was married, but his marriage was in trouble, with the prospects for its survival dim. He had no children. Gary, the youngest son, had taken a degree in economics but had not yet settled on a vocation. Stuart was troubled that Gary seemed to be drifting, with little sense of direction. Lilnda, the youngest, was in college in southern California and doing well there.

Finally, all the children had left home; Stuart was responsible only for Linda's support. However, he had given a good deal of money to almost all of the others, primarily to enable them to buy homes. Despite his philosophy that children need to make it on their own, he wanted to provide for their security.

Stuart and Susan continued a work- and family-centered life. Susan now was helping Stuart in his office several afternoons a week, as well as one Saturday a month. She enjoyed the work. He saw the arrangement as productive for their future when he might cut down his practice and his staff. At the same time, he missed having Susan at home waiting for him with dinner on the table; he recognized that he had been indulged by his wife and family and by his nursing staff.

When asked how important being a physician was in determining his sense of self, Stuart replied, "It's very important that I'm a doctor. You kind of wonder after a while, what was I like before I was a doctor? Because you're always playing this role." But in the interviews, Stuart had always been far more frank and free of status concerns than most other physicians could be.

Stuart's sister had been working for him for a number of years. The independence she achieved through working helped resolve her marital problems. Stuart was still extremely busy and said he was enjoying medicine more than ever. He found new developments in his field fascinating. A particular stimulus for him had been the arrival of a new, young physician in a loose partnership.

That physician proved to be a workaholic; when Stuart had to take over his caseload, he had to work even harder than usual. The young physician was very competitive, bringing out all of Stuart's competitiveness. No allowances were made for age, he said, with considerable satisfaction. Stuart reported himself in excellent physical shape. He maintained a regular schedule of jogging and tennis, took care of himself, and felt full of energy and quite up to the demands of his profession. He expressed a very upbeat outlook in the structured interview.

In a more clinical interview on the same day but with a different interviewer, he appeared less sanguine. He thought he worried more and in a way was more insecure: "I still do things, force myself, try to prove to myself I'm alive and well. I compete in order to prove I'm all right." He wished he were more patient and tolerant and felt that his brusqueness was not his basic nature but the job. He also wanted to be more "courageous, recapture some of my optimism."

On issues of social concern, Stuart felt there had been both good and bad developments. He was rather unenthusiastic about the women's movement. His daughters often accused him of chauvinism, he said with a laugh. (He had always held strongly traditional views on sex typing; they had cost him an election in high school!) Stuart approved of efforts to enhance women's self-respect and dignity and of equal pay for equal work. On the other hand, in his practice he saw many working mothers whose children were placed in day care at a very early age. That, he felt, was sad, and probably harmful. He thought the sexual revolution had been essentially harmful for women, making sex objects of them. Although he did not feel that society should return to the guilt-ridden days of his youth, sexual license had gone too far, he thought.

Although still a skeptic and doubter, Stuart was participating in church and liked being there. His wife, who credited him with her conversion, had become more devout than he.

The Vietnam War again became a topic of discussion in this interview. It had been a cause of great conflict in the Campbell household, although less acknowledged in the 1969 interviews. Stuart and his sons had screaming fights; the smallest girl would cry, and even his third son would cry. Inevitably the situation would be adversarial: Stuart against his sons. He supported the war; they opposed it. He felt they should register for the draft;

they resisted. At one point in the interview Stuart indicated that he had supported Richard Nixon and approved of what he had done; at another he said he had little use for Nixon. In one interview he said that the United States should not have gone into the war, but having done so should have won it. In the other interview he felt that the United States should have gotten out of it sooner and saved a lot of lives. Clearly he was still greatly ambivalent. What he learned of the way the marines operated in that war changed his attitude; after that he never again recommended that a young man go into the marines.

Dealing with such issues had not been easy for Stuart. The boy who had rejected the statement, "My country, right or wrong," became a man strongly imbued with patriotism, the invincibility of America, the importance of America's role in the world. His own experiences in World War II and the Korean War had changed his attitudes toward war, the military, and America's preeminent role in defense of the free world. But by age 61 he was able to recognize, acknowledge, and even laugh about his own hypocrisy. One of his sons made that quite clear. Bill had told Stuart that in the light of the father's feelings, he, Bill, thought he should drop out of college and volunteer for Vietnam. Stuart was horrified. "You never volunteer!" he warned. He did see the contradictions in his own attitudes. In the end, his strongest conviction seemed to be that the United States should never have gone into that war and should have gotten out of it sooner. Nonetheless he did, perhaps still does, feel it "unfair" that students at the University of California should have cut classes, gone on strike, and passed out leaflets against the war, while he still supported the university with his taxes and subsidized his sons who were attending that university and doing those things that were exactly opposed to his point of view.

Despite the searing arguments, Stuart and his children maintained their closeness and were not alienated from one another. That was possible because they respected one another and argued from a position of independence—not financial independence necessarily but the independence of adulthood.

Assessed on the personality Q-sort at age 61, Stuart still showed the same salient characteristics noted from early adolescence. He was rated self-confident, intellectually invested, and highly dependable. Beyond these attributes that marked him as a man of great competence, he came closer to the ideal profile of psychological health mentioned in Chapter 2 than did any other member of the study. He was seen as modestly assertive, somewhat outgoing, and very much a warm and agreeable person.

A 1982 Interview with Susan Campbell

Again Susan Campbell gave a picture of the family, her husband, and their marriage that was consonant with what Stuart told his interviewer on the same day, when both came in together. We learned on that occasion that Susan had not contemplated having a family before she met Stuart.

> I was never going to get married at all. Didn't want to get married. I said I never want to be anybody's wife; I didn't want to be anybody's mother. That's not for me. . . . And, well, he's always been very busy. I had told my classmates that anyone who marries a doctor is an idiot. I don't want to be the last person my husband thinks about. You see? God heard all those proud statements!
>
> Stuart asked if I liked children. I said, no, I don't even know any children. I didn't want any children. Because I had a plan, you see, I was going to be a career woman. My mother said, "Never be dependent on a man." Then the conflict has been exactly that. I hate being dependent, and I used to get furious with my own dependency.
>
> I'd think, "I'll just take these children and leave and I'm never coming back and I can manage perfectly well without you." . . . And poor Stuart hadn't done anything at all! It was just that awful feeling of being utterly dependent.

But Susan continued: "I'd get over these things very quickly. He's really very nice." She described her life as very full and satisfying. She was playing the cello, teaching Sunday school, and working in Stuart's office afternoons, as well as babysitting for her eldest daughter's two children. "I'm sure I've had a richer life than I would have if I had *not* gotten married. . . . I've had a very full life. . . . I feel like I am chairman of the board now."

The children had done well, and they were a delight to her: "What makes me happy as a clam is when the children, our grown-up children, get together and enjoy each other's company, even when I'm not there. I like that." It was obvious that the family was very much in touch. Life with Stuart was still interesting and somewhat unpredictable. They were now doing more in the way of attending concerts and plays, and they still walked and talked a great deal.

Asked what kind of a wife she had been over the years, Susan thought a moment and then responded, "Obedient. I hate the word, but I've done it. Stuart has always known exactly what I'm supposed to do. And I've done it. I've yelled and hollered, but I've done it." She went on to say again how angry she would get because she had to do all the cleaning up when the boys left the house in a mess. But they had become considerate husbands, and she felt certain that her having had "temper tantrums" helped to impress on them some sense of personal responsibility about such matters.

The dining room table was still a major issue: "If we ever kill each other it will be over the dining room table.... We're going to battle on forever, I think. But we do talk. I think that's why things fall apart around our house, because we sit down and talk so much."

Susan felt that her marriage had changed her markedly, making her more open to new experiences and less rigid (though it was difficult for the interviewer to imagine that she had ever been a rigid person).

Postreview comment: On the typescript of the draft, Susan wrote: "the tamed shrew."

She had never regretted her commitment to the marriage, noting that the few of her friends who had divorced had traded one set of problems for another.

She did not express moral disapproval of unmarried couples who live togehter but thought that without a firm commitment, it is too easy to shift because of a temporary whim, and then one loses a great deal. As she described the current activities of her children, Susan's feeling of reward for her commitment was evident.

Asked if there were things she wished she had done differently in her life, she said, "Not really," but then added that perhaps she would have brought the children up differently and would have been nicer to them. Then she mentioned a conversation with one of the boys who had said, "You smile at everyone else; you never smile at me." And Susan realized "that it was a matter of time. I told him about why that was: it was because he was the one who always had buttons off and shoes untied and torn jeans, and when I was looking at him, I saw things I had to do about him, not the little kid inside, or seeing that his face was dirty and his hair was all messed up and." Here the interviewer added, "The buttons have to be sewn." "Yes, and so I explained that to him, but I think that he's the only one that mentioned it." Indeed, there is no question that the children felt their mother was loving, supportive, and fun. And so the picture that Susan Campbell provided in her interviews added color and richness to the story of Stuart's life, even as she undoubtedly had added to his life itself.

A LIFE HISTORY INTERVIEW AT AGE 63

Two years later, when he was age 63, Stuart was interviewed again, this time to review some of the salient features of his life. While as friendly, cooperative, and pleasant as ever, Stuart was found by the interviewer to be a bit more businesslike, anxious to complete the interview since it was his day off. "He seemed to me to have aged quite a bit in the two years [this interviewer had interviewed Stuart in 1982]; his face is heavily lined and when not animated as it usually is, looked rather tired, perhaps even a bit sad."

Stuart was asked to fill out a Life Satisfaction Chart, as he had done many years before. He did so quickly. The scale ranged from 1, "rock bottom," to 10, "tops." Stuart drew lines at 4 for ages 5 to 10, went to 7 by age 15 to 20, down to 3 at age 25, back to 7 at 30, and drew a straight line from 30 to 60, going up to 8 at 65 and projecting 9 at 70. The interviewer commented that the chart was pretty flat. Stuart said, "Yeah, I don't bounce around much." Age had somewhat flattened the early years, and age 17 was no longer "absolute tops," as it had been at age 38.

What was the best time in his life? "Probably right now it is about as good as any. I enjoy my family, I enjoy my wife, I like my work, and I'm probably better at it than I ever was. . . . I get a lot of respect. I enjoy that; some of it is deserved in my mind and some of it isn't. The main thing is that I respect myself. I know that I did something and saved some money and anxiety for somebody. Once in a while I save a life and that is great." The only point of dissatisfaction, depression, or unhappiness in his life, he indicated, related to the failure of his first marriage.

Stuart called himself "a pessimist by nature . . . a cautious person. With my childhood background I tend to be somewhat cynical about things." Reminded that he had called himself an optimist earlier, he amplified: "I am optimistic about myself and about life but at the same time I think I am realistic. . . . I am always predicting that hard times are right around the corner. I still believe things are going to get tough. I don't put much faith in it. I don't have any great respect for material wealth."

Stuart was still involved in civic affairs and recently was asked to be chief of staff at a hospital. He felt it was not a good time to be so involved because hospitals and doctors were in a state of ferment, with lots of problems. His feeling was that "the sooner we get on some national health [plan] the better off we'd be." He did not think Americans would fare poorly if they ended up somewhat like the English, Germans, and Swedes. He recognized that this was a switch in his position. Even so, he remained a conservative: "What I really would like is to have contracting between people. That is the only basic, efficient thing." With the trends in medicine being toward organizations and health insurance, he did not see that as likely to happen.

Stuart defined a mature person as one who

> has accepted himself or herself without too much discomfort—he likes himself. He sees his good points and is not constantly looking or being critical of himself. I think he has a value system of what he thinks is important, and to me that . . . would turn out to be somewhat similar to my own value system. He would be honest and intellectually curious, he would of necessity be somewhat of a skeptic, a seeker still, not have any final, complete answers because then I think he is out of touch with reality . . . hopefully he would have a good relationship with his wife and children and have a good deal of satisfaction in his work.

He thought he began to feel like that when he was age 30 but felt he had matured much more since then because of time and experience.

He regarded as the most important turning point in his life

when his grandmother stayed in Oakland rather than returning to Scotland and taking the children with her. He felt that was a very lucky turning point for him. The decision to go to the university came next, and possibly the decision to come to the area in which he now lived rather than stay in the first area in which he worked. He mentioned no other events or times that he saw as significant turning points in his life.

Stuart said people often asked him when he was going to retire. "Then I think to myself, 'Who are you kidding? You have been putting off so many things for so long to practice medicine and build up some equity for your family's security. What are you worried about, you might never have any time to do these things. You had better start thinking about it.'" The preceding summer Stuart and Susan spent three weeks in Germany, a trip he enjoyed, and he reported plans for a cruise to the Mediterranean, but he was not interested in esoteric travel. He would like to do much more reading, watch good television, and garden. He said nothing about actually stopping the practice of medicine.

The Scottish tradition as exemplified and taught by his grandmother significantly shaped him, he felt, to be hard working, conscientious, to keep his word and be brave. "I was raised on all that stuff." He added, "I am a pretty reserved person; in some way you could call me cold." (Very few persons would.) Stuart envied the Italians their demonstrativeness and their warmth but did not envy the Germans. He felt the Scottish are more like the Germans—more prone to riot, get drunk, get mad. "It is that militarism."

Yet when asked how he would like to be remembered, Stuart said it would be for being gentle: "I am not so sure that I can be gentle all the time. I do hurt people. I am not always so sensitive about it either . . . but I try to be a lot more gentle as I get older and I think about it a lot more. I would like to be remembered for being gentle. You can put it on my tombstone."

Lunches with Stuart and Susan in 1990 (to discuss this history) confirmed the impressions secured from the vast file of data accumulated over nearly sixty years. Stuart still maintains his practice, with his younger associate. He still runs and plays tennis at age 70. Susan still teaches Sunday school and volunteers two mornings a week at a preschool, as well as helping at the office afternoons. They walk and talk and are still engrossed with each other. Stuart corrected a couple of errors in the description of his early home situation but had no suggestions with respect to interpretations of his later development. Susan noted a number of places where the typescript of her interviews had contained errors or was ambiguous and added a few words of further interpretation or expansion.

STUART CAMPBELL: A SUMMARY

Stuart has been a cooperative, conscientious participant in the Oakland Growth Study since its inception when he was 11 years old, nearly sixty years ago. Everyone who has observed, counseled, or interviewed him over those years has liked him, enjoyed working with him, been impressed by his personality and achievements. No one ever saw him as cold or as less than admirable.

Stuart is competitive; he likes being first, at the top of his class. This does not imply arrogance or a lack of humility; quite the contrary. Stuart has been seen a bit more favorably than he sees himself. The side that he describes as having been selfish and cynical seldom surfaced. He fit his own definition of a mature individual. And no other member of the entire study group remained so consistently the same from junior high to later maturity.

Stuart's record is the more remarkable considering his deprived early years. His mother had died; his father abandoned the children and then died far from home. He was raised by an elderly immigrant grandmother who seemed to the study staff stern, rigid, and uncommunicative, but she imbued him with strong ethical standards and a sense of will. One clue to Stuart's particular development can be found in the fact that he did not experience himself or his life as deprived either of affection and guidance or in material terms. His memories of his mother were warm and loving, and he had some good memories of his father despite his grandmother's invective against him. He felt loved and even to a degree indulged by his grandmother, denied nothing he really wanted. At the same time, he appreciated their precarious economic situation. If he had to work and worry about money, so did many of his contemporaries. He said once that he felt luckier than some of his friends whose fathers were out of work. His grandmother's values were clear and strong, and she conveyed them to him firmly and unequivocally, especially concerning education. She convinced him that the United States was the land of opportunity; with hard work and tenacity, he could be and do anything he wanted. She set high standards and held him to them. Stuart believed her and lived accordingly. It also seems likely that Stuart was born with an equable disposition, one not given to moods. Finally, Stuart was able to seek out and learn from the people he needed in his life.

His need for love and approval is strong, but he has always had sufficient self-confidence to believe that he could and would arouse those feelings in others. Stuart sometimes consciously endeavors to charm and impress his interviewers and in so doing may indicate a stronger positive position on whatever question he is asked than might otherwise to true. He is not, however, manipulative or calculating; if he does exaggerate his position, he is likely to balance that response in another interview. On some issues, he is probably a great deal more ambivalent than he appears.

Over the years, some of Stuart's views have changed, though his basic values have not. In his middle years, his views on the role of the military in society, the duty of the citizen to give military service regardless of cause, and the role of America in the world were very different from those of the idealistic boy who deplored excessive patriotism. The Vietnam War and the controversies with his children around that war, as well as his own experiences with other young men and his sense of justice and fairness, enabled him to modify some of those views. Stuart is not and has never been, a rigid man.

From the Democrat in his early years with strong feelings about social justice, he has become a conservative Republican in the tradition of the self-made man, a change not inconsistent with his early do-it-yourself experiences. In his early adult years, he saw himself as more comfortable with men, less comfortable with women. In later years, he emphasized the fact that his early life as well as his working life had been dominated by women, with whom he felt more comfortable than he did with men. From an early, somewhat macho stance, he grew to emphasize the nurturant aspects of his nature demanded by his profession as a pediatrician and his own temperament. At the same time he retains rather stereotypic male attitudes toward women, though his daughters seem to be chipping these away.

Stuart's identity has been particularly influenced by two factors: his Scottish heredity and upbringing in that tradition and the insecurity resulting from the loss of his parents and the early lack of money. All his life he has opted for security rather than adventure, responsibility rather than impulsiveness or, possibly, spontaneity. Stuart, rather wistfully, noted his admiration for Italians despite the fact that he saw them as often "sloppy, lazy, and disorganized but you have to love them because they have that warmth." He may have been regretting a lack of that spontaneity in his own life. Yet in his interprersonal relations, certainly in the interview situation, he appeared much more spontaneous than most other respondents.

An enduring, dependable relationship with his wife and strong family ties have been of central importance to him, as has his role as a doctor. Being a doctor and a strong family man, a man who assumes civic responsibility, a man who can be counted on, are the major components of Stuart's sense of identity.

Stuart's need for security, to "have enough to eat" as he sometimes put it, has led to some of the contradictions in his life—contradictions of which he has, to some extent, been aware but has not changed, either because he would not or could not do so. In his middle years, for example, he often decried the subsidizing of young people, the tendency to give them too much, do too much for them and in that way limit their experiences. He believes his early experience of getting what he wanted for himself, by himself, contributed to his self-esteem, as well as the respect of others for him. He wishes that his children might have had such opportunitites. But even when they are grown, married, and working at their own vocations, he is still subsidizing them, worrying about providing security for them.

Stuart wants to be remembered as a gentle person. No doubt he will be. Predominantly, however, he will be remembered as a good man, a good doctor, a good husband and father, a good citizen. He has manifested competence and human warmth all his life. He serves as a kind of ideal illustration of planful competence enriched by warmth and humor. I shall have more to say about Stuart in Chapters 6 and 9.

CHAPTER 5

STILL LEARNING AT SEVENTY

MARY WYLIE

Mary Wylie, an attractive, vicacious, competent woman—a widow, mother, artist, student, and homemaker—has led a life of remarkable stability and consistency. Despite moves in the United States and abroad, especially during her child-raising years, as well as the loss of a beloved husband in her 40s, she seemed in many ways little changed from the girl we first studied just before she entered junior high school. In other respects, however, she seems quite different from the girl who in junior high school was seen as competent but extremely timid, very status conscious, and affected in her behaviors. What accounts for these discrepant impressions? Can we derive from the data collected over the past fifty years an understanding of the influences that have given her self-confidence, greater tolerance of others, and the resilience to launch her children and build a stable, satisfying life in her later years?

Mary has little information about her ancestry. Her paternal grandfather, born in England, was a sea captain who sailed the China Trade. Her maternal grandfather, of Scandinavian origins, became a businessman. Mary knew none of her grandparents; all had died before her birth.

Mary's father, Austin, born in England in 1875, emigrated to the United States with his parents at the age of 19. He resented having to leave his electrical engineering program to accompany his parents. He was the youngest child; his older brothers had finished their education and remained in England. Why the grandparents decided to emigrate is unknown. In his early years in the United States, Mary's father took many jobs regarded as below his capacities and "station in life," she says, but kept his disappointments to himself and never complained. For most of the years of her life, her father worked as office manager and purchasing agent for the

Denver Manufacturing Company. He always provided adequately for the family and was a hard-working, frugal man. Mary described him as "gentle, quiet, firm, dignified, an outstanding cricketer, a dedicated gardener."

Mary's mother, Harriet, nearly twelve years younger than her husband, was born and raised in San Francisco. We learned from an early interview with Mary's mother some of the circumstances of the marriage. After graduating from high school, Harriet had worked in an office for fourteen years, apparently at a quite responsible job. She had not originally been much interested in marriage because she did not care for housekeeping, but she suddenly realized that she wanted a family of her own and decided that she would marry after all. She had met her husband-to-be through the Sierra Club, to which both belonged, although they had not been at all romantically involved. We do not know exactly how the marriage came about, but it would appear that it brought together two congenial persons rather than being a love match. Within a year after their marriage, they had their first daughter, Dorothy. A second daughter, Betty, was born the following year. Two years later, in 1921, Mary, the youngest daughter, was born in a Bay Area suburb. (On reviewing the statement that her parents' marriage had not been a love match, Mary said that they had been a tender and loving couple.)

There appear to have been no significant problems in Mary's early years. At the time of enrollment in the study, when Mary was in the sixth grade, the staff member who interviewed Mrs. Wylie commented that the mother was enthusiastic about Mary's participation in the study and showed great interest in the topic of child development. She expressed some minor concerns about Mary— that she was underweight and had a poor appetite and that she did not take responsibility around the house, though she did what she was asked to do. Mrs. Wylie was somewhat concerned that Mary did not seem to concentrate or settle down to do any one thing well, but at the same time she was pleased with Mary's general social skills. She saw Mary as most like herself among her daughters. One minor annoyance was that Mary often picked poor children to play with. Here the mother expressed the concern about status that was later to be revealed as a recurrent theme. The interviewer rated Mrs. Wylie high on intelligence and mental alertness and saw her as being completely cooperative, open-minded, and somewhat excitable and talkative. The interviewer also noted that it appeared that discipline was firm, that there was much intellectual stimulation available in the home, and that the children were exposed to good music and a high level of cultural sophistication.

Staff impressions of Mary at the start of the study were very positive. On her first visit to the clubhouse where the junior high students met and participated in various activities, an observer described her as one who "leads in painting, a pretty, dainty blond, a little supercilious and condescending at times to her peers but usually interested and friendly." The year was 1932. Subsequent observations of Mary often started with the words, "friendly, as usual," though at one or two testing situations she was seen as a bit sullen or antagonistic.

THE JUNIOR HIGH YEARS

Beginning in the sixth grade and through the end of high school, Mary completed a series of inventories of attitudes, opinions, and self-perceptions. She generally gave responses in the categories most frequently chosen by her peers. In the sixth grade, however, her self-perceptions were less positive than at any later time. She saw herself as very much like "a girl who is not popular," one who is "easily upset if she has to talk with a grown-up and can't say exactly what she means." Consistently, over the junior and senior high school years, she did not see herself as "a girl who gets good grades" or as at all like "the brightest girl" (nor, she indicated, would she like to be). She characterized herself as "fun-loving," as "one who adores parties," and, for the most part, as "a girl who wants to become a happy, ordinary person." Her self-perceptions and aspirations were thus very different from Stuart Campbell's.

Throughout the high school years, Mary's responses to inventories and occasional interviews reflected close, smooth relationships within the family and especially close ties to her mother. Among a list of potential "wishes," Mary checked that she wished her mother could be happier and that she could have better health, though there was no indication that her mother's health was poor. Mary also checked that she wished she "wouldn't quarrel so much with her family," which seems to have reflected frequent quarrels with

one sister. On the whole, she seemed highly accepting of the constraints that her parents exercised and grateful to them for giving
her greater freedom as she matured.

She reported few signs of any psychophysiological problems,
though she seemed to be rather more annoyed with a wide variety
of situations described in an "annoyance inventory" than most of
her peers. Mary indicated that she generally liked school but did
not like being told by the teachers to sit still and be quiet. She liked
most of her teachers but expressed negative feelings about one or
two who were not very accepting of her. In junior high, however,
she did not display the rather extreme talkativeness that was sometimes commented on during the senior high years.

Mary's mother was again interviewed during the daughter's last
year in junior high. At this time she expressed much satisfaction
that her daughter was in one of the leading cliques in school. She
recognized, however, that Mary was seen as very much of a follower
rather than a leader of the clique. The interviewer noted "there was
a great deal of uneasiness concerning her social status running
through the mother's remarks." There was also some indication of
not being entirely satisfied with her current lot, including a number of somewhat snide remarks about respects in which she had not
gotten her way with her husband. It did not appear that there was
any substantial conflict in the family, just an expression that she was
discontented with certain arrangements around the house.

The house, which occupied a large lot with impressive garden
areas, was described as extremely attractive, and its contents clearly
reflected the parents' strong intellectual and cultural interests. Mrs.
Wylie revealed, however, that the family was not financially well off
at this time. Her husband had given up golf, and they had given up
their membership in the Sierra Club and their attendance at the-
aters and concerts in order to make ends meet.

It was clear that Mrs. Wylie's chief interest was in her girls, and
she had invested herself very heavily in Parent-Teacher Association
(PTA) activities and in attending classes on child development. In
interviews during her adult years, Mary described her mother as
"lively, energetic and quick-tempered," a woman who did not like
housework but did like gardening and active involvement in helping others. She noted that her mother was not only active in the
PTA but was for a period its president. Looking back on her childhood years, she reported that the home was harmonious, free of

conflict, warm, loving, and secure. This was certainly the impression of the staff gained from Mary's reports during her adolescent years.

Postreview comment: Mary commented that gardening was at times a source of disagreement between her parents, and here her father's views prevailed. Checking on the early interviews with her mother, we found that gardening priorities were the cause of some of Mrs. Wylie's rather snide remarks about her husband. Mrs. Wylie had reported that neither she nor her husband was a churchgoer, and the staff had the impression that the parents were indifferent to religion, but Mary noted that her father "lived by the Ten Commandments and knew the Bible inside out." Both parents had been churchgoers before marriage, but they belonged to different churches.

In general, both her teachers in junior high and the staff members with whom she came in contact found Mary attractive, likable, and competent. She was not an outstanding student, but she was conscientious. She was seen as timid, but she was liked by her peers and possessed a good deal of social skill. She accepted her parents' controls and expressed herself as very close to them. Although she reported that she quarreled with her sisters, she also indicated that they were very important to her, especially her oldest sister.

There was good agreement among the raters who summed up what Mary was like in junior high school. On the Q-sort dealing with interpersonal relationships, Mary was seen as arousing liking and acceptance in peers, as accepting and appreciating sex typing as it affected self (that is, she liked to be regarded as very feminine), and as having social poise and presence with her peers. She was seen as close to her mother, as respecting her parents, and at the same time as placing a strong emphasis on being with peers and being gregarious. She was seen as being rather highly judgmental in regard to peer conduct. The qualities considered least characteristic of her were rebelliousness with adults, displaying attention-getting behavior with peers, and being oriented toward going steady. Mary was at the extreme low end of showing an interest in boys.

Raters of the personality Q-sort agreed substantially on Mary's dominant traits. They saw her as highly dependable, fastidious, arousing liking, physically attractive, poised, and highly feminine but also as judgmental of others. Least characteristic of Mary, they felt, were changeability in behavior and attitude, pushing limits to see what she could get away with, negativism, deceitfulness, and rebelliousness. Although she was rated only average in self-confidence, she scored high on the other two components of competence, "intellectually invested" and "dependable," which put her near the top of the study group girls on our index of competence in junior high school.

THE SENIOR HIGH YEARS

It was taken for granted that Mary, like her sisters, would go to college. She enrolled in University High, along with almost all her friends from junior high. Mary's major intersts and goals were fairly clear by the early senior high years. A Strong Vocational Inventory at the age of 16 elicited a statement of those interests and goals. Her vocational choice, of which she reported herself "quite sure," was "art, a specialty in dress designing." She was sure that she wanted to marry, and in most years she indicated that her number one vocational aspiration was to be "a housewife." Her second choice was "an artist." Although she did not pursue the goal of dress designing professinoally, she maintained her interest and involvement in family and art through her life. Moreover, over the years she designed and sewed her own clothes, as well as sewed for her children.

Annual "opinion surveys" in the senior high school years revealed Mary's extremely conservative views and a rather high level of prejudice toward workers and minority groups. On the list of activities and organizations approved of or disapproved of, she disapproved of almost anything unconventional or not conservative: swearing, slang, divorce, strikes, the Works Progress Administration, radicals, and many similar items. She also disapproved of "hating" and "hurting other people's feelings," but, surprisingly, she checked that she approved of "lynching," "hating other races," and "getting even with someone." Mary believed that ability is almost always rewarded, that everyone is fairly treated in the courts, that wealth is important for a good life, and that "ministers should preach more about immortality than about social justice."

Postreview comment: Mary Wylie was perplexed to read that she had replied as she had in adolescence. She had no memory of such feelings, nor did she recall any evidence of racial prejudice on the part of her parents. She did acknowledge that she had been quite sheltered but remembered wanting her mother to do something for a poor girl whom she had met.

Mary was by no means alone in the expression of racial prejudice. It was pervasive in American society—white Protestant prejudice against the latest immigrants, Jews, Negroes, Catholics, almost anyone "different." Mary seemed, however, less consistent and a good deal more naive about social justice than most of her peers.

Mary's religious beliefs were much less conservative than her political and social views. Given a choice of concepts of God, she chose "a beautiful thought to make us live better." To characterize the concept "hell," she chose "an idea that exists only in people's minds." She reported in an interview that neither she nor her parents attended church, though at one time she had gone to Sunday school. (The reason they did not attend church, she subsequently reported, was that they lived a considerable distance from the church and did not have a car in those days.)

Mary participated in a variety of activities in senior high school, running for office and serving on committees. She had several close friends, but the six she listed in her senior year did not include any of those she had listed as a sophomore. Her list of friends in the senior year included boys as well as girls, but she was still timid with boys. The dating she did was often with boys who were friends of her older sisters; with them she felt comfortable and safe. She was rather prim and proper, sexually a late bloomer, averse to the necking and petting of her peers, not interested in a boy unless he was "interesting on the way home," by which one might infer that she meant interested in talking with her rather than in necking.

In a later interview, at age 37, she mentioned having had a long-term crush on a boy whom she did not identify. Even at that time, married with (then) three children, talking about sex was difficult for her. She had an unusually late onset of puberty, a full two years after the average of her peers. She described herself as more timid in adolescence than her sisters, especially concerning boys. Still, she apparently was both attractive and popular enough to draw the attention of her peers of the opposite sex. She did get invited to the senior prom, though she felt she "only just" made it to that event. At no time during her high school years did Mary indicate a real involvement with any boy. She seems to have been content to go out occasionally with her sisters' friends or with her family. Clearly, Mary was not yet ready to deal with sex and intimacy. Goodnight kisses were the extent of her sexual activities; sex for her would begin with and be confined to marriage.

On the whole, the senior high school years were rewarding ones for Mary. During one scheduled interview later in life when she was asked to describe turning points in her life, she mentioned the development of self-confidence in high school, changing from a timid child to a more self-assured young woman. Oakland Growth Study observational reports on Mary during her junior year support that change. She was described as

> very attractive, very nice clothes, good makeup, good figure, a leader in small groups, very assured. Distinctly less affectedly superior today, though less genuine than others in the group. Seemed well-liked, enjoyed holding center of the stage. May be a bit snobbish but friendly to observers and very expressive with friends.

In 1937, she was seen as "cooperative, good-natured, fairly gay, natural with boys." At a formal dance she was "perfectly groomed, dancing with assurance and poise, very friendly as usual, happily talkative about a lot of things."

But in 1938 the observer recorded that her "social climbing seems a change from the genuine, radiant, natural behavior of a year ago, continuing the same superior air, slightly pretentious verbalizations." Later that year, when Mary ran as a candidate for publicity commissioner, her speech was delivered with assurance. During the year, Mary appeared to observers to vacillate between more assured, natural, friendly behavior and somewhat pretentious, pseudo-sophisticated behavior, not uncommon in adolescence. To be or not to be: grown up, a young lady, or a little girl.

There was clearly a change going on, one that led to her being seen as more conventional, less intellectually involved, and less secure than the Mary who was so impressive in junior high school. Yet that seemingly negative change reflected her efforts to become more in command of her life, as her later comments revealed.

Postreview comment: At several points in this section, Mary Wylie noted that her seeming poise and talkativeness was a cover-up for nervousness and that she remembered feeling inferior and striving to overcome her earlier timidity. As the youngest child at home and as one who perceived herself as weak and skinny, she said she felt inferior to her sisters. At school she was very sensitive about her performance in spelling, grammar, and math. She remembered feeling embarrassed when PTA notices, which were signed by her mother as president, were read in school or when her themes were read aloud. She felt that everyone was looking at her on such occasions. As to being seen as "natural with boys," she reported: "I was scared stiff of the boys my age!"

Different tests and tasks gave quite divergent impressions of Mary. One projective test suggested that she was extremely imaginative and insightful; another was interpreted as showing "a strong inclination to subordination." Her "affirmative orientation and faculty for devotion" was commented on, but the interpreter of the test saw a "lack of intellectual steering." A psychologist reviewing all the data for the senior high years saw Mary as "hypersensitive, unsure of herself, which she covers up through socially correct behavior and superficial contacts. People are quite frightening to her." Another observer commented: "Her effort to demonstrate knowledgeability and sophistication tends to come through as snobbishness to some of her peers but appeals to those like herself. Anxious about impulse life, which she kept under tight control."

It will not be surprising, then, to learn that the psychologists and social workers who were given the task of assessing Mary's personality as of the senior high school years were in much less agreement than those who had rated her in the junior high years. Because of divergencies in the way they saw Mary, four sorters were used before sufficiently high reliability was achieved in the composite rating. None of the judges expressed high or even much confidence in their classifications. Two of the four judges were impressed with the potentialities manifest early in the senior high years but less visible in the last two years by virtue of her insecurities, extreme conventionality, and status striving. They wondered whether college would rekindle those potentials. All predicted that Mary would go to college for at least two years, would marry before her mid-20s, and would have three children.

Postreview comment: Here Mary wrote: "How could they make such predictions? I always thought it would take me until 29 or 30 to find the 'right man' to marry."

The judges making the assessment were, of course, guessing, but they apparently surmised that Mary's lack of strong intellectual interests and her attractiveness and femininity would make her a candidate for marriage rather than leading to any other commitment. Once married, she would assuredly want children, for motherhood was indissolubly linked with marriage in the minds of most girls in the 1930s, especially conventional girls.

On the interpersonal Q-sort, those traits now considered most characteristic of Mary were that she was sensitive to anything that could be construed as criticism by or slight from peers, accepted and appreciated sex typing as it affected herself, showed some condescending behavior in relation to her peers, sought reassurance from her peers, was selective in her choice of friends, and emphasized ingroup status to the detriment of out-group status. Whereas in junior high Mary had been seen as showing little attention-getting behavior, she was now seen as showing a good deal of such behavior. Her least characteristic attributes on the senior high interpersonal Q-sorts were "adopts a pesudo-compliant, toadying attitude toward adults," "oriented toward going steady," "perceives family situation as conflictful," and "changeable in peer attachments."

On the personality Q-sort, Mary was again seen as above all fastidious, socially poised, and feminine. For the senior high years, however, she was now rated only average on dependability. In addition, she was seen as seeking reassurance from others, as moralistic, and as engaging in personal fantasy and daydreams (a new "highly characteristic" item for Mary but surely one strongly related to adolescence). She was also felt to be affected, seen as comparing herself with others, whether favorably or unfavorably, and as valuing power or status in self and others. Thus, her senior high ratings suggest greater turbulence and uncertainty in her relationships and, in general, a somewhat less well-adjusted and slightly hostile but conforming girl.

Postreview comment: Here Mary Wylie wrote: "Right! I remember beginning to feel this. I saw it as beginning to assert myself and not always following somebody or something."

Least characteristic of her again were items related to negativism, rebelliousness, and pushing limits. In addition, she was seen as not "reluctant to commit self to any definite course of action," not explicitly concerned with philosophical problems, not "questing for meaning, self-definition or redefinition," and not fearful. She was rated low on the item "enjoys sensuous experiences (including taste and touch)." As a late maturer, Mary apepars to have been somewhat more unsettled by puberty than most of her peers. At the same time, she seemed to know who she was and what she wanted.

On the measure of planful competence, Mary was no longer near the top of the study group, but she was still in the top fourth. She had gained in self-confidence but slipped somewhat in intellectual involvement and dependability, as assessed by the Q-sorts. She scored unusually low on warmth for a girl relatively high on competence. Mary Wylie's scores on the Q-sort components and index are given in Table A4, Appendix A. At the end of high school, she was eagerly looking forward to college.

Mary said that she always knew she would go to college. By the time she finished high school, both her sisters were attending the University of California, and she also enrolled there, but not without some trepidation. Her grades had not been particularly good except in art, and she was not an enthusiastic student, again except in art. She continued to feel that decorative arts would be her field and majored in that area.

> *Postreview comment:* We learned at this point that when she enrolled in college, Mary proved to do very well: "I got my first A's in my first semester at Cal. And the interesting thing was that I was the only one of the three of us to get A's in my major!" Her major was art. Her grades outside her major were mostly C's, and academic subjects were much less interesting to her than working with her hands.

MARY WYLIE AT AGE 37

The next detailed information on Mary derives from several long interviews conducted when she was 37 years old. She said then that by her second year in college, she recognized that decorative arts was a highly competitive field and that she was not very competitive. However, with some pride she added that she had used her education more extensively than had her sisters, since she could use it in the home. That use of decorative arts in the home seems to have been implicit from an early age. Like most young women of her time, Mary said she always took for granted that she would marry and have a family.

Mary completed two years at the university and then left home and university to marry (as several of the judges of her high school record had predicted). She said that she had not expected to marry until her late 20s, but she met the right man much earlier than that. The right man was named Chester. She met him through a neighbor and friend. Both Chester and the neighbor's son were attending a military academy in the East; in 1940 the neighbor invited Chester to visit during a holiday. Mary and Chester were immediately drawn to each other. Both were reserved in some respects, especially in their behaviors with the opposite sex, but she was vivacious and he was the kind of man she could look up to as the head of a family. They shared conservative political and moral values. They saw as much of each other as they could during Chester's leaves from the academy, but the United States was on the verge of entering World War II, and leaves were limited.

Mary and Chester could not have known one another well when they married, for they had seen one another for only twenty-two days during the two years of their courtship. There was correspondence, of course, but the interviewer did not gain the impression that the corespondence contributed markedly to their knowledge or understanding of one another. Nonetheless, there seems to have been no question in Mary's mind that Chester was the man for her. Years later, she said she had not thought much about what she wanted in marriage except that it should involve the kind of shared activities and understandings her parents had. She said that she had never loved another man. She went back east for Chester's graduation from the academy in June 1942; they were married in the South at his parent's home immediately after. Mary was 21 years old. Because of the war, the two married earlier than they otherwise might have. Chester was on duty in the Atlantic soon after their marriage. It was an anxious time for Mary.

Postreview comment: Mary Wylie commented that her sisters kept telling her, "You are just too darn particular," prior to her meeting Chester. She said she had no doubts despite their short acquaintance, but that "there were a tremendous number of things to get adjusted to." Through correspondence, they had gotten to exchange views and values and had found that they "jibed very well."

Mary had lived at home during her college years and had been rather more dependent on her parents emotionally and economically than many young women, but it does not appear that marriage and the consequent move across the country posed a significant problem for her. She was intent on being a good wife and being with her husband whenever possible. She took an apartment with another wartime bride and worked in a department store, as much to keep occupied as for any other reason.

We know much more about Mary's circumstances and her life satisfaction at the time of the interview in 1958 than of the period intervening between high school graduation and 1958. But as part of the interview, she completed a life satisfaction chart, on which she was asked to plot, year by year, her level of life satisfaction, from 0, "rock bottom," to 10, "absolute tops." Mary drew a generally ascending line from level 6 in elementary school and 7 in high school to hit "absolute tops" in the early years of her marriage. (Later in this account, we shall see Mary's life chart as drawn at age 61, which will give a more complete overview of her life, so I shall not reproduce the first life chart.)

As of 1958, Mary and her hubabnd had three children—two boys and a girl. Chester had remained in the service, rising to a moderately high rank. The military life had necessitated many moves, long absences, and extensive adjustments. Mary felt that she negotiated those adjustments successfully; she was an adaptable person, cheerful in outlook, prepared to cope with whatever came along. Her life chart during those years indicated only one relatively low period after the birth of the second child. The family had just moved to a community in a region of the country new to them, and Mary suffered a postpartum depression. On the chart filled out at age 37, she indicated that she felt very inadequate for raising a family. Never a person who found it easy to talk about sex, Mary was able to volunteer only late in life to an interviewer that her depression after her second child resulted, at least in part, from her loss of sexual desire and her husband's dissatisfaction with her lack of interest. She felt that her sexual desire had never been more than moderate, while his was stronger, and she feared for a time that he might leave or divorce her. Her depression was not long term, however. She became involved in a cooperative nursery school and gained assurance and satisfaction. Life soon returned to normal, and her life chart was scored at 10—"absolute tops"—from 33 on.

At age 37, Mary described her husband as

> a tall man with a long, serious face who has a good sense of humor, a precise, methodical, careful person in speech, clothing, habits: a man of high ideals who expects you to carry them out and has little tolerance for other peoples' weaknesses, makes few allowances for such, dignified and reserved but can be friendly and lively; pouts if he doesn't get his own way (I try strongly to work this out, it's not often he doesn't get his own way). I don't always agree with him but I have to go along with him. Of course, his way is well thought out. He holds a grudge.

> *Postreview comment:* After reviewing her somewhat expanded history five years after she had commented on the original version, Mary added a few adjectives to the description she had given thirty-four years earlier. She added "jolly, teasing" after the word "friendly," and modified "work this out" to "work him out of this attitude." She also noted that his whole family tended to hold grudges, a characteristic that seemed very strange to her.

When asked what she found irritating about him, she commented that he was unwilling to admit when he was wrong and that at times he forced his opinion on the family when there might be a more logical, easier, and more relaxed way to do something. But this was not a major issue for Mary. Her major worry was keeping herself and the children up to her husband's high ideals and standards; clearly she tried very hard to do so.

Mary's cheerful, conforming nature, the security of well-defined principles, as well as the political and social conservatism of her upbringing enabled her to accept and find happiness in a traditional marital role with a husband who was rather rigid and even authoritarian in attitudes, values, and ways of living. Although she recognized his sometimes intolerant attitudes, she did her best to mitigate them without undermining his authority in the household and with the children. They seldom quarreled, and there were few disagreements. She thought her children would say that she gave in to her husband on everything, but she reported that actually they compromised often, out of the children's hearing.

Mary and Chester had a strong mutual sense of how life ought to be lived. She stated, "I thought it was very important never to put the father, the man of the house, in a position of being corrected. He was in that [head of the household] position naturally; he was a forceful personality and I liked him to be that way and it didn't bother me that I appeared weak, if that's what the children thought." Over the years Mary made many such statements to interviewers; one wonders a bit if sometimes she was not arguing against her own protests. To maintain such a committed, principled role must have been very difficult at times.

Postreview comment: "We argued over different opinions in private and he frequently came around to my way of thinking." But later she acknowledged that the role had been difficult at times.

In raising their children, Mary and her husband emphasized rules and control and tried to anticipate difficulties and define ways of dealing with them before they arose. The carryover of the military way of life into their personal life was apparent but not extreme.

There was not a great deal of demonstrative affection between parents and children. Mary felt the children did not want it and that demonstrativeness did not come naturally to her husband. The children were not close to their father. More than twenty years later, she would comment:

He was a bit formal but he could be friendly and loving. But I don't think the children had any great tender fondness toward either of their parents, really. I think they respected us but they are just not terribly, terribly fond of us and, of course, I'm sorry that this is the way they do feel, but I think we might as well admit it if you see it and that's the way it is. I think it stems from the fact, to some degree, that the youngsters did not enjoy wrestling, being tossed up in the air, being cuddled or fondled or hugged or kissed. . . . I sort of tried to do it in a mild-mannered way.

I will always remember saying, "Now Daddy and I will love you no matter what you do. We'll always love you even when you're naughty or do bad things. We love you but we certainly don't like a lot of these things that you do."

Postreview comment: Here Mary Wylie noted that "hugs followed."
Verbal reassurance rather than physical displays of affection was her
way of dealing with such issues.

Mary saw herself as hard working, conscientious, energetic,
friendly—a person who liked to help other people and willing to
figure out difficult situations. She felt that her marriage was very
happy, that she had compromised when necessary (despite her irritation with Chester about "forced opinions"), and that they had a
"wonderful life" together. She was happy that she had not had to
go out to work, other than a number of briefly held clerical jobs in
department stores when she was first married and Chester was at
sea. Once she had children, her preference was to be at home, because "I thoroughly enjoy my job of being a mother and making a
happy home." She believed in being kind, helping others, and leading a "good Christian life."

During the series of interviews at age 37, Mary's interviewer commented on what he saw as a "Pollyanna" theme running through
her life and personality—a tendency to start mentioning something
negative but then turn it into something positive, always to "look on
the bright side," a characteristic that has permeated Mary's life to a
greater or lesser extent to the present day, though not, in all later
interviews, with the same slight self-righteousness. Cheerfulness as a
way of life is a conviction of hers; she saw herself then as a cheerful
person and does so now, though in a less determined fashion.

Postreview comment: Mary felt that the attribution of a "Pollyanna"
theme was inappropriate: "I was taught by my parents to look for
good in every person and find something good in every bad situation. I remember saying that to my husband early in his career. I
know I said it many times to our children and I don't call it a
Pollyanna attitude." Mary Wylie has an extraordinary ability to abide
by the maxim, which makes her a very pleasant person to know.

The interviews at age 37 were conducted by a male interviewer
who was generally skillful and perceptive but whose philosophy of
life and general life-style were markedly at variance with the orientations of Mary Wylie. This may somewhat help to explain Mary's unwillingness or inability to disclose more of herself than she did when
asked to characterize her strengths and weaknesses. She focused on

her drawing ability and her ineptness at sports, declining to talk about her personality attributes. (On review she later added, "I was fairly good at sports!" She thought that she had said "academics," and the interviewer had written down the wrong word, which may well have been the case, since the 1958 interviews were not taped.)

In general, the picture that emerged for the Q-sorters who translated the series of interviews into personality assessments was of a dependable, highly moralistic woman with wide interests, uncomfortable with uncertainty, and strongly overcontrolled yet productive. At this time, but at no other adult period, she was also seen as somewhat fearful and aloof. Nevertheless, she was seen as markedly more sympathetic and giving than she had been in high school and also as more interested in intellectual matters. She still scored somewhat below her peers in social perceptiveness, as she had in senior high school, and was seen as placing only a modest emphasis on personal autonomy. She no longer appeared significantly status conscious, a pronounced change.

> *Postreview comment:* Mary Wylie was perplexed by the term *over-controlled*. She wondered why she was seen as overcontrolled at age 37. She did not recognize the tight grip that she had held on her feelings as "overcontrol," though this was the meaning of the ascription. The full Q-sort item specified: "Tends toward overcontrol of needs and impulses; binds tensions excessively; delays gratification unnecessarily."

There was, then, both continuity in many of Mary's attributes from the high school years to age 37 and at the same time substantial change in others. The correlation between her adolescent and age 37 personality profiles was .42, suggesting slightly more change than the average for women in the study. Marriage and motherhood had brought many constraints into her life, but she was functioning effectively and enjoying herself in the process, though there still seemed to be a rather strong measure of overcontrol and need to conform. She no longer seemed condescending toward others and no longer seemed to have the need for reassurance that was so evident in her senior high school years. She was seen as substantially warmer and more agreeable than in the last years of high school. On the measure of competence, Mary's score went up somewhat more than did the scores of most study members, despite a lower score on the component "intellectually invested." She was clearly more self-confident and highly dependable, scoring in the top 15 percent of the women who participated in the first follow-up.

Chester and Mary were active, conscientious church members, though neither had been raised in the denomination they chose and Mary had not been brought up a churchgoer at all. It was her husband's wish that they join; she agreed and remained active in the church ever after. Both also held it important to be involved in community affairs, particularly those relating to their children, such as scouting, and both took active roles. Such participation seemed to Mary and Chester especially important since military life required many moves and adjustments for both them and their children. They sought to maintain security, stability, and consistency of standards regardless of location. Their discipline of the children was strict, and they expected much in the way of chores and conformity. Their philosophy of child rearing was thus very different from that of the Campbells.

That Mary put her husband's interests first is attested by the fact that soon after the birth of the third child (several years before the age 37 interview), when her husband was transferred overseas, she left the three children with her parents and accompanied him to evaluate the situation in terms of the family needs; both she and her husband were too anxious and uncertain about the living conditions to take the children immediately. After some months, when both felt they could establish a home appropriate for the children, she returned to California and brought the three children to the overseas base, where the family lived for several years before returning to the United States. Despite the difficulty of the decision and planning to go overseas, Mary, later in life, said that her marriage was at its best during those years: "Living conditions were particularly nice, the climate was good, the scenery was wonderful, I had household help. The children were doing well. He was relatively happy [in his assignment]. I had time to do some of the things I wanted to do. We were in full vigorous health."

THE MIDDLE YEARS: MARY AT AGES 37 THROUGH 49

Our next interview with Mary Wylie came in 1970 just after a period of severe crisis. The early 1960s had been good years. A fourth child was born when Mary was 40. There was some tension in the family between father and oldest son, but Mary coped successfully as mediator. Then suddenly a series of disasters befell her.

In 1965, Chester was involuntarily retired, a great shock to both of them. The event was totally unexpected and undesired by either of them. One of Chester's superiors 'had given him a number of negative reports. Mary commented:

> Some of his commanding officers weren't easy to get along with. He had the misfortune to have the same rating officer four times who was a difficult skipper to work under and gave him bad fitness reports. So he [Chester] was forcibly retired early and it was a big shock to both of us.

For a year Chester worked as a consultant for a private company. Then in 1966 he applied for a position with a governmental agency engaged in international operations and was appointed. Both he and Mary had enjoyed their overseas assignment and hoped for another such assignment; however, the agency sent him to a remote, somewhat dangerous location with no possibility of the whole family's accompanying him. Chester left for a two-year assignment, the longest of their many separations. The last child was still very young.

Chester and Mary had both enjoyed and valued military life. Later she expressed disappointment that none of her children had been interested in attending a military academy. She felt the military life was good and worthwhile. "It's helping themselves and helping the country at the same time. And you get a good education at the military academy practically free." But by the time her two sons might have been old enough for such training, the Vietnam War was underway, and the social climate in the country had changed. Military service had little appeal to most young Americans.

The turmoil and traumatic changes of the mid- to late 1960s had a strong impact upon Mary's sons. Their relationship with their father, never very close, had become strained. This may account to some extent for the slight sense of disappointment in her children evident in her later interviews, as well as her feeling that the children were more respectful than loving in their feeling toward their parents. The war period posed problems for many parents and adolescents, and such problems were especially acute in families in which parents were strong supporters of American military actions while their children were not.

Thus, in the midst of the Vietnam War and the social changes of the 1960s, in themselves quite enough for most parents to deal with, Mary was alone with her children. She expressed little complaint about her husband's decision to go abroad, although it was apparent that when he went, the family would have to stay behind, for there would have been no schools for the children. It seems probable that besides her usual inclination to place his needs before her own and her desire to please him, she accepted his decision the more readily because she knew how damaging the involuntary retirement from the military had been to his self-esteem. Here was an opportunity to regain the authority, the respect, and the sense of accomplishment that for a time had been lost to him. He expected, as he always had, that she could and would cope with whatever difficulties arose, and she did. Nonetheless, she sometimes felt underappreciated when, on his semiannual visits home or in letters, he criticized her decisions. During those years, she had to make difficult decisions regarding the children, the house, and their finances. In the past, she had depended on discussions with Chester for such decisions. Though difficult, the experience prepared her for the years of her husband's subsequent illness and death and those that followed.

When Chester finished his assignment in 1968, both expected that he would be in the United States for three months. They would visit his parents in the South, and then he would go to Washington for reassignment. Soon after his return, however, Mary began to notice a change in her husband. One night, he suffered a grand mal seizure and then more seizures in the hospital. The diagnosis was inconclusive; Chester was released from the hospital on antiseizure medication, and the family went ahead with their plans to visit his parents in the South.

The government agency placed Chester on indefinite leave due to his medical condition. He checked into a hospital as soon as they arrived at his parents' home. The diagnosis this time was a brain tumor. For almost a year, Mary and her family remained in the South in temporary quarters near his parents while he underwent surgery and other treatment. Despite treatment, his condition deteriorated. Although Mary did not and does not complain, that year must have been frightful for her as she coped with a suffering, dying husband, her children, her husband's parents, her own grief and anxiety, and all the enormous problems of living in temporary quarters in a hot and humid climate under such adverse circumstances. Finally, she felt that they must return to California. With the aid of California friends, she bought a house, sight unseen, and moved the whole family to California in July 1969. Chester died in October. Mary was 48 years old.

Approximately a year following the death of her husband, Mary was interviewed twice. She was trying to pull together her life, and it was clear that she was succeeding. Putting aside her own grief in the light of her responsibilities toward and the needs of the children left at home, a 17 year old and a 10 year old, with determination and competence she had set about learning and doing what had to be done. A decade later, Mary cried as she said, "I feel I have made a very, very good recovery from my husband's death because it really left me completely empty." Even during the interviews a year after his death, Mary was seen as having adapted "amazingly well" to her new roles and responsibilities. From the beginning of her marriage, Mary had shown herself to be a strong, adaptable, competent woman, wife, and mother. As she had repeatedly stated, she believed that the husband should be the head of the household, his authority preeminent, but she apparently never felt that her position was subservient to her husband's. Describing him and their relationship the year after his death, she recalled:

> He was a very strong—a pleasant personality, but a very strong character and he usually got his way and usually the things he wanted me to do I wanted to do, too. It gave him pleasure for me to be doing them with him, to learn how to do it, and he always expected me to be able to excel at absolutely everything. But I kept saying . . . give me something that's within my capacities but don't ask me to balance a checkbook, to keep track of the stock market and things like that. Actually, we agreed pretty well . . . a number of our friends had ups and downs and we agreed so wholeheartedly on what we liked to do and how to do it—or we would give in to the other one—that we had so few disagreements, we were hated—I won't say hated, but disliked by a lot of our friends because we didn't have any arguments. Isn't that funny? I can remember almost distinctly the five or six fights that we had in 27 years.

Her role in their relationship was one of commitment and conviction. In each new environment, Mary had created a happy, secure home for her husband, her children, and herself. She had been forced to make difficult decisions such as the one to leave the children behind for a time, including an infant, while she went abroad with her husband to explore the possibilities for establishing a home there. And she had maintained the home in his absence for a full two years. She had, in short, learned both the expectations of her husband and the knowledge and skills to carry out her role and his.

Mary's responsibilities changed little after the death of her husband. He had carried heavy life insurance, which now guaranteed financial security for Mary and the children. She did not have to go to work outside her home, but could, in fact, continue her life much as in the past during the times of her husband's absences. She continued in her traditional roles of mother and homemaker, though her role with the children necessarily broadened without a husband to turn to for decision making. She had had to mediate strong tensions between her oldest son and his father. She did so without compromising her husband's wishes, though she recognized that both father and son had taken extreme positions that demanded some compromise.

Now she turned for advice to friends in the church, who gave strong support and occasional direct guidance in handling issues that arose for the younger son. When counseling of the youngster seemed to be called for, she sought it and participated to the degree that the counselor suggested. It was useful, and the relationship between mother and son appeared to be on solid ground. Adjusting to changed circumstances as she always did, she recognized that without a father present to back her up, she could not be as strict about rules as she had once been. She adapted, felt she was perhaps a bit too lenient with the younger children but tried to define rules and values that would give order and meaning to their growth in the face of changing social values. In the period after Chester's death, Mary's mother, still active, was a strong source of support to her daughter, available when help was needed and to enjoy the close communication that had always characterized their relationship.

After Chester's death, Mary enrolled in a home maintenance and repair course and learned how to keep their house functional. That was necessity, not choice. Given a choice, she invariably opted for artistic endeavor and reveled in it, whether in the studio, an art class, or the garden.

Despite the recent tragic loss of her husband—or perhaps because of what her coping revealed of her strengths—Mary's personality ratings at age 49 suggested great personal growth and considerable change from the assessments made at age 37. The basic picture of very high scores on dependability, productiveness, poise, and even cheerfulness remained intact. Mary was no longer seen as highly overcontrolled but as more sympathetic and more socially perceptive. The single most salient attribute that both judges agreed upon was that she had a "rapid personal tempo." She did not present herself as at all "victimized by circumstances," despite her losses, and she retained exceptionally low scores on "reluctant to act," "withdraws when frustrated," and "rebellious." Mary Wylie was fully engaged with life, and the picture that emerged from reading the interviews at age 49—that of a mature, exceptionally competent woman—struck me so forcefully that Mary's life story seemed to merit closer study.

On the measure of planful competence, Mary's score was again higher, as were scores of most women at this period. She was seen as somewhat more self-confident, more intellectually invested, and slightly less dependable (largely because she was less overcontrolled, a positive rather than a negative change). The biggest changes, however, were in the other three components of personality. Mary had become much more assertive, much more outgoing, and was now seen as warmer than ever before. Again she scored in the top 15 percent of the women.

LATER MIDDLE AGE

By the time of the most recent general follow-up interview, when Mary was verging on age 62, the youngest child was still living at home but was not expected to be there for much longer. Mary viewed her daughter's imminent departure with equanimity, for she did not expect it to make a profound change in her life. Although her children had made choices in their careers and life-styles that varied widely from her expectations of them when they were younger, she accepted their choices and their right to make them. One son changed radically several times in his adult life, from conventional work and life-style to unconventional. She did not find this easy to accept, but she declared herself well satisfied with him, feeling that he had become increasingly stable and responsible. Such minor dissatisfactions as she has expressed about her children concerned primarily their failure to live up to their potentials, as she viewed those potentials. She felt their options in life would be greater and their satisfactions more complete if they did so.

In the years since her husband's death, Mary had involved herself in community college art classes of many kinds—ceramics, painting, photography. Her art increasingly entered into her sense of identity. Her deep interest in art in all its many forms was fortunate for the life she chose because she could pursue it at home while fulfilling more traditional roles. It also gave her an avenue for expression of her personality, feelings, and needs. It had not only added brightness and beauty to her life but had given her an area of self-confident living that was her own, separate from her husband. Her sense of herself as an artist and her increasing skills in many fields of art increased her self-esteem and sense of self-worth. Though she saw herself as noncompetitive, she came to value competitiveness, encouraged it in her children, and must have felt some pleasure in her recognized superiority in artistic fields.

Mary Wylie completed another life satisfaction chart in 1982. Unlike the charts of most study members, it showed sharper dips and climbs than her earlier chart. Her husband's sea duty during World War II and her postpartum depression had not been indicated as quite such severe problems previously. There was no hint that the problems of her adolescent children or the tensions between her husband and the oldest child had caused a drop in her life satisfaction. The depth of her disappointment at her husband's forced retirement was exceeded only by his death. Yet Mary had apparently climbed back to achieve a high level of satisfaction even after these disasters.

Mary continued to be very involved in church activities and had several close friends with whom she could share her most intimate thoughts—something lacking from her life when it revolved around her husband and children. Her father died at the age of 81, but her mother was still alive in 1984 at the age of 97. Among those persons in her life who had been able to give her continuous support, Mary's mother ranked high. Margaret Mead, in her autobiography, *Blackberry Winter*, remarks on the good fortune of a man or woman who retains a parent into that parent's old age. To witness a parent's aging and changing, coping with the vicissitudes of those stages of life yet ahead, as well as continually to experience their regard, affec-

Figure 5.1. Life Satisfaction Chart for Mary Wylie, Age 61

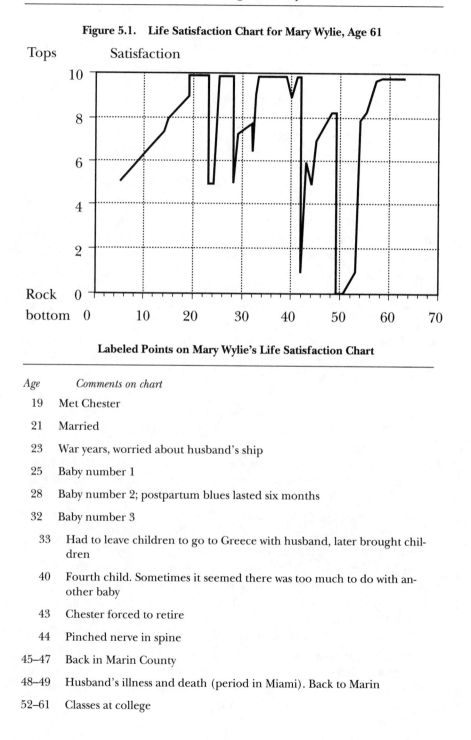

Tops Satisfaction

Rock bottom

Labeled Points on Mary Wylie's Life Satisfaction Chart

Age	Comments on chart
19	Met Chester
21	Married
23	War years, worried about husband's ship
25	Baby number 1
28	Baby number 2; postpartum blues lasted six months
32	Baby number 3
33	Had to leave children to go to Greece with husband, later brought children
40	Fourth child. Sometimes it seemed there was too much to do with another baby
43	Chester forced to retire
44	Pinched nerve in spine
45–47	Back in Marin County
48–49	Husband's illness and death (period in Miami). Back to Marin
52–61	Classes at college

tion, and support, is a blessing of no mean dimension. Mary had this good fortune. Her mother had stayed with her for the month before her husband died, a constantly supportive, undemanding presence.

Mary sometimes measured herself against her mother. She recognized her future self in her mother, whom she strongly resembled in both physical features and personality. She admired her mother's vigor and cheerfulness despite the growing disabilities of great age and she enjoyed her company. At the time of the last interview, Mary had just organized a family reunion and party to celebrate her mother's 97th birthday. She was contemplating the possibility that her mother might soon come to live with her, knowing it would mean changes in her own life and some sacrifice of her own plans and that she would experience burdens and anxieties as her mother's health inevitably failed. Nonetheless, she was not only willing but happy to take on the additional responsibilities if that turned out to be the best plan and one that her mother wanted. She also was close to her sister, Dorothy, though they did not see one another very frequently. Both had busy lives. She was less close to Betty, but worried about her since she was not well and their mother currently was living with her.

A LIFE HISTORY INTERVIEW AT AGE 63

As a consequence of her having been selected by random means for more intensive review of her earlier materials and for a life history interview, Mary Wylie was again contacted in 1984. She readily agreed to the interview, which was conducted in her home. Asked about changes in her life since the 1982 interview, she reported that the biggest one was admission to a university where she could complete her BA. After thirteen years of community college courses, she had enrolled, because, she said, "I want to finish something." She believed she finally had the time and freedom to do so. At the same time she wanted to "savor all forms of art; they are so stimulating and exciting, it makes the brightness of a day or the zest of living." The interviewer commented that Mary's home reflected that artistic savoring—comfortable and mildly disorderly, warm, full of interesting, beautiful photographs, paintings, and ceramics. It was as appealing, likable, and cheerful as Mary herself.

Her recollections of her adolescent years and of her aspirations then were very close to what we already knew of her. She remembered herself as having been more shy around boys and more fearful than she was perceived to have been. But she felt that by late adolescence, she had known reasonably well what she wanted to do and what she liked and disliked. In answer to a question about dependency on her parents, she said she had been quite dependent and had lived with them through the first two years of college but had felt "secure within myself" on leaving home to marry. She stressed that her parents could not have afforded to send her to college if she had not lived at home through this period, as her sisters also had.

On the whole, Mary Wylie's review of her life at age 63 was highly consonant with the picture derived from the earlier interviews. It was in fact striking how often she gave at each interview from age 37 to 63 almost identical reports about aspects of her early life and episodes from the adolescent years.

In 1984, Mary felt that she was "very much the same person" she had been in early adulthood: "I have had to become a more positive person while I am on my own, but I remember being that kind of a positive person at 18 or 19." She felt that she had grown a great deal in her two years at college. She reported, however, that though she had thought herself quite mature in her 20s, in retrospect she was not. In fact, she did not know if she was yet fully mature, which she viewed as "being able to handle one's own problems, helping others, creating a happy atmosphere around one, keeping oneself in a good balance of joy and sadness." In those early years, she felt, she was not particularly tolerant of other people's ways of doing things and saying things. "I wanted everything done my way because I thought it was the best." Then she laughed and added, "I still like to have things done my way!"

Postreview comment: Mary was not content to let the matter stand there. At age 70, in the final review of her history, she added in the margins and on the back of the page: "because 'my way' is derived from studying other people's ways of doing things and by asking lots of questions. Then sifting all that out and coming up with the fastest, smoothest, most direct way, that uses the least energy, motion or upset to the people or the situations involved." Mary still has strong opinions.

Her Q-sorts based on the 1982 interview did not suggest that Mary was the same person that she was in adolescence but they did suggest that she was remarkably the same person she was at age 49. The correlation between Q-sort profiles of 73 items was .76, as high as the reliability of measurement. In many fundamental respects, she was the same dependable, feminine, productive person she had always appeared to be except for the unsettled period in the senior high school years. Her scores on all components of planful competence were above the mean, much as they were twelve years earlier. No one scores lower on negativism or deceitfulness, and the aloofness that was seen in early adulthood was totally gone. Her personal tempo was still much more rapid than it had been earlier, and she scored higher than ever before on the items of personal warmth, expressiveness, giving, socially perceptive, and "values own independence and autonomy." Mary was no longer primarily a wife or a mother; she had become her own person.

Since her husband's death, Mary had mellowed somewhat without feeling she had changed markedly. Her house was probably not as neat as it was when Chester was alive, nor her attitudes quite as fixed. She seemed more self-aware as well as self-accepting. Although she had once stated that they had not been a deeply religious family, most people would characterize her as deeply religious. She felt that her life had been ordered by God, and she believed in a spiritual world: "The death of the physical body is not the end of a soul and I can feel that." Her religion had been a major source of strength despite the fact that organized religion entered her life only at marriage.

> *Postreview comment:* Mary was surprised to learn that only a few years ago she had referred to the family as not deeply religious.

When asked in 1984 how she would like to be remembered, she hoped it would be as "hard-working and cheerful, had a sense of humor, did pretty well in ceramics and has some great photographs." Mary's answer suggested a rather sharp shift in her sense of herself. In an earlier interview, in her late 30s perhaps, she might have been expected to want to be remembered as a good wife and mother; now she wished to be remembered as an individual with her own characteristics and accomplishments.

Despite many changes, moves, and the tragedy of her husband's death in middle age, Mary remained a stable, secure, cheerful woman, conventional in her views but creative, too. She had been traditional in her roles and her way of living; she felt fulfilled by her life: "a wonderful life, very full. It was exciting and different and loving and warm and trying at times and strange. And I had to bear up under a lot, at times, perhaps, but I look at it as, I think, it was a wonderful life."

Her interviewer in 1982 had failed to ask Mary for her views on the women's movement, so I posed the question after this chapter had been drafted. Mary Wylie was somewhat perplexed at having to deal with this question—over the telephone—a year after we had reviewed her history, but she attempted to explore her own feelings. Certainly she had never been a feminist, and she wished to know just what I included under the label "women's movement." Equal pay for equal jobs? Extreme demands to be treated like men? She said she had never felt oppressed or felt any need for participating in a consciousness-raising group (my term, in probing for her feelings.).

Mary noted that in a family of three girls and no boys, the girls had learned to do the chores boys usually do—yard work, washing the car, and the like—as well as helping with their mother's chores. The women's movement had had little effect on her own life. She was clearly supportive of many of its objectives but found some of the extreme adherents hard to take. Yet she thought that it was inevitable that as women became aware of the extent of inequalities through the mass media, they would become more organized in seeking greater equality. She liked the traditional role she had chosen, but she recognized that not all women would.

The patterns of stability, security, and cheerfulness were established at an early age, were augmented by marriage, and have persisted for the length of Mary's life. She has always been an active participant, committed to the groups of which she was a member. For nearly thirty years, her strongest commitment was to her role as wife and mother, but that role entailed a wide range of responsibility and opportunities for contacts outside the home. Her husband supported, indeed strongly fostered, her developing competencies. Mary never lost her ability to take a positive view of life; one might indeed say that this has consistently been one of her outstanding personal attributes. Despite the conventionality and conformity of her youth, she has been able to adapt to the changing circumstances of her life as needed and to grow in self-awareness and understanding within the framework of traditional roles and responsibilities that have provided the bulwark of her life.

MARY WYLIE'S GENERAL REACTION TO THE HISTORY

In her initial review of her history in 1985, Mary Wylie had many comments on the early years. Once the section on the middle years was reached, she had few comments beyond an occasional "Right!" in the margin. She felt that "everything seemed quite straight there." And although she had originally been somewhat concerned that classmates might recognize her because of certain unique features of her life, she concluded that she probably would not mind if they did.

In general, Mary Wylie's response to the summary of her life as we had reconstructed it was nondefensive, even when she found that our data were not wholly consonant with her own views. We had not initially offered any interpretation of her somewhat unsettled period in senior high school beyond noting that this was fairly typical of adolescence and that Mary had been a late maturer. She herself felt the need for a psychological interpretation in terms of having felt inferior. She had measured herself against her more self-assured older sisters. She perceived herself as "the youngest, the smallest, the weakest and the skinniest." She was easily embarrassed in school and had felt herself deficient as a student in junior high. Not surprisingly, then, she was resolved to change herself as she moved into the senior high years. Puberty brought stresses, and it brought efforts to achieve a new self-definition, as it does for so many adolescents. That new definition seems to have been achieved in the college years, when she discovered that she could not only do as well as her sisters but could surpass them as a student, earning A's in her major.

Mary Wylie accepted almost all of our description of her, though she could not accede to the characterization by the male interviewer who saw her at age 37 as a bit of a Pollyanna. A positive outlook, she felt, was something worth working on—for oneself and for one's children. Quite clearly there is a difference between a person who unconsciously denies (and fails to face up to) the unpleasant aspects of life and one who consciously seeks to find the good side of people and situations and to maximize the potential for positive outcomes.

A FURTHER NOTE, 1991

In 1991, I felt that Mary Wylie's life history did not adequately represent the data from the adolescent years, and I undertook a revision and sent it to her. By now, we had talked a number of times and thoroughly respected each other. Mary reviewed the manuscript, and this time she added comments at several points beyond the description of the adolescent years. Again, she was nondefensive for the most part, though she did not recall some of the attitudes that seemed manifest earlier or some of her statements along the way. This is true of most of us, of course, but no one has interview notes or tape recordings of what we said ten, twenty, or thirty years ago.

Our session together in 1991 afforded me the opportunity to view Mary's impressive gallery of her photographic art and the various types of prints—block prints, monotypes and etchings, monotones, and multichromes—that she has produced in recent years, largely in her art classes at college. She is in no hurry to receive a degree, though she is taking occasional courses to meet academic requirements for graduation. Art is her life, and it is a rich life. Prints from her plates grace a series of publications of the college. She has had work shown in prestigious exhibits, and she now feels ready for an exhibit of her own. Until recently, when her mother died, she visited daily with her mother, leaving little time for the preparations that would be required for an exhibit. As this book goes to press, Mary Wylie is having that first exhibit of her own at the university gallery. She reports that one of her etchings, entered into a larger exhibition of art, was judged "best in the show!" Life is indeed satisfying.

At the same time, Mary is an avid gardener. Dozens of potted plants are mounted on the wall or ring the edge of her patio. Her raspberry patch, tomato plants, and apricot trees were thriving, and she tends the garden entirely on her own. Her face flushed with pleasure as she showed me the sources of her deep contentment. Those who think that the later years must be dreary times should have a chance to visit with Mary. She is in her element. Loving friends, warm relations with her children, and a full agenda of tasks to be accomplished prepare Mary for the next thirty years, which is what she can expect if she lives as long as her mother did.

CHAPTER 6

ANTECEDENTS OF PLANFUL COMPETENCE

The lives of Stuart Campbell and Mary Wylie in a sense speak for themselves. Two persons with unique potentialities were born into families formed by parents having particular cultural backgrounds and socially patterned but personally evolved relational styles. They experienced a particular slice of historical time. In Stuart's case, the death of his mother and the economic deprivation caused by the desertion of his father well before the depression years certainly imposed as stressful conditions as any other encountered later. In Mary's case, her family was relatively well insulated from the effects of the depression by virtue of her father's secure job.[1]

Mary and Stuart faced common developmental tasks but quite different challenges. Before introducing the lives of other study members, it will help to have a more explicit frame of reference for analyzing those lives. This chapter examines more fully the various types of influences that serve to shape development over the life course and, particularly, considers those features of the developmental course in childhood and adolescence that tend to produce high or low competence in the later adolescent years.

PERSONAL ATTRIBUTES OF STUART CAMPBELL AND MARY WYLIE

Stuart Campbell was seen as sickly during his early years and missed much of the first grade, but by the time he was in junior high school, he seemed to be a healthy, fully normal youngster.[2] His tested intelligence was well above the average of the group, giving him almost unlimited intellectual potential. He was seen as slightly

144

more physically attractive than most of his peers in junior high school and was rated a bit higher still in senior high school, in the judgment of staff members who assessed physical appearance. He was reasonably adept in handling his body though not an outstanding athlete in any respect. Finally, his temperament seemed equable, and he was widely regarded as likable, though he showed a strong temper at times.

Stuart was about average in body build—neither tall and thin nor short and muscular and not overweight. He attained puberty at age 13½, almost exactly the average for the study group.[3] Except for intelligence and his pleasant demeanor, the attributes of the adolescent Stuart Campbell did not appear to be exceptional, but Stuart's scores on the measure of planful competence exceeded those of almost all of his peers. He scored high on all three components—self-confidence, intellectual investment, and dependability—in both junior and senior high school. He was seen as slightly below average in assertiveness in junior high school but somewhat above average in senior high school. In both periods, he was also seen as relatively outgoing rather than aloof or reserved. And in both periods he was seen as a warm person, sympathetic to others. Stuart was popular with peers and held leadership positions, but he was more oriented to adult standards than to peer standards and themes.

Mary Wylie was rated one of the most attractive and feminine girls in the whole study group. Her measured intelligence was slightly above the average for girls in the Oakland Growth Study. Although she was seen as thin and frail by her mother, and she shared that view, her health was apparently good and her physique not markedly different from the average of her peers, except for being a bit taller and thinner. Mary was quite late in attaining puberty—nearly two years behind the average of her peers. Mary, like Stuart, appears to have had an even temperament and was easy to get along with except for a somewhat condescending manner.

She did not see herself as self-confident in her junior high years, but Mary was nevertheless rated somewhat above average on the component "self-confident versus victimized," largely because she was calm and cheerful rather than self-defeating and distrustful. She scored above the mean for the group on intellectual investment and dependability in both junior and senior high school. She was seen as more outgoing than most of her peers but somewhat submissive at both periods. Like Stuart, Mary was fairly popular, and she was somewhat more immersed than he was in peer culture.

All of these attributes reported as characteristic of Stuart and Mary in their junior and senior high school years reflect the interaction of what was constitutionally given and their life experience before entering junior high school. Physical attractiveness, body build, and the age at which a person reaches sexual maturity are largely determined by birth. Intelligence is somewhat more malleable, and by the time a child has reached high school, the effects of social class position and intellectual stimulation may have substantially altered the manifest level of intellectual functioning.[4]

In the school years, however, all of these attributes, at whatever level they have reached at any time, have a bearing on the social stimulus value of the person. It is therefore of interest to look at how scores on these several attributes influenced the way the study members as a group were seen by the research staff.

PHYSICAL AND INTELLECTUAL ATTRIBUTES INFLUENCING ADOLESCENT PERSONALITY

Three attributes of the person and his or her social background are substantially related to the person's adolescent planful competence: intelligence, physical attractiveness, and the family's socioeconomic status. Of lesser importance but nevertheless having an effect on some components of personality at adolescence are one's body build, (height, slimness or fatness, muscularity, and so on) and whether puberty is attained early or late. These several attributes have different effects or meanings in males and females and at different stages of adolescence. For example, a girl's IQ is much more strongly related to her being seen as intellectually involved and dependable in junior high school then it is in the senior high years.

Table 6.1 summarizes the relationships found in the senior high school years between physical and intellectual attributes and the several components of personality with which we shall be most concerned, as well as with the index of planful competence itself. Family socioeconomic status is included because it has an influence on a number of the components.

Had Table 6.1 shown correlations with junior high school com-

Table 6.1. Correlations Between Physical and Intellectual Attributes and Competence Index plus Personality Components as of Senior High School Years

Attributes	Planful Competence	Personality Component[a]					
		1	2	3	4	5	6
Males							
Age 17–18 IQ	.59**	.26**	.19	.65**	.14	.47**	-.09
Physical attractiveness	.29*	.55**	-.25*	.11	.11	.04	.02
Ectomorphy (slimness)	.22	.07	-.14	.17	-.18	.29*	.07
Endomorphy (fatness)	-.08	-.20	.07	.05	-.10	-.02	-.19
Mesomorphy (muscularity)	-.17	.14	.09	-.27*	.23*	-.28*	.02
Early sexual maturity	.25*	.31**	-.09	.26*	.10	.02	.10
Parental socioeconomic status (-1)	.22*	-.01	.15	.25**	-.19	.24*	-.25*
Females							
Age 17–18 IQ	.29**	.02	.12	.46**	-.05	.14	-.03
Physical attractiveness	.37**	.55**	-.33**	.13	.06	.10	-.02
Ectomorphy (slimness)	.13	.10	-.03	.13	.09	.05	-.18
Endomorphy (fatness)	-.01	-.21	-.03	.02	-.15	.15	.14
Mesomorphy (muscularity)	-.10	-.01	.07	-.08	.05	-.11	.15
Early sexual maturity	.02	-.09	-.18	-.05	-.25*	.15	.11
Parental socioeconomic status (-1)	.33**	.09	.02	.35**	-.10	.26**	-.07

*p < .05, **p < .01.

[a] 1 = Self-confidence; 2 = Assertiveness versus submissiveness; 3 = Intellectual investment; 4 = Outgoing versus aloof; 5 = Dependable and productive; 6 = Warm, sympathetic.

petence rather than with senior high competence, we would have found a significantly higher correlation between IQ and competence for the girls. Instead of the girls' IQ being negligibly related to dependability in senior high school, we would have found a highly significant correlation (.35) between a girl's IQ and her dependability, as well as a substantially higher correlation between her IQ and her intellectual involvement (.60, essentially the same as for boys). Prior to the assessments in senior high school, the girls had reached sexual maturity; for many of them, boys were now a major topic of interest. In the 1930s it would not do for pubescent girls to show off their brightness, so the manifestation of superior intelligence was considerably dimmed in the service of interpersonal relationships. For boys, on the other hand, IQ became more important between junior and senior high school, and body build became substantially less important. For both boys and girls, physical attractiveness was the strongest single correlate of self-confidence, while IQ was the strongest correlate of intellectual investment.

Physical build and the scheduling of maturation are largely genetically determined, but how they affect behavior and how they are interpreted are influenced by cultural preferences for particular physical types. In the childhood and adolescent years of our study members, as in contemporary America, relatively tall, slim girls and women were in vogue, and broad-shouldered, muscular men were the prototypic cultural heroes, in sports and in the movies. Broad-shouldered, muscular men tend to be stronger and more athletic but not nearly to the extent that stereotypes suggest.[5]

How such stereotypes came into being is a topic beyond our scope, but it is relevant to ask to what extent these stereotypic notions impinged on the study members. The three studies are especially appropriate for the purpose of examining the effects of body build because William Sheldon, the originator of the most sophisticated measures of build (called "somatotypes"), assessed the somatotypes of all of the study members from nude body photographs taken each year from the time of entrance into the studies to late adolescence. Somatotypes are defined by scores on three components of physique: muscularity and squatness (mesomorphic component), thinness (ectomorphic component—literally maximum amount of skin for body mass), and fatness (endomorphic component).[6] While a person's somatotype is defined by all three components, we can relate each one of the components separately to other attributes of the individual. Those with a high mesomorphic component tend to be substantially stronger than those with a low mesomorphic and high ectomorphic component.

In junior high school, mesomorphic boys—muscular, athletic types—scored high on assertiveness and low on intellectual involvement and dependability, though they had higher self-confidence than their less athletic peers. Within the classroom and in the peer group, the mesomorphic boys were seen as daring, as fighters, and as leaders, especially by the working class.[7] They fared less well in the classroom, however. The ectomorphic (often "skinny") boys were less athletic, but they applied themselves intellectually to a greater extent and tended to be highly dependable. These attributes carried over to a somewhat lesser degree into senior high school. In junior high school, the endormorphic (fat) boys were not significantly lower in competence, but they had been rated significantly lower than their peers in self-confidence.

Girls attain puberty earlier than do boys, and most had their growth spurt and first menses while in junior high (average age 11.5). For a few years, those with earliest onset were taller and much more mature in appearance, though ultimately they would be less tall than their peers.[8] For girls, early maturing tended to be awkward and embarrassing, for they were taller than many boys their own age. Early sexual maturity also tended to attract a new kind of attention (and pressure) from older boys. This was a mixed blessing; some girls loved it, but others became less outgoing. For boys, on the other hand, to attain puberty early was to be bigger and stronger than one's peers, and hence to be advantaged in athletics and in appearing mature. Most boys attained puberty shortly before graduating from junior high school (average age 13.5), so it was in their senior high years that early maturing most enhanced social reputation and self-confidence. Early-maturing boys were seen as more poised, more comfortable in relationships with their parents, and more often achieving leadership among and liking from their peers.[9] Note from Table 6.1 that they were not only more self-confident but also more intellectually involved in senior high school. Girls who had attained puberty early tended to be somewhat less assertive and also less outgoing than their peers, though only the latter attribute attained statistical significance.

Social class membership influenced the relative importance of early maturing, muscularity, and intelligence for popularity and leadership. By the senior high school years, academic performance became more important, especially for middle-class boys who were planning to attend college. Therefore, IQ began to be relatively more important in its influence on how a boy would be seen by his peers, attenuating the importance of body build and early maturing for middle-class males.

The data from all three studies confirm the proposition that body build and the timing of attainment of puberty make a difference in how males and females are perceived by their peers and how they see themselves.[10] When we attempt to view the whole life course, however, our interest is in whether there will be lasting effects of differences observed during the adolescent years. To the extent that a person is favored in any respect—height, strength, energy level, beauty—we might expect that person to maximize his or her positive attributes and to have these become especially salient in his or her self-concept. Given two high school students with equal potential for intellectual development but grossly different potential for athletic performance—for example, one low and the other very high—we might expect the person more favored in athletic physique to put greater effort into developing physical prowess, while his athletically inept peer would concentrate on academic performance. Again, peers give a handsome boy or beautiful girl more positive feedback explicitly relating to appearance, and this clearly was reflected for both sexes in self-concept and in aspirations. But sometimes the relatively homely appearing child early in adolescence is described as attractive in adulthood, and vice versa.[11]

People sometimes seek to overcome their handicaps instead of simply shifting the focus of their efforts. In a society in which tall men are more positively viewed than short ones, the short man may be more driven to seek power than his taller peers. Noting the relationships found in adolescence between personality and appearance, we shall want to examine how physical attributes affect long-term outcomes in the life course.

We cannot say that any particular attribute caused the relationships between that attribute and features of personality. A major part of our task will be to discern how these attributes interacted with life experiences, early and late, and what the long-term consequences appear to be. Coming from the middle class or the working class modified somewhat the consequences of body build and of early or late attainment of sexual maturity. To an even greater extent, it influenced the intellectual involvement and dependability of both boys and girls. Better-educated parents tended to provide greater intellectual stimulation and firmer controls on their youngsters, enhancing both tested intelligence and an interest in intellectual matters. When we observe the magnitude of some of the relationships shown in Table 6.1—especially the very strong contribution of IQ to each of the components of competence for males, the extreme importance of physical attractiveness as an influence on the self-confidence of both males and females, and the association of family socioeconomic status with intellectual involvement and dependability—we can be reasonably sure that these will tend to have enduring effects.

SOURCES OF SOCIALIZATION AND SUPPORT

Early Socialization Tasks

Before they came to junior high school or even to the first grade of elementary school, Stuart and Mary had successfully mastered the lessons that a child must learn in order to function successfully in the social world of the school and the larger community. Parents and other agents of socialization seek to provide physical care and nurturance, train the child in bodily control, teach a wide variety of skills, from language to self-care skills, acquaint the child with the rules of social life and the important values of the society, and ultimately help the child to formulate his or her own goals through guidance, correction, encouragement, and support. The child must be able to trust those caretakers or be subject to intense anxiety and must learn to express biological impulses appropriately, recognize objects and cues, negotiate obstacles, communicate, develop an internal map of his or her home and neighborhood, develop a sense of right and wrong, learn to take the perspective of another person in interaction, and achieve a measure of self-regulation and the ability to evaluate his or her own performance. These reciprocal tasks are summarized in Table 6.2.[12] The early years of child training may be a battleground or all may go quite smoothly. When these early tasks have been well mastered, the child is far more likely to have a positive experience in school. Mary and Stuart had such experiences.

We lack detailed information about the early years of Mary and Stuart because they were in the Adolescent Growth Study, for which data collection started when the members were in the fifth or

Table 6.2.   Types of Tasks of Early Childhood Socialization in the Family

Parental Aim or Activity	Child's Task or Achievement
Provision of nurturance and physical care	Acceptance of nurturance (development of trust)
Training and channeling of physiological needs in toilet training, weaning, provision of solid foods, etc.	Control of the expression of biological impulses; learning acceptable channels and times of gratification
Teaching and skill training in language, perceptual skills, physical skills, self-care skills in order to facilitate care, ensure safety, etc.	Learning to recognize objects and cues; language learning; learning to walk, negotiate obstacles, dress, feed self, etc.
Orienting the child to the immediate world of kin, neighborhood, community, and society and to his or her own feelings	Developing a cognitive map of one's social world; learning to fit behavior to situational demands
Transmitting cultural and subcultural goals and values and motivating the child to accept them for his or her own	Developing a sense of right and wrong; developing goals and criteria for choices; investment of effort for the common good
Promoting interpersonal skills, motives, and modes of feeling and behaving in relation to others	Learning to take the perspective of another person; responding selectively to the expectations of others
Guiding, correcting, helping the child to formulate own goals and plan activities	Achieving a measure of self-regulation and criteria for evaluating own performance

sixth grade. So far as we know, neither was a difficult child in early childhood. We know from the Guidance Study that many parents are concerned in the early years about problems like enuresis, thumb sucking, temper tantrums, and other behaviors frowned upon but difficult to control. Jean Macfarlane and her staff found that almost all young children showed some behaviors that their parents regarded as problems but that most had disappeared by the time the children were of school age.[13] A few tended to persist, and these are of interest in trying to assess how important the early years are in determining the later personality or character of the adolescent and adult.

Some problems, such as nocturnal enuresis and thumb sucking, were early manifest by a high proportion of children but decreased rapidly with age, while others, such as disturbed sleep and fears, increased to around 4½ years and then leveled off, decreasing prior to the onset of puberty. Still other problems, such as nail biting and disturbing dreams, increased right up to the onset of puberty. Lying was very common in the age range 4 to 7 years and was still reported for more than a third of the boys and a fifth of the girls at ages 8 and 9, but dropped off sharply thereafter. Temper tantrums were reported to occur with some frequency on the part of most boys and girls up to age 7 and then dropped off but were still mentioned by nearly a third of the mothers when their sons were age 12, with daughters not far below this level.

Perhaps the most interesting finding for our purposes was that marital adjustment yielded more consistent and higher correlations with behavior and personality difficulties than did other family variables."[14] Where there was much marital tension and unhappiness (which may have led ultimately to divorce), children tended to be more demanding of attention, negativistic, and given to temper tantrums. As Caspi, Elder, and Bem have demonstrated, these attributes had later consequences.[15] Where the marital relationship was good, parents tended to agree on discipline. Parental education appeared to show fewer relationships with children's problems than did intrafamily relationships.

Both Stuart and Mary initially enjoyed the care of a loving mother and father, though we know far less about Stuart's parents than about Mary's. As a consequence of his mother's tuberculosis, Stuart must have been deprived of her care intermittently. We have no information about his caretakers when his mother was unable to care for him. Perhaps his father received help from his own parents, who lived in the Bay Area. It is hard to imagine Stuart's calm self-assurance as a child if there had not been some consistently loving and supportive person or persons when his mother was unavailable. We know that he exhibited no fear of depending on others, despite the loss of his mother and father early in life, as well as the disruption caused by being placed in a sanitarium for many months. Such losses and disruptions can often lead a child to hold back from establishing close ties with others, fearing that they, too, will abandon him.[16] We do not know what protected Stuart from such a feeling, but he escaped it. Without question, once his Scottish grandmother appeared, he had consistent, loving care. Although she was unexpressive and somewhat lacking in warmth, he never had any doubt that if she lived, she would care for him.

Stuart reported that a close tie to one of his peers and to that boy's parents helped to teach him how to behave in a society that was alien to his grandmother. His grandmother could provide neither the male guidance nor the sense of expected grooming and demeanor appropriate to an American boy. Stuart learned very early to turn to others who could assist him, but when he needed her, his grandmother was always there as a source of support. She insisted on high standards, and she gave him responsibilities that strengthened his self-esteem. He respected her and looked up to adult figures.

Mary Wylie was also held to high standards by loving parents. It appears that her mother maintained firm and consistent discipline, and she was supportive and attentive. Mrs. Wylie also stressed kindness to others and the importance of moral obligations. She insisted that one focus on the positive aspects of experience, not the negative. With Mary, however, popularity and social status were presented as more important than intellectual prowess. She was also more sheltered and timid than Stuart, as were most girls of her generation.

Mary had older sisters who could orient her to the world of peers and, later, to the game of dating. Mary's late sexual maturing, however, and apparently a rather modest sex drive kept her from being highly involved with boys. Popular with peers and fun loving, Mary was taught to conform to highly conventional standards by conservative parents. She did not claim the rights and privileges of adolescence but was nevertheless much more involved than Stuart in the peer group, although her friends were highly conventional and not rebellious. The standards of her parents were never supplanted by peer group standards. Mary, like Stuart, had come through early childhood and adolescence with firm controls, good social skills, and a reasonably good idea of who she was and where she wanted to go. Relative to Stuart, Mary seemed unduly sheltered from the real world—not only sexually innocent but also unaware of the meaning of poverty or minority status. Her values were those transmitted by her parents. To a much greater extent, Stuart's values in high school were achieved through his own seeking for answers from many sources.

Thus we see certain similarities and certain quite clear differences between two highly competent adolescents. Some of the differences, especially those relating to life goals, were in a sense badges of gender in the 1930s. Others were the product of family climates, temperament, and chance associations. Most of the similarities, however, were derived from the kind of parenting or socialization experiences within the family that had been experienced by the time Stuart and Mary came to junior high school.

The Effects of Parenting on Study Members' Adolescent Competence

The combination of high standards, firm controls, and loving support that Stuart and Mary experienced has been found to influence each of the components of what I have labeled planful competence. Two previous longitudinal studies—one conducted many decades ago and the other fairly recent— give firm support for this assertion, and, as we shall see, the background of Mary and Stuart is quite typical of our adolescents with high competence. The earlier study, by A. L. Baldwin and his colleagues, found that parents who employ democratic authority (high levels of communication between parent and child with consultation of the child on decisions affecting that child, and encouragement of self-reliance) tended to produce children who were above average in ability to plan and who were socially involved.[17]

More recently, Diana Baumrind has sought to identify behavioral outcomes of different child rearing practices at several periods of childhood and adolescence.[18] She found at the preschool level that "children who were happy, self-reliant and able to meet challenging situations directly had parents who exercised a good deal of control over their children and demanded responsible, independent behavior from them but who also explained, listened and provided emotional support." Baumrind then identified "agentic children" (showing social leadership and high cognitive functioning at age 8 or 9) and found that their parents exercised firm rule enforcement, especially for girls, and high demands for self-control, especially for boys. Authoritarian and permissive parents had the least competent or agentic children. Other recent studies Baumrind cited stress the importance of both demandingness and supportiveness on the part of parents.

Parental behaviors toward a child are influenced by the parents' social class, temperaments, personalities, and beliefs about child rearing and the child's appearance, temperament, capabilities, and learned behaviors. We cannot yet specify what is genetically given and what is learned. An interactive process that starts soon after birth creates patterns of relationship that tend to persist. Parental calm, control, and enjoyment of the child engender positive responses in the child. A child who is positively responsive to his or her parents tends to evoke loving support; one who is willfully disobedient tends to exacerbate tension within the relationship and perhaps to elicit harsh parental responses. As the child matures, it is desirable to have both an account of parental behaviors and some indication of how the child perceives his or her parents. Fortunately, we have both in our early data.[19]

Ratings of parental behavior for several periods in the childhood years for members of the Guidance Study and in the junior and senior high school years for Oakland Growth Study members were derived many decades later from all available data, relating to each period, using several raters. Information available on fathers was too sparse to be rated reliably except for a few general items, but information relating to mothers permitted the rating of a large number of the mothers' behaviors. These were factor analyzed to yield several more global measures. We labeled the most global "mother attentive and supportive." It includes items relating to the quality of the mother's relationship with the child, her emotional support of the child, her care for the child's needs, the use of positive reinforcement, and maternal responsiveness. (See Appendix B for further information.) A second global measure, "firm and consistent discipline," incorporates items on parental control, firm enforcement of rules, consistent discipline, rules clearly stated, and the mother's encouragement of moral values. A third cluster of items relates to the father's attentiveness. Finally, a cluster of items relating to the encouragement of achievement, intellectual achievement, and considerate behavior gives a measure labeled "encouragement of achievement."

Table 6.3 shows the relationship of these items (and others, soon

Table 6.3.   Correlations Between Scores based on Clusters of Parenting
Ratings and Interpersonal Q-sorts as of Ages 11 to 14 and
Personality Components in the Senior High Years

Parenting and Other Early Antecedents	Planful Competence	Personality Component[a]					
		1	2	3	4	5	6
Males							
Maternal attentiveness	.24*	.37**	-.33**	.03	.06	.16	.30**
Firm, consistent parental discipline[b]	.42**	.39**	—	.30*	—	.34**	—
Paternal attentiveness	.14	.33*	-.38**	-.13	.02	.13	.22
Parents stress achievement	.26*	.12	-.02	.22	.03	.27*	-.02
Nonconflicted family	.34**	.47**	-.12	.06	.10	.28*	.17
Parents respected models	.41**	.22	-.30**	.27*	-.23*	.46**	.39**
IQ	.59**	.26*	.19	.65**	.14	.47**	-.09
Parental socioeconomic status (-1.)	.22*	.01	.15	.25*	-.19	.24*	-.25*
Females							
Maternal attentiveness	.33**	.27*	-.21*	.12	-.02	.30**	.19
Firm, consistent parental discipline	.49***	.37***	-.28*	.25*	-.18	.41***	.26*
Paternal attentiveness	.31**	.40***	-.16	.05	.10	.21	.05
Parents stress achievement	.32**	.15	-.10	.21	-.06	.30**	-.03
Nonconflicted family	.26*	.42***	.00	.07	.09	.05	-.05
Parents respected models	.56***	.41***	-.38***	.27*	-.06	.48***	.36**
IQ	.31**	.01	.16	.48***	-.06	.17	-.01
Parental socioeconomic status (-1.)	.33**	.09	.02	.35**	-.10	.26**	-.07
Physical attractiveness	.37***	.55***	-.33**	.13	.06	.10	-.02

*$p < .05$; **$p < .01$; ***$p < .001$.

[a] 1 = Self-confidence; 2 = Assertiveness versus submissiveness; 3 = Intellectual investment; 4 = Outgoing versus aloof; 5 = Dependable and productive; 6 = Warm, sympathetic.

[b] See note 20.

to be discussed) to planful competence and to the six components of personality. For comparison I have included IQ, parental socio-economic status, and, for women, physical attractiveness. The effects of parenting assessed as of the junior high school years on senior high planful competence are substantial, especially their effects on self-confidence and dependability. Maternal attentiveness and support not only enhanced self-confidence and warmth but tended to produce less assertive adolescents, and for girls, it also significantly increased dependability. Firm and consistent discipline strengthened all three components of planful competence for both girls and boys.[20] Paternal attentiveness had a substantially greater effect on the planful competence of girls but again increased self-confidence and decreased assertiveness for both genders. Indeed, when we compare components 1 and 2, "self-confident versus feels victimized" and "assertive versus submissive," it appears that the influences or attributes that increased self-confidence also decreased assertiveness. The two components are negatively related. There are, however, somewhat different patterns of influence for boys and girls, competence more highly associated with both maternal attentiveness and firm parental discipline on the part of girls.

The contributions of parental attentiveness and of firm and consistent discipline to self-confidence and dependability remain strong when social class and the child's IQ are controlled. Parental social class very strongly affects parental encouragement of achievement, which in turn affects "intellectual investment," and even the item "parent encourages achievement" makes only a slight contribution to intellectual investment when social class is controlled. IQ is, of course, the strongest correlate of intellectual investment, and its relationship to parental socioeconomic status partly accounts for the strong relationshp between that variable and intellectual investment. The parenting dimensions we were able to assess were not strongly related to the adolescent's intellectual investment, but there is much evidence that an adolescent's attainment on an intelligence test is itself markedly influenced by the kind of intellectual stimulation and support the child earlier received in the family.

A separate assessment of parent-child relations from the perspective of the study members themselves, using data from the junior high school period, was carried out in the early 1960s. I drew upon this set of ratings, the interpersonal Q-sort, in reporting on how Mary and Stuart were seen in their high school years. The items rated included several relating to the children's respect for their parents, harmony in the parental home, the children's feelings that their parents treated them fairly and respected their own growth and maturity, and the children's general satisfaction with their families. These ratings were not seen by the judges who assessed the parents' behaviors. Factor analysis revealed two principal factors, which we labeled "parents are respected role models" and "non-conflictual relationships in the family" (described in Appendix B). Both were found to be strongly related to the parenting components and to the children's scores on planful competence in both junior and senior high school. The relationships to planful competence and the personality components are included in Table. 6.3. When we view parenting from the adolescent's perspective in the junior high years, we are seeing not merely what the parents have done or tried to do but how it has affected the offspring. Thus, the early adolescents' perspectives may be regarded as reflecting both the parents' behaviors and the prevailing relationshp between parent and offspring.

How much of planful competence do the antecedents account for? To assess the total contribution of the several antecedents discussed so far, both parenting dimensions and the dimensions reflecting the adolescent's perspective in junior high school have been entered into multiple regressions with IQ, parental socioeconomic status, and physical attractiveness.[21] A *multiple regression* is a means of assessing the degree of association of several independent variables in combination with a "dependent" variable. While one cannot impute causation to this association, the coefficients indicate how much each of the independent variables might be contributing to explaining the magnitude of the dependent variable for the given sample. Here, the scores on the parenting components and the adolescents' perspective components, along with IQ, social class, and physical attractiveness, are the independent variables, and the measure of planful competence in senior high school is the dependent variable. All of the independent variables except physical attractiveness are based on data antecedent to the senior high school years, which increases the likelihood that they contribute to, rather than result from, planful competence. The statistic R^2 is the square of the multiple correlation coefficient, which represents the strength of the relationship of all the independent variables together to the dependent variable. R^2 is an indication of the percentage of variation (called "variance") in the dependent variable that is "explained" by this particular group of independent variables in this particular sample.

It may be helpful to delineate step by step what each variable contributed to the total variance explained, looking first at the parenting dimensions and then at the adolescents' perceptions. For males, if we limit the independent variables to the combination of IQ and family socioeconomic status, these two account for just under one-fifth of the variance in senior high school planful competence, while for females they account for a little more than 12 percent. When physical attractiveness is added in, it increases the explained variance to 27 percent for males and 22 percent for females. The contribution of parental socioeconomic status is negligible when IQ and other variables are included in the regression equation, so it can be dropped from the predictive equation, but the parenting item, "mother attentive and supportive," adds another 7 percent to the explained variance for males.

The prediction of adolescent planful competence from antecedent variables for adolescent females is a somewhat different story. While physical attractiveness plays no larger role than for males, IQ is of much less importance when a measure of parenting is entered into the predictive equation. For females, however, the strongest contribution by far comes from "firm and consistent discipline," which accounts for the largest part of the explained variance, adding another 10 percent. The coefficients that retained statistical significance and the percentage of the score on the planful competence index that is "accounted for" are shown in Table 6.4.

Because the adolescent's junior high perspective on his or her parents already reflects some of the elements of competence (lack of rebelliousness, respect for parents, and so forth), we would expect that it would be more strongly related to competence in senior high, and that is indeed the case. For boys, the amount of explained variance reaches over 50 percent, with IQ the major contributor but with significant contributions from physical attractiveness, nonconflicted family, and parents as respected role models (again shown in Table 6.4). For girls, the amount of explained variance is roughly 40 percent, with the major contribution coming from "parents are respected role models," and lesser contributions from "physically attractive" and "IQ".

Table 6.4. Multiple Regression of Planful Competence in Senior High School on Parenting and Other Antecedent Variables as of Junior High Years (Standardized Beta Coefficients)

	Males		Females	
	Parenting Items	Adolescent Perceptions	Parenting Items	Adolescent Perceptions
IQ	.48***	.46***	.16	.24*
Physical attractiveness	.28**	.28**	.26**	.24**
Maternal attentiveness	.24*			
Firm, consistent discipline			.39***	
Nonconflicted family		.24*		
Parents respected role models		.28**		.52***
R² (Adjusted R²)	.39 (.35)	.54 (.51)	.33 (.30)	.41 (.39)

*$p < .05$; **$p < .01$; ***$p < .001$.

Note: In the empty cells, the variable was not entered.

Because of the relatively limited number of study members for whom we have data on both parenting and adolescent competence, it is not feasible to use more than three or four variables to predict adolescent competence. We know from other studies that many other experiences and circumstances influence school performance and the child's achievement of maturity. Our measurement of socialization practices within the family is reconstructed from diverse kinds of data collected long before sophisticated conceptualizations of parenting practices. Currently, available measures might considerably raise the contribution of parenting. Undoubtedly extrafamilial influences, such as school experiences and peer contacts, are also important. Differences in temperament associated with genetic factors also play a part in accounting for adolescent planful competence, as does good health.

Both Stuart Campbell and Mary Wylie reported that they were spanked as children, Stuart much more vigorously, it appears. We do not have systematic information on the use of spanking as a means of punishment by the parents of our study members, but spanking was certainly more commonly accepted by educated parents then than it is today. A number of others of our highly competent study members reported childhood spankings that were accepted as appropriate. Spanking appears to have had little effect on competence or on the parent-child relationship. The parents were, in these instances, loving, and they provided nurturant care as well as occasional punishment. Far more damaging than physical punishment was conflict between the parents.

Other Sources of Socialization and Support

The peer group is another major source of socialization, especially as an arena for learning to interact with others who do not share the same behavioral preferences and beliefs that the child has learned in the family. The child gets to try out his or her skills, to explore, to deal with hostility, to establish friendships, to negotiate in behalf of one's rights and moral beliefs. We often use the term *peer group* as though it represented a monolithic society. It does not. There are many peer groups, especially in the adolescent years. True, there is a kind of adolescent culture, first described by James Coleman, that is widely shared—a culture that revolves around hedonistic activities, inward-lookingness, psychic attachment, concern for the underdog, and a strong drive for autonomy.[22] This culture, which has emerged only with the extension of education through the adolescent years, is a response to a prolonging of the period of dependency after the attainment of a fair measure of physical maturity, as well as essentially full intellectual powers.

Partaking of the themes of adolescent culture does not necessarily entail commitment to the more rebellious elements of it. If early experimenting with the trappings of adulthood—especially sex, tobacco, and alcohol and other drugs—is one expression of the drive for autonomy, it is not necessarily the dominant one. Such experimenting certainly was not at all the dominant pattern in the 1930s, though one segment of the peer group did go in for smoking, drinking, and sex. Neither Stuart nor Mary was caught up in associations with that segment. Stuart would have been happy to be seduced by an older woman, but he was not about to seduce a classmate, nor was he attracted to girls like the study member who reported, "If you want them to like you, you might as well give them what they want." Study members who were highly knowledgeable of the peer culture and participated most fully in that part of the peer society were less planfully competent. They had less good relationships with their parents, secured less education, and subsequently had more problems with tobacco and alcohol than did those with whom Stuart and Mary got together.

The peers with whom Mary and Stuart associated were interested in both academic and extracurricular activities. They hoped to attend college. Stuart was also engaged in earning money to help out at home, so he had less leisure time, though he did not apparently feel much pressured until he was in college. Those peers who were lowest in planful competence were seldom interested in what their schools had to offer; many wanted to get out as soon as possible. They failed to realize that further education could open up occupational opportunities otherwise unavailable to them.

OPPORTUNITIES AND OBSTACLES

Historical cohorts—persons born at a particular time—and individuals differ in the opportunities they find and the obstacles they must face in trying to pursue their goals. The very process of formulating long-term goals depends on having opportunities to develop interests and abilities. In the adolescent years and in the transition to adulthood, the adolescent has to come to terms with a changing appearance, changing sexual feelings, differential rates of physical development among peers, new patterns of association in large, impersonal high schools, and increased demands for mature behavior at the same time that opportunities to escape adult controls are markedly increased. In addition, the adolescent must somehow formulate who he or she is and what he or she wants to do in the years ahead. This is a very large order, and it obviously is not all accomplished in the high school or even the college years.

Achieving a firm sense of identity is surely one of the most important tasks of the adolescent years. Indeed Erikson saw it as the preeminent task of adolescence. Identity entails not only a sense of continuity and coherence but a sense of respects in which one is unique, a set of commitments to principles that are important (values, goals, beliefs), a sense of who one belongs with and wants to be identified with, a measure of self-knowledge of one's strengths and weaknesses, and, crucially important, feelings about oneself—self-esteem—that derive from all of the above and from the reflected appraisals received from others. Despite the sense of coherence, identities are not fixed; they will be modified by experience over the life course. Identities tend to become especially linked with re-lationships and occupational careers, and they may be shattered by some experiences. Yet it is in adolescence that identity begins to be stabilized and the sense of uniqueness and the knowledge of where we belong are likely to be achieved. A knowledge of options, an awareness of opportunities, and potential obstacles will help shape that identity.

Social Class

In the 1930s Americans were just becoming aware that social classes existed in the United States. It had been common to ascribe social classes to Europe and to maintain that in the United States all men were treated as equals. (Women did not enter into discussions of such matters.) Then in the 1920s Robert and Helen Lynd con-ducted their famous study of "Middletown" and described how the working class and what they called the "business class" differed in their ways of life. A decade later, Lloyd Warner and his students de-scribed the class structure of "Yankee City," a New England commu-nity. The class structure of the United States was somewhat more fluid than that of England, but the classes differed in where they lived, how long they went to school, how their members earned their living, whom they married, the churches they attended, what they wanted for their children, how they were treated before the law, and in a host of other ways. Although we talk of upper, middle, and lower classes, the boundaries are not fixed. What we refer to is a hierarchical order, deriving from differences in education, occu-pation, social prestige, and income that make life much easier for those higher up than for those lower down in the hierarchy.

Social class has a significant effect on the child's measured intel-ligence and the resources available to assist the individual from the early stages of life well into the adult years. In our study sample, for example, the average difference in adolescent IQ between those who became professionals and those who became skilled manual workers was twelve IQ points.[23] The difference in educational at-tainment was more striking: 73 percent of the middle-class male study members ultimately graduated from college as compared with 32 percent of men from the working class. Parental social class made a greater difference for females: the percentages of college graduates were 45 and 7 for girls from middle- and working-class families, respectively.

Parents were much more eager to have their sons go to college than to have their daughters go, especially in the working class, where resources were least. Whereas a male's completion of college depended more on his IQ than on his family's class position, a female's doing so was more dependent on her father's and mother's education and occupational status. Girls' IQs were no less affected by the parents' socioeconomic status than were boys', but the family's resources and encouragement were more crucial for girls. The linkage of opportunities to social class was made more significant by the economic depression during the developmental years of our study members.

Impact of the Great Depression

In *Children of the Great Depression,* Glen Elder described the impact of the depression of the 1930s on the children of the Oakland Growth Study. He indexed deprivation by prolonged unemployment of the chief wage earner and/or income loss exceeding 34 percent of prior income. Roughly 55 percent of the middle-class families and 70 percent of the working-class families experienced deprivation by these criteria. Income loss for the deprived averaged roughly three-fifths of prior income, leaving working-class families an average income of $1,118 and deprived middle-class families an income just under $1,500 in 1933.[24]

In 1933, when the study started, most members of the Oakland Growth Study were too young to be employed, except as they might carry newspapers or act as baby-sitters. Many youngsters, especially girls, helped out at home, because families had to produce through their own efforts some of the goods and services they were formerly able to purchase. By 1936, when the highest rates of unemployment had receded but many families were still struggling to make ends meet, the children's roles in the household economy were explored in one of the interviews with mothers. At this time, two-fifths of the children were employed in part-time jobs, with over half of the boys holding at least one paid job as compared with a fourth of the girls. The girls, on the other hand, were heavily involved in providing help at home. Many of their mothers were now working part time at any job they could find in order to supplement family income. Girls employed outside the home were primarily from working-class families in which fathers were still unemployed or were absent. Not the least effect of the depression was the turmoil in the families as many struggled to meet their needs.

Involvement of the children in household tasks and employment was substantially greater in larger families than in smaller ones. As Elder points out, such participation in the family economy led the child to a greater understanding of the management of money and a greater sense of personal responsibility. In addition, Elder reports that

> all of the evidence suggests that economic loss and work roles tended to free boys from the traditional restraints of parental control. While most girls responded to family hardship by assuming household responsibilities, this adaptation had little consequence for their dependence on the family or parental control, with the possible exception of girls from working-class homes.[25]

Thus, a severe family problem was both an obstacle to be overcome and a means to enhanced competence for some, especially some of the boys. We have seen how Stuart Campbell developed a sense of having some measure of control over his own destiny. Mary Wylie was less aware and did not even realize the extent to which her parents had to sacrifice because her father had kept his job and their home was relatively secure.

That is the picture, then, of the impact of the Great Depression upon the members of the Oakland Growth Study. What of the other cohort? Here the children were still preschoolers at the depth of the depression and had far less understanding of what was going on. By the time they reached adolescence, America was engaged in World War II. Thus, the members of the Guidance Study and the Berkeley Growth Study were entirely dependent on their parents during the period of depression and would have been subject to the tensions existing in the families in which unemployment had brought severe deprivation. Elder has suggested that the roles available to the children in the younger study cohort were not such as to challenge them and make them highly competent, and we shall want to observe what we can of the depression's long-term effects.[26]

Other Obstacles and Opportunities

Social class membership and the depression created inequalities of opportunity within our study. Gender was responsible for perhaps a greater inequality. The parents of study members had different expectations for sons and daughters, and the daughters were constrained toward marriage and family as the central roles in life. Even if they sought further education, occupational opportunities were available primarily in "women's work"—nursing, elementary school teaching, and secretarial and other clerical jobs. While war industries offered a brief period of opportunity for meaningful employment, after the war there were millions of servicemen to be reabsorbed into the labor force.

For the men of the Adolescent Growth Study, World War II came at a time when they were either starting their occupational careers or just getting well along in college. Some, like Stuart, managed to finish their training because the skills they were learning were much needed. Doctors were in demand to deal with heavy war casualties, and so there was even government support for their medical training. But for most men, the war brought service unrelated to what they had done or would do subsequently. Even here, adolescent competence had a payoff value: the highly competent adolescents tended to become officers.

This is perhaps getting ahead of the story, for war service and employment take us beyond the adolescent years and well along in the transition to full maturity. The kinds of obstacles and opportunities I have been discussing thus far are those that are a consequence of where one is placed in the society and when various historical events impinged on the life course. I have not stressed race or ethnic groups because so few members of the sample belonged to the groups most excluded from opportunities in our society. African-Americans and Asian-Americans were certainly excluded from the social circles of the Caucasian study members as well as from equal opportunities of employment.[27] But others were excluded or at least subject to great handicaps for individual reasons: health, mentally ill or physically impaired parents, deaths in the family. Stuart Campbell might have been one of these, had he not had a grandmother whose determination and meager allocation from the estate left to her ensured him an education in the United States. The sources of socialization and support are themselves very closely tied to the larger social structure and to the sets of expectations, combined with life events, that open or close potential doors.

There is also the matter of chance encounters, of happy or unhappy coincidences.[28] One of them was the coincidence that Stuart's maternal grandmother was on the scene when his mother died. Another was that Stuart was in a study where a physician could take an interest in him and advise him that he could be a physician himself, despite his coming from a working-class family. There are also unforeseeable crises, such as Mary Wylie experienced when her husband was suddenly stricken with a brain tumor. Each life will have its share of such events, but some persons will be luckier than others. Some will have much heavier burdens to bear. Some crises will be self-inflicted, like Stuart's unwise first marriage. Others, such as the one Mary Wylie faced, can be ascribed only to fate or chance. Our competent adolescents had fewer self-inflicted crises than did their less competent peers, but they did face unpredictable difficulties like everyone else.

THE INDIVIDUAL'S OWN EFFORTS AND COMMITMENTS

This is the most difficult of the major classes of influence to explain. It is of necessity the product of all the others, but it must be something more. It entails the ability to mobilize resources and cope with difficulties. Some persons seem very vulnerable to setbacks; others seem to be able to handle nearly insuperable problems without giving up. The essence of what I wish to designate here is the person's sense of being able to do whatever has to be done. It is variously called "internal locus of control," "ego resilience," and "self-direction."[29]

The ability to mobilize one's resources to cope effectively depends on the resources themselves and especially on the energy level or drive that the person possesses. Some study members were passive drifters through high school years and have seemed more like spectators of their lives than masters of their life course. Mary Wylie's rapid tempo and Stuart Campbell's drive to make something of his life almost certainly derived in some part from the temperaments with which their genes endowed them. So, no doubt, did some of the passivity that less competent study members often exhibited.

Drive may be expressed in different ways: in striving for success or for justice or for the welfare of others, or for sexual or artistic expression. We have no measures of these forms of drive except for self-reports in the later years, but the highly competent study members appear to show greater drive through the life course when compared with those less competent. For example, planfully competent adolescents are more sexually active forty to forty-five years after high school than are their less competent peers.

Also entailed is the individual's ability to decide what is important to him or her, determination to pursue the goals that matter, and willingness to make firm commitments to self and others. This is an essential aspect of planful competence. As I suggested in Chapter 1, this ability is developed as a person learns to assess his or her options, to undertake activities that are challenging and to do this on one's own.

In examining the specific patental behavior ratings most highly correlated with competence, it emerged that the strongest negative ones were laxness and permissiveness. One might have thought that permissive parenting would give the child an opportunity to do things on the child's own initiative. Quite the contrary; lax and permissive parenting did not afford the combination of encouragement and stimulation along with firm guidance and control where needed. Children could not develop self-confidence when they failed to behave in accordance with prevailing expectations for someone of their age. They could not make assessments of their options without assistance from someone who could help to interpret the world they did not yet understand.

Parenting was a very important element in the child's learning how to mobilize his or her efforts and to make firm commitments. We must not think of parenting as having had all of its effects in the early years. Parents' responses to the problems of adolescence sometimes changed rather markedly the offspring's sense of his or her ability to cope. Most of the study members did not change much from the junior high to the senior high years, but a few changed a good deal.[30] Some became much more self-confident and intellectually invested. Some, especially a few of the girls who did not look forward to the roles expected for them by their parents, seemed to lose not only self-confidence but their sense of zest. One highly competent junior high girl shifted to the fun-loving peer group late in senior high once she learned that her parents

would not help her get a college education. Others managed to go
to college with only minimal aid. Influences beyond the home became important sources of guidance and support.

ADOLESCENT INTERESTS AND ACTIVITIES IN THE 1930s

The primary sources of entertainment for most high school youth
in the 1930s were radio, movies, and magazines, plus athletic
events.[31] Favorite radio programs and movie stars were topics of
conversation in the 1930s and were reported on inventories used
most frequently in the Adolescent Growth Study. In accounts of
what they did on a typical day, however, few study members reported that they listened to the radio and very few that they spent
much time on this activity. Reading magazines and books occupied
more of their time, especially among middle-class youngsters, but
for most, activities with peers were by far the most important ways
in which the adolescents spent their time outside school. Also,
more than half the boys had some form of employment in the later
high school years, as did a fourth of the girls. Many girls were responsible for household duties.

Boys engaged in sports far more than did girls, and much of the
boys' time was spent on playgrounds and athletic fields. This was especially true of the working-class boys in the study. Middle-class
boys generally had more money for crafts and equipment and more
often engaged in building model airplanes, collecting stamps, sub-
scribing to magazines, and buying books.

Girls tended to be much more submissive and limited in activities. By the junior high years, concern about appearance and dress
made such matters a more important part of a girl's life. Girls were
more interested in parties well before boys and in romantic movies
and dancing. Not until the final two years of senior high school did
many boys begin to take a significant interest in dancing, but by age
13 most girls wanted opportunities to dance.

For boys, having access to a car (or, better, owning one) became
a major concern as adolescence progressed. In the junior high
years, more than 95 percent of the Oakland Growth Study boys
wanted a bicycle, and presumably most ultimately had one. By age
15, 90 percent wanted to own a car. Considering the depth of the
depression in the mid-1930s, one might assume that few could at-

tain this goal, but a number managed to buy a second-hand vehicle. An older car in running condition could be bought for as little as twenty-five dollars, for cars were constantly being repossessed by dealers. A boy with a paper route or another part-time job could easily clear a few dollars a week if his family did not need his earnings.

Neither boys nor girls claimed to spend very much time on homework during the 1930s and 1940s. Most were apparently able to do much of their course assignments during open periods in school.

Dating was much less frequent among high school students in the 1930s and 1940s than in recent decades, especially in early adolescence. In the ninth grade, there was infrequent interest in dating or in the opposite sex as compared to the 1980s or even the 1950s. Girls began dating earlier than boys, and the "faster" girls dated much older boys. By the twelfth grade, most boys were beginning to date if they had not done so earlier.

Attitude surveys administered to students in the Oakland study revealed far less tolerance of different ethnic groups and religious denominations than was manifest after World War II, when prejudice and discrimination became much less acceptable in America, though they still existed. On the other hand, these youth seemed almost puritanical in their rejection of betting on games, playing cards for money, and disapproval of women smoking.

THE EXPECTABLE LIFE COURSE

For any historical period, there is an expectable life course in the sense that most people will follow a roughly predictable set of developmental experiences.[32] They will take on major social roles in a relatively narrow band of years and will, if they survive to the expectable age at death, have encountered a number of widely shared life experiences. True, there will be considerable variation at the extremes of social status, physical well-being, and psychological health, but in general they will be subject to common influences. Moreover, there will be something of a "normative schedule" that will let people sense that they are "on time," "early," or late." Such a schedule was certainly in the minds of most of our study members, born in the 1920s. The schedule was somewhat different for working-class than for middle-class men and women. Both tended to follow somewhat similar paths, but the paths of working-class persons more often contained obstacles—broken families, unemployment, disrupted careers—and life expectancy was somewhat shorter for those with the most meager resources.

The Adolescent-Adult Transition

By the 1930s, the childhood and adolescent years were largely structured by the demands of the school, with family, work, and leisure activities taking up the residual time. Late adolescence began the period, now much studied by psychologists and social scientists, called the "adolescent-adult transition." The transition traditionally entailed a series of changes in status but not necessarily in any particular order: the shift from student status to the status of worker or of housewife, separation from parents and establishment of an independent life, and marriage and the establishment of a new family.

At the turn of the century, the adolescent-adult transition might begin much earlier and last much longer.[33] Many children left school and began full-time work at the age of 12. They might continue to live in their parents' home for another two decades. Males might leave to serve in the army or seek work in a different region, but females more often stayed with their parents until marriage. Marriage most often came in the late 20s for men and the mid-20s for women, as it did for the parents of our study members. Not everyone followed such a schedule, of course. There were great differences between social classes, ethnic groups, and rural versus urban residents. But the adolescent-adult transition tended to be much more drawn out than in the 1930s.

In the 1930s, most adolescents in the United States completed high school.[34] Many worked at least part time while they continued education beyond high school. In the 1930s and 1940s, women were married in high proportion by their early 20s; the average age at marriage was roughly 21. For men, the average age at marriage was three or four years later, and there was greater dispersion, with a number waiting beyond age 30. Working-class men and women tended to marry earlier than their middle-class peers.

The men and women in our sample closely approximated the national norms in age at first marriage, though there was very little difference between middle-class and working-class men in age at marriage. Most had their first child within two years of marriage. More than 97 percent of the women in our study group married, and more than 90 percent had one or more children, part of their clearly expectable life course. The proportions of men marrying and fathering children were just slightly lower.

For men, especially in the middle class, establishment in a steady job had generally been expected as a prelude to serious consideration of marriage, but the Great Depression and the extension of education into the college level had begun to erode that expectation. Part-time work or almost any kind of full-time job might be combined with further education or marriage, or both, particularly if both husband and wife had some kind of employment. In general, though, the expectation was that the man would earn the family's income, and his wife would maintain the home. Until there were children, most women took jobs, often clerical jobs in retail trade or in an office. The few who sought careers were most likely to prepare for secretarial jobs, nursing, or teaching at the elementary school level.

By the end of their high school years, roughly a third of the men and a somewhat smaller proportion of the women had some idea of the careers they wanted to pursue, based on their interests and perceived opportunities (though the women almost always were more focused on marriage). The rest either crystallized occupational goals in the course of further education or, through a process of trial and error, followed up leads until they found a job that seemed appropriate. Because of World War II, many men in the Oakland study took stopgap jobs before the war. Their real careers began after return from military service.

Except for a few women who secured graduate degrees, most women did not have continuous careers until after their children were well along in school. On the average, the women in the study worked only two or three years prior to marriage and childbearing. However, in their 30s and 40s, many members of this generation gained a new perspective on their options through the women's movement. Along in their late 30s and early 40s, most women did enter the labor force, often facing initial disapproval from their husbands. The expectable life course of women was undergoing great change.

The Adult Years

Some students of the life course see school, work, and retirement as providing the major framework of the life course.[35] To a certain extent this is so, but the framework is a loose one, and each person uses it to shape a unique life. Some students of the life course purport to see stages through which everyone passes.[36] Our data do not support such a view. Men and women have a number of common experiences, and similar sources of life satisfaction or dissatisfaction that are found at almost all age levels. Asked to identify stages or distinctive periods of their lives, few members of our study felt that they could recognize such periods. If they did, it was often in terms of wrestling with some difficult situation that took years to resolve or, especially for women, periods of residence in different communities. For men, career stages or employers sometimes served as markers.

Turning points recalled as such by our study members late in life were to a surprising extent a result of early events or circumstances. Life crises did not pile up at midlife, as popular accounts have suggested, but were often related to the person's own competence and, sometimes, to external events over which the person had no control.

In each of the histories to be presented, I trace the course of development from the earliest observations available to us up to at least 1990, when the older members were verging on age 70. I focus on their relationships with others, their major commitments, and how they felt about themselves, their parents, their husbands and wives, and their children. We cannot always be sure about reported feelings. Sometimes the reports from other members of the family are highly consonant with what our primary study member has told us; sometimes there are discrepancies. Many parents see their relationships with their children in a more favorable light than their children do.[37] I shall have more to say about that in Chapter 16.

We turn now to an examination of the life history of two additional competent men, each quite different from Stuart Campbell and from the other, and then I shall present more quantitative data on all the men who have remained in the study.

CHAPTER 7

UPHILL ALL THE WAY

KARL SCHULZ

Three behavioral scientists who read Karl Schulz's entire case record forty-five years after his graduation from high school summarized their impressions (independently) in the following terms:

> A straight arrow who knows who he is and what he wants and seems to have a quite objective view of himself and those who are dearest to him—a warm and highly competent human being.

> A man who seems always to have operated within clearly defined goals and ideas and within these limits lived well—an internally-motivated winner.

> Early on he knew what he wanted professionally and pursued it, working hard for it in school and creating a niche for himself in a system that carried him along.

During his early adolescent years, Karl struck the research staff as a sad and lonely boy. At the age of 7, he had lost his father, to whom he had been close, and the staff felt that that loss had very much blighted his early years. Karl was obviously very bright but seemed embarrassed in social situations and was characterized as being largely silent in group settings; he avoided being the center of attention. Commenting on the youth's appearance when he was 15, a staff psychologist stated: "He is, and probably will continue to be, a homely fellow." But she then added, "Seems surprisingly well-liked for one so unresponsive." Nearly fifty years later, the interviewer who conducted a clinical interview with Karl Schulz when he was 61 years old characterized him as "a rugged-looking man, very masculine in appearance; could be considered handsome." In adolescence he was often characterized as unkempt; in his later years he was seen as "very neat, clean, and well-groomed."

There appear, then, to be some rather considerable differences between Karl the adolescent and Karl the retired scientist-engineer. There were indeed many changes, especially in his social presentation. At the same time, there were remarkable stabilities. At every period he was seen as highly dependable, very intelligent, productive, and straightforward. As we shall see, the most substantial changes appear to have taken place between adolescence and the first adult follow-up, when Karl was 37 years old. Since then there has been some additional mellowing, perhaps related to his retirement at age 58, but on the whole there has been remarkable stability in his personality over the adult years.

His history illustrates well how personal strengths and a supportive environment can overcome what clinicians may perceive as serious vulnerabilities. The most important supportive element in Karl's life was clearly his wife. Substantial detail about his marriage and family life has been included because the family has been the core of Karl's life and because Mr. and Mrs. Schulz have been willing to share their life very fully with us.

KARL SCHULZ'S CHILDHOOD AND ADOLESCENCE

Karl was an only child. Both of his parents were offspring of Western European Protestants who had migrated to the United States in the latter half of the nineteenth century. Karl's father was a college graduate and an engineer on the staff of a large chemical company. His mother had graduated from high school, attended business college for a year, and worked for a number of years. Both parents appear to have had strong intellectual and cultural interests. Karl's mother mentioned that prior to her husband's death, they had attended the opera as well as enjoying outdoor interests together.

From all that we have learned about them, they appear to have been loving parents. When Karl was 7, however, his father died of a heart attack. He and his parents had been out for a walk, and suddenly his father collapsed and was carried home. Karl is not sure whether he died immediately or within the next day. The event left him with a great feeling of loss.

Upon the death of her husband in 1928, Mrs. Schulz was apparently able to manage for a year or so on the proceeds of insurance and investment income, but she then took a job selling real estate. The stock market had crashed, and the Great Depression was beginning. It was the worst of times for entering the labor market, but Karl's mother had no alternative. At this time, or shortly before, Mrs. Schulz's own mother and her divorced sister came to live with Karl and his mother. By pooling resources, it was possible to make mortgage payments and hold on to the house that Karl's parents had been buying. This also ensured that someone would be there when Karl returned from school, and he reported that his grandmother had been primarily responsible for his supervision during the daytime.

The Junior High School Years

When Karl entered the study at age 11, his mother was characterized by the staff as energetic, restless, excitable, and inclined to worry. Later, at the tea held for parents of the senior class, she was described as being at ease, poised, and vivacious. Mrs. Schulz was seen as having considerable concern regarding her son's development and as interested in getting helpful suggestions from the study staff. She was always a willing participant when interviews were requested.

Mrs. Schulz's principal concern in the early years was her son's sleep difficulties. He frequently lay awake until very late at night and was resistant to going to bed when she thought he should. He himself indicated on research inventories that he had trouble sleeping, and it would appear that his reading after going to bed was perhaps the major issue of discipline for his mother. Later, she wished that he would be more sociable.

Karl spent a good deal of time in solitary activities, reading and building in his workshop, but he also participated in sports and appears to have been accepted by other boys. He was always tall for his age and, in the childhood years, quite thin. He had been seen as sickly in his preschool and early school years, and underwent three operations, including an appendectomy, before he reached age 8. Despite this, he did so well in school that he skipped a grade. His mother regarded him as overly conscientious. It would appear that she communicated to him her need for emotional support and for his cooperative behavior, and he strove to meet her expectations. Although it was she who put him to bed each night and who instructed him in moral values, the mother's real estate sales job took her away from home at the very times when most parents and children spend time together, on weekends. Karl was one of the minority of children who checked as typical of his situation the inventory items: "I wish my mother were not so busy," and "I wish my mother could be happier."

His mother reported that Karl had slept in the same room with her until he was 10 years old, possibly as a consequence of the size of the augmented household. We do not know when his sleep difficulties began, but they persisted long after he had his own room. His mother also indicated that she was still participating in brushing his teeth and bathing him when he was 11. She stated that "he would never wash his face, would wear that same shirt and socks for weeks." At this period he was rated by the study staff as somewhat more unkempt than most of his peers.

Karl attended Sunday school regularly between the ages of 6 and 15, but by the latter age he preferred to sleep later on Sunday mornings and to attend church. He had strong religious attitudes: He saw God as making us want to do good things and as the creator of all things. He saw Jesus as a great example and hell as a feeling of misery in one's self. He saw death as everlasting sleep, and he indicated that he prayed to do what his parents had taught him. His religious consciousness was far more mature and intellectually honed than that of most of his peers.

Karl always scored high on IQ tests, his scores ranging from 119 on a group test to 142 on the Stanford-Binet. Scores improved over the high school years; he had been seen as not able to mobilize his full capacity at age 13. His school grades were mostly A's with the exception of B's in English, though occasionally he received A's in that subject as well. He was seen by teachers and staff as being quite independent in his thinking but highly conventional and inhibited in his behavior.

Karl characterized himself as unattractive on early inventories. He indicated that he worried a good deal about bad things happening. He was regarded by staff psychologists as inhibited and somewhat withdrawn through the junior high years. He was described as going off by himself with a basketball and apparently working to improve his skills as a basketball player. At home he occupied himself with woodworking and reading. He cut lawns and worked at other jobs to earn spending money.

Several months before his 15th birthday, Karl took the Rorschach test, that series of inkblots that, like summer clouds, may call to mind a menagerie of beasts or evidence of hidden fears. He was described as "much interested in the test, enjoying fantasy, slightly excited." His responses were characterized as "sensitive, reactive, decidedly introverted, active fantasy [with] much originality and unique thought trends. Anxiety, worry and unhappiness are indicated in a small degree." Karl was clearly not inhibited in his imagination.

Toward the end of junior high school, it appeared that Karl was having a particularly difficult time, perhaps brought on by pubertal development. Late in his last semester in junior high, his mother reported that he and the two boys who had been his close friends seemed unable to get along, and Karl became more solitary. Staff observers also commented at this time that he seemed more self-conscious and shy and less confident of himself. He was characterized as "very inhibited and shy with adults." Yet an observer of Karl's participation with his friends a few months earlier had noted that "in a situation with friends, [Karl] is communicative, accepted and shows initiative," unlike his behavior in larger groupings. On one of the inventories during the difficult period, he acknowledged feeling "very unhappy without knowing why"—not a terribly atypical admission in mid-adolescence.

> *Postreview comment:* In reviewing this account, Karl Schulz could not recall any falling out with his friends or any special unhappiness toward the end of his junior high years. He thought that perhaps he had shifted from being involved primarily with neighborhood boys to being more involved with friends from school. Possibly this was the case, and his mother was aware only of the neighborhood situation. There was, however, indication of unhappiness.

Judges who reviewed all of the materials relating to Karl's junior high years characterized him as more adult than peer oriented. He was seen as selective in his choice of friends, respectful of his parents, and not at all likely to claim the rights and privileges of adolescence. Prior to attendance of senior high school, then, we have a boy who was somewhat withdrawn socially but clearly not rebellious, who seemed often sad but also able to manage his school work and his activities in a fruitful manner, and who was exceptionally dependable.

Karl scored just below the mean on the component "self-confident versus feels victimized" but well above the mean on the components "intellectually invested" and "dependable." His total score on planful competence put him in the top half but just out of the top third of the study males in junior high school.

The Senior High School Years

Karl's first year in senior high school found little change in either his self-perceptions or the ratings by others, but in his last two years, he seemed to become more sociable and somewhat less inhibited. In his first year, he joined the chess club and the model airplane club and occasionally participated in group activities with other members of the study sample, but by and large he made little use of the clubhouse that was available to study members. He became more involved in playing basketball and also received more respect from his peers by virtue of his academic performance.

Throughout his high school years, beginning in junior high, Karl indicated that his occupational goal was to become an engineer. He apparently always had before him the idealized image of his father and his father's occupation, and his superior intellectual ability and superior performance in mathematics and science suggested that engineering was a logical choice.

Karl was determined to learn to "do things right." Although he said that he did not like to dance, he attended a remedial class in dancing so that he would become more skillful, as he apparently did by his senior year. His conscientiousness and dependability stood out. At the same time, by his senior year he was seen as being able to relax and to acknowledge feelings denied previously. Whereas in most earlier years he had checked very few items on an "annoyance inventory," suggesting that almost nothing annoyed him, in his senior year he checked many sources of annoyance. By then he also became involved in many more social events, participating more fully in events sponsored by the research program. On one weekend trip, a staff psychologist who had observed him noted that he had addressed staff members more familiarly than previously, asked questions, kidded a girl about her ping-pong, and then took her on for a game: "His whole manner was changed into a rather light-hearted, wisecracking mood, and I thought he got along very successfully." At the senior year graduation party, he brought a tall and bright but not very popular girl and appeared to be having a lot of fun. Nevertheless, he dated very little and on the whole seemed uninterested in girls.

Psychologists who read the senior high school materials exhibited a high degree of consensus in their assessment of Karl's dominant traits. He received the highest possible rating on the traits "ambitious" and "values independence" and was only a shade lower on "prides self on objectivity," "dependable," "intelligent," and "productive." At the other extreme, he received the lowest possible score on the item "deceitful" and very low scores on "self-dramatizing," "talkative," and "poised."

Our index of planful competence showed Karl to be at the edge of the upper third of study group males. He was very near the top on "dependability" and "intellectual investment" but somewhat below the mean on "self-confidence." The last measure probably reflected his social presentation of self rather than his confidence in his abilities. In any event, he was clearly more aware than many of his peers of his own strengths and weaknesses, seemed remarkably undefensive, and had the discipline and ability needed to make mature choices, though his lack of experience with the opposite sex might make him vulnerable to a misstep when it came to marriage. Karl Schulz's Q-sort scores are given in Table A4 of Appendix A.

A staff member who wrote a detailed assessment of all of the adolescent material prior to the first follow-up predicted that Karl Schulz would become an engineer or go into some other closely allied vocation. Further, she noted, "I would not expect that he would have gone into the administrative aspects of the field but rather some aspect of it which would have allowed him independence but not great responsibility for others. For instance, research in this area would fulfill these requirements." She predicted that he would marry but probably late and that he would lead a fairly conventional and comfortable life. At the same time, this psychologist surmised that fatherhood might be "a somewhat more difficult problem because of his need for autonomy and his tendency toward inhibition."

KARL SCHULZ AT AGE 21

Three years after Karl's graduation from high school, Karl was interviewed by Judith Chaffey, a staff member who had been his counselor when he was in junior high school. The interview was not guided by any theoretical perspective or directed toward the systematic collection of data but simply sought to find out "how things were going" with former study members. Miss Chaffey characterized Karl as "more free and talkative than usual." America was now at war, and Karl was about to enter his senior year at the University of California. He indicated that he was doing well in engineering school and would enter the army upon graduation, to receive further electronics training and then enter the Signal Corps.

Reading this interview nearly fifty years later, one becomes vividly aware of social change. Karl was interested in the prospect of further training because, as he reported, they were "working out a new method of detecting the presence of airplanes." Radar was not yet widely known, but Karl hoped to be able to go to England "because the men who invented this system are working it out there." Karl also looked forward to traveling and seeing some of the world, so he did not seem apprehensive about entering the service.

As of 1942, his grandmother and one aunt still lived with his mother, but his other aunt (who had presumably lived with them for a while) had gone to Guatemala (for what reason, we do not know). Karl's mother and grandmother had planned to visit her there until the war intervened. Mrs. Schulz was still heavily involved in her job. Like many other women who had been autonomous before marriage, she clearly enjoyed using her considerable abilities. Karl said that she was essentially running the real estate office, since her boss was often away and seemed indifferent about managing. He described his mother as "too much identified with the business now" to think of leaving, even though she sometimes talked about leaving. Karl lived at home during his college years, and since tuition was free for state residents, apparently his college attendance was not a financial problem.

Asked if he was sorry he had not joined a fraternity, Karl replied that quite the opposite, he was glad because he would not have had time. He reported that he had to work hard but was in the top fifth of his class and hoped to become a member of Tau Beta Pi, the national honorary society for engineering students. He had gone skiing a few times and apparently participated in a square dancing group. He was still in touch with and getting together with several of his friends from the study group, and he asked about others in the group, both men and women. Asked what he thought about the number of his peers who were marrying before going into the service, he thought there was some danger in this "since a boy might change a lot," but that it probably depended on the circumstances. He mentioned that he was going to a different church, because he liked both its minister and the social activities of the young people there better than at the church he had previously attended. It was the church that the institute director's daughters, who were roughly his age, were also attending.

Karl's observations about the kinds of governmental controls that might be necessary after the war suggested a very conservative (keep government out of business) outlook.

Miss Chaffey noted that "his only sign of embarrassment was at first when we were talking about him. He kept looking away from me. So I changed the subject and told him what I was doing and he immediately looked directly at me and continued to do so." Karl seemed to be moving toward much greater self-acceptance and ease and was looking ahead with interest and enthusiasm.

KARL SCHULZ AT AGE 37

Nearly twenty years intervened between high school graduation and the first adult follow-up. The interviewer, who conducted a series of three interviews with Karl, characterized him as "a refreshingly undefensive, good-natured, intellectual and interesting person. He is a good-looking man who dresses casually but is well-groomed. I found [him] to be a very easy person to interview not only because of his involvement in and positive evaluation of the study, but also because he is sufficiently relaxed to be able to accept the questions without feeling threatened by them. He is somewhat shy and reserved but he related easily in the interview situation."

The initial interview dealt with recollections of adolescence, and the picture that Karl presented was consonant with what we already knew though presented rather tersely. He noted that he had been more academically than socially inclined and had been extremely shy. He remembered with pleasure playing chess with members of the chess club, playing basketball, and learning how to drive. He noted his earlier ambivalence about dancing: "Once a week they had dances that we sort of wanted to go to but always tried to avoid." He commented on the change in his attitude toward girls in his senior year: "I realized it was foolishness not to go out, and I gradually got to feeling more interested in them.... They didn't seem quite so strange."

Karl remembered himself as feeling reasonably well satisfied during his adolescent years. At the same time, when he filled out a life satisfaction chart, indicating on a year-to-year basis the level of life satisfaction, the lowest point was the year of his father's death, when he rated satisfaction at 3 on a 9-point scale, and life satisfaction gradually increased during the junior and senior high school years, rising to 7 in the senior year.

Asked how well he thought he had understood himself in adolescence, Karl replied in some detail:

> I thought I knew all about myself at that time. I understood the direction I was going, educationally and vocationally. As far as emotions and feelings, I didn't have too good an understanding of them, although I can't think of times of real confusion. We had lots of talks about the meaning of life, and religion.
>
> I think I knew my assets and limitations reasonably well. I thought I was reasonably intelligent.... I did best in math and science. I thought I was healthy and capable of taking care of myself. Felt fairly confident in myself in most situations, certainly not all. My limitations were in keeping too much to myself. I was sort of an introvert. I had close friends but I was shy with others. I didn't have too good an ability to express myself.

He felt that his mother and grandmother had respect for his judgment and he for theirs, though they were not always in agreement.

When he was asked whether there were any experiences or people who had been especially influential in his life or anyone on whom he had tried to model his own life, he replied, "No, not really, other than the projection of my father...what he might have been like....This was always kind of a guide for me and I try to do what he would have done." Thus he formulated explicitly the inference that the staff had drawn from early observations of the youth.

The 1958–1959 follow-up focused much more on the early years than on what had happened since, and it was especially deficient in getting at educational and occupational histories. To fill in the picture, data are available from a questionnaire designed for this purpose in 1964.

Karl had graduated from the University of California with a degree in engineering and had immediately entered military service. He was sent to Officer Candidate School and not long after sent overseas. The army years brought his first prolonged period of his life outside the family home, and he felt that this had been a useful experience, though he had not been enthusiastic about army regimentation.

While in the service, stationed on the East Coast, he met Kathleen, the woman who would become his wife. Their meeting was described in several of the subsequent interviews as having occurred at a dance for young officers, held in a large New York City hotel. The future Mrs. Schulz was tall, like her husband-to-be, and the two gravitated toward each other in the course of a Paul Jones, a square dance in which the dancers change partners. They saw a good deal of each other in the brief period before Karl went overseas, and they corresponded frequently. Upon his return from the service in 1946, Kathleen flew west for a visit, and before the visit ended they had set the date for their wedding, a month or two later. By then, Karl had secured a promising job in the field of aeronautical engineering.

Early Occupational History

At the time of the first follow-up, Karl was still with his initial employer. He was also taking graduate courses, part time, to prepare him for more technical work. He was about to become a scientist in the field of aeronautical research. There had been several promotions, and Karl expressed a high degree of satisfaction in his job. Not only did he find the work entirely suitable to his interests, but he appreciated the freedom to develop ideas and use his imagination, skills, and abilities. Among the aspects he liked best about the job were its general convenience for the family and the amount of leisure time that it provided.

Karl indicated that on the average he devoted forty hours a week to his job, a respect in which he was highly unusual in that nonmanual workers among those in the study reported working an average of fifty-one hours a week. The only incentive that might induce him to change jobs, he thought, would be "a tremendous salary increase for the same sort of work." The income he reported for the year was well above the national average and about equivalent to the higher levels of federal civil service or a full professorship in all but the top universities.

The questionnaire sent in 1964 inquired into the priorities accorded among work, marriage and the family, church, and community affairs. Karl indicated a very high level of involvement and of satisfaction in his family roles. He rated family activities as those that he enjoyed most, as well as those on which he was spending the most time. He also rated family activities second among those to which he would like to devote more time (first were recreation and leisure) and second in providing him with the greatest sense of accomplishment (here work and work-related activities rated first). Not given high priority in any of these choices were community affairs and church activities.

Perhaps because he himself had been deprived of the joyous interaction of parents and children, being both an only and a fatherless child, Karl seems to have relished a sense of completeness that derived from fathering and participating in a large family. The competence and agreeableness of his wife and her full enjoyment of mothering undoubtedly helped to make him more comfortable in the role of father than had been predicted by psychologists in Karl's adolescent years.

Marriage and Early Parenting

Although we did not learn the details of their early married life until later, it was evident that Karl and Kathleen had a very happy life together. Despite their brief relationship (two months) before Karl was shipped overseas, they apparently felt very comfortable and in touch through what Karl later characterized as "thousands of letters." Asked many years later about factors influencing their marriage, Kathleen Schulz mentioned her immediate positive response to Karl: "He seemed like an old frined—easy to talk to, comfortable to be with." Above all, she had been impressed with his character. In response to the same question, Karl said he "knew immediately she was the one." They had been married for ten years at the time of the 1958 follow-up.

In a later interview, we learned more about their early married life. Demobilization of the armed forces brought an acute shortage of housing. There had been very little construction of residential dwellings during the depression and war years, and the Schulzes had to settle for a furnished room near Karl's place of work. They were still in that room when their first child was born.

There had also been an acute shortage of automobiles, no new ones having been available for private purchase from the end of 1941 until the war's end in 1945. It was many months before the Schulzes could acquire a car. Although the early years were a struggle, the Schulzes managed to put money aside, and three months before their second child was born, they built a house.

Asked in 1958 what sort of person his wife was, Karl replied, with a warm laugh, "She is delightful. She is a very good-natured person ... sentimental, easygoing, and kind ... she has a good memory ... she's intelligent ... quick ... she is more interested in people than I am ... she is more extroverted ... she even wondered whether she would be interviewed ... she'd love it and it would be easier for her than it is for me, I think."

Although many of the details of his wife's background did not come out until the next follow-up, when Mrs. Schulz did participate, it is relevant to note that her background was quite different from that of her husband. She came from an Irish Catholic family in which she had experienced a happy childhood and had a close, loving relationship with her mother. Karl rather glossed over the extent to which his own mother was disappointed in his marrying a Catholic, though he alluded to this when asked if he had ever disappointed his mother. It appears that what was most problematic for her was the likelihood that the children would be raised as Catholics. This was not a problem for Karl.

Two staff members made separate visits to the Schulz home within a year of the first follow-up interview and administered intelligence tests to their four children. Both psychologists mentioned being cordially received by Mrs. Schulz, and one added, "I was introduced to all the children who appeared an eager, enthusiastic group, anxious to do their tricks for me." She went on to state that "as long as the children stayed within what appeared to be fairly firm rules about their conduct, [Mrs. Schulz] was content to let things go, but if they stepped outside the boundaries, they were greeted by a yell from her and a general admonition to behave themselves. However ... the children acted in a spontaneous and friendly manner both to their mother and me." The second test administrator found Kathleen Schulz composed and pleasant. Both staff members commented on the large, modern home, nicely furnished, into which the Schulzes had recently moved.

Karl could think of nothing specific when asked what about his wife irritated him and made it clear that any irritations were trivial. He reported that decisions were usually mutually agreed to but that each deferred to the other in areas in which the other was more competent. For the most part, he said, "our minds seem to run in the same channel and we usually come to similar decisions. There really aren't too many causes for disagreement."

The four children ranged in age from 3 to 11. The oldest and youngest were girls and the middle two, boys. Karl felt that the first and third children tended to resemble him, in being somewhat less social and more stubborn than the others, while the second and fourth children were more like his wife, "easy to get along with."

The final interview in the series dealt largely with parenting. His characterization of his strong and weak points as a parent were somewhat similar to his characterization of himself as an adolescent:

> I know some of my faults. . . . I tend still to have a temper and have to consciously work at it. . . . I get excited too easily when the kids do something they shouldn't do. Possibly I'm a bit too strict in terms of rules . . . and I'm a little bit fussy, maybe. [Then, on the positive side, he noted:] I spend as much time as I can with them and it is hard to give each one a share of individual attention. I like to play with them. . . . teach them to do things. . . also teach them attitudes, like right and wrong and fair play. I try to give them help in school work and in their scouting when it is needed. I think I probably am giving them a liking of the outdoors . . . we go camping, picnicking, hiking . . . try to stimulate their interests in many things.

Karl felt that it was necessary to discipline children but not harshly. "After a certain age I think you gain less by spanking and then it is best to deprive them of their privileges." He commented that sometimes it is desirable to give in to the children when they have strong feelings, and he noted that each child should be treated in terms of his or her own needs. "You have to use common sense and try to be reasonable."

In his discussion of child rearing, he frequently touched on the importance of such matters as tending to the children's health, providing them with attention and love, helping them to develop their capacities, and, perhaps above all, giving them a feeling for the rights of others. The interviewer noted that in talking about his children, his responses were more spontaneous and free and much longer than those given in the initial interview in the series.

When asked to compare the ways in which he had been raised with those in which he was raising his own children, he noted, rather surprisingly, that his children were more closely supervised than he had been. He pointed out that "a larger family makes a difference." But in general he felt that the basic aims he and his wife had were not different from those of his own mother and grandmother.

The only child about whom he expressed any apprehension was his 11-year-old daughter, feeling she might have a difficult time because she did not easily make friends and did not take advice easily. The expression of the first of these concerns was very similar to that of his own mother when he was 11, at the start of the research project.

From the 1964 questionnaire, we learned more about the marriage and parenting. He reported almost no significant disagreements with his wife on a large number of areas of family life where disagreements are fairly frequent. Those that were mentioned at all, with an indication of "very little" disagreement, were religious training for the children, where to go on vacation, in-laws (whom to see and how often), the use of birth control, and how strict to be with the children. The children were raised as Catholics, and they attended parochial schools for the elementary grades. By now, a fifth child had been born.

Asked about decision making, Karl indicated that he would more often make decisions on selecting and buying a car, on how the children should be disciplined, and how money is spent, but his wife would more often make the final decision relating to religious training for children, getting together with friends, and the use of birth control.

Karl's rating of his marriage was just below the "almost perfect" level. He saw mutual understanding of each other's problems and feelings as the most important element of marriage for him, with a chance to have and rear children second in importance. He surmised, however, that companionship and husband and wife doing things together might be most important to his wife, and he rated this as third in importance to himself. Standard of living, sexual relations, and the security and comfort of a home were rated lower in importance. Asked to choose the attributes most to be desired for a youngster in his or her early teens, when given a list of seventeen parental values, Karl chose the same items for a boy as he chose for a girl: that the child be happy, honest, and dependable.

He felt that the children's preschool years had been the period in which he had enjoyed them most, because they could take care of their own physical needs yet were dependent on their parents, and their problems were relatively few and relatively unimportant. The senior high school years were seen as the greatest problem, with the note that "their problems get more serious and far-reaching." He acknowledged that occasionally he felt inadequate as a parent in not being able to understand a child's attitude or to get across to them what seemed to him to be right. He felt that having children "brings parents together and keeps you interested in many things that would not touch your life otherwise. They can present a real challenge to help them achieve the most of which they are capable."

Karl completed a chart entitled "best and worst periods of my life" in 1958 and a comparable life satisfaction chart in 1981. (The latter is reproduced later in this chapter.) On the 1958 chart he rated his early years at level 6 (on a 1 to 9 scale) and dropped to a 3 at age 7, the year his father died. Ratings gradually climbed but did not reach 6 again until the junior high years and then 7 for the senior high years. Karl rated his college years (entailing accelerated training) at age 6. The first year of army life was the low point beyond adolescence, and the next year, when he met his wife, required two checks, one for the exhilaration he felt after meeting her and a second, much lower, for military life, now overseas. The high, reaching "absolute tops" on the scale, was the year of his marriage, and the subsequent years dropped off slightly though generally to only one or two categories from the top. The family had acquired their first new home when he was 29 and their second when he was 36, and both of these enhanced the evaluation of those years.

There was high agreement among the clinicians who completed the personality Q-sort for Karl Schulz at 37. The most salient features of his personality were seen as "dependable," "straightfor-ward," "values intellectual matters," and "arouses liking." He was viewed as not at all "self-dramatizing," and he also received ex-tremely low scores on the items "self-defeating" and "feels victim-ized." He was now seen as substantially more introspective than he had been, as somewhat less overcontrolled, and as more physically attractive, cheerful, and poised. His verbal fluency and initiation of humor had come up substantially. Karl Schulz still scored relatively low on the item "satisfaction with self," perhaps because of his im-pressive ability to discern the respects in which he wished to im-prove, but he had moved up on the component "self-confident versus feels victimized." The correlation between his senior high school Q-sort profile and that at age 37 was .55, suggesting a fair de-gree of stability yet appreciable change as well. Karl Schulz was now at the border of the top 10 percent of the study males on the mea-sure of competence.

The relatively young age of the children at the time of the first adult follow-up made it difficult to assess how smoothly family rela-tionships were developing. The most perceptive and skillful parents are often more aware of the respects in which they fall short of their objectives in child rearing than are neglecting or harsh par-ents, for the latter almost always deny the existence of problems. Karl Schulz was clearly more self-aware than self-protective, and the picture he gave was of a somewhat overly controlling, occasionally critical but generally supportive and never harsh father who en-joyed his children. It seemed clear that rules were very important in this family, as indeed they tend to be in larger families. (The Campbells were a notable exception.) There was no indication of parental tensions over discipline but some suggestion that Karl was stricter than his wife as well as a suggestion of anxiety involving the oldest child.

THE SCHULZES IN 1970

When Karl Schulz was next interviewed in 1970, at age 48, his wife and two of the children also participated in the follow-up. The Vietnam War was in its most brutal phase. The interviewer's intro-ductory comments to the transcription of the interview describe Karl Schulz as more reserved and highly controlled than had the interviewer who saw him at age 37. The latter was the mother of several children and nearer to her respondent in age than was the interviewer at 48. Although positively impressed by her respondent, the current interviewer felt that Karl had shown acute discomfort when attention was focused on aspects of his own personality and that the interview had been fairly stressful for him. She commented: "His way of approaching life is on a more objective, rational, intellectual basis, yet he shows warmth and genuine concern for others, but is not intuitive and as comfortable with people as he is with ideas." She noted that he seemed to take considerable satisfaction from his roles as father and husband as well as his occupational role and that "he is successful in all these roles, knows that he is, and is appropriately self-confident." She felt he had a good awareness of his strengths and weaknesses and that husband and wife appeared to counterbalance each other's personality with ease and comfort. A second rater of his personality characterized him as "the personification of the silent majority." Both saw him as conflict free, stable, and able to provide his children with many of the gratifications he lacked as a child.

The Interview with Karl Schulz

Karl's mother was now in her 70s, and age had taken its toll. She had had a series of mild strokes that left her unable to drive and markedly limited in her activities, though she was not bedridden. Her sister, who had lived with the family when Karl was small, was now looking after her. Karl was in touch with them and visited about once a month, but his mother's memory was so impaired as to make meaningful communication difficult.

The interview then turned to discussion of the children. It became apparent that the oldest daughter, Fran, now 22, had had a difficult few years when she headed off to college. Karl did not volunteer any details about the problem other than saying that they had seemed to be at odds in everything during her first couple of years in college. He did not disclose why she had dropped out of college to take a job, focusing instead on his feeling that more recently "her attitudes in general have changed, mellowed, and she's found things aren't quite as idealistic or black and white as she had believed." His major satisfaction with his daughter was that "she's adjusting finally to the world or the community as it is, not expecting all her dreams to come true overnight."

The oldest son, John, was now in college and seemed to be doing reasonably well, though it was suggested that perhaps too much of his time was spent going to sporting events and hiking and fishing. As before, this son was characterized as much more like his mother—easygoing and comfortable with people.

The second son, Scott, on the other hand, was still seen as more like Karl himself had been in adolescence—quiet, a little less self-confident, and less sociable. By everyone's accounts, the older boys enjoyed each other and did a good deal together; their father had indeed transmitted to them an interest in fishing and in the out-of-doors. It did not appear that there were any particular tensions between father and sons, as there obviously had been with the oldest daughter.

The youngest daughter, Sara, fourth child in the family, was again characterized as being like her mother—enthusiastic and sociable. She had just been selected as a cheerleader at high school and appeared to be doing reasonably well in school. Her father summed up his feelings with the statement: "She just seems to be a very delightful girl at the moment." He added, however, that "it's once they get beyond this stage that the problems start coming out, you know."

The youngest son, George, seemed to be coming along very well. His father noted, "He tends to be at the top, as far as leading or ability at playing things . . . so he's, I think, a little over-confident sometimes." But again the boy was characterized as easy to get along with. Karl felt that the younger children had learned from "taking in" all of the discussions with the older children and hearing them "yelled at" from time to time. The two younger children were in parochial school—the daughter an eighth grader and the son probably in the fifth grade. It developed that each of the children shifted to a public high school after graduation from the eight-year parochial school.

The interview next turned to family interaction and a discussion of how disagreements were handled. Despite the national furor over Vietnam, Karl indicated that national and international political and social issues were not much discussed with the children. "There's always something else we're talking about, of lower family-type levels. I'm not sure that we agree politically." He went on to indicate that he and his wife did not try to influence the children one way or another with reference to political issues. "There are probably disagreements, but they're not really discussed very thoroughly or brought out to any extent. We've had some disagreements on what the kids thought they should be able to do. Particularly I think when they get to the driving age this has been the most noticeable." Staying out late at night was again an issue in the family, though Karl felt that "as long as we feel we're being reasonable about it, they seem to accept it pretty well."

Karl felt that his wife would definitely tend to be the confidante of the children, particularly because she was available to them when they came home from school or from other activities that they would want to talk about. He did not feel that there were significant differences between himself and his wife in the rearing of the children and noted that they presented a united front both because they usually agreed and to preclude having the children play one parent against the other. He expressed their primary aims as being to produce "decent human beings basically who would contribute to the general society and at the same time be happy individuals." Asked for a basic principle of his moral philosophy, he replied with the Golden Rule of treating one's neighbor as one would want to be treated.

Karl did not feel that there had been much change from his own adolescence to that of his children in terms of getting a job, independence, or sexual attitudes. He thought that he and his wife probably understood their children a little better than his mother and grandmother had understood him as an adolescent, pointing out that his mother had had to be heavily involved in her job. Basically he felt that he had had somewhat more freedom than he and his wife were permitting their children, but this was primarily because of his mother's work. He did indicate that his mother and perhaps his aunt as well had at times suggested that they thought Karl and his wife should be somewhat more permissive with their children, but apparently this was not a major issue.

When the interview turned to the marital relationship, Karl again described his wife as easy to get along with, good-natured, reasonable, fair, and enthusiastic. He felt that she kept the family organized and running smoothly and that they were able to discuss things completely freely. His only irritation, a minor one, was that his wife was a little less tidy than he would have liked, but he said that he understood that this was primarily a matter of her sense of priorities when she was otherwise busy. He thought the two had grown together over the years, each influencing the other in desirable ways.

He saw his wife as less restrictive with the children and acknowledged that both were a little on the conservative side and somewhat old-fashioned. He considered his wife as more religious than himself, as well as being friendlier and more interested in social activities.

Asked how his wife might see him, his reply was basically as a partner in the maintenance of the family and a good provider. It was difficult for him to say in what respects his wife might be irritated with him.

Questions about decision making evoked almost identical answers to those given a decade previously: Both tended to think somewhat alike and there were seldom problems, but then he added, "If one of us feels very strongly one way or another, this might settle it, but there's usually little difference between us on most of the items I can think of." He felt his wife had helped him become a more considerate person.

Asked for his definition of love within marriage and whether it had changed over the years, Karl replied that he felt it was basically the same, though tempered with time: "As you have gotten to know a person really well, it's sort of a deeper sense of companionship, if you will, or sort of rely on the other more, because you've developed this way, you've worked together."

The assessment of Karl's personality on the Q-sort at age 48 was not much changed from that at age 37 but reflected the somewhat less enthusiastic response to him by the interviewer at this period. He was still seen as highly dependable, as valuing intellectual matters, as straightforward, and as valuing independence. He was also seen as priding himself on his objectivity and as somewhat "aloof," but he was now rated much more "giving," much more satisfied with himself, and more masculine. Ratings at this period correlated more highly ($r = .61$) with those for the adolescent years than had the previous set of ratings, suggesting less change than had the earlier assessment, and there was a close relationship between the two adult Q-sorts ($r = .66$). Again Karl Schulz scored in the upper fifth of study males on the age 48 assessment of the competence index.

The Interview with Kathleen Schulz

Like her husband, Kathleen Schulz made a positive impression on the interviewer, who saw her as "a warm, compassionate, humorous woman ... [with] good judgment and good common sense.... I find her one of the most pleasant women I have seen."

The picture Kathleen Schulz gave of the marriage and the family was entirely consonant with her husband's characterization of it, but she gave somewhat more detail, especially in discussing the children. What quickly became apparent was her much higher level of emotional concern with the problems of her oldest child. She noted something that we had not previously registered: Fran had been born less than a year after they were married, before their lives had achieved very much stability. Kathleen had wanted to breast-feed Fran, but this did not work out, and apparently the experience was traumatic for the mother. She reported an early comment by her husband that in the first six months she had cried more than her daughter had. It will be remembered that Kathleen had come from the East Coast to marry Karl and had given up all of her own ties there to move into a new community and take on a totally new role. For more than twenty years, Kathleen had been faced with child rearing, and she was just beginning to contemplate greater freedom for herself.

Kathleen Schulz agreed with her husband that Fran had definitely matured in the last couple of years, but the first two years of college had been a terrible wrench for both mother and father. Fran had gone to the University of California campus that spawned the student rebellion of the 60s, and had arrived there when turbulence was at its height. She had joined a sorority but relatively early had established a liaison with a male student who ultimately persuaded her to quit college at the end of her sophomore year and to take a job. The relationship had broken up some months thereafter, with the young man having indicated that he was not really interested in a permanent kind of relationship. This had been extremely traumatic to Fran, though it appeared that she had recovered well and was now working toward her college degree in addition to holding a job. Kathleen was pleased with her eldest daughter and felt that Fran "would make a fine wife and mother."

Kathleen Schulz described each of the other children in terms of personality and interests. She delighted in the special qualities each possessed. She was clearly the close confidant of both sons and daughters and they and their father were at the center of her life. She characterized her oldest son as like Karl—"about as steady a husband as anyone could find anywhere. . . . Karl is really a soft-spoken, tremendous father." Although apprehensive about the epidemic of drug use by adolsecents, she felt reasonably confident that her children would not succumb, for they did "not need a crutch or to prove something." At a time when long hair and adolescent rebellion were most fashionable and were problematic for many parents, neither of her adolescent sons had presented any problems. Both had received leadership and scholarship awards in the high school they attended.

Both parents had been active in attending school functions such as basketball games and other activities that their children took part in. Although the children were reported to have sometimes chided their parents for being "uptight" about marijuana, Kathleen Schulz retained a strong aversion to drug experimentation.

Although there was no mention of the Vietnam War, Kathleen did indicate that the older boys resented the prospect of being drafted, and one assumes that they may have strongly disapproved of what was happening in Vietnam. There was no indication, however, that the war was a matter of strong disagreement within the family.

Data from Questionnaires

In addition to the interviews conducted with the study members and their wives and with children between the ages of 14 and 18, questionnaires were distributed at the time of the second follow-up touching on job attitudes, political and social participation, preceptions of the marital partner, and objectives and assessments of parenting. It asked specifically about relationships with children between the ages of 14 and 18. Neither Karl nor Kathleen Schulz claimed to understand the children "very well," but both felt that they understood them fairly well in most respects. Asked to indicate the degree of agreement with the children in a number of areas that were frequent sources of intergenerational disagreement, especially in the 1960s, Karl indicated that he did not know his children's political attitudes or where they stood on civil rights and race relations, while Kathleen checked that she did not agree with the children's views in these two areas. Both parents reported that they discussed issues of right and wrong to help their children become good persons, but, as Karl had already reported in the interviews, political issues and issues of race relations were not part of such discussions.

Both parents saw themselves as middle of the road but more conservative than their children. It is highly relevant to recall that a major issue of the 1960s was the generation gap, yet neither of the children who was questioned felt that such a gap existed in their experience.

Both parents indicated that they had enjoyed the children most in the earlier school years, when any problems posed were relatively easy to handle. As a consequence of their experience with Fran, both reported that after high school was the most difficult period, noting that once the children were away from home, parents could have only slight influence upon them.

The Schulzes showed substantial consensus in the values they chose as the most important attributes for an adolescent child, both feeling that being dependable ranked first for boys and girls, and both also chose considerate as one of the three most important attributes of a girl. Karl rated ambition somewhat higher than did his wife, who chose self-control as extremely important for a boy, and for both boys and girls Kathleen chose being a good student as extremely important, while her husband chose popularity.

On the whole, the two children who were seen had high respect for their parents and considered their parents, and especially their mother, to have had the strongest influence on them and to be the people whose ideas and opinions meant most to them. Yet neither parent had seen himself or herself as being that influential. Moreover, while Kathleen had felt that she understood her children only "fairly well," both children felt that she knew them "very well." This reverses the more usual finding in which parents think they understand their children very well but the children feel differently. This is not to say that the Schulz children viewed their parents as perfect models to follow, but rather that whether they agreed or disagreed on various issues, their parents mattered very much to them and both children saw their parents as strongly supportive of them.

As the family was approaching the empty nest stage, it appeared to be functioning well but with some parental apprehension as to what would happen when other children left home. Among the study families, this one rated exceptionally high in marital satisfaction and consensus between the parents, showed no appreciable coalitions, and there was very high parental involvement in the lives of the children.

THE SCHULZES IN 1982

We saw both Karl and Kathleen Schulz some thirteen years later. Again, the interviewers were enthusiastic in their descriptions of the Schulzes as extremely pleasant, competent persons. In the interval since our previous contact, both of their mothers had died. Karl had retired three years before the interview at age 58. He had advanced in his field of engineering research to the top level that he could occupy without having major administrative responsibilities. His whole career had been spent with a single employer, and it had been highly satisfying, both intrinsically and in the convenience, income, and retirement benefits it carried. Asked in what ways his job had been important in determining his sense of self, Karl Schulz replied: "It was a good part of it. It gives you an identity in terms of what you're contributing and where you fit into the picture of the world aside from your family." Yet when asked which aspect of life had most influenced his sense of self, it was not the job or career but, rather, family relationships and activities. The job took second place.

In retirement, he missed some of the long-term relationships with his former associates, whom he characterized as a friendly group. Yet he did not feel any different sense of self since retiring, for he had the satisfaction of knowing what he had contributed. And what pleased him most about not working was not having to get up early in the morning, noting that he was "a night person."

The Schulzes had been in complete agreement on when he would retire and what they would like to do. They had been making impressive progress toward their objectives, but in the previous year Kathleen had had a fall, suffering a broken leg and, more seriously, a detached retina. Karl was concerned about his wife's sight, as indeed she was, for efforts to repair the retinal damage resulted in the loss of sight in the affected eye.

Fran, the oldest daughter, was now 34, and employed at a rewarding job in the Midwest. George, the youngest child, was, at 21, a senior in college. He had been away but was about to spend six months at home on an internship arrangement that would bring him back to the Bay Area. The intermediate children had graduated from college, though only the oldest son, John, had married. Scott was working at a job that he very much enjoyed, one for which his college education had specifically prepared him, and he was living several hundred miles away. Sara had a job in the publishing business and had an apartment in a city fairly near to her parents' home, so she could visit frequently. Although Sara's life-style was not entirely to her mother's liking, on the whole the Schulzes were very pleased with the way their children had turned out. Kathleen would have liked to have some grandchildren and was beginning to wonder how long she would have to wait.

The 1982 clinical interview afforded an opportunity to learn more about Karl's earliest experiences in the family and a bit more about his parents' marriage. Very little of this information had been elicited earlier. Among his early memories were going camping with his parents (apparently from infancy), going fishing with his father and sitting on his father's lap, and holding the steering wheel of the car while driving out in the country. Karl said that his mother had been an adventuresome young woman who went to Alaska, then considered the last frontier. It appears that she had gone with a friend from the midwestern state where she had grown up. At a time when very few young women would have ventured to Alaska, there was apparently a demand for their services, and both took jobs in a bank. It was in Alaska that Karl's parents had met. His father was there on an engineering assignment. We do not know how long it was before his parents married, but it was after they had returned to the contiguous forty-eight states, in San Francisco. Perhaps, like Karl and his wife, his parents had corresponded and deepened their knowledge of each other. In any event, there is every indication that theirs had been a happy, rewarding relationship and that they were competent and caring parents. Karl's distant memory of his father was vague, but beyond his own memories, his mother must have presented a very positive picture of the father he knew so briefly.

Karl's mother became a very involved businesswoman, whose success was apparently sufficient to provide her with a comfortable income in later life. She had suffered further strokes beyond the previous follow-up, which made it very difficult to communicate with her, and there had not been a great deal of interaction between his mother and her grandchildren as they grew older.

Although he regretted that he had missed his father's guidance, companionship, and teaching, Karl thought that as a consequence he had become more independent, "probably because I had to." He noted that his mother had given him a great deal of freedom rather than being overprotective, as might have been expected under such circumstances. He felt that both his mother and his grandmother had given him a lot of encouragement: "You can do this, you can do that." His mother had encouraged him to go to college and to set his sights high, but he did not feel that she had pressured him. Here we see clearly the importance of high standards for the development of early planful competence. Thinking back on what it had meant to be an only child, he had not felt particularly deprived. Having to play by himself and come up with his own activities had not been all bad, although it did not improve his social skills.

From Kathleen's clinical interview, we learned more about her enduring close relationship with her own mother, a strong, independent woman. Kathleen's mother had died only a few years before, having outlived her husband by twenty-five years. Mother and daughter had been in close touch until the end, and indeed Kathleen had been with her mother on the East Coast during the last few weeks of her illness, until she entered a hospital and it was necessary for Kathleen to return to her own family commitments on the opposite coast.

We learned a bit more about their early married life in California. Kathleen described with considerable humor the problems of living in a furnished room through her initial pregnancy. When she had the baby, there was nowhere for her mother to come and stay, so she and Karl managed on their own. Looking back she commented: "There were tears and gnashing of teeth, but you survived. And you look back and think, 'gee, maybe this is where you get your strength.'" They not only survived, but as she noted, their coping together brought them closer.

In their interviews, both the Schulzes commented on the relatively meager social life in the early years of their marriage. For both of them, the community into which they moved was one in which they had no previous contacts, and except for social activities connected with Karl's employment, it took some time before they acquired friends with whom they would get together socially. But because both were highly autonomous persons and were fully available to each other, it does not appear that there were major strains at any time.

Both Karl and Kathleen remained as enthusiastic about their marriage as they had been earlier. Neither had ever thought seriously of divorce, nor had they ever been separated. Asked in the structured interview, "What has kept you together?" they gave rather similar replies. Karl spoke of their "willingness to share and confront problems and take care of the children ... because we still love each other." Kathleen noted "our commitment when we married, our attitudes and expectations." Both wanted their children's marriages to be like theirs. Kathleen commented, "I would hope that they would marry someone who would cherish them." Karl's formulation was: "To have the same support, family life. I think it's been great."

Both Karl and Kathleen felt that their level of satisfaction in the marriage had remained constant over the years. There were differences in emphasis over the years, but both found it hard to say when the marriage was at its best or worst. Karl summed up his feelings: "When you're young it's romantically wild and then you have children, which is fun, and then you have yourselves, which is fine, too. Probably when we were first having our family, probably the first child was most exciting. Doing things together."

As part of the 1981–1982 follow-up, Karl Schulz filled out another life satisfaction chart (Figure 7.1). As was the case with Stuart Campbell, whose life chart at 39 was shown because it was much more informative than his 1981 chart, Karl Schulz's chart at age 61 was a smoother curve, with somewhat less variation. The same events in the years up to age 37 accounted for the lows and highs, as had been the case in 1958, but only the death of his father was scored below the midpoint of the scale. Army service was a modest blip in the chart, but the year he met Kathleen was now rated higher than the adjacent years. Again marriage was "tops." In the years beyond age 37, there were just two temporary drops of a point, reflecting the turmoil of Fran's first year at college and his mother's death. The chart ended with a very slight drop caused by concern about his wife's eye injury.

Figure 7.1. Life Satisfaction Chart for Karl Schulz, Age 61

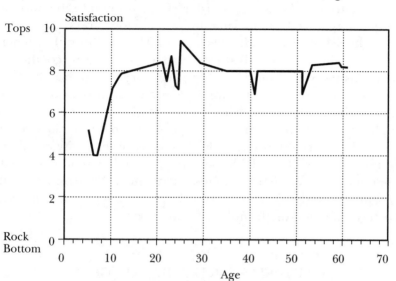

Labeled Points on Karl Schulz's Life Satisfaction Chart

Age	Comments on chart
6–9	Sick a lot, operations, Dad died
16*	Got a car (rated 8, the high point of adolescence)
21	Army duty
22	Met Kathleen
21–24	Army duty
25	Married
26	First child
41	Had mononucleosis; two and a half months in bed
51	Mom died
53	Son married, two children graduated; got boat and place at lake
58	Retired

*Labels and values from 1958 "best and worst periods" chart.

The personality assessment of Karl at 61, based on another round of Q-sorts, suggested minimal change over the adult years. He again received the highest possible score on "dependable" and was only a shade lower on "straightforward," "productive," "has wide interests," and "warm." Again, the attributes deemed least applicable to him were "deceitful" and "feels victimized." Equally inapplicable was the phrase "disorganized and maladaptive when under stress or trauma." Both of the Schulzes were effective copers. The stability of Karl's personality over the adult years is attested to by the correlation coefficient between his age 37 and age 61 profiles, .75, which is as high as the average reliability of the Q-sort composite at any given period. He still scored high on all of the components of the competence index though relatively lower than previously on dependability, perhaps because he was more relaxed and because most of the study members were now seen as dependable persons. His higher scores on "self-confident versus feels victimized" more than offset this drop, and at 62 Karl Schulz scored well up in the top 10 percent of the participating male study members on the index of competence.

A LIFE HISTORY INTERVIEW AT AGE 63

I conducted the life history interview with Karl Schulz at his home, the home that the Schulzes had acquired in their mid-30s. It was in a pleasant upper-middle-class community, on a block of very well-maintained homes on relatively spacious grounds. We reviewed recollections of adolescence, as had been done nearly thirty years earlier, at the time of the first intensive follow-up. Asked how well he knew himself and understood himself—his goals, his needs, and his values—at the end of adolescence, Karl Schulz again noted that he knew both where his problems lay and what his strengths were. When I explained my interest in trying to ascertain how lives get organized, Karl noted that his early goal of going into engineering "was a big help in making decisions and getting things organized...you were not floundering around."

I observed that it was unusual for a man to be as successful as Karl had been and at the same time not to be so involved in the job that he had to stint on the family's time. Karl noted that there was very little pressure in his job to work overtime and his being in a car pool had helped to define his hours of work. One aspect that he had liked was that there was a good deal of leeway in setting his own schedule for tasks that needed to be accomplished. He noted that his research-oriented job was very different from production engineering: "It wasn't pure science, but you had a lot of personal choice of what you could do or how you could do things."

Asked when he felt he had become fully mature—intellectually and emotionally mature—Karl Schulz thought that this occurred a few years after he had married. His wife had brought new perspectives, and the children had made him aware of previously unrecognized aspects of life. He saw his military service as also having contributed to making him mature. Asked to define what maturity meant to him, he replied: "[Being] able and willing to take charge of your life and taking responsibility for your actions whatever you do."

Karl Schulz did not think he had ever experienced any period of depression, and certainly no midlife crisis. His life, he said, had been "pretty even." Asked to look back and say whether he had remained pretty much the same person that he had been or whether he might have changed, he said that he did indeed think that he had changed. "Hopefully you grow and change and adapt a little bit." On the other hand, his general moral values had not changed, though he might have different attitudes than he had held earlier. Asked in what respects he felt he had changed, he replied: "I think I am more understanding of people and their problems. After you've been through some yourself, you realize how people have to behave or do things in certain cases." He felt that he had become more comfortable with people and friendlier than he had appeared earlier. His philosophy of life, however, was little changed: "You try to be a good person and do what is morally right and try to bring your family up that way."

How would he most like to be remembered? "As a good husband and father, I guess. Maybe a good neighbor and someone who has made a little contribution toward the good of mankind in the work you've been doing, although I don't think any of my efforts have been that overwhelming. . . . Basically, that you have lived a good life."

A REVIEW SESSION WITH THE SCHULZES

When I had prepared a draft of Karl Schulz's life story up to 1982, I sent a copy to Mr. and Mrs. Schulz with a request for permission to present it at a seminar on family dynamics. They were asked to suggest any corrections, modifications to preserve anonymity, or other changes that they deemed desirable, and a review interview at their home was arranged for. Karl and Kathleen Schulz received me cordially, and we entered into a wide-ranging discussion that continued for more than four hours, with lunch at midsession. Karl suggested dropping a few descriptive phrases that would tend to identify him but otherwise did not so much suggest changes as indicate where his memory was not quite consonant with certain details presented. These have been specified in the foregoing account.

All of the children had completed their transition to full adult status, and the Schulzes brought me up to date on the status not only of their children, all of whom were now married, but of their grandchildren. Their oldest daughter, Fran, had indeed married and was now happily at home with two youngsters. Two of the sons had wives who were employed full time, but they had taken time off to have children and then returned to the job. Their husbands were apparently sharing child care and home duties on an equitable basis. Moreover, the data we had secured from two of the children in the past three years (by mail questionnaire) suggested happy marriages and high job satisfaction. Although only one of the children now lived within an hour's drive of the parents, all five were bringing their families to their parents' home for Christmas.

The offsprings' family patterns are different from those of Kathleen and Karl. There are fewer children, wives tend to be employed, and husbands and wives share in the same tasks rather than having a sharp division of labor. Despite such changes, the several types of information that we have about the offsprings' families is that they shared attributes that Kathleen and Karl valued in their own marriage: cherishing their partners, providing mutual support, and feeling strongly committed to each other.

In the course of the interview, we discussed in some detail the early years of the marriage. There were difficult days, they recalled, but they shared whatever problems existed. Karl commented that his wife was never demanding, that she was willing to put up with a modest style of life. Moreover, "we depended on each other; if either had blown our tops, we wouldn't have lasted." Each knew that the other could be depended upon. Kathleen commented that if she had had a bad day, she knew that shortly after 4:30 Karl would be home and that he would take over. He would feed the little ones, play catch with the older ones, and generally take charge so that Kathleen could retire to read a book, rest, or do whatever else she felt like doing.

Because Karl had to be at work very early in the morning, Kathleen generally tended the children if they needed attention at night, but she regarded this as appropriate. Although at the start they had relatively little, once they managed to rent a small house, life was much more pleasant, and they managed almost immediately to begin saving. They both noted that when things were roughest, they knew that their general progress was going to be "always up." Kathleen observed that rough going prepares one for future coping and wondered whether the lack of struggle of the current generation of young adults would not make it harder for them to cope if they ran into difficulties subsequently. As she noted, their children had many more possessions when they got married. She and Karl had each other and a determination to build a family and a life together. She also noted that although there had been rough going in terms of living arrangements initially, "we never had any emotional rough going."

When I asked whether either Karl or Kathleen had ever experienced a period of depression in those early years, both immediately said "no." The only period of depression for Kathleen was when she fell and broke her leg and suffered a detached retina, which led to the loss of sight in one eye.

The Schulzes could think of no major issue that had been especially difficult for them, though one candidate that came to mind was the question of whether they needed a larger house in the early years of family growth. They built their second, larger house only seven years after having built their first house, and Karl had been rather reluctant to take on this financial burden. However, Kathleen had pushed for the house, and he acceded. As they both noted, it was the best investment they had ever made.

I inquired about Karl's retirement, which had come when he was only 58. He reported that he was finding work less exciting and that he was enjoying getting up early in the morning less and less. It was not that there was anything he specifically wanted to do, but there were rumors that the retirement program would be changing for the worse, and apparently a substantial number of Karl's colleagues decided to retire at the same time. Since retirement income would be reasonably adequate and since Kathleen had qualified for social security by working the necessary six quarters, there were no financial constraints requiring continued employment.

The Schulzes planned to stay in the area as long as they can. They enjoyed their home (they had just remodeled several rooms) and their yard, and they noted that their closest friends were in the community. Asked how they had made these friends, Kathleen commented that some were neighbors, some had come through the church, and some through work but the largest number were through the activities of their children. Parents of the children's friends often became their friends. It was clear that they were strongly rooted in the community and were good citizens of that community. Thus, the Schulz family might be considered not a "haven in a heartless world" but a haven in a warm and friendly world where there are opportunities for one to shape one's own life.

OVERVIEW

Karl and Kathleen Schulz retain a traditional view of the family, especially in their emphasis on the importance of children and relatively traditional gender relationships. In many traditional families, however, husbands have not been as fully available to their wives and children as Karl has been. And in many families of their age peers, women who were raised to espouse traditional values have been influenced to a substantial extent by the women's movement and have reevaluated the child-rearing years, when they were confined to the home, often with considerable resentment. One finds no such resentment in Kathleen Schulz. One finds rather the satisfaction of having raised five children who are competent, decent human beings. Relatively few of our study members have managed to bring large families through the 60s without suffering at least one casualty to the "drop out, turn on" generation.

One might wonder how a man who had been a somewhat inhibited adolescent, not at ease in social situations, could establish so thoroughly intimate a marital relationship as Karl and Kathleen share. One answer is Kathleen, who could at once put Karl at ease. Another is that Karl had enjoyed close friendships with several of his classmates. He was not lacking in the ability to relate closely, even if his emotional expression had seemed constricted. Certainly his emotional expression concerning Kathleen was not constricted. There had been, in his words, a "mad romantic phase" to the early years of marriage, and each partner always expressed genuine enthusiasm in talking about the other. Above all, they were best friends from the start.

In an era before children were regarded as burdens and seen by many feminists as a source of oppression of women, both Karl and Kathleen looked forward to the opportunity to nurture a family. They were willing to take on the responsibilities of parenthood, although they knew that their own freedom would be limited; they had strong convictions that parenthood was an essential part of the lives they wanted to live.

From all the data reviewed, they appear to have been warmly accepting of their children, but they set limits for the children and held them to those limits, perhaps being a bit overly strict in the earlier years but relinquishing controls and encouraging the children in a wide variety of acceptable activities. From questionnaires received from three of the children and from the Schulzes' most recent reports, all seem to be doing well, and all regard their parents with considerable affection. The values they espouse for their own children are very close to those espoused by Karl and Kathleen. In their 30s, they still see their parents as having been highly supportive and their own developmental years in the family as not at all stressful. Karl and Kathleen have not only been competent persons; they have raised competent children.

In considering this family history, we cannot ignore the importance of potentialities and proclivities genetically acquired. The patterns of personality resemblance within the family show amazing consistency from early childhood to the most recently available data. Two of the children most clearly resemble Karl, in being less socially outgoing, and two more clearly resemble their mother, with the youngest child less clearly similar to either parent. All have superior intelligence, as evidenced by testing in the early years and more recently. The boys' tall stature made them obvious recruits for a basketball team, and they were successful athletes, not only in basketball but in other sports as well. Throughout their childhood and adolescent years, they received love and guidance from parents who had sufficient resources to provide them with intellectually stimulating opportunities. All were assisted to go away for their college experience. Finally, all seem to have been imbued with motivation to do something significant with their lives.

CHAPTER 8

DESTINED FOR THE LAW

HENRY BARR

Whereas Stuart Campbell and Karl Schulz both suffered the loss of a loving parent in childhood and felt the direct impact of economic deprivation, Henry Barr came from one of the more affluent families in the three studies. Moreover, his parents were both loving and long-lived. Henry was enrolled in the Berkeley Growth Study before his birth and was seen every few months during the first three years of life, as was his mother. They were repeatedly seen over his first 18 years. He was a healthy baby, relatively placid, and a child with whom his parents were extremely content. Henry, like Stuart Campbell, was an exemplar of very high planful competence in adolescence and at every period of adult life when we were in touch with him.

Henry Barr has had a stable and successful career as an executive in the legal division of a large corporation. He has wide intellectual interests and a disciplined will that owe a great deal to his childhood environment and his parents' very high standards and expectations. Yet throughout his career and particularly in his late 30s, there was a hint (sometimes not wholly recognized on his part) of ambivalence about his work. In a very real sense, his career was chosen for him by a somewhat domineering but also supportive father in whose footsteps Henry traveled; from childhood he was driven not so much by internal desire as from a sense of duty. At 60, however, we see changes that bespeak a resolution of his ambivalence.

We have relatively little information about Henry Barr's ancestry, except that it is of old American stock. His maternal grandparents were Bostonians. Henry's father, who played such a dominant role in his life, was born in a state farther to the south, a few years before the turn of the century. He worked his way through a prestigious college and law school at a time when less than 5 percent of the population attained a college degree. After running a Bay Area branch of a New York law firm, he opened his own business in 1926. He worked hard and played little. He became a member of several exclusive clubs, an indication of his high social and financial status. Brought up a Protestant, in adulthood Henry's father belonged to an interdenominational church.

The elder Mr. Barr was an individualist with strong opinions. Slow and methodical, he was bent on having his own way. His wife described him to an interviewer in 1941 as a man who was never well adjusted—either to himself or to people around him—though they were a devoted couple. He lived in an inner world, which made him seem inaccessible to others. When his talkative, irritable, and demanding mother came to live with the family (1933–1941), he became even more taciturn.

In 1965, Henry described his father as warm inside but with a donnish, almost forbidding exterior, so that none of the family felt close to him. If they told him their problems, they received a lecture instead of a sympathetic ear. As a consequence, they seldom turned to him when troubled. Yet it was evident that he cared very much for them and was intensely interested in them.

Henry's mother, about five years younger than her husband, was born in New York State in 1898 and attended a leading woman's college. She later took music, writing, and psychology courses while living in the Bay Area. She was brought up as an Episcopalian. A staff interviewer in 1941 described Mrs. Barr as an attractive, well-poised, and gracious woman. He thought her good-natured, with a sense of humor. The interviewer also speculated that she would be tactful yet insistent on voicing her full opinion on a subject. She was the organizer of family activities.

The interviewer inferred a probable clash of personalities between wife and husband, but on the whole their relationship was very good. The elder Barr's incommunicativeness, however, made his wife "frantic" at first, she reported.

The first growth study contact with the Barr family began just before Henry's birth in 1928. At that time the family, consisting also of a brother four years older than Henry and a sister two years older, lived in a large rented house, but Mrs. Barr mentioned that they owned a lot in an exclusive residential suburb where they planned to build. We do not know exactly when they built their home, but the family had apparently been occupying it for some years in 1941 when a staff member conducted a lengthy interview there with Henry's mother.

The house was that of a well-to-do family, as the interviewer characterized it. It was a large, vine-covered, masonry house set on a terraced lot, with substantial lawn and garden. The paneled living room, with a high-beamed ceiling, contained a scattering of oriental rugs, a grand piano, large built-in and well-filled bookshelves, a large fireplace, and an enormous picture window that afforded a sweeping view of hills and bay. The interviewer learned that each of the boys had a suite to himself—a sleeping porch, bedroom, and bath. Mrs. Barr indicated that the entire house was used freely by all family members and that the children frequently brought friends home. Maintenance of the home was a cooperative venture, for Henry's parents believed that responsibility should be learned early. The children not only cared for their own rooms but helped with the gardening; the allowances they received seemed quite ample to the interviewer, though not as great as many of their friends in the neighborhood received.

If the depression had any effect on the family's life-style it was not apparent, though Mrs. Barr said that they would do more traveling if they had a greater income. Looking back at his childhood and adolescent years at age 56, Henry could not recall that the depression had any impact at all on his life.

We learned from an earlier interview with Henry's mother that both parents had very much wanted children and wished them to have every advantage they could be given. Despite his somewhat forbidding and critical ways, the elder Mr. Barr was extremely interested in the children's activities and development but was not highly involved with them. There are indications that the oldest son was raised with unusual strictness, and perhaps as a consequence he was ill at ease socially and failed to perform up to his father's expectations. Henry, on the other hand, was extremely adaptable and showed a good deal of social ease.

The Barr children were regularly tended by nursemaids during their early years, an arrangement fairly common among affluent families but rare in the study group. Although Henry's mother stated in the 1941 interview that she was fully in charge of the children, she commented later in the interview that they were with the nursemaid so much of the time that they would not have missed her. In any event, it was clear that she planned their activities in great detail and saw that her plans were implemented in a quiet but firm way. In 1930, when the oldest of the three children was age 6, she commented that taking care of them required all of her time and left her exhausted. Yet at that time a staff member remarked on the great tact and firm purpose she employed in dealing with the infant Henry when he was brought to the institute for testing.

Henry seemed an unexceptional child during his preschool years insofar as physical and mental development was concerned, although he was characterized as relatively independent, stubborn, and self-confident. At age 4, his mother described him as lacking in persistence, and under test conditions, he was reported by the study staff to give up readily on difficult tasks, withdrawing into himself. A few years later, however, the staff noted his high level of effort and his persistence in seeking to master any tasks given him. It would appear that his parents' efforts to motivate him toward achievement had had considerable success even before he entered school.

At the age of 7, Henry was characterized by the research staff as showing a high level of effort and drive and performing very systematically at tests. He seemed to strive for success in whatever he did. During the elementary school years, Henry performed well in school, but the staff commented that his impulse to succeed appeared to originate less from within than from a sense of duty. Henry himself confirmed this interpretation when reviewing his childhood more than forty years later. The premium he placed on successful performance is well illustrated by his responses to one of the Thematic Apperception Test (TAT) stories that he made up at age 11½.[1] Henry told of a mad scientist who thought he could bring the dead back to life; he killed himself when he failed to do so.

Henry's intelligence test scores varied somewhat during childhood and adolescence, but his IQ clearly put him in the upper 5 percent of the general population. Perhaps because he attended a school in which so many bright children of academics and other professionals were enrolled, his superior intelligence occasioned little note on the part of study staff during his school years. In institute testing, Henry often required some urging to respond when he encountered difficult problems. He seemed cautious about trying new tactics unless he felt reasonably sure they promised success. During this period, the staff characterized him as deliberate but somewhat passive, moderately self-critical, and sluggish.

At age 12½, he was viewed as reserved and compliant, well mannered and strongly on the controlled side. Yet he was also seen as highly adaptable—even a social chameleon of sorts. He was able to make himself acceptable to adults and at the same time make friends easily among his peers. His friends were frequently older than himself, indicative of his social maturity and perhaps prestige as well, and he sometimes imitated their behavior. When for several years he had a somewhat domineering older friend, the usually quiet and reticent youth himself became talkative and high-spirited like the older boy. By early adolescence, he evidently tried out somewhat different personae. His father expressed admiration for the boy's social skills and his disciplined behavior.

ADOLESCENCE

Although characterized by the study staff as "sluggish" in school, Henry liked sports and did well in them as both a preadolescent and an adolescent. He swam, played tennis, and enjoyed other activities at the country club to which his parents belonged. He also had a great succession of hobbies, including chemistry and a butterfly collection; he passed from one to the next as his enthusiasm waned but showed great interest in understanding the world around him. He had a good deal of mechanical aptitude and enjoyed building. He was a member of the Boy Scouts, as were many middle-class boys at that time, but he said, "I didn't work at it very hard."

Henry had a decidedly masculine build—tall, broad shouldered, and muscular—as he achieved physical maturity. He reached puberty at about the average age for boys in the study group. In senior high school, he played on several varsity teams, among them swimming, tennis, and basketball.

Through the high school years, study members filled out inventories that indicated how they felt about particular kinds of peer behaviors and how they regarded themselves. Henry saw himself in general as a boy who would rather agree than fight, though toward the end of high school he placed his preference midway between the two extremes. Despite his being seen as very independent, he indicated that he preferred following another's directions to doing things his own way. Yet he also saw himself as someone who usually knew what he wanted and as a leader. Nevertheless, he seems to have shown little interest in student government, though as a successful athlete and a good student one might have expected him to be a strong candidate for student office.

Henry's general social and political views as of his senior year in high school are revealed by his responses to a questionnaire in 1944 administered to all members of the study. They showed him to be generally conservative, pro–big business and anti–labor unions and big government, as one might have expected of a successful lawyer's son. He favored obedience and respect for authority yet agreed with the statement that "society improves when young people with rebellious ideas continue to fight for social change." He strongly agreed with the statement that "no weakness or difficulty can hold us back if we have enough will power." He strongly subscribed to some views that tend to characterize authoritarian persons, such as that "some of the goings on in this country would make the wild sex life of the old Greeks and Romans seem tame" and that "most people don't realize how much our lives are controlled by plots hatched in secret by politicians." At the same time, however, he favored permitting all loyal Japanese-Americans to return to California right after the war, and he strongly disagreed with the statement that "if Negroes live poorly, it's mainly because they are naturally lazy, ignorant and without self-control." In these responses, he was far more tolerant than most of his peers. Nevertheless, he agreed that "it would be a mistake ever to have Negroes for foremen and leaders over whites" and that "it would be best to keep Negroes in their own districts in schools and to prevent too much contact with whites." We do not know how many of these views Henry shared with his parents, but they were shared by many middle-class American youth at the time. However, Henry was more inclined to see the world as a dangerous and wicked place than one might have expected of a bright 17 year old.

We later learned from Henry that toward the end of high school and throughout college, he worked summers at a variety of essentially full-time jobs. He had gone to summer camp in earlier years, but at age 16 he took his first away-from-home full-time job, working on a fire prevention crew for the U.S. Forest Service. He had held various part-time jobs from the time he was 12—gardening for neighbors, working as a stock boy, selling mistletoe at Christmas.

There was a strong work ethic in the Barr family, and the sons were urged to earn spending money to supplement their allowances.

We have only meager data on Henry's occupational aspirations during his high school years, but those data suggest that such plans were beginning to jell prior to his university enrollment. The stories he made up in response to the TAT frequently involved lawyers, yet on inventories relating to job choice, he thought of law as something he did not wish to do. Early in his high school years, he saw as attractive possibilities becoming a scientist, an engineer, a draftsman, or a machinist. From 15½ on, however, he indicated his first choice was to be a lawyer and his second to be a businessman. It is interesting to note how he perceived the law in the stories he made up in response to the TAT. In some of these stories, the boy protagonist carries out the intent of laws and regulations against antisocial forces or forces that are arrayed against him and his family. In some of them, he tries to protect his family and his family's wealth. It may be noted that at 13, Henry was described as valuing money highly and being good at saving. The boy in the stories either locks up the antisocial forces or chases them away. But in Henry's story the boy's father was a lot better at doing this than the boy himself. Thus, his responses again suggest the perception of the world as a dangerous place and a desire to fight against evil forces but also seeing his father as a more powerful person than himself.

Except for the 1941 interview with Henry's mother, we have little information on relationships or the division of labor within the Barr family during Henry's childhood and adolescence. In an interview at age 37, Henry, however, indicated that both parents had been active in disciplining the children, though his mother took the more prominent role. His father had a forbidding manner and could become upset with them, but he seldom was openly angry, and he never spanked the children. His mother had remarked many years before that there had been few occasions for finding fault with Henry. She added that he did not harbor a grudge when he was reprimanded, which was seldom. Henry indicated that his parents had kept after him to complete projects he had started, and they provided him with many rules for guidance. He felt that they always appeared interested to hear his point of view and gave him considerable freedom in both work and leisure. Thus, his recollections at age 37 meshed well with his responses to earlier inventories and his mother's earlier report. He felt that his father had tried more than his mother to change him but that both had been satisfied with him and both expressed love and praise, his mother to a greater degree.

We learned from Mrs. Barr that during their school years Henry liked his older brother and got along well with him. He frequently imitated him and tagged after him, despite the fact that the older brother loved to tease him. The siblings did not engage in prolonged quarrels, for Henry seemed to prefer to avoid quarrels and would give in rather than have a continuing struggle with his brother, who seemed never to let a quarrel die down. There appears to have been less closeness when Henry entered adolescence and some suggestion that he rather enjoyed noting his brother's lack of social ease.

Judges who carried out the personality Q-sorts uniformly rated Henry as dependable, productive, intelligent, and valuing intellectual matters. He was above average in self-confidence and was seen as not at all self-defeating or negativistic. In general, there were few changes from junior high school to senior high school scores, though two items stand out as showing appreciable change: Henry went from being seen as not at all submissive to somewhat more submissive than average in senior high school and from somewhat irritable in junior high school to very low irritability in senior high school. Other attributes on which the psychologist-judges gave him high ratings during his senior high years were "cheerful," "fastidious," "ambitious," and (somewhat) "power-oriented." At the same time, he was seen as not at all self-dramatizing, talkative, or rebellious. In short, he manifested the traits that in general are characteristic of highly competent, mature males, except for the indication of somewhat greater submissiveness (largely attributable to one judge). Perhaps it was the lack of self-dramatization and talkativeness that led to Henry's being perceived as submissive; he was not aggressively assertive, nor was he very outgoing. He scored just a bit lower than Stuart Campbell on the index of adolescent planful competence. Henry Barr's scores on the Q-sort components are given in Table A6 of Appendix A.

The history reported thus far was based almost entirely on materials available from Henry's childhood and adolescence, except as noted. We did not see Henry from the time he left high school until he participated in a follow-up at age 37, though he responded to a brief questionnaire about his physical status at age 21, when he was a student in college. From the two interviews conducted when Henry was 37, we learned of his experience in the intervening twenty years. This period has been reviewed in later interviews as well, and the several descriptive reports seem entirely consistent. Nevertheless, we must recognize that the information on his marriage and early career are based on retrospective reports from Henry alone covering a period of nearly twenty years and on inferences made by the interviewers. I draw on all subsequent interviews for descriptive details but will note variations if they were apparent.

EARLY ADULTHOOD

At age 37, Henry Barr was interviewed twice (at his law office) by a soft-spoken, slow-speaking man, who was a psychotherapist. Listening to the tape-recorded interview, it would be difficult to imagine two less similar personalities except that both men were quiet and thoughtful. The pace of the interviewer's questions was laboriously slow, and he frequently allowed long pauses after Henry had answered his questions. Henry, on the other hand, would often anticipate the completion of a question and begin to respond before the interviewer had finished. Perhaps this led initially to some irritation in the respondent, who was under much greater time pressure than the interviewer. Toward the end of the first interview, when another appointment was requested, Henry Barr wondered whether that would be a terminal interview, "because it seems that this program can go on and on." He noted that as he became busier, it was more difficult to participate (he had already transported his daughter to the Institute of Human Development for several testing sessions).[2] At the same time, he expressed willingness to continue.

In addition to securing information about developments in his life after high school graduation, the interviewer sought to review with Mr. Barr his earlier years. The latter's description of life in the family was highly consonant with what we had learned from his mother and from himself more than twenty years before.[3] Harmony, control, a highly moral (not religious) sense, strong guidance from his father and loving support from both parents—these elements of family climate were again highlighted. Nevertheless, just as his mother had sought to convey the idea that there was nothing exceptional about her children, Henry Barr now seemed committed to the presentation of self as a somewhat colorless, not particularly gifted person.

Reading the transcript of the two lengthy interviews conducted in his office at age 37, one is struck by the thoughtful effort Henry Barr made to explain himself and his life to date. He was frank even when it was painful for him to address certain topics, yet there were places where he seemed not to face up to the degree of his own discomfort. There was never a note of enthusiasm about his life.

Asked to chart the high and low periods of his life year by year, Henry Barr said he felt such a chart would not be meaningful. "I don't really have any wide swings in my life. It's been fairly [pause] very uniform....There are individual moments or periods, short periods....I'll draw the graph right across." (He did so, drawing the straight line at 8½ on the 10-point scale.) No other study member appeared so reluctant to acknowledge that some years were more satisfying, more exciting, and fuller of promise than others.[4]

Discussing his school days and the consequences of following an older brother and sister through the same school, he commented, "We were ordinary children. We didn't have any bizarre characteristics or anything pretty outstanding. So we were, sort of, reasonable, average, except we were better students." At 37, he could not remember any of his teachers in grammar school, nor could he recall the transition to junior high.

Henry's recollection at age 37 of his high school interests was quite different from the responses he had given to inventories while in high school. Although he now reported that he had been interested in the humanities and "certainly not in science or mathematics," he had earlier expressed much interest in science. This kind of reconstruction of the past to correspond to the present is not at all unusual, even for persons with excellent memory. It seems to be a normal feature of the human personality, whereby we preserve our sense of continuity by not recognizing that we have changed.[5]

From high school, Henry went to the University of California, as he and his parents had taken for granted he would. Henry lived at home during this period, though he belonged to a fraternity and took many of his meals there. We know less than we would like to about his college years. He had always gotten reasonably good grades in school, and university courses posed no problem for him, though he said that he had to work hard for his grades. He felt that he could study better at home than at the fraternity, and he knew that good grades would be important if he decided to go to law school. He was uncertain as to the career he might pursue and was not highly enthusiastic about courses he took in his business-oriented major. He had particularly enjoyed humanistic studies and read widely in English and history.

Henry had played on the freshman tennis team but found varsity sports participation too demanding of time for someone intent on getting good grades, and he confined his play to fraternity intramurals. He dated but never became seriously interested in his girlfriends. During the summers, he worked at manual labor in logging camps, along with his brother. It was hard physical labor, but he apparently enjoyed the activity. Most of his co-workers were far less well educated, but Henry and his brother learned to communicate with and work shoulder to shoulder with men of diverse backgrounds.

Not only Henry's father but both his paternal and maternal grandfathers had been lawyers, and Henry's father had hoped that his older son would follow him into the profession. But Henry's brother was much more interested in science and engineering and in many respects was resistant to his father's efforts to mold him in the father's image. When it became apparent that his older son would not go into law, Henry's father expressed the hope that his second son would. As Henry put it later: "My father made it fairly clear that he hoped I'd become a lawyer. But he didn't push it. I really think it was taken for granted in a way. I'm not sure I would have become a lawyer by natural inclination. So I was really pointed toward that."

In his senior year, Henry applied to the eastern law school that his father had attended. He subsequently reported that once he applied and was readily accepted, "it was the first time I was fully committed to go to law school." In the semester between graduation from college and enrollment in law school, he took courses in political science, courses that his father suggested would be helpful later.

Henry began law school just before the start of the Korean War and had completed his first year when he was called up for military service. He was in the top third of his law school class and could have avoided service at that time had he chosen to request defer-ment. He felt, however, that he would ultimately have to serve, and because he still had uncertainties about pursuing a career in law, he decided to enter the service. Thanks to his having enrolled in ROTC when he was in college, he was called to duty as an officer. Through his father's influence, he was assigned to serve in the same regiment in which his father had served in World War I. A brief refresher course in Officer Training School brought him a first lieutenant's bars, and he then served for a period at a base in the United States. He regarded his service there as akin to prison, and he was happy to be ordered to serve in Korea. Looking back on his army service, Henry observed:

> I enjoyed the Army more when I was in Korea because it was difficult being in the Army here, particularly at Fort Ord (just beyond the Bay Area), when all my friends were out of the Army. There wasn't much sympathy for military service at the time. Korea was just at the wan-ing stages.
>
> The most difficult time of my life was at Fort Ord, because down there I felt like I was in prison. I'd get released [on a weekend pass] and come up here and then have to go back. That was all removed when I went to Korea, because then you were in a completely mili-tary situation. I enjoyed it when I was overseas, but not here.

Henry arrived in Korea soon after the cease-fire, and he served for about a year as commanding officer of an infantry company. Much of the time they lived in bunkers on the edge of the demilita-rized zone and patrolled it, with occasional exchanges of fire. "It was, uh, interesting," Henry said at 37. Later he volunteered that he had experienced occasional nightmares as a result of this military service. At the same time, he viewed his responsibility for the men in his company as a maturing experience. He felt that his service had probably enhanced his patriotic feelings. But perhaps more im-portant, he stated, "I returned to law school with a great deal of en-thusiasm, more than I might otherwise have had."

He knew that he did not want to spend his life in the military, and indeed military service had made him see more clearly what he did not want as an occupational career. Being a veteran had an-other advantage; his educational expenses were now defrayed by the GI bill. He was discharged from the service somewhat early, just in time to reenroll in law school. After a few weeks of feverish review of his first-year notes, he diligently applied himself to his studies and graduated from law school two years later. He returned to California to take the bar exam, which he passed without difficulty. He had no special goal in legal work, but his father was a strong believer in the desirability of a private law practice, and the son followed his father's suggestion.

He joined a small, private law firm soon after admission to the bar. Almost as soon as he began practicing law, his uncertainty about career vanished, he later said. He realized that he was suited to the profession and would enjoy it, but he was not enthusiastic about the adversarial aspects of law practice. After several years, he was offered the opportunity to enter the law department of a large corporation. A friend who worked for the corporation had told him how satisfying he found it to do legal work that he felt had real social significance in that much dealth with environmental issues, a matter of keen concern to him. Henry had not felt that the kind of law practice he had been doing had such significance, and although he realized that as a corporate lawyer he would probably not make as much money as in private practice, he decided to make the shift.

Marriage and Family

During his first year in law school, Henry had met through a mutual friend the woman he would ultimately marry. The daughter of a physician, Molly was the same age as Henry. She came from a financially comfortable background but from a somewhat less culturally sophisticated family than his own. She had not gone to college and was not particularly intellectually inclined. Molly was nominally a Catholic, but religion was not a salient issue for either of them, so the difference in their religions did not seem important.

Henry had begun dating in high school, and he dated through the college years but ruled out marriage until he completed his education. He corresponded with Molly while he was in the service and after his return to law school and saw a good deal of her during summer vacations, but both continued to date others. Once he had returned to the Bay Area, they saw much more of each other;

they were married less than a year later. Looking back, twenty years later, he thought he had married Molly because "it was the traditional thing to do" at age 28.

Henry's characterization of the marriage nine years later, when he was interviewed at age 37, suggested severe problems. Although he rated his marriage as "fairly happy"—a 5 on a 1 to 9 scale—this rating put him in the lowest 10 percent of study members in their assessments of their marriages. Henry said that he particularly enjoyed the companionship that marriage afforded, and he viewed his home life as a warm, comfortable haven, but his more detailed characterization of the relationship suggested great tensions.

Henry Barr found it extremely difficult to describe his wife to the interviewer or to say what there was about her that had attracted him. The word *love* never was mentioned. He finally indicated that they enjoyed each other's company and seemed to have quite a bit in common, including a lot of friends. Asked to describe Molly, he started by observing that she was not a particularly complex individual. He characterized her as full of goodwill and "kind to other people, but she's not an intellectual." Less interested in ideas than he was, she was much more gregarious and more interested in people. He thought that she was reasonably satisfied with her situation in life and that she did not have any great wants or desires. Asked to describe a person just the opposite of his wife, he thought it would be "someone who is hard-driving, anxious to achieve great social distinction." Then he added, "someone who is more brittle and less concerned about people's feelings."

He felt that he had known his wife well when they were married, partly through their correspondence and partly through their being together during the summers while he was in law school. They had become engaged soon after he took his bar exam just after law school.

Molly had been working in the San Francisco office of an international firm when they married, and she continued to work for a year and a half after their marriage. She left at some point in her pregnancy and remained out of the labor force thereafter. She was not markedly confined to the home, however; she was involved in volunteer activities such as those of the Junior League once their daughter started nursery school. She and Henry had apparently worked out a satisfactory division of labor, for he helped around the house, and when their daughter arrived, he was an involved father.

Perhaps it was when he described himself that he gave the clearest indication of problems in the marriage. He characterized himself as a

> perfectionist . . . much more demanding than my wife, less relaxed . . .
> wanting to get things done and getting them done right . . . a much
> more tightly wound individual than she is. . . . There are times when
> my major source of irritation in our marriage is the fact that she isn't
> as well organized. I recognize that this is a failing, probably, on my
> part more than hers, but when a person tends to be the hyperorga-
> nized type that I am, they get impatient with people who are not that
> way. Particularly when I feel that things should be done *now* or soon
> and she is more willing to let them go by.

It was evident that his wife had not been imbued with the same set of priorities and compulsions that Henry had and that deep dissatisfactions were almost inevitable. Yet at the time, he said he felt quite sure that the marriage would endure; there had been adjustment problems earlier, but he thought that their relationship was going much smoother now. He was able to give a quite frank and insightful statement of how he thought his wife perceived him—as overly impatient and fretful. It was evident that he saw her as deficient in intellectual depth and ambition, as well as their having very different temperaments and interests.

Henry at first said that he and his wife had similar interests, but when he began to describe those interests, he commented with a laugh: "They're not as similar as I thought they were before we were married." Henry was an active tennis player and enjoyed a variety of athletic activities as participant or as observer; his wife was not particularly interested. He played the classical guitar; his wife was less musically inclined. But they did go to symphony concerts often together with friends, and both liked to entertain on a small scale. Henry was unenthusiastic about cocktail parties and the small talk they engendered. "I'd much rather have a quiet dinner party where you can sit down and discuss things with people." What might one discuss? "I'd rather get in a hot political conversation or philosophic discussion than discuss run-of-the-mill daily activities."

On the score of temperament, he revealed a good deal more after filling out an inventory that asked for comparison of personal orientation of husband and wife:

One of the principal differences between my wife and me is that I tend to be much more self-contained and self-sufficient. As far as other people are involved, I can go for weeks and be perfectly happy, virtually alone. She, under similar conditions, would be quite miserable and want to be with other people. ... I'm happy with my little projects, at home, and she tends to be less happy when we don't have an active social life.[6]

Nevertheless, he acknowledged feeling down at times. Asked whether he ever had felt blue in his life, he replied:

Oh, sure, all the time. I mean, many times, for no reason I can explain to myself or understand. I'm despondent or don't feel as resilient as other days. Some days I come down here and feel I can lick the world, and there are many days that I feel I have difficulty with the most common, simple problems. ... I've had arguments with my wife or disagreements about major decisions—a period of despondency can evolve.

He went on to say that frustrations and emotional turmoil in connection with trial work had tended to carry over into other activities, and he was now shifting out of trial work. He was more involved in negotiating and drafting agreements, which he found satisfying and less stressful. The adversarial nature of trial work was not to his liking.

The Barrs' daughter, Betsy, was age 6 at the time of the interview, and her father had high hopes for her. Asked, "What would you say you most want in life for your child or children?" he said he hoped that his children would become "significant people, make some contribution, however small, to the society in which they live." He specifically ruled out what he thought many people might opt for: "Not happiness," he said, "because happiness is a fictitious goal." Focusing on his daughter, he would "like her to get as good an education as she can take ... and do something significant with her life. I'd love to have her be a writer or a physician, a professor...."

On a questionnaire asking what attributes he regarded as most important in a young son and in a daughter, Henry Barr checked the same three (out of seventeen) attributes for both boys and girls—ambition, honesty, and being curious about their world—all attributes that he possessed to a high degree. The first and third were attributes that required both good constitutional potentialities and proper nurture. There would appear to have been every reason to assume that these requirements would easily be met. But there was already some evidence that Betsy had a problem that was later revealed as severe dyslexia.

Henry Barr described his daughter as "fair, tall, Nordic-looking and fairly large for her age." In temperament he saw her as ebullient, very excitable, and either very happy or very unhappy. In kindergarten she had been assessed as insecure and in need of help before entering the first grade. He felt this was "ludicrous" but acknowledged that Betsy "doesn't have much in the way of concentration." This he attributed to the recency of their move from a somewhat isolated, idyllic suburban location to the city (a year previously). He thought she might be a "late bloomer" academically, as he reported himself to have been. But he also reported that Betsy was regarded as the lowest performer in her kindergarten class of twenty, and he may have had some anxiety that she was to a degree retarded.

Henry denied that he and his wife differed significantly in their philosophies with reference to the child's upbringing, but he would have preferred sending her to a public school while his wife opted for a nonsectarian private school. Betsy tended to turn much more to her mother when she was unhappy, and it appeared that Henry Barr was willing to let his wife make the decision as to which school it would be. In general, he felt they were trying to raise their daughter the way they had been raised, except that he wanted a closer relationship with her than he had had with his own father.

The Barrs were somewhat concerned that Betsy would be spoiled or otherwise disadvantaged as an only child. Both were eager for additional children, but none had appeared after their daughter was born, despite lack of contraception. At the time of the interview, the couple was considering adoption.

Occupational Career

At the time of the interview, Henry had been with his corporate employer for six and a half years and had moved ahead in its law department. He described his job and the complexities of the cases that he handled, which largely had to do with such matters as securities and regulatory work. At the time he was heavily involved in

legal matters relating to major expansion of corporate activities beyond the home state. His description of his activities was detailed
and made clear the heavy responsibilities that he carried, but he
did so in a very low-key way, never suggesting his own importance.
One of the aspects that he particularly liked about his work was that
a younger lawyer like himself could be entrusted with more important matters than he normally would in a private law firm. He also
liked the fact that he did not have to entertain clients socially and
that it was a job that paid reasonably well but one that he could
leave back at the office at the end of the day.

While he expressed general satisfaction with the job and indicated that it had those attributes that were most important to him,
he subsequently gave some indications that he was less than totally
committed to the job. Asked whether he had ever thought of writing about legal issues for publication (after he had indicated that
he would have liked to see his wife write short stories and would
like to see his daughter be a writer), he stated that he was not a
legal scholar. He went on to add that although he could turn out
good legal work when he had to, "I'm not a spontaneous or volun-
tary legal scholar....When I leave here, I pretty well leave the law for
the day. I'd much prefer to read about history or almost anything
else. To me the law or at least parts of it are pretty dull and I'd
much rather engage my mind in other things."

On the other hand, when the interviewer asked further about
philosophical interests, Henry Barr felt that "some of the great
philosophic questions are involved in constitutional law" and that
his "real interest" ran to that branch of the law. He was by far most
enthusiastic when talking about this topic.

Other Activities and Interests

In 1965 Henry reported that his relationships with his brother
(with whom he had taken many camping trips) and sister were
good. He had very close ties with his parents, whom he saw at least
weekly. Henry also reported that since practicing law and having a
family, he tended to see friends less often—perhaps once or twice a
week—but that was agreeable to him. He preferred having a few
good friends to many casual ones. These were people he grew up
or went to college with, and together they went on picnics, to the

beach and symphony, and entertained one another in their homes. He also enjoyed political and philosophical discussions with them.

In 1965 Henry was a political independent who had done Republican precinct work, but he was tending toward the Democratic party more and more. He agreed with his father, who also became more politically liberal as he grew older, in opposing U.S. involvement in Vietnam, and he attended antiwar rallies. Henry felt that the unreasonable fear of communism led U.S. foreign policy into many problems. He deplored the U.S. invasion of the Dominican Republic, noting some parallels with the Soviet Union's invasion of Hungary. He was far better informed about international political developments than the great majority of study members. He felt that America had made a serious mistake in going into Vietnam without the sanction of the United Nations, and he rightly noted, long before the full facts on the Vietnamese debacle came out, that the majority of Vietnamese did not want the United States in their country.

Henry was a strong supporter of civil rights, with a desire for more equality and even a belief in the desirability of breaking unreasonable restrictions or laws. He had "no doubt that our greatest internal problem is the racial problem." He believed that America was too properous and smug for its own good. There were, in his opinion, more important goals than earning great amounts of money. Thus, in certain respects he had become much less conservative and more humanitarian than the adolescent Henry. Although he saw himself as not at all religious, he had strong moral convictions, and he followed them.

In his self-descriptions, Henry was generally self-aware—far more self-aware than most of our other study members. He recognized the parallels with his father's life, his own perfectionism, and the attendant anxiety that made him relatively difficult to live with. He saw himself as a hard worker, of not exceptional intelligence, and a tightly organized planner with lists. He hated having unsolved problems and tended to make relatively quick decisions (usually not to his regret). He was so energetic that he could not sit still when there were tasks to be done; he felt he had to be doing something constructive—the result, he thought, of a puritanic guilt complex. Almost certainly there were elements of basic temperament involved here as well as learned life-style.

Henry Barr's personality Q-sort profile showed less change than that of the average study member between the senior high school years and age 37, but there were some changes. While still seen as highly dependable, intelligent, productive, and valuing intellectual matters, he was seen as less sociable and less warm than earlier (or later). He was rated much less "gregarious" and as somewhat less "warm," "giving," and "sympathetic" than the average male in the study group. It was only in this period that he dropped below the average in the item "arouses liking." Henry was seen by the Q-sorters as having a less rapid tempo in early adulthood and as being less introspective, less socially perceptive, less cheerful, and less poised than at other periods, though my own current review of the interviews suggests both a more rapid tempo and a more introspective and socially perceptive quality than the raters recognized. Henry Barr was not cheerful, but he appears to have been quite accurate in his assessment of his strengths and problems. Nevertheless, he seemed unaware or unwilling to acknowledge that he was at times quite depressed about his marriage and his daughter's apparent learning disability.

Henry Barr was rated as slightly above the average study member in basic hostility but was not seen as extrapunitive. He was seen as more assertive and yet more fearful at age 37 than at any other time. The impression may well have reflected the dilemma stemming from his high aspirations for his wife and child and the great uncertainties and ambivalence that he felt.

When he had been asked to describe a person who was the opposite of himself, Henry characterized "a very relaxed, unconcerned sort of individual who worries about tomorrow tomorrow, and doesn't particularly plan ahead or have any particular objective in mind, but is living for the sake of living without giving it too much concern." Thus, he made evident both the exemplification of planful competence and the costs that such competence could entail if not leavened by an ability to relax and enjoy "living without giving it too much concern." At age 37, Henry Barr did not seem to be enjoying his life as much as a man of his talents and integrity should be enjoying it.

Through her husband, Molly Barr had been invited to become a participant in the research, but she declined the invitation. This was hardly surprising, considering the tensions in the marriage and the potential awkwardness of being asked to make disclosures that could be embarrassing to both.[8] Betsy, however, was periodically brought to the institute by her father, for testing as a second-generation study member. The staff characterized Henry Barr as a supportive, involved father, but there was not further follow-up of members of the Berkeley Growth Study until 1982, so again we have a long gap to be covered largely by retrospective report.

HENRY BARR AT AGE 54

Henry was still with the same corporation, but he and Molly had divorced, by mutual agreement, in 1981, about a year before we talked with him. Henry had risen high in the corporate structure and felt he had reached his ceiling. He had been passed over in the selection of chief counsel, though he was just a step below. This did not seem to be a major source of disappointment, and at age 54 Henry Barr seemed much more relaxed and satisfied than seventeen years earlier.

Family and Children

Soon after the previous contact, the Barrs had adopted a son, Paul, who was 4 days old when his new parents picked him up at the hospital. By then it was becoming evident that their daughter, Betsy, had severe dyslexia, and the Barrs must have been somewhat apprehensive as to whether Paul would be "normal." Paul seemed a normal infant, but he was late in talking, and his impaired motor skills early in childhood suggested neurological damage so severe as to limit his mature performance. Two years later the Barrs adopted another boy, again a few days old when he joined the family. He ultimately proved to be not only normal but exceptionally bright. The rearing of the children added a good deal of stress to the couple's life.

Betsy had attended a private girls' school and had required tutoring and therapy. It took her father a long while to accept the severity of his daughter's handicap. Determined to have closer ties with his children than his father had had with him in his early years, he spent much time trying to help his daughter:

> I worked with Betsy, just worked and worked and worked with her on arithmetic and reading and that was frustrating because—she never

put it together. . . . With the first child, I expected the child to be terrific. It was hard for me to understand why she couldn't put those numbers together. I knew intellectually why she couldn't do it, but . . .

The meaning of this child's problem to a father who above all else valued significant achievement was intensely painful: "She's the first child—the first adult in our family who's not graduated from college, of all the cousins and nephews and nieces, which, of course, she feels."

Paul's problems were even more acute. He was hyperactive and had multiple learning disabilities requiring that he attend special classes. Moreover, his physical ineptness kept him from being a full participant in peer activities. Henry tried to give the boy a lot of attention; they went fishing and cycled, for example. The divorce had cut down sharply on their time together, but Henry saw him once a week and talked with him on the telephone almost every day. The younger boy, Perry, was both intellectually and athletically gifted and had less need for a special pal. But Henry felt that Perry understood and did not resent his greater attention to Paul. He felt very close to both sons.

The problems of the older children required a lot of thought and involvement by the parents. Paul spent one academic year in a diagnostic school. Henry thought Paul should return to special classes in public school, but Molly opted for a small, private school where Paul would get loving care. As so often happens if there are tensions between husband and wife, the children's problems added enough stress to make their relationship more difficult. Henry said that they had both come to realize that the marriage was less and less gratifying, but apparently neither wanted to say anything because of the children. When the matter was finally discussed, they were in agreement that a divorce would be liberating for both of them. Indeed, it was Molly who proposed the timing; Henry said he was willing to stay longer, but Molly did not want to. In retrospect, he felt they should have ended the marriage sooner.

Henry felt himself happier since the divorce. For years he had been frustrated at not being able to share with Molly discussion of topics that were important to him but of little concern to her. Tensions between them had increased as they disagreed on the best course for the children. Neither felt satisfaction or self-realization in the relationship. He now felt freer, and one suspects that Molly did, too. He was free of the disagreements and tensions that their married life had evoked and free to engage in the activities he liked best: going to the opera and the symphony, getting together with friends, reading. Even his attitude toward age had changed; he was thinking of himself as much younger than his mid-50s, and he was dating a much younger woman.

He realized that he was more fortunate than Molly; she was past the age where she would be likely to become romantically involved, and her social life was markedly curtailed by her responsibility for the children, though Betsy was now in the job market. Henry felt sorry for Molly's lack of social life but thought that she too had been happier since the divorce. It had been an amicable divorce, with arrangements worked out between Henry and his wife's attorney. He expected to marry again and had a woman in mind, but he was aware that if he did marry someone much younger, the age discrepancy might be a problem two decades hence.

Henry Barr's financial status made it easier to arrange a mutually satisfactory divorce settlement, but his sense of fairness and personal responsibility just as surely entered into the arrangement. When asked in 1982 to select from a list of reasons for his marital choice the most applicable one, he selected, "We had been going together so long that marriage was inevitable." It was, he said, "the traditional thing to do," a somewhat atypical response for a planfully competent man. It would appear that because they had been going together over a period of years, he felt an obligation to marry, but he also found Molly an agreeable person and both wanted children. The first ten years, he thought, had been fairly happy, though this was not how he had described the marriage when it was in its ninth year. His sense of responsibility seems to have militated against a mindful assessment of their probable compatibility over the years. That same sense of responsibility prevented him from facing up to his dissatisfaction much earlier. A high score on the component "dependable and responsible" occasionally had high costs as well as benefits.

Occupational Career

Henry Barr's corporate position now entailed a good deal of supervision of other lawyers in addition to his own practice. He enjoyed his legal practice more than the time he spent supervising others. Asked what he did not like about his work, however, he answered, "Very little." If free to go into any job, he said he would not choose to change, and although he had been somewhat diffident about his legal career seventeen years earlier, he now saw it as very important in determining his sense of who and what he had become: "Much more than earning a living. That's incidental. I'd probably do this if I didn't earn anything. It's a profession, and done right it's a demanding profession. It demands a high degree of excellence; at least I demand that of myself. I sometimes achieve it." He saw his work as the primary source and his family as the next most important source of his identity. He reported himself as enthusiastic about going to work but noted that despite his heavy involvement in the job, he did "not spend 80 hours a week there," as some colleagues did. He felt that he could be earning much more in private practice though probably with less satisfaction. In any event he noted that he would have a very comfortable income when he retired: "I'll be very secure financially, so I'll be free to do my thing, whatever I can find that is useful. Whether I'm paid or not, I want to do something that is not only useful but that's a real challenge, so it's a kind of second career starting at 65."

Retirement was still more than a decade away in his plans, but he had thought a good deal about it. His idea of retirement was, as is evident from the statement just quoted, anything but a settling into a comfortably relaxed life-style. He wanted to contribute, and he felt that he should be able to function effectively into his later 70s, as his father had.

Perhaps one reason that Henry Barr thought of himself as much younger than his years (as did our interviewers) was that he participated actively in sports—jogging, cycling, and playing tennis. Keeping himself fit seemed a basic principle in his philosophy of life, though he never phrased it that way to our staff. It was another aspect of his sense of personal responsibility, but it was one that he obviously enjoyed.

Reviewing the important decisions of his adult years with an interviewer in 1982, there were few he would choose to reverse. If he had once been ambivalent about law school, he now saw the decision as appropriate. While he still felt his father had influenced him somewhat more than was desirable, he said that he had been independent enough so that he could have resisted if he had truly felt negative about law school. He saw his involvement in his work as a major stabilizing force in what had become an unhappy marriage.

Even the marriage, he felt, might have been a good deal worse. It had been a mistake, but perhaps the biggest regret was that they had not divorced somewhat earlier, when both realized they did not want to spend the rest of their lives together. In the early years, there had been rough spots, but there was happiness, too; in time, their differences in interests and educational backgrounds could no longer be suppressed, and the problems of the children added to the stress.

Although he saw himself as something of a loner, one might more accurately say that he was to a very high degree self-sufficient. He certainly seemed to have no problems in relating to others, and he struck both the interviewers who saw him at age 54 as an appealing person, with an air of vitality and an ability to respond freely and frankly to their questions. He commented that he had the facility to be "able to talk with anybody about anything." But he valued a few close friendships above a highly diversified social life, and he liked to protect time for reading and for music.

Politically, Henry Barr had continued his move away from the conservative positions of his early years—and of most of the corporate lawyers with whom he worked. His corporation was very conservative: "They'd much prefer I be active in the Republicans. . . . I'm not encouraged to be active as a Democrat." One wonders whether his having been passed over for the position of chief counsel for this large corporation did not in part derive from his concerns for government action to ensure social justice and environmental protection. But Henry was more interested in specific environmental issues and in the control of nuclear arms than in political action per se.

This time Henry Barr did fill out a life satisfaction chart that deviated just a bit from the straight line he drew seventeen years earlier. There was a slight drop at the point where he was passed over for the position of chief counsel. Despite his reported dissatisfaction in the marriage and his much greater satisfaction now, he did not register these variations on his chart, so it gave us only that one clue as to the importance of his having reaching his ceiling in the corporation.

Asked whether he had changed over the years, he said he thought he was "the same person—incorrigible." He felt he dealt with stress somewhat better than in the past. His self-description accorded well with the personality assessment made by the study's clinicians. As always, he was seen as responsible, productive, and, above all, a man who valued intellectual matters (quite apart from his intellectually demanding occupation). But now he was seen much more positively in terms of interpersonal warmth and sympathy, as a "giving" person who aroused liking, had a rapid tempo, was poised, cheerful, and valued his independence. At 54, his personality profile was remarkably similar to what it had been in high school except for the higher scores now on items connoting warmth and positive affect. He scored among the very highest on the component "intellectually invested" and high on "self-confident," but, like Stuart Campbell and Karl Schulz, his score on "dependable" was now just average, as a consequence of his more relaxed attitude. Nevertheless, he scored near the top in mature competence.

A LIFE HISTORY INTERVIEW AT AGE 56

Two years after the 1982 follow-up, when we conducted our life history interview with Henry Barr, we asked whether as an adolescent he had given any thought to what he wanted in marriage and a family of his own. "Not the slightest," he replied. As to the kind of person he wanted to marry or the kind of relationship he wanted, he thought it would have been "somewhat like my own family where there seemed a similarity of background and a compatibility for that reason." Yet ultimately he seemed to drift into marriage that lacked precisely that similarity and compatibility.

In 1982 Henry Barr had said he expected to remain with the corporation until age 65 and then find a new career. At that time he expressed his deep satifaction in what he was doing, but two years later he felt he was getting stale. Moreover, he stated that some of the sense of satisfaction with his career had begun to "tarnish" a few years before when he was passed over for the top job in the legal division.

Asked whether he had ever experienced a time of dissatisfaction, of wanting to make a change (a question designed to elicit any evidence of a "midlife crisis"), Henry Barr replied:

Only now am I experiencing a feeling that I want to make a change in my career or in what I do. That is not so much that I am dissatisfied with what I do now, it is just that I have freedom to do what I want to do and I think a change for me in the next few years will be a good thing. It is more of a positive thing. It is probably good after doing one thing for thirty years. It is a new challenge.

Unlike the majority of study members, Henry Barr said he had been well aware of the options and opportunities available to him from a very early age: "If anybody had a situation in which they could succeed in whatever they chose to do, I was certainly well up on the spectrum. My parents believed very strongly in education and they would have made any sacrifice that was necessary if I got the grades for whatever I wanted to do." He regarded his father as having been also his mentor, guiding him and serving as a role model. His father was a perfectionist who expected everything to be well done, and so was the other person who served as a mentor, one of the partners in the law firm that he had first joined.

Henry Barr dated his having become mature at about the time that he started work, at age 28 or 29. In this respect he felt mature somewhat earlier than most other men did. His view of maturity was more multifaceted than that of most other respondents. To be a mature person, he felt, was to "realize your limitations, accepting reality, that life is not perfect, that you are not going to achieve all your goals." But it also entailed an awareness of the needs of other people and a willingness to subordinate one's own gratification to make someone else happy.

Reviewing his career and career satisfaction, he expressed somewhat more ambivalence at age 56 than he had at 54 and was in fact surprised when he was told that he had appeared to be deeply satisfied at 54. He commented that once he began thinking of what he wanted to do with the rest of his active life, the kind of change he might want to make, his satisfaction in the job began to diminish rather rapidly. He was becoming impatient to make the change, and he felt sure that he would be making it within the next year or two. Marriage also was on his mind, but he was having a hard time making the decision.

When asked whether he had a theory of how his life was shaped, Henry Barr said he did not, but then he added a statement of precisely the kind of informal theory we were looking for: "I think my life was shaped a lot, my early life, by the family in which I grew up." He knew precisely where his high standards and sense of responsibility came from. He was, to a considerable degree, the realization of what had been expected of him.

Many people begin to experience a shift in time perspectives—from thinking about past accomplishments to thinking about time remaining to do what one wants to do—as they get well along in their middle years, and Henry Barr acknowledged that such a shift had come upon him in the past three or four years. It was this sense of urgency that now made him eager for the change, for arriving at a final decision on "how I want to spend the rest of my active life."

Toward the end of the life course interview we asked: "When you think of your life as a whole and the difference it has made, how would you like to be remembered?" His reply was different from what one might have expected a few years earlier but was very much in keeping with the man we were interviewing: "I think as a good person, a sympathetic, feeling, and compassionate person, that more than a competent lawyer. If I made any change in recent years, I think it is more in understanding and emphasizing the human values as opposed to merely the factor of competence in a profession." He dated this realization to around the time of the divorce and noted that the divorce itself had been a big factor in making him realize how important the human aspects of life are.

One might say that at 56 Henry Barr was breaking out of some of the constricting patterns that had guided his life. He was no less responsible, but he was beginning to think more about what *he* wanted. Moreover, he seemed to see the world somewhat differently. Always concerned with the social significance of his work, he had found the adversarial aspects of legal practice unsatisfying. He had started out with rather conventional conservative views on many social issues, but he had moved in his middle years to have far more concern with civil rights, protection of the environment, and other issues that were generally a part of the Democratic rather than the Republican platform. As a consequence he felt the divergence of his views from those of most of his corporate associates, though there was no indication of tension on this score.

Henry Barr maintained a close relationship with his parents throughout his life. He had seen them at least weekly and he was on the telephone with his father—nearing age 90—daily at the time of our previous contact. His mother, whose health had been excellent, suddenly developed cataracts and had become blind in one eye, leading to profound depression. His father needed emotional support, and Henry provided it unstintingly. As his responsibilities for the children diminished with their adolescence and the divorce, his concerns for his parents became more acute. Yet the Henry Barr we saw at age 56 was by no means weighed down. Rather, he was competently coping and at the same time moving toward the new career that would incorporate the goals and themes he had chosen for "the rest of [his] active life."

HENRY BARR'S REACTION TO HIS LIFE HISTORY

I had felt reasonably comfortable in selecting Henry Barr for one of the life histories to be presented because he had always been thoughtful and had shown an awareness of the problematic aspects of his own development and personality. All of the interviewers and other staff members who had contacts with him had a decidedly favorable impression of him; both physically and in his style of relating to others, he evoked positive responses. At the same time, we knew that it would be difficult to ensure his anonymity if a life history were to be published that presented his occupational history and family history in accurate detail. Often it is possible to conceal true identities by changing attributes that are not important but that would serve to be identifying. But in the case of Henry Barr, there were many details that could not be changed without distorting the history of his development and the forces shaping his life.

I had some trepidation in sending him the draft of a history that presented his life as we understood it from the study records. That apprehension, however, was quickly relieved when he phoned to say that he had received the history, had read it, and in general approved of it. He stated that he thought the account accurately described his development and himself as a person, and, indeed, he had shown it to a close friend, who agreed that it presented a generally accurate picture.

There were, however, a few details that he felt needed slightly revised emphasis. He noted, for example, that his father was not only somewhat forbidding in his ways but was an extremely critical person. At the same time, however, Henry noted that we had attributed a "quick temper" to his father, which he felt was an incorrect description. He observed that his father seldom became openly angry and was not a man to lose his temper. Indeed, the only time he could recall his father really becoming angry was when he was faced with death at the age of 90, just a few months before we spoke. His father had asked what a much younger man might have asked: "Why me?"

Clearly the elder Mr. Barr was a dominant force in his son's life—if not the dominant force. One might surmise that in the high standards he set and the model of achievement that he presented to his son (whom the father had greatly admired even as a child), coupled with a rather forbidding manner and a tendency to be highly critical, both spurred the son on and yet constrained him from flights of fancy or expression of sheer joy. Adherence to high moral standards and responsibility to others always seems to have kept a lid on his ability fully to let go. His identity, like that of so many other professionals, was largely lodged in his profession, although that profession had been primarily of his father's choosing. His identity was even more tied to the thoughtful boy who did his best for the father whom he admired but could not get very close to. But Henry Barr is himself a warmer person, a less forbidding person than his father, and a devoted father despite the divorce.

POSTSCRIPT, 1990

At the time of editing the life history that had been prepared in 1986, I asked Henry Barr if he would be willing to bring his history up to date. He was. We had lunch together and talked about lives, and especially about his in recent years.

Henry Barr retired in 1987 at the age of 59. He had not planned to leave the job quite that soon, but unexpectedly the company offered a favorable early retirement program, and Henry decided to take advantage of it. He not only retired but made a complete break with his profession. Rather than asking that his license to practice law be relegated to inactive status, he resigned it. In this way, he unequivocally gave up the practice of law. He was set to make a real change in his life patterns. He felt that some of the recent trends in the practice of law as a commercial enterprise had cheapened the profession, and he wanted no more of it.

When we had last seen Henry Barr, he was trying to decide

whether to marry a woman lawyer twenty years his junior. He had been ambivalent, recognizing that in another twenty years he might be an impediment to her life enjoyment. They resolved his dilemma in a way that would not have been feasible a generation ago: they bought a house together. She practices law; he reads, travels, and has been studying French. A great disappointment in his marriage had been the inability to share intellectual interests with his wife. Now, Henry reports, he and his friend can discuss such interests for hours. At least once a year, they take a trip together, and in between Henry is seeing some of the places he never got to see in his years of disciplined work.

His children are doing well. Despite the unfortunate deficits that the two oldest were dealt at birth or before, they have found niches where they can achieve satisfaction and a sense of accomplishment. His daughter, Betsy, was upset about the divorce but came to understand that it had been a necessary step for both parents. She is, Henry said, "a good person," and she was moving toward complete independence as a preschool teacher. The older boy, Paul, despite his more severe handicap, is also on his own. He is no longer living with his mother but working as a part-time gardener and getting further training through a state agency in preparation for a full-time job. Younger son Perry has now graduated from the University of California at Los Angeles and is looking for a job in the business world.

Molly has not had as easy a time as Henry. Her more intense involvement with the children and her somewhat more circumscribed economic situation had curtailed social activities, and to Henry's knowledge there has been no romantic involvement. But Molly has close women friends and has worked part time in a shop whre she used to volunteer many years ago. As in many other divorces that occur in the middle years, the resolution entailed relatively greater costs for the woman than for the man.

Henry Barr talks of his life now as self-indulgent, but he is not a man to indulge himself. In fact, one might regard his current activities as not mere self-indulgence but rather self-realization. He has been savoring some of the riches of the Western cultural heritage and clearly expanding his vision. He enthusiastically described some of the breathtaking qualities of the Hermitage in Leningrad. Soon he will be going to visit yet other societies and cultures vastly different from his own, on this occasion India and Nepal.

Henry Barr knows that he will eventually have to find some activity that will give a greater sense of purpose to his life, but he is not yet clear as to what it will be—perhaps a volunteer program. It will be just a part-time activity, in any case. He does not need additional money. Or perhaps he will find that a program of study and intellectual exploration will meet his needs. For now, he seems comfortabel with his program of "self-indulgence."

As of the late fall 1990, Henry Barr reported in a questionnaire that he was serving as a volunteer for a health association, soliciting funds and distributing materials. He rated his health "excellent" and his feelings about life "Enthusiastic, life is very good." As this book goes to press, a final telephone call found that Henry Barr had volunteered to serve on a civil grand jury, which will keep him anchored in the Bay Area and considerably occupied for a full year. There will be less self-indulgence this year.

CHAPTER 9

COMPETENCE IN MEN'S LIVES
AND CAREERS

Stuart Campbell, Karl Schulz, and Henry Barr were planfully competent adolescents, and they are highly competent men. They illustrate my argument. They do not constitute merely anecdotal evidence, such as is presented in so many recent best-sellers that purport to describe the problems in men's and women's lives. Systematic evidence follows.

In this chapter I want first to note some of the similarities and differences among the three men whose lives have been presented. Then I describe a few of the men who were at the other end of the index of planful competence in their high school years and the general attributes of these men. Beyond such descriptions, I shall draw on the intensive life history sample to provide a brief decade-by-decade overview of the involvements and satisfactions of the men in their major life roles, comparing or contrasting those who had been above with those who had been below the mean level of adolescent planful competence. The remainder of this chapter will then give a somewhat detailed analysis of the men's occupational careers.

THREE COMPETENT MEN: A SUMMING UP

Henry Barr, Stuart Campbell, and Karl Schulz have had satisfying and productive lives. In adolescence, each knew in a general way where his intellectual and occupational interests lay, and each had a reasonably clear idea of who he was and the kind of person he wanted to become. They have been occupationally successful by almost any criterion. More important, they are esteemed as responsible men of goodwill by their peers and, especially, by those who know them best.

All three men ranked high on the measure of competence at every period when they were seen. All of them showed substantial continuity in personality, though two appreciably increased in their social skills and sociability over the years. Nevertheless, all have known difficult times, and two have experienced failure of a marriage. None, however, has been devastated by life crises or, to our knowledge, caused the devastation of others. All are loved and respected by their children, and all are in stable, satisfying relationships in later maturity. All look back on their lives with a sense of fulfillment; they have pleasant memories. These attributes tend to characterize the lives of other men who were planfully competent in adolescence, though there are exceptions.

There are differences among the three men whose lives have been depicted, as well as similarities. Stuart Campbell is obviously more outgoing, dynamic, and competitive than are Henry Barr and Karl Schulz. The latter are more reserved, but they differ from each other markedly in their intellectual interests and life styles. There were both similarities and differences in their early experiences. Henry Barr came from an affluent family, where he had not only economic resources but the guidance of two highly educated and attentive parents. His options seemed unlimited, while those of parentless Stuart Campbell and fatherless Karl Schulz seemed relatively meager in the early years. Parental loss and depression deprivation enforced a call for high responsibility on the part of Stuart and Karl, and both responded with a will. Henry Barr's sense of responsibility came not from economic demands but from his parents' conviction that a child should learn to be a responsible contributor to the household from his early years. All three men were held to high standards of performance by loving caretakers. Perhaps it is not irrelevant to note that all of those caretakers were products of Northern European cultures that put a high value on educational attainment. All three men internalized those values and standards very early. All were good students, not in the sense of seeking grades but in being genuinely interested in learning.

Like most of their peers, the two men from the Oakland study served in World War II, but unlike most, they had completed their professional training before serving. They were able to use that professional training in their military assignments as officers. Henry Barr was in law school when the Korean War began and could have opted out, but he chose to serve. He, too, became an officer. Military service had a different meaning for each of the men, but in every instance they seem to have performed admirably.

Henry Barr's career as a lawyer was to a large extent patterned on his father's views, and his father remained a role model until his death at age 90. Stuart Campbell, on the other hand, stands in marked contrast to the father who abandoned him. Stuart is the nurturant father par excellence, despite the lack of a male role model in the family. His choice of profession and the knowledge and skills it has imbued certainly have helped. Karl Schulz had only the idealized vision of his father, but that image helped to shape not only his career but his self-conception. However, it did not provide him with the assurance or social ease that a living father might have provided.

Perhaps nothing differentiates the men more sharply than their marital histories. Karl Schulz was not much interested in girls in high school or even in college, and he seemed inhibited, but he had had genuinely close relationships with friends. He may also have had an image—perhaps out of awareness—of the kind of person that he wanted to marry. At least it took very little time once he had met his wife-to-be to become attached. A chance encounter brought a new goal and a dominant influence into his life. Still, he felt that marriage during the war was unwise.

Stuart Campbell was more interested in girls, but in high school he lacked the skills to get highly involved with them. In college, he formed a close relationship with a female classmate, though apparently with no thought of marriage. It eventually led to marriage, largely because of feelings of guilt about sex outside marriage. Stuart was far more impetuous than Karl and less planful where marriage was concerned. The marriage lasted only a year, before both parties realized that it had been a mistake. It did not take Stuart long to establish another relationship, to fall very much in love and quickly to marry, despite his military commitment.

Henry Barr, on the other hand, did not let himself be tempted by thoughts of marriage until his education was completed. He married later than most competent men. When he did, it was more out of a sense of obligation after a long period of association than as a consequence of being in love, as the other men were. Perhaps because we did not see him early in his marriage and we have only retrospective reports after the marriage had been going downhill for some time, one senses none of the exhilaration in his relationship with his wife that Karl and Stuart have reported. However, one gets much more of a sense of deep satisfaction when Henry Barr talks about his current companion. His thoughtfulness is reflected in his decision to share life with a much younger professional woman but not to marry so as not to limit her later options.

All three men are firm in their commitments. None is strongly religious, but all are highly ethical. All are seen as straightforward and not the least bit deceitful or moralistic. They differ in the degree to which they are seen as assertive and talkative but hardly at all in the attributes that mark them as effective, likable persons. All score high on a measure of psychological health in later maturity.

The dominant attributes of these men are prototypic of those who scored high on my measure of adolescent planful competence. They are markedly different from the attributes of men who scored toward the bottom of the scale.

MEN LOW IN ADOLESCENT PLANFUL COMPETENCE

There are far fewer similarities in the life histories of most of the men who were low in planful competence in adolescence. Some less competent adolescents discovered who they were and where they wanted to go early in adulthood, and they, too, have tended to lead satisfying lives. However, most have been somewhat less successful occupationally. Those who had scored in the lowest third in adolescent competence, as compared with those in the top third, far more often experienced recurrent life crises and a sense of frustration and failure in their careers and their family relationships. They do not in general report themselves as less well satisfied with their current lives, but they report far more past difficulties, and they tend to present themselves more defensively. Most are less able to acknowledge shortcomings than are Stuart Campbell, Henry Barr, and Karl Schulz.

If the lives of less competent men were to be presented as fully as those of the three just mentioned, there is a danger that some would be devastated by knowing how they were and are perceived by others. The loud burly man who tries to dominate every setting in which he finds himself, fancying himself a princely fellow, would find it unsettling to know how widely he is perceived as a bore and how little respect his former wife and his children have for him. In adolescence he was always on the outskirts of every group, lacking in self-confidence, disinterested in school, and unpredictable. His blatant self-presentation today, which some might see as epitomizing self-confidence, makes him seem the diametric opposite from the adolescent whom we studied, yet the underlying dynamic may still be very much the same. He is not at peace with himself. As a result, it is not feasible to present a detailed history of the lives of such men. Instead, I briefly describe how these men were perceived by their interviewers at the last follow-up, when they were in their mid-50s to early 60s. The descriptions can be compared with the interviewers' impressions of Barr, Campbell, and Schulz. Subsequently, in connection with specific aspects of their lives, I shall draw upon fragments of the histories of the men who had scored low.

I cannot give 1982 descriptions of the four men who received the lowest scores on adolescent competence; all four ended their participation with the first adult follow-up. All had still scored in the bottom third on the index of competence as of ages 30 to 39. They were not at the very bottom at this point, but a couple were not far from it. As might be expected, those whose life experience was most dismal tended to drop out. Therefore I shall take the five men who had scored lowest in adolescence among those who remained as participants, providing a brief characterization of background, marital history, and occupation plus the interviewer's descripton:

1. A middle-class, semiprofessional from a broken home, raised by his middle-class father and stepmother. He has had three marriages, none of them satisfying to him or his wives. The interviewer described him as

    a very tense, anxious individual who seemed to need control in the interview at all times.... He maintains distance by excessive rambling. In a number of statements he contradicts himself and it was difficult for him to remain within reasonable boundaries on most questions.... He is extremely immature in relation to his wife.

2. A salesman, son of a salesman, raised by warring parents. He has had two marriages.

Anxiety and uncertainty hung around this subject like a cloud....His whole emphasis, the whole theme and content of the interview related to his view of himself as an alcoholic and a desire to have me understand his rejection of himself as an emotionally immature person while alcoholic, and his satisfaction that he was now sober and had been sober for almost six years....He is a man who feels enormously inadequate.

3. A truck driver from a working-class family not valuing education and one with considerable conflict between parents. He has had one marriage, with no children.

His shoulders were hunched and his body was in an attitude of vulnerability and sadness.... He immediately began discussing his unhappy marriage. He said that he always saw himself as "the lowest of the low."... He has no friends.

4. A civil engineer from a middle-class home, father professional, parents compatible but extremely undemonstrative. He is in an intact marriage but one with extreme problems for some decades.

His life has contained a good deal of turmoil, but he glosses over a number of dark corners and crises in work and in marriage....He is at this point a somewhat lonely man who gets his satisfactions from doing things with his hands and from tackling practical problems. He steers clear of relationships that entail the exchange of feelings. [It should be added that this man had become much more competent in middle adulthood and his marriage has greatly improved.]

5. A successful salesman and investor from a lower-middle-class background. He has been stably married. The interviewer commented:

He was entirely cooperative, friendly, anxious to respond as well as possible to the interview questions.... He seems to see himself as a man who has not made a great success of his life. He described himself as somewhat bitter.... In a way, he sees himself as a "weak sister" and I could not disagree with that characterization.

These men have not all been failures, but they do not look back with a sense of fulfillment. For the most part, they have married and supported their families in reasonably comfortable style, but both their occupational and their family lives have been stormy. Most are now seen as dependable, but they are neither interested in intellectual matters nor self-confident. The average IQ scores of these men were somewhat lower in adolescence than were those of our most competent men, but the differences were slight except for the third man. Only the last two of these men are in marriages that they and their wives regard as satisfying; the others range from not happy to miserable.

Some men found it difficult or painful to look closely at their own lives. One such man, asked if he had ever had a mentor, replied:

> I went through life without ever knowing what the hell was going on....If somebody would explain to me why I am what I am, it would be like somebody saying how a movie came out. It ruins the movie for you. If somebody would tell me why I do what I do, it would ruin my life....I don't ask "why do I feel this way?" To try to analyze it I would have to go to a psychiatrist, and I wouldn't go to a psychiatrist for all the tea in China.

The planfully competent men (or women) were much more open to self-knowledge and to exploring new possibilities for enriching their lives.

Contrast the descriptions of the less planfully competent and that self-defining statement with the interviewer's characterization of the study member who had scored highest on planful competence some forty years before; call him Harold Able. The interviewer had not heard of my concept of planful competence, for it had not yet been formulated, but her description of Harold Able epitomized the concept.

Harold Able was a very successful professional, the son of upper-middle-class, warm, supportive parents. He has had a very happy marriage and an exemplary relationship with his son. He was retired at the time of the life history interview, when he was 64:

> He is a man of precision and planning, stable, who has followed a clear-cut course of action....I had rarely heard a man who indicated so little dissatisfaction with his life....He indicated without complacency that he thought he had been lucky. His interests are broad—gardening, fishing, bird watching, and, above all, literature.

It is apparent from these descriptions and the earliest characterizations of Barr, Campbell, and Schulz that their adolescent competence scores gave very strong clues as to how interviewers might perceive men who had been at two extremes on planful competence thirty-seven to forty-five years after they had graduated from high school. Rankings on the competence index showed substantial continuity over most of the adult lifetime.[1] Most men who had scored low on planful competence increased their scores as they matured, but men who had shown early competence managed to maintain an edge by virtue of their ability, preparation, and early successes.

Study members whose lives were most unhappy or unsuccessful or who were engaged in illegal activities were likely to drop out of participation. The four whose scores on adolescent competence had been lowest dropped out after the first adult follow-up. Personality Q-sorts of adolescent data were carried out only if a study member was seen in his or her 30s. It is therefore quite likely that a number of those study members who did not participate in any adult follow-up would have scored even lower on adolescent competence.

Low Adolescent Competence: A Rebel with a Cause

There were a few rebellious adolescents who for one reason or other enjoyed participating, including at least one who engaged in a variety of criminal activities. The son of prominent, well-to-do, and intellectually gifted but embattled parents, he was bright, witty, physically small, and not athletic. He was early aware of his parents' conflicts and his mother's alcoholism. His mother favored his sister and all but ignored him, and his father was apparently unavailable. As an adolescent, he delighted in pranks, in breaking rules, and in pursuing sexual favors. He so epitomized rebelliousness that I shall call him Reb. Reb was often obnoxious, bragging and derogating others, especially in his senior high years. On an inventory he stated, first, that he did not trust people and, second, that he did not want to trust them. He cut school frequently and finally was expelled in his senior year. Beneath his rebellious exterior was a very hurt adolescent.

In junior high, Reb had scored roughly in the middle of the

study group on planful competence, but by senior high he was well down in the lowest third. He scored almost exactly in the middle on intellectual investment (largely because of high intelligence and high verbal skills) but was near the bottom on self-confidence and was rated in the bottom 10 percent on dependability.

Reb's mother had a career of her own, and it apparently took priority over her children and her husband. She was holding a party in the home while his father lay dying of a heart attack in an upstairs bedroom. "Go up to be with your father; he's dying," she told him. The party went on. Reb recited an account of this episode at the time of the first adult follow-up. His bitterness suggested that the episode must have shattered what little trust he had in adults.

That first follow-up entailed a series of interviews, and Reb went on a long alcoholic binge between the first and second interviews. He seemed determined to report to the interviewer the worst of his behaviors: armed robbery that landed him in jail in the Philippines (when he had served as a crew member in the wartime merchant marine), assault with a car upon a man who resented Reb's having run off with his wife, and then an account of his own brief marriage. He clearly did not like himself and seemed to be struggling to change, yet there was a boastful tone to his sorry recital of misdeeds.

Women apparently found the adult Reb fascinating at first. Artistically talented and extremely radical politically, he was intense and forceful in his rejection of the status quo in almost every sphere. He expressed his views with such flair that he must have seemed a hero to many with leftist leanings. One professional woman was so taken with him that she proposed marriage, to give him time to return to college years after he had dropped out and to fight for the rights of the downtrodden. (He only briefly held regular jobs beyond the end of World War II, though he later dealt in a wide variety of illegal drugs.) He occasionally had the assignment of providing care for his wife's autistic child by a previous marriage. Reb loved the boy, but one of his experiments in caring for him was to teach him to smoke marijuana. His wife did not appreciate this, and a divorce quickly followed.

When we last saw Reb at age 62, he had just been released from a mental hospital where he had landed after a heavy dosage of angel dust. He had earlier served time in state prison for drug sales. By then a member of Alcoholics Anonymous, he was largely being cared for by other members. He still wanted to argue political issues and flout convention, but his intellectual ability was much impaired.

Perhaps nothing better epitomizes Reb's general attitude over the years than his answer to the question, "How would you like most to be remembered?"

> REB: Just like anyone else. The only kind of immortality that anyone ever gets is to [have] left an unforgettable memory some-where. . . . So I hope people will remember some very good things I have pulled off, some beautiful capers.
>
> INTERVIEWER: What comes to mind?
>
> REB: The blowing up of the munitions train.

There were other capers as well, several somewhat similar. Reb seems to have known that he was near death, but he poured it on. When asked, "Do you have a theory of how your life was shaped?" he thought for a long pause and then, with a smile, replied:

> "There once was a girl, quite mild
> Who kept herself all undefiled
> By thinking of Jesus, infectious diseases
> And the dangers of having a child."
> —Something like that, sure.

The interviewer did not know what to make of this. As she tried to put additional words in his mouth, he ended the final interview with: "If a man asks for bread, don't give him a stone."

Reb lived a few years after we last interviewed him. By then he was in a board-and-care home for former mental patients. We cannot say with any assurance that anyone fully understood the boy who was so small, so bright, and so insecure.[2] But some of his subsequent hostility could be more readily understood once we had learned how his parents had treated the boy from an early age.

Another Type of Low Competence: Lack of Focus

Most men who had scored low on adolescent competence and remained in the study were not rebellious. Some had been rebellious in adolescence, but most were simply unfocused and unaware. Asked about his self-understanding and preparation for adult life in adolescence, Fred, a 56-year-old who had scored low in adolescent planful competence, commented:

> I always felt that I understood myself.... Now as far as aims towards later life, I did not prepare myself. I didn't understand where I was going at all. I was kind of drifting from one period to another, probably thinking that each step was going to take care of itself.... I didn't [plan] until I was almost 37, and then I began to plan.

Fred had been seen as lacking motivation, low in both self-confidence and intellectual interests in high school, despite the fact that both of his parents were college graduates and his father was a highly respected business executive. They had not challenged him or given him any real responsibility. Fred was certainly bright, but he used his intelligence sparingly. "I always felt that I didn't have to work today because tomorrow I could make up for it, and that was my biggest mistake. I think that too many people make that mistake today."

Fred never approached his father's occupational status, though he ultimately spent nearly three decades in a sales job. Before that he had made a near-disastrous attempt to find a new career in his early 30s. His marriage has been badly strained as a consequence of his drinking and inability to mobilize his resources.

THE ADOLESCENT-ADULT TRANSITION

Because we did not interview study members in their 20s, we have to rely largely on their reports at ages 30 to 38 on their transition to full adult status. That transition was complicated for the Oakland men by the onset of World War II (1941–1945) and for the younger cohort of study members by the Korean War (1950–1953). The first of these wars began in Europe in September 1939. When the German army overran the armies of France and England in 1940, America began to arm and to draft men into the military services for the first time since World War I.

Men who had entered college or had married before the Selective Service system went into effect tended to be deferred

prior to actual entrance into the war, as were those whose employment was deemed essential to the national interest. A few Oakland
men entered the army soon after finishing high school, but most
did so in 1942 and 1943.[3] By 1942, when the average member of the
study would have attained legal majority, roughly a fifth of the men
had married, most of them, like Stuart Campbell, soon before entering the service. Men whose college majors had high relevance
for the military, like prospective physician Campbell and engineer
Schulz, were often deferred, but their education programs were
speeded up to make them available for service in the shortest possible time.

From all the evidence available through the entire series of interviews and the final life history interview with our subsample of
study members, it appears that very few men (or women) had a serious problem of breaking away from the parental family.[4] Men
from the Oakland study often lived at home even if they attended
college, and these men and many who were employed were living
at home when they entered the service. Some married while in the
service; others, like Karl Schulz, married shortly after their return.
A few, who married late or not at all, remained in the parental
home until their late 20s. However, the median age at marriage for
the Oakland men was just under 24, despite the fact that roughly 90
percent served in the military during the war.

The military draft continued after World War II. By the end of the
war, men from the younger study cohort were being drafted, and by
1950, when the Korean War began, nearly half of the Guidance
Study and Berkeley Growth Study members had served or were serving. That proportion ultimately increased to roughly 70 percent.[5] As
Glen Elder has noted in his research focused on the effects of military service, the men who entered the service first were those who
had tended to do poorly in school, came from deprived families, and
scored lower on a measure of social competence (not the measure
used here) than their peers who entered the service later and those
who never served in the military. Men who had married young and
who had children were less likely to be drafted until late in the war
unless they had commissions in the reserve. The early entrants were
most likely to return to college or to a specialized training program
after the service and to marry later than their peers.

Thus, there was no standard sequence of the events that marked
the transition from adolescence to adulthood for the men in our

study. Leaving home for college or for military service usually preceded marriage, but many of the men worked for a time prior to military service, especially among the Oakland men. The great majority were out of the service by age 26 and were married, though most did not have children until two years after marriage. A few were still in school or in job training programs under the GI Bill after their first children had been born.

A DECADE-BY-DECADE OVERVIEW OF THE MEN'S LIVES

Work, family, and other role involvements can markedly affect each other. A sequential description of the experience of our study members decade by decade seemed essential, but this required reading through all of the information available and creating a historical summary for each person. The task could be accomplished for only a segment of the total study group—that subsample of sixty members already described as the life history sample. The life history sample consisted of thirty-two men and twenty-eight women randomly chosen from those study members living within fifty miles of Berkeley. Percentages based on this small number of cases are bound to vary—at times substantially—from those for the whole study. Nevertheless, trends tend to be very similar wherever we can compare the sample with the larger group. The value of the smaller sample is that every study member's history was studied as an entity, decade by decade to age 50, and his or her involvements and satisfactions coded by two highly trained professionals.[6] Neither knew my hypotheses regarding competence because they had not yet been formulated, and no study member had yet been classified according to competence. Therefore, any differences that appear cannot be attributed to biased coding.

The Twenties

In their 20s, more than half the men were seen as more heavily invested in their jobs than in any other role. Those who had been above the mean in adolescent competence tended to be more intensely involved in their work and somewhat less involved in their marriages than their peers who had been less competent. Although men who had been on the low end in adolescent competence were slightly more likely to be divorced in their 20s, most appeared to be more available to their wives, and the life history readers felt there was less tension in their marriages, compared with the highs, but both of these differences could be due to chance variation in the small samples. Among the men high in adolescent competence in the smaller sample, only Stuart Campbell was divorced.

Most men were fathers before age 30, but involvement in the parental role was seldom intense, as the men were struggling with both occupational and marital adaptation. As would be expected, those who had scored high on planful competence were better satisfied with their occupational roles. Nearly half the lows but less than a fifth of the highs appeared to have been substantially dissatisfied when they described the jobs they had held in their 20s.

We sought evidence of turmoil or crisis in the lives of study members decade by decade and found substantial differences associated with adolescent planful competence. In their 20s, nearly three-fifths of those with low planful competence (the "lows") but only a third of those with high competence (the "highs") experienced disruptions, turmoil, or real crises. No highly competent man experienced a crisis that seriously disrupted his life, but a third of the men who had scored low on adolescent planful competence experienced such crises. The data to age 50 are summarized in Table 9.1.

Table 9.1. **Discontinuity, Turmoil, and Crisis in the Major Roles of the Men, by Decades, by Adolescent Planful Competence (Life History Sample)**

	20s		30s		40s	
	Low PC	High PC	Low PC	High PC	Low PC	High PC
No apparent discontinuity or turmoil	33	43	27	57	36	67
Minor discontinuity or sense of turmoil	7	21	7	22	21	7
Sense of turmoil, dysphoria	7	0	7	7	7	13
Considerable discontinuity in major role, no crisis	20	36	20	0	29	7
Severe discontinuity, sense of crisis	33	0	40	14	7	7
Total (percentages)	100	100	101	100	100	101

Early planful competence had little bearing on men's attitudes toward gender roles or how they fselt about their wives working: half of the men had strongly traditional attitudes about differences between the sexes in temperament and appropriate life roles. These men essentially felt that women belonged at home, caring for children and looking after their husbands. One-fourth believed in equality between the sexes and expressed willingness to honor that concept, while the remaining quarter were more traditional than egalitarian but showed some appreciation that traditional roles might not be a completely fair deal for all women.

The highly competent men appeared to feel somewhat more negative about the appropriateness of their wives' working, and somewhat fewer of their wives were employed. By and large, this was by the wives' own choice, since there was less need for additional income in the families of the more successful men. Most women at mid-century were eager to have children and expected their husbands to be able to support them.

The Thirties

In their 30s, larger differences in favor of the men who had been more competent in adolescence became apparent. Three-fifths of the highs stayed with a single employer, usually with several promotions, as against one-fifth of the lows, a statistically significant difference. Three-fourths of the highs had orderly careers (staying in the same line of work) through their 30s, as against two-fifths of the lows, and job satisfaction was almost exactly parallel to orderliness.

In this decade, marital tension among the highs seemed greatly reduced: nearly 90 percent remained in an intact and satisfying marriage through the decade, and none divorced, though one man was considering divorce. By contrast, only half the low competents were in intact and happy marriages. A fifth divorced, and more than a fourth of the intact marriages reflected tension and turmoil. Now it was the highs who were relatively more involved in their marriages, despite high occupational involvement as well, and they were more satisfied, as would be expected. High job satisfaction and greater financial security undoubtedly reduced stresses on the more competent men and their wives.

The highs were also more involved in the parental role, though not markedly so. No man in either group was more involved in parenting than in any other role (as many women were), and only one in ten seemed as involved in parenting as in work or in the marital role.

Turmoil and crisis in the 30s again showed a significant difference in favor of the high adolescent competents. Three-fourths of the highs appeared to escape all but minor discontinuity or turmoil, but only a third of the lows were equally fortunate. Again, two-fifths of the lows as against 13 percent of the highs experienced serious crises in their lives. Turmoil and crises associated with the occupational role accounted for more than half of the acute problems faced by the lows.

In their 30s, the two groups did not differ in availability to their wives and families—a third had revealed themselves as feeling guilty on this score—though less than a fifth reported serious problems as a consequence. However, there was a role in which the men who had been low in adolescent competence appeared both more involved and much better satisfied: friendships. Two-thirds of the lows but only two-fifths of the highs reported having close friendships. Spontaneous references to satisfaction with friendships appeared in the early interviews of four-fifths of the low competents but only in a fourth of interviews of the highs, one of the most extreme differences found. Thus, the greater involvement in job and family was offset by a lesser involvement with close friendships. More than a fourth of the highs expressed some dissatisfaction with their not having close friends available. One of the costs of high competence in men may be a tendency to give friendships lower priority than obligations to the job and to family. Planfully competent adolescents were not seen as less gregarious or less outgoing than their peers.

The Forties

Age 40 has long been seen as a watershed year.[7] A man should be well settled in his occupation and enjoying a satisfying family life by his early 40s. Perhaps one reason for the impression that 40 (often termed midlife) is a period of crisis is that a man who has not found his niche by 40 is likely to feel he faces a crisis, though his situation has not changed. One of the men in the life history sample (who had been quite low in adolescent competence) commented when seen at 38, "I'm not a failure—yet." In the next decade he found his niche and indeed was not a failure. By the end of the decade, nearly all the highs and three-fourths of the lows had experienced a decade of stable, orderly employment. Now, however, it was the lows who were rated most involved in their jobs. Many of them recognized that they had fallen behind their peers. Unsatisfied with what they were doing and how far they had advanced, they were working longer hours, trying to catch up.

Marital continuity continued to favor the highs but only slightly. Three-fourths of the highs were in happy, intact marriages, according to our raters' assessments, and two-thirds of the lows showed comparable stability and satisfaction (a trivial difference, given sample size). The only divorce at this period, in our life history sample, was of a high competent. One additional man in each group was contemplating divorce.

Our raters sensed a substantial drop in the men's involvement in the marital role, despite the general level of satisfaction. Now involvement in the parental role was much more substantial. For several of the highs, we felt that involvement with their children became as important as was their work or their relationship with their wives. For a clear majority, the parental role was highly important, but nearly a third of the men (high competent and low alike) were rated only "somewhat involved" with their children.

Discontinuities, turmoil, and life crises dropped off in the men's 40s. Most men's lives had become more stable, but there was again a difference favoring those who had been more planfully competent in adolescence. And again the difference was largely attributable to occupational setbacks experienced by the lows. Now, however, these were more often disappointments and not a source of major crisis or turmoil. Only one man in each group faced a severe crisis during his 40s. Those sources of turmoil that did occur more often came toward the end of the decade rather than early in it, though the difference is not statistically significant. It does provide further evidence that the idea of a midlife crisis around age 40 is largely a myth. The recurrent crises that occur in the lives of men low in adolescent planful competence far overshadow any evidence for a midlife crisis.

MEN'S OCCUPATIONAL CAREERS

Getting on the Occupational Ladder

No other role is more important in giving structure and content to the lives of most men than their occupational role.[8] Children may wonder what they will be when they grow up, but most adolescents have only a vague idea about the occupational options that exist as possibilities for them unless parents or other adults have reviewed those options with them. As Henry Barr's experience suggests, parents who are college graduates can generally transmit much more accurate knowledge about occupational requirements than parents with more limited schooling. In the working class, emphasis is more likely to be placed upon immediate local job opportunities; in the middle class future and geographically remote possibilities are more likely to be considered. As counseling has become a service of high schools, knowledge limitations due to class should have diminished, but counselors may themselves be unable to see the potentials in a working-class boy and especially one from a minority or seriously deprived background, with none of the polite polish of a middle-class youngster.

Several working-class study members ruefully reported, "The school counselor said I should work with my hands." Working-class adolescents who did well in school were more often counseled to "be what you can," as Stuart Campbell was. Today, the availability of community colleges has somewhat attenuated social class differences in educational attainment, but working-class youth are still much more locally anchored. Study members from working-class backgrounds have tended to live nearer their parents than those from middle-class families, and the same tendency holds for their offspring. Going to college opens up wider perspectives, as well as a wider range of opportunities.

Working-class youth more often took the first job they could get after graduating from high school, while middle-class youth more often either went to college or into a family business or looked for a job that might offer longer-term prospects. Some had made rough assessments of their talents. All had taken inventories that were designed to gauge their vocational interests, but few seem to have been much influenced by what the inventories showed. When we checked the occupational choice inventories completed by Oakland study members in adolescence, approximately a third mentioned a specific choice. Those who were rated in the top half on competence were no more likely to say they had settled on a specific occupation than those who were rated in the bottom half, but they were more likely to say they had some idea of what they wanted to do, often mentioning two or three possibilities. Many of the less competent adolescents said they had no idea of what they wanted to do, while others named specific occupations that seemed unrealistic choices. Many very competent adolescents were interested in several possibilities but did not know enough about them to make a decision. Stuart Campbell felt pretty sure about medicine in high school, but Henry Barr was interested in literature and science, and even when in college he was not yet at all sure he wanted to be a lawyer. The choice was perhaps easiest for Karl Schulz, since he had both his father's example as a role model and his own demonstrable ability in mathematics and science. Also, he lacked literary and social skills. In a sense, the more diverse an adolescent's interests and talents are, the harder it is to make a decision before the completion of college.

The competent adolescents were much more likely to enter the occupations they mentioned in high school than were their less competent peers. They had been more likely to prepare themselves by learning what kind of educational program they needed to follow and then by undertaking such training. Some shifted out as they learned more about the demands of a particular field or learned about other possibilities. One student enrolled in a top engineering college because he had enjoyed and gotten high grades in math and science, but the college did not allow him any opportunity for humanistic or social science courses—literature, psychology, philosophy, sociology. He shifted in midstream and ultimately chose sociology. Many study members made such shifts once their interests were aroused by a good teacher or an influential book.

Thus, the key to effective and satisfying choice of a career is not so much an early choice as an informed choice. Competent adolescents later reported that they were aware of their options to a considerable degree. Their less competent peers had very seldom been aware of theirs, usually because they were not asking the right questions but sometimes because they had much less assistance in knowing what to ask.

Men who became professionals largely made their choice of occupation before they had finished their academic training, except for the small number who went back to universities after having tried some other occupation. This is not to say that some of the highly competent men did not shift their choices relatively early in the career, but more than half were convinced they were in the right occupation by the time they had reached age 30. Thus, one might say that they had settled down occupationally by age 30. For men who had been rated lower in adolescent competence, many did not find the right niche until their 30s or 40s. Among those with middle-class origins, fully half of those who had scored below the mean on adolescent competence reported they had *never* found the right job. The comparable figure for the top half was 12 percent.

All three of the men whose lives have been presented in detail had given much thought to career choice by the time they left high school, although two still had some uncertainties. Henry Barr did not resolve those uncertainties until his late 20s, but he reported that as soon as he started practicing law, he knew that was what he wanted to do. Karl Schulz stayed with one employer for his whole career. He found his job highly gratifying, even if not as remunerative as it might have been. Stuart Campbell never looked back once he finished his medical training. Very few men who had scored low in adolescent competence felt they were in the right niche from the start. Those few for the most part pursued occupations for which they had special talents, largely in art, music, and the use of craftsmen's skills.

Occupational Attainment

Occupational attainment may be conceptualized in many ways. Most widely used by social scientists is the prestige rating of the occupation.[9] In general, occupations that carry high prestige are those that entail a high degree of knowledge and skill. They are high in substantive complexity; that is, they are highly demanding in the tasks to be carried out, whether that demand has to do with people (e.g., supervision and mentoring) or data (e.g., synthesis) or things (highly skilled technical manipulations).[10] Prestigious occupations also tend to pay well, though some persons with very rare talents in athletics or entertainment may receive higher monetary rewards, as do many who successfully manage or manipulate financial transactions.

Monetary reward may, in fact, be the criterion that most members of the general public think about when the term *occupational attainment* is mentioned. But whether we use prestige, substantive complexity, or pay matters only slightly when we are talking about groups of people, because the three are highly correlated.[11] The members of our study sample have in general done well by any criterion, but there are nevertheless great variations in attainment. It would be a serious mistake to assume that high job attainment is necessarily a badge of success and happiness. Such attainment tends to be bought at the cost of much hard work in preparation, deferred gratifications, and often a slighting of family responsibilities and relaxed leisure. But high attainment also tends to bring greater security and comfort for the family and the possibility of earlier retirement—matters explored further in this chapter and the next.

Most of the men in the study sample equaled or excelled the occupational levels of their fathers. In part, this performance was related to a marked change in the occupational distribution in the United States between the years before World War II and the 1950s to 1970s, when most of the study members attained their highest occupational status.[12] Professional, technical, and administrative occupations constituted a greater proportion of the labor force in 1970 than they had in 1930 or 1940. Our study members also had another advantage that many of their fathers had not enjoyed: higher educational attainment. College and university enrollments had greatly increased, especially after the war, when the GI Bill permitted many veterans from less well-off families to go to college. In addition, the location of our study sample, in an area with several excellent colleges and universities, was a special boon for our study members' educational attainment.

Let us now consider more closely the antecedents of occupational attainment, especially those that have been found in larger studies focused on the topic. High educational attainment tends to be a prerequisite for high occupational attainment, and this was certainly demonstrated by our study members.

Predicting Educational Attainment

Parental socioeconomic status and IQ are predictors of both adolescent planful competence and educational attainment, but planful

Table 9.2.   The Relationship of Adolescent Attributes to the Ultimate
Educational Attainment of Study Males ($N = 70$)

Adolescent Attributes	Zero-Order Correlations	Standardized Beta	
		Model 1	Model 2
Parental socioeconomic status[a]	.44**	.15	.11
Age 17–18 IQ	.56**	.25	.23
Planful competence in high school	.68**	.54	
Self-confident	.33**		
Intellectually invested	.63**		.31*
Dependable	.61**		.34**
Variance explained (adjusted R^2)		.55	.56

$*p < .05$, $**p < .01$.
Note: The empty cells indicate that the variable was not entered.
[a]Hollingshead scale, reflected.

competence in the senior high school years is by far the strongest predictor of educational attainment. Table 9.2 shows for the several antecedents of educational attainment both the zero-order correlations (that is, association between single pairs of variables) and the contribution that each of the antecedents makes in a multiple regression. Whether we use the total index of competence (Model 1) or intellectual investment and dependability (Model 2), the two components that contribute most to the explanation of educational attainment, adolescent competence is shown to be a far more powerful influence than parental socioeconomic status and IQ combined. A boy's being intellectually invested—that is, interested in intellectual matters—was more important for his ultimate educational attainment than was his measured intelligence. That is not really surprising, when one considers that Reb and other boys whose IQs matched those of our most competent adolescents did not show much interest in academic or intellectual matters in their adolescent years and most did not do well in high school. It is not that high grades were very important. They were not, except as they made possible admission to a university, graduate school, or professional school. But it was important to be both motivated to learn

Table 9.3.   Predicting Occupational Attainment from Attributes
Assessed in Adolescence (N=64)

Adolescent Attributes	Zero-Order Correlations	Standardized Beta
Parental socioeconomic status[a]	.20	.05
IQ at age 17–18	.57**	.06
Educational attainment[a]	.57**	.23*
Planful competence in high school	.71**	.60**
Self-confident	.46**	
Intellectually invested	.59**	
Dependable	.66**	
Variance explained (adjusted R^2)		.54

*$p < .05$, **$p < .01$.
Note: The empty cells indicate that the variable was not entered.
[a]Hollingshead scale, reflected.

and disciplined enough to study and to do well enough to continue
with one's education. Additional education tended to enhance intellectual investment.

Predicting Occupational Attainment

Sociologists have conducted much research on the study of occupational attainment. The most critically important predictors are family socioeconomic status, IQ, and educational attainment.[13] Beyond
these, variables such as family income; family intactness; parental,
peer, and teacher encouragement; and the person's own motivation
to attend college and to achieve high occupational status all appear
to make a contribution to high occupational status in the early years
of the career and subsequently. Roughly half of the variance in occupational status is accounted for by all these variables together.[14]

Adolescent competence is as powerful a predictor as are all of
the aforementioned characteristics combined (Table 9.3). It accounts for roughly half the variance in occupational attainment
over the whole career, measured thirty-seven to forty-five years later.

Figure 9.1
Occupational Attainment at Successive Periods
Relative to Father's Occupational Status at Birth,
by Adolescent Social Class and Planful Competence

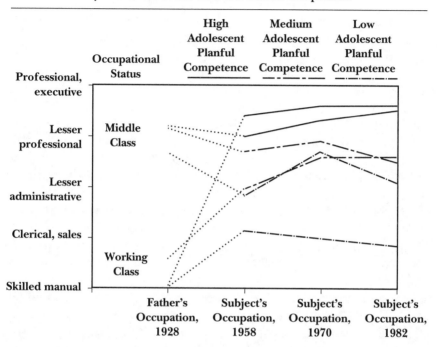

Each of the other variables entered into a predictive equation makes some contribution, but the measure of competence apparently reflects not only the effects of parental socioeconomic status, IQ, and educational attainment but many more of the factors contributing to occupational attainment.

Figure 9.1 indicates the father's occupational status at the time of the study member's birth and then, at successive age levels, the son's occupational status for six groups, differentiated on the basis of the family's social class position (middle and working class) and the son's adolescent competence (high, medium, low). On the average, boys who were high in competence exceeded their fathers' occupational status and that of boys lower in competence. Parental socioeconomic status has little influence on ultimate occupational attainment when adolescent competence is controlled. The family's social class makes a difference only for boys who were low in adolescent competence. Here, coming from a middle-class background tended to produce both higher educational attainment and higher occupational attainment. Middle-class parents could provide more resources and more assistance, including influence in getting better jobs. Of course, the benefits of a middle-class background significantly increased the proportion of adolescents who scored high on planful competence. Relatively fewer working-class boys scored high, but if they did, they found no more obstacles to achieving high occupational status than did their middle-class peers.

On the average, working-class boys exceeded their fathers' occupational status by their 30s. That they did so is largely a result of changes in the occupational structure over the intervening years rather than superior performance. Those who had scored low on adolescent competence actually declined in occupational status in the later stages of their work life.

By the time of the most recent follow-up, 60 percent of the men from middle-class backgrounds who had been high in competence occupied professional or top executive positions, and another 36 percent were in responsible managerial or semiprofessional jobs. Among those middle-class boys who were in the lowest third in adolescent competence, on the other hand, only one in ten had become a professional and another one in ten was in a semiprofessional or managerial job. By and large, these more successful men from the lower group in adolescence had become much more competent by their 30s.

Our sample from working-class backgrounds is relatively small, but more than half of the working-class boys who were high in planful competence occupied professional jobs; not a single one of those who had scored low in competence in their adolescent years did. To become a professional, one must at the least be a college graduate. For those from a working-class background, higher education was largely dependent on having been highly competent in adolescence.

Income Differentials Associated with Competence

Many of the men in our sample have been highly successful in terms of occupational status and were rewarded with incomes substantially above the national average. The one extremely wealthy member of

Figure 9.2
Percentage with Income above $50,000 in 1982,
by Senior High Planful Competence and Class of Origin

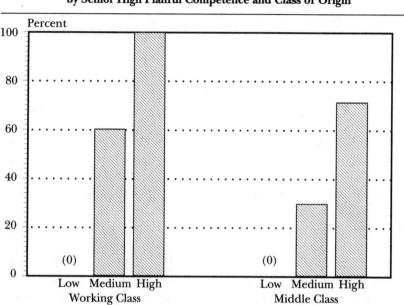

the Adolescent Growth Study made his money in oil and was, to all intents and purposes, retired abroad at the time of the first adult follow-up when he was 37. In a questionnaire distributed to study members at the time of the last follow-up, we asked for current annual income and income expected after retirement, by $10,000 increments up to $50,000 and then incomes above $50,000. Figure 9.2 illustrates the striking differences among the groups classified on the basis of social class of origin and competence level in adolescence. Among men with middle-class origins, 71 percent of those who had scored in the top third on adolescent planful competence, 30 percent of those intermediate, and no one in the bottom third reported earning more than $50,000 a year in 1982–1983. Among the small sample of men with working-class origins, the respective figures were 100 percent of those in the top third on competence, 60 percent of those intermediate, and no one in the bottom third. The differences between middle- and working-class men merely reflect chance variations because of the small number of working-class men who were high scorers on planful competence. Thus, class of origin made little difference in earnings when adolescent planful competence is taken into consideration.

Orderliness of Careers

The ideal career, from the standpoint of orderliness, is one in which a person builds upon prior training and skills and proceeds through a succession of levels of responsibility and prestige to the career's end. A person may shift employers when moving up but continues to draw on skills and experience that are directly functional to the new, higher-status job.[15] Thus, a civil servant who progresses from clerk to administrator or a college faculty member who moves from instructor to assistant professor and ultimately to full professor are examples of orderly careers within bureaucratic organizations, where orderly progress is most visible. The progress of a physician, architect, or lawyer who is self-employed is more difficult to assess in terms of distinct steps, but increasing professional stature and income are likely markers of orderly careers as the practitioner draws on the large store of technical knowledge required by the profession.

Men with successful careers are likely to have orderly careers, though this is not necessarily the case. For example, although for many years Andrew Carnegie was cited as an example of a man who rose from stock clerk to chief executive, his career actually entailed moving across occupational fields.[16] He started as a bobbin boy in the textile mill where his father had worked but got training to become a telegrapher, and then was employed on the Pennsylvania Railroad where he subsequently achieved managerial status. Through shrewd investments, he was able first to secure control of several small steel mills and ultimately to build the largest corporation in the United States for the production of steel. One might say that he built on his prior experience and skill, but he followed a course that would be far more difficult today and, in any event, would hardly be called orderly.

An orderly career was closely tied to getting in to the "right" field of work relatively early in one's occupational life and then rising in the hierarchy. An adolescent did not have to know what he wanted to do after college, but he had to realize that adolescence is a time of preparation, and not merely a period of experimentation or psychosocial moratorium, to use Erikson's term.[17] Failure to come to this realization often led to reverberations over the rest of the life course.

Our highly competent adolescents were much more likely to have orderly careers than were their less competent peers. They knew where they were going or where they wanted to commit themselves more or less permanently much earlier than their peers. The less competent far more often tried a variety of jobs in their 20s. For them, the settling-down phase often did not come until well along in their 30s, though there were certainly exceptions. For example, at least two of the men who came from seriously troubled families and scored quite low in adolescent competence decided very early in life that they wanted more than anything else to be artists. The two were among a surprising number who had superior drawing ability, which was noted by the junior high school counselor who worked with members of the Adolescent Growth Study. In both instances, she encouraged them, and both have spent their entire careers in some form of artistic endeavor that uses their skills. Those careers have not been outstandingly successful, partly because neither man had enough self-confidence to take the steps that might have led to much wider recognition of their talents. Instead, they settled for relatively modest but secure positions. These men have had the satisfaction of enjoying what they do, although their early socialization experience had persisting costs for their relationships with others.

Perhaps no one better illustrates a disorderly career than Ralph, the son of an upper-middle-class business manager. Ralph had worked as a paper boy in grammar school and in a cannery summers during his high school years. Bright but seemingly not much interested in academic subjects, he dropped out of high school to take a job. After two months, he left and worked as a laborer for eighteen months. At this point he returned to high school and graduated six months later. He then worked in a factory for two years but was fired for insubordination. He next entered military service as a volunteer soon after U.S. entry into World War II.

Following the war, in which he displayed exceptional courage and was wounded several times, he found it hard to settle down. He became for a time a bouncer in a nightclub. Subsequently Ralph had a series of jobs—too many for him to remember in any detail. He married, and he was a devoted husband. Controlled at home, he lost control on the job. At one period he had ten jobs in twelve months. Looking back, he reported, "I'd work and then I'd go on a binge or

something and then I'd have a fight with the boss and then I'd quit."
(As a youth he had felt his father did not care about him, yet he
greatly admired his father.) He worked at driving trucks, stacking
lumber, driving a cab, and as a clerk in a grocery store.

Subsequently, he returned to school under the GI Bill. Then he
found a job in which he received further training and began to develop technical skills in a rapidly expanding field. He had several
promotions and within a decade was supervising men with college
degrees. No other study member had a more disastrous early employment history, and few were more pleased once they found the
right niche. This man had been rated in the lowest 10 percent on
adolescent competence. Nevertheless, he matured, with the help of
a loving wife, and as a consequence he seemed a totally different
person thirty to forty years later.

For men in the Adolescent Growth Study who went to two-year
colleges, the propsect of being drafted led many to take temporary
jobs, so that prewar jobs should probably not be considered as part
of their careers. For those who left high school in 1938 or 1939,
however, nearly two years passed before the military draft came into
effect. It was not unusual for men who had scored low in adolescent
competence to have worked at three or four different jobs during
this period. After wartime service, some settled down relatively
quickly, but most made shifts along the way, some of them in their
late 30s or even into their 40s, before settling into the job that they
finally stayed with. Men who had scored low on adolescent competence tended to have many more jobs over the life course than did
their more competent peers. Many of these men stated that they
had never found the right job. They becamse reconciled to their
occupational status, but most said they would not choose the same
career again.

Occupation and Identity

As Stuart Campbell noted when we interviewed him late in life, his
identity was lodged in his occupational role: "It's very important
that I'm a doctor. I sometimes wonder, 'What was I like before I was
a doctor?' because you're always playing this role." It was primarily
among the professionals that identity was lodged in the occupation.
When asked how important the occupational role had been in de-

termining their "sense of who and what they are," men who were highly competent in adolescence were far more likely than others to report that their identity derived from their occupation. When, however, they were then asked which aspect of their experience— job, relations with spouse, family, other activities—was most important in determining their sense of who and what they are, there was far less difference between the men high and low in competence. Occupation tended to win out, but marriage or family was chosen almost as often.[18]

Among professionals, their occupational roles, and not merely their heavy investment in the job provided the sense of identity. We must keep in mind that some of the men who were low in adolescent competence had become highly competent later in life, and many were heavily invested in their jobs. They frequently stated that the job gave them a sense of being effective, but they did not report the kind of role identity that Stuart Campbell did.

Men for whom the job was in no sense a central life interest nevertheless indicated how their self-image was involved when we asked how important their jobs had been in determining "your sense of who and what you are." A car salesman replied:

> It's enabled me to get what I want out of life as far as money is concerned. It's enabled me to be recognized in the industry as one of the top people, and when I go into other organizations, they know who I am.

Yet this man attributed his sense of identity first to his marriage— that is, his wife—and second to his children. Often we found that the job was the place where a man felt he had proved himself, even if he had not been highly successful. But where he clearly had been a success, identity more often was involved. One of the architects in the study commented:

> It *is* who and what I am. Unfortunately for my family it has probably been one of the most important things in my life in that I've proven that I am somebody by being a success at that I'm doing.

This man said he had been sure at 16, when he had a part-time job with an architectural firm, that he wanted to have a place in that profession:

> I really loved from the very beginning the thrill of being able to say I had something to do with that structure standing there for a long time. Everywhere I go in the Bay Area, I see things that I had something to do with. It's an ego trip. Maybe that's what the whole thing is, one big ego trip.

There were some nonprofessionals who reported that their jobs were the most important element in their sense of identity, but they couched their rationale differently. An insurance adjuster commented, "Ninety-nine percent of my job is where I am in life, the amount of money I make, and so on." Then he noted that he "wouldn't be worth much without my good wife." But which was more important to his sense of who he was? "My job, obviously."

Job Satisfaction

Every occupational career has some ups and downs, as does every marriage, though the downs may not be serious. Men in corporate positions might be assigned to locales that were not congenial to them or to their families. Men in almost any organization might encounter superiors or associates who were abrasive. Even among top executives, the merger of two companies might lead to uncertainties for a period or even to termination of one's job. Therefore, a man might report himself less satisfied with his job or with his career at one time than at another. Nevertheless, when we asked for retrospective reports on sources of satisfaction or dissatisfaction in their lives, decade by decade, job dissatisfaction was clearly greatest in the 20s and 30s and diminished thereafter.

Nearly a third of the men, looking back from their 50s and 60s, characterized their jobs as the primary source of dissatisfaction in their lives during their 20s and 30s, but less than half that proportion reported major job dissatisfaction during their 40s. Dissatisfaction was greatest among those who never found what they considered the right job. Once they reached their mid-40s, however, most men became reconciled to their jobs and to the likelihood that they would not find a better opportunity elsewhere.

When we administered standard scales of job satisfaction to study members, we found very little relationship between their total satisfaction scores and their level of occupational attainment.[19] There was, however, a significant tendency for those who had scored high in adolescent competence to be more satisfied than those who had scored low. For example, 60 percent of those from middle-class backgrounds who had scored above the mean in planful competence said that if they had another chance, they would take the same job as the one they had, but only 25 perent of those scoring below the mean would choose to do so. The same tendency exists in our small sample from working-class families. Moreover, when we asked a series of specific questions about what they liked and did not like about their jobs, it quickly became apparent that early competence led to higher levels of satisfaction with both the current job and the career.

A number of features of the job were viewed more favorably by men who had been competent adolescents than by those who had been less competent. No feature showed the opposite tendency except "convenience of travel to or from work." It is probable that more competent, and hence more affluent, men chose more often to live in more remote areas. As might be expected, men who were highly competent and who occupied higher-status jobs reported superior job security, more pleasant physical surroundings, and more co-workers who took an interest in them. In both the middle class and the working class, men who had scored high on adolescent competence more often said that they had "a chance to do things that [they] do best on the job" and that their promotions were fairly handled. When asked what aspects of their work made the job most satisfying to them, intrinsic features of the job were mentioned by more than two-thirds of the middle-class men and slightly less than half of the working-class men. Here, however, there were no differences between those who had been highly competent and those who had been less competent. Extrinsic features such as pay, on the other hand, were mentioned more often by the men who had scored low on adolescent competence. The feeling of being in a job that made a useful contribution to society was far more often mentioned by men who had been competent adolescents.

Most of the differences in specific facets of job satisfaction just reported are associated with the higher level of occupational attainment, although the global measure of job satisfaction shows no such relationship. Higher job satisfaction is also associated with a more positive affective style—with being cheerful, optimistic, outgoing rather than negativistic, and pessimistic, as reported elsewhere.[20] Two of the personality components used in this set of analyses produce the same result. Men who as adolescents were both self-confident and outgoing were substantially more likely to report high job satisfaction thirty-five to forty-three years later, even when job level was held constant.

In the early and middle stages of their careers, a number of the highly competent men had shifted employers to take advantage of offers that would improve their status. During the decade prior to the last adult follow-up, however, 71 percent of the middle-class men who had been highly competent adolescents remained with the same employer they had had a decade before (or remained as self-employed professionals) as against 45 percent of the men who had been low in adolescent competence. Almost all working-class men remained with the same employer. For them, security in the later years was a major concern.

Work Involvement

Men in demanding occupations, especially professionals, are likely to be highly involved in their jobs. But high involvement was by no means limited to professionals and upper executives. At every adult follow-up, most men said they were highly involved. In their 40s, male study members reported an average of more than forty-eight hours a week devoted to the job, with the younger cohort (at age 40) working a bit more than the older one. A major complaint of the wives of members seen at this time was the amount of time their husbands spent on the job or on the road for the job, making them unavailable to the family.

At every period, the men in high-status jobs worked longer hours. A few professionals, like Karl Schulz, could limit themselves essentially to a forty-hour week, but most could not. The blue-collar workers, on the other hand, consistently averaged forty hours a week or less. While high job status was associated with a greater work investment among the 48 year olds, seen in 1970, the 40 year olds who had been less successful as of 1970 were putting in longer hours and struggling harder to get ahead than were their more successful peers. It appeared that many of them recognized that the time for "making it" had almost disappeared.

By their mid-50s and 60s, more than half the men said they were somewhat less involved in their jobs than they had been a decade previously, though fully three-fifths said they were still heavily involved. Most said there had been no change in their responsibilities. There was a tendency, however, among all of the subgroups to be somewhat more relaxed about their responsibilities. In Chapter 15 we shall discuss more fully the consequences for their families of men's heavy work involvement earlier in their careers. Both husbands and wives later agreed that such involvement had been a problem and a source of tension in more than half the families. For the most part, men's work involvement was not problematic by the time the children had left home and many of their wives were employed.

Career Change and "Midlife Crises"

There is a widespread belief that many men who are successful by midlife find that their striving has resulted in an empty victory: Their jobs are no longer satisfying. Some are said to seek self-expression by turning to totally different careers. In *Holding On or Letting Go: Man and Career Change at Mid-life,* Stanley Osherson describes twenty men aged 35 to 50 who had made career changes.[21] He had advertised in arts and crafts journals to recruit such men, so there was no way of knowing from his research how common this pattern of career change is. Our research suggests that it is rare.

Within our sample, several men made career changes after considerable success, but they did so for health reasons. Most men made such changes because they had neither substantial success nor real satisfaction. Two men who first held white-collar jobs decided around age 30 that they wanted outdoor work. Several men worked in their father's businesses for ten or more years and then became disillusioned with the opportunities afforded there. Most of the men who made career changes had not prepared themselves for a career. Several had severe problems with alcohol.

Men who had scored low on adolescent competence accounted for more than twice as many career changes as a consequence of dissatisfaction than did their more competent peers. Consider, for example, Bill, a man who had worked in a company of which his father was an officer. He found himself blocked and frustrated in his mid-30s. At 54, Bill commented about the years that he worked in that company:

> I was boxed in. I wasn't going anywhere. I was extremely unhappy. My wife and my brother were after me to leave the company. . . . I wasn't going to make a great deal of money. So finally after cocktails one Saturday night, I [decided to] quit.

He commented that everyone else thought he was the "fair-haired boy" because his father was a company officer, but "actually, I had to work twice as hard." He had learned a good deal of the business, but this knowledge did not seem to help. Then he observed:

> Well, it's my own fault. I liked to drink. I'd party at night and come in with a hangover, but I happened to be my father's son and you can't do that. So I maneuvered myself into a corner.

Next Bill tried a totally new line of work, selling insurance:

> [A neighbor] talked me into going to work, promised me a managership. This type of thing is like having your own famiy business. . . . But I didn't do well. It was an intangible. I couldn't sell it. I ended up drinking seven days a week, took diet pills. . . . They couldn't find me three days in a row.

Bill was let go and finally found a more congenial job in which he has been reasonably successful, but his career is not one that he regards as ideal. He acknowledges that he "blew his chances" early on.

As earlier noted, the age 40 has a special significance in American society. A man is expected to "make it" by 40. An academic almost has to get tenure by age 40 if he or she is to have a stable career in a university. We found that expectations of advancement in one's job markedly diminished beyond age 40. However, there is little indication that any substantial number of men experienced a mid career crisis as age 40 approached. Although Gail Sheehy popularized the concept of a midcareer crisis and Daniel Levinson claimed to find it in the men he interviewed around age 40, our longitudinal research finds no significant increase in occupational crises at this period of life.[22] Far more occupational shifts occur before age 35 than between 35 and 45. Those that did occur after age 40 were more often due to health problems (a heart attack, severe asthma, back problems) or to personal incompetence than to a feeling that one's occupation has been unrewarding after achieving a substantial measure of success.

One type of career change that did occur with some frequency was for a man to start his own enterprise, using the knowledge and skills he had developed as a member of another organization. Some were successful, but more ultimately went back to being employees in a larger business. The stresses on the family often proved very great in small business enterprises.

There were men who shifted emphasis in their careers without completely changing occupations. High levels of administrative responsibility brought to bear different skills than the more technical ones required in specialized occupations. Another example would be the kind of change that Henry Barr made in the area of law that he specialized in—from a private firm handling court cases to corporate law and its policy implications. Many men made such shifts as interesting opportunities became available or as they found themselves feeling stale in their jobs. But very few completely threw over their careers in midlife unless they had been experiencing repeated failures and changes in the preceding decades. Men and women may certainly have crises in midlife, as at any other time, but there is no crisis that is unique to midlife.

"Topping Out"

In 1980, Jane Bryant Quinn observed that baby boomers (the children of our study members) faced a career problem more acute than had their fathers, because recession was cutting back on the number of jobs at the top. She wrote in *Newsweek:*

The stalled-executive problem is nothing new. At some point, usually in their 50s, all but a few managers top out and can hope only to hang onto their jobs creditably until retirement. What *is* new is the number of managers now likely to top out in their 40s under the pressure of massive peer-group competition for a limited number of higher jobs. Most of these stalled workers will be people of adequate talent and ability.

Quinn's general assessment seems a sound one except for one point; even in the previous generation, many men in managerial jobs tended to top out in their 40s, according to data from our study members (and from a number of other studies).[23] At ages 37 to 40, when we interviewed them, most men in jobs that entailed a measure of management aspired to and expected further advancement. When we saw them a decade later, a third had realized their aspirations; most of the remainder had lowered their expectations, if not their aspirations. By 1982, when we last interviewed the men, many in the older cohort had retired, and even in the younger group—then ages 52 to 54—most were thinking of retirement, not advancement. Recall that Henry Barr had advanced far in a major corporation but was contemplating retirement at 53. Most men beyond their mid-40s were, as Robert Dubin has noted, "anchored downward."[24] That is, they looked at how far they had come, not at how far they still might go.

Men who did not make it to the top were seldom bitter, except perhaps about their own shortcomings. The vice-president of a large corporation reported at age 48: "I think it would be a disaster for me, to be president. . . . I couldn't give the corporation what they want in that job. Very few people could. We've got a remarkable man as president and when he leaves, it will take another remarkable man."

Earlier, I mentioned the interviewer's characterization of Harold Able as an exemplar of planful competence in adolescence and subsequently. He, too, was a vice-president and had indeed achieved this status in a major financial institution by his late 30s. He was on the board of directors and very near the top of the hierarchy at 48, but he had other interests and he retired in his mid-50s. At 62, he reported:

Since retirement, my wife and I have embarked on a new way of life. Pursuing interests, doing things we couldn't do before—birding, outdoor activities, doing literary things, collecting rare books at fairs.

Harold Able had pursued an economics major in college, had early found his niche, and had spent thirty years with the same organization, moving just one level below chief executive officer. He characterized his job as

> a major factor in life—very rewarding—lots of money—got status and prestige, traveled all over the world, met interesting people . . . but I didn't let it get in the way of my relationship with my family or leisure activity.

It would be a serious mistake to assume that all highly competent men want to go to the top. Indeed, it appears that the men most bothered by stalled careers are those who were stalled much further down the ladder; they aspired to rise but had not adequately prepared themselves to compete with more competent peers. This is not to say that some competent men are not blocked or that the baby boom, coupled with recession, has not made the problem more acute. Rather, many men are content to be getting along reasonably well and enjoying family, friends, and other activities.

The Contemplation of Retirement

Expected retirement incomes were again strongly related to early competence, but even those who had been low in adolescent competence did not expect any problem after retirement. Those who had been highly competent, and who would have by far the most ample retirement resources, were, however, those least likely to be looking forward to retirement. Only 38 percent of the men from middle-class backgrounds who had been in the top third in competence said they were looking forward to their retirement, as against 100 percent of those who had scored in the lowest third in adolescent competence. There were no differences in planned age at retirement, however, and it does not appear that the more competent men wished to continue working, but clearly they were ambivalent. Many of these men felt that their identities derived in substantial part from their jobs, so giving up their jobs may well have seemed a threat to their identities. We discuss this matter more fully in Chapter 16, but there is substantial evidence that despite their concerns, men who had been competent adolescents and continued to be competent had resources to maintain their sense of identity even after leaving the job.

CHAPTER 10

MEN'S LIVES:

BEYOND THE JOB

Although their jobs often seemed to be the primary focus of their lives, most men rated their family life—their relationships with their wives and children—as of nearly equal importance for contributing to their own sense of who and what they had come to be. Half of the men were married before age 25 and over 90 percent by age 30. Both military service and high educational attainment led to somewhat later marriages, though a few Oakland Growth Study men married earlier than they would have if they had not served in World War II.

Many family researchers have come to the conclusion that rating a marriage in the abstract can be deceptive; one must recognize "his marriage" and "her marriage."[1] Here we deal with "his marriage" as viewed by male study members, husbands of female members, and researchers. (In Chapter 13 we look at "her marriage" and in Chapter 15 at "their marriage" and the interplay between work and family relationships.)

How are men's marriages influenced by the men's own attributes, including their parental family backgrounds? What led to their marital choices and to their later satisfaction or dissatisfaction with their marriages? What attributes were associated with stable, satisfying marriages, with persisting but unsatisfying marriages, and with divorce? What kinds of fathers were our study members?

This chapter also examines the men's involvements and interests, the turning points and crises in their lives, and their personality change or stability over the life course. Every life has some periods of crisis and some critical decision points or turning points. Turning points are often hard to discern at the time, but in a searching review, a person can frequently say, with some conviction, that this or that event or decision marked a turning point. Perhaps the turn was sudden—a reversal of direction—or perhaps it was the start of a gradual redefinition of oneself. Closely related is the question of whether people stay about the same or tend to change over the life course. I shall present the evidence on who changes and how much, along with a report on how the men view their own lives and how they were shaped.

We turn first to the men's marriages and their family lives. In the last chapter I presented brief decade-by-decade examination of the data collected to age 50, as coded sequentially for the thirty-two men in the life history sample. A more detailed accounting is afforded by the sequence of statistical snapshots of the study group as of the time of each follow-up, looking at marital tensions and satisfactions, concerns with parenting, and so on. Finally, I shall present the men's retrospective accounts of how they view their marriages and their satisfactions in various roles from the vantage of later maturity.

MEN'S MARRIAGES

No marriage enjoys constantly smooth sailing. Every marriage entails negotiation between the partners if it is to meet their individual needs, and at times those needs will entail opposing views and tension.[2] The highly successful marriages among study members, like those of Mary Wylie, Stuart Campbell, and Karl Schulz, were most often satisfying at every period when we talked to them, but even these marriages had tensions and difficult times. Above all, however, the men and women became committed to each other. We more often had reports from husband and wife (both study member and spouse) when this was the case. In most of the good marriages, the spouse became a participant in the research at the time of the 1969–1971 follow-up. In marrriages that entailed considerable tension, like that of Henry Barr, the husband or wife more often did not wish to be interviewed. Overall, nearly two-thirds of the initial marriages lasted over twenty-five years, whereas fewer of their children's marriages lasted ten years.

Their Parents' Marriages

For most of us, parental marriages are our initial model of what a marriage is, though not necessarily a model of what it should be.

Slightly more than half of the men said they had thought their parents' marriage worthy of emulation. About 15 percent said that, on the contrary, they wanted to avoid the problems of their parents' marriages. Roughly the same proportion reported both good and bad features of their parents' marriages that they felt had some influence on the kind of marriage they themselves wanted. Another one in six said that their parents' marriage had had no influence at all on their own marriage.

We do not have complete information on the state of parental marriages through our subjects' adolescence, particularly for those who dropped out of the research prior to the completion of high school. For those who were seen during most of their adolescent years, 15 percent had lost a parent through death, and 17 percent had experienced a breakup of the parental family as a consequence of desertion, separation, divorce, or the long-term hospitalization of a parent for mental illness. Beyond this, perhaps a third of the parental families were the scene of recurrent conflict, and in some, alcohol and temper led to violence.

Among those study members whom we have seen in their adult years, the proportion from broken families is much lower, especially from those families in which the break was for reasons other than death of a parent. I have noted that family conflict and divorce constituted a significant deterrent to the acquisition of planful competence. The children of divorce are often torn by conflicting loyalties.[3] They tend to receive less attention when the custodial parent remarries. They tend to do less well in school, to drop out earlier, and to suffer from markedly diminished self-confidence. Given such difficulties, they were more likely to drop out of the study before their adult years.

There is reason to believe that study members who participated in the research during their adult years, despite unhappy childhood experiences in the family, managed to achieve greater success than the dropouts in gaining control of their lives. A few became competent adolescents despite family turmoil. Others managed to reorganize their lives by the time of the first follow-up. Even so, the men and women who had come from homes in which there had been much conflict tended to have less happy marital experiences than those from nonconflicted family backgrounds. Among men who were seen as adults, 53 percent of those whose parents had divorced or deserted the family, 13 percent of those who had lost a parent to death during their childhood, and 25 percent of those from intact marriages were themselves ultimately divorced or separated.

Age at Marriage

The earliest marriage among the men came at age 18, the latest first marriage at age 42. Men who married very early were slightly less likely to have an intact first marriage through their middle years. Among those who remained in the study up to the 1982 follow-up and for whom we knew their age at first marriage, 30 percent married before their 23d birthday, 43 percent from age 23 to 25, and 27 percent at age 26 or later. Thus, nearly half the men's marriages came within a period of three years, strong evidence that a social norm was operating. Further evidence was the frequency with which men said, in essence, that they married when they did because "the time to marry had come": 46 percent mentioned this as one reason for marrying when they did. Recall that Henry Barr gave this as a reason for his marriage.

There were only slight differences in age of marriage, rates of divorce, and number of children between middle-class and working-class men and between those who had scored above and below the mean on planful competence, but middle-class men who had been below the mean on planful competence had more divorces and middle-class men who had been above the mean had more children. Theirs was a generation that valued children and was not much concerned about the population explosion.

Adolescent planful competence was not significantly related to age at marriage, but a high rating on the component "self-confident" was conducive to early marriage, and this offset the tendency for greater educational attainment to delay marriage. An even stronger tendancy toward early marriage was a high rating on the adolescent Q-sort item, "interested in members of the opposite sex." Those so rated had considerable dating experience in high school and were much more likely to report (later) that they had engaged in intercourse while still in high school.

Unique circumstances almost always entered into the decision to marry, and most men reported several reasons for their choice and the timing of marriage. Feelings of compatibility, mutual physical attraction, and personality attributes of the partner led the list of reasons, but often situational factors and social pressure were cited as well.

The men who married earliest most often wed their childhood sweethearts. Sometimes there was an urgent reason for an early marriage—pregnancy. One man explained his marriage at 18, noting "We went to high school together. She was special. She went with other fellows and I went with other girls, but we always ended up going back together. [*Interviewer:* What other factors influenced you?] She was pregnant." This was not a frequent response, however. Far more often, the premarital pregnancies of which we became aware had ended in illegal abortions or in giving up the infant to be adopted or to be raised by the girl's mother. Marriage in the face of pregnancy often meant that the pair was in love and had already made a commitment to each other. The man just cited was still happily married forty-three years later. In general, however, when the pair married primarily to legitimate a birth, they were not likely to remain together.

Another man who had married in his teens said that he had always wanted to get married and raise a family and "I wanted to be young enough where I could grow up with my children." Although he had been rated in the bottom quarter of male study members on planful competence, he had an athletic talent that permitted him to earn a relatively high salary by the time that he was 18. He married a 16-year-old high school student who was both beautiful and an effective coper. He saw them as the "All-American couple." His work required him to travel a good deal, but he and his wife had four children well before he was 30. She was left with the task of raising the children. Ultimately she rebelled, secured a divorce, and made a more satisfying life for herself and her children. He remarried; she did not. His second marriage was threatened by his proclivity for affairs with other women.

The men who married latest appear to have been uncomfortable with the opposite sex and to have had little dating experience. If they subsequently held jobs in which there was no contact with women, they were not likely to have many opportunities to meet the opposite sex unless they went to dance halls or bars. Such was the situation of Joe, a man of Southern European extraction who married at 42. Joe's parents had loved each other, he said, but they quarreled a good deal, especially over his mother's drinking problem. Joe had scored very low in planful competence in high school.

He felt rejected by both his siblings and his peers, had very low self-esteem, and showed no intellectual interests. Joe had never felt comfortable with girls and had not known any well in high school. He went to work immediately after graduating. His work, driving a garbage truck (as a partner in a business inherited from his father), was largely carried out in the very early morning hours and did not bring him into contact with anyone else. He was not a man to visit bars, as his brothers did, but occasionally, he went to dance halls, and in his late 20s he met a woman, ten years older than himself, who "flashed her smile and I fell." She seemed younger than her actual age, but she had been married and had grown children. It was roughly fifteen years, however, before the couple married. By that time, both his mother and father had died. Joe had been ambivalent about his mother (he remembered how even when he was a child on her lap she had reeked of alcohol), and he said he had felt closer to his father. Nevertheless, he married an older woman who was in many ways like his mother. His wife had not gone beyond grade school, and he later commented that she was not much help to him. Why had he chosen her?

> I didn't know any [other women]. . . . I was looking for someone to be with, you know. I was getting older. I didn't want to be by myself. . . . It was one of those Reno deals. I rode up to Reno and I said let's get married. The first time I bought her the ring she refused it. And then the second time I asked her she accepted it.

The marriage was apparently a disaster from the start.

Marriages at the Time of the First Follow-up

There appears to have been a good deal of tension in many of the marriages during the early years. This was especially true of the men who had rated high on the measure of adolescent planful competence, occupied jobs of high status, and were heavily involved in their work. Nevertheless, most of the men reported themselves as well satisfied with their marriages at the time of the interviews conducted in 1958–1959. About one in ten of these men had already divorced and remarried.[4]

As of the time of the first follow-up, 90 percent of the men had children. Roughly 10 percent of them expressed dissatisfaction with their wives' performance in the parenting role—about the same percentage as saw themselves inadequate in that role (though, of course, not the same individuals). Only 10 percent claimed to feel completely comfortable and adequate as parents, but three-fourths saw themselves as generally adequate but as having some shortcomings in the parental role.

To the extent that men discussed the early years of their marriages, those years, and especially the early months, required a good deal of adaptation. As part of the interview, the study members were asked to fill out a life satisfaction chart on which they were to rate their satisfaction, from 1 to 10, for each year from age 5 on. Despite the need for adaptation following marriage, the year they wed was very often a high point on the chart. Immediately following that high, however, there were many dips as adjustment problems, and particularly the arrival of children, adding economic pressures, brought down their recollected life satisfaction. The life charts, on which they labeled the reason for their highs and lows, would suggest a greater level of tension and dissatisfaction than would the replies to direct questions on the interviews themselves. I shall have much more to say about this in Chapter 15, when we examine the marriage from the perspective of both participants.

The Marriages in 1969–1970

The second major follow-up, when the Oakland men were aged 48 to 49 and the Berkeley men aged 40 to 41, found nearly a fifth of the male study members divorced. The rate of divorce was nearly one in four for the Guidance Study group. All of the Oakland men had married, but five of the Guidance Study group (among 60 seen) had not married. The Berkeley Growth Study sample was not included but had been seen three or four years earlier and had a divorce rate of roughly one in five, with three men unmarried.[5] Because Arlene Skolnick has described and analyzed the marriages of the study members in a chapter of the book *Present and Past in Middle Life,* which viewed various aspects of the lives of our study members in their 40s, I shall merely touch upon the highlights of her analysis and add a few further observations.

Although no single measure of the state of a marriage is adequate by itself, the level of satisfaction of the participants is one of the most significant measures one might draw upon, whether assessed by judges or directly by self-report. Two measures were available: self-reported satisfaction on a thermometer-type scale, from 1 to 10, and judges' ratings made from all available data secured from husband or wife. The two correlated only fairly well (.58); differences in the ratings were sufficient to indicate that subjects and judges did not share the same criteria. For those who had been rated a decade before, the 1969–1970 average self-rating was slightly higher. If the couple stayed together, the men were slightly more satisfied at age 40 or 48 than they had been at age 30 and 38.[6]

At the same time, Skolnick noted that nearly half the ratings changed markedly. Men who had been highly satisfied tended to remain a little more positive than those who had been highly dissatisfied, but the correlation between the two self-ratings was only modest. Many of the men who had reported low marital satisfaction in their 30s had now divorced, but some who stayed married reported themselves much more satisfied. Most of those who had divorced had remarried, some for the second time.

Men's marital satisfaction was significantly related to their occupational status and their age at first marriage (the later it occurred, the better satisfied they were). Those who married late tended to be better educated and better off financially. Marital satisfaction was also related to their personality attributes as assessed currently, especially to self-confidence, to being seen as warm or nurturant rather than hostile, and to intellectual investment. As a consequence, competence at age 40 or 48 was strongly related to both self-reports and judges' ratings of men's marital satisfaction. Adolescent planful competence was only slightly related to the self-ratings. Some of the men who had scored high on planful competence but were aloof and lacking in warmth had difficult marital lives, while men who had scored low but were "late bloomers" had more satisfying marriages.

Skolnick compared the personalities of males in stable marriages that were positively rated by judges with those in more negatively rated stable marriages and those who had been divorced. The men in positively rated stable marriages were (and had been over the course of the study) more cognitively invested and more self-confident than the men in stable marriages who were less well satisfied. The most substantial differences were found when she examined the attributes of the divorced:

> Eroticism is the characteristic most clearly distinguishing divorced men and women from the more stably married, regardless of degree of marital satisfaction. By early adolescence, the divorced men were more interested in the opposite sex, undercontrolled, eroticizing, talkative, gregarious, self-indulgent and self-dramatizing.[7]

As Skolnick notes, we do not know whether these attributes were most important in influencing marital selection or in their effects on marital interaction. Perhaps both were involved. My own reading of individual cases suggests that those for whom sexual involvement was a very high priority in adolescence were substantially more likely to have affairs outside the marriage. It should be noted that the attributes characteristic of the multiply divorced were also substantially related to heavy use of alcohol. They were not attributes of the planfully competent.

The Oakland sample had been asked somewhat more directly about early sexual experience at the time of the 1958 follow-up. In keeping with Skolnick's finding on eroticism and divorce, early sexual experience was associated with both a higher divorce rate and lower marital satisfaction at midlife (and again twelve years later).

Above all, Arlene Skolnick's examination of the marriages of the study members at midlife indicated the great variety of patterns that might be seen as satisfying by some couples but as intolerable by others. She stressed that stable marriages were not necessarily happy, and many marriages underwent substantial change from early adulthood to midlife. Some of the families in the older cohort were now at the empty nest stage, while most of those in the younger cohort were struggling with adolescents whose high school years were spent in the mid- to late 1960s in a period variously called the age of Aquarius, the blossoming of flower power or the hippie era, and the Vietnam era. For both husbands and wives, the junior and senior high school years of their children were reported as the most difficult for them to cope with as parents. Often husband and wife did not agree on how to handle the rebellious adolescent. When asked if they had ever felt that their current marriages would not work out, nearly two-thirds of the men said that they never had, but another fifth at one time had considered divorce, and more than 10 percent had apparently seriously considered divorce several times over the years. Nevertheless, most of those who had made it through to their 40s in an intact first marriage seemed committed to the marriage.

The Marriages in 1981–1982

In the 1981–1982 follow-up, the study members were interviewed at some length on the circumstances of their initial and current marriages and their satisfactions and dissatisfactions. In addition, most completed a questionnaire (sent to them at home prior to the interviews) relating to aspects of the marriage. Thus, we have both retrospective reports on the earlier years and an assessment of the current state of the marriage. Table 10.1 shows the status of the marriages in 1982. By their mid-50s and early 60s, 27 percent of the men had divorced and 8 percent had been widowed.

Of men in intact marriages, their self-rated level of marital satisfaction had increased once again, and the amount of increase approached statistical significance. Of those who had previously scored their marriages below a 6 on the scale of 1 to 10, most had divorced (Henry Barr being one of this group), but a few had resolved their discontents and scored their marriages much higher. Self-ratings for those who had been planfully competent in high school were not higher than scores for their lower-rated peers, nor were they significantly higher among men currently (1981–1982)

Table 10.1. **Marital Status of Male Study Members at 1982 Follow-up, by 1982 Competence Level (Percentages)**

	High Competence	Low Competence	Total
Currently married to first wife	73	53	65
Married to different wife	19	29	22
Divorced or separated, not married currently	6	12	9
Widowed after 1969, not remarried	3	2	3
Never married	0	4	2

Note: Percentages total more than 100 because of rounding.

rated higher on competence. On the other hand, judges' ratings of the men's marriages were again positively, though modestly, related to adolescent planful competence and were related to current competence at a very high level of statistical significance.[8]

Men's ratings of their marriages in 1981–1982, while higher than in 1969–1970, were not appreciably correlated to the earlier ratings. Thus, as Skolnick had found a decade earlier, the amount of change in self-ratings was so great as to suggest great instability in the day-to-day assessment of satisfaction. Judges' ratings suggested somewhat more stability. The correlation between the two periods was a highly significant .42.[9]

Asked to look back on their marriages and to report when the marriage was at its best or its worst, 10 percent said there was no best time, and 15 percent said there was no worst time. The great majority, however, felt they could identify a best and a worst period, even if they did not regard the worst as a period of serious difficulty. Most men identified the best time in terms of the stage of the marriage or time period, though a fifth mentioned situational factors, such as when job pressures were least, when the family lived in a particular location, or before some event that had caused great suffering. Almost exactly half the men said that the marriage was at its best "now," while a fifth thought the early years, before children arrived, had been the best time. The men who scored below the mean on competence more often mentioned situational factors— often job problems or other crises—rather than family stage or period.

More than one reason might be offered to explain why marriages were at their best. Most often mentioned were the quality of the husband-wife relationship (63 percent), the satisfactions and pleasures of parenting (41 percent), and/or the amount of involvement of the family members with each other (21 percent). There were only slight differences related to the current or earlier competence of the men.

When the men described their marriages at their worst, they less often talked about the stage of the marriage and more often mentioned situational factors that caused problems. When they did mention stage, the early years were most often the least satisfying, especially among the more competent men. Fully a fourth reported that the first few years had been the most difficult, with second place going to the period when the offspring were adolescent.

Thus, their replies accord well with the ratings we had made of the marriages when the men were in their 20s, based on the life history data, where the highly competent had appeared to be experiencing somewhat more tensions in the marriage. They were also in accord with the responses that the men had given to questionnaire items relating to the easiest and most difficult times of parenting when questioned in 1969–1970.

The reasons given for feeling that the marriage had been worst at a particular time were relational problems entailing conflict, arguments, inability to communicate (38 percent), parenting demands (sometimes related to family stage and sometimes to a particular problematic situation—35 percent), and heavy work involvement of the husband (34 percent). Financial problems were mentioned by only one in seven of the men as a reason for marital stress. On the other hand, roughly 15 percent mentioned extramarital affairs (most often attributed to their wives but sometimes acknowledged by themselves) as a cause for the worst period of difficulty in the marriage. Such affairs were slightly more often mentioned by the men in the lower competence group, but the difference was not statistically significant. Alcohol abuse was mentioned as the cause by about 10 percent of the men, this time most often acknowledged as the consequence of their own heavy drinking.

A few examples of the men's responses to the questions on best and worst periods of the marriage may be helpful. A man of intermediate adolescent competence who had married very early reported that his marriage had been at its best "the first couple of years. We went out and did a lot more things." It was at its worst "when the kids were 5 and 6 and we were hassling about different things. I beat her up a couple of times and she packed up the car, took the kids and left me." Yet they were still together (not amicably so) more than forty years later. To our question, "What kept you and your wife together?" he replied, "Mainly the kids, I guess. If we had not had them we would have been long gone." Unfortunately, "the kids" had been deeply scarred by their parents' conflict. Drug and alcohol abuse were one consequence.

Another man, a professional in his second marriage, contrasted his current "unhappy home" with his parents' very happy home. This second marriage had endured for over twenty years but had never been a success. The early years had been the best and the current time the worst period of the marriage. Husband and wife seemed to inhabit different worlds. She was much younger than her husband, from another culture, and berated her husband as a male chauvinist. She made demands her husband would not meet and had attempted suicide. What had kept them together?

> Well, it's probably been because it's an easier way to go. I think my presence around has had some influence on the children. I don't like the idea of changing my entire financial structure.

Not infrequently, the reasons for staying together had little to do with the relationship itself.

By contrast, another man (of high planful competence) in his second marriage for nearly twenty years reported the early years best because he and his wife were able to travel extensively with the children. Once the children were adolescents,

> they won't go with you anymore, because they're not interested in the things that you're interested in. Yet you can't go off and leave them either at age 15 or 16. So in the last 10 years or so we haven't had as many opportunities to get around as we did in the first 10 years.

What had kept them together?

> Sharing all kinds of things—home, hearth, children, a mountain community that we love, sports and games that we play together.

Another of planfully competent adolescent, subsequently married for nearly forty years, reported what had kept him and his wife together:

> We respect each other and we have a real affection for each other. And I think sexuality keeps you together—which took a while in this marriage to be really good (but now is very good).

Few of the men were enthusiastic about the women's movement: nearly three in ten were basically negative and a comparable number generally favorable, leaving two-fifths who saw both pros and cons. Very few, however, felt that the women's movement had had an effect on their marriage. Three-fourths said their wives shared their views and less than one in six thought there had been any effect on their marriages at all.

In general, there were only modest differences between men who had been planfully competent in adolescence and their less competent peers in response to questions about the current or past status of the marriage, but the differences almost always favored the more competent. The planfully competent reported higher levels of companionship and shared activities with their wives in their 40s, 50s, and 60s. They also reported greater satisfaction in their sexual relationships and greater involvement in sexual activity than their less competent peers.

The interview conducted in 1982 asked only about the relative frequency of intercourse and sexual satisfaction. Almost all of the older respondents acknowledged some decrease in the frequency of intercourse, but very few acknowledged that they were not sexually active. The marital questionnaire asked more specifically about the frequency of intercourse within the past six months. Here striking differences emerged, and they were more highly related to adolescent planful competence than to current competence. Because men who had been rated less competent were only half as likely to return the questionnaire as were those rated more competent, the number of cases available for the less planfully competent was small, but the difference between the groups was so large as to be highly significant. Not one of the twenty-nine men who had scored above the mean in adolescent planful competence and who returned the marital questionnaire reported a complete cessation of sexual activity, but five of the thirteen men who had scored below the mean reported no sexual activity in the past six months. The same picture was presented in the reports of the men's wives on frequency of intercourse, which agreed remarkably well with their husbands' reports.[10]

There were also substantial differences in the extent to which the men reported, in the interview, with its much larger number of respondents, that where there had been problems in the sexual relationship they had attempted to work them through. The planfully competent more often said they talked about them, laughed about them, and dealt directly with them (43 percent of the planfully competent versus 17 percent of the less competent adolescents). The less competent men more often said they had simply been unable to deal with such problems. Thus, adolescent competence appears to be related to sexual behavior in marriage roughly four decades after the high school years. Part of the difference between the higher- and lower-competence groups appears to be related to the adolescent social class of the study members, with men from working-class backgrounds less sexually active and less well able to communicate with their wives about sexual activities. Nevertheless, planful competence proved to be more highly related to later sexual activity than did childhood social class membership.

Again in 1982 we asked the men in intact first marriages whether they had at any time thought about divorce. Roughly one man in five who was in an intact first marriage acknowledged having at one time or another thought about divorce. The proportion is slightly related to planful competence but much more significantly related to competence as evaluated in later adulthood. Men above the mean were only half as likely to have thought of divorce as those below the mean. Some were opposed to divorce on religious or moral grounds, even though they were very unhappy in their marriages. Asked what had kept the couple together (whether or not they had ever thought of divorce), nearly half the men credited the strength of their mutual relationship and their feelings for each other as the primary factor. Perhaps the most colorful expression of the importance of the relationship was uttered by one of the highly competent men: "At this point, I can't think of anything my wife could do—have an affair, empty our bank account, almost anything—that could end my love for her and our marriage." Moral or practical considerations having little to do with the relationship— such as opposition to divorce, the welfare of the children, inconvenience, or the cost of divorce—were mentioned by roughly a fourth of the men as the main reason that their marriages had held together. California's law requiring that a divorcing couple's assets be divided equally was clearly a factor in preventing some divorces of men who found little satisfaction in their relationships with their wives but did not want to change their style of life.

The Marriages in 1990

In 1990 I sent a questionnaire to all study members for whom we had a current address and received replies from nearly two-thirds of those whom we had seen in 1981–1982. In the interim, at least an additional 7 percent of the study members had died, and others had moved after retiring, without reporting the new address.[11] The response rate was much lower among men who had scored below the mean on planful competence, introducing a greater bias than was found in the 1982 interviews.

We did not learn of any new divorces, but it was apparent that at least one couple had separated and that a few of the men were very dissatisfied and contemplating divorce even at ages beyond 65. Nevertheless, the average self-reported level of marital satisfaction was considerably higher than at any other time since we had first administered the self-report scale, partly reflecting the more selective response, with competent men much overrepresented.

The men's self-ratings of marital satisfaction in 1990 were substantially related to their ratings in the previous follow-up, the first time that a considerable degree of continuity was evident in the self-ratings. Most men felt that their wives were accepting of them and were supportive of them.[12] More than four-fifths indicated that their wives were their closest confidants. As we shall see shortly, however, their wives were much less likely to claim their husbands as closest confidants.

Among the men who now rated their marriages a 9 or a 10 ("near perfect"), many reported that their marriage and the relationship with their wife was the best part of their life now. When asked in the questionnaire, "In general, how do you feel about your life these days?" most of these men checked "Enthusiastic, life is very good." In a few instances, a man might rate the marriage a 9 or a 10 but not be enthusiastic about life. Most often, the reason was his or his wife's poor health. Here we might find the answer not in what is best but rather, "What is the least satisfying thing in your life?" A fairly typical response was, "My wife's poor health."

Men who rated their marriages below a 7 seldom reported themselves enthusiastic about their lives. Two men rated the marriage a 1, reporting that the marriage was the least satisfying aspect of their lives. One added, "I made a most unwise selection of a spouse."

Especially for the men who had retired by 1990—most of the Oakland men and about half the Berkeley study members—either the marital relationship had become much more the central focus of their lives or they had a markedly attenuated marital tie. In Chapter 16, we shall look more closely at life satisfactions in the later years.

OTHER ROLES AND ACTIVITIES

Work and family roles were, for most men, the main substance of their lives. A major complaint of the men in the early adult years and later, in looking back on those years, was that they had too little time for recreation. We had no systematic data on the subject, however, until we asked the Oakland sample about their activities in a questionnaire when they were in their early 40s. We asked what activities they now spent the most time on, what they enjoyed most, what gave them the greatest sense of accomplishment, and what they would want more time for. Work clearly received the highest priority; the more successful men were, the more they tended to indicate that they enjoyed work, spent more time on it, got a greater sense of accomplishment from it, and (often) wished to be able to spend more on it. Family clearly came next. Men who had experienced deprivation during the Great Depression rated their families especially high as a source of enjoyment and the place where they would like to spend more time.[13] Recreational activities came next but well behind work and family. Recreation received its highest ratings from men in less demanding and less rewarding jobs. These men spent much less time on the job in general, and as Wilensky has noted, they tended "to park their job concerns at the place of work" while the more successful men often brought those concerns home.[14] Very few men were involved in community activities, which were rated lowest in priority.

In 1970 we supplemented the interviews with a questionnaire that inquired more specifically about various leisure-time activities. Most frequently mentioned were watching television or going to movies, outdoor activities, visiting with friends and relatives, and reading. Nearly a third said they went out to dinner at least once a week, and more than 90 percent said they went at least once a month. The great majority of activities tended to be family centered or at least carried out at home.

Political Involvement and Orientation

Relatively few men were appreciably active in political activity. More than 90 percent said they had voted in both the 1960 and 1964 elections, and a third said they had been politically active, but the

main activities mentioned were contributing financially to a candidate or party or signing a petition. Less than 10 percent mentioned
precinct work, circulating petitions, poll watching, or fund raising,
all of which were listed for checking if one participated in these activities.

On the whole, our study members have become somewhat more
politically conservative over the years and are rather more conservative than the average American. Economic status, personality, and
professional affiliations tend to influence political views, but the relationships are not strong. Henry Barr, a successful lawyer, might be
expected by virtue of his income and work affiliates to be conservative, but his concern with equality and justice as well as for the environment led him to question the conservative agenda. On the
other hand, Stuart Campbell's caring attitudes did not preclude his
conviction that people should get what they earn by their own efforts or his strong patriotic commitment that extends to military action. Henry Barr was strongly opposed to U.S. involvement in
Vietnam; Stuart Campbell was solidly behind the war effort, though
he came to see some of the terrible consequences. Karl Schulz was
less concerned about political issues and civil rights; he had
definite conservative views but did not attempt to change the views
of others.

An analysis of the relationships between personality and political
ideologies of a subgroup of study members when they were in their
40s found that consistent liberals had been, since adolescence,
more independent, more philosophically concerned, more tolerant
of ambiguity, but also more rebellious, less sympathetic, and less
cheerful than consistent conservatives.[15] Thus, each group scored
higher on some of the items that were positively associated with
competence and lower on others. We can say that personality had
some bearing on political views, but the effects were modest except
at the extremes.

Rebelliousness was a dominant trait of the adolescents who became extreme radicals. One way to flout convention is to oppose
the whole system. No one was more opposed than Reb, the middle-
class boy whose sad history was briefly told in the previous chapter.
His closest friend in high school and college shared both the early
rebelliousness and the radical philosophy but was less autonomous
and ultimately chose a conventional career.

Some radicals became conservative. Most of those who had

thought in their 30s that the Russian experiment was a noble one or for whom American capitalism was anathema became ardent supporters of capitalism long before the collapse of the Soviet Union. In general, those who were most competent in adolescence were less likely to say they had become more conservative and more likely to say they had become more liberal since adolescence. Those who became professionals were especially likely to see themselves as more liberal, though they, like the majority of our sample, and indeed of the population, tended nevertheless to have voted for Republican candidates for the presidency.

Religious Involvement

We did not always inquire about religious involvement, but at no stage of life did such involvement seem important to most of the men. In the interviews conducted in 1969–1970, when the study members were in their early or late 40s, they were asked about church attendance, religious orientations, and their belief in an afterlife. Roughly a fifth indicated they were active participants in a church, with the high competents about three times as likely to be participants as those who had been low in adolescent competence. A number of the lows wanted their children to be involved in the church, but they themselves were not. Altogether about a third of the men said they attended church at least once a month, and a few said they attended church on special occasions such as Christmas and Easter. Most men had no regular church affiliation, and in this respect they were typical of their peers in the society as a whole.

Nevertheless, among those without a church affiliation, more than a third of the planfully competent said they experienced religious or spiritual feelings that were related to a supreme power in the universe or to the mystery of life, the unity of the universe, and similar abstract ideas. Fewer of the men who had been low in adolescent competence had such feelings; a fourth of them reported not only that they had no religious involvement but that they had no experiences that they would identify as religious or spiritual. Thus, formal religion played little role in their lives.

One man in five believed strongly in an existence beyond death; an equal number felt sure there was no afterlife. Another one in ten thought there might be life after death, but they were balanced by the same proportion who thought that there probably was not an afterlife. The remaining two-fifths said they did not lean one way or the other or just did not know what to believe. Here, there was no difference between those who had been planfully competent and their less competent peers. Despite the low level of church participation and limited belief in religious dogma, few men characterized themselves as either agnostic or atheist. Moreover, for a small group, religion was extremely important. Some had been planfully competent adolescents. A number of others came to religion through Alcoholics Anonymous.

The questionnaire sent to study members in 1990, when they were in their early 60s or approaching their 70s, revealed that those who had been highly competent in adolescence were again much more likely to have some involvement with the church than those who had scored low in adolescent competence. More than four-fifths of those who had scored low in planful competence had no church involvement whatsoever, as against approximately half of the highs.

Friendships

Close analysis of the life history sample revealed a greater importance of friendships for men who had been rated low in adolescent competence than for those who had scored in the top half, and this finding was confirmed for the larger sample of subjects. The most complete data were secured in the interview with the study members in 1969–1970, when they were in their 40s. Those who had been rated low in planful competence were more likely to say that friends were important to them and more likely to say that they had one or more intimate friends or confidants than were those rated high. Half the highs reported they had no closest friend as against less than a third of the lows. The implications of this finding showed up in their reported activities with friends and their relative involvement with family and friends. More than two-thirds of the less planfully competent reported that most of their activities with their friends were informal shared experiences, such as going to the theater, playing golf or cards, or having dinner together, but less than one-third of the more planfully competent reported such activities. The more competent men more often reported formal activities such as meetings of clubs and other organizations and business-related activities or discussions.

When asked about the degree of their involvement with family and with friends, both highs and lows indicated greater involvement with family, but those who had been rated low in competence were more than three times as likely to say that their involvement with friends equaled or outweighed that with family. As earlier noted, we are dealing in part with a difference between middle-class and working-class life-styles, with working-class men more likely to spend leisure time with other men rather than with their wives. In general, middle-class American men are seldom highly involved with friends. As Levinson reported in *Seasons of a Man's Life*, "friendship was largely noticeable by its absence."[16] Clearly, many highly competent American men do not have intimate friends with whom they share many activities, and a number express regret that this is so. Dedication to career and family have their costs.

STABILITY AND CHANGE OVER THE LIFE COURSE

All lives have ups and downs, and very few study members had difficulty in identifying when the high and low points in their lives occurred and why. Yet most men (and women) said that they themselves had changed little beyond adolescence, apart from being more "mature." At the same time, in 1970 more than half the men thought their wives had changed since they had married, and more than half the wives thought their husbands had changed. Apparently we cling to a sense of identity that says "there may be some superficial changes, but the real me has remained the same."

Over the years from adolescence to the first follow-up, most men changed a good deal, as evidenced by the Q-sort data on their personalities. The average correlation between men's personality profiles in the high school years and at the time of the first follow-up was .33, suggesting substantial change.[17] From the first to the second follow-up, it was .46, and from the second to the third, .55. Thus, the big change occurred between adolescence and the initial adult follow-up. Over the adult years, most men changed much less than they did from their high school years to the first follow-up, but they did change as life circumstances changed.

Adolescent Planful Competence and Personality Change

The first question to be addressed is, Who changes most, and why? Instead of referring to stability as opposed to change, I shall refer to personality resemblance—one's resemblance to an earlier self—over time.

Change or resemblance from the high school years into and through the adult years is best predicted by adolescent planful competence. Table 10.2 shows the mean resemblance score between high school personality and each of the three adult personality assessments by level of planful competence as assessed in senior high school. Recall that the resemblance score is the correlation between the individual's profile on the seventy-three most reliable Q-sort items at any two periods. The levels of adolescent planful competence are the top third, middle third, and bottom third on the measure described in Chapter 2. At each period, personality resemblance is substantial for those in the top third, minimal for those in the bottom third, and intermediate for those in the middle third.

Another way of assessing the relationship between adolescent planful competence and personality change is to correlate the resemblance score with the person's score (or ranking) on planful competence. The correlation between competence in senior high school and later resemblance to adolescent personality is .56 to the early adult years. That to the middle adult years (1969–1970) is .54, and the correlation to later maturity (1981–1982) is .65 for the men. This means that nearly half of the amount of resemblance or change in personality in the forty or so years from the completion of high school to the mid-50s or early 60s is accounted for by the index of adolescent planful competence, incorporating the three

Table 10.2. Mean Resemblance Between Personality Profile in Senior High
School and Profile at Successive Adult Follow-up Assessments, by
Level of Adolescent Planful Competence (Males)

Adolescent Planful Competence	SH-1958	SH-1970	SH-1982
Mean for all males	.33	.32	.30
Highest third	.49	.52	.50
Middle third	.28	.21	.21
Lowest third	.20	.17	.11

personality components "self-confident," "intellectually invested," and "dependable." The lower resemblance to adolescent personality in the men's 30s and 40s was at first puzzling. Resemblance usually decreases over time; however, personalities do not necessarily change in the same way over different periods of the life course. In analyses conducted after the 1970 follow-up, Peskin and Livson detailed how tendencies in adolescent personality may be drawn upon and enhanced at one period and suppressed at another.[18] Specifically, they argued that in the early adult years, when establishing their careers, males draw less on the dominant traits they showed in adolescence than they will at a later age. As Peskin and Livson put it, "Selection of past modes of responding is determined by relevance, not recency."[19] Personalities are neither stable nor do they change consistently in the same direction.

Each of the components of adolescent planful competence is itself related to personality resemblance over each period of time. However, they relate to a different degree at each period as personalities change. All three of the components—self-confidence, intellectual involvement, and dependability—continue to cohere in a meaningful way and to be mutually reinforcing. Yet the components themselves shift considerably over time, and their interrelationships change. In the adolescent years, the highly competent boys were seen as especially warm but only slightly outgoing, while in the adult years they were somewhat less warm and much more outgoing. (See Table A.2 in Appendix A showing the intercorrelations of the personality components in the senior high years and in 1982.)

Consider the nature of the changes that made the less competent adolescents so different in their adult years. For the most part, they moved toward more effective functioning, toward using better judgment and becoming more competent. At the time of the first adult follow-up, by their 20s or 30s, many men had gained markedly in self-confidence and dependability and now more closely resembled those who had been planfully competent adolescents.[20] On the other hand, a few men like Reb, who was still rebellious, insecure, and irresponsible at age 38, showed almost as high a level of personality resemblance as the competent men. Reb remained true to his adolescent self, which meant that he remained largely self-defeating. Stuart Campbell had shown very high personality resemblance in every period, the measure of resemblance actually being higher than the reliability of the measures used. Henry Barr, on the other hand, showed the more typical pattern. In the middle years, he seemed somewhat changed from the personality he had presented in adolescence, but in his 50s he more closely resembled the young man who had been studied nearly forty years before.

The Prediction of Resemblance or Change

In attempting to account for change into and through the adult years, can one find which life experiences or other aspects of personality influenced change? High educational attainment and orderly occupational careers both seem to contribute to stability rather than change but only slightly.[21] Being divorced seems to have had no effect on whether a man's personality changed. Neither parental social status nor IQ, both contributors to adolescent planful competence, add to resemblance when adolescent planful competence is itself used as a predictor. On the other hand, another contributor to adolescent competence, a high degree of maternal attention to the son in the years before attendance at senior high school, does add significantly to the prediction of resemblance. Having been outgoing in adolescence made no contribution to predicting resemblance at earlier periods but does in later maturity. (See Table A.3 in Appendix A.) Together with planful competence, these variables bring the amount of variation "explained" from the senior high years to later maturity up to over 60 percent. Because of the relatively small number of cases for which we have all of these measures, it is not possible to include more than four, or at most five, variables in a predictive equation. A larger sample might find that a number of other experiences contribute to personality stability or, conversely, lead to greater change. Undoubtedly, there are other, unmeasured life experiences that bring about change in some contexts but not in others. Physiological change, situational change, and chance events undoubtedly enter into personality changes over the years.

Change in the middle years, between early adulthood and later maturity, was related less to planful competence and more to life experiences, especially occupational experiences. High occupational success appears to have increased later competence ratings more than anything else. Here one must consider the possibility that high occupational success unduly impressed the raters. The level of competence attained at the time of the first follow-up was a more powerful predictor of change through the middle years than was adolescent planful competence. Together with occupational attainment, it accounted for nearly half of the variability in men's resemblance scores from their 30s to their 50s and 60s. (See Table A.4 in Appendix A.) Nevertheless, adolescent planful competence better predicted resemblance from high school to later maturity.

Many unexpected events occurred over these years: job loss, death of a parent, spouse, or child, serious illness, conflicts with and over rebellious adolescents, self-doubts, bouts with alcoholism. We know from the examination of individual histories that such events may lead to emotional and mental breakdowns. They may have only temporary effects—which seems to be the case with divorce for men but not for women—or they may have more permanent effects. The life satisfaction charts reflect such events. However, there are not enough instances of any particular kind of event, other than divorce, to permit a systematic assessment of effects in our small sample of lives. All I can say is that the planfully competent adolescents and the men who became competent by early adulthood changed least over the middle years of life. They were more effective copers, but also they brought fewer crises on themselves. Adolescent planful competence accounts for a large part of the variability between adolescence and each later period.

One other measure of personality proves to be a powerful predictor of personality resemblance over the years, especially to the later years: the measure of psychological health.[22] It was not until late in the analyses that I incorporated this measure into my data set and discovered that it was strongly related to planful competence at all periods, but especially in later maturity. In the senior high years, the profile of psychological health was most strongly related to the component "self-confident versus feels victimized" and least strongly related to "dependable," a tendency found at every period. Being dependable in adolescence was a crucial element in both educational and occupational attainment, so that planful competence is a far more potent predictor of success in men's careers than was psychological health when assessed in adolescence. But in the adult years, when self-confidence and being somewhat outgoing were strongly related to personality resemblance, psychological health became a very good predictor as well. In later maturity, the index of competence and the measure of psychological health are so highly correlated as to be measuring essentially the same phenomena.

Insofar as there are differences between the two measures, men who were planfully competent adolescents were in their mature years less gregarious, less self-indulgent, less interested in the opposite sex, less warm, and less likely to express hostility directly than the model template for psychological health. The planfully competent were seen as more intelligent, more verbally fluent, more aloof, and more uncomfortable with uncertainty. However, the more outgoing of the highly competent men scored as high on psychological health as on planful competence, that is, in the top rank. Indeed, planful competence in senior high school is a better predictor of mature psychological health than is the psychological health template when applied in adolescence. Recall that Stuart Campbell scored higher on the index of psychological health in 1982 than any other man in the study.

Continuity in the Index of Competence

From the junior high to the senior high years, scores on the components of competence changed only modestly. The reliability of the index is roughly the same as the correlation between the junior and senior high school years, and in my earlier analyses I combined the junior high and senior high scores to increase reliability. Over the adult years, however, each component shows less stability than the total index (Table 10.3). In other words, one or another component may change or all may change, but the aggregate that indexes competence will change less. Moreover, for men, the three components that make up the index of competence show less change over time than do the components "assertive versus submissive," "outgoing versus aloof," and "warm versus hostile." These three show very little continuity beyond senior high, and even self-confidence drops off markedly in the later years. This is not because planfully competent men become less self-confident but because those low in adolescent competence increased their scores on self-confidence markedly in their adult years. Nevertheless, planful competence in adolescence substantially predicts competence at all periods.

Table 10.3. Continuities in Men's Competence Ratings and Other Personality
Components (Correlation Coefficients for Constant Sample)

	Junior High to Senior High	Senior High to:	
		Early Adulthood	Later Maturity
Index of planful competence	.76***	.64***	.56***
Self-confidence	.72***	.44***	.29*
Intellectual investment	.68***	.57***	.44***
Dependability	.67***	.50***	.45***
Other personality components			
Assertive/submissive	.48***	.12	.13
Outgoing/aloof	.66***	.32**	.27*
Warm/hostile	.46***	.02	.13

*p < .05; **p < .01; ***p < .001.

Each of the components of planful competence contributes about the same amount to competence in the early adult years, and together they account for somewhat more than a third of the variation in men's competence in their 30s. This means that two-thirds is accounted for by other factors, primarily experience in the intervening years: the effects of further education, marriage, war experience, occupational experience, and so on.

What of the final assessment of competence, when the men were in their 50s and 60s? Here the components of competence from early adulthood are the best predictors, with "dependable" making by far the greatest contribution, followed by "intellectually invested." The three components together, as of ages 30 to 38, account for roughly two-fifths of the variance in competence as of later maturity. If occupational attainment is added in, it contributes another fifth.

Examination of the planfully competent men who changed the most indicates that they differed from the dominant tendency for the planfully competent to be warm, sympathetic persons in adolescence. The changers tended to be seen as dependable at all periods but to decline in self-confidence and to score lower on "intellectually invested" in their adult years. It may be that judges placed too much weight on school performance in assessing the attributes that together represent the component "intellectually invested." However, these men also tended to have interpersonal problems in the early years of their careers (and subsequently), which led to defensive maneuvers and sometimes to increasing hostility, as well as diminished competence. The few planfully competent men with drinking problems were among this small group.

Planful Competence and Rigidity

High competence in adolescence, requiring self-control and serious consideration of one's options, may suggest the likelihood of overcontrol, compulsiveness, and rigidity. In general, however, highly competent adolescents were seen as warmer, less conventional, and more interesting than those low in competence. Nevertheless, a person could score high on planful competence even if he was conventional and overcontrolled. Indeed, although a substantial amount of impulse control is needed for dependable performance, there can be too much of a good thing. One cost is potential rigidity.

An instance is afforded by a man I shall call Eugene Goode. In junior high school he was seen as extremely uncomfortable with uncertainty, cheerful, likable but emotionally bland, somewhat aloof, and with a tendency to feel guilty and to withdraw when frustrated. By senior high he seemed much less bland and aloof, much more intellectually invested and productive, and much less likely to give up when frustrated, though he still had a tendency to feel guilty. Eugene knew by the time that he was a junior in high school that he wanted to become a financial expert, and he planned a college program that prepared him for the job. He joined the staff of a large corporation soon after graduation. Eugene was never seen as self-dramatizing or self-promoting, but he could be counted upon to do a very thorough job in anything he undertook. In several interviews, he characterized himself as a workaholic. He rose gradually through the ranks in the central offices of the corporation, exercising both technical skill and supervision over other professionals. He received more and more responsibility but in his 50s began to feel that his technical skills were not as great as those of some of his subordinates, and he became apprehensive that he was not up to the demands of the job. There was apparently conflict with one of his subordinates as well. A period of profound depression immobilized him for a time and required his hospitalization. Then he returned to the job.

Eugene requested a less demanding position in which he functioned adequately, at a somewhat lower salary, until his retirement ten years later. He had commented, in connection with stresses on the job, that part of his problem went back to early training: "My mother taught me, when somebody tells you to do something, you do it, you don't question it—which has its disadvantages." Eugene Goode is retired, and he and his wife and children are close. For the most part, they are content, and they are good citizens and good neighbors, but Eugene's planful competence was counterbalanced by his tendency to feel guilty if he did not excel and a compulsion to conform that made it difficult for him to relax and adapt flexibly.

Turning Points

Some men and women experienced turning points where their lives took quite a different direction from that in which they had been heading. We have seen some evidence of turning points in the lives of the men described previously, especially the men who had been less competent in adolescence. Career change as a consequence of heavy alcohol use or finding a challenging and satisfying job after a decade of failure in a wide variety of types of work were turning points.

I had thought that a knowledge of turning points might provide another clue to personality change, so in the 1981–1982 follow-up we asked study members if they had an experience in which their lives "took a different direction." Almost all answered yes, and most could identify more than one. Since the men were now in their 50s and 60s, I assumed they would tell us primarily about events in their adult years, perhaps in their middle years. Some might mention turning points related to a "midlife crisis." That was not the case. Many of the events or circumstances that constituted turning points had been experienced in childhood, adolescence, or young adulthood. Indeed, some had occurred too early in life for the boy to be aware of their importance until later. Stuart Campbell thought that the most important turning point in his life had been his grandmother's decision to stay in the United States and not return to Scotland. She wanted to ensure a good education for her grandchildren. Surely his life course was profoundly affected by her decision. His other big turning point was when Dr. Stolz, the pediatrician director of the Institute of Human Development who examined the boys every year, encouraged him to think about a career in medicine.

In general, however, the events or circumstances reported did not have such a critical influence on the direction of the man's life. Most often the turning points mentioned were transitions that were expected yet gave a different meaning or feeling to a man's daily life. The two most frequently mentioned were career events and marriage. Neither event, however, was necessarily seen as representing a new direction. When questioned on how his life took a different turn at marriage, one man asked incredulously, "How can your life possibly *not* change when you marry?" The turning points associated with jobs were as often as not getting into the right job or getting a promotion or other opportunity that produced greater satisfaction and self-confidence rather than a change in direction. Of course, there were setbacks as well and also real changes in direction for men who were blocked in their early career aspirations.

Career events—starting in a chosen profession, a major promotion, a change in line of work, or loss of a job—were mentioned by two-thirds of the men and marriage by more than half. Divorce was mentioned by nearly everyone who had been divorced, and parenthood was seen as a turning point by more than a fourth.

Military service was seen by many men as a turning point, but it seldom led to a change in direction.[23] It was a profound experience for many—sometimes with positive overtones, sometimes primarily negative ones. A professional recalled his army experience:

Not so much a turning point as an influence. Got drafted at 18 right after graduation from high school. I had quite a few harrowing experiences in the infantry, thought I'd never live to see the day I'd come home. I killed some people and saw my buddies get killed. It left an impression on me that has never really worn off. Took a long time after getting out of the Army to not jump when someone said "boo" to me.

For a number of men, military service was something of a revelation:

> Going into the Army was the first time I was totally away from my family. Had to do the best you can, make the best of it. Shipped overseas, even worse. But before I went I became engaged; that was the best part. Coming back was another best part.

> [*Interviewer:* "How did it change your life?"] I met all kinds of different guys from all over, all had the same problems. It taught me more tolerance. I had to get along with people and work with people. Going into the Army made me more independent.

For other men, especially those who did not see combat, the military was something of a lark:

> I went into the Army and that affected me. Fulfilled my desire for travel, adventure.

The variety of meanings attaching to any particular type of perceived turning point was found even in such stressful events as the death of close relatives. Most often such deaths brought negative changes to the life course, but sometimes deaths thrust men into challenging new roles, as when a man had to take over the family business when his grandfather, father, and uncle all died within less than six months.

The data on turning points do not serve as a basis for systematically assessing change. Rather, they afford further insights into the course of personal development and changed perspectives on the self. As we shall see when we examine the turning points reported by women, these were most often precisely those experiences that led to new self-perceptions.

Turning points that did lead to a sharp turn in the direction taken were most often a consequence of unexpected and unwelcome events or circumstances—an injury or illness, death of a spouse, divorce, unemployment. A promising college athlete had been scheduled to play professional ball but was seriously injured and unable to pursue his dream. A cabinet maker developed such severe asthma that he had to give up his work. A man who divorced his wife found that he lost not only a wife but his relationship with his children and the respect of his parents and siblings. Cut off from all his closest ties, he has lived a lonely life ever since.

There was little difference in the number or general classification of the turning points reported by men who had been planfully competent adolescents and their less competent peers except in one respect: Far more of the latter reported turning points that entailed life crises.

OTHER RETROSPECTIVE VIEWS FROM 1982

All members of the study were sent a Life satisfaction chart on which they were asked to plot the high and low points in their lives, using a scale of 0 ("rock bottom") to 10 ("absolute tops"). We had used the charts at the time of the first follow-up, and most people could plot, year by year, the course of their lives to that point. When they were in their 50s and 60s, however, they tended to flatten out their charts and, indeed, to show primarily extreme experiences. There were still a few who went from top to bottom of the chart several times in the course of reviewing their lives, though men were a bit less likely to do this than women.

I have used the chart for two purposes. First was to try to ascertain the peak experiences in people's lives and the nature of the sharpest drops. The life chart afforded a basis for defining a life crisis: any drop of four points or more or any drop that took the respondent more than halfway to the bottom of the scale within a five-year period. The second use, which I comment on in the last chapter, was to give a very general assessment of level of life satisfaction at a particular time.

As expected, the death of a parent, spouse, or child was the most frequent cause of a sharp drop in life satisfaction. Deep distress as the consequence of a death was indicated on the life chart by roughly a fourth of the men. A fifth showed a similar though not quite so sharp a drop where severe marital problems or divorce were concerned. Another fifth of the men labeled at least one sharp drop as due to career problems. Sources of deep distress might be seen as turning points but often were not. They were, nevertheless, times when many men looked more deeply within themselves, trying to make sense of what had happened or to come to terms with an enduring sense of loss.

The systematic analysis of the data collected over the past sixty years strongly supports the impressions gained from the life histories of men who had been rated planfully competent in adolescence and those who had been less competent. While in high school, some study members had made known their plans to go to college; for others,, there was no indication one way or another. Nevertheless, planful competence produced a high level of college attendance, some of it after military service. It "predicted" high levels of occupational achievement over the next forty years. Education and occupation were uppermost on the minds of the planfully competent adolescent males. They thought of where they wanted to get in life and how they might get there.

On the other hand, very few of the planfully competent men gave much thought to the kind of person they wanted to marry. Here they differed little from their less competent peers. Most took marriage for granted. Yes, they would marry and have children, all in due time. But here they would tend to drift, assuming that they would meet someone with whom they would fall in love. All of the planfully competent males did marry, and most made well-considered choices.

Very few study members seem to have had the problem of feeling they were not "real" men—that they missed the initiation rituals extolled by some popular writers. The men who had the greatest difficulty in becoming effective males tended to have ineffective fathers who were not involved with them and to have mothers who were either relatively unavailable or overly permissive. There was frequent conflict in their families. Where there had been parental harmony and an interested father—or a mother who could give the boy an image of what was expected of a mature male (and mature males he could relate to outside the home)—the men of our study did not need special help to attain manhood.

Planful competence appears to have led to effective planning among both men and women primarily in those aspects of life that were central in their own concerns. It not only served to make them more responsible, but in general they were more flexible in coping with the inevitable sources of stress and turmoil that careers and family present.

We turn now to look again at additional individual lives—the lives of women. The women who were children of the Great Depression were subject to far greater changes in role expectations than were their male peers. They tended to change in different ways than the men did, and planful competence in adolescence influenced other features of their lives than the ones most affected for men. It seemed important to examine the lives of women who experienced major changes, and the two women selected for additional full life histories were not models of adolescent planful competence. They are women who became competent. For now, Mary Wylie will represent adolescent planful competence, but in Chapter 13 I describe another woman who scored very high on adolescent planful competence as well as on adult competence, and I shall contrast the lives of the planfully competent with those of women at the lower end of the distribution of scores on planful competence.

CHAPTER 11

PROGRAMMED FOR MARRIAGE

ALICE NEAL

Alice Neal illustrates how a woman who was immature and lacking in purpose as an adolescent could reshape her life even after mothering three children. She became a successful businesswoman, yet as we shall see when we consider women's careers, she was far more typical of her adolescent peers who stayed home with their families or entered the labor force to only a very limited degree. Her life has not been easy, but she is now far more comfortable with herself than in the past.

Alice Neal was born in Berkeley in 1928, the fourth child, and third daughter, of a family of six children. She was a lively, energetic child. When she was 3, the family moved to another Bay Area county, where Alice has lived all but those early years of her life. She has been a faithful, cooperative participant in the Guidance Study all of her life.

Alice's mother was interviewed every year from the time Alice was 2 1/2 years old, and Alice herself was interviewed repeatedly from the age of 6. We have a picture of a girl who was quite changeable from year to year but who was always fun loving. Her family was warm and close, but it had its stresses and strains as its members sought their places in relation to each other and to the world beyond.

FAMILY HISTORY AND EARLY LIFE

Alice's ethnic background is essentially Irish. Her mother was born in Ireland; her family emigrated to the United States when she was 12 years old. Alice's father was of mixed Irish and German heritage, though he was born in San Francisco. His mother was born in Ireland. This grandmother lived with Alice and her family for more than two years, at severe emotional and financial cost to the family. She was uneducated and superstitious and must have created an atmosphere inhospitable to intellectual achievement.

Study records did not indicate Alice's father's educational attainment, but Alice later told us that he had attended college for a time. His job never provided quite enough income for savings but permitted the large family to live comfortably, if always at the limit of their means. Mrs. Neal told the interviewer that her husband liked gardening, while she enjoyed playing the piano.

> *Postreview comment:* Alice commented that her mother had not really played the piano. She could play only one piece and had not learned to read music.

Mrs. Neal's own education had not gone beyond the eighth grade, but she was a person of considerable substance. Although she devoted most of her energies to the children, she was politically aware and was less conservative than her husband. It appears that she was most often the one who decided major issues, though she expressed great pride in her husband's accomplishments.

Alice's family was seen very favorably by the Guidance Study staff. Her parents were characterized as having an "unusually happy marriage" and being emotionally very stable. They were also stable residentially. After having spent eight years as renters of the large, pleasantly situated house that they first occupied when Alice was 3, they decided to purchase the house. In these years, Mr. Neal went from being a bookkeeper, to accountant, to manager of a department in a large commercial organization. He also became a leading citizen in the community, serving on several local commissions over the years. It does not appear that he was ever interviewed by a member of the study staff during the nineteen years that intensive interviews were carried out. He seems to have been relatively uninvolved in disciplining the children, but when they were young, he played with them. Mrs. Neal reported, when Alice was 11, that all of the children regarded their father as "the grandest person in the world."

CHILDHOOD YEARS

A major factor in Alice's development was her placement in the family. The third of four girls, she had to compete both forward and backward to find her place and identity within the family. Her eldest sister, Theresa, five years her senior, suffered from asthma but was avowedly her mother's favorite. Her second sister, Martha, three years older than Alice, was a troubled girl, the child her mother said she least understood. Martha was very close to Theresa—the two were "tight," Mrs. Neal averred—and excluded Alice from their activities. Susan, the youngest, was seven years younger than Alice, too young for companionship.

When asked whom Alice most resembled, her mother laughed and said, "I don't know where I got that one; she's different from any member of the family. She's got more spunk than anyone else in the family." The interviewer felt that Mrs. Neal, though she favored Theresa, actually considered Alice most like herself.

Unable to find the sibling closeness and acceptance she wanted and needed, Alice sought friendship outside the family. There she was more fortunate; a neighbor child, Gert, whom she met right after the move, became her lifelong friend. The two did everything together. Alice thought Gert was smarter, but Alice was physically and socially more advanced. Gert's name came up again and again from early childhood into the adult years.

In the first interview with Alice, at age 6, she was seen as friendly, relaxed, and self-confident, despite having expressed a wish to be "very blond" and "more good-looking than I am." Asked what age and gender she might prefer, she thought she would like either to be younger (about age 2) or be her younger brother. The reason was the same: so she would not "have to do any work." She mentioned frequent bad dreams and said she did not like to dream. Disturbing dreams and a poor appetite were recurrent complaints, but the latter seemed to be primarily a reflection of her not having the enormous appetite of her older siblings and overconcern on the part of her mother.

On later occasions Alice thought she would like to be a newborn baby. She acknowledged tattling on her older sisters, for whom she expressed dislike. Almost from the beginning of school, she stated that she did not like school, though occasionally she liked a subject or a teacher. In the first grade at her parochial school, Alice's teacher was a severely disturbed nun who had to be hospitalized by the end of the year. Her experiences with this teacher gave her very negative feelings about school itself. By age 8 she acknowledged that she liked being sick so she could avoid school. What especially impressed interviewers was her ability to be frank in acknowledging her problems and faults, not making excuses for them.

Personality evaluations of Alice at ages 8 and 10 showed considerable variation, suggesting either that she changed a good deal in this period or that the psychologists were unable to make reliable assessments. At both ages, she was seen as having a rapid tempo, expressive, talkative, and as tending to show "anxiety and tension in bodily symptoms." At 8 she was seen as thinking very conventionally, dissatisfied with herself, having very narrow interests, and seeking reassurance but also dependable and straightforward. Two years later, she appeared more rebellious, pushing limits, lacking in poise, and apparently felt victimized. Earlier self-confidence gave way to insecurity, bragging, and signs of considerable tension.

On several occasions the young Alice told her interviewer that her mother was "too busy" to spend much time with her. Her assistance to her mother gave her a sense of closeness and satisfaction that her sisters may not have had. Her mother almost always characterized her very positively, as independent, helpful, and self-reliant, through the years of childhood and early adolescence. Her mother noted that Alice at age 8 was demanding of attention and enjoyed being sick because it brought her attention. But at 9 Alice was said to be "the most pleasant of my children," and at 11, her mother characterized her as "the shining light of the family." At this time, she was said to be her father's favorite, except for her older sister. Eight years later, Mrs. Neal stated that her husband had never had a close relationship with Alice, but Alice expressed great satisfaction at her father's willingness to listen, nonjudgmentally, to whatever she said, and she felt he had been very understanding of her problems.

Whereas both her mother's reports and her own responses to the annual interviews reflect a friendly, mostly happy, and very helpful girl, especially up to age 10, the projective tests (and some of her dreams) suggest a good deal of underlying anger, resentment, and aggression. Periodically Alice was reported to be attention seeking and given to showing off, sometimes to the embarrassment of her older sisters. Nevertheless, except for occasional displays of temper, she was not only controlled but basically quite conforming. Her ministering services to the rest of the family—helping with household tasks, serving breakfast in bed to her mother, caring for her younger siblings—may well have been a way of handling the ambivalent feelings of which she was only vaguely aware.

What did her parents hope for and expect of Alice? Early on, her mother reported her as the bright one, and her IQ of 120 was certainly high enough for her to plan for college, but there is no indication that either parent ever thought in such terms. Both were said (by the mother's report) to "want her to grow up to be a good mother and housewife." In this, they were undoubtedly typical of most other American parents in the lower-middle and working class and of many upper-middle-class parents as well.

The Guidance Study staff mentioned, approvingly, that the parents had "no pushing ambitions" for their children. They tended to "take things as they come." They were also glad for guidance in handling the inevitable problems that must be confronted when a couple has six children, two with severe asthma. But one wonders whether the children were ever challenged to develop their full potential. Alice showed few indications of such challenge.

In an in-depth assessment when Alice was 13, Erik Erikson noted that her mother had persistently tended to favor the most recent child. He felt that Alice's isolation from her older sisters led her to take on the position of assistant mother to the younger siblings. She appeared to have overidentified with the maternal role, and in her fantasy life she was preoccupied with the maternal body. She had expressed an interest in becoming a nurse "because I want to see what people's guts look like."

Alice frequently mentioned that she resented her oldest sister and the attention she received. Theresa's asthma was, in fact, the reason the family moved away from Berkeley; her doctor had strongly advised them to do so. Whenever Theresa had an attack, her mother waited on her hand and foot; through her asthma, she dominated the family. As Alice approached adolescence, Theresa began to recover from asthma, and her attacks apparently ceased. It is not without significance that as soon as Theresa's attacks ceased, Alice took her place as the family asthmatic. At age 12 she suddenly developed acute asthma and was very ill, frequently requiring hospitalization, since the asthmatic attacks seemed often to result in pneumonia.

Now it was Alice's turn to dominate the family with her asthma. She herself said, in late adolescence, that if she had not felt so ill she would have thought that she developed asthma on purpose to dominate the family and get the privileges and cosseting Theresa had had. Alice's asthma persisted through her high school years and into her marriage and did not begin to diminish until she was in her 30s, after her children were born and she had begun working again.

ADOLESCENCE

In early adolescence, Alice was seen during her institute interviews as "frank, open, relaxed" despite the fact that her nails were bitten to the quick. She was regarded as independent, generous, and friendly but also constricted and very peer oriented. According to her mother, Alice was well liked by the neighbors, who found her sympathetic.

Alice was in high school during World War II, but assessing the effect of the war on her is not easy. Certainly men in uniform abounded on the West Coast, and the heightened tension of the times pervaded the atmosphere. Such factors may have contributed to Alice's extreme "boy craziness" during the years from 15 to 19. At 15 1/2 Alice was described by her mother as boy crazy despite never having gone out with a boy. Commenting on those years later, Alice said that she chased boys constantly, but if they became interested in her, she backed off. Her interests in general were social, limited, and superficial: boys, clothes, movies, loud music, dancing, her girlfriends.

Alice's mother worked approximately four hours a day as a telephone operator. Her sisters had gone to work after high school and now contributed to the family exchequer. Everyone was expected to help with the housework; Alice cleaned house on Saturdays and was a willing worker, considered by her family and those who interviewed her as independent, self-confident, and capable. We later learned that she had also been regularly employed during the summer months in the later years of high school.

By 13 Alice and her friend Gert were playing a good deal with the neighborhood boys. Alice still wanted to be blond and, especially, to be taller than her 4 feet 10 inches. But she was glad to be a girl and now reported that "my mother spoils me all the time." She was interested in her sisters' boyfriends, often to her sisters' annoyance.

Alice told the interviewer she would have preferred to attend public school, but her mother, a devout Catholic, insisted on parochial school. This became a major source of discontent during the high school years, though Alice accepted her mother's decision as impossible to change. Repeatedly she continued to express resentment against her older sisters, whom she accused of bossing her around, and about not being allowed to go to a public high school. When there were family arguments—for example, over what radio program to listen to—the older girls sided with their father, while the younger ones sided with their mother. According to Alice, their mother usually won. Thus, despite some resentment about school, Alice never rebelled against her mother.

By age 14, Alice had grown three inches and felt more secure. She was highly excitable and talkative in the interview. Tension was manifest in her closely bitten fingernails but not otherwise. She appeared more attractive and reported much better grades than she had in previous years. The next year, however, she called school a "drag," and it turned out that several of the final grades she had received were marginal (D's). The whole interview at age 15 was pervaded by her complaint that her mother would not let her attend public high school. This year, both asthma and a broken arm cut into her high school studies. Her wishes were for "a tall, dark, and handsome sailor" and a new wardrobe (described in some detail).

By 16, Alice "wouldn't want to be any other age." She was now as tall as she had wanted to be and was described by her interviewer as "rather a 'cute' girl." She was dating one sailor and writing to another, but her relationships with boys were apparently quite controlled. She and Gert did not approve of necking, but both were much interested in boys.

Alice no longer considered nursing as a possible career. One visit to a hospital apparently convinced her that there were unpleasant duties that would make her very uncomfortable. But what she might do was a puzzle. She did not think she ought to marry until she was 22, which meant that she would have to find something because she did not consider college an option. Had she thought about the kind of man she would like to marry? she was asked. "Oh, sure, I've thought about that lots of times. I want him to be 6 feet 2 inches tall, blond, tanned, and lots of fun and [to] have 'personality.' "

In a very long, detailed interview held with Alice as she approached high school graduation, she said she could not stand the thought of growing older, because, she realized, life would be less carefree. For the first time she reported many similarities between herself and Theresa, who had become engaged to a sailor about whom Alice was also enthusiastic. Better still, Alice herself had a new flame, though she said that he paid little attention to her. The topic of fun and dating came up intermittently but by no means dominated the interview.

Asked what changes she would make in herself if she had her life to live over, Alice said she would want curly, blond hair "more than anything else in the world." She would have a more pleasant disposition—not get mad as easily—and a better figure. Her major assets, she felt, were a sense of being capable, good clothes, and friends, all of which gave her confidence.

The values she would instill in a child included several most typical of persons who tend to be strongly conforming: obedience, neatness, to be a good student, and not to be a sissy (in the case of a boy) but also to be self-reliant and ambitious.

Reviewing all of the material available on Alice during the senior high school years, the clinicians who carried out the personality Q-sort reached a high degree of consensus on Alice's personality. She received very high scores on "talkative," "feminine," "conforming," "gregarious," "self-dramatizing," "uncomfortable with uncertainty," and on the tendency for anxiety and tension to find outlets in bodily symptoms. She received low scores (that is, these were not typical attributes) on "fearful," "aloof," and "rebellious" but also on "wide interests," "values intellectual matters," and "ambitious." She ranked just above average on the component "dependability," roughly average on "self-confidence," but very low on "intellectually invested." As a consequence she placed toward the top of the lowest third on the measure of adolescent planful competence. Her scores on the components of personality are given in Table A9, Appendix A.

Alice's strong involvement in the fun-loving peer group and her preoccupation with dating were quite typical of girls who scored low on the measure of planful competence. However, her conventionality and strong sense of moral controls kept her from getting sexually involved, as did so many other girls who were as strongly peer oriented. It appeared most likely to the clinicians who evaluated her adolescent personality that Alice would become a wife and mother in relatively short order, despite her having regarded 22 as the best age to marry. All predicted marriage within a year or two.

Looking back from the vantage of nearly forty additional years, Alice felt that she had not really understood herself "at all" in adolescence. "I never really thought about the future . . . I just worked and drifted into what happened." Insofar as she had any goal—and it was one just taken for granted—it was to marry and have a baby—which is exactly what she did at 19. The clinicians were quite correct.

A Report on Later Adolescence

Our first report on Alice beyond her high school graduation came from her mother, who was interviewed in 1947, when Alice was on the verge of marrying. After high school, both Alice and her friend Gert got jobs—in the same building but not the same office—in San Francisco. Alice had worked in San Francisco during her summer vacations and the Christmas season from the time she was 15, sometimes for a federal agency and sometimes a private company. She enjoyed the clerical job with a private company that she secured after graduation. She continued to work after marriage but quit when she was five months pregnant. Alice's marriage and pregnancy had followed the most difficult and traumatic period of her entire life.

Although Alice had mentioned several boyfriends in earlier adolescence, her first serious attachment to a young man occurred when she was 17. This was Lee, whom she had mentioned at the previous interview. It was for her a grand passion; although she did not use the word, she later described herself as infatuated beyond reason, and her mother so characterized her.

Mrs. Neal said she had taken an almost instant dislike to Lee, a soldier at a nearby military base. She considered him "shifty, essentially dishonest, and out to get anything he could for himself."

> *Postreview comment:* Alice wrote in the margin, "She liked him at first." Alice said that her mother had not only been favorably impressed with Lee at first but had encouraged her in the relationship. But her mother's views of him changed as Alice became more infatuated and his behavior toward Alice became more problematic.

He treated Alice abominably, but apparently the worse he treated her, the more devoted she became. They went steady for a while, Alice totally faithful to Lee, while he frequently took out another girl behind her back. Suddenly he proposed that he and Alice become engaged, gave her a ring, and insisted on an engagement party that would be announced in the papers. Mrs. Neal felt that he did so in order to send a clipping from the paper to his home town in the Midwest, to a girl he presumably wanted to spite.

The final blow to Alice's hopes for a future with Lee came when Alice's mother became certain that Lee had stolen her purse, in which she always kept a good deal of money since it was the family "bank." The day after the theft, Lee was reported to have taken another girl out dinner-dancing, despite his having supposedly been broke.

Alice's mother said nothing about her suspicions to Alice but went directly to the priest at the military base where Lee was stationed, whom she knew, and sought his help. Lee was confined to barracks and then sent to Alaska on the next troop shipment. Alice, according to her mother and her own subsequent description, went completely to pieces, though Mrs. Neal initially told her nothing of her own involvement in the affair. That relationship and its outcome were a turning point in Alice's life. Alice suspected that her mother had been involved in Lee's transfer, and her relationship with her mother was strained for a time. The trauma of her relationship with Lee has remained engraved in her memory to this day.

Six months later, on a blind date, Alice met George, the man who would become her husband. George was very different from Lee—attentive, stable, and kind. He was a high school graduate, had completed his military service recently, and now had a job and a steady income. At first Alice was not interested in him—he was unexciting and too dedicated to her—but for the first time in her life, she truly enjoyed the companionship of a man. Her mother was enthusiastic about George even though he was not a Catholic; she was anxious for Alice to marry him, feeling he was just the kind of man Alice needed as a husband. Suddenly Alice decided that she did in fact want to marry George.

Theresa, the first daughter and still her mother's favorite, was also marrying, and the big wedding with all the trappings was to be hers. Mrs. Neal thought Alice and George might elope, and in fact it was clear from the way she talked that she rather hoped they would. Even if they did not, Mrs. Neal said that the plan was for the two sets of parents to accompany the young couple to Reno, to be married quietly there. The reason she thought Alice might elope was that she felt Alice "for some reason" wanted to be married before Theresa.

> *Postreview comment:* Here Alice wrote: "This I never heard of." She said that it had never occurred to the couple to elope, nor was she aware of any desire to be married before Theresa. She observed that Theresa had been scheduled to marry on three earlier occasions but each time put off the wedding. Also, she noted that because George was not yet 21, California law required that he receive parental permission to marry, and elopement was hardly feasible. Thus, the mother projected her wish onto her daughter.

Alice and George were indeed married soon after but in a local church, not in Reno.

ALICE AT AGE 30

Alice's interviewer summarized her impression of Alice at this stage of her life as follows:

> Very young for her years, open, friendly, talked freely. She seems to be much less mature than her mother was at the same age when we first saw her, in spite of the fact that she is the mother of three children. In many ways she seems like an open, friendly child who tells all.

Asked about the high and low points in her life after she had completed graphing them on a form provided by the interviewers, Alice reported:

> The highest period in my life was when I got married. It was a very exciting period. The lowest period in my life was my previous boyfriend to whom I was engaged. Mother broke it up . . . I was desperate, although as I look back on it I know she was absolutely right. It would have made a mess of a marriage. But at the time, the bottom of the world dropped out for me.
>
> From 15 to 19 I was just crazy in the head. I pursued boys wildly, never had a moment when I wasn't chasing some boy, trying to get him to like me. And the minute he did, I was frightened and liked him no longer. I had no sense whatsoever. As I look back on it now I don't know how the family put up with me . . . I think maybe the ma-

jority of adolescent girls are flighty and interested in having boys pay attention to them but I think I was far more extreme than most kids that I knew in high school.

Nineteen was the most tempestuous year of my life. I became engaged to a boy at Hamilton Air Field and was completely involved with him to my mother's and father's great consternation.

Alice's account of her relationship with Lee essentially corresponded to her mother's 1947 account of the same relationship, except that Alice's account is more extreme and self-dramatizing: "I was getting increasingly unstable and jittery during this period and completely defiant of both parents while still living at home." Alice adds to the tale of Lee that she wrote to him without her mother's awareness. She reported that he ultimately got a free flight down from Alaska, and she saw him in San Francisco.

Somehow it was a great disappointment. This period of separation had done something to both of us. I was crushed that I wasn't as infatuated with him as I had thought. I felt I had no loyalty, and I think he was as fed up with me as I was with him. . . . Mother later told me about going to Hamilton Field. She had felt that I was so at loose ends, so absurd, so infatuated that I didn't have good sense. And of course she was right.

Postreview comment: Here Alice Neal wrote: "This never happened." She said unequivocally that she never saw him again after he was sent to Alaska. Two possibilities exist: Either the interviewer reported as a direct quotation something that had become garbled in recording, or Alice had at the time of the age 30 interview reported an imaginary meeting that served to resolve the issue by suggesting that when she saw him she was no longer infatuated but rather "fed up." The second alternative seems the more likely, for if she had seen him and no longer was attracted, one suspects that relief rather than a residual of emotional involvement would have been evident. In any event, in this interview Alice seemed frequently to dramatize events and to exaggerate their consequences.

Alice talked of her marriage to George, the fun they had together, and their active social life. She continued working for nine months after marriage until she became pregnant.

> Then occurred my miserable ill health that's been the only thing to
> mar our marriage. I really got awfully sick about the fifth month and
> had to quit my work, was hospitalized, had all sorts of complications,
> and began running up the big medical bills that have characterized
> our life ever since.

> *Postreview comment:* In recollecting on this account, Alice said that she
> had been sick, even hospitalized, before the pregnancy. In the fifth
> month of her pregnancy, the company for which she worked moved
> to New York, and her job ended. Actually, she said, her health im-
> proved after she stopped working.

Alice and George's first child, Sandra, was born in 1949. The
young couple bought a new house the same year. Fifteen months
after Sandra's birth, Alice was pregnant again, sick again, and beset
with medical bills again. That year, 1951, she described as the lowest
point in their marriage. Jane, the second child, was born prematurely
and contracted diarrhea in the hospital; Alice's mother was very ill;
Alice had asthma and pneumonia, and had fallen during her pregnancy. They recovered from that bad year, and her husband got a
raise. He had been very helpful throughout her illness and pregnancies, and she felt she was "darn lucky to have married the nice guy
that I did. I sometimes feel he's gotten the very short end of the deal."

In 1956, when Alice was 27, the couple decided to risk having another child. Alice said she was sicker than ever before this time: "I
had pernicious vomiting, vomited day and night for five full
months. I was completely exhausted and if it hadn't been for his
family and my family helping out with the care of the two children
we already had, we really would have been desperate." The third
child was a son, Gary.

In 1959, on a chart plotting "best and worst periods of your life"
on a yearly basis, Alice put her current morale at a fairly high level
but said it was not as high as it might be because of three factors:
her health, feeling sorry for her husband and the load he had had
to bear, and a poor relationship with her 10-year-old daughter,
Sandra, which had her baffled. She did not describe her problems
with Sandra.

We bought a new home in 1958 . . . and it was also in 1958 that I had the worst asthmatic attack I've ever had. In fact, my asthma dominates our present household in the same way that it used to dominate our home life when I was growing up, or Theresa's asthma used to dominate our home life. It's tough on the kids and particularly tough on my husband who never complains, is calm, helpful, but has a tremendous burden to bear . . . If I could only get my health straightened out so he didn't have both me to put up with and the medical bills to put up with, and I could get a better relationship to Sandra than I have, my [life satisfaction] rating would go up to 9 because I have three nice kids and a husband who's a saint. When I'm not sick we have a good time together. We have a boat. We do a lot of things with the kids.

The interviewer felt that implicit in her recital of her health problems, particularly with asthma, was the thought that it had a psychological base, that she exploited others with it—first her mother and the family at home, and now her husband.

In spite of her verbalized statements about how tough it is on her husband, there's something immature and little girl about her which makes us feel that she uses her asthma to get the protection and love that Theresa used to get when she was a child growing up. She has partial insight or is on the threshold to having insight, and therapy might be extremely helpful.

One other thing that should be added is her relationship to her family. She said, until she married, she didn't have a comfortable relationship, really, with any member of the family because she was so wild and impossible that it was out of the question. She really seemed nurturant and protective and very friendly when she was talking about her troubled sister, Martha.

The "best and worst periods" chart revealed that Alice saw her early years as not very satisfying because of feeling excluded by her older sisters and because of a very negative initial school experience. She noted on the chart that her first teacher (a Catholic nun) was a terrifying person, subsequently committed to a mental hospital as psychotic. One wonders whether Alice might have had a very different orientation toward school had she had a sympathetic and stimulating teacher at the very start or if she had not been forced to attend a parochial school.

At 30 Alice seemed very much the same person she was as an adolescent: warm, friendly, open, conventional, given to self-dramatization and overexaggeration of such difficulties as she had with her parents and siblings. She appeared a rather typical "feminine" housewife whose interests resided strictly in home, family, and social activities. Despite her self-characterization as "wild and crazy" as an adolescent, she had never gotten into real trouble; Alice was a virgin when she married. Moreover, she had not seemed wild to the research staff but extraordinarily peer oriented rather than being adult oriented.

Alice's mother, also interviewed at this time, was seen as essentially unchanged: frank, open, certain of herself and her points of view but friendly toward her children, although probably still managerial with them. Alice's father, now retired, had had several severe heart attacks, as well as high blood pressure. According to Alice, he had changed from a generous and friendly to an irritable and crabby person, unable to tolerate his grandchildren's noise and totally dependent on her mother, who spent much of her time trying to keep him happy. Alice found the change in him very sad.

Alice described her husband, George, as a very handsome man who had briefly modeled for ads for the company for which he worked, though he disliked being reminded of the fact. He was less quick tempered than she, Alice reported. Both were social and outgoing and enjoyed others—friends and relatives alike. They led a family-centered life.

George's family, approximately the same size as Alice's, was seen by both as less close and more adult oriented. Alice described her mother-in-law and father-in-law in sharply contrasting terms. She saw her mother-in-law as the "most unfeeling, unemotional, tight—what other words can I think of? She's a trouble-maker, stirs things up. She's two-faced, even her own daughters told me so. And my father-in-law, he's really a dear. How he lives with her I'll never know. He's just, well, he never says an unkind word about anyone."

George, just a year older than Alice, was also interviewed in 1959. Their views of themselves and each other coincided remarkably well in the traits just mentioned. His brothers were much older than he was. While not as critical of his mother as Alice, he indicated that he had been frightened of her as a child, though she had never spanked him.

George considered himself quite dependent on Alice; he

thought she was the more independent and certainly the more dominating of the two. Nonetheless, he felt they shared most interests and activities; they liked to be together and do things together. He thought he was somewhat "set in his ways," as was Alice. Neither of them liked too many children around or too much noise. It bothered Alice, he thought, to have children mess up the house, which she kept immaculate. She was quite nervous, he said, and took tranquilizers. Occasionally she had nervous spells, when she would be very upset. The interviewer thought George sounded irritated, anxious, and protective when he spoke about Alice's illnesses.

Alice, George, and their three children were living a conventional, family-centered, married life—worrying about bills, the children's development, and health, but enjoying their family and their social life. Their family life exemplified that 1950s watchword, *togetherness*.

At 30, Alice had changed in a number of respects from the girl last seen at 17½ but was about average in the balance between change and continuity for females at this period. She was at the extremes in showing tension through physical symptoms (somatizing) and in bodily concern but was nevertheless seen as more attractive and more fastidious than the average of her peers. She was rated high in assertiveness and femininity but also in conformity and in underlying hostility, the latter representing a considerable change from adolescence and childhood. Alice was still friendly, but she seemed moralistic and not at peace with herself.

ALICE NEAL AT AGE 42

The interview occurred in June 1971 when Alice was 42½. George was also interviewed, and both husband and wife completed questionnaires to fill out the picture of their lives. The turbulent 1960s had taken its toll of the nation and left its mark on Alice. At 30, despite her illnesses, she had been seen by the interviewer as looking younger than her years—somehow a little girl still. At 42, her interviewer thought she looked older than some other women in the sample though not unattractive: "She is very expressive, with hand gestures and a good deal of laughter, a sort of a damn-your-eyes, no nonsense, female attitude in approaching the various

sorts of questions . . . that she discussed. I would say that she neither enjoyed nor disliked the interviewing process but saw it as
something she would do because she committed herself to it some
years ago."

It was during this decade, between ages 30 and 40, that Alice
changed markedly. The upheavals of the civil rights movement, the
violence and disillusionment of the Vietnam War, student strikes,
and the hippie movement may have had an impact on this family,
as on others with growing children, but we know primarily about increased tensions with her daughter Sandra, who became rebellious
as she entered adolescence. We also know that a turning point occurred for Alice.

In 1961, when Sandra was 12, Alice took a job. She had not intended to do so; going to work was fortuitous. A sister-in-law told
her that a large chain was opening a new store just before the holiday season and had part-time sales positions available. Why didn't
she apply? Alice and George had bought a new home in 1958 and
found themselves financially "in over our heads," she said. Her husband was "dead set against" her going to work, but she applied anyway and was hired in the children's department. A neighbor
woman was happy to take care of the children. When the opening
period that required extra staff was over, Alice remained on call for
part-time work and was called frequently.

After a few years of part-time work at that store, Alice was asked
by a friend to apply for a job at an exclusive children's shop. She
did so, got the job, and enjoyed the work very much. After three
years, the shop went bankrupt. Alice claimed that she had not been
dissatisfied with this outcome; now, she thought, she could stay
home and collect unemployment insurance. But the owner of another children's store offered her a job. She turned him down,
telling him that she wanted to stay home and collect unemployment compensation. He had responded, "You can't do it. You won't
get it once you've been offered a job. Besides it's Christmas time
and they'd just insist that you take another job, if not this one."
Alice took the job. By 1971, when she was interviewed, she had
been there for seven years, working four days a week. She had become general manager.

It's turned out to be the best deal I could possibly find. I do all the
buying and managing, and, as I say, am paid extremely well. He's re-

ally a doll to work for. So it turned out to be very good. I've got my daughter working for me. My daughter, Jane, my sister, my next-door neighbor, my sister's son; we've got a family affair now. . . . Let me put it this way, if you have to work, it's a fun place to work. And we all get along really well and I enjoy it . . . it couldn't be more pleasant. I would be bored to tears if I were home everyday.

Alice's work combined most of her interests: contacts with people, involvement of family members, children, clothes, the use of the managerial skills no longer much needed at home. Alice seemed to have created in her work a family, and a set of family relationships, more satisfying than her relationship at home with her own immediate family. She still liked to do housework and enjoyed her home most when it was immaculate, but that was no longer enough. She now did her cleaning on Friday when off work. The "work family" allowed her to employ Jane, her second daughter, with whom she had a very close, warm relationship, "as close as a mother and daughter can be," she remarked. She had employed her sister Martha full time and thus had been able to help her, divorced and beset with problems. She even employed Martha's son and friends. She enjoyed the company of the young college girls she employed part time. They talked to her more freely than they would to their parents, she felt. Her employer obviously trusted and respected her, giving her a free hand to run the store as she wished. She had been successful in markedly increasing the business, to everyone's satisfaction. And she was more than happy to have the additional income; as she said, she was well paid. Without her income the family would not have been able to live as well as they did.

Alice's work also made less pressing an increasing ambivalence about her husband and his work. During this interview Alice again described her husband as nice and gentle, pleasant, and solicitous of her well-being. But this time she repeatedly stressed his immaturity:

He's immature for his age. He will never, ever, ever grow up. On the other hand he is probably the easiest person in the whole world to live with…he seldom gets mad and is easy going. Financially, as long as he has clothes on his back and enough to eat and drink that's all he cares about, life just goes on. . . . He's had the same friends since he was in high school. When you listen to them they might as well be in

high school as far as they're concerned. He can't stand any unpleas-
antness, he just completely shuts it out from his mind. I can't force
him to talk about unpleasant issues. He hasn't gone to see his
mother since April; she's in a rest home 2 miles away.

Three years earlier, George's mother had had a breakdown. She
tried to commit suicide and then tried to kill George, Alice explained. He, too, nearly "flipped out," and she thought she might
have to put him in the hospital. His mother had recovered, but he
refused to see her or talk about her. "He just can't face any unpleas-
antness."

Although as "nice" as ever, George seemed to Alice no longer the
supportive husband he once appeared to be, nor did they now appear to agree about most things, as they once did. Alice implied
that she had changed and George had not. There was an edge of
dissatisfaction in Alice's voice, perhaps with herself as well as with
him, when she described the way she manipulated George into
agreeing with her decisions. She made the decisions and then convinced him they were his ideas all along. Otherwise, she said, they
would still be living in their first, small apartment.

Alice's marriage appeared to have followed the pattern of her
parents' marriage: a dominating, energetic woman married to an
easy-going, passive man, though George was not as successful as her
father had been. On their relationship, Alice commented:

> He knows where to find me every minute of the day and night and
> the same for him. We never like going out anyplace, we never, ever
> do. [On reading this, Alice added a phrase implicit in the original
> quote: "unless it's together."] Sometimes I think we have such to-
> getherness that it's unbelievable. . . . We always go out on weekends,
> but it's always together. It's perpetual togetherness."

Clearly this "perpetual togetherness" was not altogether satisfying.
Nevertheless, both marital partners continued to feel and demonstrate the reliability and loyalty each needed and valued.

George's work had changed during this decade. When Alice first
met him, he was working in a semiskilled capacity for a heavy equipment company. Then the owner, who had no children but did have
a large estate, asked George to work exclusively for him on the estate with the promise that he would leave George something in his

will. He said he looked on George as a son. George agreed, and George's employer kept his side of the bargain. However, after a year, his employer died; since then George had been working strictly for the widow, with whom he did not get along very well. (Although this had been Alice's earlier assessment, she later said that George and his employer's widow subsequently got along very well.)

He went to work at the usual time but got off at 3:30. Alice said he told her what he did, but she still did not understand what kept him busy. They paid him well, and "as far as I can see," she said, "he's got himself a nice easy deal." George's hoped-for inheritance they considered their retirement, though Alice did not have much confidence that it would materialize. She implied that there probably would be little money left to inherit. She thought it better that his employer stay alive and George earn his pay. But what a "horrible thing to talk about anyway!" she added.

The most painful and difficult problem for Alice during this decade had been her relationship with her oldest daughter, Sandra. It had never been an easy relationship from the day Sandra was born. Alice said Sandra always had a mind of her own, was always her "rebellious" one. She was the brightest of the children—an A student in parochial school who never seemed to have to study. Alice fervently wanted Sandra, and her other children as well, to go to college. At this stage of her life, she had changed her views of college. She now regretted that neither she nor her husband had gone to college because they would have gotten much further ahead if they had.

Sandra had enrolled in a nearby university at the time that student strikes against the Vietnam War began. Her boyfriend was a leader of the local strike, and he and Sandra were both arrested. She also began spending most of her nights with the boyfriend. Alice strongly disapproved of this behavior and told Sandra that if she persisted in it, she would have to move out of their home. Sandra left immediately and moved in with her boyfriend. His father, a prominent professional, was happy enough to support the two of them while they continued college.

In a couple of years, however, Sandra suddenly quit college and left with a friend for a small town in Colorado. In the three years since then, Alice had not seen Sandra until the night before this interview, when her daughter turned up at their home unexpectedly.

Even though she had been very angry with Sandra, Alice had kept in contact with her, and Sandra occasionally had visited her mother before leaving for Colorado. They had talked on the phone from time to time after Sandra's departure from the area. George, however, wanted nothing to do with his daughter. Alice reported:

> When Sandra left, he wouldn't talk about it. That was it, she left. He cut her off, and when she would come back, he wouldn't even talk to her. He just put her out of his mind completely.

Sandra's quitting college perhaps made Alice most unhappy of all. She felt she had come to terms with her hurt and unhappiness over Sandra, but clearly it still affected her. Drugs? Yes, Sandra certainly used marijuana and was high on LSD on one occasion when she telephoned. Otherwise Alice just did not know. Sandra had telephoned her just two weeks before she came home, collect, which was unusual. Sandra said she had to keep talking because she was in a telephone booth and it was hailing and she did not have on shoes. Alice's first thought had been to send her a check. "But I thought to myself she's got two arms and two legs and if she wants shoes she can sure get a job and get some. . . . Before I used to send her money and I just thought to myself, 'no more.'" She added, "Last night I was sitting there talking to her and I said, 'Gee, I'm awfully sorry, Sandy, but it's 11 PM and I'm pooped and I have to go to work tomorrow morning.' And she said, 'Boy, I sure couldn't get with this house, having to get up and go to work every morning,' and I said, 'Yeah, we put you through private schools getting up every morning and going to work, you know?'"

With Jane, her second daughter, Alice had a very close relationship. Jane seemed not to have been affected by the changing times and life-styles. She worked with Alice at the shop, helped at home, went to college, and in every way was a model daughter, for which Alice was grateful. Her son was more of a problem.

Gary, the youngest, was now 15. Alice laughed and said, "He's a pain—but he's getting better." She added that she was at fault with Gary:

> I babied him to the point, I guess, of being ridiculous, gave him a bath until he was 10 and dressed him until he was 12. I'm sure I'd be dressing him yet except for the fact that Jane would stop me. And so

he's immature. He's helpless. He can't do a thing for himself . . . but
he's a good kid as far as no behavior problems or anything. He's a
good boy. A know-it-all right now, we call him our "reliable unin-
formed source."

When asked how having children had changed her, Alice was not
sure how to respond. Her discussion showed other clear and important, even profound, changes, in part at least due to coping with
her children and the times in which they all lived. For instance,
until this decade a devout Catholic who attended church regularly,
she now virtually never went to church, to the distress of her husband (who was not even a Catholic). George's anxiety about Alice
and the children's failure to attend church amused Alice, and she
teased him about it. Clearly change of any sort unsettled George.
Alice said that she used to make the children go to church every
Sunday until Sandra refused to do so. At that point, she wondered
why she, herself, continued to go; church had bored her for a long
time, so she stopped going. Furthermore, she made clear that she
had used birth control pills for years and believed in birth control.
She also strongly believed in legalized abortion.

As of 1971 Alice was opposed to the Vietnam War, a change of
position for her. Alice no longer gave unthinking obeisance to authority. She had learned to distrust authority, including governmental authority, and to make up her own mind on an informed basis.
Even her health had changed. Although she did not claim to be
cured of asthma, she had not had an attack for two years and no
longer took allergy shots. In general, her health was good, and she
had, she said, more energy than might be good for her.

The Alice of 1971 was in many ways a very different person from
the Alice of 1959—stronger, more independent, more liberal, more
mature. The clinical formulation of the interviewer in 1971 stated
that she felt Alice was depressed about her marriage and her
daughter but could not face her own feelings "for fear that no one
will come to her aid." Perhaps. In the questionnaire Alice filled out
prior to this interview, she noted that her years of greatest satisfaction were from 20 to 30 because "you have hope that things are all
going to turn out perfect." She reported least satisfaction with the
years over 40 because "you know it's too late and nothing is going
to turn out the way you hoped." Nevertheless, to the staff it appeared that Alice Neal had come a long way in the previous decade

and might well find her 40s much more satisfying than she anticipated.

The personality assessment of Alice Neal at 43, based on the Q-
sort, reflected the sharp turning point that occurred when she
found satisfaction in an occupational role. Fewer than 10 percent
of the female study members showed as sharp discontinuity in overall personality as Alice did between ages 30 and 43. Whereas she
had been seen as somewhat below average on dependability at age
30, by 43 dependability and assertiveness were seen as her most
salient features. She was now seen as highly productive, poised, and
protective of others, all representing great change over the
decades. Attributes seen as not at all typical were "reluctant to act"
and "rebellious." She was still talkative and expressive but seemed
much more self-assured, less moralistic, and much more mature.
Despite some dissatisfactions, she had coped with her problems in a
positive way. She rated well above the mean on the index of competence though she was not seen as intellectually invested.

ALICE NEAL AT AGE 54

In 1982 Alice came to the Institute of Human Development for several interviews. In addition she filled out two questionnaires, one
on marital relationships and one on employment. The year 1982
had not been easy for Alice. Just a week before the interview, her
mother had died. It was a blessing, Alice felt, since her mother
faced a second leg amputation after having had one removed. She
would probably have had to go into a convalescent home. Alice felt
that she and her mother had always been close and had a good relationship. During this last period of her life, Mrs. Neal had lived
with her youngest daughter, Susan. Alice had telephoned her every
day and had seen her as often as she could. Her death was an important loss to Alice.

At the beginning of the year, Alice's older daughter, Sandra, her
husband, and their 5½-year-old son had come to visit. They ended
up staying for five and a half months, due to circumstances beyond
their control. First, Sandra's husband's father, who also lived in the
same county, died of cancer. Then Sandra's brother-in-law's home
washed down a hill during local floods. For five months, Alice and
her husband housed not only Sandra and her family but her

brother-in-law and his family of four. It was a stressful time for everyone, but as Alice said, they all survived. "She was my rebellious one," Alice said, but now they were getting along fine. They did not share the same beliefs in all cases, but they respected one another. Sandra and her husband had gone to a remote area of the Northwest, where they built their own house and started a school. Alice admired their industry.

Jane, her second daughter, had had a baby recently. Jane was still in the same town, not fifteen minutes distant, and Alice saw her frequently. They were close, as they have always been.

During this decade, problems with Gary caused Alice much grief and wrenching anxiety. Gary was a teenage alcoholic. He drank nothing but beer and that only on weekends, but the results were devastating. "Spent hell with him for years," Alice said. Frantically, she tried everything—Al-Anon, counseling, and she even committed him to the psychiatric ward of a local hospital once. The counseling sessions continually made clear to her that she was supporting his drinking by giving him a car, paying for his education, supporting him, and letting him live at home. She was advised to "throw him out," but she felt she could not; he had no place to go. Furthermore, her husband threatened to leave if she threw Gary out, but she finally did it.

> The last time, my throwing out day, he gave the car away. . . . I said "Where is it?" He didn't remember. He did things like he would drive home stark naked and walk in the door and he wouldn't know where his clothes were or anything. It was just horrible. So then I threw him out.

Gary moved in with "one of the kids who worked with me." He did not stop drinking then. It took two drunk driving arrests and a $1,000 fine to do it, but he had not had a drink in a year, and he had had the same girlfriend for four years, a young woman Alice dearly loved, and now Gary was employed. "It's so much more than I hoped for," Alice said. She felt he was pretty independent now, and needed to be. "I think half his problem was being too dependent, really."

What of the marriage of Alice and George? Alice felt that her marriage had been at its worst during the time she threw Gary out five years ago, though her husband did not leave, despite his threats. Other than that period, she felt that the marriage had been at its second lowest ebb since the first of this year, no doubt exacerbated by the crises. She said she and George were "almost more like friends than husband and wife at this stage of the game." Their sexual relationship had been the "pits" lately; sex was much more important to her than to him and always had been. They would discuss their sexual problems; then George would go to the doctor who tells him he's fine and for awhile things are better. But not for long. Alice felt that part of his problem was that he drank too much, which worried her: "He's not an alcoholic, that's for sure, but he's working his way there." She had not seriously thought of divorce or separation; they still did everything together. What had kept them together? she was asked. "We love each other," she explained. And she indicated that she would like her children's marriages to be as durable as theirs. On a scale of 1 to 10 Alice rated her marriage a 6. Faced with a list of important aspects of marriage, she assigned "companionship" the top place, rated "security and the comfort of family life" second, "sex" third, "mutual understanding" fourth, and "being a parent" fifth, the last category.

> *Postreview comment:* On review, Alice was surprised at her earlier responses. But remembering the turmoil that being a parent had caused in her life, her rating of that aspect of marriage last was not surprising to us. Now, with her children's lives going well, she would probably have revised her ratings.

There was much contradiction in Alice's discussion of her marriage. She indicated on a checklist of items descriptive of the respondent's marriage that she and her husband hardly ever laughed together but also that they frequently had a good time together. She checked that one of them frequently became angry and that she did not feel she could completely be herself around her spouse. Yet she indicated that he appreciated her just as she was. She checked that she could not talk with him about things that were important to her, and she agreed with the statement that her marriage did not give her enough opportunity to become the sort of person she would like to be. But she indicated that he was affectionate and spent money wisely.

Postreview comment: The preceding paragraph struck Alice Neal as quite wrong when she read it. She and George did laugh together a good deal, she said. Yes, they had fights, but she could talk with him about the things that were important to her, and certainly she could be herself with him.

In response to a question as to whether on the day of that interview and questionnaire the relationship had been strained for some reason, she recalled an argument that had been emotionally upsetting. Yes, she thought, she might have given more negative responses than would otherwise have been the case. In general, she felt, our account did not do justice to her husband; it highlighted the problematic aspects of the relationship. Her explanation helped us to understand why the report she had given was so lacking in internal consistency and so self-contradicting. It reflected her ambivalence—her recognition of both the positive and the negative aspects of the relationship on a day when the negative aspects had been activated.

Throughout the thirty-five years of her marriage, Alice's perception of herself, her husband, and her own needs had changed markedly. At this stage in her life, she described herself as a strong person, a statement she would not have made in the early years of the marriage. She knew her husband to be the less dominant, more dependent person in the marriage, the one less able to support the family financially. They disagreed now much more than they had earlier and had less in common, and he was less supportive emotionally, but he remained the kind, thoughtful person she first knew, who was usually good-humored. Now, though, that often made her furious, and he talked too much.

Alice married George at 19 following a passionate infatuation with a boy her mother considered unsuitable. She probably recognized at some level that marriage to Lee would be disastrous for her. Nonetheless, even in her 50s, she sometimes grieved a bit for that passion she once felt and never felt again. George was suitable and a good companion; he offered security and reliability. Alice wanted to marry; it was time, both she and her mother felt. One can speculate that she wanted desperately to be in love, that George loved her, and that she decided that she must be "in love" with him—and clearly she came to love him. Their marriage has endured and probably will endure. Alice values loyalty and lives it; she is intensely loyal to her husband, her family, her children. Her need for acceptance and security is still marked; despite her frustrations and dissatisfactions with the marriage, she has no intention of leaving her husband.

Asked about turning points in the life course, Alice identified "going to work" as the major turning point. She went to work because she needed money, she said, but once she started, knew she could never stay home again because she so much enjoyed working. Otherwise, she would have been "nothing but a bored housewife, and fanatically cleaning." The job influenced her sense of who and what she is more than anything else in her life. She placed her marriage second in influence. She was still very heavily involved in her work and continued to be allocated more responsibility. On a questionnaire dealing with occupational involvement, she agreed with the statement, "My main satisfaction in life comes from my work." She also felt that even if she had enough money to live comfortably for the rest of her life, she would still work regularly.

Alice did not look forward to retirement: "The very thought of being retired to me is just strictly putting yourself in the grave and being so bored to death....I'm not looking forward to it [retirement] at all. Right now if I had all the money in the world I wouldn't retire I don't think. I'd go crazy."

Alice indicated that she would like to travel. George did not like to travel and in fact would not. Finally she went to Hawaii without him, to his surprise. Then, she decided to go to Mexico with her brother; George, despite his protest, went along. He enjoyed the trip, she thought, but he subsequently refused to go to Europe, a dream of hers. She was tired of spending all their vacations at Tahoe. The preceding year, she and George had had a fight about that, but she finally gave in and went along, resenting the money spent there that might have been used for a plane ticket to somewhere more interesting.

In assessing Alice Neal at age 54, the clinicians who carried out the personality Q-sort again found her to be highly dependable, productive, expressive, and assertive. She was seen as little changed over the twelve or thirteen years in which her children had themselves entered adult status. She seemed somewhat less introspective than she had been at 40 and was rated very high on valuing independence, an attribute that was noted at age 10 but never appeared salient again until this assessment in her mature years. She also received a very high score on "appears straightforward, forthright, candid in dealing with others." Rated well above the mean on self-confidence and dependability but somewhat below on intellectual investment, Alice Neal had made it to the top third of the distribution on our index of competence.

A LIFE REVIEW AT AGE 56

In preparation for assembling all of the materials available on her childhood and adult years, an interviewer went to Alice's home in 1984 to conduct a life history review interview. The interviewer described a very neat and attractive home, inside and out, one to which several rooms had been added over the years. Alice was gracious and, as ever, frank and earnest in dealing with present and past, even with painful issues.

We asked her to review her adolescence, telling us how well she understood herself then and what she wanted to do with her life. She told us that she had never really thought about the future but had just drifted. More positively, she noted, "I think I was pretty responsible in spite of the fact that I am sure everyone else would say the opposite." Of course, everyone else had not said the opposite, although in her period of being completely preoccupied with boys, she seemed less responsible than she had been earlier. Alice noted that she had been very dependent on her mother after high school and had lived at home until married. Indeed, she had been away from her parents for only a few days in her whole life up to the time of marriage.

Asked whether she felt she had known what she wanted to do with her life, she responded, "I know I wanted a baby and I got pregnant on purpose and that was still being an adolescent but that is what I did." In general, the replies that Alice gave about her adolescence were quite consonant with what we knew about her. She now regretted that she had not been a better student and secured further education, but she knew that her own attitude had dictated what she did. She knew now that it would have been better to wait until she was 22 to get married, and she did remember accurately that that was what she had told us thirty years previously. She did not think that either the depression or the wars that followed it had had any impact on her life.

Because Alice had been so immature in adolescence and early adulthood, we were especially interested in her placing of the time when she became "intellectually and emotionally mature." Her reply, given with a laugh, was equivocal: "Probably never. Oh, golly, I don't know. I would say probably in my forties. By 35 I've got kids in high school. . . . I would say probably 35. I don't know."

Asked why she had picked 35, Alice replied, "I was working then and I knew I enjoyed working and I knew that I was good at what I was doing and I knew I was going to go someplace in my job." Now asked to define what it meant to say that a man or woman is a mature person, Alice had no difficulty in defining what she meant by the term: "To be able to make decisions, to be responsible for the decisions that you make, to be able to manage your finances, to be able to entertain and meet people without feeling that you have an inferiority complex and to feel like you can bluff your way through things that you don't know anything about." Alice clearly met her specifications for being a mature person.

There were some residual dissatisfactions in Alice's life, but there had been no major crises in the last couple of years. Her son was now married to a woman whom Alice liked very much. Alice did not feel that she had changed appreciably as she looked back over her life, apart from having matured. She noted that among other friends, she still had the same friend whom she had had since she was 3 years old, Gert. She thought she still had a good sense of humor but also still had a tendency to be sarcastic, something that she said went back a long ways. But then she added, "How can you not change and be almost 60 years old? It is ridiculous. The older you get, the smarter you get, that's for sure."

Asked, "When you think of your life as a whole and the difference it has made, how would you most like to be remembered?" Alice replied, "Oh, as generally being cheerful and helpful. . . . I am concerned about people and I would like to be remembered as, like everybody I guess, being a nice person."

Alice Neal completed a life satisfaction chart on which she plotted the high and low points of her life as she recalled them (Figure 11.1). It shows great variation from one period to another, most often related to the tenor of her most intimate relationships—fiancé, husband, children—and periods of great stress. In general, the chart shows dramatically the effects of the events in her adult life as described both in earlier periods and at the time of the most recent interview.

Figure 11.1. Life Satisfaction Chart for Alice Neal, Age 56

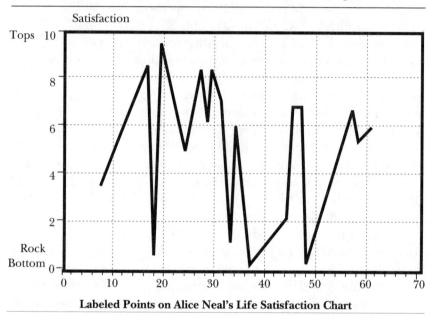

Labeled Points on Alice Neal's Life Satisfaction Chart

Age	Comment on Chart
7	Did not like school, nuns mean
12	Had fun, enjoyed childhood
16	First engagement
17	Engagement broken
18	Met and engaged to husband
19	Married
20–21	First two babies
24	Bought first house; financially overextended
28	Birth of son
29	Financial stress
30	Present home; financial stress followed
32–34	Problems with Sandra

34+ Job brought satisfaction

38   Sandra left home

44   Sandra married

45   Jane married

45–48 Gary's drinking; asked him to leave home

52   Grandchildren (on the way up)

54   Gary married (again up)

56   Uncertainty about George's job

When compared to the chart she had filled out in 1958, however, her recollections of the junior and senior high school years led to much higher ratings than she had given them at age 30. The current chart shows a steady climb from relatively low satisfactions in the early school years up to the time of her first engagement; the earlier chart showed a drop in satisfaction from level 5 (ages 5 to 10) to a 3 at ages 11 to 15, when asthma dominated her life and that of the family, and then wild gyrations between levels 3 and 6 during her flighty later adolescence.

ALICE NEAL: A SUMMING UP

It was only after a colleague and I completed an article on the personality attributes associated with occupational careers for the women in our study that Alice was selected as a subject for a chapter of this book. Although she was more feminine and more strongly oriented toward the opposite sex in high school than most other women who chose careers, she was typical in most other respects. She especially exemplifies women who found in an occupational career a new affirmation of self—women who became more competent and, especially, more self-confident as a consequence of their occupational experience.

Alice was again interviewed in her home briefly in early 1990 after she had given us permission to prepare this chapter (though she thought her life was "too boring" to report). Life was still progressing smoothly at that juncture; it was no longer crisis ridden. She and George remained the only residents of their home, though Jane, who now has three children, still lives close by. Gary, married with two children, is employed as a carpenter and works on very expensive homes. Alice believes his alcoholism, caused in part, she thinks, by severe acne, shyness, and social insecurity, no longer exists, although he does drink. Her eldest daughter, Sandra, continues to live in the Far North but is now spending part of each week in a large city 300 miles from her home in order to attend college in a paralegal program. All her children are doing very well, Alice feels. She is satisfied with each of them and with her six grandchildren.

On the whole, Alice's health now is excellent. Three years ago she had a severe asthma attack after having been free of such attacks for years. Tests determined that she was extremely allergic to cats, a new allergic reaction for her. Since they got rid of their cats and cleaned all the carpets and upholstery, she has had no further difficulty.

Alice is still working four days a week and continues to enjoy her job. There are now two stores, both doing well. The only real change in her job is that she is no longer doing the buying for the stores, a part of the operation she said she was glad to give up. She has a part in the store's profit-sharing plan and has no thought of retiring until she must. Alice still dreads retirement. She does not know what she will do with herself. She likes to read—reads constantly whatever comes to hand—and likes to work in the yard, weather permitting. A profusion of flowering plants brilliantly decorate the breezeway of her house. But those activities would not take up all her time. She knows that both she and George will have to retire at age 70. The prospect worries her.

George's long-time employer (the widow of his first employer) died in 1984. Since then he has had his own gardening business. Now he works for just two people, both wealthy with large yards. Unlike past years when he and Alice were home together only one day a week, they now have two and a half days together each week. That amount of togetherness is driving Alice crazy, she said; seven days a week constantly together she does not think she could stand. But she does not know what, if anything, to do about it.

Alice remains as committed to her husband and to her marriage as ever; she has no thought of separation. Yet it is clearly her area of greatest ambivalence and dissatisfaction. George tells her everything he does. If she is taking a shower, he will interrupt to tell her he is going out to put the car in the garage. "Fine," she said, "but why tell me about it?" She has to make every decision. "I honestly don't think he knows how much money we have," she commented with irritation. Her friends do not understand her irritation;

George is so good-natured, kind, and thoughtful. "In the mornings he is up first and holding my bathrobe for me. He meets me at the door with my martini when I come home from work. If I am five minutes late he is looking at his watch and tells me I'm late." She agrees that he is like one of her children. When it was suggested, lightly, that George made a good "wife," Alice did not disagree but did not like the implication of the role reversal.

While work has given Alice satisfaction, pleasure, a better income, self-confidence, and knowledge of accomplishment, it also seems to have aggravated the reversal of roles that perhaps was implicit in their relationship from the beginning. While enjoying some of the benefits of George's dependence and passivity, she also resents his clinging demands. He will not travel and told her after a trip to Canada she recently took with a sister that she "could not" take such a trip again. Alice said that that would not stop her, but his attitude clearly saddens her; she wishes he was more adventurous and independent.

While most areas of Alice's life seem quite satisfactory at this point, nonetheless she conveys a sense of dissatisfaction, restlessness, and uncertainty about the future. Alice is a little bored with her life and fears that she will be much more bored when she is no longer working. She will postpone retirement as long as she can but knows it is inevitable ultimately and has no idea of how she will cope with it. Her long working career, unanticipated as it originally was, has filled important needs in her life and provided equally important satisfactions. She will see it end with great reluctance.

In Alice Neal's life story we see the intersection of changing social contexts, expectations, and personality. The relaxed atmosphere of Alice's family, with little intellectual challenge for a bright girl, and indeed no expectation of any roles but marriage and motherhood, failed to prepare her for effective functioning in other adult roles or even for making a well-considered choice of what she might want as an adult. As a little girl, she wished not to grow up; as an adolescent, she said she dreaded becoming an adult, with responsibilities. An orientation toward having a good time made her a pleasant, friendly girl, but the lack of any substantial intellectual interests left her with only superficial, romantic thoughts about a prospective husband. At the same time, she was a willing worker at home and, in general, a dependable person. As a wife and mother, she was far more responsible than her adolescent

statements would have led one to expect, despite her persistent illness.

Alice's potential for growth began to be realized more fully after
she took a temporary job, for a little extra money. It gave her a
sense of accomplishment and then of challenge. Alice is no feminist, but she has become a self-reliant person—the self-reliant person that she wanted her own children to become, when she was
asked at 17 what she would want for a child.

ALICE NEAL'S REACTION TO HER LIFE HISTORY

Alice Neal read her life history at a difficult time, when she was
under considerable stress as a consequence of her husband's serious illness. She mentioned over the telephone that there were
some points that needed correction, so the researcher visited her at
home. She was, as expected, gracious but at the same time businesslike. Her specific comments and corrections have been noted.

We did not specifically discuss any of the interpretations made
except as noted in the postreview comments. Presumably, they were
accepted, although they must have aroused some painful feelings.
Alice Neal now has the strength and the insight to handle painful
feelings. She has the ability to accept her own life course, with its
ups and downs, and to face the future with a steady determination,
if with some apprehension.

CHAPTER 12

AGAINST ALL ADVERSITY

BETH GREEN

Beth Green is the only study member whose life is here depicted in detail who did not remain in the study through adolescence. She dropped out when she was 16 and did not again participate until the 1970 follow-up, when she was 49. She provided us with much additional information about her childhood and adolescent years at that time, and she has participated in all of the data collection since then.

No one in the study came from a less favorable family setting and set of early experiences than did Beth. The study staff knew only a part of the story of her childhood years. Her mother had been effusive in praise of Beth and expressed enthusiasm when her daughter first entered the study. Beth's mother had been the daughter of a midwestern banker and his Christian Scientist wife. They had four children, of whom the oldest, a son, died at 15 of acute appendicitis when his mother refused to call a doctor. Two years later, a daughter died at 13, again for lack of medical care when acutely ill. At this point Beth's grandfather left everything to his wife and moved out of the home. The grandmother then moved to California (shortly before World War I) with her remaining two daughters. She had a house built to her specifications in the area served by one of the schools from which study members were drawn. Beth's mother had been 12 at the time of the move.

Beth's mother was married at 17 and then attended college for a semester. She dropped out when she learned she was pregnant. Within the five years following Beth's birth, according to study records, she had divorced her first husband (by whom she had a second daughter, Edith), married a second husband (after having borne him a son, Jim), divorced her second husband, and moved with her three children back to live with her mother. It subsequently developed that Beth's mother was severely mentally ill, although she was not hospitalized until decades later.

Much of the time up to age 7, Beth and her mother lived with her grandmother. Then her grandmother died, and the children were totally at the mercy of their mother. It was not until she was interviewed at age 48 that Beth reported in some detail what life had been like in this family. Asked to describe her mother as a person, she commented that the interview would be like talking to a psychotherapist, which she had been doing for the last two years.

> Well, it was an extremely painful situation all the time I was growing up. Very bad. I think she was going insane from the time I can remember. She had very sick thoughts. She felt that everyone was against her. We weren't allowed to talk to any neighbors. We had to cross the street if we saw someone coming. I don't think there was hardly a day went by when we didn't get some sort of physical beating. And usually we didn't know what it was for.
>
> I don't remember her ever cooking a meal for us. . . . When I was 2, when my father and mother were divorced, my mother went to live with her mother, whom I remember with a great deal of love— my grandmother. In fact, I don't remember living with my mother too much before the age of 7. I just remember mostly my relationship with my grandmother and my grandmother's son. My mother must have been away part of the time. She met this PG&E [Pacific Gas and Electric] repairman and she became pregnant and had a child, and then he married her after the child was born. We lived in Arizona for a year perhaps.

> *Postreview comment:* On reading this twenty-one years later, Beth crossed out the reference to her grandmother's son, noting, "Her son died in South Dakota before she came to California." She also noted that her mother had met the repairman at her grandmother's house. She recalled at this time visits from great aunts and one aunt who was married in her grandmother's house. Beth was the flower girl. She recalled the bride coming down "the wide curving staircase in my grandmother's home." It was, then, a residence of some elegance.

> My grandmother died when I was 7. I was the oldest. I had to have complete responsibility for the housework, the meals, my little brother and sister had to be taken care of and cook their meals. My

mother didn't seem to be capable of doing this. She was an extremely unhappy person, very bitter. She hated men of all kinds, especially prejudiced against any nationality except her own.

Beth went on to fill in her history over the intervening years, and we shall return to what she reported at age 48 but first fill in a bit more of the years before she entered the study. At age 61, she elaborated:

I was probably 10 or 11. I was very isolated. I was afraid. I was ashamed and also I did not want to bring anyone to my home, so I didn't cultivate any friendships. I was a very prolific reader, and I loved to play with my doll. I had a little doll and I had a little garden of my own.... I can remember being very happy when I was left alone but there was constant fear when my mother came home, not knowing, you know, what was going to happen.

Beth's father left her mother with no support other than her occasional jobs and welfare payments. It soon developed that she could not hold a job, constantly creating havoc wherever she was employed. The family was deep in poverty, living in the most wretched circumstances, often without enough to eat. Beth's description of her preadolescent years continues:

We were extremely poor. I know we were forced to go around and steal milk off porches and go down to the local fruit stand and go through the half rotten fruit and bring it home, and carry the garbage down in my little red wagon when it got dark and dump it in the street garbage can [several blocks away].... I was just so embarrassed. And we didn't have toilet paper and we didn't have Kotex pads.

Reviewing those early years brought tears to her eyes, but she never completely lost her composure. She could think of positive experiences, too:

I got a lot of satisfaction out of school and a lot of good feedback from my teachers.... I was a good student and I think they were my substitute mothers. had several that really did some very special things for me.

Because data available from the later adolescent years had been lacking and Beth Green had not been included in the life history sample, I conducted a series of interviews with her after preparing a preliminary draft of her story. She both commented on what had been written and elaborated on what had happened in particular periods. In addition, she subsequently wrote out further elaborations, many of which are reported as such rather than as comments on the draft.

Postreview elaboration: "Sometime before I entered junior high school my mother obtained a player piano for a very small sum as she told it. That was my priority from then on. A teacher paid for me to have lessons from a young woman neighbor across the street from us. It was to be for only a very short time (possibly three months) and then my mother became very upset with this neighbor and I was forbidden to speak to her or have any more lessons. I was heartbroken."

And I functioned so as to please them, you know. And yet I was never able to go to anyone [that is, to seek help or guidance]. Nowadays there's a million sources out there you can go to.

Postreview comment: "I never felt that I could get or ask for help from anyone because if I did and it didn't happen *immediately,* my mother would have been furious for our 'tattling' and I would have feared for my life.

"I suspected very strongly when I was about 10 (and felt upset with myself because I felt I didn't love my mother—doesn't everyone love their mother?) that my mother was dishonest and told lies about people that liked me and tried to help me, in order to influence me to turn against them. This did not work. But I learned not to look directly at her or try to appear that I agreed with her.

"I was my mother's confidante—she had no friends or neighbors that she talked with except a Hungarian lady next door, Mrs. K. I spent many an hour forced to sit quiet and attentive while she would go on and on in her disturbed way. Edith and Jim were too restless and did not give her attention—I was the one who had to listen the most."

Given these terrible early years, most psychologists and psychiatrists would predict severe damage to the child, and they would not be wrong. Would it be possible to overcome the shame, the fear, the lack of maternal love that so devastated this preadolescent girl? Not entirely, but Beth has found the strength to cope with her past, and that is why she has allowed me to tell her story. We begin with what we had learned in the early years of her participation in the study.

ADOLESCENCE

The Junior High Years

When initially interviewed in February 1932, Mrs. Green was taking care of a neighbor's child, her only source of employment income at that time. She gave permission for Beth to be in the adolescent study, saying that it would be good for Beth because it would lead to contacts with other children. Beth, she reported, was very shy and had few contacts with others. There is no indication that the interviewer sensed any sort of problem with Mrs. Green, though a report of a visit to the home a year later indicated extreme inconsistency in the mother's statements. Mrs. Green reported herself very pleased with Beth and praised her highly. The degree of the mother's pathology was not recognized until two or three years later. By then, Beth was well known to the study observers.

One of the study observers gave the following description of Beth when she was first brought to the institute for testing and observation, along with a number of other girls in her class. She was 11 years old and about to enter junior high school:

> Beth is small; she has very rosy plump cheeks, attractive eyes, a serious face. A plump little body tapering to slender arms and legs; stands very straight. Wore faded cotton dress, soiled from several days' wear. She was extremely interested in all the toys, examining them and trying them. She asked the observer how to play with several. Very intent. Seemed terribly impressed with the attention she got from Mary Jones and doctors. Talked about it to others (who weren't much interested). In the bantering conversations of [two other study members] she was at a loss because she answered seriously. She was more interested than any of the others in the toys and the strange friendly people. Paid little attention to the girls.

Repeatedly over the four and a half years that she remained in the study, Beth was seen as "not belonging." Phrases that appear in the observational accounts over the years include "stays with the group even though ignored most of the time," "has a grimy, greasy, unkempt look," "she is bedraggled, unkempt as usual." But at age 14 1/2 was a notation, "She has made rather noticeable steps in grooming (though still at the extreme in general unkemptness). Her skin looks clean and she has a permanent. Again today she stayed with a group but was no real part of it. Other girls were pleasant but uninterested and took little notice."

> *Postreview elaboration:* "In those days it was not common to wash one's hair except every two weeks and especially if you had your period. I had a crush on a neighbor boy, my age, 14, and did not realize it until after he was gone most of the summer. Before that we could talk easily about most things. I liked to sit on his front porch cement steps because his much older physician father also played the piano and I could hear it through the closed door. Anyway, I started washing my hair (which was on the oily side) every day and I still do to this day. When school started I found myself afraid to talk to the boy because I felt he would suspect I had a crush on him, and so when he came to pick me up to walk to school with him as we had before, I would not answer."

So far as I could establish, Beth never talked to the study staff about the beatings she received at home. She did, however, reveal the feelings that the home situation left in her in several of the inventories and tests. When asked to tell whether certain types of events were usual or not usual, she designated as usual that "the woman quarreled with her husband every day," that "when the children are at home they fight like cats and dogs," and that "the children drive their mother wild with their noise." Asked to find the word that most nearly describes father, she underlined "sympathetic"; for mother, "cross"; for house, "cold."

> *Postreview comment:* "I had a fantasy that my father would come and rescue me even though my mother spoke so badly of him and men in general. Though I wanted a husband and family, I wondered if I could ever get one because I believed my mother some. I felt I would never be able to accept a date."

A few months short of her 12th birthday, Beth was given a Stanford-Binet intelligence test. At that time, she reported that she had started school in Arizona before coming back to the Bay Area. Apparently this was a brief period when she had lived with her mother apart from her grandmother, after the mother's second marriage. The intelligence test revealed a superior level of intelligence but a very unhappy child. The tester jotted down the following notes as direct quotations from Beth: "I can't make friends. I try and try but I can't find anything to say to them." She asked the tester what she could do. She said her mother had advised her to play jokes on the other girls, but she did not like this advice. At the same time, she said she was happier to be receiving lunches in the cafeteria; before the new cafeteria opened, she seldom had anything to eat for lunch. (She later noted that she had been given the job of serving lunch to the faculty in their lunchroom and her "pay" was her lunch.) Moreover, one of the teachers had given her a new dress, and she did not have to feel as if people remembered who had worn the dress before, as she usually felt. (Most of her clothes were handed down.)

She talked about her younger sister, with whom she played most often. Her sister had no friends, she said, because she still wet her pants, though Beth was sure she did not do it on purpose, as her mother alleged. Beth thought her mother was not fair and acknowledged that at times she did not like her mother. She said she could not talk to her mother because her mother did not seem to understand or take any interest. She mentioned seeing her own father last year, the first time she remembered having seen him. She did remember that they lived with her younger brother Jim's father longer (he being the one whose last name the family now used).

At the age of 12, Beth filled out a questionnaire that asked who performed each of a number of household duties that would normally be performed by parents, often with the help of children. She indicated that the mother's task was to earn money to support the family, but her own tasks were to get the meals, set the table (with her sister), get herself ready for school, wash the dishes, clean the rugs, clean the house (with her sister), look after the children when they got home from school, open the door when the doorbell rang, and serve the meals. She indicated that the children "put ourselves to bed" and "we each wash our own clothes." The clothes, we learned, were largely second hand. No other child in the study carried even half this load of work to maintain family life.

In April 1934, when Beth was 12, a visit was made to the home to assess the nature of the family environment. The family then consisted of Mrs. Green and the three children. The home they lived in had been owned outright by Mrs. Green's mother, so the major expense for housing was the tax bill. Whatever other inheritance there may have been from Beth's grandmother had apparently been exhausted some time before this, having been divided between Beth's mother and her mother's older sister. The interviewer described the exterior of the house as being about average but the interior as being in dreadful condition, with threadbare furniture, springs broken and protruding, and everything disorderly and dusty.

At the time of the interview, Mrs. Green was not working. She had been cleaning apartments the month before but stopped because of "housemaid's knee." She noted that she had done office work as a stenographer and private secretary but "hated working for men" because they "got fresh" with her.

The report on the economic situation of the family was grim. They received aid from the Community Chest—thirty-five dollars a month for food, light, and water. Clothing was "always supplied by church and friends," with an indication that shoes were the greatest problem. All insurance policies had been sacrificed. The only piece of electrical equipment was an iron. There was no telephone. The house had no heat and no hot water, since no money was available to pay for gas. As a consequence, bathing was feasible only when it was warm in the house and one could tolerate a cold bath.

Beth's mother had strong cultural interests that had been developed in her own relatively favored early years. She read articles in the better magazines, when she could get hold of them, and liked to go to museums and occasionally to the theater. She noted that it was necessary to give up food for such luxuries. She disparaged her former husband's interests and noted that he had dropped out of high school. She claimed to have had a year at the University of California, after she was married. Given the economic status of the family, it was startling to learn that Beth's mother identified a sailboat as their most needed expenditure.

The home visitor gave the mother high ratings on "mental alertness," "comprehension of and cooperation in the study, frankness in discussion," "self-esteem," "trustfulness," and "cheerfulness."

However, Mrs. Green was seen as deficient in "accuracy of thinking" and received a low rating for her personal appearance. It appears that despite the extreme incongruity of some of Mrs. Green's statements, the interviewer was almost oblivious of the extreme problems that this disturbed woman presented. Perhaps the utter poverty of the family overrode everything else in the interviewer's perceptions.

The data file contains two poems that Beth wrote in the eighth grade when she was just beyond her 13th birthday. Their imagery is striking. "April Wind" imagines the various effects of a soft breeze—on flowers, on ripples of a lake, on clouds—while "I stand alone in a silent pose." "The Sea" envisions huge breakers, foam-tipped, illuminated by the sun at dawn. "While I sit—by myself, watching them all the while." Equally striking are some of the drawings that Beth did in art class or for the study. Her talent impressed her teachers, and she was very much interested in the possibility of getting further training in art.

At 14½, a Rorschach test was administered. The summary report characterized her as showing "high intelligence activated by an affect turned inward." Other phrases included "markedly introversive, vivid imagination, some withdrawal from environment"; "much originality, freedom from stereotypy"; "emotionally restricted, not suggestible, and independent of surroundings to some degree."

In experimental situations, Beth impressed the tester with the intelligence of her questions. She was characterized as "the ideal subject," and she did very well. She persevered and was not bothered when she made a mistake.

In the summer of 1935, Beth and her mother were seen at a guidance clinic. The report of their visit was made available to the institute staff some five months later, when the staff was trying to formulate a plan to help Beth. We do not know what had precipitated the clinic assessment or who had arranged for it. In any event, Beth was the focus.

She was seen as very superior intellectually and friendly but shy and lacking in self-confidence. A psychoneurotic inventory suggested extreme insecurity, withdrawal, feelings of persecution, nervous instability, and supersensitivity. A personal interview revealed that Beth liked school and felt that her teachers helped her very much. She wanted to be a musician or an artist, but most of all she wanted to have a nice home and raise a family.

The clinic staff made a home visit and again characterized the interior as showing years of neglect. The family doctor reported that Beth's mother was "impulsive, incoherent and unreliable, but responsive to kindness." The attorney who had settled the estate of Beth's grandmother characterized the mother as "mentally unbalanced."

Postreview comment: "Dr. McFarland was our family doctor although I don't remember seeing him much. Sometime around age 12–13 he came to our home and the breakfast nook was set up to perform tonsillectomies and also have our adenoids removed. My brother needed this done but he did all three of the children on the breakfast nook table and carried us to our beds. His daughter, Madelaine, was his nurse. I believe he did all of us for the fee of $50. He had been my mother's physician while she lived with her mother, and I remember him as very kind.

His daughter was beautiful and took a warm interest in us. She asked my mother if she could take each of us shopping and buy us some new clothes. My mother agreed and Jim had the first turn. She brought him back dressed in a fancy suit (he was a very cute child) with shoes, underwear, pajamas, etc. My mother became very abusive to her because she had not bought 'practical' clothes—and she took them back and exchanged them. Edith and I never did get our turn—I felt badly."

The clinic report saw as the most "significant factors" in Beth's unhappiness "poverty; unfair, inconsistent and too severe punishment; lack of recreation, adequate clothes and companionship; her mother's emotional instability; and an inadequate and unbalanced diet."

Occasionally the observers who commented on Beth's appearance and behavior thought they saw a measure of improved ability to relate to her peers, but there was no consistent trend. Increasingly she became a focus of concern for the study staff.

Perhaps the best summary of Beth during her junior high years is given by a counselor's report, written just after she had entered senior high, as part of a staff assessment of how they might best assist the girl in her difficult struggle. It began, "Beth is probably the most unhappy child in this group." The problem was seen as directly a result of her family situation. The mother's inability to keep a job was noted. This time, the assessment of the mother was quite different from the staff's first observations:

> The mother would impress you with the happy family life they have together, in spite of poverty, and with the maternal concern over Beth. However, when giving Beth clothes, it is necessary to take precautions that the mother does not take the clothes and wear them herself, leaving Beth still in the old ones. The mother staged a scene for me once that makes me think she is a slicker. In any case, Beth hates her mother and is ashamed of herself for hating her. Beth thinks very ill of herself as a person, too, full of quiet complexes about something. It is this feeling of inferiority and this ingrown attitude that no one can possibly like her or want to know her that makes people ignore her, rather than anything disagreeable in her own personality.
>
> Beth has done excellent work in classes and has made it look to her classmates as if that is all she cared about and didn't want friends. She has been in the special art class right along and has talent also in writing. She did exceptionally good work in the only play I saw her in and lost her self-consciousness completely. Her creative ability introduced her to a little social life this last year.

> *Postreview comment:* "Someone gave me some material and I made myself a dress—since we had no sewing machine I sewed all the seams by hand with a back stitch and it turned out well. When my mother saw how nice it looked she immediately commandeered the dress and cut off the bottom and down the back so it would fit her as a blouse. She wore a sweater over it so the cutting/hacking wouldn't show. I was very distressed. I never made another until I was living alone and then I bought a machine and taught myself how to sew. I made many clothes, too, for my husband and girls."

The Senior High Years

Our data for the senior high years extend just into the first half of her junior year. There were somewhat fewer inventories and observations in this period, but the record begins with the staff's assessment of how they might best help Beth cope with her own unhappiness. Some of the staff members felt that Beth's proficiency in school work reflected the wrong priorities; they believed that it was more important that she hone her social skills rather than her intellectual skills. One staff member, who had visited the home and talked with Beth's mother, wondered aloud whether the tasks of adjustment were not becoming much more difficult, now that adolescent parties were a favorite social activity. She noted that Beth's biggest worry was being left alone at a party or dance. On the other hand, she also noted that Beth "has certain substantial qualities which, as she grows older, will be appreciated more by mature persons than by her present associates." Some of Beth's positive attributes—for example, that she never attempted to deal with her problems by making herself obstreperous—constituted favorable signs.

The meeting appears to have ended with the posing of several questions:

> The findings seem to indicate that Beth is atypical in nearly every category in which observations have been made. How much of this is due to the fact that her family is what it is? What changes would occur if she were taken away, or is it too late for such a change to be of any value? What kind of a situation could we put her into that would do her any good?

There does not appear to have been any attempt to come to a resolution with reference to these questions. Staff members continued to be attentive to Beth and concerned with her situation, but nearly eighteen months would pass before there was further special notice in the records.

On a "Rating of Personal Abilities and Characteristics" as part of the Strong Vocational Inventory, Beth checked "yes" to just two items as applicable to herself: "gets rattled easily" and "am inclined to keep silent on confidential matters." She saw herself as lacking not only social skills but abilities in which she was actually seen as outstanding by her teachers, such as the ability to persevere and to have novel ideas.

Opinion tests during the first year of senior high showed her to report good health, no problems with eating or sleeping, and little evidence of any psychosomatic disorder.

On a reputation test, she was still seen as at the extreme in unkemptness and lack of popularity, as a follower, as one who avoided the center of attention, and as habitually silent. On the other hand, she moved from being seen as sedentary in junior high to being average in activity by her junior year in senior high. She was also seen as average on enthusiasm, femininity, and assertiveness as against submissiveness.

The inventories filled out in the first half of her junior year showed little change in Beth's activities or general orientation. An interview on school programs indicated that her two favorite courses in senior high were art and social living, in which she had learned about heredity. The course she liked least was physical education, except for getting acquainted. She had made friends with a girl she met in class. She indicated some frustration at not being able to take all the art and music courses she was interested in and also take both business and college preparatory courses.

Asked about sex education in school, she felt that it would be "all right" but should not start before tenth grade. As to when she herself had begun asking questions, she replied that she did not have to ask; her mother had told her everything when she was about 12. The interviewer noted, "She talked in a matter-of-fact way when pinned down but resisted questioning. Evasive, wished to change the subject."

> *Postreview comment:* "I had no prewarning of menstruating—when this happened to me away from home and I told my mother she immediately made fun of me and tormented me that I had done something wrong. She told my brother and sister and encouraged them to torment me, too. After I had cried awhile she finally made the effort to explain it to me. One evening, late at night, she woke me up and was in ecstasy because the minister who had been visiting her had been attracted to her—'we grabbed each other,' etc. . . . and on in graphic detail."

Toward the end of the term, a crisis occurred for Beth and her sister. We learned later that Mrs. Green had repeatedly told her daughters that she hated them and that when they became 16, she was going to "throw them out." Apparently she did not wait until then. We did not learn the details until Beth Green read the first draft of this chapter.

> *Postreview comment:* "My mother went to pieces on Edith's [13th] birthday, in her anger at all of us, especially Edith. She found an old suitcase, dumped Edith's clothes in it and had to tie it up with a rope as the clasp was broken. I was given a nickel [streetcar fare] and was told to accompany Edith to the streetcar and be sure she got on it

and did not try to run away. Our aunt's name and address was written on a piece of paper and Edith had only that to help her locate
the house. It must have taken her some time as I had put her on the
streetcar in the afternoon. We both felt very bad but I don't remember us crying—we were beyond that."

The first that the research staff knew about the crisis came when
a male faculty member affiliated with the study met Mrs. Green on
the street. She said that she was in need of help and wished that
someone from the institute would call on her. One of the two staff
members most closely familiar with Beth and the family made a visit
the next day. Mrs. Green cleared a chair for the visitor to sit on (the
couch and chairs were littered with papers, kittens, and toys) and
started her story. Beth came and sat beside the institute staff member as her mother talked, and her younger brother came in later.
The mother's complaint was that Edith had been "stealing again"
and therefore the mother had "sent her to her (paternal) grandmother's with a note saying that she was to be sent to her father
who was in Florida." Mrs. Green now wanted Beth to be sent along
with her sister, or, if her sister had already left, Beth was to follow.
No attempt had been made to learn whether their father wanted
them or to look for possibilities of a placement in the Bay Area.
Mrs. Green said she was on the verge of a breakdown and had to
have a rest from the children. The younger daughter was "impossible," and Beth was now characterized by her mother as "sassy and
selfish." Besides, said Mrs. Green, the younger girl needed Beth to
look after her.

The staff visitor tried to get Beth to talk, but the girl said that she
guessed everything was all right. She never contradicted her
mother or spoke up at all unless spoken to. Mrs. Green said she
had walked out on her WPA job the previous week. Her boss had
been grouchy, so she just left; she did not wait for her belongings
but sent Beth back for them the next day. Everything lay where it
had been dumped the day before. Mrs. Green had not "had time to
pick them up yet."

The staff member described herself as aghast at Mrs. Green's
headlong procedures in making arrangements. She asked about
the possibility of the younger girl's going back to a home in which
she had been placed previously, but Mrs. Green said that the child
had learned some very bad language there and that she did not

want her associating with that family. The mother's conversation was rambling and excited. She thought Edith ought to be in a Catholic convent. The staff member tried to review possible alternatives for having the girls cared for. The mother then gave her the names and addresses of the father's mother and sister. When the aunt was contacted, she indicated that she was eager to be of help immediately.

Beth's aunt reported that her brother had married Beth's mother when the latter was only 17 years old. The groom was young, too, and the marriage was looked upon by the family (who worked to break it up) as a youthful indiscretion on his part. He had initially said he would help with the children's support but found his wife impossible to deal with. Subsequently he had lost his job and was unable to help. (We later learned that Beth's paternal grandfather had been born in Germany. He was a successful architect, who married an American-born wife. Around the turn of the century, he was commissioned to carry out a long-term architectural project in Latin America and settled there for some years. Ultimately the family was displaced by a revolution and came to Berkeley when Beth's father was 14. Beth's father was reported to be a high school dropout, but his siblings persisted in their education and attended the university.)

The aunt reported that a week or so previously, she had been telephoned at 11:00 P.M. by people in their former house in downtown Berkeley, who reported that 13-year-old Edith was there with a tattered suitcase. She had been sent out earlier by her mother to look for her grandmother's residence. The child was dirty and bedraggled, her clothing a bundle of rags. Edith said that her mother had accused her of stealing but denied that she had stolen anything other than some milk bottles some time ago. She felt that her mother disliked her and was unfair to her, and she hoped she would never have to live with her again.

Edith was now staying with another of her father's sisters, according to the aunt, and they felt she was well behaved and rather nice. It appeared, however, that the aunt had been in touch with the girls' father and that he was willing to take both girls away from their mother if he could obtain custody. He had remarried and was living in the Bay Area, not in Florida.

Two months later, Beth and her sister were reported to be staying with their father and stepmother in San Francisco. A staff member from the study visited as soon as the information was received. The stepmother was out shopping and the father was at work, but the two girls were at home. They were radiant about their new home and very fond of the stepmother. Sometimes they called her "mother" and sometimes they called her by her first name.

Then they heard that Mrs. Green was looking for her daughters, something that alarmed and puzzled Beth, who asked, "Why is she looking for us? She didn't want us to stay." Both Beth and her sister appeared to like their new school. The visiting staff member reported: "Altogether she was the most natural and happy I have ever seen her." The move to San Francisco was the end of Beth's early participation in the Adolescent Growth Study, since much of the data collection was through the school in Oakland. There were no adolescent or early adult Q-sorts for Beth Green, but her 1970 and 1982 component scores are given in Table A10 in Appendix A.

Her mother did ultimately find them and visited their school. She tried to get the girls to return with her and did convince Edith, by now less happy in the new home, to do so.

> *Postreview comment:* Edith had felt restricted in her father's and stepmother's home. She was much more rebellious than Beth, and although she had fought against her mother, she preferred her relative freedom after school to the close restrictions placed on her by her stepmother. Beth refused to return home with her mother, who had accosted the girls in the schoolyard during gym period: "My mother claimed that she had not wanted us gone—only long enough to get clothes and other necessities out of our father and then we were supposed to come back home. I said, 'No, Mom, that wasn't the way it was at all' but she gave me such a furious look I shut up. Edith decided to return with her that day and left with her. The school was very upset about that since she had been in school and it was like it was their responsibility and they had failed."

Although she was expected to do all the chores, including preparation of dinner for her father's household, Beth probably remembered more acutely than her sister what life with her mother had been like. She also felt that there were many benefits to living with her stepmother.

> *Postreview comment:* "Though I was not happy at being a drudge I also realized I at last had a chance to learn how to dress, take care of my

skin and hair and have relatives and friends to communicate with and not be afraid any more. I worshiped my stepmother—she was very pretty, petite, dressed beautifully, had lots of friends, a mother and dad who loved her dearly—she was everything I wanted to be. And most of all when she first saw me she came and hugged me and held me close—I felt very welcome. I could never remember my mother hugging or kissing me."

BETH GREEN AT AGE 49

It was 1970 when Beth Green reentered the study. We do not know for certain why she had not been seen at the first adult follow-up. Most likely it was because her address was unknown at the time. She had married, had three daughters, and then been widowed when she was age 45. Devastated by her loss, she felt that she wanted to see the people from the study who had taken such a strong personal interest in her. She had called Judith Chaffey, who had immediately remembered her when she mentioned her first name. There had been a happy reunion dinner with Judith Chaffey and Mary Jones and many contacts since.

The 1970 interview with Beth Green required two sessions, one at the institute and one at her home. The transcript runs to more than a hundred pages, indicating something of the travail in her life and the full, frank report she provided. The interviewer described Beth as an attractive woman, "nicely groomed in a blue and white knit dress, short curly hair and very twinkly eyes, pleasant smile. She speaks in a very soft voice, almost inaudible at times, thinks over questions carefully, and handled her feelings quite well. Talking about her parents was especially painful, yet her feelings don't seem to block her responses to any extent."

The interview started with questions about the parents, and here—to the complete surprise of the interviewer—came the first full report of Beth's early history. She characterized her father as very proud, very selfish, and very sarcastic: "I really don't have too much good to say about him." She noted that he had completely neglected her as a child, and she had no memory of him in the early years except for a two-hour meeting when she was about 10. He provided no support for the two children he had fathered. Moreover, when she went to live with him, she found herself used as "a drudge." "I did everything and was made to feel very inferior and stupid. I wanted very much to go to college but they wanted me to get a job and start paying my own board. Which I did."

We learned much later that Beth's father had continually made caustic remarks about her being overweight. She tried to cut down on meals but then would be ravenously hungry and would eat voraciously at times. In desperation, she would make herself vomit, a practice that persisted episodically for many years.

Beth had a reasonably good relationship with her stepmother, despite feeling exploited. Although she was not allowed to have friends come to the house and was expected to do all of the housework, she felt that her stepmother had tried hard to be a good mother. Her father made this difficult and continually put down his new wife. Ultimately, she committed suicide, after Beth had left the home.

It developed that her father had not only exploited and humiliated her but had also molested her sexually at about the time of her 16th birthday. She learned to keep out of his way. Fortunately, he traveled and was only home on weekends.

When asked to describe her mother, she said she thought that her mother had been on the verge of psychosis from as early as she could remember. It was then that Beth reported the recollections of her early years that were quoted initially. After she had left her mother's home, she had seen her mother only twice. One was when her mother had come to the school she was attending in San Francisco and tried to get her to come home, along with Edith. Her mother became quite violent when Beth refused, but a teacher intervened and her mother left. Mrs. Green had written a number of letters to the Institute of Human Development at this time, accusing the staff members of plotting against her and trying to destroy her life. Mrs. Green appeared to be actively psychotic. She reportedly sold the house for a small amount of cash, took the money, and traveled with Jim until she ran out of money (in a midwestern state). She then took a job as housekeeper for a farmer and subsequently bore him a child.

After Beth had graduated from high school and was employed full time, while still living with her father's family, she had not only been expected to pay for her board and room but to do all of the housework. When she received a fifteen dollar raise on the job, her father raised her rent to forty-five dollars a month. At the time, she was earning sixty dollars a month. She had discovered that for thirty dollars a month she could get room and board at a boarding house and would not have to do any work. This, she said, was "the happiest day of my life." She was 19 at the time, and she was making friends both on the job and through a social club that she had joined at the Y.

She began to date at age 19. Soon thereafter, at a dance, she met Bill Jones, the man whom she would ultimately marry. Bill had already enlisted in the air corps and was about to be shipped overseas. He was away for over four years, during which Beth dated to some extent, but it was always Bill whom she thought of. She began to write to him quite regularly, and they became engaged while he was still overseas.

Somehow her mother learned of Beth's engagement and returned to the area to try to destroy Beth's relationships with her fiancé and her employer. She came to Beth's residence and broke into her mail. She tried spreading rumors about her daughter. And, as she had done much earlier, she tried to kill her daughter by choking her. At this time Beth was 23 years old. She recalled that on several occasions her mother had choked her almost to the point of unconsciousness, but something made her stop before she killed her daughter. Some years later, Mrs. Green was finally hospitalized for the first time with a diagnosis of schizophrenia.

Within six weeks of Bill's return home, he and Beth were married. We did not learn anything about Bill or about Beth's marriage to him until a dozen years after the 1970 interview. In 1970, her loss was too recent for the interviewer to feel comfortable in asking about the marriage, especially after the rather traumatic review of her early years. But when she was interviewed in 1982, Beth gave a summary of her life in the intervening years and she enlarged upon this in 1990.

When Bill had enlisted in the air corps, America was starting to build up its military forces, in the year preceding entrance into World War II. He had hoped that he would receive training in photography but instead was given training as a hydraulic specialist. He was en route to the Philippine Islands when Pearl Harbor was bombed, so his unarmed ship turned back to the West Coast. Then he was sent to the South Pacific in a convoy.

After four years of service in the South Pacific, often in malaria-infested areas, Bill was returned to the United States in the late spring of 1945. He and Beth hoped that he would get out of the service immediately, but he had to wait for the start of formal demobilization. In any event, they were married while he was still in the service. Beth recalled how emaciated Bill had been then and how green he looked from his long-term dosage of Atabrine to control malaria. Beth felt that Bill had been kept in the air corps unfairly after some men were being released because of the need for hydraulic specialists. In any event, he was discharged soon after the conclusion of hostilities in the Pacific following the bombing of Hiroshima.

Once Bill was discharged, he returned to his former job as a projectionist in the small Oregon town where he had lived with his parents before entering the service, because they wanted him close by. Bill and Beth were able to make a down payment on an older house (for which the total price was $4,000). Bill still hoped to become a photographer, and after a year, he was accepted in a professional photographic school in Los Angeles under the GI Bill. The stipend for living expenses was inadequate for two persons in Los Angeles, so Beth took a job as a secretary. She continued to work until well along in her first pregnancy.

Beth reported in the 1982 interview that Bill had not been enthusiastic about having children. She hoped to have children and realized that Bill's parents very much wanted a grandchild, but Bill seemed to be frightened by the prospect of childbirth for his wife. Beth then learned that Bill's mother had died when he was born.

After four years of photography school, Bill and Beth returned to Oregon, where Bill then got a job as purchasing agent, feeling that he was not ready to venture into photography. Their second child was born during this period, and they purchased their second home. Bill now entered a photo print shop where he was able to use some of his knowledge of photography.

Postreview elaboration of initial draft: "Bill felt he could design and develop equipment that would reduce the tedious process of developing color matrixes in three different colors (all hand done at that time). His boss would put up the space and equipment needed—Bill would develop and invent *after* hours without any additional pay—he came home late or after midnight a great deal of the time. He was promised that his salary would double if he was successful. This occurred within about nine months and his salary was doubled. The work that came in after this new process was introduced to the public made it necessary to hire an additional man. It took Bill about two months to train him. At that time Bill came home with his paycheck reduced in half or to his original salary. It was sickening and more than Bill could bear to be used that way. There was nothing in writing to protect him—Bill was far too trusting and this happened other times on his jobs, too. He quit and left for the Bay Area in search of another photo job and stayed with a relative for about four months. I stayed behind to get the house prepared to sell. As soon as it was sold I joined Bill in San Francisco with our two small daughters."

Bill found a job closely similar to the one he had left, and within six months of their move, the couple was able to make a down payment on their third home, using the proceeds from the sale of their Oregon home. Beth subsequently noted: "We budgeted very carefully, and had no debts except for mortgage payments. No major purchases were made until we had saved for them. Bill was raised on a farm and his early training impressed upon him never to buy on credit cards. I was very comfortable with this."

Once again, however, after Bill was successful in introducing new methods at the shop, he was let down by his employer, who had his son take over the operation. In his several jobs in small shops, Bill never had any benefits such as health and pension plans, sick leave, or vacation time. Now he felt the need for more security. Beth had been working at an airline that did provide benefits, and Bill decided to take advantage of his military training as a hydraulics specialist. He was hired by a major airline and retained this job for the last nine years of his life.

Shortly after Bill's shift in jobs, their third daughter was born. Once again, Beth returned to work, this time as a typist in a "letter shop." She subsequently had several secretarial jobs and worked almost continuously.

From the questionnaire Beth completed at the time of the 1970 follow-up, there was a suggestion that her marriage had entailed a good deal of tension, for she rated her satisfaction well below the average. The major problems she indicated were her husband's workaholic tendencies and his inability to communicate his feelings. We discussed these matters in our 1990 interviews.

Asked in 1990 to describe Bill as a person, Beth characterized him as "very intelligent, very kind." She added that he did not have much self-confidence, that he had been put down a great deal as a child. Bill's father remarried when Bill was 9, and his stepmother was a nervous and unaccepting person. Beth and Bill thus had in common the feeling of having been rejected, though Bill's father and stepmother had positive feelings toward him. Beth said that Bill had a lot of talents, but he was "used" by others and eventually became very discouraged.

Beth described the early months of the marriage as a very happy period. They lived off the army post and she enjoyed "playing wife." Beth did not remember any serious problems of adjustment, but there must have been some. Both were totally inexperienced sexually and quite naive, and with their early backgrounds, both had considerable inhibitions relating to sexual expression—a persistent problem over the years and one they were unable to discuss. Other than this, the only other topic that Beth felt unable to discuss with her husband was her own early years and family background. In general, they had similar goals, and both were devoted to the children.

The one area of major conflict in the marriage related to Bill's workaholic tendencies. Bill was intent on supporting his family well, and he took on more than the expected level of work involvement throughout his married life. As a consequence, he was available to Beth and the children only on one weekend day, and this was the source of a good deal of stress.

Ultimately, they bought a piece of property in a not-too-distant scenic area, where they went to camp as a family for recreation. Here Bill could relax and enjoy the children. He talked of cutting down his work schedule, and Beth said he was on the verge of doing so when suddenly his life ended. The family had been on a camping holiday at their property and were just packing up to return home. Bill had a fatal heart attack.

Beth managed to deal with all the decisions and arrangements that had to be made and to be available to the children immediately after Bill's death. A few months later, however, she had suffered a complete collapse of self-confidence.

Postreview comment: "My feelings of inferiority and that no one could possibly like me or want to know me returned full bloom. I had always had a fear that maybe my mother was right—I was mentally ill like her. I had never talked about it because the one time I had—Bill had asked me a few days before we were married, 'Is your mother alive? You have never talked about her'—I told him briefly about her mental illness. To my shock Bill said, 'If I had known that I never would have asked you to marry me.' I kept it buried from then on."

We do not know what lay behind Bill's reaction to Beth's disclosure about her mother. Did he believe that her mother's illness might be hereditary, and did this partly underlie his fear of Beth's having a child? Or did he feel that she herself must have been damaged? We only know that he had placed a great gulf between them, one that does not seem to have been completely bridged by their years together. Yet he did not try to withdraw from the marriage. One must assume that his death brought not only grief but also a sense of guilt and despair.

We return now to what we learned in 1970. At the time of her interview at age 49, she was in psychotherapy and had been for more than two years. Her interviewer noted that Beth was

> in a highly transitional phase of development, the seeds of which are widowhood and role reversal between mother and daughter, additionally facilitated by several years of psychotherapy. . . . [There are] unmistakable strides toward psychological health and personality growth. . . . She is using her insight to establish more meaningful, mature relationships and seeking a new style of life more congruent with the knowledge of self.

The interviewer then explored Beth's current relationships with her parents and siblings. Beth had not attempted to see her mother again in the twenty-five years since she had married, and her mother was now in a mental hospital in the Midwest. Her father had died, without any reconciliation between them. Asked to describe her sister, Edith, and their relationship, Beth said that she enjoyed seeing Edith but that it was difficult to be around her very long: "She's got a very good heart. Very daring, very brash. She'll walk into any situation and just take over. . . . She reminds me a lot of my mother." Edith had married and had three children, with whom she was frequently upset. She refused to cook for her husband and treated him somewhat contemptuously: "She'd go out and buy a house or put a down payment on a car without ever consulting her husband. Just bought it. And then if he'd get upset and say 'No,' she'd say, 'I'll leave and take the children.' And he loves his children." From Beth's report, it appears that Edith probably had a genetic vulnerability that, coupled with her early experience, led to the same sort of behaviors just short of overt psychosis that had so long characterized her mother. Beth dated the onset of her sister's more extreme behaviors from the birth of her first child.

Much of the interview dealt with Beth's relationships with her daughters, which had become strained after Beth's emotional collapse. Her oldest daughter, Jan, now 20, a beautiful girl (the winner of a local beauty contest), had apparently been given a lot of responsibility for her sisters and household duties while her mother worked, and to some extent she had taken over the maintenance of the household at the time of Beth's collapse. At this time there were serious problems with her second daughter, Liz, who at age 17 was in rebellion on the fringe of the drug culture of the 1960s. As Beth put it:

> I became extremely unsure of myself, so I guess that out of self-defense Jan took over with some other people and I became much worse. I just kept feeling less and less like a parent who was in charge. They really could do just beautifully without me. They didn't need me at all. And she just didn't seem to be able to understand me too well. I think the first few months after my husband died I was leaning on her too much—I don't think, I know I was. And I guess I sort of became panicky. There was a lot of family argument and I would get extremely despondent. I would usually end up going to my room and just staying there and crying. 'Cause I felt I was coming through all wrong and I was failing them. This is when she started to really take over and, as I say, someone had to be a parent. Then once other things started happening it was hard for her to let go.

Subsequently, Jan left to be with her boyfriend at college.

Beth and Jan had always done painting together, and now her daughter was heavily involved in her art. Beth approved of Jan's boyfriend, though she had been somewhat concerned with the prospect of a premarital pregnancy. Now her daughter was "on the pill" and Beth noted, "She can get married—or not get married." The young couple did many things together and were very much in love but said they did not want children for a long time, certainly not before he finished college.

Beth's second daughter, Liz, was a source of both joy and concern. At 17, she had already twice thought (mistakenly) that she was pregnant. She had run away from home on several occasions and had apparently contemplated suicide on one of them. Yet her mother characterized her as a bubbly person in general. Liz was a junior in high school at the time of the interview. Although she was described as attractive and vivacious and the kind of person that her friends come to when they are in trouble, she herself seemed often to pick losers, according to Beth. Both of the older girls had experimented with LSD and marijuana, though neither appeared to take drugs regularly. Obviously the friends the girls picked had been a problem for their mother and continued to be.

Liz also seemed to have a good deal of artistic talent, and her mother hoped that she might ultimately attend a Bay Area college specializing in the arts. She felt that she wanted all of her children to go to college but that for economic reasons they would have to live at home when they did so. The youngest child, Mona, was 14. Beth enjoyed "the fact that she accepts herself so well and is happy and she doesn't seem to have any hang-ups or be uncomfortable." She worried that since she was not home when Mona came home from school, she never could be sure that something would not happen:

> I try to keep certain rules and standards. I guess I've lagged a little bit behind what my husband would have done. But because of some of the things that happened when Liz was having problems, I wonder if Mona will say, "Well, Liz did this and Liz did that." She might feel that she can kind of follow along the same way, if there are the same temptations, which there could be. . . . I should say I did have a full-time job and then I quit it when Liz ran away, because I felt I should be home when she came home from school. And so I took a part-time job. . . . Then I decided I wasn't really getting by too well on just Social Security. And I told the children I had to feel I could trust them, because I had to go back and work full-time and I wanted to see how they felt about it. And I feel that they have been pretty good about this.

Beth had been seeing a psychotherapist regularly for two years prior to the 1970 interview. This was a time of great turmoil in her life, particularly because of the problems with Liz but also in her own efforts to come to terms with her past and her typical patterns of relating to others. Psychotherapy can lead to changed perspectives and enhanced social skills, but it can also lead to extreme dependence on the therapist and intense preoccupation with self. This was certainly the case for Beth Green. She not only attended therapy sessions regularly (sometimes twice a week) but was preoccupied with understanding herself and pleasing her therapist.

> *Postreview comment:* "I had no idea what psychology was about, or a psychiatrist, when I went into therapy. When I went into a strong transference a few months after entering therapy I was very frightened because I thought I was a lesbian (my therapist was a woman). (I had just recently had that explained to me by my daughters—they knew far more than I did.) I stopped by the library on the way home and picked up half a dozen books on the subject. I stayed up very late most nights—I read everything I could find and took many notes. Perhaps now I would find an explanation for my feelings of inferiority and feeling so inadequate when I was with a group of people. I suspected that this was caused by the sick things that had happened in my childhood but I didn't know how to get over it—I didn't have the skills.
>
> "Though it was extremely painful it was still like a magic key to finding out what was wrong with me. I still have to fight the bad feelings (but I think most people do) but not nearly as often or as strong. This made me very introverted for a long period of time. It took a lot of energy to go through this and I was still trying to function as a good mother and employee.
>
> "I felt suicidal many times and like I would just pack a few things and leave for a strange city—I knew my children would be much better off without me and would function well. I never did this but I gave it some very serious consideration. When the therapy was finished, I felt that this had helped me a great deal to feel "normal" and I still think so.".

At night she frequently wrote about her therapy sessions and her dreams. We later learned from Beth that her emotional dependency on her therapist had been extraordinary, and it must have been seen as very problematic by her children. Beth wanted desperately to be accepted not merely as a patient but as a friend. She would ruminate on what her therapist was doing and whom she was seeing. At times she would drive by her therapist's residence to see if she was there. The therapist herself, a divorced woman with adolescent children, appears to have been rather unstable; she had severe interpersonal problems and moved her residence every few months. At times she seemed to be reversing roles with her patient as she described her own situation and sought Beth's emotional support. She had proposed her son's dating one of Beth's daughters, hardly a desirable linkage. Ultimately, Beth recognized that her idol was not an ideal role model, though she continued to see the therapist. Finally, she said, she took her therapist to dinner and called an end to the experience. On the whole, therapy had served its purpose, despite deficiencies in the therapist.

The second interview was conducted in her home, some three weeks after the first interview. It came at a time of great turmoil, for her relationship with Liz had been near the breaking point in recent weeks. At issue were visits to the home by a boyfriend whom Beth perceived as treating Liz unfairly and checking up on her. He dated other girls but did not want Liz to date other boys. He frequently came to the home to spend the evening, and often Beth felt displaced in her own living room. She liked to read in the comfort of her favorite chair but felt she had to withdraw. Beth had at first been accepting, but on one occasion when the young man came by at 11:00 P.M. to check up on Liz, she vented her anger upon him. This led to smoldering tensions and occasional flare-ups between mother and daughter that had reached the point of a major explosion the night before the interview. Beth had been unable to get across to her daughter the reasons for her concern about the boy. The action she had taken in speaking her mind to him had been advised by her therapist. Ultimately she decided that the best way to try to communicate her feelings and explain her actions was to show Liz the description of that therapy session as she had written it down right afterward. Beth reported:

> All of a sudden she really listened to me. She said, "Mom, I just don't understand why you didn't tell me this before." She says, "I accept it and I feel so badly that this has gone on so long without knowing the reason why you were doing this, but why wouldn't you tell me?"

Discussing her efforts to change her ways of relating to others, Beth noted:

I always tried to be what other people wanted me to be, and I think that's what caused an awful lot of my depression. And I'm beginning to know now that I have to be able to express myself and let other people know how I feel. And so the therapist I went to, she finally made me realize this by saying that Liz would be identifying with me, since we were so close. If she would see that I didn't think my feelings counted for anything, that I would always just put myself in the background, she would adopt this same attitude toward the important things in her life.

The world of the adolescent had changed enormously in the generation separating Beth from her daughters. Her own early experience was such as to lead her to withdraw into herself and relate to others primarily in terms of trying to please them. Her daughters' world was one in which adolescents sought more largely to please themselves. Beyond this, Beth had not yet learned how to express feelings before they became overwhelming. Thus, her efforts now to express herself may have been much more confrontational than she would have wished. In any event, it appears that she could not fully understand the world of her daughters, and she did not see why they were not content to sit at home and read with her in the evening.

Beth was very proud of her daughters. She stressed that they could cook and sew and they had artistic abilities. She had tried to provide a role model for them, as had their father, and she stressed that she wanted them to be honest, considerate, and responsible. She wanted to be a warm and accepting mother, but she acknowledged that it was difficult for her to hug her daughters and show affection that way. Indeed, she recalled how when her stepmother had approached her to hug her as a 15 year old, she had shrunk from her father's new wife. When her own mother had closely approached her, it was almost always to hit her or threaten her, never to hold her. Beth had herself used physical punishment on her daughters, especially Liz, until one day she realized how much aggression she had felt, and she burned her "spanking stick."

At the time of the 1970 follow-up, then, Beth Green was in transition but still under extreme stress. Having three daughters at a time when drugs and easy sex were in vogue and lacking the support of a husband, she faced a daunting task. She hoped that ultimately she could marry again, for she did not like being alone, but prospects did not seem particularly bright. The several meetings of Parents Without Partners she had attended had not been congenial. Although she had several friends with whom she shared interests in art, her relationship with her therapist was the only one that seemed to have high intensity. She did have other interests—painting, singing, and playing the piano—and she was an avid reader.

The psychologists who made overall assessments of Beth Green's personality as of 1970 were in fairly good agreement, despite the turmoil she was experiencing. The one most salient feature that all agreed upon was her introspectiveness. Undoubtedly her involvement in psychotherapy at the time accounted for both the depth of her self-searching and her very high rating on talkativeness, an attribute that is not usually found in introspective persons. Beyond this, she was seen as a warm person, giving, as arousing liking, but also as moody. There was general agreement that she was dependable, had wide interests, and was socially perceptive. She scored above the mean on dependability and intellectual investedness. She was seen as definitely not aloof or rebellious; she did not tend to withdraw when frustrated. On the whole, then, she had many of the attributes associated with competence, and she scored slightly above the mean on the competence index, though she clearly lacked self-confidence, and for good reason received a high score on "tends to feel cheated and victimized by life."

Postreview comment: When she read that she was seen as highly talkative, she wrote: "I believe that my talkativeness was caused because finally there was a group that had known part of my history from early childhood and after being silent so long I now had a chance to 'put the record straight' sort of—being in psychotherapy had opened the doors and I felt freedom in exposing the childhood situation."

BETH GREEN AT AGE 61

When she was interviewed in 1982, Beth had remarried. She and her second husband, Fred Casey, came to the institute together. Beth had known Fred's wife, who was a fellow artist, and had been close to her when she was dying of cancer. When Fred was widowed, she had tried to be helpful to him. She seemed more firmly in control of her life now and more at peace with her early years. Her mother was still in a mental hospital in the Midwest. Beth's therapist had written to the hospital to secure information on the mother, and she advised Beth to confront her fears of her mother. Beth then went to visit her mother in the hospital and found that her mother had a useful role there and was able to function well within the institution. She had set up a library and assisted in care of the chapel. But she could not function outside the hospital and continued to write "poison pen" letters.

The visit helped Beth to realize that her mother had not been in command of herself and that her mother's behavior toward her was not something she had brought on herself. The interviewer, totally ignorant of Beth's early experiences with her mother, asked, "Have you ever thought about having your mother come to live with you?" Beth replied, "Absolutely not. It would be a fiasco. She is schizophrenic and paranoid and is very dominating and angry. I still have some basic fear of her physically, so I wouldn't be able to handle that." Subsequent to the visit, Beth had found it impossible to correspond with her mother except to send birthday and Christmas cards, which were not acknowledged.

Questions about Beth's sister and half-brother revealed that their relationships were not close. Edith had always been highly independent and somewhat rebellious, and she remained so. She did not write or send greeting cards, but when Beth had had surgery (prior to her remarriage), Edith had come to help her. Beth said she would enjoy an occasional day with Edith but not much more. Her sister "learned to cope in her way, and I think she's quite content."

Their half-brother, Jim, sent occasional letters or phoned and seemed to be getting along reasonably well, but Beth felt she had little in common with him. She had the impression that he wanted to let her know how well he was doing but was not much interested in her. He had been her mother's favorite and had been less traumatized by her sick behavior, and this must inevitably have colored Beth's perception of Jim.

Beth felt most warmly about her youngest half-sister, who was roughly twenty years younger than herself. Mary had been born to her mother and her midwestern employer shortly before the mother's hospitalization, and Beth had not met her until she had gone to the Midwest a decade earlier to see her mother. Mary had also been traumatized by the mother, and she, too, had had intensive psychotherapy. The half-sisters had established a warm relationship and kept in touch with occasional phone calls.

When the 1982 interviewer asked for a review of satisfactions and dissatisfactions over the years, Beth reported that her relationship with her husband had been the most satisfying aspect of her 20s and her children had been the major source of satisfaction of her 30s and 40s. In her 20s, lack of leisure had been the major source of dissatisfaction; in her 30s it was her husband's having to work with swing shift (in airplane maintenance); and in her 40s, it was health problems. Her chief satisfaction in her 50s had come from intensive psychotherapy, partially related to her source of dissatisfaction—problems with her daughters, especially with her middle daughter. These aspects of her life, and particularly the current situation, were explored at some length in her clinical interview. Beth expected life satisfaction to go up. She said she had become more assertive and no longer ran away to avoid unpleasant confrontations.

The 1982 interview also reviewed turning points. Beth's biggest turning point had been leaving her father's home, to be on her own. She felt she had entered a different world, where she could have friends and be free. She later told us of other turning points as well. Becoming a mother had certainly been one, for it gave her a sense of deep satisfaction and competence, at least while her husband lived. Therapy had been another major turning point, for she became much better able to make choices and not slavishly to seek to please everyone. Beyond that, her increased self-confidence and technical skills led her to be very positively valued as a secretary, and this added to her self-esteem.

Beth's second marriage had brought a period of intense stress when she moved into her husband's home. Fred was several years younger than Beth, and two of his five children were still living at home, though in early adulthood. They appear to have resented their stepmother. Fred's children pulled him one way and Beth the other, and Fred, a gentle person except when angry, found it difficult to resolve the conflict. Prior to their marriage, Fred had asked Beth for help in dealing with the problems of his 15-year-old daughter, but after the marriage, he tended to defend her inconsiderate behavior. Fred had a son, two years younger still, who was at home several years after the marriage. He had been a pleasant, helpful boy but turned to drugs soon after the marriage. He had subsequently gotten on top of the problem, but it had added to the turmoil and stress. After a great deal of acrimony, the daughter subsequently went to live on her own. She still was receiving financial help from her father even though employed. Beth later commented that as long as the children remained, "I was in their territory. I would come home from work, the furnace would be turned up to 85, clothes and shoes all over the house, the kitchen a mess. I'd have to clean it up before I'd fix dinner, with no help from her. And then I'd have all these glares and this unhappiness from her."

Beth did not find the layout of Fred's house congenial and argued for finding a different place, but to Fred it was home. She objected especially to the organization of the kitchen, and she felt uncomfortable with the portrait of her husband's first wife that looked down on her from the living room wall. Finally, after realizing that Fred could not give up the house, Beth suggested remodeling, and he agreed. Beth had learned to be more assertive. She was prepared to terminate the marriage if she could not be happy in it. This extended to venting her anger and throwing plates on one occasion. The picture of Fred's first wife came down soon after, and life returned to a somewhat more tranquil level. Tensions remained, however, especially over the question of inheritances. Beth had been financially better off than Fred and wanted to be sure that the resources she brought to the marriage would go to her children, not to his, if she should die before him. She knew that Fred himself was well protected by health insurance and retirement resources. Ultimately she had a lawyer draw up an appropriate will, but this must have added tension.

Despite the stormy period that they had gone through, Beth enjoyed doing things with Fred and was pleased to have been able to improve his financial status. She felt that he had helped her to grow and she had helped him to plan for the future. At the time of the interview, both Fred and Beth seemed committed to make their marriage work. And if throwing plates can hardly be considered a mature way of handling conflict, it had at least helped to define the situation.

During this same time period, Beth answered the telephone for three years at Suicide Prevention and an additional three years for Parental Stress, a demanding but very rewarding emotional involvement.

Beth's daughters were all married, Jan for the second time. She had married the boy with whom she had lived a decade earlier, but the marriage had not worked out. Of all the girls' husbands, this had been the one Beth most admired and felt closest to, but he became a philanderer after marriage. Fortunately there had been no children. Jan's second marriage had brought a child and seemed to be going well.

Liz married a man who was "a terrific provider," and the marriage was going well, but Beth was not comfortable with him. He tended to be very abrupt with her, and the relationship was strained. Beth was pleased that Liz was happy in the marriage and had a husband who loved his family and provided well for them. They had, she said, a lovely home and the funds to travel and engage in a variety of recreational activities.

Fred, like his wife, enjoyed painting. He was shy about his talent and would hide his paintings, but Beth felt that he had considerable ability. Together they had enrolled in a watercolor class. Both enjoyed it and felt their techniques had improved substantially. They also visited for dinner with some of Beth's friends and with neighbors. Fred was often a reluctant participant, but he usually seemed to enjoy himself. The couple ate out a good deal.

Beth's job kept her busy, as did Fred's. She was now a senior stenographer in a government agency and had become a proficient word processor operator. She especially enjoyed the people she worked with and "the fact that I can handle all these different things at one time." She felt that her job had contributed to her sense of identity, though she put "friends" in first place as having given her a new identity over the years.

Beth reported that she was "heavily involved" in her work, more so than previously. She was satisfied with both the features of the job itself and her salary. Fred, too, was heavily involved in his job, but he talked about it far less than Beth talked about hers. She wished he could talk more about his experiences. She was very pleased with the way in which he shared household tasks such as dishes and heavy cleaning. Asked about retirement plans, Beth reported: "We want to do a lot more traveling. He wants to work until he dies, at least part-time. I kind of want that, too."

Fred's health worried her. He had a pacemaker, and his health seemed precarious. The one thing she would most like to change in her marriage would be for her husband to give up smoking. Since their marriage, they had done things together, and Beth felt that the future would be better if their health remained good.

Beth felt positive about the future of their marriage and about her daughters. She felt her children were becoming closer, and in general she reported herself satisfied with how they had turned out. She saw Jan as a competent but somewhat dominating person who still treated her mother as she did when she had to take over more than a decade before. Relations with the two younger daughters were good, but she characterized Mona as being very passive. Mona reported herself bored and did not like being tied down by a child, but she was not willing to take any initiative. She had seemed extraordinarily "unconcerned" with any public issue and unwilling to address any serious matter when interviewed a decade earlier, and we had wondered whether she would subsequently become a more active and zestful participant in life.

Between her interveiws in 1970 and 1982, Beth showed overall stability in her personality ratings, but there were substantial changes in the ratings of certain attributes. She was rated more satisfied with self in 1982, but she still received a somewhat higher than average rating on "feels victimized." She was seen as somewhat more vulnerable to becoming disorganized when under stress or trauma at this time, perhaps because of her report of the turmoil in her recent marriage. At the same time, she was seen as strongly sympathetic with others, warm and oriented to being helpful to others, and she was rated near the lower extreme in extrapunitive behavior, that is, in transferring or projecting blame on others. Despite her slightly below average rating on the personality component "self-confidence versus victimized," Beth was now rated high enough on the components "intellectually invested" and "dependable" to score in the top third of all women in the study on our index and competence as of later maturity.

REACHING TOWARD SEVENTY

It was not until eight years after the 1982 follow-up, when I was reviewing the lives of study members who reported a mentally ill family member, that Beth Green Casey came to my attention. Because the 1982 interviews suggested that she was coping effectively, I asked her if she would be willing to have her story told. She was most gracious and tentatively, but warmly, assented. I sent her a copy of a completed history so that she would know what would be entailed. After reading it, she agreed to be interviewed further.

By the time of the first interview, I had prepared a description of her adolescent years and had sent it in advance of our conversation. When we met, she noted that in a few respects our records appeared to be in error and filled in some of the gaps in the adolescent history, as well as in the later years. A second draft was prepared, incorporating everything through the 1982 interviews, and again we talked. Beyond this, Mrs. Casey had typed several pages of comments, many of which have been reported. In these 1990–1991 interviews, we went into considerable detail on the circumstances of her first marriage and the lives of her daughters. I also met her husband, Fred, and had a chance to see the impressive array of paintings, many done by themselves, that decorated their home.

Both Fred and Beth had retired a few years after the last intensive follow-up of the whole study group. Fred had not intended to retire, but a disabling stroke had totally paralyzed his left side and had markedly impaired his functioning. Beth had continued to work for a couple of years longer, and then she decided that it was time to enjoy more free time. Each has been involved in occasional volunteer activities, as well as in their shared enjoyment of painting.

Despite his inability to use his left arm, Fred has occupied himself with crafts. He developed amazing skill using a vise to hold the objects that he was working on. He made a model sloop, each plank and fitting shaped with exquisite care. Fred was also making tiny easels on which he mounted paintings, little larger than a postage stamp, yet beautifully precise. Additionally, Fred serves as a volunteer on a telephone committee for the American Association of Retired Persons. Thus he is substantially occupied, despite his impairment. Beth, too, has occasionally participated as a volunteer, serving as secretary for an art group.

After more than a decade of marriage, Beth and Fred seem to have worked out a reasonably satisfying relationship. Both feel appreciated and supportive, though neither feels completely free in discussing everything important to them. Beth's health is considerably better than Fred's, and her chief concern is for his health. She reports herself "generally satisfied" with her life at present. What is best about life, she said, is having fairly good health and enough funds to travel and help out with her children, as well as having friends and satisfying hobbies. Just before our interview in the fall of 1990, Beth had been to Spain on a tour. A couple of months later, during the Christmas holidays, she and Fred took a cruise around the Hawaiian Islands. They are enjoying new sights and experiences together.

All three of the daughters are now parents. Her children's acceptance of her is very important to Beth. She wants to be close to her daughters and their children and is generally satisfied with their relationships. There are some strains with one or two of her sons-in-law, but Beth is pleased that her daughters' marriages seem to be on solid ground. If at times she feels not wholly comfortable with her daughters' husbands, she appreciates that they are strong "family men." She tries to be supportive and not to interfere with the raising of her grandchildren.

Beth is closest to her youngest daughter, who is the one most likely to provide assistance should she require it. Mona would like Beth to move closer to her, but Beth prefers to be independent and to maintain her own place. She feels that she can count on love and emotional support in her later years.

CONCLUSION

At times, Beth is in full command. She knows that she is bright and capable, that she was a valued employee, that she has considerable artistic talent, that she has many friends. She is able to enjoy being with her friends, music, painting, traveling to new places. At other times she is assailed by doubts and depression. Still, she manages to cope. Earlier she tried to deny that there were problems in her relationships with her daughters, and inevitably she regrets that closer ties to one are precluded by the attitudes of her son-in-law. Now, however, she seems quite realistic in her assessments of future developments and resigned to the likelihood that she will be alone in her later years. She hopes to become more involved in volunteer activities. At the time of writing of this history she is especially enjoying a new electronic piano that graces the living room.

Asked when she felt she had become fully mature, Beth smiled and said, "I'm still working on it." She felt that she was there when she completed her therapy but she still has occasional periods of doubt and depression. "They come and go," she added, "and I'm sure that's going to be going on in my life forever." And what did maturity mean to Beth? "One who accepts things the way they really are. One who makes responsible decisions...accepts their life pretty much the way it has come forth. There's not too much you can do to change life's circumstances. If you can live with them without falling apart, you're probably doing pretty well."

The most unhappy girl in the Adolescent Growth Study of the 1930s was above average in our ratings of competence in 1982 and is far more satisfied with her current life than many of the women who were carefree girls sixty years ago. She scored particularly high on intellectual investment and the personality component originally labeled "warm" but which seems to me more appropriately to reflect a prosocial orientation (being helpful to others). Considering the devastating experiences of her childhood and adolescence, she has managed to take charge of her life in a way that few of us would have predicted. She has not merely survived but has achieved the ability to accept her life—not without sorrow but with the realization that she is the one who must deal with whatever comes, and she is confident that she can do so.

EPILOGUE TO THE LIFE OF BETH GREEN

Beth Green was by no means the only study member who was abused as a child, though the severity of abuse and deprivation that she experienced was extreme. Readers familiar with Richard Rhodes's *A Hole in the World* will recall that Rhodes, a Pulitzer Prize–winning author, had to struggle for decades to come to terms with the early loss of his mother and the brutal cruelty of his step-mother during his preadolescent years. Rhodes's mother had committed suicide when he was an infant, leaving him and his 2-year-old brother with a father who had treated his mother rather harshly. His father at first tried to care for the children himself but then married a woman who was a cruel tyrant and whom the father feared but could not leave. Rhodes, like Beth Green, found the means of maintaining his sanity and a source of recognition and respect by virtue of his pursuit of knowledge in school and his escape through reading. But even decades after he and his brother had been removed from the home where they had been brutalized and put in a well-run institution for homeless boys (the Andrew Drumm

Institute), Richard Rhodes struggled with the torment of his early years—the hole where a mother should have been, the hunger and pain inflicted by a violent woman and a cowardly father. He writes of

> a predicament I struggled desperately to resolve: how to calm and to rescue the lurching monster of overwhelming, intractable, involuntary rage that my mother's suicide, my father's neglect and my stepmother's violence instilled in me. Turning anger inward creates depression; that was the despair that I found it necessary to "sustain," fearing that if I allowed my enormous anger release I might murder someone.[1]

Rhodes won a college scholarship and began to write, but he felt blocked except when he drank heavily. Ultimately, after a difficult marriage, heavy drinking to quell anxiety, a severe eating disorder, and suicidal impulses, he entered psychotherapy. He began to function and to write effectively. Like Beth Green, he was not able to be the kind of parent he would have liked to be, but he loved his children. At 50, he wrote the story of his life, not as the novel that he had contemplated but as the ultimate effort to come to terms with the past.

Many of the other study members who were abused or neglected were alienated from school as well as from home. Receiving no encouragement to develop their intellectual skills, they turned their anger outward or (especially in the case of girls) sought love in any way they could get it. The results were often devastating, as we shall see.

CHAPTER 13

PLANFUL COMPETENCE IN WOMEN'S LIVES

For the girls of the Oakland Growth Study, the junior and senior high years were years of severe economic depression. If their fathers were unemployed or markedly underemployed, and the family experienced real deprivation, their mothers often did whatever they could to earn money. As Glen Elder has documented in *Children of the Great Depression,* under such circumstances the adolescent girls were likely to take over some of the mother's domestic duties.[1] We have seen the most extreme example of this in the case of Beth Green, but a measure of domestic involvement on the part of girls in deprived families was quite general. Even where the girls were not called upon to take household responsibilities, their parents urged upon them the desired roles of wife and mother.

Except in families in which the girls' mothers had attended college or had come to appreciate that a daughter might have greater opportunities by virtue of a college education, far fewer parents urged their daughters to attend college or assisted them than was the case with their sons.[2] Insofar as most of the girls expected to be employed, it was primarily as a prelude to marriage, not as the initial step toward a career.

The outbreak of World War II and America's mobilization for war afforded opportunities for employment that had not existed a few years before and at the same time posed a critical question for the young women who were a year or two beyond high school: to marry before their male friends went into the service or to wait? Some married earlier than they had planned; others put off marriage.

After the war, there were some 10 million or 11 million men to be absorbed into the civilian economy. Except for traditional "women's jobs"—such as elementary school teaching, nursing, typing—there was little acceptance of women in the labor force.[3] By the 1950s, when the Guidance Study members were coming of age, America was basking in "normalcy"; the traditional family was exemplified by Ozzie and Harriet Nelson and a dozen other television and radio families extolling domesticity. As Arlene Skolnick has so aptly commented, "The version of Freudian theory being purveyed at the time insisted that the proof of healthy femininity was to be found in feelings of emotional fulfillment in carrying out the roles of wife and mother."[4]

But the 1950s were, as Skolnick points out, an aberration. Women had been moving toward equality and a greater measure of personal autonomy in the early decades of the century. The 1920s had brought a sexual revolution that was not to be overthrown as contraceptive methods improved, and in the labor force clerical and service jobs increased enormously.

Each decade therafter saw more women entering the labor force and more general acceptance of the idea that a woman might legitimately have a career of her own. With the advent of a general women's movement, calling for consciousness of gender even as Karl Marx had called for consciousness of class, the women of our study were now subject to quite different pressures from those earlier experienced.[5] Many were not sympathetic to the more extreme exponents of the women's movement, but almost all recognized some of the restrictions, irritations, and at times humiliations that their gender had been subject to. Many were ambivalent. They had made choices decades before that they might not have made if given another chance.

Traditionally, women's lives have been contingent upon the lives of their husbands. To a considerable extent, they still are, though the lives of the daughters of our study members are far less contingent upon their husbands' careers and whims than were their mothers' lives. It is not surprising, then, that women's self-conceptions, their aspirations, and their personalities show much more change over the life course than do men's. Forty to fifty years ago, a woman attained high status by marrying a man who had the potential to achieve high status. She aided him in the process. She bore and reared children, and the task was a challenging and demanding one. But this regime afforded less opportunity to participate in the larger world and less intellectual stimulation than was afforded her husband. As we shall see, early planful competence led to marrying a husband who would be a good provider, but the assignment thereafter was not one to nurture all of the components of competence as I have defined and measured competence. To be a competent mother requires dependability, self-confidence, and warmth but perhaps a somewhat different kind of intellectual investment than does success in the occupational world. Moreover, success as a parent is, I suspect, less predictable than is success in a chosen occupation. In general, women who are planfully competent adolescents appear to have been more successful parents, but they have had less control over their offspring than they might have had over their product in almost any occupation.

Of the three women whose lives have been portrayed, only one was rated in the top third in planful competence as an adolescent, but all have scored above the mean in their later adult years. Even the most competent, Mary Wylie, changed more than did most competent men in the course of their lives. From the start, all three of the women had a common goal: to marry and have children. As adolescents, none expected to have a continuing occupational career. One, Beth Green entered the labor force soon after she finished high school and remained employed during most of her married life. At the other extreme, Mary Wylie was only briefly in the labor force, during World War II, and never was employed for pay after her children were born. Alice Neal, like Mary, had not intended to be employed after she married. Her goals and sense of self changed sharply after she experienced the challenge of work outside the home, and of the three she became most invested in employment.

I briefly characterize the woman who was rated highest on planful competence in senior high school in order to give an example more comparable to those of Stuart Campbell and Henry Barr. I then describe several women who had been rated very low. Change will be a frequent theme.

BRIEF ILLUSTRATIVE HISTORIES

Judith Judd

In junior high school, Judith Judd was a quiet, self-conscious, and shy girl. She was bright and did well academically, and she was highly dependable, so she was well above the average in the rating she received on planful competence, despite not being seen as highly poised. She was still somewhat shy during her senior high years, but she nevertheless had a good deal more self-assurance, and she was seen as friendly, intellectually invested, and highly dependable. Indeed, she was ranked higher on planful competence than any other girl in the life history sample. She was a favorite of many of her teachers, popular with the peers, and highly regarded by the older women who were so important to the Adolescent Growth Study.

Judith's father was a university professor (in agriculture) and her mother a homemaker who had become a secretary after her first husband had died. Both parents had been widowed, and each had children from that previous marriage. Judith was the only child of this second marriage for each. They were a happy couple, quiet, calm persons who enjoyed the same cultural activities and the out-of-doors. They were devout churchgoers, firm in their standards for their children. They were also loving and supportive and created an environment in which their offspring flourished. Judith looks back at her youth with happy memories.

The voluminous records relating to Judith's high school years reveal a girl who did not conform to peer group standards but one who expressed strong religious and ethical beliefs. She disapproved of racial prejudice, groups that preached hate, war, and also of "poor losers," "hurting other people," "laughing at other people," and "being superstitious." She clearly had positive feelings about school, although she felt most enthusiastic about her art classes. Judith had four close friends throughout the high school years, was moderately active in high school clubs and activities, and generally had an upbeat outlook.

Many of the inventories that she filled out in high school presented questions with multiple-choice answers—alternative responses to questions such as, "Do young people worry about the future?" or "What do you think that God does?" Judith almost always checked responses that suggested thoughtfulness and maturity. She frequently provided original responses when the ones offered were not appropriate to her views. Both in response to one of the inventories and on several other occasions, Judith expressed much deeper religious involvement than most of her peers. She saw the Bible as "God's own words to man," and she indicated that she prayed "to feel closer to God." As a definition of hell, she checked, "A feeling of great misery within oneself." She reported that she had gone to Sunday school and church throughout her life and that this was a very important and meaningful experience to her. At the time she was in high school, her mother sang in the church choir.

Projective tests given during the last two years in high school suggested a certain degree of emotional suppression and preoccupation with herself. A psychologist who interviewed her about her views on sex education characterized her as "frugal in using words," reticent but not tense, and having a good emotional orientation." She was seen as quite conventional in her thinking (and she certainly was on moral issues), but she was not a conformist. She apparently dated more than Mary Wylie but was not much involved in the "fun-loving peer group."

Judith early showed talent in drawing and was strongly encouraged by her teachers. Well before her senior year in high school, she decided she would like to be a commercial artist. However, one of the study staff had persuaded her that it would be desirable to have at least two years of college before she shifted into full-time art training. She had already decided where she would attend college—a small, highly regarded coeducational college about 500 miles from her home. She enrolled six months after she had graduated from high school at the age of 16.

The psychologists who rated Judith on the personality Q-sort were impressed with her intellect, the goals she had set for herself, and, as one put it, "the way she has been able to participate in adolescent activities without becoming frantic." She scored high on all three components that make up the index of planful competence and had the highest total score of any of the female adolescents. (Her scores are given in Appendix Table A11).

When Judith came in for an interview nearly twenty years later, we learned that she had married at 22, was widowed by World War II, was now married to a professional, and had three children. Describing her adolescence, Judith noted that although she had been shy during her high school years, she had been both athletic and an avid learner. She described a happy family situation that had provided solid satisfaction, even if it had not endowed her with great poise. Her parents, she said, were

quite consistent in their discipline and they carried through. If they said we were to get something done and we didn't, we couldn't go to a show or something. Not so much punishment as just learning the-consequences. We all had jobs, and sure, we balked at times. We alternated dishes and the table—used to have hilarious times! We all had our rooms to clean and Saturday morning we helped clean the house. Boys, too. We all had an allowance—not a reward—we could count on it.

There had seldom been friction between her parents, who enjoyed the same activities. She said they held high expectations for the children, though she did not sense any pressure. On the other hand, she said that her older sister had felt more pressure to excel. Judith was close to both parents but perhaps closer to her father, who sometimes took her on field trips. She later said they had explored every back road in California in connection with her father's visits to farms. Sometimes they went fishing together. He taught her fly casting, as well as a love of the out-of-doors. She said her father was very humorous, and it was a joy to be with him. At the same time, however, it was her mother to whom she turned when she needed certain kinds of information or support.

Judith looked back on her adolescence as a period of constantly questing for meaning:

> I was wondering and questioning where I was going and what it was all about. That's probably typical of teenagers, I suppose. Questions like that are more acute in adolescence; it's a transition stage. You know you'll eventually have to be out on your own without the help of parents or anybody else. In our group there were lots of bull sessions and discussions.

Judith had such a good experience at college that she stayed for the full four years, graduating in 1942. Soon after, she married a man whom she had known for some years, just before he was sent overseas in World War II. He was killed in action several months before their son was born. Judith and her sister, also married to a man in the service, teamed up together, both holding jobs and sharing care for their two children during the war years.

Judith was remarried at 25 to a chemist employed in industry. She yielded her plan to become an artist, but she retained her interest in art and continued to draw and paint. She and her husband had two daughters within the next few years.

Remarriage posed some problems of adjustment. We know very

little about the early years of the marriage, but at age 37, Judith rated her life satisfaction very low for the first year after marriage, tersely noting "different adjustment." Asked, "What sort of person is your husband?" she replied:

> He's a scientist and he thinks that way—very orderly thinking and in his activities. He would remind you of the typical absent-minded professor, although he knows what he's doing.... He's well liked, I think. He has a number of people working under him and they all seem to have great respect for him. We're alike in not particularly liking social activities and it works out real well. We usually agree on what we enjoy doing.

Judith saw her husband as very considerate of people's feelings but not inclined to talk out problems that "need hashing out." That she found very frustrating at times. Moreover, he was not at ease with his children, feeling that he did not understand them. This undoubtedly had a good deal to do with the further decline in Judith's life satisfaction when her son reached adolescence.

Judith recognized that the family she and her husband created lacked the kind of family spirit and teamwork that she had enjoyed in her parents' home. She realized that it had been difficult for her husband to have acquired a child along with a wife, apparently it was difficult for the boy as well. Judith's main worry was the unhappiness and rebelliousness of that son, now age 14. She felt that she was inconsistent as a parent, but it appeared that her inconsistency probably reflected a lack of parental consensus. Nevertheless, she enjoyed motherhood.

At 49, Judith and her husband were both interviewed at their home in the midwestern city where his company had moved him. The interviewer described the attractive, large house in which the family lived as tastefully and impressively decorated with Judith's paintings and drawings and with her husband's craft work. Judith and her husband were gracious hosts. The couple missed the outdoor life of California, particularly backpacking in the Sierra, as the whole family had frequently done. Her husband's job was less rewarding that it had been, and he was looking forward to retirement, when they hoped to return to California.

Judith had been very active in her church while still living in the Bay Area. The minister of that church and the minister of a largely

black congregation in the inner city discussed the possibility of establishing an interracial camp that would give an experience of outdoor life to the inner-city children. A facility was available in the
foothills of the Sierra, and Judith was asked to organize and manage such a camp. She served in this capacity for its initial period of
operation, and her children were also involved, first as campers and
later as counselors. Wherever she lived, Judith was an active, contributing member of the community but not a joiner in the social
whirl.

In the Midwest, the couple were enjoying closer relationships
than ever before, doing many things together yet each having some
separate interests. The children were now gone but not entirely
problem free. Judith recognized that each of her children would
have to work out his or her own life-style, and she was not judgmental.

Judith observed that she and her husband had been strict with
the children—he stricter than she. She later noted that the children's years in junior and senior high school were probably the
most stressful ones for the marriage. There had been tension over
the demands her husband made on the children. He had been a
perfectionist, and Judith wished for a more relaxed regime. This
tension must certainly have been experienced by the children.
From her description of current relationships, however, Judith appeared to be emotionally close to her offspring and they to her.

When we next saw Judith Judd, she was back in California. Her
husband had retired, and they had found a house in a small city on
the fringe of the Bay Area, where they could again enjoy the out-of-
doors for most of the year. Judith was heavily involved in volunteer
activities and in art, and together she and her husband had
planned to travel and to engage in community activities. But even
as they were setting roots down, he was stricken with cancer and
died after a series of hospitalizations. It was only a few months later
that Judith came in for the interview.

She was still grief stricken, but she was composed and she was
looking ahead as well as seeking to integrate the loss of her husband in her own life. Her children had been lovingly supportive,
and their lives gave her a sense of fulfillment.

Judith had decided in her 20s that being a wife and mother was
what she wanted as her main role in life, and in her 60s she still
stated that she would not change that choice. However, she has also

been much more. In recent years, she has been a volunteer in a hospice for cancer patients. Currently she is on the board of directors of the prestigious art society in the county where she lives. In addition, she paints.

Asked at 62 whether she had thought in adolescence about the kind of person she had wanted to marry, she replied that in marriage she wanted "companionship, mutual interests, some security—I was big on security."

She remembered how important Judith Chaffey (the junior high teacher who joined the study staff) had been as a source of influence in her adolescent years: "You could pour out your soul to her, where you wouldn't to your family or even your friends." Their close friendship extended for nearly forty years, until Miss Chaffey was seriously impaired by old age.

Asked when she had become fully mature, Judith Judd replied: "I haven't the vaguest idea. I am still growing. I hope, still maturing." Her definition of maturity was one of the briefest we received: "Coping with life—dealing with every-day living ups and downs." She had experienced more misfortunes than most of her peers, but she had coped with them. Few of her peers so well exemplified maturity by almost any definition.

How would she like to be remembered? "As a person who has done the best they could at any particular time, giving it their all."

She had no doubt as to how her life had been shaped: "As a member of a very close, warm family. Very supportive, very strong family ties have certainly shaped my life." Given firm guidelines and that loving support in addition to a superior physical and intellectual inheritance, Judith Judd had all the basic ingredients of planful competence.

The interviewer who conducted the life history interview with Judith commented: "She radiates a quiet kind of peace and sanity that is rare." Judith Judd has manifested competence as long as we have known her. At every point she was rated in the top 10 percent on the index of competence. Her personality changed little from period to period, though she was seen as more outgoing (here a very large change) and warmer in her later years. More than most women, she has maintained her sense of identity and her ability to keep growing despite a considerable amount of disruption and turmoil in her life, for reasons largely outside her control.

When I reviewed this account with her nearly ten years after the life history interview, she was still maintaining her garden, still serving as a volunteer eighteen hours a week, and still demonstrating the competence she had manifested in high school. She was analytic in her thinking, somewhat reticent, definitely in control of her life, and at peace with herself and others.

General Attributes of the Highly Competent

Judith Judd, Mary Wylie, and the other girls who had been highly competent in adolescence resembled their male counterparts in seeking a college education if they possibly could. They were far more likely to attend college than were their less competent peers. However, relatively few competent girls had a professional career in mind, though many had an interest in some occupational specialty. Most expected to marry and to have families, and this is precisely what they did. In college or soon after most met their husbands-to-be.

Not one of the wives of our highly competent professionals whose life histories were presented had been employed for pay during their children's preadolescent years. None felt any need to earn additional income, and all found the maternal role rewarding, though each had other interests and involvements. The more competent adolescent females tended to marry men of higher educational and occupational attainment. We do not, of course, have data on their husbands' adolescent competence, but it appears that there was a fair degree of mutual choice on the basis of competence.

Girls rated highly competent also tended to be rated high in warmth and cheerfulness. They were seen as more attractive than their lower-rated peers, perhaps less because of physical beauty than because of their more pleasant demeanor. They stood out as more interesting and more dependable, if somewhat less peer oriented. They were, on the whole, less manifestly interested in boys and in having a good time, more interested in literature, art, and music than many of their peers. The highly competent adolescent girls might or might not be concerned with social and political issues, but they tended to be better informed and more aware of the world.

In their adult lives, the girls rated highly competent in adolescence were somewhat less likely than those rated lower to be employed for pay, they were likely to have larger families, and they were less likely to become divorced. They were more likely to be well satisfied with their marriages and their lives generally.

WOMEN LOW IN COMPETENCE

There appear to be two chief orientations, in the adolescent years, among girls who were seen as very low in adolescent competence: they tended to feel either very inadequate and helpless (having extremely low self-esteem and strong feelings of victimization) or rebellious (having extremely low scores on the "dependable" compontent of personality).[6] Both extremes tended to be strongly associated with multiple marriages resulting in divorces, because both led to being vulnerable to and/or attracted to and by men who were eager to exploit them.

Martha Jones

Feelings of inadequacy characterized Martha Jones, the daughter of a somewhat domineering mother and an occupationally unskilled father. The family provided little emotional support and almost no intellectual stimulation. As a child and adolescent, she felt totally inadequate. She was of average intelligence but never much interested in school. She had few interests and few friends. While she was in high school, she started having sex with the boy next door, and they married at 18. She subsequently was not sure why they had married, but she later told us he was "very nice." She had a son when she was 19. She was then told she should not have any more children, at which point she left her husband. Again she was not sure exactly why, though she later said that it would not have been fair to him not to be able to have more children.

Martha returned to live with her parents, took a typing course, and then secured a secretarial job. She worked intermittently, leaving her son in the care of her mother. She then married "an educated man" with a good job, but he left her within a year. Again she returned to live with her parents. With their encouragement, she next married a man she knew only slightly and brought her child to live in the newly established household. He abused the child. At this point, Martha had an acute psychotic break and was hospitalized. Her husband was subsequently arrested for molestation of another child.

Following her hospitalization, Martha returned to work and secured a divorce. Her fourth marriage was to an alcoholic who beat her. Again she secured a divorce. She wanted to have a home and be a proper wife and mother, but she always made a bad choice.

Marth's fifth marriage lasted longer, but this time she found herself married to an embezzler who ultimately went to prison. Commenting on her marital history, she wondered if "it's possible that the abuse is something that I invite on myself." Her sixth marriage was again a disaster, but this time she was widowed. Martha needed someone to depend upon but never could find the right person.

The multiply married women who were rebellious often had a close relationship with their fathers and a highly conflictual relationship with their mothers. They tended to dislike school and to be oriented toward having fun. Many were sexually precocious with older men. They often married for the first time to escape the conflicts of their parents or conflicts with their mothers, giving little thought to what they wanted in marriage other than a home and, often, babies. But caring for a child beyond having one to cuddle had not been contemplated. In this respect they were not unlike the many girls who currently have premarital pregnancies. An example of the rebellious girls—an extreme one, it is true—is afforded by Janice.

Janice Rice

Janice Rice was the only child of her father but the second child of her mother, who had been previously married and had an adolescent son when Janice was born. Her parents' marriage was not a happy one; they quarreled incessantly. Her father owned a store and was a good provider and a doting father. Janice and her mother competed for the father's love and attention, and Janice won. He adored her and satisfied her every whim, and she idolized him.

The parents separated for a time when Janice was young, but

they went back together, presumably for her sake. Janice was an un-enthusiastic participant in the Adolescent Growth Study. Of average intelligence, she was totally disinterested in school, had only limited interests, and scored very low in adolescent competence. In her junior high years, the staff viewed her as "a show-off, bold, active, with extreme interest in the opposite sex, adult in appearance." In senior high, she was characterized as "coarse, common, unkempt; looks and acts tough. Seems to have thrown overboard any allegiance to conventional, nice-girl respectability." She was in full rebellion against conventional society.

In her late 30s, Janice reported, "I only went to high school because I had to. . . . I didn't like it, wasn't happy there at all." She felt that she was not accepted by her peers, "and if you didn't belong [to a clique] you weren't anything." So she turned to older associates and to meeting men at dance halls. "I was popular where I went, but not at school." She saw herself as a follower: "I do what the other guy wants to do." This was true in reference to her behavior with the men she met at dance halls. Asked if she necked or petted much when in high school, she replied:

> Most of the time I'd go all the way, and I got in trouble. Then my mother bought me a diaphragm and made me wear it—even if I went to the movies with a girl friend, because "you never can tell." That's what I'd do with a daughter, get her a diaphragm. . . . Once you've gone all the way, it's hard to stop. . . . I didn't want to stop. . . . If they don't get it from you, they will from someone else, and you don't want that to happen.

An early pregnancy was almost inevitable; it resulted in an abortion while she was still in high school. Nevertheless, she ultimately graduated. She had no special plans and was at loose ends for some months after graduation. When her mother suggested that she learn a trade, she considered business school but took a job as a cocktail waitress in a lounge that dressed its waitresses in sexy costumes.

Between the ages of 19 and 38, Janice was married and divorced five times. She was hard-pressed to explain to herself later what had led to these marriages. It was even difficult for her to recall some of her husbands. Her husbands were ne'er-do-wells, heavy drinkers content to have Janice support them. One turned out to be an ex-pimp, and another aspired to being a pimp. She had a child by her second husband, after having had a second abortion somewhere along the way. The child was cared for by her mother. Much of the time, Janice and her husbands lived with her parents. Her father continued to be supportive of her until he died, a devastating loss to her. When Janice bore yet another child, her mother refused to accept its care, and the baby was placed up for adoption. The child's father had not been her husband, who was seldom at home.

Finally, in her late 30s, Janice found a man who could provide some stability and even a home, the replacement for the father she had lost. They met through a mutual friend. A somewhat older man who had not previously married, Gil was a steady worker. He found in Janice the spark he had been seeking. After briefly dating, she moved in with him, and a year later they were married. Now she wanted a child but was unable to conceive. They tried to adopt a child, but social agencies would not approve of Janice as an adoptive parent. For a few years, they shared a happy life together, traveling and enjoying recreational activities whenever Gil could get away. Then Gil took ill, and their activities became markedly restricted. When he died, Janice was left in a bleak world, devoid of interests, overweight, spending much of her time in front of a television set. Her life was not at all what she had envisioned. Her outlook was starkly despairing.

While we have too few cases to delineate clear-cut types of multiple divorces, it appears that the girls who were rebellious in adolescence more often ultimately achieved a reasonably happy marriage than did those who felt totally inadequate. Nevertheless, most had rough sledding in their early and middle adult years. An example of a woman who turned her life around after a very rebellious adolescence is given by Louise.

Louise Dolin

Louise Dolin was the second child of a couple who had a stable but often conflicted marriage. Her mother was a woman with an enormous need to be socially recognized and admired. She was active in the PTA and in a number of community organizations. A research staff member characterized her as "always on the go" but commented that she found little time to play with her children. Mrs.

Dolin and her husband were described as "querulous and over-excitable," and each could easily outrage the other. The mother was seen as both lax and inconsistent in dealing with her children. At times she could be extremely harsh with them, though she usually tried to give the research staff the impression of being understanding. When Louise was a preadolescent, her mother described her as "a sweet, adorable child." From about age 13 on, however, Louise did not feel that her mother understood her at all.

Louise had a distant relationship with her father, who was usually immersed in work, either at his business or at his home workshop. Mr. Dolin left the rearing of the children to his wife. Mrs. Dolin continually involved herself in her children's affairs, intruding into many situations rather than letting her children manage for themselves and making demands on teachers and very great use of the services of the Guidance Study. Louise was viewed by the staff as an extremely dependent and docile child in the preadolescent years. Somewhere between the ages of 9 and 13, however, she began to rebel and to make clear in the interviews held with her that she no longer was her mother's sweet, docile child. At the age of 17, Louise was interviewed by a staff member who characterized her in this way:

> She is extremely rebellious against her parents and the home situation in which all three participants are loaded with conflicting feelings and hostility. She seems to be harassed by the impulsive acts of her parents, wants freedom from restraint without also assuming responsibility.

In junior high, Louise had been in the lowest 25 percent on our measure of competence, and by senior high she had the lowest score of any girl in the three studies. She had matured physically early in junior high. Louise was attractive and fun loving and uninterested in school. Her intelligence test scores were somewhat lower than the average for the group, but she appeared to be brighter than the scores suggested. The tester thought her "unmotivated." Her mother tried unsuccessfully to restrict her and seemed "Victorian" to Louise, and there was constant conflict.

When Louise was later asked whether she felt she had known herself and understood herself in high school, she replied: "I think I was the kind that just jumped off the cliff and said, 'Here I go.'"

Her jump entailed marrying a man more than ten years older than she, who had been her riding instructor. He offered the escape from her mother that she had been waiting for. As she later said, "He was glamorous and very charming . . . He wasn't a little 17-year-old kid, and that influenced me." But he proved to be sarcastic and psychologically sadistic in dealing with his immature child bride. He put her down to the point where she felt utterly worthless.

Louise had a daughter, Gerry, a year or so after her marriage, but then she sought the love she desperately wanted outside her marriage. Her husband suggested a vacation in Mexico while his aunt cared for the child. He then dropped off Louise to visit her parents while he said he needed to make a few last-minute arrangements. Instead he phoned her to say he was filing for divorce and that she would never again see her daughter. The ensuing court battle for custody of the child featured lurid accusations not only against Louise but against her parents. Her father died of a heart attack before the court finally awarded Louise custody of Gerry.

Louise stayed on with her mother after the divorce. Her mother cared for the child while Louise took a job. Within two years, she met Roger, who would become her second husband. He was related to one of her friends. She later reported, "He seemed as unselfish and kind and thoughtful as my first husband had been harsh. I still was escaping my mother, I'm sure, when I married him, but I was really touched by his devotion to his illegitimate child that he was attempting to raise." It soon developed, however, that Roger, too, had hidden problems far more serious than the illegitimate child whose mother had rejected it. She found that her husband was treating his little girl, Mimi, as if she were an adult female and his wife.

> He was very passionate in the fondling of this little girl and this was a horrible shock to me. I raised Cain, partly because I was revolted I think by what this meant and partly because I resented his not paying attention to me. I pointed out to him what he was doing to the kid. He knew it was true and was horrified. At this time he joined [a fundamentalist religious group] and went overboard about religion, trying to atone.

In the first two years, they had a son, David, but Roger became more and more disturbed. He became terrified of anything sexual and terminated relations with his wife. At times he was quite abusive of his daughter, Mimi (who had come to love Louise as her mother), though he tried to be a good father.

> When Mimi was about 7 or 8, he started hitting her. And it got worse and worse. It got to the point where he'd corner her in the bathroom and beat her. And of course I would get involved, trying to get him off her. And of course he'd turn around and beat me. And she'd go to school many times with black eyes. And I kept saying to myself, "God, I hope her teacher notices and does something about this." . . . But not one teacher ever said a thing.

Louise might have left her husband at this point, but she felt that with his illness he needed her, and certainly Mimi needed her. Perhaps more important, when she threatened to leave he said he would follow and kill her and the children. Louise wished to adopt Mimi, but her husband would not hear of this. As she summed matters up at the age of 30: "So here I am, almost 31, having three children to mother, a sick husband, and in many ways a very unsatisfactory life. I don't see people much. The only satisfactions I get are doing a good job by the kids."

Louise thought then if Roger became more dangerous, she would have to leave him, but it was not until fifteen years later that she took action. At 18, Gerry had moved out to live with her grandmother, because she could not bear to stay with the wild man her mother had married. Somewhat later, Mimi, who had finished high school and had gotten a job as a secretary, also moved out, after her father had been extremely harsh to her. Roger was furious.

When Mimi had been on her own for several years, she met a young man whom she loved and planned to marry. She discussed her plans with Louise, who approved but felt that Mimi should inform her father of her forthcoming marriage. Mimi decided to do so by telephone, sensing that he would disapprove. He exploded with rage, calling her every vile name he could think of. If she married, he demanded, she was not to engage in sex with her husband. He became more and more upset. He was furious with Louise because she had approved of Mimi's marrying. Louise reported:

> He got me on the floor and he was choking me and I've still got the scars on my head. You know, I looked in that man's face and there

was nothing there. His eyes were just blank. I don't to this day know what made him stop, but I thought he was going to kill me. So I wouldn't go home after that. It was the worst beating he ever gave me. I decided I wouldn't go home [after work] unless my son came with me. He was 19, and he was working as a carpenter. At that point, he said, "Mom, I can't take this any more." He'd already told his father he'd kill him if he ever touched me again and I thought, "What a thing for a son to have to say to his father." So he said, "Ma, I'm going to leave and I want you to come with me. ... Don't worry, I'm earning money. You've got time, you'll find something. I'll take care of you."

Louise was terrified as to what the consequences might be if her husband found her, but they hired a truck and took all of the furniture, silverware, pots and pans, dishes, linens—everything that Louise needed—and she and her son rented an apartment together. She took a menial job and went back to night school, studying secretarial work and bookkeeping. Then she got herself a job as a bookkeeper.

Louise credits her son with having saved her from her husband's psychotic rages, but she says that she had gotten a new perspective on herself somewhat earlier, and that was the most important turning point in her life. It came when she read a column by former first lady Eleanor Roosevelt, who had written that persons dissatisfied with their lives had only themselves to blame; they should take action to change their situation. Although Louise had not taken action until her son urged her to, she had come to see herself in a different light, as capable of action when required.

After I had drafted a brief sketch of her life and asked her permission to publish it, Louise told us of a critical event that she regarded as responsible for her early lack of self-confidence and of competence. In early childhood—at age 5 or 6, she thought—her mother had found Louise and her brother engaged in sexual play (or one might say that he was molesting her), and her mother had called her a filthy child and berated her as no good. Louise believes that this event markedly changed her and her relationship with her mother. Our data are not helpful here, for her mother never discussed this matter with the staff psychologists. Until at least the age of 9, the child seemed very dependent on her mother and docile, which could reflect her having suppressed her feelings. Clearly it was her mother, far more than her brother, who had violated her, imputing blame to the daughter, not to the son.

In her early 60s, when we discussed these events and recollections, Louise could look back on the previous decade and a half as being the period in which she had finally come to enjoy life. She did not remarry, but she eventually did find a congenial man with whom she set up both a small business and a household. Gerry, David, and Mimi are all married. Louise enjoys her grandchildren, and she feels good in knowing that even though her partner is gravely ill, she has basically taken control of her own life and has made his life more bearable. The focus of her life and her self-esteem is her concept of herself as a mother, but she has demonstrated her competence as a manager, as well. She has friends again, a pleasure long denied her. The girl who was rated lowest in planful competence in senior high school now stops and thinks about what she is going to do before doing it. As a consequence, she was rated above average in competence at the last follow-up. No other person in the study appears to have changed as much in basic personality from adolescence to later maturity as Louise has.

If some girls who were low in adolescent competence proved later to be highly competent, there were others who had rated high in adolescent planful competence but whose competence somehow eroded away or was demolished. Lucy Proteus was such a girl.

Lucy Proteus: From Competence to Disaster

Lucy was a bright girl who did well in school; she was reasonably popular and self-confident in junior high (though overly dependent on her parents and very conventional). In senior high she was rated average on self-confidence and dependability but quite high on intellectual investedness, putting her just within the top third on the index of planful competence. She was rated much above average on assertiveness and on being outgoing.

Lucy's parents were warm and accepting but perhaps overly directive. They encouraged her to attend college, and her high school grades were good enough to get her into almost any university. She dropped out of college in her last year to marry a man whom she had met when he was in Officer Candidate School during World War II. He was a graduate of a top-flight university with a degree in business administration. He proved to be a capable and very decent person. When we saw her at age 37, Lucy had four children and seemed very pleased to be a mother. She felt no need or desire to complete college but preferred to devote herself to her family. She reported that she had lost a child at age 6 months after having had the first two children. The experience devastated her, and she said she had lost all sense of being in control at the time and became much more dependent on her husband.

In the interview, she seemed pleasant but very unsure of herself. She acknowledged complete dependence upon her husband, who had been very supportive when she "fell apart." She appeared to be happily married and satisfied with her life but revealed that her mother, her brother, and her sister all had problems with alcohol. She stated that she herself was a light drinker, having only one or two drinks before dinner. Often she answered questions obliquely and seemed to be fencing with the interviewer. Asked about friends, she reported, "Everybody is my friend," but she had no close confidant.

Lucy was a practicing Catholic and had considerable concern that she had evil as well as good within her makeup. Asked, "What kind of person do you think you are now?" Lucy responded: "Oooh, I'm a slob—I don't have a high opinion of myself. . . . I'm not an evil person but neither am I good. I have both propensities. I hope the good is greater than the evil. I try feebly. . . I'm not stupid—not terribly stupid." Then she went on to say that she knew she was above average in intelligence "but no genius." She quipped that she called herseld "a cute kid" and "a living doll" but then immediately commented that every so often she said the wrong thing and was laughed at. Lucy characterized herself as lacking in willpower and as afraid of many things—of dying, "of making mistakes . . . like doing away with my kids, of my husband dying." But especially she seemed afraid of what she called the evil in her. The interviewer noted that "she had talked so much about the evil in her, the bad. It was difficult to know what to make of this."

Lucy Proteus avoided sharing any intimate information, making defensive jokes and sparring with the interviewer. She was a heavy smoker and said she saw no need to stop. She had started to smoke at 17, she said, in rebellion and to build up courage, yet she also reported that her mother had not objected. Her father had objected, and it had pleased her to be able to go against his wishes in some way.

Her husband had been able to give up smoking; Lucy had not. At age 37, Lucy was seen as markedly less competent than she had been in adolescence, and her personality profile hardly resembled the profile in senior high school. She scored very low on self-confidence, average on intellectual investedness, and low on dependability. Now she had fallen into the lowest third on the index of planful competence.

A dozen years later, at age 49, she was again seen as markedly changed. She resembled her adolescent personality somewhat more in certain respects, but she scored very low on all the components of competence. She seemed less defensive, but what she revealed showed serious problems. She acknowledged difficulties with her children, the youngest well along in adolescence. She said she had a drinking problem but had overcome it through therapy. She still had "a problem," she said, but she could not describe it. Again there was a good deal of bantering with the interviewer and occasional expressions of annoyance at questions that probed into matters that she had somewhat tossed off. It was clear that there were some difficulties with both her daughter (a lesbian) and her second son. Asked to indicate "the hardest part of your children's growing up for you," she wondered, "Are they grown up yet?" (laughter). Then, "Just plain old growing up."

Lucy characterized her husband as "a nice person." She saw him as less flexible than herself, more conventional, a hard worker. "He has a great deal of will power, I don't. I have a better sense of humor, though." Although at first she denied that there was anything that she found irritating about him, she then commented that he was a compulsive worker and that he could be very sarcastic, as indeed she herself could be. Asked about their sexual relationship, she first fended off the question and then indicated that after having had three Cesareans and as a Catholic opposed to birth control, she had put severe limitations on their sexual life. One felt that there must be great tensions in the marriage, and her husband's interview made clear that there were, but Lucy would not reveal the whole story. Asked what kind of a marriage she would like to have in fifteen years from the time of the interview (at age 48), Lucy said, "Up in heaven, dearie." Lucy was now smoking more than two packs a day, and she ultimately acknowledged that her drinking was not under control despite having earlier said that the problem had been solved through therapy.

Lucy's husband was much more open in discussing the marital

relationship. He was seen by the interviewer as highly controlled and polite, pleasant but quite unassertive. He reported that his wife had initially wanted him to be dominant but now was in full rebellion. It would appear that she resented much about her current life situation, perhaps feeling trapped by the choices she had earlier made. He reported that she had originally wanted to be a doctor but was told that girls don't become doctors; they become nurses. Although she had not expressed any great appreciation of the women's movement, it appeared that she was rankled when she considered the path that she had followed. Her husband characterized her as never having accepted life as it is,

> so life's real tough on her. She hates [the town where they live], she hates me, she hates the kids a good part of the time, she hates the weather. . . . She doesn't like to camp, she doesn't like to fish or hunt, so now she hates the camper. And she has to drive that instead of having a car. . . . Life's a real burden for her. . . . The last two years have been real tough. . . . She denies that she has an acute problem with drinking, because instead of being a happy drunk, she's an unhappy drunk. As she increases her consumption, things become more unbearable. She can get extremely bitter about the whole situation.

Her husband was committed to the marriage but said he did not know what he could do. He felt that he would stay with her at least until his youngest son had finished high school. He did not seem to realize that if she did not like camping, fishing, or hunting, there were alternatives. They camped. It was, perhaps, a way of fighting back, but it had not helped the drinking problem.

Lucy died when she was in her 50s of a combination of emphysema and alcoholism. Her husband described the difficult last years as a form of suicidal behavior on his wife's part. She clearly hated herself, and, as she had earlier said, "If I hate myself, I hate everyone else." She had acted out that hate toward her husband and her youngest son, who was still at home. At times she became totally destructive. She behaved in a psychotic fashion, preventing her husband and youngest son from sleeping in the house. She hacked her husband's car with an ax and destroyed the interior of their camper. Her husband still tried to care for her, though he sometimes had to sleep out of doors. Ultimately she discovered that she could drink herself into oblivion.

We learned later that Lucy's youngest son developed schizophrenia when he was in his 20s. Lucy herself may have had a vulnerability that did not fully manifest itself until midlife. Given the alcoholism that was pervasive in her mother and her siblings, there may well have been some genetic vulnerability that was triggered by the terrible stress of her loss of a child or by her inability to deal with the children's problems. She had felt the "evil" within her and she could not tolerate living with that feeling. Her life had not taken the course she thought she was choosing.

DECADE BY DECADE: THE LIFE HISTORY SAMPLE

Many of the correlates of early competence, or the lack thereof, will already be apparent, but a brief overview of how the higher- and lower-rated adolescents differed over the decades from their 20s to age 50 will give a further perspective. The life history sample of women consisted of twenty-eight women, so we shall be talking about very small groups when we compare the experiences of those who had been above with those who had been below the mean in adolescent competence.[7] Nevertheless, there are consistent and sometimes large differences between the groups. For example, when we compared their adolescent vocational goals, we found that no girl low in competence had a particular vocation in mind (as against expecting to get a job and to work for a while before marriage). It will be recalled that Mary Wylie wanted to be a dress designer, and Judith Judd, a commercial artist. In all, roughly two-thirds of the competent adolescent girls had a vocation in mind. Half of them appeared to have achieved a fair degree of emotional and intellectual independence from their parents by late adolescence as against a fifth of the less competent girls.

The 20s

Looking back from their 30s, twelve of the less competent saw themselves as having been extremely immature in adolescence as against half as many of the more competent. Both groups held strongly traditional views of women's roles, with only two girls (both highly competent) expressing egalitarian views of gender roles.

Roughly 90 percent expected to marry and, we inferred, expected marriage and parenthood to be their primary roles. In their 20s, two-thirds held one or two jobs before marrying, while a fourth married without having been employed. Two women in each group appeared substantially involved in their jobs, the rest being only slightly involved.

Only one woman in the life course sample remained unmarried through her 20s, but five had married two or more times. Four of the five had been among the less competent adolescents, and all of their remarriages were problematic. Among them were Janice Rice, Martha Jones, and Louise Dolin. The one divorced woman among the more competent adolescents appeared to be happily married the second time. Three of the women lost a husband—two in World War II. Of those continuously married, the more competent group was twice as likely to be judged well satisfied in their marriages, and their husbands held higher-status and better-paid jobs. The more competent were also more fully involved in the parental role—all but two had children—and better satisfied with their mothering activities.

About a fifth of the women were significantly involved with the church in their 20s (as contrasted with only a couple of the men in the life history sample), and the great majority of the more competent group were involved to the extent that the church was a source of emotional investment. About a fourth were involved to some degree in artistic expressive activities—painting, music, drama.

For the women in our life history sample, the 20s were a time of considerable discontinuity and turmoil, and the war was certainly a major factor, especially for those who married early. For the less competent, marital problems predominated; for the more competent, the main sources of turmoil or crisis were illness or death of the husband or worries occasioned by the husband's military service. About a fourth of the women expressed some discontent with the extent of their husbands' work involvement, but most expressed understanding of the pressures their husbands experienced.

The 30s

In their 30s, two-thirds of the women who had been rated less competent were in the labor force at least half-time—twice the proportion of the more competent. In general, the husbands of the less competent women were in lower-status jobs than were the husbands of the more competent, and like Alice Neal, wives of the former felt a need for more income. Four-fifths of the more competent women were stably married, though a fifth of the marriages were characterized by a certain amount of tension. Among the women who had been less competent, only two-fifths were stably and happily married. Again there was more discontinuity and turmoil in the lives of the lower-rated groups (Table 13.1).

Table 13.1.   Discontinuity, Turmoil, and Crisis in the Major Roles of the Women, by Decades, by Adolescent Planful Competence (Life History Sample)

	20s		30s		40s	
	Low PC	High PC	Low PC	High PC	Low PC	High PC
No apparent discontinuity or turmoil	29	36	36	43	29	57
Minor discontinuity or turmoil	7	7	7	36	7	7
No discontinuity but turmoil	14	28	7	7	7	
Discontinuity, no turmoil or crisis	7			7	7	7
Severe discontinuity, crisis	43	29	50	7	50	29
Total (Percentages)	100	100	100	100	100	100

In their 30s we could not discern any differences in the degree of involvement of the women in their marriages or in parenting, their top priorities, even for the women who held jobs outside the home. Those high in planful competence were somewhat more satisfied with their marriages and much more satisfied with their ability to cope with the demands of parenting. As full-time parents, they clearly had an advantage. They also enjoyed somewhat more recreation, though very few were able to involve themselves in substantial recreational activity.

Roughly two-fifths of the women were unhappy about their husbands' lack of availability at home, and for half of them there were serious tensions as a result. The problem was experienced equally by those who had been rated more competent and their less highly rated peers.

The women were far more involved with friends than were the male members of the study. Two-thirds had intimate friends with whom they could share their feelings, mutual aid, and joint activities. There were very few who had only casual friends or who felt cut off; these few were women who had been rated low in adolescent competence and especially in self-confidence. The high-competent group reported greater satisfaction with their friendships in general.

The 40s

By their 40s, some additional members of the high-competent group had entered the labor force, but two-fifths remained out. Three of the twenty-eight women were widowed, and another five were divorced (two for the third or fourth time) during their 40s. The presence of adolescents put a strain on many marriages. Again, however, disruptions and crises occurred more often in the families of the women who had been less competent (see Table 13.1).

Now for the first time a number of women—a fifth in both groups—appeared to be more involved in their occupational role than in their families, and another fifth appeared to be equally involved in job and family. Recall that the women were in their 40s in the 1960s and 1970s, and the climate of gender relations was rapidly changing. Most women expressed satisfaction in their jobs. Indeed, they appeared more enthusiastic than the men (especially the less competent men).

Involvement in parenting had become less intense, despite turmoil with adolescents, but the high competents were much more satisfied with their parenting activities than were those who had been rated lower (85 percent versus 42 percent). Fewer women were at all involved in the church, perhaps as a consequence of their children's nonparticipation. On the other hand, more women were now participating in volunteer activities in the community, especially those rated high in competence. Recreational involvement increased markedly, especially among the women who had been rated less competent in adolescence.

Husbands were somewhat more available to their wives in their 40s, and the husbands' work commitments were less often problematic. Again, most of the women reported several intimate friends and substantial satisfaction with their friendships.

EDUCATIONAL ATTAINMENT
AND OCCUPATIONAL CAREERS

Parental social status had a much stronger influence on the adolescent planful competence of the females than on that of the males in the study. Moreover, very few working-class girls were able to graduate from, or even attend, college. The higher the family's socioeconomic level was, the greater were the girl's intellectual investment, dependability, and, above all, educational attainment.[8] Middle-class girls were not, however, more self-confident than were working-class girls, nor was self-confidence related to educational attainment.

The best predictor of educational attainment was not adolescent planful competence but the family's socioeconomic status followed by the component "dependable" and then by the girl's IQ. Together these explained nearly half the variance in educational attainment (see Table A.12 in Appendix A). Whereas for the males, "intellectual investment" was a more powerful predictor than IQ, it would appear that many very bright girls managed to hide their intellectual interests in the service of gender stereotypes. For girls, IQ was a better predictor of true intellectual investment than were psychologists' ratings.

Women's Careers[9]

Many large-scale studies have documented the various influences on a woman's labor force participation, and a fuller analysis of the careers of the women has been published in a professional journal, so I merely touch on the main themes that are evident in the work histories of the women in our study.[10] Economic need, which fluctuates with marital status, family size, children's ages, and husband's occupational status, is a major factor in any period. Occupational opportunities are also important, and these depend not only on attitudes toward women working and economic conditions in a local area but also on the woman's own occupational skills. The more highly educated she is, the greater is her potential in the labor market. But competing role demands, such as those of wife and mother, may keep a woman at home, especially when the children are young.

Adolescent planful competence was very little related to women's careers. The majority of the young women were oriented to marriage. The higher their competence, the higher was their husbands' occupational status and the less need was there for them to work. Moreover, in an era when children were greatly valued, the higher an adolescent female's rating was on competence, the more children she tended to have.[11] Both her husband's occupational status and the number of her children were among the very highest correlates of low labor force participation.

We obtained the work histories of the women most completely in the 1982 follow-up, but we secured basic data on labor force participation at each of the contacts we had with them. At the first follow-up, in 1957–1958, less than one in seven of the Oakland women was employed as against 30 percent of the younger Guidance Study women. When the Oakland women were age 48, however, the two groups showed similar proportions employed—44 and 43 percent. By the 1982 follow-up, many Oakland women had retired, but nearly two-thirds of the Guidance Study women were employed (Table 13.2).

Roughly two-thirds of both cohorts of women had been briefly employed before marriage. The average duration of employment was just over two years, and only a fourth remained in the labor force more than three years prior to marriage or the start of childbearing. Then most withdrew from the labor force. Of those who resumed working, half came back (usually part-time at first) by age 34. Many were in and out of the labor force repeatedly in the next

Table 13.2.   Proportion of Women in the Labor Force
at Successive Follow-ups

	1958–1959		1969–1970		1981–1983	
	Modal Age	Percentage Employed	Modal Age	Percentage Employed	Modal Age	Percentage Employed
Oakland Growth Study	37	13	48	44	61	31[a]
Guidance Study	30	30	41	43	53	63
Berkeley Growth Study	37[b]	39			53	67

[a]An additional 13 percent had retired
[b]This follow-up took place in 1965–1966.

twenty to thirty years, depending on family circumstances and available opportunities. If a husband was transferred to another location by his employer, his wife almost always had to give up her job and investigate opportunities in the new location.

Roughly two-fifths of the women worked more or less regularly after reentry, with no break over five years. Four percent did not marry and had more or less continuous work histories. Women who started college but did not graduate were less likely to have been employed at all after marriage than were either college graduates or women with only a high school education, and they were much less likely to have worked regularly. At the other extreme, of twelve women with graduate training, nine worked regularly after reentry and two never married. Members of this group were in the labor force 87 percent of the years between completion of education and the last follow-up. Otherwise, the educational groups differed little in the percentage of years they spent in the labor force, ranging from 37 to 42 percent.

I shall report two summary measures of a woman's work involvement, "work attachment" and "percentage of years in the labor force." The latter consists of the percentage of years after completion of her education that a woman was employed up to 1982. "Work attachment" on the other hand, indicates behavioral commitment to the work role as measured by consistency and duration of labor force participation and coherence of career.[12]

Percentage of Years in the Labor Force

Women in the study who were employed for a high proportion of years tended to come from parental families of lower socioeconomic status, to be married to men whose jobs were of somewhat lower skill levels, and, most important, to have fewer children than those who were employed for a lower proportion of years. Educational level was little related to the percentage of years of employment. In part, this was because of the high proportion of years in the labor force on the part of women who had graduate training, and in part it resulted from the countervailing influences of the husband's job level and the wife's educational level. The two tended to go together but to have opposite effects on labor force participation. When these several interrelated factors are controlled statistically, a woman's educational attainment becomes slightly more important as an influence on her labor force participation (a positive one) than either the number of children she had or her parents' socioeconomic status in her childhood (see Table A.13 in Appendix A).

Personality attributes were not important influences on amount of labor force participation, nor was divorce, although divorced women usually reentered the labor force earlier than women in stable marriages. The divorced were more often in and out for short periods. When we examine work attachment—consistency and coherence of work experience—we find a different story.

Work Attachment

The adolescent antecedents and the experiences that were most strongly related to a woman's work attachment were aspects of personality and of how the adolescent had been seen by others. The highest of all correlates was physical attractiveness; the more attractive she had been in adolescence, the less likely she was to have a consistent career of long duration. Attractiveness was part of an interrelated cluster of the Q-sort items descriptive of personality that included "feminine," "conventional," and "self-confident." In general, the girls who scored higher on these attributes were also seen as more knowledgeable of and involved in peer culture and more interested in the opposite sex. Girls who were pretty, feminine, and conventional would in general have been popular in the peer culture and, other things being equal, would have had reason to feel self-confident. They would also have been predominantly oriented toward marriage and family life rather than careers, for they were the prototypes of traditional women forty to fifty years ago.

The other most significant correlate of a woman's labor force participation was her husband's occupational level in the middle years of his career; the higher the husband's occupational level was, the lower was the woman's ultimate work attachment. Divorce was also a negative correlate of a woman's work attachment, largely because the divorced women often remarried and were seldom stably employed. Again, there were many countervailing influences upon the women's work attachment, requiring that we examine the net effects of each attribute when others are controlled for. Table 13.3 shows the net effects when different combinations of variables are

**Table 13.3. Life Course and Personality Predictors of
Women's Work Attachment**

	Zero-Order Correlation	Standardized Regression Coefficients		
		Model 1	Model 2	Model 3
Parents' Socioeconomic Status	-.14	-.14	-.06	
Adolescent IQ	-.11	-.04		
Educational attainment	.08	.40**	.38**	.31**
Husband's occupation, 1970	-.31**	-.37**	-.26*	-.28*
Age at first marriage	.02	-.19	-.09	
Number of children	-.18	-.17	-.10	
Adol. physical attractiveness	-.44**		-.38**	-.36**
Adolescent status seeking	-.33**		-.24*	-.31*
Number of cases		65	65	65
R^2 (Adjusted R^2)		.21 (.13)	.39 (.32)	.38 (.34)

*$p < .05$; **$p < .01$.

examined simultaneously. In the most efficient model, Model 3, adolescent physical attractiveness remains the most potent predictor of a woman's low work attachment, while her educational level is the strongest positive antecedent. However, adolescent status seeking, associated with marriage to a man of high status, remains significant even when husband's occupation is also included and is a significant influence. Thus, two adolescent attributes, coupled with a woman's educational attainment and her husband's occupational level, serve to explain slightly more than a third of the variation in her commitment to an occupation over the rest of her life for this group of women born in the 1920s. Today we would expect a much stronger contribution from her choice in adolescence and much less from her physical attractiveness.

Women's Occupational Attainment

The antecedents of women's occupational attainment for this group of women are quite different from those for the men in the study. Because their parents' socioeconomic status was so important for their educational attainment and because women who had been highly competent adolescents spent less time in the labor force, planful competence was only marginally associated with occupational attainment. Unless the percentage of years in the labor force is entered into the predictive equation, one can explain less than a fourth of the variability in the occupational level the women attained by the time of the last follow-up or their retirement, if that came earlier. But when percentage of years in the labor force is taken into account, adolescent IQ and educational attainment are the primary contributors to attainment, with percentage of years next in importance. (The data are reported in Table A.14 in Appendix A.) These findings are closely in accord with other studies of women's occupational attainment in finding IQ and education as the prime contributors. The addition of percentage of years in the labor force roughly doubles the amount of variability explained and in this respect goes well beyond other attempts to account for a woman's ultimate occupational attainment.

I shall discuss the effects of a woman's occupational involvement on her marital satisfaction and on her personality change over the life course in the next chapter, but here I stress the importance of their occupational experience to many women. We have seen that importance in the life of Alice Neal. For many other women, their job experience marked a turning point in how they saw themselves.

At the time of the 1981 follow-up, we asked women who were employed, "Some people feel that their jobs are the most central feature of their lives. Others feel that their jobs are just a means of earning a living. In what way has your job been important in determining your sense of who and what you are?" This question was asked not only of the original subjects but of the wives of male subjects in the study, yielding a sample of 128 women who had been employed to a substantial degree. Of these women, one-fifth said that their jobs had been the most important element in determining their current sense of who and what they are. Another two-thirds said that the job had been important but not critically so, leaving only 15 percent who saw their occupational involvement as having been relatively unimportant in determining their sense of identity. Their jobs had been particularly important to the women who were college graduates; 36 percent of them cited their jobs as the primary basis for their sense of identity, as contrasted with only

10 percent among women who had not completed college. The college graduates in general occupied jobs of higher status and clearly had been more involved in their jobs once they entered the labor force.

A few examples of the women's responses to the question on identity may give a clearer indication of how their jobs affected their sense of themselves. Alice Neal had answered this question by affirming that her job had been most important and her marriage somewhat less so in determining her sense of identity. She added:

> I think I would have been nothing but a bored housewife, and frantically cleaning the house. I would have been an entirely different person. [*Interviewer:* So it has given you a new dimension, new meaning?] More self-confidence. When you meet as many people as I meet every day, solve as many [problem] situations.

A divorced woman with four children, now remarried and operating a small shop, reported:

> My job used to be the central part of my life. I put my whole being into my job because my husband and I argued a lot and I enjoyed my job more than I did my home. The job made me feel more confident. I bettered myself at my job.

A professional answered the question on identity crisply: "It's it. I *am* a landscape architect." The second most influential aspect of her life was her marriage.

Thus, many women were thinking differently about themselves after being employed outside the home, particularly if they held demanding jobs. They managed to juggle two or three major roles, and their own sense of competence grew in the process. In the next chapter we shall look further at the consequences of occupational involvement for personality change, but the primary focus for us, as for the women born in the 1920s, will be on marriages.

CHAPTER 14

WOMEN'S LIVES:

MARRIAGE AND CHANGING ROLES

Whereas planfully competent males had been preoccupied with the issue of occupational choice and occupational preparation, planfully competent young women tended to see themselves primarily as preparing for marriage, though they often had career interests that they later yielded. When we asked women, in the life history interview, whether in adolescence they had thought about the kind of man they wanted to marry, those who had been planfully competent were likely to have thought in terms of qualities that would make a man a congenial companion and a good father. If their less competent peers had thought at all about the kind of man they wanted to marry, it was more often in terms of appearance, dancing skills, and fun on dates, as Alice Neal and many other peer-oriented girls told us both in adolescence and subsequently. The planfully competent girls tended to hold a different set of values from their less competent peers.

In this chapter, we look at some of the influences on women's marriages, the course of the marriages as they perceived them, and some of the reasons for and consequences of divorce among women in our study group. Then we examine their participation in other activities and roles, such as organizational participation, social activities, recreation, and friendships. Finally, we look at the turning points in women's lives and the extent to which they stayed the same or changed over the adult years.

WOMEN'S MARRIAGES

Whereas 15 percent of the men in the study felt that their parents' marriages had no influences on their own, only 1 percent of the women saw their parents' marriages as irrelevant to their own. On

420

several occasions over the adult years when we asked about parental conflict and how they saw their parents' marriages, we found that women were somewhat more likely to report tension or conflict in the parental marriages than were the men in the study. Daughters tend to be more aware than sons of their mothers' dissatisfactions in marriage, by virtue of much closer mother-daughter communication. In any event, more than a third of the women felt that their parents' marriages were not a good model for what they wanted their own marriages to be. In this respect, there was a substantial difference between those who had been planfully competent and their less competent peers, with only a fourth of the high scorers but fully half of the low scorers seeing their parents' marriages as representing what they wanted to avoid. Most of the planfully competent women saw their parents' marriages as a positive model, though a number also mentioned positive and negative aspects of the parental marriage. The same pattern had emerged when we had asked about parents' marriages twenty-four years earlier. Substantial conflict was reported as characterizing the marriages of parents of the less planfully competent: 42 percent versus 11 percent for the highly competent.

If there had been alcoholism or abusive behavior on the part of their fathers, women had a definite idea of what they wanted to avoid when they married.[1] For example, a woman whose father died when she was age 10 later reported of her parents' marriage: "I don't remember them together. [*Interviewer:* You don't have any memories at all?] A few, but they weren't pleasant. One time that he hit my mother. Other than that it was him drinking." What she derived from her parents' marriage was that she did not want to marry a man who was violent or had a drinking problem. Nevertheless, she did want to marry, and to marry quickly after she finished high school. She said that after high school she had felt "all out there by myself." Her first marriage was to a man older than herself, one that she had qualms about, but, as she said, "I didn't want to [marry him] but I did anyway. It was the thing to do. He was older than I, and he had been around. I really don't know why I married him." She knew at the time that she didn't love him, but she felt that her life would be more complete if she was married. The marriage did not last. Asked about her second marriage, she said: "There's no comparison. I fell madly in love soon after we met. It was romantic and exciting and I knew right away, this was it."

With women as with men, we found that those coming from families broken by divorce, separation, or desertion were themselves much more likely to become divorced: 56 percent as contrasted with 24 percent of those from intact families. Those from homes broken by divorce, separation, or desertion were also far more likely to drop out of the study in their adolescent years, as were those who lost a parent through death. If they stayed in the study, however, those who had lost a parent through death had no higher divorce rate than did those from intact families. Again, then, it is likely that women who continued in the study had more positive experiences than those who dropped out.

Age at Marriage

A few of the girls married at age 17. Two-thirds married between the ages of 18 and 23.[2] Among those who did not plan to attend college, becoming a wife and mother was, after all, the primary goal toward which they had been told they should strive. If they had engaged in necking and petting or in intercourse during high school, sex was a major reason for getting married. Contraception was not readily available to adolescents, and those forms that were most available tended to offer the least protection.

The wife of a study member recalled the period of courtship when, if she and her husband-to-be parked outside the house and necked in the car, her mother would flick the porch light switch on and off. If the daughter did not come into the house then, her mother would come out and yell and stamp her foot. The pair was strongly attracted physically: "And then we got married, because you couldn't sleep together unless you were married." Here the interviewer asked: "You got married because you wanted to sleep together or because you wanted to marry him?" She replied, "It was all the same thing. Nobody slept together unless they were married. There wasn't any question. Not with my mother, there wasn't." But some girls did have sex before they married. Roughly a fourth acknowledged later that they had, and a few married because they were pregnant.

Of the correlates of early marriage, none was stronger than interest in the opposite sex as expressed during the high school years.

Just behind this, and undoubtedly related to it, was age of puberty; the earlier a girl had attained puberty, the more interested the opposite sex was in her. If she was equally interested in the opposite sex, she tended to become less interested in academic achievement, and this often produced tensions within the parental family and rebellious behavior on the part of the adolescent. Girls who were more controlled and responsible in their behavior scored higher on our measure of dependability, and their educational attainment was substantially greater.

When all of these influences are put into a predictive equation so that their interacting effects can be examined, interest in the opposite sex turns out to be most important, with age of puberty second and the senior high school score on dependability coming third. Educational attainment does not add to the amount of variability predicted once dependability is taken into account. Together, these attributes accounted for more than a third of the variability in women's age at marriage (see Table A.15 in Appendix A). More recent studies indicate the importance of hormone levels for a girl's early sexual behavior.[3]

Early marriage was itself one of the strongest predictors of divorce. The reasons were summed up by a divorced wife who had married at age 16. In her late 30s, she commented:

> At 16, what do you know? You're young and suddenly you have babies to care for and, you know, this is what you wanted to do—take care of children—and you cook and wash and clean house and there isn't much left of the day after that and you don't know anything else. How much have you been exposed to?

Once the children were in school, she had taken a job and left a husband who was loud, aggressive, and seldom available when she needed him.

There were a few girls who had not planned to marry. They tended to have a greater sense of autonomy and to want to do things that interested them until someone changed their minds about marriage. One member of the older cohort (she had not been seen at the first adult follow-up and therefore had not been rated on planful competence) noted that getting married was the most important turning point in her life. For her, it really was a change in direction: "I wasn't going to get married. I was planning to grow angora rabbits and to hell with men. I was 26 when I married—lived alone in an apartment until then. [*Interviewer:* What decided you to get married?] I was sick and he got me to the hospital." It developed that *he* had kept asking her, and she finally gave in once he had shown how much he cared for her. For each decade of her life, she reported that her child and her husband were her primary sources of satisfaction. Of her 40s, she reported that satisfaction came from her husband, child, job, and friends. The interviewer askid, "In that order?" "No," she replied, "the whole ball of wax was wonderful." Asked about dissatisfaction in each decade, this woman reported, "None." Husband and wife collaborated and communicated.

For most women, whether they had been eager to marry or not, eventually someone came along to whom they either were strongly attracted or who became so strongly attracted to them that they ultimately acceded to marriage. Most of the women who started college but did not complete it married older classmates or other men they had known, and then they dropped out. Many of them have completed college in their later years, and a few, like Mary Wylie, are still enjoying the role of student.

Why They Married Their Spouses

Most women could think of several reasons for their choosing to marry the man they did marry or for acceding to having been chosen by him. None was more frequently mentioned than exemplary attributes of the person they married, such as his kindness, his sense of humor, his compassionate nature. Nearly three-fourths of the less planfully competent girls mentioned such attributes, as against two-fifths of the more competent. Next in order of mention was the existence of a strong emtional or physical attraction to each other—that attraction called love by many women but fewer men. Those who had been rated above the mean on planful competence were almost twice as likely to report such attraction than their less competent peers (59 percent versus 33 percent). Another difference between the groups was in the importance of a sense of compatibility—similar interests and getting along well together—mentioned by two-fifths of the highs but less than one-fifth of the lows.

Planfully competent women and those less planfully competent did not differ in the proportions who attached considerable importance to a man's ambition or desire for achievement in deciding whom they would marry, but it was only among the less planfully competent that any woman deemed ambition "not important"— and more than a fourth of the less planfully competent gave that response. Alice Neal was one who did, as were several of the women described in the previous chapter.

Women who had been less planfully competent were also almost three times as likely (36 percent versus 14 percent) to mention situational or opportunity factors: pregnancy, not knowing anyone else, or not having been asked by anyone else. Asked if they had been ready for marriage when they had taken that step, one in seven of the less planfully competent reported retrospectively that they had been immature or too young to make a proper decision. None of the planfully competent gave this response. One has a sense, then, that the planfully competent girls were more in command and entered into marriage with more zest and more understanding of what they were doing than did their less competent peers.

In general, it appears that more competent women chose to marry and were chosen by more competent men. We cannot say for certain that the men were more competent in adolescence, but they had attained higher educational and occupational status as of the time of marriage and at each follow-up. A woman's own educational attainment at the time was the most powerful predictor of her husband's occupational level at the first follow-up.[4] Planful competence in senior high school was, of course, a predictor of educational attainment, and it was significantly related to her husband's status but to a lesser degree than her educational attainment. Many women met their husbands-to-be in college. Another significant correlate of the husband's occupational attainment was the socioeconomic status of the woman's parental family. Most marriages brought together persons of roughly equivalent status, except that planfully competent adolescents frequently married spouses from families of somewhat higher status.

In the whole study sample, a woman's physical attractiveness was only slightly associated with her husband's occupational status and at first glance seemed far less important than her educational attainment. It became most important for girls who did not attend college. When we control for the interacting effects of these several influences, two dominate in their effects on the husband's occupational status: the woman's own educational attainment and her physical attractiveness.[5] Educational attainment reflects intelligence, socioeconomic status of the family, and planful competence (especially dependability). That attainment, together with physical attractiveness, accounts for nearly 40 percent of the variability in the occupational status of the men whom the women married. (For the data, see Table A.16 in Appendix A.)

The Marriages in 1958

Our data on the marriages in 1958 were relatively meager. Although the marriage was touched upon in the interview of Oakland study members at several points, the primary emphasis was not on the marriage itself but on the psychological dynamics manifest in the discussion of the parental marriage, the subject's own marriage, and parenting. The coding that was undertaken did reveal one rather startling finding: In 52 percent on the parental families of women who had been rated low on planful competence, there was evidence of either pathology or extreme conflict (or both) in the parental family. This contrasts with only 16 percent of the families in which pathology or conflict (or both) was noted among those rated high on planful competence. Given the relationship of family turmoil to competence, it is hardly surprising that the women who had been rated planfully competent were considerably more favorably oriented toward marriage and more likely to express themselves as very well satisfied in their marriages than were their less competent peers. The number of cases available from this Oakland subsample is relatively small, but quite consistently the competent expressed themselves as better satisfied with almost all aspects of their marriages and families. Overall, roughly one woman in six was significantly dissatisfied with her marriage, and a slightly higher proportion expressed themselves as somewhat dissatisfied with their husbands in regard to the rearing of children. Over half of the women reported that they and their husbands shared equally in decision making within the family, while another fifth reported that husband and wife were each dominant in their own areas. Less than a fifth reported their husbands dominant.

None of the men in our sample had acknowledged that they themselves were dominant in decision making within the family.

The Women as Mothers

By the time we first saw them as adults, the great majority of the women were mothers. More than a fourth of those who had scored low in competence had divorced, and almost all had remarried. Roughly three-fourths of the Oakland women, interviewed at ages 37 to 38, said they preferred the role of wife and mother to that of worker, and only about one in seven was then employed.

Most were highly involved with their children and seemed to feel reasonably adequate, if at times at a loss as parents. Roughly one mother in ten acknowledged more troubling feelings of inadequacy. However, no mother said she felt entirely inadequate in dealing with her children's problems. The question about parenting elicited considerable self-searching on the part of many women. A very competent mother noted:

> At times I think I'm a lousy parent. We do the best that we can—what we believe is the best way of bringing up children. I enjoy my children in spite of difficulties. I have a reasonable amount of patience with them. I think enjoyment of the role of parent is pretty important. I try to offer encouragement.

Most mothers saw themselves as not permissive but also as perhaps less strict than their own parents had been. Those who had been more planfully competent tended to stress discipline and responsibility. As one put it: "All children need discipline and would be bewildered if they didn't have it. The matter of establishing good habits, a good routine of living is the result of discipline." Her formulation is certainly in accord with our findings regarding the antecedents of planful competence. The majority of Oakland study members felt that warm acceptance coupled with firm guidance made for effective parenting, but a third stressed only the qualities of warmth and acceptance. Half saw themselves as somewhat like their own parents in their child rearing efforts, but the rest split equally between those coded "very like their parents" and those coded "unlike their parents." Nearly all the mothers said they wanted their children to be self-reliant, to have a strong sense of right and wrong, and to be happy, but as we have seen in the families described in detail, their ways of dealing with the children were not always recognizably linked to these objectives.

The Marriages in 1970

In 1970 we had much more adequate data on the marital relationship, including the two sets of ratings earlier reported—judges' ratings and self-ratings. As in the case of the men's data, there was relatively little relationship between women's ratings of marital satisfaction in 1970 and the way they had rated themselves in 1958. Additional divorces had taken place, though in the case of women, relatively more of the divorces that occured during their late 30s and 40s were second or even third divorces. Marriages of women who had been planfully competent were rated significantly higher by judges and were rated higher by the women themselves than were those of their less competent peers. Most women reported that in general they and their husbands spent most of their leisure-time activities together, and here there was little difference between the competent and the less competent. Roughly 50 percent of the women felt that their marriages had grown closer over the years, with less than a fifth feeling that theirs had become less close. Although the competent were favored somewhat in this comparison, the differences were not great. Nearly two-thirds of the women felt that their husbands had changed since their marriage, and for the most part, the changes appeared to be favorable, because women who said their husbands had changed rated their marriages more positively than others.

Nearly half the women said they had at one time considered divorce or separation, but a fourth felt that the problem had been resolved. For more than a third of those who had scored low on adolescent planful competence, however, the problem had not been resolved; they were still considering the option. Among the planfully competent, more than two-thirds had never thought that their marriages would not work out—almost twice the proportion who gave this report among the less competent.

The contemplation of divorce undoubtedly would have been far more frequent if members of this generation of men and women had had fewer children. (They averaged roughly three.) For example, a woman who rated her marital satisfaction quite low responded in the following way to the question of whether she had ever worried whether her marriage would work out:

> Well, yes and no. I feel where children are involved I really would never consider divorce. I would feel that there was enough good in the marriage to try to work things out, and I think with five children and a good father, that I would never seriously consider divorce. There have been uncomfortable times in the marriage.

There were problems with several of the children that she saw as "reflections of our unresolved conflicts," but keeping the family intact was paramount in her thinking.

Asked to rank the importance of five aspects of marriage, women ranked them in almost the same order as men, except for their top choice, which was "mutual understanding of each other's problems and feelings," ranked first or second by 68 percent of the women as against 57 percent of the men. Next, ranked first or second by 60 percent of both men and women, came "companionship, in husband and wife doing things together." "Being a parent," "sexual relations between husband and wife," and "security and comfort of family life" followed, ranked in that order by both men and women. "Being a parent" was chosen by more women, while sexual relations and the comfort of family life were chosen by relatively more men, but the latter two still ranked below "being a parent" for men.

There was little discussion of the sexual relationship unless the study member brought it up, but there was a question about "problems in the sexual relationship" and which partner was more interested. While in general men were said to be more interested, and this had been the predominant response of male study members, a number of the women noted that their husbands no longer seemed as much interested in sex as they themselves were. Perhaps the biggest difference between competent and less competent women came in their reports of problems in their sexual relationship with their husbands. Eighty-seven percent of the planfully competent women reported that there had been no significant problems, as against only fifty percent of the women who had been less planfully competent.

On balance then, most marriages that had survived into the 40s were reasonably satisfying, but certain problems were reported with some frequency. Among them was the problem of the husband who seemed not interested in anything but sitting around at home while his wife wished to get out of the house and, often related, the husband who could not or would not communicate with his wife. One wife reported: "Conflicts get handled by not being handled. He won't fight about it. I mean, he won't discuss it. He makes it very clear what he thinks, and you could beat your head into the ground and he would feel that he's right." This wife and many others were most distressed by their husbands' inability to talk about feelings. This was a problem in the family of Judith, the planfully competent woman whose life was briefly described in the previous chapter. Women often had such complaints when their husbands were in highly technical occupations (engineering and science, for example) in which they had relatively superficial relationships with other persons. Men who chose such occupations had tended to be less outgoing and less introspective.

Parenthood

In 1970, many of the study members had adolescent or young adult offspring. The Vietnam War was winding down, but it was still a major issue, especially for the better educated adolescents and young adults who saw the attempt by Western nations to control Vietnam as imperialist and racist. Domestic turmoil over the war was not merely evident on the political scene; it destroyed tranquility in many families. So did drug use and the younger generation's freer sexuality.

When there was strife, mothers were usually the peacekeepers. Stuart Campbell and his sons might shout at each other, each knowing he had the truth on his side, but it was Susan Campbell who had to try to calm down the rhetoric. In that family, the members respected each other, so while there was much heat, there was little rancor. How to handle the rebellious adolescent was a major issue between parents in some families, especially in the Guidance Study, as in the Neal family. Fully half the Guidance Study mothers mentioned that the major area of disagreement with their husbands was over dealing with the children. We have seen how both

Alice Neal and Beth Green struggled with the problem of their daughters' sexual freedom. Very few parents escaped the tensions that generational change had brought about. Being a parent in 1970 was a difficult role to perform.

Mothers were more likely than fathers to say they enjoyed their children at all ages, but if they had a preference, it was for the preschool or elementary school age. The period seen as the most difficult ranged from junior high to after high school. No mother reported herself sorry that she had had children, but the independence of the adolescent offspring, their lack of respect for parents, and their lack of discipline were a source of perplexity and discouragement. Nearly half the women acknowledged that they were fairly often angry with their children, but two-thirds nevertheless saw themselves as basically affectionate toward the children. They saw their husbands as somewhat more often angry and less affectionate. Women who had been planfully competent more often approved of their husbands as parents, and their higher rating of family harmony was reflected in the children's positive perceptions of their parents in questionnaires administered and interviews carried out with the children in 1970.

The Marriages in 1982

By 1982, another tenth of the women had divorced and a like number had been widowed. Less than three-fifths of the women who remained in the study were married to their first husbands, while nearly a fifth were in their second, third, or fourth marriage. Roughly one in twelve (none among the planfully competent) had married three or more times. Only one of the planfully competent women had remained unmarried, and nearly two-thirds were still in their first marriage, in contrast to less than half of their less competent peers. The distribution by marital status for those for whom adolescent planful competence had been assessed and the total sample of female study members is shown in Table 14.1.

Whereas men's self-ratings of their marriages went up somewhat between 1970 and 1982, the average of women's ratings stayed almost exactly the same. Moreover, women who rated themselves satisfied in 1970 tended to rate themselves satisfied in 1982. The relationship between periods was modest but suggested substan-

Table 14.1.   Marital Status of Female Study Members in 1982, by
Adolescent Planful Competence Level (Percentages)

	High Competence	Low Competence	Total
Currently married to first husband	64	44	57
Married to different husband	14	31	19
Divorced or separated, not remarried	5	14	12
Widowed, not remarried	15	8	9
Never married	3	4	4
Total	101	101	101
(Number of subjects)	(37)	(38)	(129)

Note: Percentages add up to more than 100 because of rounding.

tially greater continuity in women's assessments of their marriages. Women who were well satisfied with their marriages indicated that they felt their husbands were accepting of them as persons. Planfully competent women were six times as likely as their less competent peers to "strongly agree" with the statement, "My husband brings out the best in me." To a somewhat lesser degree, satisfied women—and planfully competent ones—reported that they felt there was a good deal of reciprocity in the relationship—for example, that their husband did not expect more of them than the husbands themselves were willing to give.

Some of the women who had previously acknowledged considering divorce had actually divorced, and a few others apparently were now sufficiently satisfied in their marriages to forget that they had told us they had once thought of divorce as a way out. Only a sixth of the planfully competent said they had ever considered divorce as against more than a third of the less planfully competent.

Nearly a third of those who had been less planfully competent said their mutual satisfaction had decreased in recent years, but fewer than 10 percent of the planfully competent reported a decrease in satisfaction, and nearly three-fifths reported an increase in satisfaction. The planfully competent women, like the planfully competent men, again reported in the interview a higher level of satisfaction with the sexual relationship than did their less planfully competent peers, though the difference between the groups was less marked for the women than for the men. More than half the planfully competent reported that sex was as important to themselves as to their husbands, but less than a fourth of the women who had scored low in adolescence reported themselves equally interested in sex. Thus, there is again evidence of a greater zest for a full marital relationship on the part of those who had planfully competent adolescents forty years earlier. On the questionnaire inquiry as to the frequency of sex, 70 percent of these women reported at least weekly intercourse as contrasted with only 30 percent of the women who had been less planfully competent. However, when we compare women classified by competence scores based on 1982 assessments, the percentages differ much less. Roughly half of each group reported at least weekly intercourse, but among the less competent in 1982, more than a fourth mentioned no intercourse in the previous 6 months.

How could it be that an orientation or set of attributes assessed more than thirty-five years earlier predicts sexual satisfaction in later maturity better than the same attributes assessed currently? One possible reason relates to the study members' early attitudes toward sex. The planfully competent girls were more focused on responsible preparation for adulthood. Responsibility ruled out casual sex, but it in no way ruled out the full enjoyment of sex in marriage. Many of the women (and men) who were precocious and engaged in casual sex never came to understand the deeply satisfying quality of sexual love between two partners whose intimacy extends into all aspects of their lives. Those who became bored with sex in their 40s and 50s had probably never known such an experience. Another possible reason is that the planfully competent adolescents had married more competent men.

The Empty Nest

At the time of our first follow-up, most of the study members had young children, though some of the Oakland cohort's offspring were entering adolescence. Eleven years later, many children of Oakland study members had left the parental home, and others were away at college. By 1982 almost all the children had left home. We had expected that women who had not been employed would find the departure of their children difficult to adapt to. A few did, but more seemed relieved that they had more freedom. We did not ask specifically how they felt about the children's leaving, but the topic often came up in the interviews. Only two women mentioned the children's leaving as representing a turning point in their lives.

Some women noted that their relationship with their husbands went more smoothly after the children left home. The couple could be freer sexually than they had been at home for many years. Mothers still talked frequently over the telephone with their children, especially their daughters, and most were involved with grandchildren if the children lived nearby.

Menopause

In the 1982 follow-up when the study members were all over age 53, women were asked about their experience with menopause in a questionnaire relating to health. Roughly a fifth of the women in the younger group were still going through this physiological stage, but all of the older women were well beyond it. A full third of the women reported that they had had hysterectomies. The average age of menopause in the study population was 48, with the range running from 34 to 54.

Among those who had experienced menopause or were in the process, very few—just 8 percent—had found that it caused much pain or discomfort, while 36 percent reported no pain or discomfort at all. In all, two-thirds of the women found it caused no more than "a little" discomfort. Some women who had passed beyond this stage commented in the clinical interviews that they enjoyed sex a good deal more once the fear of pregnancy was past. As in studies that have focused specifically on this topic, our data support the view that most women do not regard menopause as a major problem or as a definition that they are no longer sexually attractive.[6]

The Marriages in 1990

By 1990, roughly one-fifth of the women had been widowed, and most widows were living alone. About 5 percent of the sample had a child, grandchild, or friend living with them in their own residences.

The questionnaire sent out in 1990 to all study members for whom we had current addresses was most often returned by the best educated and most competent members. Relatively fewer members from working-class families returned the questionnaire. This bias resulted in a marked increase in the level of marital satisfaction reported by the members, because the planfully competent women (more often from middle-class families) had consistently rated their marriages substantially higher than did their less competent peers. For the women who did respond, most rated their marital satisfaction the same or slightly higher than they had eight years earlier. As with male subjects, there was a much higher degree of consistency than ever before. Moreover, to the extent that questionnaires were received (in separate envelopes) from both husband and wife, agreement was substantial; the coefficient of correlation was .67.

Women who rated their marriages "very happy" to "nearly perfect" again saw their husbands as highly accepting of them and felt that their husbands expected no more of them than the husbands were willing to give. There was a fairly strong relationship between the acceptance scale scores of wives and husbands but a much weaker relationship between the reciprocity scales of husbands and wives, suggesting that husbands and wives perceived their own behavior and their spouses' quite differently. Items on the reciprocity scale related to whether the spouse "acts as if he/she were the only important person in the family" or "insists on having his/her own way." Women who rated their husbands low on acceptance and reciprocity were much less satisfied. They frequently expressed their dissatisfaction in the portions of the questionnaire that asked for comments.

No other aspect of their lives had as much influence on their reports of life satisfaction as did their feelings about their husbands and the relationship they had with them. When asked, "What is the best thing in your life?" more than a fourth of the women wrote in "my husband," and another third wrote "my family," presumably meaning husband and children. On the other hand, when asked, "What is the least satisfying thing in your life?" one woman in seven named her relationship with her husband. This response was most often given by women who had not been planfully competent (and who had tended to marry less competent men).

With many husbands retired and therefore at home much of the time, the marital relationship was put to a different kind of test. When it was functioning smoothly and rated highly, everything else seemed to go well, and most women, if in good health, checked that they felt enthusiastic about life.

Women Who Divorced

For many women, divorce was an escape from a very unpleasant relationship. It often represented a sign of health, even if it suggested that the marriage had represented a mistake in judgment. Some women made such mistakes repeatedly; they married men who exploited and abused them. The most common reason for divorce, however, appears to have been marriage before the young woman was ready for it. Repeatedly we heard statements like this one:

> [After high school] I was anxious to be married and start a home of my own, because one thing my parents did not believe in was education for girls. . . . And one of my friends was getting married, and I thought, well, maybe this is the answer. And the fellow I married was just about in the same position. So we met and got along just fine and married. I think we both found out that we weren't what we had thought we were.

He was even more immature than she was, and he was unable to settle down, so she secured the divorce. Fortunately, there were no children. She married again a couple of years later and had a happy second marriage and several children, as well as a job that enhanced her feelings of competence. This woman, like so many others who married before they knew what they were doing, had scored in the lowest fifth on adolescent planful competence. In 1982 she scored above average on the competence index.

The strongest antecedents of divorce were high interest in the opposite sex while in senior high school, early marriage, and a low score on the component "dependable" when in senior high. Planful competence was a predictor, but the single component "dependable" was more powerful than the index itself. Neither self-confidence nor intellectual investment was significantly related to divorce. Together, three attributes—interest in the opposite sex, early marriage, and dependability—accounted for something over one-fifth of the probability that a woman would become divorced by her middle years, with almost all of the influence coming from "dependable." (See Table A.17 in Appendix A.) Thus, the contribution to divorce of each partner's attributes was considerable, but a major factor in the probability of divorce was the compatibility of the attributes of both spouses and the values, religious or moral, that they held.

Women who had three or more divorces tended to be extremely rebellious and/or to have very low self-esteem. They tended to have been pampered by their fathers and in conflict with their mothers, and overwhelmingly they came from families in which pathology and conflict were manifest.

Highly competent women who divorced were much less likely to remarry unless they were quite young at the time of their divorce. No woman who had been above the man on the component "dependable" married more than twice. This is not to say that competent women may not have multiple marriages. Men and women much in the public eye, especially creative persons whose occupations entail much traveling and a great diversity of personal contacts, are far more likely to find themselves intrigued by new relationships and to divorce. But most of the women born in the 1920s did not have such temptations or opportunities. Very few divorced because of a new love interest unless there was serious trouble in their initial marriage.

Several divorces were reported to have come about when the wife realized she "did not want to spend the rest of my life with this man" and courageously took the step to establish a life of her own. Sometimes it required the contrast with a more satisfying relationship to precipitate consideration of an alternative to an unsatisfying marriage (a theme beautifully depicted in the movie *The Wash*) and also exemplified by this reported turning point:

> The first time I really took a step that was totaly different was when I started having an affair, when I was in my early 30s. My marriage was turning out not to be the way I wanted it to be. I met this man who thought I was terrific. We started meeting at lunch and it drifted into a full-fledged affair. It lasted for 15 years.

Finally taking stock after participating in an encounter group program, she decided to leave her husband, and when we last saw her she was relishing living by herself in an apartment, not yet divorced but on the way.

OTHER ROLES AND ACTIVITIES

Women who were in the labor force and were also mothers, as most were, had limited recreation time until the children were well along in high school. Family outings on weekends and visiting with friends and relatives were among their chief sources of enjoyment. So was reading, when they had spare time, and three-fourths of the women reported that they read something daily and with considerable enjoyment. Roughly a third played a musical instrument or sang, and those who did took considerable pleasure from this pastime, though they might get to do so only once a week.

Nothing surpassed going out to dinner as a source of pleasure in the reports women gave us in their 40s, though for most women this was a somewhat infrequent occurrence. Their husbands usually had two days off from work, but the wife who prepared the family dinner and other meals seven days a week had no respite. Less than a third said they went out for dinner as often as once a week. The frequency of such activities obviously depended largely on family income, and since planfully competent girls had married men who became more successful, they benefited in being able to participate in activities that required sizable expenditures.

Only about a third went to concerts, theater, opera, or museums as often as once a month, but these were a source of much greater enjoyment than the more frequent television that almost everyone watched and the movies they attended. A third of the women engaged in crafts and hobbies—painting, knitting, gardening, and a wide variety of types of collecting—at least weekly. Thus, in their early 40s, when most still had children at home, they engaged largely in activities that they could carry on at home.

Once the children had left home, a number of women enrolled in college or in adult education classes, taking art classes, learning languages, or working for the degrees they had not earned before marriage. More of them entered the labor force.

Women's Religious Participation and Beliefs

When interviewed in 1958, nearly half the Oakland men had said they had no religious affiliation, whereas more than three-fourths of the women mentioned at least a nominal placement of themselves as Protestant, Catholic, or Jewish. Protestants outnumbered all other denominations by two to one. More than half the women reported that they attended church at least twice a month but that their husbands went to church less often. A third of the women were classified as "very religious" and another half as "moderately religious," leaving only one in six indifferent or negative (as contrasted with two-fifths of the male study members). However, the wives ascribed much greater devoutness to their husbands than the study males claimed.

A dozen years later, only about half as many said they were attending church regularly, yet nearly two-thirds expressed belief in a traditional Judeo-Christian concept of God. Only a fourth, however, felt at all certain there was an afterlife. Half seemed doubtful that there was, differing little from the male study members in this respect. Particularly when one spouse was Catholic or Jewish and the other Protestant, there was a tendency for at least one member of the pair to be relatively nonreligious. If both were fervently religious, they would have been less likely to marry outside their own denomination. We have seen how Kathleen Schulz maintained her strong religious involvement while her husband did not, and religion did not become a major issue where their children were concerned.

Some persons who had been quite religious in their earlier years became less so, like Stuart Campbell. Others, like his wife, found religion in their adult years. Women who did so tended to become strongly involved as members of church congregations and to take great comfort and satisfaction in their feeling of a personal relationship with their God. As with the men, the more competent women were somewhat more likely to have a religious affiliation and involvement.

Stuart Campbell's wife perhaps best expressed how several women felt about their having become believers in a religious tradition: "I've become a Christian, and life is just wildly interesting. It's an opening to a great breadth of experience, youthfulness and excitement."

Political and Community Activities

Although in adolescence boys had been more interested in politics than girls, it was the women in our study who were more likely to take part in activities in support of political issues and candidates. The women more often reported that they circulated and signed petitions, served as poll watchers, and in general volunteered their time. It was obviously easier for them to devote their time to such activities if they were not employed full time, and it appears that a fourth to a third of the women became politically involved on occasion. A third of the women regarded themselves as more liberal than their husbands and more liberal than they themselves had been at age 21. Only a few were more conservative than their husbands. Nevertheless, two-thirds said they were more conservative than their children (and their children agreed, in their questionnaire responses).

We did not ask about participation in PTAs or other educational and community service activities except on a questionnaire in 1970, but many women represented the family in relation to their children's schools. Many others served as den mothers for Cub Scouts or Brownies. Above all, the mother of several children became the family chauffeur, taking the children to dancing lessons, gym, music lessons, and the dozens of other places that preadolescent children go to. When the offspring were old enough to drive themselves, there was relief but also a new source of worry: "Will they come home safely?"

Friendships

Women were twice as likely as men to report friendships as highly important to them in their 40s. About three-fifths said their friendships were important or very important. The proportion reporting various activities with friends was not, however, much greater than for men. As in the case of men, planfully competent women reported friends to be slightly less important. They did somewhat fewer things with friends and more with families. The reason for the difference was that divorced and widowed women who had not remarried were substantially more likely to turn to friends for emotional support, as were women who found it difficult or impossible to confide in their husbands. Thus Mary Wylie, widowed, had answered when asked how important friends were: "Very, very important. I just spill over to them very easily, and I realize that I need it." Another widow, who had served in the Women's Naval Reserve (WAVES) in World War II, and for whom friends were very important reported: "I have kept in touch with my WAVE friends and our former neighbors. Have made trips and been visited by WAVE officer friends. . . . Our WAVE group has every volunteer area covered in senior programs." For her, friends are the essence of an active, fulfilling life.

If women do not report an even greater margin of difference in the importance of friends, compared to men, I believe it is because they tend to refer to much deeper relationships than do men. Men only occasionally report confiding intimate details of their lives to other men. Many women appear to take for granted that that is precisely what one does with a close friend. As Carol Gilligan and Deborah Tannen have so well documented, women work above all to preserve smooth relationships, while men more often seek to attain their ends with less regard for their relationships with others.[7]

WHAT IF ONE HAD ANOTHER CHANCE ?

"If you could live your life over again, would you change any of the decisions or choices you made regarding education, marriage, having children or employment?" This question was posed (only to women) in the 1982 interview, at the end of a set of questions on the women's employment experience. In their 50s and early 60s, most women would not change very many of their choices, even when some of them had not turned out well. For example, most said they would not change their marital choice, though a fourth (regardless of level of planful competence) wished they had waited until they were somewhat older. Only one woman in forty of those who had children wished she had not, while twice that proportion among those who did not have children were sorry that they had not. A fourth would have changed the number (mostly opting for more) and an equal proportion the spacing of their children.

The major changes they would make had to do with education and employment. Those who had not graduated from college most often expressed regret that they had not continued with their education; only one-fourth said they were satisfied with their education.

Less expected was the response of nearly two-fifths of the college-educated women who wished they had had training or education relevant to an occupational field or profession. Once they had discovered what they were capable of, they began to see the possibilities that had not been envisioned earlier in life. Planfully competent women were somewhat better satisfied, as befitted their greater educational attainment.

Women who had not reentered the labor force after marriage were almost equally divided between choosing the same dedication to family again and opting for a career after children were grown. Among those who had reentered the labor force and been employed for some years, most were either satisfied or wished they had started to work earlier or had worked longer. In other words, far more women would now choose some kind of occupational career in addition to raising a family. The planfully competent and the less competent differed little in this respect.

TURNING POINTS IN WOMEN'S LIVES

The turning points in women's lives, like those in men's lives, related most often to marriage and employment, but they had somewhat different meanings. Again, many of the turning points were expected role transitions—leaving the parental home to take a job, marrying, having children, and reentering the labor force when the children were older—but they more often appear to have made a difference in a woman's sense of identity.

When asked in the life history interview to elaborate on the somewhat superficial questioning about turning points that had taken place two years before, roughly half the women mentioned events or circumstances connected with employment. For some, their initial employment was an affirmation of their autonomy. For example, one woman's turning points were "graduating from high school and going to business school and getting a job in San Francisco. I felt like I was a person on my own." Her parents had discouraged her from going to college or taking nursing training, "so the next best was business. My mother also discouraged my interest in math, but later I found I was good at it." She went from being an unconfident, submissive, not intellectually challenged adolescent to a much more competent woman.

More often the employment-related turning points were consitituted by reentry into the labor force once the children were old enough to be somewhat responsible for themselves. Three-fourths of the women were in their 30s and 40s. Many other mothers who did not enter the labor force agonized over whether they should. The decision was especially difficult for women who were college graduates but were untrained for any specific occupation. Most did not have to work—their husbands occupied upper-level jobs—yet many felt they ought to make use of their education. Some engaged in volunteer activities. Others turned to painting, music, or a variety of hobbies.

One of the planfully competent women affords a good example of an unexpected turning point in returning to work when several of her children were in private colleges, putting considerable pressure on family income. She was ambivalent about going back but had a chance to take an administrative position and decided to do so:

> I felt I could and it would be OK to do so and I'd work a few years and help tide us over this period. . . . It was sort of an ego trip to think I could go back to work . . . and it was just totally amazing to me that I could do this after being home. I had been a scout leader and PTA president and such things, but never on this gradiose scale.

The "scale" was becoming president of a state association in her field of work and "flying places at somebody else's expense." She commented that she had had a profession but not a career, having raised a large family.

Most women mentioned marriage as a turning point. It meant a much greater change in their daily lives than it did for men, especially after the birth of children. It may be recalled that 92 percent of the women had children—most more than one. Marriage meant a new identity, a new set of responsibilities, although very few women mentioned this aspect of taking on a new name as well as a new way of life. There were some women who had not expected to marry, and for them marriage was truly a turning around of their lives. Far more often, marriage and parenthood was a turning point in the sense of entry into a new phase of life, whether envisioned accurately or not. Sometimes a first marriage had not worked out, and it was the second marriage that was the real turning point, because, as one woman said, "Our life together has been just great."

Few men mentioned a geographical move as a turning point, but a third of the women did, and often the move was a source of major disruption in their lives. Karl Schulz's wife noted how difficult it was to leave all her friends and relatives on the East Coast when she married a Californian and settled in a community where she knew no one but her husband. A low point in Mary Wylie's early married live was the move to a new area just as she was about to have another child. Judith Judd found her husband's transfer to the Midwest a jarring experience. If it was difficult for women who cared for their families, it was especially so for women who had satisfying jobs they had to give up. At least a couple of them did not give up their jobs; their turning point was a divorce from a husband who made the move without them.

Occasionally a move could be an enriching experience, as it was to a study member's wife from a small northeastern town:

> When I graduated from high school I went to college in New York City. I had a real learning process. [My home town] was a very backward society and there was a lot of racial prejudice there. New York had so much to offer. I found out that I had options.

Marriage cut short her exploration of those options, but once her children were well along, she went to graduate school, received a professional degree, and has been practicing her profession.

On occasion, events that at first seemed shattering turned out to have positive consequences, and this seemed more often so with women than with men. Having to deal with a very difficult problem gave a sense of strength and a new perception of possibilities in future living. These were true turning points. Consider the response of a study member's wife who reported that she had been on the verge of suicide:

> When I was 23 I got pregnant without being married, and that was the big turning point in my life. I thought life would end and that when I was six months pregnant I would commit suicide. But I never had the courage to do it. After the child was born, it actually turned to the best. My values changed completely.

Her aim previously had been to be "independent and free and

never get married." Subsequently she married one of the most competent men in the study, and they have both been very happy.

Another study member discovered that she had breast cancer not long after her husband had died:

> That day, 14 years ago, was a low and a turning point for me. It seemed unfair at the time after [husband's] death. Looking back, it was, as he might have put it, a "blessing in disguise" for it motivated me as nothing else had done to start living again.

Even a husband's severe depression became a test that revealed strengths not previously realized: "It strengthened my faith, which I always had. It gave me an opportunity to see that I could handle something really serious." Her husband's recovery and subsequent enjoyment of their life together made the illness a turning point for him as well.

For at least two women who had been acknowledged alcoholics, the great turning point was when they were able to give up their addiction. As one put it: "When I stopped drinking. It didn't all happen at once, but I haven't had any [alcohol] for six years. My life has been different since then." It had been a very sad life. Raised by devout fundamentalists who objected to dancing, lipstick, cigarettes, and many other activities of her peers, she had always felt inferior. Although not overtly rebellious, she had tried to be like the other girls when away from home by wearing lipstick and smoking. She married a man who drank, but he could control his drinking, and she could not. She lost her child (to an illness not connected with her drinking), and the alcohol problem became more acute. Ultimately her husband left her. After more than two decades of alcoholism she joined AA and found in its social supports and religion the strength to stop drinking.

PERSONALITY CHANGE THROUGH THE ADULT YEARS

On the average, women show about the same degree of personality resemblance over the life course as do men, which is to say that they show only a little. When one compares their personality profiles at successive periods, one finds much change from adolescence to their 30s and then greater stability in the middle years,

Table 14.2. Mean Personality Resemblance from Period to Period
and Correlation of Individuals' Resemblance with Adolescent
Planful Competence

	Mean Personality Resemblance[a]	Correlation with Planful Competence
Senior high–1958	.34***	.56***
1958–1970	.46***	.25*
1970–1982	.53***	.41***
Senior high–1970	.29**	.67***
Senior high–1982	.28**	.53***

*$p < .05$; **$p < .01$; ***$p < .001$.

[a]Perfect resemblance would be 1.00; no resemblance, .00.

again similar to the findings for men (Table 14.2). The respects in
which women change much and in which they change relatively little are quite different from the findings for men, but again it is the
most planfully competent who change least and the least competent who change most.

When ranked by adolescent planful competence, the median resemblance score (coefficient of correlation) in the top third of
women over the forty or so years beyond high school was .46, while
in the lowest third, the average resemblance was .18. In their adult
years, most of the women who had been lowest in planful competence gained greatly in self-confidence, intellectual investment, and
warmth, while becoming less assertive. The women who were rated
most planfully competent became more outgoing but were seen as
somewhat less dependable in later adulthood than they had been
(as were the men), though they still were rated highest in dependability. In the later years, then, differences between the ulitmate
adult personality profiles of women who had scored high or low on
planful competence had diminished somewhat more than in the
case of men.

There was much less stability in the three components of competence beyond high school than we noted for the men. Moreover,
while for men the overall index of competence showed more stability than the individual components, the opposite was true for
women. The components changed in different directions; they did

**Table 14.3. Continuity in Women's Competence Ratings and Other Personality
Components, Selected Periods
(Correlation Coefficients for Constant Sample)**

	Junior High to	Senior High to:	
	Senior High	Early Adulthood	Later Maturity
Index of planful competence	.65	.31	.32
Self-confident	.51	.34	.39
Intellectually invested	.66	.45	.34
Dependable	.56	.38	.22
Other personality components			
Assertive/submissive	.52	.60	.38
Outgoing/aloof	.55	.45	.45
Warm/hostile	.55	.37	.11

not cohere as an index to the extent that they did for men.
Whereas girls who scored high on dependability in senior high
were seen as significantly above the mean on "warm" and below the
mean on "outgoing" and "assertive," by their later adult years they
were about exactly average on "warm" and "outgoing" but well
above the mean on "assertiveness." (See Table A.1 in Appendix A
for the correlations between the components in senior high school
and in 1982.) The greatest changes over the years were in the ratings of "dependable" and "warm," largely as a result of a conver-
gence of most women at higher levels (Table 14.3).

At each follow-up in the adult years, planfully competent adolescents differed from their lower-rated peers on a number of scales of
the California Psychological Inventory (CPI). The CPI provides an
independent source of validation of the hypothesis about planful
competence, since it does not require an interviewer or raters and
therefore avoids the possibility of judges' ratings being biased by
virtue of the superior socioeconomic status of the more planfully
competent.

Although the differences between the high and low groups on
the various components of personality had decreased by virtue of
the maturing of the low scorers, those who had been planfully com-

petent in adolescence were classified on the CPI in 1958 as more responsible, as superior in achieving both by conformance and by independence, as more intellectually efficient, and as more psychologically minded that their less planfully competent peers.[8] Moreover, most of the scales showed even greater differences in 1982, when the study members were in their 50s and 60s, than they had shown twenty-four years earlier.

The correlations between adolescent planful competence and personality resemblance at later periods were lower for women than for men, but they remained substantial, accounting for roughly a third of the greater resemblance of the planfully competent (shown in Table 14.2). There was considerable variation from period to period, as might be expected in view of the finding by Peskin and Livson that the salience of particular aspects of personality at a given time depends on the demands of the period.[9] In the early adult years, when women were focused on the care of small children and marital adaptations, Peskin and Livson proposed they were carrying out the activities for which their adolescent and socialization had presumably prepared them. Once the children had gotten well along in school, the women became more focused on achieving a greater sense of autonomy and a somewhat different personal identity, one that would give rein to tendencies long kept in check by maternal concerns.

There were several kinds of experiences intervening between adolescence and the time when they were first seen as adults that appear to have led to personality change. Women who were divorced by the time of the first follow-up showed significantly less resemblance than would be expected, even when their initial (lower) level of planful competence was taken into account. And women who were in the labor force most consistently showed different patterns of personality change over the adult years than those who remained full-time wives and mothers. High lifetime labor force participation significantly increased women's self-confidence, assertiveness, and intellectual investedness when compared with those having low labor force participation.[10]

As they moved along in the middle years, women became more outgoing and warm (or prosocial) than they had appeared early in adulthood. The components "self-confident," "outgoing," and "warm," as assessed in high school, take on increased importance as predictors of personality resemblance. Planful competence remains important, but when "outgoing" and "warm" are added to the predictive equation, along with whether a woman has been divorced, they account for more than half the variation in women's personality resemblance from adolescence to the 1970 and 1982 follow-ups. (See Table A.18 in Appendix A for the regression coefficients.) Divorce clearly caused personality change, which showed up most strongly in the initial period, during which most of the divorces took place, but the effect of divorce on personality resemblance was still evident in 1982. Being relatively outgoing and warm in adolescence were not in themselves as strong predictors of resemblance as planful competence, but when paired with planful competence, these two components ultimately contributed strongly to the prediction of who would show high personality resemblance and who would show much less resemblance—or, in less careful terminology, more stability of personality over the life course. Labor force participation also had an effect, but for the whole sample, it did not reach statistical significance. To have been planfully competent, outgoing, and warm (that is, to have a prosocial orientation toward others) in adolescence and to have remained in an intact marriage over the adult years was to retain to a large extent the personality profile one had in adolescence. Many women who had not possessed these attributes changed in the direction of acquiring them by later adulthood; hence, they were the ones who changed most.

Planful Competence and Psychological Health

In adulthood, for women as for men, the summary score or ranking that members received on the scale of psychological health developed by Livson and Peskin was very similar to the ranking they received on the index of competence.[11] Indeed, for the adult women the correlation between scores on the two measures in consistently above .8 and above .9 in later maturity. Thus, the index of competence (the same items and weightings used in adolescence but scored as the person was rated in adulthood) and the measure of psychological health are essentially the same in the middle and later years. Insofar as high scorers differ, it is in the planfully competent being less rebellious, unpredictable, and interested in the opposite sex and more cheerful, protective, and likely to arouse liking.

The two measures had quite different meanings in adolescence, however, though even then the correlation was substantial. The measure of psychological health was highly related to the components "self-confident" and "intellectually invested" and much less related to "dependability." As a consequence, the index of psychological health in adolescence was not a strong predictor of educational or occupational attainment, for which dependability was an important prerequisite, nor did it predict personality resemblance between adolescence and the initial follow-up nearly as well as planful competence. Beyond the first follow-up, however, the measure of psychological health was as good as or better than planful competence alone in predicting women's personality change or resemblance. The measure of psychological health gave greater weight to being outgoing and self-confident, and this was the direction in which women changed. (In adolescence, both planful competence and psychological health went with a high score on the "warm versus hostile" component.)

The coalescing of competence and psychological health in the later years might well have been expected, but the level of agreement between these two totally dissimilar measures, devised to serve quite different objectives, still came as a surprise.

Recollections of Satisfaction, Dissatisfaction, and Life Crises

As they looked back at the earlier decades of their lives, both in filling out life history charts and in answering questions about their satisfactions and dissatisfactions in each decade, the women were clearly most emotionally involved in family relationships. Their husbands were a major source of satisfaction for nearly three-fourths of the planfully competent in their 20s and for nearly three-fifths in every subsequent decade, being crowded out of first place only in the women's 30s, when three-fourths named their children as a major source of satisfaction. Women who had scored below the mean on planful competence took substantially less satisfaction from their husbands, with 20 to 30 percent fewer finding major satisfaction in the marital relationship. During their 30s and 40s, one in six among the less planfully competent indicated that her husband had been a major cause of dissatisfaction.

Children were predominantly a source of satisfaction, especially in the 30s of their mothers, when satisfaction exceeded dissatisfaction by ten to one. By their 40s, when the children were adolescent, they were less often a source of satisfaction, and dissatisfaction was expressed by roughly one woman in six, regardless of level of planful competence. In general, however, the planfully competent expressed a higher frequency of satisfaction with their children, and, of course, they had more of them.

Fewer of the planfully competent women were in the labor force full time, and only in their 40s did more than a quarter of them name their jobs as a major source of satisfaction. By their 50s, their jobs took first place as a source of positive satisfaction for the less planfully competent, while it dropped off markedly for their more competent peers.

Before their 50s, no woman mentioned good health as a source of satisfaction, but poor health became an increasing source of dissatisfaction in each decade. For some it was their own poor health—a life-threatening illness or a debilitating one like Alice Neal's asthma—but by their 40s concern about their husbands' health began to be mentioned with some frequency. And in their 50s, fully a third of the less planfully competent and nearly a fifth of the more competent reported that either their own or their husband's health was a major source of dissatisfaction. The less planfully competent were much more likely to smoke and to drink to excess at times, which may help to explain the difference between the groups.

The life charts study members filled out in 1982 (unfortunately, by only about two-thirds of them) give another indication of major sources of crisis or of distress. Recall that any sharp drop that showed a loss of more than half the scale score at a given period was coded as a crisis. The most frequent such crisis was caused by the death of a parent, spouse, or child. Many study members lost their parents in their 40s and 50s, and when they had very strong attachments to them, the loss, especially for the women, was acutely distressing. More distressing still was the loss of a husband, and by 1982, more than a fifth of the women in the older cohort had been widowed, some for the second time. The life chart that Mary Wiley filled out in 1982 had shown a drop all the way to the bottom when her husband died. Particularly when a woman had preadolescent and adolescent children, the loss of a husband not only deprived her of love and emotional support but also gave her a new set of responsibilities to be carried out alone. When husband and wife had had a close relationship, as in the case of Mary Wiley and Judith Judd, the loss left a great gap in their lives, but at least they could look back on many happy times. When there had been more struggle and less closeness, as in Beth Green's first marriage, the loss could be even more devastating, for it almost inevitably brought feelings of guilt as well as grief.[12]

Perhaps no event in the lives of our study members was more traumatic than the loss of a child, whether the child died in infancy or as an adult. Some women managed to cope, maintaining happy memories as well as an abiding sense of loss. Others were devastated and turned to alcohol or to self-blame and bitterness. We have seen how Lucy Proteus was devastated, though there is no evidence that she perceived herself as being in any way to blame for her child's death. Nevertheless, her husband reported that after the child's death, she had seemed completely shattered.

Another mother, who lost two children, one to leukemia and one to an accident, commented: "I block these things out—this is the only way that I can—you know, just draw a blank—put it out of my mind and forget how I felt, how anybody felt. You know, forget it." She could say no more. There were two other children, who were a source of great pleasure.

A mother whose low self-esteem and exposure to a heavily drinking husband had led her to become an alcoholic in her 20s lost a child to an infectious illness when she was 40. She reported in a letter, which she authorized me to quote, "A couple of days before Billy was gone, he said, 'I sure like you.' What do you think that did to me? Guilt, guilt, and more guilt."

No one expressed a more poignant account of the loss of a child than the mother of a boy who developed leukemia when he was 7:

> I don't know if they're perfect when they're little or if you just begin to think so. It doesn't really matter. Leukemia is such as odd disease because you aren't sick with it. It was like he had a little virus, and then we went to the doctor and they said, "He has acute lymphatic leukemia and he may have three months to live." And then they give them cortisone and they go home, they go to school and they go to parties and they swim and they ride bicycles and you see them out there and you think, "He's going to be dead in three months?" That three and a half months was the longest three and a half months of my life.

Somewhere along the way, roughly a fifth of the women had had an illness severe enough to cause a sharp dip in the life chart, and fully a fourth showed deep distress as a result of marital problems or divorce. As might be expected, marital problems showed up on the charts most often in the 20s and 30s and illness in the 50s. There was no evidence of a piling up of problems around age 40.

In 1970, we had not asked the study members to fill out a life chart but had asked them to indicate the most satisfying and least satisfying periods in their lives. Half of the 40-year-old Guidance Study women named the previous decade as the most satisfying in their lives, as did a third of the Oakland members at age 48. The 20s were chosen by roughly a fourth of each group, as were the 30s for the older cohort. There was even greater consensus as to the least satisfying period: roughly half the women chose adolescence and a fourth, childhood.

Thus, the idea that the 40s are a period of despair for many women received almost no support. Only 5 percent of the female study members regarded their 40s as the least satisfying period, and they tended to be women who had faced crises, such as the loss of their husbands, in this period. In their middle years, some men and women undoubtedly were dissatisfied with the quality of their lives or deplored their lost youth. By and large, however, if our study members experienced midlife crises, they were more often caused by the deaths of loved ones or by having to deal with adolescent offspring than by either their marriages or their jobs.

CHAPTER 15

FAMILY RELATIONSHIPS

The critical importance of family relationships to the development of planful competence and to quality of life has been evident in all of the histories presented. In the earliest years, the family is the source of protection and nurturance. Then it becomes the shaper of values and of self-esteem, orienting the child to the larger world—to the need to take others into account, to learn skills and acquire knowledge. As the child and then the adolescent acquires skills and knowledge, parental controls diminish, and parental encouragement and support become important aids to the offspring's own transition to adulthood.

During the early adult years, one's parents may be close by, readily available for help and guidance, or they may be thousands of miles away, available only occasionally. As we shall see, there was great variation in the role that parents played during the study members' early adult years, but once a person married, parents were not generally a major preoccupation unless either they or the study member was in great need through illness or other life crisis.

In this chapter I want to focus first on the study members' relationships with their parents over their own middle and later adult years, next on the husband-wife relationship in terms of their interactions in marriage, then on the relationships of the study members with their own children and on the children's perception of their parents. Finally, I shall briefly characterize the offspring themselves as they enter their middle years.

RELATIONS WITH PARENTS

The planfully competent men and women I have described tended to have good relationships with both parents. A cluster of items evaluated as of the junior high years—which I have named "parents are respected role models"—was one of the strongest correlates of planful competence in senior high school. By and large, the men and women who scored lower on planful competence came from more conflicted homes and had less comfortable relationships with their parents.

How did the study members feel about their own parents as they matured? How close have they been in their parents' later years? We began to collect systematic data on the topic in the 1970 follow-up, when the study members were in their 40s and their parents ranged from the early 60s to the mid-80s.

More than half the study members in their 40s lived within a hundred miles of their parents and saw them several times a month. At the other extreme, 10 percent saw their parents only once or twice a year, and nearly as many had not seen their parents at all in the previous year. Contacts with parents were much less frequent, of course, when the parents and children lived far apart, which was most often the case when the study members were college graduates who had taken jobs or married outside the area of parental residence. Marital conflict in the parental home and parental divorce were associated with less frequent later contacts between children and parents, especially with the father, but by far the most important influence on frequency of contact was the distance separating parents and offspring.[1]

In their 40s, only 7 percent of the women and 2 percent of the men were seen as highly involved with their parents, such as depending upon their parents for help with decisions and being emotionally involved in their daily lives. Roughly a third were seen as substantially involved; their parents' well-being was important to them, and contacts, even if not very frequent, were a source of pleasure. Two-fifths were classified as being moderately involved with their parents and one-fifth, very slightly—their parents mattered very little to them. There were, in fact, a few women—but no men—who had not seen their mothers in more than a year and said they had no intention of ever seeing them again. All were from conflicted homes, with parents mostly divorced. Beth Green was one of these women.

Many more fathers had died than mothers. When only one parent was living, there was a tendency for the study member to visit somewhat more frequently and to be more involved with that parent than otherwise, and this was especially true of mothers.

Asked about the quality of their relationships with their mothers, currently or in the past, three in ten women characterized the relationship as predominantly negative. Half of this group mentioned extreme stress or conflict and half mentioned chronic tension as characterizing the relationship. Men were much less likely to mention extreme conflict with their mothers, but one in six mentioned that there had been chronic tension. Another four in ten men and women reported that their relationships with their mothers were mixed—a source of both satisfaction and dissatisfaction. The remaining three in ten women and nearly four in ten men reported good to excellent relationships with their mothers, either currently or in the past, if their mothers had recently died.

The sexes differed less in reported relationships with fathers. Twice as many reported good relationships as reported poor ones, with about two-fifths again reporting a fairly close balance of positive and negative aspects. Female study members, however, tended to report that they had grown closer to their mothers and less close to their fathers, while males reported that they had grown closer to their fathers and were equally likely to have grown either closer or less close to their mothers.[2] Half of the men and women reported no change in the relationship with either parent.

Typical of a man with low involvement with his parents (also low on planful competence) was one whose parents lived about an hour's driver from his home. He saw them "three or four times a year or something like that." His father he characterized as "the dominant one of the two," and as to their relationship, he reported:

> We argue all the time and he thinks I'm a radical at times, but otherwise, why I just let him think what he wants. It doesn't bother me that much—once in a while I irritate him but other than that, no big thing.

Asked about the most satisfying part of his relationship to his mother, he replied:

> I don't think there's anything particularly one way or the other except I appreciate them as being parents and that's it. One way or the other—they're there, I realize—I don't have any qualms one way or the other.

He reported that he had no worries about either parent, though he was annoyed that one wished to be buried and the other cremated, and both planned to disregard the other's wishes (that is, the survivor would take the matter into his or her own hands).

Contrast this with the response of a man whose mother had been widowed and lived nearby. He saw her regularly on weekends and occasionally in evenings:

> She's very independent. She does a lot of things on her own, but sometimes on weekends she has something for me to do or she wants me to take her someplace. I call her once or twice a week and if I have to cut the lawn or do the painting or take care of anything that has to be done, why, I'm always there.

Representing a woman who greatly admired her mother and maintained a close tie with her despite being separated by a thousand miles was the response of this planfully competent study member at age 40. She characterized her mother thus:

> I guess she'd have to be the most exceptional person that I've ever met.... She likes everybody else to have a good time and she likes gaiety and fun and she therefore likes younger people.... I don't mean that I lie awake and worry about it, but it crosses my mind that once she goes, you know, my really true soul mate in the whole wide world will be gone.

When we examine the relationship between planful competence and involvement with parents, all of the women who were very much involved and emotionally dependent on their parents in their middle years fall into the group classified as low on planful competence. Most of them had never become autonomous, competent adults. On the other hand, three-fifths of the women who were high in planful competence reported themselves substantially involved with but not emotionally dependent on their mothers, as against one-fifth of those below the mean in planful competence. In other words, comfortable, positive relationships between the study members and their parents were much more typical among the planfully competent women than among their peers. Highs were twice as likely to report good relationships with their mothers and half again as likely to report good relationships with their fathers as those who had scored lower on planful competence. The same tendencies were shown by male study members, but the differences by level of planful competence were not quite as great.

In 1970, and indeed for at least the next decade, most study members were more concerned about and involved with their adolescent and young adult children than with their parents. By 1982, most of the parents of the Oakland study members had died, and those of the Berkeley study members were in their 70s and 80s, but four-fifths of the survivors were still in their own homes, and even among those surviving parents of the Oakland study members (most over age 85), more than half were still in their own homes.[3] Only among women over age 85 did as many as 15 percent live with one of their children, but almost one-fourth of this older group were now in nursing homes.

Very few of these aged parents needed financial help from their children, but by 1982 many did need help around the house and in managing their affairs. The older women, in particular, were often partially incapacitated physically. Moreover, roughly a fifth of them were suffering from some degree of senility, and another fourth were sufficiently forgetful as to need help at times. Even among the younger mothers, a fourth had fairly severe health problems, and a fifth were suffering from occasional confusion or memory loss, which demanded a measure of assistance. Far fewer fathers were living; those who had survived were much more often in reasonably good health and many fewer were mentally impaired.[4]

Both male and female study members reported a greater feeling of obligation to visit their mothers than their fathers in the parents' later years, largely because both more often saw their fathers as less needy than their mothers. Because of Social Security and retirement programs, most of the elderly parents were able to live reasonably comfortably in their own homes well into their later years. A few widows needed financial help, but less than 5 percent of the study members indicated financial strain as a result of their parents' needs. Far more—roughly a third—said they felt emotional strain in attempting to deal with those needs, especially when the parent showed mental deterioration.

It will be recalled what while Henry Barr managed to see his mentally intact parents frequently and was emotionally close to both of them, Karl Schulz found visiting his mother in a nursing home stressful, as did Alice Neal's husband, whose mother was in a similar situation. Especially when the parent suffered from Alzheimer's disease or had had strokes that impaired communication (as Mrs. Schulz had), there could be little pleasure in such visits. While almost all children felt some sense of obligation to their parents, women reported that the pleasure of interacting with their mothers was very important to them—more than twice as often as did men. Men seemed particularly uncomfortable if they could not communicate easily with their mothers; they more often reported that the pleasure of interacting with their fathers was an important reason for visiting.

It was obviously much more pleasant to visit an intact parent than one who was suffering from senility. Mary Wylie's mother remained mentally intact up to her death at 102, and Mary spent a part of almost every day with her at the nursing home where she resided in a neighboring community. When parents were nearby, daughters or daughters-in-law frequently provided a measure of personal care, though very few were the primary caretakers of their elderly parents.[5] Undoubtedly, the superior financial situation of most of the parents relieved the burden their children would otherwise have faced. Even among parents who had been members of the working class, steady employment had led to adequate Social Security benefits and the possibility of independence for most. Most had indicated to their children that they preferred to maintain their own residences as long as possible. When they did move, some widowed parents went to live with their children, but more often, if they were impaired, they went to nursing homes. It was here that visiting was most difficult for the children. A wife whose mother-in-law was senile commented:

> It's very sad and painful. The doctor explained it to my husband: "There's two things that can happen. There's one where their mind's all right and their body is wracked with pain. That's very hard on a person. The other is where her body's all right. It's old. But her mind has just said, 'See ya.' You are much better off."

Most of us do not feel much better off under these circumstances, especially when we ourselves are in our 60s and 70s. A person whom we loved and respected has ceased to be, and yet a hollow replica remains.

Even in the years when their parents were declining and were a source of deep concern, it was the offspring of our study members who caused more concern and required more of their resources. But before looking at the relationships with the younger generation, let us look at the relationships of husbands and wives over the years.

THE MARITAL RELATIONSHIP

A few of the couples have now celebrated their fiftieth wedding anniversary. Many have been widowed and even more divorced. By the 1982 follow-up, roughly three-fifths were still married to their original partner, among those who participated in the follow-up. Since then, a number of the older study members have died, and many more of the Oakland women, most of them married to men a few years older than themselves, have been widowed.[6]

Most husbands and wives were within five years of being the same age, with men about three years older on the average, yet women who wed early often married men ten or more years older than themselves. Study members and spouses tended to have similar IQs ($r = .50$) when both were tested in their 40s, though males averaged a few points higher than females. This difference reflects both the lower socioeconomic status of girls than boys in the Oakland Growth Study and the more substantial educational attainment of the males among persons born in the 1920s, both affecting measured IQ. Analyses of IQ change from adolescence to age 40 or 48 suggest that when there was a substantial difference in the study member's and the spouse's IQ at this time, there was a significant tendency for the study member to have increased or decreased in IQ in the direction of the spouse's level.[7] As Eichorn and her colleagues put it: "Like foreign travel, living with a spouse who is brighter than oneself may be intellectually stimulating. Unfortunately, the inverse influence also occurs."

Far more important, however, was the influence of the marital relationship on the emotional well-being of both partners. We have already noted some of the major sources of conflict and dissatisfaction in their marriages, as perceived by men and women. The self-reports of husbands and wives as to their marital satisfaction at any given time show a measure of agreement, but it is modest agreement at best, each one's assessment accounting for only about a fourth of the variation in the other's. (Table A.19 in Appendix A shows the correlations for each period for which we have self-reports from husband and wife, and the relationship of self-reports to judges' ratings.) Recall that spouses were much less likely to participate when the marital relationship was strained, and this was especially true if the spouse was the more dissatisfied partner.

Causes of Tension: Differing Backgrounds and Values

Major differences in values—the priorities attached to different goals, styles of life, standards for children's behavior and attainment—were often at the root of marital conflict. When two persons with different basic values are attracted to each other and marry, they face many hurdles. Not infrequently they fail to surmount their differences. Mary married Tony, a popular athlete, while she was still in her teens. She described the early years of her marriage and why she and her husband ultimately divorced:

> I would read sometimes in the evening, and Tony would say, "What the heck do you want to sit there and waste your time reading for?"—why don't you do this or that, or he'd be watching television and then I would go into the bedroom or the kitchen. I'd rather read than watch the television. I liked music and he was always telling me, "Turn it off!" because he'd be listening to the ball game or "Dragnet" or something.
>
> I liked the theater, I liked the symphony and I was—we're just different, I guess. His interest was always in ball games and, not that I dislike that because I enjoy that myself, but it's nice to go out to a good restaurant or to the theater. . . . So it was just different interests all the way down the line.

Her husband's report was far less detailed. He never understood how she could like the activities she preferred. Early on, she had gone to games with him and had been the pretty wife he could show off. He had, above all, wanted a family, and they had several children before his wife began to wonder whether there might be an alternative to this way of life. Tony was a pleasant, seemingly relaxed man. He could not understand why she wanted a divorce. He remarried to a woman who had much the same tastes as he did.

Early in any marriage, partners discover differences in what was taken for granted in their parental homes. A woman may expect her husband to appreciate the qualities her father appreciated; a man may expect his wife to wait on him the way his mother waited on his father. If they can discuss their priorities and adapt to each other's most important needs, they may experience a certain amount of tension, but, given a genuinely intimate relationship, they are likely to achieve a reasonably satisfying set of mutual expectations. They do not have to meet anyone else's expectations if both members are satisfied. Of course, either may change in time, and then new adaptations have to be made.

Except as reported by the study members themselves in the first follow-up, we had no data on the spouse's perceptions until the 1970 adult interviews. We did learn how the study member thought the spouse felt, and often these reports provided a good picture of the marital situation. Henry Barr conveyed his disappointment at his wife's lack of intellectual vigor and portrayed her inevitable dislike of his critical response to her, while Stuart Campbell, Mary Wylie, and Karl Schulz gave more positive depictions of their marriages. In Henry Barr's case, personality differences were more important than cultural ones. That was often the case.

Spouses' Personalities and Marital Satisfaction

By and large, husbands and wives came from fairly similar cultural backgrounds, shared similar interests, and felt a considerable degree of compatibility, and this was especially true of the planfully competent. This did not mean that they were temperamentally similar or that their personality profiles resembled each other, but there were respects in which husband and wife showed similarities on particular components of personality. In 1970, when we had the first comparable personality assessments of both study member and spouse, resemblance was greatest on the components "intellectually invested" and "dependable," each correlated above .3. In addition, husband and wife resembled each other to a statistically significant degree on the component "outgoing versus aloof."

In 1982, spouses also resembled each other in self-confidence, but the correlation on dependability was no longer significant, perhaps because a number of the study members had retired and a major basis for assessing dependability was no longer available. In any event, the spouses did resemble each other to a significant though modest degree on the index of competence in both 1970 and 1982.

A question that immediately comes to mind is whether those who were most highly satisfied in their marriages were more similar to or different from their spouses. To answer this question, I computed the mean level of marital satisfaction for both husband and wife, combined the data for the two follow-ups, and then compared the top half in marital satisfaction with the bottom half in terms of personality resemblance on the various components. The results are somewhat mixed, especially for the 1970 follow-up, but in general couples who were in the top half on the measure of marital satisfaction showed greater resemblance in the components "intellectually invested" and "outgoing versus aloof," as well as in the index of competence for both periods (Table 15.1). In addition, husbands and wives who were more highly satisfied with their marriages were more likely to resemble each other in self-confidence in 1982, though not in 1970.

Resemblance on "assertiveness versus submissiveness" and "warmth versus hostility" appears to have no bearing on level of

Table 15.1.   Personality Resemblance of Husband and Wife on Q-Sort Components, by Marital Satisfaction, 1970 and 1982

	1970		1982	
	High Marital Satisfaction	Low Marital Satisfaction	High Marital Satisfaction	Low Marital Satisfaction
Self-confident/victimized	.09	.05	.34***	.15
Assertive/submissive	-.08	.09	.01	.15
Intellectually invested	.40***	.31**	.34***	.08
Outgoing/aloof	.35***	.01	.32***	.07
Dependable, productive	.30**	.35**	.01	.03
Warm/hostile (friendly)	.16	-.04	.11	.11
Competence index	.31**	.22*	.25**	.09

*$p < .05$; **$p < .01$; ***$p < .001$.

marital satisfaction. We cannot, of course, say that marital satisfaction is greater because husband and wife resemble each other. It would be just as reasonable to say that husband and wife tend to resemble each other on certain attributes when their marriage proved highly satisfying. There is certainly reason to assume that if one member of the pair is intellectually invested and they have a good relationship, the other is likely to become intellectually invested. We have the model of Henry Barr's marriage to suggest the reverse action: low marital satisfaction caused by gross differences in the extent of intellectual investment. There is, in any case, a dynamic process whereby both satisfaction and features of personality change over the years.

Work Roles and Family Roles: Unavailable Husbands

Tension could arise from many sources, but one of the most common, especially in the first ten to twenty years of the marriage, was the husband's involvement in his job. Three-fifths of the husbands acknowledged in 1982 that they had not been as available to their families as would have been desirable, and three-fifths of the wives reported that their husbands' lack of availability had been a problem for them.

The most frequently mentioned problem was the husband's giving priority to peak work demands, and here the planfully competent were perhaps a bit less available than their less competent peers and over longer periods. The second major category accounting for unavailability to the family was that of men whose jobs required a great deal of travel, largely corporate salesmen and men in the military services. These men were slightly less often numbered among the planfully competent. Their absence could be especially problematic because they were so seldom with their families during the week.

In discussing the problem, men often deplored that they had missed seeing their children grow up. A fourth of the men who had not been available recognized that there had been serious problems for their wives and children, but many others merely mentioned that their wives had complained. Only when problems were so serious that they could not be ignored did some men appreciate what their wives had experienced.

Several wives whose husbands had traveled away from home most of the week mentioned the tremendous stress they had experienced. Dave's wife commented:

> I had to do everything on my own, and it was rough. It was hard on Billy [son] because he never saw Dave. When Dave came home on the weekend, I'd had kids up to here and wanted to get out. He was so tired of eating out that he wanted to stay home, so that was a big conflict.

How did she deal with the problem? "I just had to bear with it and hope he wouldn't have to keep traveling." Another wife compared her stint of caring for five children while her husband traveled to being in prison.

Wives of men in the military faced similar problems for long periods. When the husband did come home, children could sometimes be cared for by grandparents, giving the wife a bit of a break, but child care in the relatively large families of our study members was a grueling task for many women whose husbands were not available much of the time.

Some men often did not get home for dinner or when they did were preoccupied with problems they brought home from the job. Their wives also had a difficult time. A tense, irritable husband was no help with the children, and the atmosphere might even be calmer without him. In all, seven men blamed the failure of a first marriage on their lack of availability to their wives or their inability to be sufficiently aware of their wives' difficulties when the husband was away, physically or psychologically, because of work. Many more mentioned serious consequences for their wives and their children in their current marriages, especially depression, alcohol, and drugs.

Asked what the consequences of his total dedication to his profession had been for his wife, one man said simply: "Well, you know about her drinking." Others told of bitter arguments and alienated children. The wives' fatigue was most acute when the children were young, but adolescence posed problems that demanded more attention.

Almost exactly the same proportion of husbands and wives reported some tension in connection with the husband's unavailability, and almost the same proportion reported serious consequences (one in four of those not available), but, surprisingly, the husbands and wives often disagreed on both the matter of unavailability and its consequences. The husband of a woman who said she had been at her wits' end, feeling she was imprisoned with her children, said he was seldom unavailable. He did acknowledge that he wasn't much of a father—"constitutionally unsuited," was his comment. The children look back on a dismal family life characterized by little love, less fun, and much tension. Another man was aware only of his own regrets:

> In my first marriage I made myself pretty scarce around the house. I short-changed myself by not being able to notice the progress of my children's growth. But I don't think they suffered. Kids can have a heck of a good time in the right environment without being supervised.

In time, his wife had given an ultimatum, and he said he had "tried to spend a Sunday with them," but apparently that had not been the answer. In his second marriage the problem of unavailability continued, but his wife reported:

> He's totally immersed in his work. It doesn't present a problem because we don't allow it to present a problem. It's like a flat tire. It's inconvenient and it's a real problem but either you fix it or you catch a taxi. I just accept it.

A number of wives did "just accept it," while others complained. Sometimes their husbands managed to achieve a better balance in their lives, and sometimes the problem went on indefinitely. Clinical interviews in the wives' 50s and 60s elicited deep-seated resentment from many women.

While most professionals were heavily involved in their jobs and were often not as available as other men to their wives, their wives were also more likely to be understanding. Commenting on the problems caused by her husband's lack of availability, the wife of a university professor explained:

> They haven't been serious. My husband really makes a lot of time to spend with the children. He's home a lot, but there are things that interfere. I mean there are times when he's working nonstop for

weeks to get something done. At that point we just stay out of his way. But he's not like that all the time. He's a very conscientious father and does a lot with the children. Every week we do something. They count on it, too.

Asked at what period in marriage the problem was most difficult, she replied:

I think when the kids were babies, when they were from a year or two, two and a half or three. I think he deliberately worked a little later. He'd deny that, I'm sure. But it was a new job and we just moved to [a new university] and he wouldn't get home until after 7 or so and that period between 5 and 7 used to be just hell. And it would have been nice to have somebody to share the burden with at that time.

She complained and "wished he'd come home earlier, and gradually he has come home earlier."

When a man was preoccupied with attaining occupational success, he might feel devoted to his wife and family and yet slight them by failing to allocate time for close involvement in his wife's and children's activities. At home and in our interviews, he talked more about the challenges of the job and less about his feelings in other respects, though often we heard apologies for his not having spent more time with the family. In their 30s, such men appeared less warm and less nurturant of others than they had appeared to be in adolescence. Manifestly they were less nurturant, yet many were not unconcerned. Often they were seen rather negatively by their children. When adolescent offspring were asked to characterize their fathers in the questionnaires they filled out in 1970, many not only saw their fathers as overinvolved in their jobs but as relatively unhappy. The father who daily came home with complaints about his stressful day did not radiate good cheer, nor was he likely to be as interested in what his children were doing at the moment.

Some men could be highly involved in both work and family, as Stuart Campbell was. His children often stayed up to be able to share experiences with him when he had to be out in the evening. Stuart's wife was far less enthusiastic. She knew (in theory) what she was getting into when she married a physician, but many times she felt sorely taxed. Karl Schulz was a rare professional whose job did not demand more than a 40-hour week; he was available to his wife and children to a much greater extent.

Wives and Husbands Working Together

In a chapter of the book *Present and Past in Middle Life,* dealing with men's occupational careers, I noted that when men worked in their father's businesses, there was often tension over the amount of responsibility the son was granted as he gained experience. A number of the descriptions given by study members "suggested that a son's involvement in a family business is likely to precipitate a battle of the generations and a wife's participation in her husband's business is likely to precipitate a battle of the sexes."[8] Vivid descriptions of conflict can lead to wrong inferences, and I now think that *likely* is too strong a word, if it suggests that this was a frequent outcome.

In 1982 we asked specifically if wives had worked for their husbands and, if so, in what capacity, for how long, and how they felt about the arrangement. Twenty-eight percent of the wives had worked for their husbands at one time or another, a few in family businesses but most often doing bookkeeping and other clerical work (especially for self-employed men in small business ventures), serving as receptionist or typist, or providing other direct assistance to their husbands. Three-fourths of the men and more than two-thirds of the women questioned said that they had liked the arrangement, and only about 10 percent reported significant tension, the rest giving reports of mixed feelings. Where husband and wife were close confidants (and the husband was not a tense perfectionist), the wife's working with and for her husband was satisfying to most of the couples. Wives who were least well satisfied tended to say that they preferred to work for a regular salary in a situation with less personal involvement. Satisfaction was not related to a woman's educational attainment, but the proportion who at some period worked for their husbands was highest among college graduates and lowest among women who had not gone beyond high school.

Many wives helped their husbands' careers in other ways: by offering understanding and emotional support when there were problems, by informally providing directly relevant help or advice without being employed, and by entertaining their husbands' work associates or potential clients. More than half the men felt that their wives had been supportive of their careers, and women who were college graduates appeared to be most supportive, though wives were less likely than men to mention emotional support as an aid to their husbands. Roughly a fourth of both husbands and wives mentioned directly relevant consultations and discussions of issues, and an equal number mentioned entertaining for their husbands. Frequently, however, husbands and wives had different perceptions of the help provided by the wives. A man's report of his marital satisfaction was significantly related to his statement that his wife had been helpful to him but not to her report of helpfulness. In other words, good feelings about the marriage tended to produce good feelings about career support, though influences may well be reciprocal. It is likely that a wife's expression of her feelings about her husband's lack of availability—especially if she had expressed strong resentment—had more influence on her husband's perception of support than did the actual amount of help she provided over the years.

Effects of a Wife's Employment

While there were young children in the house, most couples agreed that it would be best for the wife to stay at home with the children and not return to work. The chief exceptions were women who had taken graduate degrees or who had married late and had skills or experience that provided them with challenging or rewarding jobs. Some husbands objected to their wives working even after the children were well along in school, but the number reported as objecting decreased with each follow-up, even as the proportion of women with children who were in the labor force was increasing rapidly. National surveys had found that only 15 percent of the population approved of the employment of married women in the mid-1930s, but by 1970 50 percent did, and by 1978 nearly three-fourths did.[9] Thus, as they reached their 40s, the women in our study had much more external support if they wished to enter the labor force. Nevertheless, there were in every period some men who objected to their wives working, as Alice Neal's husband did. A few women appear to have sought divorces from husbands who insisted they stay at home, but most women seem to have changed their husbands' minds, as Alice had.

When the husbands were asked at the last major follow-up interview if their relationship with their wives had been affected by her working, slightly less than half said that it had, but they split evenly as to whether the difference was positive or negative. Husbands who felt that their wives' working had had a negative influence on their relationship occasionally acknowledged that they resented their wives' independence and the added demands placed on them at home, but more often they cited diminished opportunities to do things together or said their wives were less relaxed and more diffi-cult to live with. An equal number of men, however, said their wives were happier and their relationship was more interesting after their wives began working. Very few men thought that their wives' rela-tionships with the children suffered as a result of the wives' work-ing, though somewhat more of their wives feared that this was the case.

The wives' reports of their husbands' reactions to their labor force participation suggested that their husbands were presenting to us a more positive, accepting account than the responses they had given to their wives. At no period was there a significant rela-tionship between a woman's work attachment or labor force partici-pation and her own or her husband's reported marital satisfaction, but when the women were asked whether their relationships with their husbands had been positively or negatively affected by their working, roughly three times as many reported negative effects as reported positive ones. Negative effects were most often reported by women with at least some college education as compared with those with only high school education (42 percent versus 21 per-cent). Moreover, of those who reported negative effects, one-fourth indicated that their husbands resented their working. Conflict over division of labor in the home was mentioned by only a few women, all of them college graduates whose husbands had high-status jobs.

Even where there was not conflict over a wife's working or over a husband's being expected to take over a greater share of homemak-ing duties, there was often a degree of tension. One wife com-mented, after she had given up her job:

> I think it [the marriage] changed a good deal after I quit work, be-cause it's natural that when a wife works she's involved in her job and her husband is involved in his job... and in the evenings nei-ther one wants to listen to the problems that the other had during the day. It's much nicer now. I like it!

From these analyses, it would appear that in this cohort of

women who had been oriented toward domesticity, labor force participation by itself did not seriously affect their marital happiness but caused some tensions and was more problematic for the marriages of college graduates whose husbands were reluctant to share household chores. However, most of the study members who entered the labor force did so when their children were well along in school. Their daughters are now in the labor force when the children are still preschoolers. While husbands in the offspring generation may help at home more than their fathers did, most of their wives work a "second shift," as Hochschild has so convincingly documented in her book, *The Second Shift.* Those who must do so are often less satisfied with their marriages.[10]

Alcohol Abuse and Marital Relations

There were only slight differences in the reported alcohol consumption of planfully competent and less competent men and women when we have asked them periodically if they drank alcoholic beverages or smoked and how much they drank or smoked. In the case of both men and women, those who never smoked at all or never drank alcohol scored somewhat lower on planful competence in adolescence and in mature competence than did those who were moderate smokers (and later quit) and those who drank in moderation. As a consequence, correlation coefficients do not give an adequate indication of the relationships between smoking and drinking and planful competence. It appears that many of the persons who never tried cigarettes or alcoholic beverages tended to be high on the component "dependable" but relatively low on "intellectually invested" and on "self-confident versus feels victimized." Many were less venturesome; some might be called inhibited or rigid. On the other hand, those who became heavy drinkers (and heavy smokers) tended to be undercontrolled and to score substantially lower on the components "dependable" and "intellectually invested" though not necessarily lower on "self-confident." The men and women who had scored highest on adolescent planful competence tended at least to try cigarettes and to be moderate drinkers, but they also were much more likely to give up smoking by their 50s.

Reports on smoking levels were, we believe, quite reliable, for those who were heavy smokers tended to smoke when interviewed. Reports on amounts of alcohol consumed were less trustworthy. Sometimes, however, spouses or children revealed what the original study member would not: that the study member was an alcoholic. It is difficult to establish how many study members have had serious problems with alcohol. Drinking patterns can change sharply, and recent research suggests that some people who have been extremely vulnerable to alcohol abuse at one period can drink in a controlled way at another.

We can say with confidence that at least a fifth and possibly a third of the study members have had a problem with alcohol at times, although far fewer currently have a problem or did at any particular time. Some planfully competent men and women have had drinking problems, but a listing of known alcoholics during the middle adult years—using all sources of information—suggests that at least three times are many alcoholics had scored below the mean on the index of planful competence as scored above the mean.

Reporting on research she carried out in the 1960s, Mary Jones delineated "problem drinkers" on the basis of the study members' reports of heavy drinking plus evidence that the person's drinking was a problem for self or for family members or led to difficulties on the job or elsewhere outside the family.[11] Several study members had lost their driving licenses because of drunk-driving convictions. In their adult years the problem drinkers, male and female, scored high on many of the negatively weighted items in the component "self-confident versus feels victimized"; that is, they felt victimized. They were seen as self-defeating, basically anxious, self-pitying, and tending to become disorganized under stress. They also scored low on the items making up the component "dependability," although the components had not yet been delineated at the time Dr. Jones prepared her report. In adolescence, however, the most substantial differences between those who became problem drinkers and those who did not were almost all related to dependability and control.

Some of the problem drinkers who had been planfully competent, like Lucy Proteus, declined markedly in competence scores and underwent considerable personality change. Others, particularly if their drinking was related to heavy stress and was of relatively short duration, have not appeared markedly impaired or changed by the experience. Those with a long history of problem drinking, almost all among the less planfully competent, have been among the most crisis prone.

An adequate analysis of alcohol abuse in the study population is beyond the scope of this book. A few members (almost all of whom had scored low on planful competence) started drinking heavily before marriage, but heavy drinking on the part of many of the men and most of the women appears to have begun after marriage, either as part of a shared cocktail hour, social drinking connected to the job, or drinking to escape feelings of extremely low self-esteem or inadequacy in the face of heavy stress.

Alcoholism was a major source of tension in many families, whether only one or both husband and wife were heavy drinkers. Often one partner could put the brakes on, and the other could not. Violence was most often found in heavy-drinking families—violence against the spouse and children or on occasion against the parents by alcoholic sons. A sad instance was afforded by a couple who came to their interview from a motel because their drunken son had beaten up his father and thrown him out of his own home the night before.

Some marriages ended in divorce well before the late middle years as a result of a man's alcoholism and his behavior toward his wife and children, or because of a woman's inability to function adequately as a mother when living in an alcoholic stupor much of the time. Others were still tenuously together after years of threats by the less impaired spouse to seek a divorce.

Highly competent persons were less likely to drift into alcoholism through social drinking. One of the women who had ranked toward the top in planful competence began to drink when she had five small children; her husband was in a job that took him away from home for ten days and then brought him home for four. Her doctor prescribed tranquilizers, and she took them intermittently. A couple of years later, she also had a brother's two children living in the home, along with her husband's mother, who was both senile and diabetic. Looking back at age 62, she commented:

> I think I learned then that you could use a chemical to take the pressure off and I didn't know how to do it any other way. And then I realized that it was a lot handier to have a glass of wine than it was to go looking for tranquilizers and I started using it that way.

For the next ten years, she was an alcoholic:

> I felt sure that our marriage and our family life was dissolving, and I
> know that alcohol was probably the largest percent of that problem.
> All marriages have trouble sometimes, but you don't make it any bet-
> ter by sticking your head in a bottle. So it took a while for me to get
> straightened out.

Ultimately she did get straightened out but only after some terrifying experiences, including driving her car some distance in a complete alcoholic haze. Subsequently, she became a speaker for
Mothers Against Drunk Driving.

Alcoholism of one or both parents almost always led to turmoil
and difficulties for at least some of the children. In several instances,
mothers began to drink heavily in their middle years, and their older
children had to take responsibility for maintaining order in the
household. Husbands and children could be supportive when the
mother made an effort to stay sober, but they could take only so
much. One daughter said of her alcoholic mother (a successful businesswoman), "It makes the whole family crazy." In many of the families in which a parent had a problem with alcohol, one or more
children had a serious problem with alcohol or drugs, or both.

A husband's drinking could more often lead to violence, but
even if it did not, persistent drunkenness was most often associated
with loss of the children's respect and often with their early departure from the family home. A woman who complained in 1970
about her husband's drinking problem saw it then as merely something that made him unattractive and unavailable to communicate.
He drank two six-packs of beer in an evening and felt that was the
only way he could relax. A dozen years later, she was ready to leave
him. She reported that her only real dissatisfaction in life was her
husband's drinking. She made tape recordings of his drunken behavior, but he refused to listen. Not surprisingly, their oldest son
had a drinking problem before he left home.

Continued Heavy Smoking

Although it was only occasionally a major issue with their spouses, continued heavy smoking on the part of study members was often a concern of their children, who had become aware of the dangers of smoking. Subjects who had scored low on the index of adolescent planful competence and high on the component "outgoing" tended to smoke at a much earlier age than their more competent peers, and they tended much more often to become heavy smokers (more than a pack a day). In an earlier report on smoking among Oakland subjects, I noted that the antecedents of smoking were different from males and females and that smoking apparently served somewhat different functions.[12] Girls who smoked had received much higher ratings on needs for recognition, control, and escape than had boys who smoked. The latter scored significantly lower on need for achievement but higher on the need for autonomy. In their late 30s, the heavy-smoking males had secured much less education and were less successful occupationally.

Three-fourths of the men who became heavy smokers quit prior to the 1982 follow-up, but only one-fourth of the women who had smoked heavily managed to do so. The men who continued to smoke are primarily distinguished by lower educational attainment and high scores on "outgoing versus aloof"—they are highly sociable. They also tend to drink more heavily than their nonsmoking peers.

The women who continue to smoke differ little in current personality but tend to have had less education and are much more likely to have been divorced. They differ most sharply from their peers who no longer smoke in their adolescent scores on dependability. Low adolescent dependability is the strongest correlate of reported difficulty in stopping smoking ($r = .50$, $p < .001$). Where both husband and wife had been heavy smokers, it was extremely difficult for one to stop or even cut down on the amount smoked if the other continued to smoke. When one wanted very much to stop or was ordered to stop by his or her physician and the other continued to smoke heavily, this was an occasional source of tension, though we never collected systematic data on the topic. Among both men and women, smokers are more often drinkers, and heavy smokers are more often heavy drinkers, especially among males. Fifty percent of the men who are reportedly heavy drinkers (not necessarily problem drinkers) are still smoking, in contrast to only 17 percent of the men who drink moderately or not at all.

Marriage as a Changing Relationship

As the role of women in American society has changed, many couples have had to adapt to a very different set of beliefs from the ones they took for granted at marriage. Some women—both study members and their daughters—hold to the traditional views, and it appears that the great majority of husbands like this arrangement. Other women became aware of potentials they had not been able to develop and of the gratifications possible when one is more autonomous. If their husbands were unwilling to grant their wives greater autonomy, tension levels increased, even when the pair stayed together. It appears that planfully competent men and women were better able to adapt. The planfully competent women had more often chosen the traditional family role when they married, because it was then seen as the norm, and they were, by our definition of planful competence, neither rebellious nor strongly conforming. Those whose parents were eager for their daughters to experience their full potential were more likely to carry through in preparing for a profession, but they were a small minority. In general, however, planfully competent girls tended to secure more education and as a consequence were more likely to value autonomy. They and their husbands more often engaged in discussions about changing roles, they were more often close friends, and one might say that they relied more on diplomacy than on war in renegotiating relationships, whether they entered the labor force or not.

Someone to Confide In

In the 1982 interview, we asked whether there was anyone "other than your spouse" with whom the study member could share their innermost thoughts and feelings. Women were much more likely than men to say "yes." Most often they were relatives or friends they had known for some years, and the confiding was a two-way process.

In 1990 we did not include the phrase "other than your spouse," and as a consequence we learned that fewer than half the women confided primarily in their husbands. On the other hand, their husbands, if they had a confidant, overwhelmingly confided in their wives. Even when the men rated their marriages 5 or lower on a 10-point scale, half said they confided primarily in their wives. Only one woman among the twenty-eight who rated their marriages that low indicated that she confided in her husband. Instead, these women confided primarily in their daughters or in friends.

Among women who rated their marriages at 8 or above, as 70 percent did, slightly less than half mentioned their husbands as their confidants. Those who did were also likely, when asked, "What is best in your life?" to name their husbands. The women who did not explicitly mention their husbands most often turned to friends or to their children. Where women did confide in their husbands, it appears that the two were "best friends." This was much less often the case when only the husband confided in his wife.

Over the years, the marital relationship took some unexpected turns. Most often, extramarital affairs led to extreme tension, and sometimes to the breakup of marriages, but they apparently helped to offset other problems in at least a couple of marriages. A highly expressive, gregarious wife who had earlier complained bitterly of her husband's inability to talk about feelings and his unwillingness to pursue an active social life found a lover in her middle years. The children were largely out of the house, and she was able to take occasional trips with him, as well as with other friends. The pattern suited both husband and wife. On the verge of 70, both rated their marriage higher than they had twenty years before. Her closest confidant is her lover, but, asked what is best about her life, she mentions her "good health, dear husband, exceptionally good children and good friends." Her husband pursues his own interests but enjoys his wife far more than he did in the first thirty or so years of marriage. And the children, who had been seriously alienated twenty years ago, now enjoy warm relationships with their parents. Such arrangements are rare, but they do occur.

RELATIONSHIPS WITH CHILDREN

We had asked the study members about their children at the time of the first follow-up and about their views on parenting, but the first systematic data on relationships with specific children were not obtained until the second follow-up in 1970. At this time, in both questionnaires and the interviews, we asked about specific children in the age range 14 to 18. The interviews with the children were largely done by women graduate students in psychology and sociology who were much less skilled than the interviewers who had seen the parents, but they were much closer in age to the adolescents, and for the most part they give a fairly good idea of the self-presentation and views of the children who were seen. In some instances, especially in the case of adolescent males interviewed by attractive young women, the respondents were rather laconic. In other instances, the interview situation became one in which the 17- and 18-year-old males tried to appear sophisticated to their slightly older interviewers.

The questionnaires presented parents and offspring with identical questions asking how well they agreed on a number of issues and values: personal philosophy, political attitudes, religion, choice of friends, civil rights, moral values, and dating and sex. The correlations for various combinations of parents and children suggested a fair degree of similarity in views on a number of issues, with correlations running between .4 and .5, but in general children reported less agreement with their parents on these items than the parents reported.

There were substantial differences in the level of agreement on different topics, particularly as related to the age of the adolescent. For example, only 10 percent of 14- and 15-year-old girls said they did not agree at all well with their mothers on the matter of dating and sex, while 43 percent of the 18-year-olds said they did not agree at all well with their mothers. Age was much less related to the level of agreement between boys and their mothers, as reported by both the boys and the mothers. Disagreement between parents and adolescents was greatest in the areas of political views and, for males, religion.

Asked in the questionnaire how well they felt they understood a particular child, only 5 percent of the fathers and of the mothers checked "not well"; from two-fifths to half checked that they understood the child "very well." In response to the same question, a fifth of the daughters and slightly fewer sons rated paternal understanding "not well" and a slightly smaller proportion checked "not well" for their mothers.

Most parents felt that they had been a strong influence on their children, as indeed they had, but fewer of the children acknowledged the level of influence that the parents claimed. As I noted in discussing the highly competent parents, some of them were less likely to claim strong influence than their children were to report that the parents had indeed exerted strong influence. In the 1970 questionnaires, the daughters of study members were especially likely to report less parental understanding and less parental influence as they moved into later adolescence, having been much more in tune with their parents at age 14 than at age 18.

As any parent of adolescent offspring learns, by midadolescence the offspring choose to participate much more with peers rather than with family. While 85 percent of the girls and 77 percent of the boys at age 14 to 15 reported they accompanied their parents on vacation trips, the figures had dropped to 36 percent and 41 percent by ages 17 and 18. The older adolescents ceased going out to dinner with their parents and instead got together with peers. This was, of course, perfectly normal, but it complicated the assessment of adolescent personalities, since very different matters were going on in the lives of the younger and the older adolescents in the study.

There were, however, some consistent patterns in the relationships of offspring with their parents, and those patterns were influenced by both harmony in the families as they had been constituted in 1970 and the competence of the parents, which were themselves related. High marital satisfaction, approval of the spouse as a parent, and a positive emotional climate in the home as rated from the parental interviews in 1970 were all significantly related to parental planful competence and to the adolescent's feeling of being understood by both parents (but especially the father) and the amount of influence attributed to both parents by the offspring at ages 14 to 18. Many of the correlations were above .3 and a few above .4, all highly significant statistically. Fifteen years later, in 1985, when I sent another questionnaire with many of the same questions to the offspring, now varying in age from 27 to 34, the same correlations were found. A question specifically asking about closeness to parents found that harmonious relationships between the parents in 1970 predicted greater feelings of closeness, especially on the part of the sons and daughter toward their fathers. Parents whose marriages had been harmonious had sons and daughters who saw their parents as having been more influential and as having encouraged and helped them to reach their goals.

What of the effects of parents' planful competence on the relationships of the young adult offspring with their parents in 1985? Here our samples of offspring matched with parents from whom we had measures of planful competence were small, especially off-spring of parents who had been rated low in planful competence. Nevertheless, the differences between offspring of those study members who had scored high on planful competence and those who had scored low were very similar to the differences found with harmonious families. Only among the offspring of men who had been planfully competent did any offspring report that their fathers had had the strongest influence on their own development, but well over one-fourth of this group did. Children of a planfully competent father or mother more often said they had known themselves reasonably well in adolescence. It appears, then, that family harmony and having at least one parent who had been planfully competent had roughly similar positive consequences for their offspring.

Study Members' Views of Their Adult Children

Study members were asked in the 1982–1983 interview to comment on their level of satisfaction with each of the children—the respects in which they were most satisfied or dissatisfied with them—and to discuss the exchange of services with their offspring. Roughly three-fifths of fathers and mothers reported themselves "very well satisfied" with each of their children. Less than 5 percent described themselves as "very much dissatisfied" with any child, and roughly 10 percent reported themselves to be "somewhat dissatisfied," with the residual expressing themselves as "pretty well satisfied."

Most seemed to like their children as persons. More than two-thirds mentioned the child's personality as a source of satisfaction, while a fifth mentioned the child's personality as a source of dissatisfaction, often feeling that the child was selfish or had other unpleasant attributes or was unable to establish friendships. Roughly two-fifths expressed pleasure, but one parent in six expressed disappointment with the offspring's achievement, and roughly one in ten reported a degree of dissatisfaction with the kind of relationship they currently had with any particular child.

At the time of the 1982 follow-up, when study members were in their mid-50s and early 60s, about one in seven reported offspring over age 22 still (or again) living at home. Parents were much more likely to express disappointment and dissatisfaction with offspring then living at home than with those who were on their own. Less than half the mothers and less than a third of the fathers expressed high satisfaction with sons or daughters over age 22 who were still living at home, and over a third expressed significant dissatisfaction with these children.

To our knowledge, among our subjects only one woman and one man were admittedly homosexual. Among their children, there are at least a half-dozen. I was unaware of the sexual preferences of the offspring, and few, if any, parents had mentioned the topic in our interviews. When I sent the 1991 questionnaire to the offspring, however, I included as a category under the question on marital status, "Unmarried but in an intimate relation with a member of the opposite sex." I received two or three indignant letters, asking why I limited intimate relationships to the opposite sex. Several other respondents crossed out "opposite sex" and wrote in "same sex."

Those who acknowledged that they were gay were, for the most part, college graduates. So far as I could tell, they appeared to have reasonably good relationships with their parents. We do not have enough information to draw any inferences beyond this. Clearly a son or daughter's preference for the same sex is a problem for most parents, at least initially, but many parents not only love their gay offspring but respect him or her.

According to the study members' reports in 1982, more than two-fifths of the offspring aged 22 and older were to some degree financially dependent on their parents. Such dependency was another source of parental dissatisfaction, especially if it represented the offspring's inability to cope with normal expenses. On the other hand, many parents seemed to be happy to be able to help their sons to manage a deposit on a house or to help out sons and daughters who were having emergencies but were normally self-supporting. If regular financial aid went especially to those with whom parents expressed dissatisfaction, emotional and moral support went much more often to those whose parents were satisfied with them, at least as reported by the parents.

Parental reports of satisfaction with their adult children almost certainly overstate the degree of satisfaction and mask some tensions that exist in the relationships between many parents and their children. A major source of parental dissatisfaction that sometimes surfaced in other parts of the interview was discontent with a son's or daughter's marital choice and, even more acute, dissatisfaction when a child's marriage was dissolved by divorce. Many of the off-spring developed life-styles that were not at all congenial to their parents. For a few parents, a generation gap still exists, but most parents have been able to accept that their children's values may be different without necessarily being any less based on moral princi-ples. A number of others, whose life-styles twenty years ago were the despair of their parents, had returned to more conventional roles, and parents who could not accept the alternative life-styles have been grateful that they could reestablish closer relationships.

The dissatisfactions that parents express generally have little to do with the issues that led to the widely proclaimed generation gap of the 1960s and early 1970s. Once the Vietnam War was over, most Americans realized that it had been a mistake, and surely it had been the most heated issue of the era. If there is an issue between the generations today, it more often has to do with living within one's means. The children of the Great Depression learned to be frugal, unless their families were very well off. They often see their children as having had a much easier time and having gotten used to living well without having to work for it. Even when parent-child relationships are very good, as in the Campbell and Schulz families, the parents feel that their children have lost something by not hav-ing to struggle as they did. The issue, however, is not one that causes conflict so much as bemusement.

The Younger Generation in 1991

In 1991, I sent a questionnaire to all offspring whose parents pro-vided their children's current addresses in response to our request at the time of the 1990 survey. Roughly 70 percent of the study members for whom addresses were known had returned the 1990 questionnaires. The response rate was considerably higher for those who had scored above the mean in adolescent competence and much lower for those who had scored below the mean. This re-sulted in a more highly select group of offspring, and there is rea-son to assume that those whose relationships with their parents were closest and who were themselves doing well would be more likely to return questionnaires than other sons and daughters of the study members. Thus, one must be aware of the probability of considerable bias in the 1991 sample. Of roughly 500 questionnaires sent to offspring for whom we had a valid address, 330 were completed and returned.

Nearly three-fifths of the offspring were in their 30s, 10 percent in their 20s (some of them children of second marriages of the male study members), and the remainder in their 40s, with a few verging on 50. On the whole, the offspring have done well. Fifty-six percent of the daughters who were over 20 years old had graduated from college, as had 65 percent of the sons.[13] The rate of graduation for women in their 30s and in their 40s was identical—57 percent—but men in their 40s were substantially more likely to have completed college than men in their 30s—72 percent as against 59 percent.

For both sons and daughters, educational attainment was significantly higher if the offspring reported a happy childhood family experience (more frequent and interesting activities, loving relationships, less frequent tension), saw the parents' marriage as a happy one, indicated in 1991 that they had been aware of their options in adolescence, and had not had significant problems with drugs or alcohol. It was also higher if their parent who was a study member had scored high on adolescent planful competence.

We know that planfully competent men had higher occupational status and higher incomes and that planfully competent women married men who attained high occupational status, so it comes as no surprise to learn that far more of the children of the planfully competent had graduated from college. Although we have relatively small groups of children matched with parents who had scored low on planful competence in adolescence, there were sufficient in every pairing except father-son to make comparisons of educational attainment by parental competence. Whereas only 41 percent of the daughters of men and women who had scored low on adolescent planful competence graduated from college, 68 percent of the daughters of planfully competent adolescents had graduated from college, and more of them had secured graduate degrees. Overall, more than a fourth of both sons and daughters had secured graduate degrees—the daughters more often master's degrees, while nearly 10 percent of the sons had secured doctorates.

The occupational attainment of sons in their 30s and 40s is similar to that of the larger cohort of study members at a comparable age, despite the experience of many of the younger generation with the counterculture and drugs in the 1960s and 1970s. Among sons in their 30s and 40s, the proportion who responded to a question on career satisfaction by checking, "It truly represents what I have wanted to do," was 40 percent—10 percent higher than the reports of their fathers at the same age. More are unmarried than their fathers were in their 30s (35 percent), but 90 percent in their 40s are or have been married. At all age levels, many are living in an intimate relationship without marriage (36 percent of the men in their 20s, 12 percent in their 30s, and 5 percent in their 40s). Of those over 40, half have been divorced.

For the daughters, the contrast with their mothers' lives is even more striking. Their educational attainment is a little less than that of the sons, but many more are college graduates than was the case with their mothers. Of daughters in their 20s, a fourth report themselves as single and not in an intimate relationship, while a third report themselves in an intimate relationship with the opposite sex; the rest are or have been married. Of daughters in their 30s, however, four-fifths are or have been married, and among those 40 and over, 52 percent have divorced. Thus children's divorce rates as they enter the middle years are nearly twice as high as the life-time divorce rates of their parents. Divorce rates are substantially higher among sons and daughters from broken or conflicted homes.

Whereas only about a third of their mothers had been employed by their late 30s, in 1991 85 percent of the daughters were in the labor force, most of them employed full time. Those in the labor force are equally likely to have children but tend to have fewer children than those not in the labor force. However, almost all of their mothers had had their first child in their 20s, but many of the daughters are still childless in their 30s (30 percent) and their 40s (20 percent).

Planful Competence and the Offspring

Our original study members had been observed, tested, and questioned over a period of six to fourteen years by the time they finished high school. Their offspring who were interviewed in 1972 at ages 14 to 18 were seen for only a hour or two. Many were still in junior high school. The interviews gave us some feeling for the adolescents and their problems, but they did not afford an adequate basis for assessing the personalities of the respondents. The interviewers, for the most part graduate students, often had their own agendas, and the interviews with the male adolescents sometimes revealed more about the behavior of a particular pair in interaction than about the boy's personality.

There is evidence from the series of questionnaires, however, that those who knew the general direction they wanted to take, those who had planned for higher education, and those who saw their parents as helpful and supportive of their efforts to attain their goals had much more often graduated from college and had attained higher occupational status. This was as true of females as of males. Those girls who had planned a career or career and marriage were as likely to be married as their peers who had chosen marriage and family as their primary roles. When both were employed full time, as most women were, those who had planned a career had much higher status and higher-paid jobs.

It seems not unreasonable to assume that adolescents who had a significant problem with alcohol or drugs had been less planfully competent than those who did not have a problem. Drug use to a problematic degree—as against mere experimentation—is a sign of undercontrol and in general occurs most often when adolescents are rebellious or their lives lack meaning, or both.

Among the offspring of study members, alcohol and drug abuse was often a serious problem. Both genders were equally vulnerable, with one in six reporting that they had had a "significant" or "serious" problem with either the legal drug, alcohol, or the illegal drugs so available since the late 1960s. Another 30 percent of the sons and 17 percent of the daughters acknowledged having had a "slight problem" with drugs or alcohol. Perceiving their families in childhood and adolescence as relatively less happy was slightly associated with problematic drug use, but the most significant antecedent was a parental problem with alcohol.

Again this takes us back to parental planful competence. When we link parental planful competence (for the small sample where parental planful competence can be paired with a son's or daughter's 1991 responses) with the offspring's acknowledged problems with drugs and alcohol, the children of planfully competent parents far more often report that they never had a problem with drugs or alcohol.

Alcohol and drug use were associated with lower educational attainment, lower occupational attainment, and lower career satisfaction and job involvement (the latter three probably as a consequence of the educational deficit).

The sons and daughters of study members clearly tended to benefit if their mothers and fathers had been planfully competent adolescents. It appears that parental competence contributed to the child's competence. Certainly the more harmonious families had sons and daughters who liked their parents and were emotionally closer to them. Whether those sons and daughters will themselves be better parents, more successful occupationally, and happier persons in their later lives remains to be seen, though it appears that they are on the way to being all these things. The children of the planfully competent have less often divorced, but their divorce rate is nevertheless very high compared with that of their parents.

SUMMING UP

When we have reports from several members of the family, we become aware that each tends to see family relationships from a different perspective and that it is very difficult to label any one perspective as the objective truth. Husbands and wives, even when from similar backgrounds, had different expectations, and as they faced the problems of their jobs, their children, and their mutual adaptations, they had different needs. It appears that men and women who were planfully competent in adolescence or who became more competent in early adulthood were better able to appreciate and adapt to each other's needs. They may also have come to resemble one another, for there was greater resemblance at later maturity than a dozen years earlier in the attributes of husbands and wives who were most satisfied with their marriages.

Where there were severe conflicts between parents, children tended to have more problems. There is also a good deal of evidence from the intensively studied cases that the problems of the children exacerbate problems between spouses. Sometimes there is blame, sometimes merely disagreement as to the best course to be taken. We saw some of this in the families of Henry Barr and Alice Neal. By and large, competent parents seem more often to raise competent children. At very least, the children seem to have better opportunities and better relationships with their parents.

CHAPTER 16

THE LATER YEARS

LOOKING FORWARD AND BACK

In recent years, the costs of bringing back the study members for interviews and testing increased markedly, while the funding available for such research became more scarce, and the mortality rate began to increase as well. It seemed imperative to secure some information on the current status of study members when the older cohort was beginning to reach age 70, and a mail questionnaire was the only feasible means of doing. An eight-page questionnaire was sent out to all study members and spouses for whom we had addresses in November 1990. By then at least 20 of the study members seen in 1982 had died.

Ultimately we received questionnaires from 188 study members and 126 spouses. As was anticipated, the planfully competent were again much more frequently responsive than their peers. Lacking resources for a systematic check of current addresses and lacking adequate information on recent deaths, we cannot accurately ascertain the reasons for nonresponse, but there was a tendency for those who had scored higher in adolescent planful competence and who were better off in 1982 to respond in higher proportion.

In this chapter I draw primarily from three sources: the 1982 interviews and questionnaires, the life history interviews (1983–1985), and the 1990 questionnaires (along with a few items from the 1991 survey of offspring). We look first at the men's and women's decisions with reference to retirement and the circumstances of retirement, then at their thoughts about aging, as reported in 1982 and subsequently elaborated on by many, and at their current life satisfaction, health status, and activities. Knowledge of the chief sources of their satisfaction, the aspects of life that are irksome, and their summing up of how they would like to be remembered give additional clues to the shaping of personal identities.

RETIREMENT

Roughly two-thirds of the male study members had retired by 1990. The proportion was over 80 percent of the Oakland members, by now in their late 60s, and almost exactly 50 percent for the younger group, averaging 62 in late 1990. Only 6 percent retired because they had reached mandatory retirement age. More than half those who had retired said they did so because retirement conditions were favorable and they had many things they wanted to do. Some companies wishing to cut back on staff had offered extra years of work credit to induce early retirements, and many of the men had taken advantage of such offers. Some men, like Henry Barr, had found their work less interesting or challenging than it had been. Poor health was mentioned by 7 percent as the reason for retirement. The proportions retired and reasons for retirement were very similar to those found in major studies of retirement in the United States.[1]

About half the women who had worked for at least ten years in the not-too-distant past had retired. Some, who had not worked beyond age 50, also called themselves retired, but most had worked only briefly. Among women, too, favorable retirement terms and the desire for more leisure, especially if their husbands had retired, were mentioned most frequently as the primary reasons for retirement. A few women retired because of unfavorable work conditions or poor health.

Among men who had retired from their primary job, one in ten had another regular full-time job and a similar proportion had a regular part-time job, while one in seven was self-employed. Thus, more than a third of the "retired" men were still occupationally involved. Somewhat fewer retired women were working regularly and none full time, though several were self-employed, usually in craft activities.

Nearly two-thirds of those who had retired indicated that retirement had worked out well, and that they were able to do almost everything they had planned to do. A fifth had partially realized their plans, but the remaining sixth had done so to only a very limited degree. Health problems, most often the husband's, financial problems, and other obligations—for parents, siblings, or children—had precluded the realization of their retirement plans. Several study members had lost their wives or husbands soon after retirement, and for them future prospects had been completely changed.

We asked about the timing of retirement when both husband and wife had been employed. Surprisingly few had retired at the same time.[2] More than two-thirds of the wives who had worked regularly retired either earlier or later than their husbands (in equal proportions) in intact couples, and a fifth of the retired men reported that their wives had not yet retired. Some of these men had younger wives, having remarried a younger woman after divorce.

Living Arrangements and Financial Status in 1990

In 1990, more than 90 percent of study members who returned questionnaires were living in their own home or condominium. There was little difference between retirees and those still working in their reports of residential stability. Roughly three-fifths of both groups were living in the same quarters that they had lived in ten years previously and expressed the intention of staying there indefinitely.[3] About a third had moved in the previous decade, leaving less than 10 percent who were planning a move in the foreseeable future. The one difference between groups was that retirees were somewhat more likely to be living in condominiums, most having moved some time prior to retirement.

Women were nearly twice as likely as men to be living alone—20 percent versus 11 percent. More women than men had lost a spouse, and older women were less likely to remarry. Nearly a third of the women who were still working were living alone, many of them divorced and a few widowed. Of women who had not been employed in recent years—most of them not having had careers of their own—96 percent were living in their own home or condominium, either with their husbands or alone. The women who had not worked recently reported somewhat higher annual family income than those who were still working, and the latter reported much higher income than women who were retired. A third of the retired women reported family incomes under $30,000, roughly twice the proportion found among women who were still working and those who had not worked in recent years. Nearly half of the women who had not yet retired reported family incomes above $50,000 a year, as did women who had not worked. Thus, the study members who responded to the questionnaire were on the whole very well off.[4]

Retired men also reported much lower annual family incomes than men who continued to work, and this was especially true in the older cohort. Among both men approaching 70 and those in their early 60s, those continuing to work tended to occupy jobs of higher status and to have been more highly involved in their jobs and satisfied with their careers at the time of our previous contact. They also earned substantially higher incomes, with roughly half reporting total family income over $50,000 a year. In both cohorts, the planfully competent were more likely to be employed than their less competent peers.

The Meaning of Retirement

The 1990 questionnaire gave little opportunity to explore the meaning of retirement to men whose jobs had been the primary source of their sense of identity and who had still been engrossed with their work up to the point of retirement. In 1982, however, when only a fourth of the older group of men had retired, we had asked about retirement plans, communication between husband and wife regarding retirement, and, for those who had retired, their feelings about being retired. I draw upon these data as well as the more recent data to give some sense of how early retirees differed from those who continued to work into their late 60s and what retirement meant to the men and women after long occupational careers.

Men who had retired by 1982 for reasons other than poor health had, in general, more than merely adequate retirement incomes. Although most found the prospect of retirement more attractive than continued employment, the great majority had stated that their jobs had been of major importance to their sense of who and

what they were, and a third had named the job as the most important source of identity. Would they soon find themselves feeling differently about themselves once retired? Nearly a third of the early
retirees did say they felt somewhat differently about themselves, but
of these, seven-eighths said they felt more positively about themselves because of the freedom they now enjoyed. Two-fifths acknowledged that at times they missed participation in social
activities that they had enjoyed while still working, a fourth missed
relationships with co-workers, and a fifth missed some job activities,
but only one in eight felt that the loss of the occupational role left
them feeling more negative about themselves. Men in the latter
group tended to take on other jobs after retirement.

Some men had stated in 1982 that they did not intend to retire.
For the most part, these men held to their intentions; as of 1990
even those in the older cohort, approaching 70, had not yet retired.
This was especially true of professionals who could somewhat meter
the amount of energy they wanted to put into their work. Others
had jobs that gave them enough flexibility so that they did not feel
under great pressure. A teacher commented:

> I'm not going to retire. We can't stand each other around the house
> that much, literally so. I think a relationship can really deteriorate if
> you're just hanging around. When I go off to school in the morning at
> 7:30, and I come home at 2:30, then the relationship is refreshed.... I
> don't feel that I'm ready at this point to just go out and play games
> all day and find that that's a fulfilling part of my life. I can do that
> after 2:30. I really need something meaningful.

This man supplemented his teaching with running a ski lodge and
a summer camp, so he had provided a great deal of flexibility for
his involvement in the later years.

Self-employed professionals, like Stuart Campbell and other
physicians, often lessened their work involvement somewhat but
still worked essentially full time. At age 69, one physician reported
that he had no plans to retire but was "enjoying several new experiences, among them becoming an accomplished cook and taking instrument training for private flying." He rated his health
"excellent" and his marriage "almost perfect." Not surprisingly,
when asked how he felt about life at this point, he had checked,
"Enthusiastic, life is very good."

Although only a fifth of the men in the older cohort continued to work beyond age 65, those who did had more often been highly involved in their work and well satisfied with their occupations in 1982, and most of them were enthusiastic about life as they approached 70. Men still working in the younger cohort had also been more involved in their work in 1982, but more of them were continuing to work out of necessity rather than out of choice. Most were satisfied with their lives, but fewer were enthusiastic.

THOUGHTS ABOUT GROWING OLD

On successive weeks in 1992, *Newsweek* magazine featured articles about aging. The first celebrated how good life can be in the later years. The second deplored how miserable it is to grow old. The exponent of the "golden years" wrote about freedom to pursue one's interests, explore new experiences and relationships, and enjoy relaxation and contemplation. The decrier of life in the later years wrote about aches and pains, loss of loved ones, and a lack of a sense of real accomplishment. Each made valid points, so far as our study members were concerned.

In the 1982 structured interview, we asked a number of questions relating to a life review and to aging. For the most part, the questions were open ended, so that responses represent what came to mind, not necessarily what responses would be to questions about a particular facet of aging. For example, three-fifths of respondents in their 50s and 60s had indicated that they had made plans for the future. When this wide range of plans (or sometimes vague wishes) was classified into major categories, the most frequently mentioned plans fell into the category "leisure activities, including travel." Nearly half the study members and their spouses mentioned such plans, but less than a fifth mentioned retirement planning and fewer still mentioned making a will or other plans having to do with death. Had we asked specifically about such matters, we would certainly have found much higher proportions saying they had made financial plans. The responses to the open-ended questions suggest that a substantial number of study members had few concerns about the future or preferred not to think very much about potential problems. When they did think of plans, it was most often in terms of pleasant activities.

When we asked the two-fifths who said they had not made any plans why they had not, the majority of those over 60 gave responses such as, "I prefer to live one day at a time" or "I just don't like to plan my life," or they said they really didn't expect their lives to change very much. The men, and especially the women in the younger study group, more often said, in effect, "It is too early to make plans," though the younger group as a whole was no less likely to have said they had made plans. As would be expected, planfully competent men and women were more likely to have made plans and much less likely to indicate that they did not like to plan their lives.

Planfully competent men and women were more likely than their less competent peers to say they had thought about aging, though the difference was not quite statistically significant. The more competent ones who had not given the matter much thought often said that it was a current concern, while their less competent peers explained that thinking about aging "didn't help" or was "too depressing."

How They Saw Themselves As They Approached Old Age

The most detailed questions about aging were asked when the older subjects were on the average age 62 and the younger ones age 53 or 54. There are surprisingly few differences in the way members of the two age groups saw themselves and their aging in 1982. Indeed, the only respect in which there was an appreciable difference was in relationship to plans and to retirement. Moreover, there were only relatively modest differences between men and women in their views on aging. To the extent that there were differences, I focus on the older group, since our concern is with the effects of aging upon them.

At age 62, more than three-fourths of our study members saw only minor signs of aging when they looked in the mirror: a few wrinkles, hair balding or greying, stature a bit less erect. Only one man in ten and one woman in six felt that there had been major changes in appearance. One man, an outdoorsman in excellent condition, commented: "I can look in the mirror and see things happening, but I'm not really very conscious of them. I'm not willing to let the mirror dominate the way I really feel." He felt himself to be in excellent health.

Many people also mentioned aspects of health, such as having less keen sight or more difficulty hearing. Asked specifically about health problems, roughly three-fifths of the men and women mentioned minor problems, while one in six saw their health as unchanged and nearly 10 percent of the women felt that their health had improved in the previous decade. Nevertheless, roughly one in seven had a serious health problem that affected what they could do and how they felt. Relatively few had to limit their activities at age 62, but two-thirds indicated that they had to limit some activities by the time they were 70. In 1990, arthritis was the most common complaint of the women, and heart trouble or stroke had afflicted nearly 10 percent of the men. Back injuries, knee and hip injuries and replacements, and cancer were each reported by 3 to 5 percent of the study members or spouses.[5] Two-thirds of our subjects reported some loss of energy by 1990, with the other third dividing equally between those who saw no change in their energy level and those who reported a major decrease.

At age 62, most men and women did not think that their interests had changed significantly since their 40s. Those who said their interests had changed often mentioned new activities made possible by more leisure, but most attributed changes to the effects of aging, as in reporting "the end of backpacking days." For some, the loss of favorite activities was of considerable importance, but most study members seem to have taken for granted that at some point they would have to shift away from strenuous activities. A number were surprised at how much they could do, rather than disappointed because of what they could not do. This tendency to have a positive view of themselves was manifest again in 1990, when they were asked to compare their current energy level to that of most people their age. Fully 56 percent saw themselves as having much more or somewhat more energy than most people their age. Only 10 percent saw themselves as having less energy than their age peers, despite the high proportion who acknowledged energy loss.

Nearly half the group felt in 1982 that there had been no change in their relationships with others as a result of their age, but a fourth mentioned change in their relationships with their children. Predominantly, the latter entailed the recognition that the children were now their equals, and communication was much more a two-way street. Many reported closer ties with siblings and other relatives than they had had in earlier years.

The great majority saw no change in how others treated them, although some felt that they were now more likely to be accorded a little greater deference, such as young people opening doors for them. Very few saw any fundamental change; at age 62, they did not see themselves as yet representing the aged, and many of them at age 70 still did not see themselves in this light. Many of those who are retired are still jogging, like Stuart Campbell, or playing golf or taking tours that require a good deal of stamina.

Concerns About Aging

When asked in 1982 to name the "bad things" about getting old, both men and women most frequently mentioned fear of becoming a burden to others. Study members in their 50s were actually more likely to mention this than were those in their 60s, perhaps because the older ones now felt somewhat surer that they would not become a burden. Declining health was viewed as one of the negative aspects of aging by about a third of the men and women, and a fourth also mentioned restrictions on physical activities. The largest difference between the two age groups—and between men and women—was that one-fourth of the older men expressed concern about mental deterioration, twice the proportion among younger men or among women their own age. This was one of the few statistically significant differences.

In his 60s, a highly competent professional whose father suffered from Alzheimer's disease during his last two years of life commented about the father:

> His behavior was quite bizarre—strange paranoid ideas. He became a terrible burden to Mother because he would wander off, was incapable of making decisions but would not accept decisions others made—like if we took him out to eat, he'd decide not to leave the restaurant. Mother finally agreed after two or three years of this to put him in a nursing home. Shortly afterwards, he died.

Later this man commented:

I worry a little bit I'll end up like my father; that's a recent concern, seeing how he ended up. When you live by day to day exercise of your mental faculties, it becomes a threat that might become more difficult. I suppose that's my only real concern.

Men (predominantly those who had not been planfully competent) were also a bit more likely than women to fear social isolation, despite the fact that they were much more likely to have a spouse living than were women. A few men and women mentioned the loss of friends or of a spouse as one of the bad aspects of growing older, but it would appear that most preferred not to think of this possibility.

There were positive aspects of growing older as well, and the most frequently verbalized one was put in many different ways that seemed to amount to the same thing: freedom, fewer responsibilities, and lack of persistent pressures. Freedom to do some things was, of course, the consequence of less demands to do other things. A variant way of regarding the later years was that one no longer burdened oneself with demands to accomplish this or that. As several people put it, one no longer has to prove oneself. Thus, in 1982, many men and women mentioned as positive aspects of aging the kind of life that retirement would make possible. Once retired, they expressed their satisfaction that they were free agents in much the same terms.

An effort to construct an index of concerns about aging yielded little of interest. The planfully competent men and women tended to give fuller, more thoughtful answers and therefore reported more aspects of old age that might be considered concerns than the less planfully competent.

Men who scored high on competence in 1982 were more likely to feel that they would receive all the support that they needed, and they expected their life satisfaction to go up rather than down in their later years. The components of competence were less closely related to expected positive outcomes for women, however. For both men and women, the best predictor of an optimistic anticipation of life ahead—expecting greater satisfaction rather than less— came from those who were currently rated high on both self-confidence and being outgoing. It will be recalled that these two dimensions of personality predicted greater job satisfaction. They appear to index a personality orientation that looks at and for the bright side. Other correlates of an optimistic orientation toward the future were few. Neither men's self-reported health status in 1980 nor their income was related to optimism about the years ahead, though their marital satisfaction showed a marginally significant relationship to optimism. Women's self-reported health was modestly but significantly related to an optimistic outlook for the years ahead ($r = .22$, $p<.01$), and their reported marital satisfaction was also marginally related to an optimistic outlook.

ACTIVITIES

Except for a relatively small group who were impaired by reason of health, the study members and their spouses were an active group. Predominantly middle class, with quite good retirement incomes, they were for the most part able to travel and participate in a variety of leisure activities. Men and women had somewhat different interests, and they differed in the frequency of those activities that were not joint activities.

For women, getting together with friends was the most frequently mentioned activity, and most women did so at least weekly—60 percent of the women as against 42 percent of the men. Women were almost twice as likely to visit with relatives several times a month—45 percent versus 27 percent for the men. Most were going out to dinner more often than they had twelve years earlier. Women were likely to participate to a greater extent in church activities, but they were less likely to be involved in lodges, associations, and other formal social groups or to attend sporting events than were men. A quarter of the men attended sporting events at least a couple of times a month as against half that many women. Women were slightly more likely to say they cared for their grandchildren, but since this was for the most part a joint activity, the differences were not great.

Beyond visiting and going out to dinner, the most frequent activity both men and women mentioned was participation in crafts and hobbies, with nearly half of the men and women saying they were involved every week. At the other extreme, nearly a third indicated that they participated in crafts and hobbies not more than once a year or not at all. Less than a third checked that they participated in community or political activities, but then many contradicted themselves by reporting that they were serving as volunteers in churches, schools, and hospitals. Women were more likely to be involved in drama groups and in artistic expression than were men.

I had assumed that it would be the retired persons who were most involved in almost all kinds of activities, by virtue of their greater amount of time available. I had especially expected that many more retired persons would be involved in activities as volunteers for community betterment. More than half the women were so involved, but this was as true of women still working as of those who had not been recently employed. Men were slightly less likely to serve as volunteers, but there was only a slight difference in favor of the men who were retired. Many of those who had not retired had told us in 1982 that they had slackened their job involvement and were doing more in the community. They had served as volunteers for years.

Among both men and women, those still employed were more often involved in political and community activities than were those who had retired. Not surprisingly, they also went out to dinner more frequently and attended movies and plays more frequently. Women who were still working participated in crafts to a greater extent than those who were retired. Part of the explanation is that many of the women involved in crafts were selling their craft products, and hence were serving both their interests and their pocketbooks. Men's involvement in crafts and hobbies was much greater, however, among the retired than among those still working.

As would be expected, visiting with friends and relatives was much more frequent among the retired, as was caring for their grandchildren. Women who were retired were more likely to go to sporting events (probably with their husbands) than were women who were continuing to work or those who had not worked, but men who were still employed were as likely to go to sporting events as retired men. Retirement also had very little to do with the frequency of travel reported, though it would appear that the kind of travel being done by the retired involved much greater distances and time.

I posed only one question about watching television, and that asked the number of hours per week that the study members watched. Men and women reported very similar means and ranges: on the average, about seventeen hours of television watching per week (standard deviation 11 to 12). A few did not watch television at all; a few others watched more than forty hours a week, with one woman reporting sixty hours and one man fifty-five. Those who were retired watched somewhat more than the men and women still working, but long hours before the television set tended to accompany the study member's own poor health or the spouse's poor health, low life satisfaction reported by husband or wife (or both), and low scores on intellectual investment in 1982.

There was only a modest, marginally significant relationship between adolescent planful competence and the report of hours of television watched, yet there was a more significant relationship with the spouse's planful competence, when husbands and wives of study members are included in the analysis: −.42 for men's watching, correlated with wife's planful competence ($p<.01$) and −.38 for women's watching, correlated with husband's planful competence ($p<.03$). I cannot explain why there was not a stronger relationship between the study members' planful competence and their hours before the tube. If we had systematic data on the content of programs watched, there would almost certainly be substantial differences associated with both planful competence and current competence. A number of the highly competent study members mentioned that they regularly watched programs that analyze the news in depth and occasionally watched a variety of educational and cultural programs. As might be expected, those who were housebound or who had few interests to pursue most often watched almost anything on television.

Sources of Pleasure, Satisfaction, and Dissatisfaction

Given all of these activities, from which did they derive the greatest amount of satisfaction? Both men and women mentioned travel most frequently as having given them the greatest pleasure during the previous year. For men, participation in active sports—primarily golf—was a close second, and for women a number of other activities were essentially tied as sources of pleasure—visiting with friends, working at hobbies and crafts, active sports, and care of grandchildren. For men, too, hobbies and care of grandchildren came high on the list though well below travel and sports in the frequency of mention.

An old popular song suggested that "the best things in life are free." When we presented in the 1990 questionnaire an open-ended question, "What are the best things in your life?" our study members' responses suggested that, with the exception of travel, the best things in life—their families and relationships with their spouses, their children, and their grandchildren—were indeed largely free. Friends were not far behind, especially for women. Thus, while they told us about activities that had given them pleasure, the best things in life were seldom the activities but rather the relationships they had, the freedom they enjoyed, and, for many, the good health that they enjoyed. Those who were most enthusiastic about their current life situation in 1990 tended to be in intact marriages in which they enjoyed good relationships. They also tended to have been somewhat more planfully competent in adolescence. The planfully competent reported themselves to be in better health, financially better off, and more likely to have someone to confide in but only a little better satisfied with their current lives.

Many individuals, in describing what was most satisfying and least satisfying in their current lives, echoed the recital of what they said was good or bad about aging eight years earlier. The 70-year-old husband of one of our study members wrote in his questionnaire that what was best in his life was "living without the urgency to do things at a certain time" and what was least satisfying was "heart and hip problems." He added: "Mentally, life is better; physically, it's all downhill. My life is happy but time is taking its inexorable toll. Nobody has ever figured out a way to postpone the inevitable. Please work on it!"

A planfully competent man who is retired but works ten hours a week and in addition volunteers for his city government five hours a week wrote that what was best was "opportunity to do the things I've wanted to before, but time available and other obligations precluded." Least satisfying was that "several offspring and families live more than 500 miles distant; less than perfect health; less physical ability and endurance." He noted in a space for additional comment, "We're very proud of our four offspring and enjoy seeing them and our grandchildren. Also meeting others in our age group undertaking similar things and having enough money to do most of the things we'd like to do."

Many report what is best in life quite succinctly: "a strong marriage," "my wife," "being in good health—having my husband and great children close by." When a husband or wife rates the marital relationship a 9 or a 10—"almost perfect"—they are very likely to say that they are enthusiastic about life. When they rate their marital relationship much lower, they are likely to tell us that what is good about life is "a nice home," "grandchildren," "my young son," or, in the instance of a man who rated his marriage as "very unhappy," "health and hobbies." Not surprisingly, this man rates his life "in some respects good, others not so good."

In response to the question, "What is least satisfying in your life?" more than a tenth of the study members reported no dissatisfaction, but most had some sources of dissatisfaction or disappointment, some of them quite serious and others relatively trivial. More than a few found that time was finite, and the things they hoped to accomplish seemed infinite. Even retirement did not give one enough time.

Among the more serious problems were health, especially health problems of the men, which were reported by almost a fifth as well as by an eighth of the women in 1990. Even more important for women were relations with their husbands; 14 percent reported that what was worst in life for them was their husbands' behaviors or attitudes or the state of their relationships. Nearly one woman in ten and somewhat fewer men mentioned loneliness, most often people who had lost their spouses in recent years after long and happy marriages. Where husband and wife had looked forward to enjoying each other's company in activities that both valued highly, the loss of either partner was a bitter disappointment, but some, like Judith Judd, managed to find rewarding activities such as volunteering services to others that brought them emotionally close to the people they served and gave a solid sense of meaning to their lives.

The character and problems of their children could also lead to feelings of disappointment and self-blame. Nearly a third of the offspring had had problems with alcohol or drugs, though most had surmounted the drug problems by 1990, but the life-style of their children and the high rate of divorces were sources of unhappiness, especially for the mothers. Being deprived of close ties with grandchildren when a son had been involved in a hostile divorce action was a bitter pill to swallow. Knowing that a son or daughter was engaging in criminal behaviors or was in prison could be even more devastating. Most often, of course, we did not hear from parents whose children had most disappointed them, but a few parents were courageous enough and sufficiently devoted to the research to keep us informed, even when it hurt.

Unless one has some serious chronic illness, health is something that is usually taken for granted, at least during the first fifty years of life. In their 50s and 60s, however, health begins to become problematic for many people, and good health then becomes prized. Fully 20 percent of the study members mentioned their good health as one of the best aspects of their lives, but 15 percent of the men and 10 percent of the women mentioned poor health as the least satisfying part of life. Recall that two-thirds of the older cohort reported that they had had to give up some activities, and they were often prized activities. People whose health was less good tended to watch substantially more television than those who had no impairment. Good health for men was modestly related to their planful competence, more substantially related to their marital satisfaction and also to the health of their spouse. Women's reported health status was modestly related to planful competence but not to marital satisfaction.

REVIEWING LIFE

In later life, most of us tend to look backward more and more.[6] We take stock of where we have come from and how we have come to where we are. Planfully competent men and women appear to do such stock taking along the way, especially when facing problems when a review of past experience can be helpful, but in the later years, particularly after retirement, looking back is one way in which we sustain the identity we had achieved. The so-called life review is a special feature of old age, though by no means confined to it.

In the life history interviews conducted in 1984, we focused on aspects of a life review: adolescent development, turning points, the attainment of maturity, time perspectives, how study members would like to be remembered, and how they felt their lives had been shaped. A few men in the life history sample found the task distasteful. Most of them had scored relatively low on planful competence and had not been highly successful occupationally, nor had their marriages been outstanding. Some, however, had reported much greater marital satisfaction than judges accorded them, suggesting one reason that judges' ratings of the marriages were more highly correlated with planful competence than were self-ratings. In any event, the men who did not want to look back might make derisive remarks about the questions or say they "didn't relate to such questions." They defended themselves from facing up to their lives.

Looking Back on Adolescence

Asked in 1984 whether they now felt they had understood themselves in adolescence, very few men and women felt that they had known themselves at all well during the high school years. The few men who said that they had known themselves "fairly well" or "had reasonably good self-understanding" had scored in the bottom half on planful competence, and no woman thought she had reasonably good self-understanding in adolescence. When we probed for different aspects of self-understanding or self-knowledge, however, some were more positive. Half the planfully competent men reported that to some degree they had known who they were (that is, their sense of identity), while the other half said that this was one respect in which they had not known themselves at all. Planfully competent and less competent men did not differ in reported self-knowledge of values and beliefs, of their own longer-term interests, or their goals. Roughly two-fifths to half of both highs and lows said in later maturity that they had had at least a fairly good knowledge of where they stood in each of these areas. Yet our data from adolescence suggest that the planfully competent had been far more realistic in their adolescent self-concepts than were most of their peers. The more planfully competent, for example, had proposed occupational goals that were much more consonant with their abilities than had their less competent peers. They were more likely to have known something of both their strengths and their weaknesses, but from the vantage point of later maturity they were less cognizant of the extent to which they had already been formulating who they were in adolescence. When seen in their 30s, they had more accurately remembered what they had believed and known in adolescence.

The women were more likely to say they had known their values in adolescence, but fewer claimed self-knowledge regarding their interests or their identities. In one respect, however, women who had been planfully competent clearly excelled their peers: they were far more likely to say that they had known their goals. They were much more likely to have had clear educational and occupational goals even if they did not pursue the latter beyond marriage, almost always the ultimate goal. Nearly two-thirds of the more planfully competent respondents to the life history interview mentioned a specific occupational goal they had held, but no woman in the bottom third of the group did. Three-fourths of the women in that bottom third said they either had no idea or had marriage as their only goal. Even among the top third in planful competence, only one woman (in eleven) felt that she had been adequately aware of her options in adolescence. Three-fifths of the women felt they had been *not at all* aware of their options. This was true of the less planfully competent men as well, but among the planfully competent three-fourths said they had had a fairly good awareness of their options. Here was a highly significant difference that precisely corresponded to the concept of planful competence.

A third of the women, most above the mean in competence, said that they had thought about the kind of man they would like to marry, but only one man in thirty-two said that he had thought seriously about the kind of wife he wanted. Thus, viewing the responses of the men and women looking back on their early years, one gets the impression that the highly competent tend somewhat to underrate their own adolescent maturity but that at times it comes through in their recollections.

It is of interest to note that neither men nor women felt that the Great Depression had had much effect on their lives. A third of the women and more than half the men said they had been essentially unaware of it. This was especially true of members of the younger cohort. One of the men, whose father had been steadily employed in a manual trade, said that he guessed the depression was over when he was born in 1928! (It did not really become acute, of course, until the early 1930s.) The most frequent effect mentioned by those who had been aware was that they developed a "depression mentality": the women learned to make do with less and not to throw out leftovers (as so many of their sons and daughters do), and the men were cautious with their expenditures and their investments. Less than a fifth mentioned significant effects on the family's life at the time, though some had learned only years later how their parents had shielded them from a knowledge of the sacrifices and hardships the depression brought. Yet Glen Elder has demonstrated with data from their adolescent years that their general orientations, the patterns of relationship in their families, and their own early career involvement had all been substantially influenced by the extent of their families' deprivation in the years of the Great Depression. Clearly, awareness is not a necessary condition for an event or set of circumstances to have had a strong influence on aspects of the life course.

The long term effects of the Great Depression, when the family's predepression economic status is taken into account, were in any case relatively modest. They were too slight to produce statistically significant differences in outcomes at later maturity with our small sample. Men from deprived families secured slightly less formal education than their peers from nondeprived families, but their occupational attainment was negligibly less than that of nondeprived men, as were their scores on the index of competence and the measure of psychological health in 1982. There is a suggestive tendency for deprived men of the younger cohort to score slightly lower on a number of outcome measures, but none approaches statistical significance.

I could find no evidence of a deficit associated with depression deprivation in any of the attainments or level of satisfaction of the women study members. Women from deprived families tended to secure less education, to work longer before marriage and to return to the labor force sooner after their children were born, but all of these tendencies are due to the lower socioeconomic status of their families in the predepression years. Again, the only effects of which the women were aware were attitudinal, and although we did not measure them systematically, such attitudes as a tendency toward frugality clearly differentiated the generation that experienced the Great Depression from their offsprings' generation.

How Men and Women Summed Up Their Lives

Most of the planfully competent men and women not only continued to participate in the study but to remain open and not overly defensive. We have seen in the life histories how several summed up their lives. Some study members, however, were resistant. One of the men most resistant to looking back and reporting on the earlier years had scored very high on planful competence. At 65 he was stably but not happily married and he had been occupationally successful, in terms of prestige and income, but his relationship with others, including his wife, had not been close. He had been a heavy drinker for some time. In 1982 he had been seen as aloof, as hostile rather than warm, and as having much less self-confidence than in adolescence. Unlike most of the highly competent, his personality at age 62 had almost no resemblance to his adolescent personality. His flip answers to our questions revealed a man who could not face the aspects of his own life that did not comport with success.

By contrast, one of the men who had scored low on planful competence—the man with the very disorderly career mentioned in Chapter 10—who had served his younger siblings as a substitute father when his own father was away on long overseas trips, a man who was wounded three times in World War II but twice returned to his unit until permanently put out of action and temporarily blinded by a bullet wound, and who was a loving husband and father, could look back on his early years and take pleasure in his relationships. He was not part of the life history sample, but in the 1982 interviews and in the 1990 questionnaire, he presented an identity that one could only admire. He was a man who had always put family first. Perhaps that is why he did not receive a higher score on dependability in the high school years. When his father had been away, he had served to keep his brothers and sisters in line, to help them with their school work, and to help his ailing and rather ineffective mother run a large household. He was less dedicated to school, but in 1982 he said that coming into the Adolescent Growth Study had been an important turning point, "one of the big changes in my life. . . . Prior to that, I didn't want to learn. They interested me in books and I've become an avid reader. I owe this study a lot. Also it's given me a tie to my past that not many people have." At the time of the first follow-up, Judy Chaffey, the school counselor, again helped to mobilize his potential:

> Judy was talking to me, wanted to know why I hadn't done more with my life—why not doing what I'm capable of—anyway, I found out that I'm not the dope I thought I was, so I started to live up to what

she thought I should be, and it made an immediate difference in my income and my attitude.

He had apparently never known that in tested intelligence, he was in the top 5 percent of this somewhat superior sample. He had been treated as if much less gifted, largely, I think , because he was a member of a somewhat devalued ethnic group. A youth of magnificent physique—the favorite of the examining physicians—his facial features did not appeal to the standards of the dominant ethnic group, and he was seen as unattractive. His self-confidence was low. His father, whom he characterized as "the toughest man I ever knew," had not been supportive of his son's aspirations, and the son much undervalued his own strengths.

He had married soon after returning from World War II and had been a dedicated husband and father. His wife commented that when there was a conflict between the demands of job and family, "he has always put family before the job, almost to the point of being fired." She also noted that she had been advised not to marry him, because they were direct opposites. But," she said, "I liked the way he got along with his family, his closeness and devotion to his mother. I knew he would be a good husband." They are "best friends." What has kept them together? "Mutual admiration society," she laughingly responded.

If success came late, he is very proud of it. Nevertheless, looking back, nothing pleased him more than the trophy cup that his siblings had presented to him at Christmas a few years back. Inscribed on it were the words: "To the world's best brother—the father we never had." In 1990, he and his wife had been married for nearly forty-three years. They treasured each other. Each one's primary concerns were for the other.

Erik Erikson proposed that the two great tasks for the middle and later years are to achieve generativity—"interest in establishing and guiding the next generation"—and integrity, to ward off despair. Integrity he defined as the full engagement in and "the acceptance of one's one and only life cycle."[7] I have not tried to classify our study members by Erikson's categories, but it appears that it is on the whole easier for the planfully competent to accept their more smoothly organized and successful lives—easier, certainly in the sense of having ended up in more comfortable circumstances, with fewer immediate concerns. Yet the ultimate criterion of success may be the tenor of memories and relationships carried into the later years. Here again the planfully competent—and especially the ultimately competent—have an advantage, and being outgoing and friendly adds considerably to that advantage. Planfully competent adolescents who had been somewhat aloof often seemed less comfortable if they had not become more outgoing or if they became less warm in their later years.

One of the small number of African-Americans in the Guidance Study looked back on a stable working-class family life with parents who emphasized the importance of conformity and of hard work. He reported at age 55 that he had had little idea of his options as an adolescent:

> My parents were satisfied if you worked and had a job, provided for yourself, but opportunities were not discussed. I don't think they really thought of opportunities then as we do now, and I am sure that one of the reasons they felt that way was because to dream of being a fireman or policeman was not possible, so we didn't think of it.

He noted that he had once, in 1942, been arrested for picketing, with a predominantly white student group, a local bowling alley "because they wouldn't let Blacks or 'Negroes' in to bowl ... and my mother couldn't understand how I would get arrested for doing that." He was fully aware that his life might have been different, "but circumstances didn't come across that way." Circumstances did permit him to hold a low-status but highly secure job, to marry happily, and to raise two children. There was no note of bitterness as he reviewed his life. He had good friends—old friends for the most part—and a loving family. When he was in his mid-30s, he had a chance to work with high school students, and he credited this experience with his having become fully mature. His definition of maturity was "to be independent, sure of yourself, able to make decisions that affect you personally, and carry them out."

He reported that he had never experienced any time, beyond the early years of his employment, when he had been dissatisfied with his life. As to whether he had changed, he mused: "I would like to say I was the same, but I think that maturity gives you more confidence and more patience. But basically, I don't think I have changed that much." How would he like to be remembered? "I haven't given that much thought, because I don't plan to go right away! I think I would like to be remembered as honest, someone you can depend upon. I don't think you can ask much more of a person." As an adolescent, he had scored just about in the middle of planful competence. The mature and sensitive woman who had conducted the life history interview commented: "He seemed to me thoughtful, pleasant, and dignified. He also gives the impression of being a happy man, well controlled, self-contained, satisfied with himself, without arrogance." As a caring adult, he scored well toward the top.

It would seem appropriate to report the summing up by someone who had been much influenced by the women's movement. The daughter of a dominating mother and a gentle father whom she adored, this study member from an upper-middle-class family graduated from a prestigious college. Although she dreamed (rather idly) about a career with the United Nations, she knew she wanted to marry and have a large family, and marry she did right after finishing college. Looking back, she says she was unaware of her potentialities: "I don't think I became aware of my power and what I could do to affect my life and change my life and get what I wanted from my life until much, much later." Like many other women (more than men), she felt that she was still maturing. To her, maturity entailed "capacity to love, to be accepting, to be compassionate." Mobilized to see herself in a different light by the women's movement, she had entered the helping professions, securing a master's degree once her children were grown. She had had considerable psychotherapy, and her discourse reflected a psychotherapeutic orientation. Although in an intact marriage, she had had to face difficult problems with a child who suffered a serious deteriorating disease, and the marriage itself had been "rocky." Now, in later maturity, she felt that marital problems had been resolved.

Asked if she had changed, her response was emphatic: "Oh, God, I don't even recognize myself!" She then described in some detail the respects in which she really had changed very little, until brought back to indicate "the respects in which you've changed most?" "I think in my capacity to live in the moment and to enjoy what is happening," she replied. "And maybe the biggest thing of all is just the size my heart has grown to. (laughing) It's that capacity to care." She would like to be remembered "as a person who has been an agent for change in people's lives whose lives were not working well for them....And I would like my children to remember me as a friend, rather than as a mother." She mentioned the importance of an early mentor and of her long-term psychotherapist in her own development. But as she thought of how her life had been shaped, she gave top billing to her parents:

> My father, because he taught me about softness and gentleness. He taught me everything I know about mothering. He taught me to enjoy beauty—beautiful things, literature, poetry, music. My mother taught me how to be a man in the world. Neither parent taught me how to be angry or how to express my anger, and I regret that.

How we see ourselves in our later years depends on many things—on our personalities, our experiences and relationships, and our daily moods. These determine what we focus on. Often the self-perceptions will be a reflection of the way we are seen by others. Self-perceptions almost always reflect unique self-knowledge, but they are also responsive to the set of defenses and other ego mechanisms established over the years.

Late-Life Losses

The 1990 questionnaires brought news of tragedies in a number of families. A mother writes of the loss of her son:

> The loss of our son was a terrible disaster. He committed suicide. He telephoned me the night before and told me he was going to. I thought he would be OK. I wish I had gotten in the car or done something right then. His widow has been impossible, hiding the children to punish us for God knows what. Our other children have all moved and we miss them....I don't think I know who I am any more. I feel lost.

At least three other study members lost a child to suicide in the past few years and are tortured by regrets. Other offspring have been lost through accidents, alcoholism, or cancer. A father writes: "Having lost our only son just a few years ago makes me reflect back on so many times we didn't communicate more and spend more time together when we had the opportunity." This man finds him-

self living on the edge of poverty as a consequence of bad investments, and he grieves over many things that have gone wrong.

Sometimes the loss of a loved one can be accepted without devastation. The husband of a study member who took her own life a few
years ago wrote that what was best in his life was "good health, my
two daughters and son, memories of 40 years of marriage to your
study member—at 70 I'm still capable of love." Least satisfying in
his life is the loneliness that he sometimes feels. At the end of his
questionnaire he added:

> What else can I say that would have value to you and your study?
> Your study member, my wife of 40 years, was a wonderful lady. A
> saint? No. Perfect? No. Because of illness—pain—loss of life qual-
> ity—she finally took her own life. She discussed it with me and some-
> what with the kids. Because of her helpless condition, she did it
> more for us than for herself. Scared—you bet. Brave—you bet.

And finally he added:

> She told me one time how she used to cheat on your manual dexter-
> ity tests! What a fun lover. Hey, she's been gone for five years. I still
> think of her 20 times a day. Lovely memories. I can't find her clone.

His wife had had back injuries that required the insertion of steel
rods into her spine. When we had last interviewed her at her home,
she was in excruciating pain, but she was trying to hold on as long
as she could.

The Difference a Life Has Made

In Chapter 1, I suggested that one criterion by which a life can be
evaluated is in the difference it has made for others. Perhaps most
of us have not given much thought to this matter, except as we have
made a difference to husbands, wives, or children. Toward the end
of the life history interview, we posed this question: "When you
think of your life as a whole, and the difference that it has made,
how would you most like to be remembered?" The interviewers
were instructed that if asked for explication of the question, they
were not to suggest any particular aspect or dimension such as rela-

tionships or achievements but just what image the respondent hoped others would retain. I wanted an indication of what our subjects regarded as having core importance in their sense of who and what they are or were.

The responses were diverse. Some people mentioned personal traits, some relationships, some achievement. A few thought their lives had not amounted to much; all but one of them had scored below the mean in planful competence. Leading all other categories was the choice of some phrasing that connoted friendliness and loving care for others. Here we would place Stuart Campbell's wish to be remembered as a gentle person. Karl Schulz, true to his identity as a family man, wanted to be remembered as a good husband and father. Henry Barr's thoughtful response bears repeating:

> As a good person, a sympathetic, feeling and compassionate person, that more than as a competent lawyer. If I made any change in recent years, I think it is more in understanding and emphasizing the human values as opposed to merely the factor of competence in a profession.

Thus, the highly competent lawyer is classified primarily as a caring, compassionate person, but his professional achievements are certainly not irrelevant to his view of himself.

Mary Wylie's choice was to be remembered as "hard-working, cheerful, with a sense of humor," and above all as a creative artist. The latter element was a less frequent one and was found almost exclusively among those who had scored in the upper half on planful competence. Alice Neal, our successful business woman, gave an answer that was perhaps closest to the "caring" category but not entirely in it: "As generally being cheerful and helpful; I am concerned about people and I would like to be remembered as being a nice person."

The summary of how study members would like to be remembered is given in Table 16. Our study members—highly competent and less competent—most often see themselves as friendly, caring persons, and most of them are. It is no surprise to find three-fourths of the women gave this response. Being a good parent or spouse takes second place; to be held dear in the memories of those with whom one has shared the greater part of life and those whom one has nurtured may not give a sense of immortality, but it

Table 16.1.   How Would You Like To Be Remembered?
(Percentages)

	Men	Women
As a friendly, caring person	50	75
As a good parent or spouse	25	32
As a moral, responsible person	22	25
As creative, innovative, artistic	16	14
As productive, effective	28	7
Not memorable—"nothing"	9	14
(Number of respondents)	(32)	(28)

Note: Many responses fit into more than one category.

should permit one to go peacefully. As might be expected, highly successful men more often wanted to be remembered for their productiveness and competence—"for making things happen"—than did women.

For men who had done less well, particularly those who had not been planfully competent, there was often more than a slight tone of bitterness when we asked them how they would like to be remembered, when they consider their lives as a whole, and the difference they made. After a long pause, a man who had not made the best use of his opportunities commented:

> I guess there's not much I can be remembered for. I don't know. I haven't won a Nobel Prize. [*Interviewer:* Most of us haven't!] I am kind of like the guy who sticks the Coke bottle in the automobile door. There is really nothing in this life that people will remember me for. But this poor guy on the assembly line says, "At least I have done something in this life that some place, somewhere, somebody is going to remember me when they hear it rattle." A Major in the Army—well, the glory is gone.

Contrast that with the identity of Marie, a woman of intermediate planful competence whose violent, dictatorial father had made her feel worthless as a child. Through employment following high school, which included mentoring by her employer and guidance by co-workers, she began to think by her 30s that marriage might

be a possibility for her. Before that she had felt no one would want
to marry her. Then her life was completely turned around when
her brother, who recapitulated his father's explosive temper, killed
both his wife and himself, leaving an adolescent son. Marie raised
the boy. At the same time she took increased responsibility at work
and served as confidant to many of her co-workers and superiors.
How would Marie like to be remembered? It was as "Aunt Marie":

> All my nephew's friends and some of my grandnephew's friends are
> starting to call me Aunt Marie. I think I always want to be remem-
> bered as Aunt Marie. I never wanted my nephew to call me mother,
> because I am not his mother, but he feels that I was a mom and dad
> to him and Mother's Day he always remembers me. But I am still his
> Aunt Marie and that's the way I want it, just plain old Aunt Marie.

The interviewer commented, in summing up the interview: "I
thought it a very apt description of both the kind of person she
seemed to me to be and the kind of values she holds. Everybody's
favorite aunt, the responsible, dependable, reliable person of the
family." Aunt Marie needed no one to tell her that her life had
counted. She had been neither beautiful nor extremely bright, but
she had a loving mother who had somehow survived her husband's
violence and imbued her daughter with the will to persevere. Self-
confidence came much later.

Life Satisfaction in the Later Years

The later years bring more unpredictable events into the lives of
most people. At any given time, many older persons will be dealing
with losses and with difficult decisions. Life satisfaction is somewhat
more fragile. Yet most do recover from their losses unless they are
physically infirm, and they find activities that bring satisfaction.

I have alluded to the question on general life satisfaction contained in the 1990 questionnaire. It came late in the questionnaire,
after questions about specific satisfactions and dissatisfactions,
health, and the state of the marriage, and it was posed in a very
broad way: "In general, how do you feel about your life these days?"
There were five categories of answers: "Enthusiastic, life is very
good," "I'm generally satisfied," "In some respects good, others not

so good," "Fair to poor, I'm not really satisfied," and, "Disappointed, life is very poor."

Only 4 persons among the 307 who responded to the question checked the most negative category and only 6 the next to lowest. Seven of those 10 were women. A fifth of the women and a sixth of the men chose the middle category, while nearly a third of both sexes reported themselves enthusiastic. Thus, more than three-quarters seemed generally satisfied with their current situation.

Whether men and women were retired in their 60s was far less important to their life satisfaction than the state of their health and that of their spouse and the state of the marriage itself. For women, marital satisfaction was by far the strongest correlate of general life satisfaction, with a correlation coefficient of .59. Next in strength of correlation was her husband's report of life satisfaction, .49. Women's self-rating of health followed, with a coefficient of .38. Almost as strongly related to her satisfaction was her husband's self-rating of his health. Adolescent planful competence was correlated with life satisfaction fifty or more years later at .26, just verging on significance ($p<.06$), because of the small number of cases for whom adolescent planful competence had been assessed. Their 1982 measures of competence were not quite as highly correlated to women's life satisfaction, but the correlation coefficient was highly significant statistically. Dissatisfaction with one or more children, as reported in 1982, was also significantly related to lower life satisfaction eight years later.

When these several measures were entered into a multiple regression equation, adolescent planful competence, marital satisfaction, and the women's own health rating accounted for more than 70 percent of the variance in the life satisfaction score for the thirty-two women for whom we had the measure of planful competence, although the direct effect of planful competence itself was not significant. For the larger sample of women who had been seen in 1982, but for whom adolescent planful competence had not been assessed, their marital satisfaction, self-rating of health, husband's health rating, and their own competence as of 1982 accounted for nearly two-fifths of the variability in the measure of life satisfaction (see Table A. 20 in Appendix A).

Men's life satisfaction was most closely linked with their wives' separately reported life satisfaction (as noted for women, .49). Marital satisfaction was a substantially less important influence on reported life satisfaction in 1990 for men than for women but came next in size of effect, followed by health. Having had to cut down on activities because of health had almost as high a correlation with life satisfaction as had health itself but added nothing when entered with health in a multiple regression. Wives' ratings of their health were as strongly related to men's life satisfaction as were the men's own health ratings. Both adolescent competence and competence at later maturity were modestly correlated with men's life satisfaction, but when health and marital satisfaction were controlled, they no longer contributed to satisfaction.

Current income was not at all related to life satisfaction in this reasonably well-off sample (which nevertheless has a fairly wide range of incomes, from under $15,000 to well over $100,000, although our cutoff category in the questionnaire was $50,000). However, a man's satisfaction with his career, as expressed eight years earlier, was related to life satisfaction even when other variables were controlled for.

In a multiple regression, roughly a third of the variability in men's life satisfaction is accounted for by the level of his wife's satisfaction, his rating of his own health, and his degree of satisfaction with his career as assessed in 1982. Their own marital satisfaction proved to be less important than their wives' level of life satisfaction and did not contribute to explained variance in men's life satisfaction.

Thus, it appears that both partners tend to be satisfied with their lives in the later years when their marriage is a source of mutual support and satisfaction, when both are in good health, and when the man can look back on his career with the feeling that it had been what he really wanted and when the woman does not feel dissatisfied with her children.

CHAPTER 17

EPILOGUE

The life course is a series of transitions in which different roles and responsibilities are managed together, some having greater priority at one time and others at a different time. There are discontinuities; some roles come to an end, others are redefined. Regularities exist in the ordering of roles at different periods, but there is no clear-cut set of stages beyond late adolescence or early adulthood.

Boys and girls born in the 1920s were taught from an early age to expect different lifelines. For some, their expectations were informed by guidance that permitted consideration of a wide variety of options and the necessary steps for pursuing such options. For others, there was perhaps little more than the expectation that a male would enter the occupational world and find a job after completing schooling, while a female would seek an appropriate husband and raise a family. For millennia, some parents have recognized that a woman's potentialities are as great as a man's and have urged their daughters to make the most of their talents. Until recently, they were a rare breed. It took women who were educated, aware of their own potentialities, and sufficiently "maladjusted" to the constricting norms of their society to call for a mobilization of women to achieve a measure of equality. Equality means freedom to choose, not that one gender must do what the other does. Not all women wanted to have their consciousness raised, but almost all the women in our study, even the most traditional, think that women should be paid the same salaries for ding the same work as men. Almost all believe that women who want to work should be permitted to work, though a few still see a home-bound career as the only appropriate course for a woman. Far fewer of their daughters would so limit a woman's potentialities.

It did not seem to make much difference, for our study members, whether they married before completing their education or afterward, provided they secured the same amount of education. In the cohort of men and women born in the 1920s, a large number entered the occupational world and some the marriage world just after completing high school. A somewhat lesser number graduated from college, sometimes after they had served in the military. The breaks in their education were not primarily by their own choice, but most of the men completed their education before age 30, even if they had served in the military.

The offspring of these children of the Great Depression have had much more discontinuous educational experiences. They did not feel that their education had been completed when they entered the occupational world. Many returned to college well beyond their 20s, and a third of the young men and women in their 30s said they were seriously considering further education, either to complete college or to undertake graduate work. Sometimes one must work to finance further education. Sometimes the education will be preparation for a new career line. In short, they seem likely to have less orderly careers and less continuity in their lives. It was hard to see any set of clearly demarcated stages in the careers of our original study members, and it will be much more difficult to find such stages in the lives of their offspring.

The structure of the occupational world changed markedly in the past century and is changing even faster now. At the turn of the last century, more than a third of the American labor force was employed in agriculture. Blue-collar jobs in manufacturing, transportation, mining, and construction employed a similar proportion of the labor force. Less than a fifth of all workers were in white-collar jobs—professionals, managers, clerical, and sales workers—and service jobs employed less than 10 percent of all workers and were predominantly in private households.[1] Today more than half the labor force is in white-collar jobs, many of these jobs requiring a high level of education and trained expertise. Employment in manufacturing, mining, and transportation has declined, relative to employment in government, finance, trade, and technical services, all of which now provide greatly increased job opportunities. The rate of change has increased as technology has made ever more rapid contributions to efficiency, often replacing workers with robots or computers. The great increase in the proportion of women in the labor force has been concomitant with these trends.

Our study members secured more education than their parents. Their children went further still, though not nearly as far beyond the parental generation. Male study members also exceeded their father's occupational attainment, for the most part. They enjoyed economic growth over much of their careers. The male offsprings' careers are already somewhat less orderly than the careers of their fathers, while the reverse is true of the female offspring. The biggest difference for women is that most now have both families and occupational involvements essentially through the adult years.

Divorce rates were still relatively low in the period prior to World War II. Recall that only about a sixth of the study members' parents had divorced during the subjects' childhood and adolescence. The study members themselves doubled that proportion of divorces, and more than half of their children over age 40 have already been divorced. The trend seems to be leveling off, but it is hard to predict the future of the family other than to note that most of the young still marry and still have children. At the same time, more and more of those children are being raised by a single parent, a much rarer phenomenon early in the century. When a family was broken by death or divorce early in the century, a grandmother or an elder daughter frequently served as a surrogate mother or mother's assistant, the daughter often giving up hope of establishing her own family. That seldom happens today.

THE MEANING OF COMPETENCE FOR MEN AND FOR WOMEN

To the extent that the central roles of men and women differ markedly, as they did for the generation born in the 1920s, we would expect different attributes to be associated with success in those roles, and that was indeed the case. My use of planful competence, comprising self-confidence, intellectual investment, and dependability, as an organizing principle for the life course was obviously from a male-centered perspective. Planful competence made for high educational and occupational attainment. Nevertheless, the concept had considerable applicability to women, although the three components were much less related in the adolescent years. For both men and women, planful competence predicted greater educational attainment, but for women, all of the

effect came through the component "dependable." Being dependable meant knowing the basic rules and expectations that allow for
smooth social interaction—being nonrebellious, controlled, and responsible. Being dependable meant not being swept along in the
hedonistic current within the peer group. It meant keeping in
mind what one wanted to achieve in marriage and in family life.

Intelligence was almost as important in educational attainment
for women as for men, but most young women did not parade their
intellectual investedness, so it was IQ and family socioeconomic status rather than being "intellectually invested" that teamed with dependability to predict educational attainment. Today's adolescent
girls, by contrast, are much more fully engaged in intellectual life,
and I suspect that we would find it much easier to assess their intellectual investedness.

Young women clearly gave more thought to the kind of person
they wanted to marry than did young men, and planful competence made more of a difference in how they thought about marriage and family life. Despite less continuity from adolescence to
adulthood in the measure of competence, women who had been
planfully competent tended to have happier and more enduring
marriages. Almost all the young women wanted to marry and have a
family, but the planfully competent invested themselves more fully
in the family just as the more planfully competent men invested
themselves more fully in their occupations. The competent
women—and men—had more children than their less competent
peers. Why these competent men and women wanted more than
two children is somewhat of a mystery, but many did. The less competent tended to be more often daunted by children. Highly competent men and women were in general somewhat more satisfied
and successful parents than their peers.

Perhaps because of their greater commitment to their families,
perhaps because of wiser choices, perhaps because of negotiating
skills, planfully competent women were less likely to become divorced. This was not the case with the planfully competent men,
though very few had more than a single divorce, and this was usually followed by a successful marriage. The highly competent men
were more involved in their jobs in the early adult years. They had
much greater occupational success and satisfaction in their careers
than did less competent men.

For both men and women, early competence meant fewer crises

in every decade up to their 50s. The highly competent men were more likely to find the right job and to remain in the same line of work. The highly competent women were more likely to find the right husband and to feel rewarded in their family roles. Both choice and selection were involved: choice of attractive opportunities and selection permitting the more competent to take advantage of the opportunities.

COMPETENCE AND CUMULATIVE ADVANTAGE

Thus there was payoff for high early competence—smoother, faster sailing—but rough seas for those who were very low in competence. In a paper entitled "Competence and Socialization" that strongly influenced my thinking about competence, M. Brewster Smith contrasted "vicious and benign circles" of development.[2] The same basic idea has also been called the Matthew principle: "To him who hath shall be given; from him who hath not shall be taken away that which he hath." As Smith noted: "Launched on the right trajectory, the person is likely to accumulate successes that strengthen the effectiveness of his orientation toward the world while at the same time he acquires the knowledge and skills that make his success more probable."[3] That is the benign circle. The vicious circle is more briefly characterized: "Off to a bad start, on the other hand, he soon encounters failures that make him hesitant to try." In other words, early advantages become cumulative advantages; early behaviors that are self-defeating lead to cumulative disadvantages.

One of the readers of this book when it was still in manuscript form wrote repeatedly in the margins, "cumulative effect." That is a crucial element in my argument in behalf of planful competence. At the same time, neither experiencing a vicious cycle of repeated failure nor being on a roll in a benign cycle of success is an inevitable consequence of low or high competence. People *can* change their lives, as many of our subjects did. Sometimes a premarital pregnancy or abortion jolted an adolescent girl into taking stock and changing course. Our study members were more fortunate than those who live in poverty in urban slums. Those with resources to draw upon could more readily avoid vicious cycles. Recall that while adolescent planful competence was the best predictor of men's educational and occupational attainment and of men's and women's personality change from the high school years onward, a better predictor of change through the adult years was afforded by competence at age 30 or 37. Early competence does not guarantee mature competence; it merely makes it more likely. Current competence at any given period was usually most strongly correlated with both satisfaction and effective performance at that period. Individual determination can bring about change throughout the life course.

In Chapter 1, I discussed a number of criteria by which a life might be evaluated as well lived: success, mental health, life satisfaction, caring human relationships, and successful parenting. There is great diversity in the degree to which our study members met the criteria. Very few persons rank at the top in all respects, but those who tend to do so were predominantly seen as planfully competent in adolescence or as competent in early adulthood. Yet I hope that the emphasis on planful competence has not detracted from seeing all our study members primarily as human beings, seeking to build a life in a world not always hospitable to their wishes and their needs.

ELEMENTS WE COULD NOT TAP

Many of the lives of our study members could provide the story lines for exciting and revealing novels. A novelist could bring into the story the perceptions and feelings of lovers, young and old, the mental turmoil that a man endured when he lost a job because he had acted unwisely, or failed to act when he should have. She could depict the exhilaration a woman felt with the attainment of her Ph.D. or the birth of her first child, or that a man felt when a major promotion told him, "You've got it made!" We were not there at the time. We could not enter into the mental processes of our study members as a novelist could enter into the minds of characters. We could only register what had happened and how the men and women felt about it later. And we learned, as others with longitudinal data have, that both the recollection of what happened and how a person felt about it can change over the years.

Each of us faces common issues as we develop and age, and yet each has different concerns that we carry over from our early years. We may be supremely confident of ourselves in some situations and relationships and quite unsure of ourselves in others. How much do we owe to others, how much to ourselves? What we learned in our families has given us skills and values but perhaps also blind spots and vulnerabilities when faced with particular problems or persons. One child starved for affection may reach out, like Beth Green, to help others, so they will be appreciative. Another may become completely rebellious and self-indulgent, like Reb, whom we met in Chapter 9.

All of us have to deal continually with how we are responded to by others, how we feel about our own actions when they have gone awry. We have to deal with our aging, our losses, future uncertainties. These are problems everyone faces, competent or not. The more competent appear to be better able to cope, especially in the earlier years, and they have less acute problems to cope with. Nevertheless, some of our least planfully competent adolescents were able to grow and to become self-confident, intellectually invested, and dependable persons who made a contribution to the lives of others. Not having been able to monitor them through their 20s, not being able to get inside their minds as they dealt with the transition to adulthood, we cannot say how or when they achieved mature competence, but we know from a few of our briefer histories that this can happen at any age.

There is a danger in the message conveyed when we rank individuals and compare those high and low on the ranking of competence. Most study members who are in between the very highs and very lows are nevertheless competent, mature human beings; they are no less warm and agreeable persons than are the highly competent. They are, by and large, no less happy, and only a little less well satisfied with their current lives, only a little less psychologically healthy. Indeed, some of them are happier and healthier than their more competent peers, and they have contributed to the happiness of others.

FURTHER THOUGHTS ON THE CONCEPT OF PLANFUL COMPETENCE

It is important to distinguish my concept of planful competence from the three components employed to measure it. The components, as measured, were an approximation of the personality traits that should lead to effective, successful lives. The aggregate measure served me better than I expected, especially in predicting personality change over time, but the components do not fully capture the concept as I now envision it.

In adolescence, a measure of dependability, of ability to exercise control and responsibility, is crucial, but control can be overdone. Just as there is a happy medium between being assertive or submissive, so there is a happy medium between overcontrol and undercontrol. In scoring the component "dependable," however, the more overcontrolled one is, the higher is the score on dependability. It is striking that relative to their adolescent personalities, every one of the highly competent men and women scored lower on dependability in later adulthood. They had not become less productive or dependable, but most had been rated less overcontrolled. At the same time, many of their peers had become less undercontrolled, less rebellious, less self-defeating, and therefore they had moved up in their scores on "dependable." The scoring was dictated by the data generated from the Q-sorts over time, but the concept of planful competence does not require this mode of scoring. Ideally, we want flexible responsibility: people who can be counted on to do their part, who will not act out rebellious feelings when they have an assignment to carry out or otherwise be self-defeating, but people who are neither conforming nor rigid.

In first describing my idea of planful competence, I noted that it entails knowledge, abilities, and controls. Above all, competence demands a fair measure of self-knowledge, of knowing one's strengths and weaknesses in order to build on the strengths and overcome the weaknesses. Some of our most competent men in later maturity, such as Karl Schulz, had not been rated very high on self-confidence in high school, but they realistically assessed their strengths, and as they built upon those strengths they became much more self-confident. Valuing intellectual matters, having wide interests, and being open to new experiences also rank high among desired attributes. The component "intellectually invested" captured this orientation and tended to offset the emphasis on overcontrol in the component "dependable."

The component "self-confident versus feels victimized" clearly connotes much more than self-confidence. It is highly correlated with the clinical psychologist's profile of psychological health. The items defining the negative pole might in fact be considered a scale of psychoneurotic tendencies, and so the component does double duty. A measure of satisfaction with self alone would not have served the index of competence nearly so well. Some very successful, very self-confident individuals are given to feeling victimized when they do not get their way and are distrustful and wary of conspiracies. They may be shrewd dealers, but more often such tendencies lead people to defeat themselves. Therefore, I would add to my specifications self-directedness, ego resilience, and friendliness.

Planful competence is certainly not the whole story. It is merely a convenient way to sum up certain attributes that appear to be highly useful for effective functioning in modern society and for making more realistic and appropriate choices in life. A critical question to be considered is: How does one produce planfully competent adolescents? How does one raise children to become self-confident, intellectually invested, dependable, and warm, friendly beings? Here our data give at least a partial answer: Children need families who love them and nurture them but also put demands upon them, set standards for them, and challenge to do their very best.

PRODUCING PLANFUL COMPETENCE

A recent book comparing parental expectations of school children in the United States and in Japan and China notes that most American parents tend to be pleased if their child does average work.[4] They assume that this is good enough to show the child's ability. Chinese and Japanese parents assume that good performance comes from effort, not from native ability—that effort, in effect, makes ability. They expect the child to do his or her utmost—not merely to obtain good grades but in preparing for life. Perhaps the Chinese and Japanese expect too much. Perhaps, but their children do learn how to learn, and they markedly outperform American children in mathematics and science. Moreover, in the early years, at least, they appear to observers to be happy and self-confident. They become determined to do their best. Our most competent study members developed such determination in their formative years.

An initially surprising finding from the analysis of the Guidance Study parenting data was that among parental behaviors rated when the sons were 6 to 10 years old, one of the strongest predictors of adolescent planful competence for boys was having parents rated "overdemanding." Behaviors that the raters saw as reflecting overdemanding parents in the preadolescent years seem in fact to have contributed to all three components of competence by challenging the youngster. Once the boys performed competently, the parents had less need to be demanding in subsequent periods. After age 10, parental demand had a different meaning; it connoted that the child was not performing adequately. The more competent the son was, the less need there was for high parental demands. By the senior high years, parents who were seen as overdemanding tended to have less effective, often rebellious sons, and the parents were now often battling with their offspring.

A child must be loved, given authoritative views of appropriate behavior, and motivated to put forth the effort to do the best he or she can. Competence does not derive primarily from high IQ or from the high socioeconomic status of one's family but from the combination of firm guidance and loving support that the child receives. High intelligence and high socioeconomic status, with their attendant educational benefits, make it easier for parents to know what is needed and to provide what is needed—but they do not ensure that this will be the case, nor does their lack necessarily lead to inadequate parenting.

WILL PLANFUL COMPETENCE STILL MAKE A DIFFERENCE?

What can we expect in the generation of our study members' grandchildren, many of whom are now adolescent? Certainly there will be less difference between men and women in the kind of choices they make. Marriage is likely to be deferred until the couple has a chance to get to know one another by living together. Sex will have no mysteries for them. Improved contraception should prevent unwanted pregnancies. Will this lead to more enduring marriages or partnerships when the couple does have children? We do not know. Almost certainly the more planfully competent will have smaller families, not larger ones. Already in 1970 the study members' adolescent offspring were talking of having a single child or, at most, two. They were aware of the world population problem to a surprising extent.

There is good reason to believe that planfully competent adolescents and young adults in the 1990s are less likely to engage in promiscuous sex and thereby become victims of AIDS and other sexually transmitted diseases. There is good reason to believe that planfully competent adolescents and young adults in the 1990s are less likely to be binge drinkers, smokers of cigarettes, or regular drug users.[5] Those who think before they act, who ease up on the gas pedal before a dangerous curve and put on the brakes when they realize they are going too fast on a strange road, are much less likely to crash.

The young of the 1990s have different options available than did the young of the 1930s and 1940s. Whether they have more or fewer options remains to be seen; there are many economic and social uncertainties, and it may be difficult to know where one will fit into a society that is chaotic. Surely under such circumstances, those who make the most careful assessments will more often make the best choices.

The capacities and early experiences in the family that make for adolescent planful competence also make for higher scores on a measure of psychological health at every period when study members were assessed. Consider these very strong correlates of adolescent planful competence: both males and females who scored high on the competence index were seen as "interesting, arresting persons," as "calm," "straightforward," "productive," "giving." They were not seen as more conforming than their peers, but they were much more predictable. They were not "thin-skinned," "fearful," or indecisive.

Can one doubt that these attributes will still give an advantage to the adolescent so characterized today? Can one doubt that a person who is calm, straightforward, and giving will tend to be a better spouse and parent than one who is excitable, deceptive, and unwilling or unable to be giving? Can one doubt that "productiveness" and having wide interests are desirable attributes for occupational success, especially in a climate of occupational instability?

Nevertheless, the critical issue for the future as for the past is the kind of socialization that a child and adolescent experiences in the home, the school, and the local community. Our research casts light only indirectly on children who grew up in poverty, deprived of the kind of opportunities that were available to members of stable working-class and middle-class families during and after the

Great Depression of the 1930s. Anyone who has looked closely at the fragmented families of urban ghetto dwellers, struggling to maintain minimal shelter, many turning to drugs or alcohol to escape endless feelings of hopelessness, knows that the children in these families will be neither positively challenged nor emotionally supported. Our data have shown how important family harmony can be for a youngster's sense of self-esteem and becoming a responsible adolescent. It would be naive to assume that any substantial number of youngsters from the most chaotic and deprived backgrounds will become planfully competent by the criteria that have been here proposed, yet a few of them somehow will make it, thanks to loving, firm parenting.

That said, I believe that the conditions making for planful competence within stable working-class and middle-class families are not likely to change markedly. Both early and recent studies of parenting agree on the importance of emotional support and firm and consistent discipline. This does not mean any specific regime. The Campbells and the Schulzes differed in the extent to which they invoked rules, but both presented their children with high standards and solid support. These parents were highly involved at all ages. At the same time, they were not intrusive. They allowed a good measure of autonomy.

A FINAL NOTE ON THE RESEARCH

Three studies were undertaken in an era when systematic research on human development was just beginning. They were directed by men and women who had limited theoretical formulations to draw upon and none of the technology we now possess for collecting detailed data—no tape recorders, video recorders, or computers. The staff interviewed mothers and children and wrote notes on what they said, administered tests, gave physical exams, measured subjects' growth year by year, and observed adolescents in their interactions with other adolescents and with staff. More than a decade after the study members had graduated from high school—nearly two decades for the Oakland sample—some of the same staff interviewed, tested, and gave physical exams to a substantial proportion of the sample. Two more adult follow-ups followed. They incorporated more sophisticated measures and recorded interviews. In all, nearly sixty years worth of data were compiled. Mere storage of the raw data is a problem.

For several decades, some critics said that the research would never pay off beyond the discoveries of the early years. The methods of data collection and early conceptualizations were too crude and too far behind the cutting edge of the behavioral sciences. But raw data that were secured in many different contexts, using a variety of methods, can sometimes be recoded or re-rated to serve concepts not originally envisioned. Without the computer, the analyses contained in this book would have been impossible. As a research assistant more than fifty years ago, I spent weeks doing a single multiple regression on a Monroe calculator. Every individual's score on each variable had to be multiplied by his score on all the other variables in the regression, each had to be squared, and all had to be entered into the regression equation. Each of the multiple regressions presented in this book took less than a second of the computer's time. The data set used to carry out these analyses contained several thousand variables that were assessed over the past fifty years.

It would have been impossible, in the late 1920s, to envision a research product that encompassed such a range of data, but it became possible because the original investigators cared about the quality of the data they were collecting. They were painstaking in their efforts to describe accurately and to maintain systematic data files as well as close ties with their research subjects.

We know now that no matter how accurate one's representation is of an interview on audio- or videotape, one cannot control the premises held or the feelings that interviewer and respondent have for each other or the effect of those premises and feelings on what is subsequently learned in the interview. We have seen such effects in the detailed histories of several of our study members. There is no absolute verity in research on human lives, but I believe that what has been presented captures some major realities of our subjects' lives.

There is more to tell about these study members. Most have been faithful participants. They tell us that the study has meant much in their lives. Some say they turned their lives around by virtue of the attention and guidance they received and the self-searching that periodic questioning entailed. Others were threatened or felt they did not measure up and dropped out. Many of the dropouts had the cards stacked against them: They came from conflicted families, had parents who were lax, or were deprived in other respects. What is perhaps most impressive to us who have been involved with them is how resilient so many have been and how dedicated. We owe them a great debt.

The lives of the children of the Great Depression inevitably bear some imprint of that depression and of the wars and other major events of their historical era. Nevertheless, the influences of their early experiences in the family, the school, and the peer group upon their choices and performances as they made the transition from adolescence to adulthood have clear implications for the lives of their successors. Each generation faces unique constellations of historical events, even as each individual experiences a unique combination of genetic potentials, parental guidance and support, and critical life events, yet the processes that shape individual lives appear to remain essentially unchanged.

APPENDIX A

SUPPLEMENTARY TABLES

Table A.1. Intercorrelations of the Millsap-Meredith Q-Sort Components
(Males above the diagonal, females below)

	Self-confident/ Victimized	Assertive/ Submissive	Cognitively Committed	Outgoing/ Aloof	Dependable	Warm/ Hostile
Senior High School Years						
Self-confident/ feels victimized	—	-.15	.45***	.39***	.37***	.30**
Assertive/submissive	-.25**	—	-.12	.24*	-.15	-.65***
Cognitively committed	.31**	.05	—	.16	.55***	.33**
Outgoing/aloof	.38***	.20*	.06	—	-.20	-.15
Dependable	.17	-.23*	.28**	-.34***	—	.31**
Warm/hostile	.27**	-.52***	.45***	-.18	.35***	—
As of 1982						
Self-confident/ feels victimized	—	.12	.43***	.49***	.39***	.40***
Assertive/submissive	.20*	—	-.08	.03	.22	-.47***
Cognitively committed	.42***	.11	—	.36***	.09	.40***
Outgoing/aloof	.55***	.12	.46***	—	-.11	.41***
Dependable	.41***	.41***	.01	.15	-.11	-.08
Warm/hostile	.33***	-.43***	.34***	.23**	-.13	—

*p<.05; **p<.01; ***p<.001.

**Table A.2. Mean Planful Competence Scores and Scores on
Personality Components**

	Senior High	1958	1970	1982
Males				
Planful competence	51	60	79	71
Self-confident/feels victimized	6	4	15	15
Assertive/submissive	23	26	27	29
Intellectually invested	–6	–8	1	–3
Outgoing/aloof	4	7	15	20
Dependable	51	64	62	59
Warm/hostile	–1	–14	–7	0
Females				
Planful competence	34	51	66	60
Self-confident/feels victimized	5	4	11	11
Assertive/submissive	14	12	16	11
Intellectually invested	–18	–8	–1	–2
Outgoing/aloof	18	19	30	26
Dependable	47	55	55	51
Warm/hostile	–20	–3	5	22

Note: See Appendix B for complete scoring descriptions.

Table A.3.   Competence Scores and Personality Component Scores for Stuart Campbell

	Senior High	1958	1970	1982
Planful competence	145	123	116	124
Self-confident/feels victimized	25	26	27	34
Assertive/submissive	35	37	38	27
Intellectually invested	42	30	38	27
Outgoing/aloof	20	27	40	38
Dependable	78	66	51	63
Warm/hostile	10	20	−6	36

Note: See Appendix B for complete scoring descriptions.

Table A.4.   Competence Scores and Personality Component Scores for Mary Wylie at Successive Periods

	Senior High	1958	1970	1982
Planful competence	66	93	109	86
Self-confident/feels victimized	7	20	24	32
Assertive/submissive	8	4	25	20
Intellectually invested	−9	−23	13	5
Outgoing/aloof	30	11	52	53
Dependable	67	95	71	49
Warm/hostile	−68	−19	5	5

Note: See Appendix B for complete scoring descriptions.

**Table A.5. Competence Scores and Personality Component Scores
for Karl Schulz at Successive Periods**

	Senior High	1958	1970	1982
Planful competence	93	114	118	111
Self-confident/feels victimized	7	27	30	37
Assertive/submissive	40	19	21	12
Intellectually invested	4	23	–6	17
Outgoing/aloof	–31	12	–1	25
Dependable	82	64	95	56
Warm/hostile	26	43	9	36

Note: See Appendix B for complete scoring descriptions.

**Table A.6. Competence Scores and Personality Component Scores
for Henry Barr at Successive Periods**

	Senior High	1965	1982
Planful competence	135	124	132
Self-confident/feels victimized	39	18	30
Assertive/submissive	8	29	27
Intellectually invested	18	11	35
Outgoing/aloof	8	–8	24
Dependable	79	96	67
Warm/hostile	–5	–20	24

Note: See Appendix B for complete scoring descriptions.

Table A.7. Regression of Personality Resemblance on Planful Competence and Other Antecedent and Intervening Variables, Males (Standardized Regression Coefficients)

Antecedents and Intervening Variables	Senior High to 1958	Senior High to 1970	Senior High to 1982
Senior high planful competence	.53***	.36**	.55***
Senior high outgoing	−.08	.16	.21*
Junior high maternal attentiveness	.17	.11	.21*
Orderly career	.09	.29*	.11
R^2(adjusted R^2)	.41 (.36)	.46 (.41)	.64 (.61)

*$p<.05$; **$p<.01$; ***$p<.001$.

Table A.8. Regression of Men's Midlife Personality Resemblance in the Adult Years (1958–1982) on Antecedent and Intervening Variables

	Standardized Regression Coefficient
Competence in 1958	.58**
Occupational status	.23*
Divorced	−.10
R^2(adjusted R^2)	.49 (.46)

*$p < .05$; **$p < .01$.

Table A.9. Competence Scores and Personality Component Scores
for Alice Neal at Successive Periods

	Senior High	1958	1970	1982
Planful competence	9	−17	94	80
Self-confident/feels victimized	10	−12	23	27
Assertive/submissive	8	34	37	53
Intellectually invested	−43	−58	2	−20
Outgoing/aloof	48	25	48	36
Dependable	42	54	68	73
Warm/hostile	−38	−66	−37	4

Note: See Appendix B for complete scoring descriptions.

Table A.10. Competence Scores and Personality Component Scores
for Beth Green in 1970 and 1982

	1970	1982
Planful competence	80	84
Self-confident/feels victimized	0	13
Assertive/submissive	9	11
Intellectually invested	25	29
Outgoing/aloof	45	35
Dependable	54	43
Warm/hostile	20	65

Note: See Appendix B for complete scoring descriptions.

Table A.11. **Competence Scores and Personality Component Scores for Judith Judd at Successive Periods**

	Senior High	1958	1970	1982
Planful competence	135	91	122	106
Self-confident/feels victimized	31	11	31	24
Assertive/submissive	24	8	24	7
Intellectually invested	3	40	35	36
Outgoing/aloof	-7	-14	26	27
Dependable	100	40	55	46
Warm/hostile	-14	42	18	57

Note: See Appendix B for complete scoring descriptions.

Table A.12. **Regression of Women's Educational Attainment on Antecedent Variables**

Independent Variables	Zero-Order Correlation	Standardized Regression Coefficient
Parental Socioeconomic Status	.62**	.36**
IQ at 17-18	.52**	.29*
Planful competence	.40**	
Self-confident	.09	
Intellectually invested	.42**	.02
Dependable	.47**	.30**
Adjusted R^2		.45

**p < .01.

**Table A.13.   Regression of Percentage of Years of Women's Labor Force
Participation by 1982 on Antecedent and Intervening Variables**

	Zero order correlation	Standardized regression coefficients		
		Model 1	Model 2	Model 3
Parents' Socio-economic Status	−.30**	−.21	−.29*	−.29*
Adolescent IQ	−.20	−.21	—	—
Education	.02	.47**	.30*	.30*
Years worked before marriage	.19	.25	.25	.24
Age at first marriage	−.01	−.33*	−.25	−.26*
Number of children	−.36**	−.31*	−.28*	−.28*
Husband's occupation, 1970	−.21	−.13	—	—
Adolescent prosocial orientation.	.21	—	—	.21*
R^2 (Adjusted R^2)		.31 (.23)	.26 (.20)	.30 (.24)

*p < .05; **p < .01.

Table A.14. Regression of Women's Highest Level of Occupational Attainment on Antecedent Variables (*N*=45)

	Zero order Correlation	Standardized regression coefficients	
		Model 1	Model 2
Parental Socioeconomic Status	.43**	.08	—
IQ at age 17-18	.50**	.17	.40**
Educational attainment	.58**	.21	.32**
Adolescent competence	.20	—	—
Self-confidence	.01	—	—
Intellectual investment	.35**	.20	—
Dependability	.05	—	—
Percentage of years in labor force	.17	—	.22*
Adjusted R^2		.23	.45

*p < .05; **p < .01.

Table A.15. Regression of Women's Age at First Marriage on Antecedent Variables

	Zero order Correlation	Standardized Regression Coefficient
Educational attainment	.26*	.06
Dependability	.26*	.21†
Interest in opposite sex (senior high school)	−.36***	−.37**
Age at puberty	−.32**	−.29*
R^2 (adjusted R^2)		.39 (.34)

†p < .10; *p < .05; **p < .01; ***p < .001.

Table A.16. Regression of Husband's Occupational Status in 1957 on Wife's Antecedent Attributes

	Zero-Order Correlation	Standardized Regression Coefficient
Senior high planful competence	.29***	−.17
Educational attainment	.49***	.49***
Physical attractiveness, senior high	.10	.43**
R^2 (adjusted R^2)		.40 (.35)

**p < .01; ***p < .001.

Table A.17.   Regression of Marital Instability (Number of Marriages and Divorces) on Antecedent Variables

	Zero-Order Correlation	Standardized Regression Coefficient
"Dependable," senior high	–.35**	–.27*
Interested in opposite sex, senior high	.26*	.20†
Age at first marriage	–.19*	–.18†
R^2 (adjusted R^2)		.24 (.21)

†p < .10, *p < .05; **p < .01.

Table A.18.   Regressions of Personality Resemblance from Senior High to Adult Assessments on Antecedents and Life Course Variables at Successive Periods (Standardized Regression Coefficients)

Antecedent variables	1958	1970	1982
Adolescent planful competence	.48***	.55***	.25**
Adolescent outgoing vs. aloof	.15	.43***	.44***
Adolescent warm (prosocial)	.15	.23*	.48***
Divorced	–.28**	–.10	–.28**
R^2 (adjusted R^2)	.45 (.43)	.62 (.60)	.59 (.57)

*p < .05; **p < .01, ***p < .001.

Table A.19. Correlations Between Husbands' and Wives' Self-ratings of Marital Satisfaction and Between Judges' Ratings for Each at Successive Dates

Year of ratings	Self-ratings	Judges' ratings	Self versus Judge	
			Husbands	Wives
1970	.34**	.36**	.60***	.61***
1982	.53***	.44***	.50***	.51***
1990	.51***			

**p < .01; ***p < .001.

Table A.20. Multiple Regression of Men's and Women's Life Satisfaction in 1990 on Concurrent or Recent Circumstances (Standardized Coefficients)

	Men	Women
Self-rated marital satisfaction		.45***
Spouses' reported life satisfaction	.42***	
Rating of own health	.32**	.13
Spouses' rating of own health		.19*
Competence index in 1982		.23**
Satisfaction with career	.19†	
R^2 (adjusted R^2)	.35 (.32)	.40 (.37)

†p < .10; *p < .05; **p < .01; ***p < .001.
Note: The variable was not entered in the empty cells.

MAJOR SOURCES OF DATA
AND MEASURES

Over the childhood and adolescent years, each of the three studies used many different kinds of instruments and techniques for data collection, resulting in literally thousands of categorizations of the study members' attributes, interests, and behaviors. To list all of these sources of data would require another book the length of this one. Here I wish to indicate the major sources of data that were drawn upon for the Q-sorts and the most important classifications of data used in the analyses reported in the text. More complete information on the materials available to Q-sorters, the procedures followed, and the complete listing of items in the adolescent Q-sort and the interpersonal Q-sort are included in Block and Haan (1971). Additional information on the separate studies is included in Eichorn, (1981).

All three studies employed repeated physical examinations, anthropometric measurements, intelligence tests, interviews on family backgrounds, ratings of the subjects' mothers, teachers' ratings from the schools, opinion ballots, and vocational inventories. The primary additional source of data for the adolescent Q-sorts of Guidance Study members was the sequence of interviews conducted with the child annually from age 6 through 17.

Subjects of the Berkeley Growth Study were seen frequently from birth through age 3 and at least semiannually from 8 through 18 years. Behaviors of the child and the mother were rated and recorded in narrative notes, which were subsequently re-rated and available to the Q-sort judges.

Data on subjects of the Oakland Growth Study were more largely secured through inventories and observations rather than interviews. Much of the data was collected in the classroom, since the study members constituted substantial portions of the students in particular classes. Data taken in classrooms usually included all members of the school class present in order to provide the complete context and to avoid discrimination. In addition, participants came to the the Institute of Human Development semiannually through the six years of junior and senior high school and were observed and rated in a variety of situations during this period. Also available were narrative notes made in such social situations as dances, picnics, and athletic events or on trips.

All of these sources of data have been drawn upon in the life histories presented. In the Q-sort, data from parents and certain ratings have been excluded from the materials reviewed by the sorters, in order to provide independent validation of some of the classifications made (see Block and Haan, 1971, pp. 121–125). The adolescent form of the personality Q-sort was directly parallel to the adult form but with items worded so as to be more appropriate for adolescents. For example, the adult form, "Is a genuinely dependable and responsible person," is rendered in the adolescent form by, "Behaves in a dependable and responsible way." Here I reproduce only the wordings for the seventy-three items of the adult form of the personality Q-sort that had the most consistently high reliability. These were used for the Millsap-Meredith components and for the profiles of personality resemblance and change.

ITEMS OF CALIFORNIA PERSONALITY Q-SORT USED FOR PERSONALITY COMPONENT ANALYSIS AND FOR RESEMBLANCE PROFILES

1. Is critical, skeptical, not easily impressed.
2. Is a genuinely dependable and responsible person.
3. Has a wide range of interests. (N.B.: Superficiality or depth of interest is irrelevant here.)
4. Is a talkative individual.
5. Behaves in a giving way toward others. (N.B.: Regardless of the motivation involved.)
6. Is fastidious.
7. Appears to have a high degree of intellectual capacity. (N.B.:

Whether actualized or not. Originality is not necessarily assumed.)

8. Is uncomfortable with uncertainty and complexities.

9. Anxiety and tension find outlet in bodily symptoms. (N.B.: If placed high, implies bodily dysfunction; if placed low, implies absence of autonomic arousal.)

10. Is protective of those close to him. (N.B.: Placement of this item expresses behavior ranging from overprotection through appropriate nurturance to a laissez-faire, underprotective manner.)

11. Is thin-skinned; vulnerable to anything that can be construed as criticism or an interpersonal slight.

12. Basically submissive.

13. Is introspective. (N.B.: Introspectiveness per se does not imply insight.)

14. Behaves in a sympathetic or considerate manner.

15. Seeks reassurance from others.

16. Has a rapid personal tempo.

17. Arouses nurturant feelings in others of both sexes.

18. Extrapunitive; tends to transfer or project blame.

19. Prides self on being "objective," rational. (Regardless of whether person is really objective or rational.)

20. Tends toward overcontrol of need and impulses; binds tensions excessively; delays gratification unnecessarily.

21. Is productive; gets things done. (Regardless of speed.)

22. Shows condescending behavior in relations with others.

23. Tends to arouse liking and acceptance in people.

24. Is turned to for advice and reassurance.

25. Gives up and withdraws where possible in the face of frustrations and adversity.

26. Is calm, relaxed in manner.

27. Overreactive to minor frustrations; irritable.

28. Has warmth; is compassionate.

29. Is negativistic; tends to undermine and obstruct or sabotage.

30. Is guileful and deceitful, manipulative, opportunistic.

31. Has hostility toward others. (N.B.: Basic hostility is intended here; mode of expression is to be indicated by other items.)

32. Thinks and associates to ideas in unusual ways; has unconventional thought processes. (Either pathological or creative.)

33. Is vulnerable to real or fancied threat, generally fearful.

34. Is moralistic. (N.B.: Regardless of the particular nature of the moral code.)
35. Reluctant to commit self to any definite course of action; tends to delay or avoid action. (Uncharacteristic end indicates quick to act.)
36. Is facially and/or gesturally expressive.
37. Has a brittle ego-defense system; has a small reserve of integration; would be disorganized and maladaptive when under stress or trauma.
38. Tends to feel guilty. (N.B.: Regardless of whether verbalized or not.)
39. Aloof, keeps people at a distance; avoids close interpersonal relationships.
40. Is basically distrustful of people in general; questions their motivations.
41. Is unpredictable and changeable in behavior and attitudes.
42. Genuinely values intellectual and cognitive matters. (N.B.: Ability or achievement is not implied here.)
43. Behaves in an assertive fashion in interpersonal situations. (N.B.: Item 12 reflects underlying submissiveness; this refers to overt behavior.)
44. Tends toward undercontrol of needs and impulses; unable to delay gratification.
45. Emphasizes being with others; gregarious.
46. Is self-defeating.
47. Responds to humor.
48. Is an interesting, arresting person.
49. Is concerned with own body and the adequacy of its physiological functioning. (Body cathexis.)
50. Tends to be rebellious and nonconforming.
51. Judges self and others in conventional terms like "popularity," "the correct thing to do," social pressures, etc.
52. Is socially perceptive of a wide range of interpersonal cues.
53. Characteristically pushes and tries to stretch limits; sees what he can get away with.
54. Is self-indulgent.
55. Has high aspiration level for self.
56. Overconcerned with own adequacy as a person, either at conscious or unconscious levels. (N.B.: A clinical judgment is required here.)

57. Appears straightforward, forthright, candid in dealings with others.
58. Feels cheated and victimized by life.
59. Tends to ruminate and have persistent, preoccupying thoughts (either pathological or creative).
60. Interested in members of the opposite sex. (N.B.: At opposite end, item implies absence of such interest.)
61. Is physically attractive, good-looking. (N.B.: The cultural criterion is to be applied here.)
62. Has fluctuating moods.
63. Is cheerful. (N.B.: Extreme placement toward uncharacteristic end of continuum implies gloominess.)
64. Is power-oriented; values power in self or others.
65. Has social poise and presence; appears socially at ease.
66a. Behaves in a masculine style and manner.
66b. Behaves in a feminine style and manner. (N.B.: If subject is male, 66a applies; if subject is female, 66b is to be evaluated. N.B.: Again, the cultural or subcultural conception is to be applied as a criterion.)
67. Expresses hostile feelings directly.
68. Tends to proffer advice.
69. Values own independence and autonomy.
70. Is emotionally bland; has flattened effect.
71. Is verbally fluent; can express ideas well.
72. Is self-dramatizing, histrionic.
73. Does not vary roles; relates to everyone in the same way.

Q-SORT ITEMS AND THEIR WEIGHTS
FOR THE MILLSAP-MEREDITH COMPONENTS

Self-Control/Feels Victimized			
	Positive Weight		Negative Weight
Satisfied with self	1.05	Feels victimized	0.85
Calm	1.02	Fearful	0.77
Cheerful	0.81	Self-defeating	0.70
Arouses liking	0.71	Ruminative	0.69
Straightforward	0.64	Brittle ego	0.61

	Positive Weight		Negative Weight
Gregarious	0.53	Thin-skinned	0.59
Turned to for advice	0.53	Distrustful	0.58
Dependable	0.49	Basic hostility	0.56
Productive	0.47	Irritable	0.53
Warm	0.47	Somatizes	0.52
Sympathetic	0.44	Moody	0.45
		Negativistic	0.43

Assertive/Submissive

Assertive	1.00	Submissive	1.15
Values independence	0.91	Overcontrolled	0.69
Rebellious	0.89	Conventional	0.68
Directly expresses hostility	0.75	Seeks reassurance	0.62
Pushes limits	0.69	Reluctant to act	0.62
Rapid tempo	0.59	Fearful	0.62
Skeptical	0.56	Withdraws when frustrated	0.54
Undercontrolled	0.46	Fastidious	0.50
Thinks unconventionally	0.45	Arouses nurturance	0.49
Power oriented	0.44	Uncomfortable with uncertainty	0.49
Interesting	0.41	Emotionally bland	0.46
		Sympathetic	0.45

Cognitively Committed

Values intellect	0.81	Uncomfortable with uncertainty	0.63
High IQ	0.65	Conventional	0.60
Fluent	0.64	Submissive	0.48
Introspective	0.63	Brittle ego	0.44
Ambitious	0.59	Withdraws when frustrated	0.40
Values independence	0.59		
Wide interests	0.59		
Interesting	0.53		
Thinks unconventionally	0.52		

	Positive Weight		Negative Weight

Outgoing/Aloof

Cheerful	0.60	Aloof	0.90
Warm	0.59	Distrustful	0.58
Talkative	0.57	Emotionally bland	0.56
Gregarious	0.57	Reluctant to act	0.54
Straightforward	0.51	Fearful	0.52
Rapid tempo	0.50	Overcontrolled	0.49
Initiates humor	0.50	Withdraws when frustrated	0.48
Expressive	0.50	Feels victimized	0.46
Assertive	0.50	Ruminative	0.41
Arouses liking	0.44		
Poised	0.43		

Dependable

Dependable	0.62	Rebellious	0.56
Productive	0.59	Undercontrolled	0.52
Overcontrolled	0.51	Self-defeating	0.47
Satisfied with self	0.44	Pushes limits	0.44
Calm	0.43	Unpredictable	0.43
Ambitious	0.43		

Warm/Hostile

Sympathetic	0.69	Negativistic	0.60
Warm	0.65	Pushes limits	0.59
Dependable	0.59	Deceitful	0.55
Giving	0.59	Condescending	0.54
Arouses liking	0.52	Conventional	0.54
Protective	0.51	Extrapunitive	0.53
Calm	0.48	Basically hostile	0.53
Straightforward	0.48	Distrustful	0.52
Submissive	0.47	Irritable	0.45
Arouses nurturance	0.41	Self-dramatizing	0.41
		Self-indulgent	0.41
		Skeptical	0.41

GENERAL CODING AND RATING PROCEDURES

Codes for open-ended questions were devised after listing at least twenty to thirty responses and seeking the most common broad categories. Where there were multiple dimensions involved and the possibility of multiple choices, each was allocated a separate sequence, with specification of unique subcategories or simply with the indication of evidence or no evidence for a given category's applicability. For example, in classifying crises from life chart data, we first ascertained the most frequent sources of crises—love or marital circumstances, occupational setbacks, illness, death, and so forth—and then within each major source the specific character of the crises—for example, broken engagement, extreme conflict in marriage, divorce. Residual responses would be assigned to "other" but listed as well. When it became clear that some responses not originally specified were sufficiently frequent to be included, we added categories and then recoded cases previously contained in the "other" category.

All coding of responses in the 1982 interviews was checked over and discrepancies resolved by senior staff. All responses to questions in the life history interview and all items in the life history summary were coded twice, and discrepancies were resolved by discussion. Except for the coding of the 1970 children's interviews, reliabilities were satisfactory in general. However, it was necessary to recode the occupational history data from the 1982 interviews because the original coders were inadequately trained for this demanding task. All ratings were based on assessments by at least two judges and their scores combined.

SPECIFIC MEASURES AND CODES

CHAPTER 6

Individual and Family Attributes

Intelligence quotient (IQ), age 17–18: Guidance Study and Berkeley Growth Study: Wechsler-Bellevue at age 18. Oakland Growth Study: Stanford Binet (1937 version) at age 17, scores reduced by 5 points to be equivalent to Wechsler-Bellevue.

Family socioeconomic status: Hollingshead education and occupation scales for fathers, plus education scales for mothers, weighted. Scores under 65 = middle class; 65 and over, working class. (Reflected in tables so high score equals high status)

Family deprivation in Great Depression: Income loss of 35 percent or more. (See Elder, 1974, p. 45.)

Body build: Scores on ectomorphy, mesomorphy, and endomorphy from 1 to 7 assigned by W. Sheldon based on nude photographs of postpubertal subjects in last two years of high school. (See Sheldon, 1940.)

Sexual maturity: Age at attaining 90 percent of mature height (previously established as most reliable indicator of primary and secondary signs of sexual maturity).

Parenting Measures

A. *Core items in Honzik Parenting Scales**

All items scored 1 to 7

Mother attentive and supportive

Adjustment of home: mother with subject

Mother provides emotional support

Mother cares for child's needs

Mother is concerned

Mother responsive to child's needs

Mother uses positive reinforcement

Firm and consistent discipline

Mother firmly enforces rules

Mother's discipline is consistent

Rules are clearly stated

(–) Mother maintains lax discipline

Parents encourage achievement

Mother encourages achievement

Mother encourages intellectual achievement

---

*These items were utilized for preliminary factor analyses once measures were available from two or more raters but before systematic assessment of reliabilities and incorporation of the items in the data archive (a task only now being undertaken, thanks to a grant from the Spencer Foundation in 1992). Therefore these scores and item combinations are subject to modification.

Mother encourages considerate behavior

Father encourages achievement

Father encourages intellectual achievement

B. *Core items in the Interpersonal Q-sort scales on parent-child relationships*

Parents are respected role models

Subject feels that the pattern of his (her) life is laid down by his (her) parents

Subject respects his (her) parents

Subject feels mother is a respected woman as judged by societal standards

Subject views other as an attractive woman

Nonconflictual relations between parents and child

Subject perceives parents as being happy people

(–) Subject perceives family situation as conflicted

(–) Subject perceives parents as restraining of his (her) activities

CHAPTER 9
Coding of Discontinuity or Crisis

All material relating to a decade was reviewed and coded or rated with reference to involvement in and satisfaction with each major role occupied in the decade: marital, parental and occupational, plus recreational, religious, community service, and artistic or cultural activities. For the major roles, coders looked for evidence that the person had "experienced any sharp discontinuity in major role involvements or in general perspective that might be considered a crisis or a turning point—a time when he/she had to face critical decisions with reference to his/her future in work, marriage or other spheres." The categories were:

1. No discontinuities or real turmoil.
2. Only minor discontinuity or sense of turmoil.
3. No discontinuity but sense of turmoil.
4. Considerable discontinuity in at least one sphere but no sense of crisis or major turmoil.
5. Considerable discontinuity in at least one sphere and with real sense of crisis of turmoil.

6. Substantial discontinuity, turmoil, or crisis.

For Table 9.1, categories 5 and 6 were combined.

Coding of Orderliness of Career

The coding, which follows, was taken from complete work histories:

1. All jobs in same field, with increasing level of responsibility or skill (include one or two jobs over career, if increasing responsibility).
2. All jobs in same field but little or no evidence of increasing responsibility or skill.
3. At least half of career in same field, with no more than one sharp break or shift—second half more orderly than first half.
4. At least half of career in same field, with no sharp breaks or shifts—second half less orderly than first half.
5. Considerable shifting but some measure of continuity for at least a decade.
6. Frequent shifting, with little continuity in occupational history (do not count frequent shifts in first five years).
9. Not ascertainable.

Job Satisfaction Scales

We employed the Quinn and Staines (1979) scales for both facet-free job satisfaction (three items) and the intermediate-length scales (eighteen items) on job facets such as challenge, relations with co-workers, and financial rewards. The facet-free items are:

1. All in all, how satisfied would you say you are with your job?
2. Knowing what you now know, if you had to decide all over again whether to take the job you now have, what would you decide?
3. If you were free to go into any type of job you wanted, what would your choice be?

Scoring was done according to the weights given in Quinn and Staines (1979).

CHAPTER 10

Self-rating of marital satisfaction (used repeatedly in questionnaires) was obtained by asking, "In general, how happy is your marriage?"

1	2	3	4	5	6	7	8	9	10
Very unhappy				Fairly happy				Almost perfect	

Marital Acceptance and Reciprocity Scales

These are the obverse of two of the scales of marital strain developed by Pearlin and Schooler (1978), with an additional item added to each. They are scored from 1, "strongly agree," to 4, "strongly disagree."

Marital Acceptance

1. My husband (wife) appreciates me just as I am (–).
2. My marriage doesn't give me enough opportunity to be the sort of person I would like to be.
3. I cannot completely be myself around my husband (wife).
4. My husband (wife) is someone I can really talk with about things that are important to me (–).
5. My husband (wife) seems to bring out the best in me.

Reciprocity in Give and Take

1. My husband (wife) insists on having his (her) own way.
2. My husband (wife) usually expects more from me than he (she) is willing to give.
3. My husband (wife) usually acts as if he (she) were the only important person in the family.
4. Generally, I give in more to my husband's (wife's) wishes than he (she) gives in to mine.

CHAPTER 13

Women's Work Attachment Index

The work attachment index is the sum of the following two items (scores shown in parenthesis):

Orderliness of Work Career After Schooling

0. Never employed.
1. Frequent shifting, with little continuity in occupational history.
2. Considerable shifting but some measure of continuity for at least a decade.
3. At least half of career in same field, with no sharp breaks or shifts—second half less orderly than first half.
4. At least half of career in same field, with no more than one sharp break or shift—second half more orderly than first half.
5. All jobs in same field but little or no evidence of increasing responsibility or skill.
6. All jobs in same field, with increasing level of responsibility or skill.

Work History After Marriage or Childbearing

0. Never employed regularly after marriage.
2. Employed occasionally or intermittently.
4. Employed regularly for at least five years, but in and out of labor force in middle years.
6. Employed more or less regularly after reentrance in labor force, with not over five years out of labor force after reentry.

CHAPTER 15

Availability of the husband to the family was ascertained in a structured interview in 1982 by asking husband and wife:

a. Some men are at times so heavily involved with the demands of their job that they are not available to their wives and children. Have there been times when this has been a problem in your family?
   (If answer was "yes":)
b. What have been some of the consequences and how serious have they been?
c. At what period in your marriage was the problem most difficult for you?
d. How have you dealt with this problem?

NOTES

Chapter 1

Introduction

1. For descriptions of the ideals held in a number of Eastern and Western cultures, see the spring 1976 issue of *Daedalus*, "Adulthood," edited by Stephen R. Graubard, especially the chapters on Islamic, Confucian, Japanese, and Rajput conceptions of maturity.
2. See John Stuart Mill, *Utilitarianism*, chap. 2.
3. John Stuart Mill, *On Liberty*, chap. 4.
4. See, for example, Campbell (1981), who used indexes of both happiness and satisfaction in large-scale surveys.
5. This formulation of positive mental health was originally developed by Jahoda (1958).
6. Vaillant (1977). Vaillant's subjects were all male and much more highly selected than ours, but his findings and our own for males are in general quite consonant.
7. In the 1920s, for example, parents in "Middletown" (Muncie, Indiana) reported as the primary value for their children "loyalty to the church." See Lynd and Lynd (1929, pp. 143–144).
8. The classic formulation on the effects of generational change was that of Karl Mannheim in his essay, "The Problem of Generations," (1952), but more recent sociologists, such as Norman Ryder, Matilda Riley, and Glen Elder, Jr., have stressed the greater relevance of the cohort, a concept developed in the field of demography. A cohort is a group of people who move together through historical time, experiencing the same events at about the same age.
9. Skolnick (1992, p. 4).
10. Between 1950 and 1980, the participation of married women in the labor force increased greatly at all age and educational levels, with the greatest increase among women with young children. See Oppenheimer (1982).
11. For a discussion of the persistent discrimination against blacks in the labor market of the United States, see Lieberson (1980).
12. Bellah et al. (1985). Bellah and his associates interviewed a small number of respondents, each interviewer choosing "particular communities, groups or

sets of individuals who vividly illustrated his or her particular focus" (p. ix). A major danger in using such an approach is that the respondents may be far from representative.

13. de Tocqueville (1835) saw religion as "the first of [American] political institutions," observing that "the Americans combine the notions of Christianity and of liberty so intimately in their minds that it is impossible to make them conceive the one without the other."

14. Howard and Bray (1988, pp. 165–168).

15. For a review of current research in the field now called "behavioral genetics," see Plomin and Thompson (1988). A major source of heated conflict arises when racial and ethnic differences are imputed to genes rather than to culture.

16. It is, of course, much easier to show relationships between parental socialization practices and child behavior than to show the effects of genetic impact, but we seldom can rule out genetic influences even here.

17. Ultimately, of course, it depends on how gross the differences in available opportunities are between segments of the population. There is no single answer to what source of influence is more important.

18. Several major studies have followed children of divorce for a number of years. See Wallerstein and Blakeslee (1989) and Hetherington (1989).

19. The resilient child (sometimes referred to as "invulnerable") has been a source of increasing interest. See Garmezy (1981).

20. All in a complex environment. See Bronfenbrenner (1979, 1986).

21. The choices are influenced by one's social class and ethnic membership, parental guidance, personal strengths, and many other factors, but none of these *determines* either choice or outcome.

22. The research literature on stress strongly supports the conclusion that unscheduled and undesired events are a far more devastating source of stress than expected transitions. See, for example, Pearlin (1989).

23. For a fuller exposition, see Mayer (1986).

24. One sees this blocking of mobility especially in organizations like hospitals and research laboratories, but it is typical of all large-scale bureaucratic business organizations and governmental agencies as well. To move up, the lower-level employee must secure higher education.

25. Research conducted in the 1960s found a substantial consensus among American adults as to the most desirable time to marry, to have children, to become established in one's occupation, and so on. There is no such consensus in the 1990s.

26. Langer (1989).

27. For example, Levinson (1978) asserts that a person's life organization "is always flawed in some respects. It contains contradictions and gaps which can be modified only by basic changes in the structure itself" (p. 54). My own view is that most people change when they perceive that they need to, most often in limited respects, not basic transformations entailing frequent crises, as Levinson maintains.

28. See Featherman (1980).

29. Ibid.

30. The following paragraphs, with minor editing, are from Clausen (1991, pp. 811–813).
31. Skolnick (1981, p. 279).
32. The details appear in Chapter 9.
33. Indeed, Levinson (1978) maintains that his postulated "sequence of eras and periods exists in all societies, throughout the human species, at the present stage in human evolution" (p. 322). Our sixty-year study suggests that no such sequence is typical even in the United States. Thomae and Lehr (1986) came to the same conclusion in a German-based study.

Chapter 2

The Studies, Their Context, and the Data

1. Lawrence K. Frank was a major instigator of organized research in child development and gerontology. He also wrote the first book on projective techniques in the study of personality and, in 1928, one of the most influential papers on the topic of social problems.
2. For the full statement, see Macfarlane (1938).
3. A few families continued to bring in their children for interviews after they moved outside Berkeley. Working-class parents, however, were somewhat less likely to continue to bring in their children. Those in the control group dropped out in much higher proportion, especially in the adolescent years.
4. For more details, see Bayley (1933).
5. The test she developed, the Bayley Scales of Mental and Motor Development, became a standard for assessing infants and is still widely used.
6. For many years Dr. Eichorn also served as associate director of the Institute of Human Development.
7. A description of the early objectives and the methods employed is given in H. E. Jones (1938).
8. Mary Cover Jones remained active at the institute until this time, contributing a chapter on the midlife drinking patterns of the study members to *Present and Past in Middle Life* (1981).
9. Above all, Jean Macfarlane was a clinician rather than a scientist. Every study member was in a sense her child, to be understood as an individual. Her writing attests to this emphasis.
10. Dr. Frenkel-Brunswik had earlier studied the personality dynamics of the adolescent study members. Her monograph, *Motivation and Behavior* (1942) was a major contribution to the study of the relationship between underlying motivations and manifest behavior.
11. Because there had been no contact with OGS members from the early war years into the 1950s, addresses were not available for many who had left the area. Some of the men were almost certainly killed in World War II, but it was not possible to get in touch with many families that left the Bay Area before 1950.

12. Grant MH-5300, for the project "Personality Continuity in the Oakland Growth Study," supported a variety of projects over the next eight years.

13. This project was supported by grant MH-8135 from the National Institute of Mental Health.

14. The grant, HD-3617, provided for both data collection (which entailed transportation costs as well as staffing costs) and some data analysis.

15. *From Thirty to Seventy* (1974) was written by Henry S. Maas and Joseph A. Kuypers. *Present and Past in Middle Life* (1981) was a product of many authors and was edited by Eichorn, Clausen, Haan, Honzik, and Mussen.

16. This was a collaborative project, designed by senior staff under institute director Paul H. Mussen. The data collection and initial phase of data reduction were coordinated by Dr. Carol Huffine.

17. Grant AG-4178 provided primarily for data analysis but also permitted filling in gaps in data for a subsample of study members whose lives were then summarized.

18. This grant, from the National Science Foundation, provided for judges to read and rate the materials in the files bearing on parenting practices at successive periods from infancy through the high school years.

19. This figure appeared in a report on Oakland schools in the 1930s.

20. Elder (1974, p. 18).

21. When Franklin Roosevelt was inaugurated, many banks had failed, and a national bank closure was in force.

22. Elder (1974, p. 19).

23. Linkages between the university and state and local agencies were very close in the period before World War II. For example, Herbert Stolz, the first director of the Institute of Child Welfare, held the position of medical director in the State of California Department of Education.

24. It would be unusual today for public school faculties to be so fully involved in a research project of such scope.

25. The school had its own publication, in which faculty and invited experts reported on the latest developments nationally and locally. Quoted from Hunt and Chaffey (1934, p. 232).

26. In recent years, behavioral geneticists and developmental psychologists have become increasingly convinced that the genetic similarities of parent and child affect the social environment that the child will experience. Moreover, genetically given tendencies also affect the individual's choices of and in relationships. For detailed discussions, see Scarr and McCartney (1983) and Plomin and Bergeman (1991), along with commentaries following the latter article.

27. The rationale for and application of the set of items in the California Q-sort is given in Block (1961).

28. An experimental design to verify that this was indeed the case was devised by Professor Lee Cronbach of Stanford University in 1980. We are much indebted to him for his assistance in answering a question that reviewers of a pending grant proposal had posed. Ratings not constrained by the Q-sort instructions, which assessed each attribute in terms of the range of variability in the population, revealed negligible differences from those obtained through Q-sorting procedures.

29. Block with Haan (1971, p. 51). For those unfamiliar with statistical concepts and terminology, the *reliability* of a measure or a rating is usually assessed by the average correlation between pairs of comparable assessments of the same individuals over a relatively short time (so as to preclude the likelihood of substantial change). When the measure consists of combined ratings of two or more judges for each subject, those combined ratings would be correlated with the ratings of other, similarly trained groups of judges for the same individuals.

The correlation coefficient itself may need explanation for some readers. A *correlation coefficient* is a measure of association between two variables, such as weight and height or (as in this case) two sets of scores on the same variables. The correlation coefficient can range from -1.0 (a perfect negative relationship, such as one might get from a measure of "tallness" compared with a measure of "shortness") through 0.0 (no relationship) to +1.0 (a perfect positive relationship, so that every step up the scale on one variable would correspond with an exactly equivalent step up on the other).

Correlation does not imply causation. Two correlated variables may be responsive to some common cause or combination of causes. The correlation coefficient may suggest causation, however, if one of the variables is an antecedent of the other and if, in various circumstances and controlling for other potential causes, the correlation remains substantial, of such magnitude that it is highly improbable that the relationship is due to chance.

The probability of the coefficient's being due to chance is called its *significance* and is highly dependent on the number of observations on which the coefficient is based. Significance will be indicated where appropriate in parentheses, as in $(p < .01)$, which means that a correlation coefficient—or other statistical measure of this magnitude—would not occur by chance more than one time in 100. Often the measures that are reported far exceed this level of improbability, but where the number of persons under consideration is only a small segment of the total, "significance" will be more modest.

30. In *Present and Past in Middle Life,* (Eichorn et al., 1981), a technique known as PARAFAC was used. Most of the factors revealed were somewhat similar to those derived by the procedures Millsap and Meredith developed which are employed here, but the latter technique yields much more powerful predictions from early data.

31. See Millsap and Meredith (1988) and Haan, Millsap, and Hartke (1986). The Millsap-Meredith components closely approximate at least four and overlap the fifth of the "Big Five" dimensions of personality that many psychologists now regard as the basic elements of personality. Here are the components, along with the names frequently applied for the "Big Five." For more details on the "Big Five," see Digman (1989).

Longitudinal Study Components   The "Big Five"

1. Self-confidence/feeling victimized ⎫
2. Assertive/submissive   ⎬   Neuroticism (anxiety)
                                ⎭
3. Cognitively committed   Intellect (openness)
   (intellectually invested)

4.	Outgoing/aloof	Extraversion/introversion
5.	Dependable and productive	Responsible, conscientious
6.	Warm/hostile (prosocial orientation)	Friendliness/hostility (agreeableness)

32. It is probable that the assessment of both dependability and intellectual investment in the high school years was unduly influenced by a knowledge of school performance, increasing the correlation, especially for males. In the later years, these two components were less highly correlated with each other, but both became more closely tied to self-confidence, especially for men.

33. In earlier publications introducing the concept of adolescent planful competence (Clausen, 1991a, 1991b), I used a slightly different index. I added the raw scores for the components and combined the scores for the junior high school years with those for the senior high school years. Combining the scores had the advantage of increasing the reliability of measurement in cases in which no marked changes occurred from early adolescence to mid-adolescence but the disadvantage of obscuring the fact that real changes often did occur, especially for the girls. In this book, only senior high scores are used. For the most part, the relationships of planful competence with other variables are only slightly changed, with "adolescent" planful competence showing somewhat higher correlations in some instances and "senior high" planful competence showing the higher correlations in other instances.

34. See Sternberg and Kolligian (1990).

35. An excellent exposition of the concept of mindfulness is given by Ellen Langer in a book bearing that title. As she has noted in a personal communication, my "planfully competent" study members are "mindful"—open to new information, aware of more than one perspective, and can develop new categories to organize experiences not adequately handled by the old categories. See *Mindfulness* (1989, pp. 61–79).

36. Some items proved to be difficult to assess reliably, especially in the adult years, when we had far more limited information on which the judges based their assessments. All of the items used in the Millsap-Meredith components had adequate reliabilities.

37. See Livson and Peskin (1967).

Chapter 3

Introduction to the Life Histories

1. Our current attitudes about issues and our current feelings about people can cause our recollections of past events and relationships to be quite the reverse of what they were a decade or two before. See Yarrow, Campbell, and Burton (1970).

2. A particularly insightful discussion is given by Cohler (1982).

3. In a few instances, persons who lived in other areas returned frequently to the Bay Area and had indicated their willingness to participate, so they were included in the pool of eligibles. The selection of particular individuals was determined by a table of random numbers, the last three digits of which were matched with numbers that had been assigned to study members. Thus, no person was selected because of any foreknowledge of his or her attributes. This procedure resulted in the selection of thirty-two male and twenty-eight female study members. Four men and three women subsequently were unable or unwilling to participate at the time the interviews were scheduled. In every instance, we took the next higher numbered study member of the same sex who had given permission for preparation of a life history.

4. Betty Webster, a mature social worker who had been one of the clinical interviewers in the 1982 follow-up and whose warm personality and superb interviewing skills made her an ideal choice for life history interviews, prepared initial drafts of the histories of Stuart Campbell, Mary Wylie, and Alice Neal. Dr. Hal Gelb, who had taken a leading role in the preparation of life history summaries from the archives, conducted several interviews, among them the interview of Henry Barr. Dr. Gelb wrote the initial draft of the Barr history. It was only after preparation of the initial drafts of the Wylie and Schulz histories that I formulated my concept of planful competence and decided on a measure.

I subsequently reworked each of the life histories, adding data on personality classifications and filling in what I felt had been gaps in the original drafts (including my own drafts for Karl Schulz and Beth Green). In every instance, I subsequently met with the study members and sometimes their spouses to secure needed bits of information, their views on the accuracy of the material presented, and their approval of publication of the only slightly disguised histories. Where they had a different recollection from the picture represented in our data, I have presented both versions.

5. An amplified version of the formulation presented in this section is contained in Clausen (1985).

6. See, for example, Elder, Caspi, and Van Nguyen (1986) on abuse of less attractive daughters by unemployed fathers.

Chapter 6

Antecedents of Planful Competence

1. Her mother's account suggested considerable stress upon the parents, however.

2. The death of their mother from tuberculosis may well have led to both Stuart and his brother's being seen as sickly.

3. A variety of observations and measurements of the sexual development of the study members (nude) were made during the childhood and adolescent years. Attainment of sexual maturity was best indexed by attainment of 90

percent of mature height, and it is this index that I employ in analyses relating to early or late physical maturity.

4.　Intellectual stimulation is substantially related to social class as a consequence of the superior educational background and generally greater availability of parental guidance and of books and other cultural resources in the home. Psychologists generally agree that the difference between an impoverished intellectual environment and a stimulating one may account for a change of twenty IQ points. For a thorough discussion, see Bloom (1964).

5.　For a more detailed discussion and analysis, see Clausen (1975).

6.　Sheldon developed the most systematic system for assessing body build, but his insistence on the determinative importance of physique for personality and behavior is not borne out either by our data or any other study of which I am aware. For the method and the claims, see Sheldon (1940).

7.　The data are reported in Clausen (1975).

8.　Body build is not related to the scheduling of sexual maturity for males but is substantially related for females, with the shorter, sturdier mesomorphs maturing earlier than the tall, thin ectomorphs and thus having an earlier growth spurt. See Livson and McNeill (1962) and McNeill and Livson (1963).

9.　The early research of Mussen and Jones (1957) on data from the Berkeley studies has received support in other longitudinal and survey studies.

10.　Maturing often brings changes in relative proportions, if not often in bodily structure. The "skinny" Mary became a nicely proportioned mature woman, a change that added to her self-assurance.

11.　See, for example, the life history of Karl Schulz in Chapter 7.

12.　The subject receives much fuller treatment in Clausen (1968), from which Table 6.2 has been reproduced.

13.　Described in Macfarlane, Allen, and Honzik (1954).

14.　Ibid. (pp. 211–216).

15.　Caspi, Elder, and Bem (1988) have traced the intergenerational interaction of the parents' problems and the early behaviors of the child.

16.　The most basic of the tasks facing the child, according to the eminent child psychoanalyst Erik Erikson (1950) is the development of trust in his or her caretakers. Children subject to abuse and abandonment in the early years are likely to lack a capacity for empathy and too often are found to be purveyors of hate and violence in their later years, as was true of Charles Manson and several members of his murderous group.

17.　The Baldwin research was not concerned with competence per se but with the development of social involvement. See Baldwin, Kalhorn, and Breese (1949).

18.　Diana Baumrind has followed children from the preschool years to early adulthood. See especially Baumrind (1973, 1991a). For a review of other studies, see Baumrind (1991b).

19.　We used both parent and child reports to make two sets of independent ratings: one to describe what the parents did (ratings developed by Dr. Marjorie Honzik in the 1980s), and the other to represent how the child reacted to the parents' behaviors and how he or she felt about the family and the parents as persons, the latter as part of the interpersonal Q-sort, developed in the early 1960s.

20. Because of a scoring error in the original scale for males (based on preliminary data no longer available), in Table 6 I have employed the single item "consistent discipline," which was the defining item for the scale, but the correlation coefficients are available only for the components of competence. The final ratings of parenting are being entered into the archive as this book goes to press.

21. For a fuller account of the procedures and meanings of multiple regression, see Pedhazur (1982).

22. For a restatement of these features of adolescent culture, see Coleman (1974, pp. 112–125).

23. Clausen (1981, p. 346).

24. Elder (1974, p. 20).

25. Ibid (p. 79).

26. Elder and Rockwell (1979). My own analyses do not suggest that the members of the younger Guidance Study Group were any less competent than members of the Oakland cohort, but the parents of the Guidance Study were encouraged by Professor Macfarlane to be more relaxed with their children and the children were perhaps less strongly motivated toward achievement.

27. There were several African-Americans in the Guidance Study, and they were subject to a largely segregated existence. One of them, whose intelligence test scores were among the very highest in the study population, had little opportunity to capitalize on his high intelligence through higher education and never achieved an occupational level consonant with his superior ability.

28. For an interesting discussion of the importance of chance encounters, see Bandura (1977).

29. A large literature exists on this topic. A good review of the central ideas underlying these terms is given in Rodin (1990).

30. The average correlation between personality measured in junior high and that measured in senior high was .77 for males and .75 for females.

31. This brief sampling cannot do justice to the great body of information on the interests and opinions of the Oakland study members. In 1955 Mary Cover Jones compared the interests and activities of students then in junior high school with those of our Oakland study members roughly twenty years earlier. See Jones (1960).

32. The concept of the expectable life course was, to the best of my knowledge, first advanced by Bernice Neugarten, who with her colleagues noted the degree to which a consensus existed as to the age at which various events like marriage, parenthood, and settling into an occupation ought to occur. See Neugarten, Moore, and Lowe (1965).

33. See Modell, Furstenberg, and Hershberg (1976).

34. The Great Depression encouraged staying in school, partly because there were so few opportunities for full-time employment.

35. See the discussion in Chapter 1, pp. 17–18.

36. The most influential stage theory is that of Erik Erikson, first proposed in *Childhood and Society* (1950) and somewhat elaborated in his subsequent writings. More recently Levinson (1978), in his *Seasons of a Man's Life,* has proposed a set of stages, each lasting roughly a decade, from the "early adult transition" at ages 17 to 22 to the "late adult transition" at ages 60 to 65. Our longitudinal data provide no support whatsoever for Levinson's hypothesized stages.

37. Since parents feel that they are to a considerable degree responsible for the kind of persons their children become and because they love their children, it is natural that they tend to see their children in a relatively favorable light and that they want to regard their relationship as a close one. Children, on the other hand, have no responsibility for their parents as persons and to a degree have had to try to distance themselves from their parents to achieve their own identity.

Chapter 8

Destined for the Law: Henry Barr

1. The TAT consists of a set of pictures presenting somewhat ambiguous scenes, and the person taking the test is asked to make up a story that will explain each scene. The test thus serves as a medium through which the person's motives, concerns or interests are "projected" in the response given.

2. The children of Berkeley Growth study subjects were given intelligence tests throughout their childhood years.

3. Often a person's recollections of attitudes, values, and even relationships is modified by intervening shifts of which the person is not aware, but for the most part our highly competent study members had accurate recall of the dominant aspects of their early family life. This was especially true in families in which harmony and loving relationships had prevailed and had persisted as they did in the Barr family.

4. In general the life charts of highly competent study members showed less variation—fewer sharp peaks and deep valleys—than did those of their peers who had been much less competent in adolescence, but almost everyone recalled sources of satisfaction or of disappointment that made particular years seem better or worse than others. Henry Barr denied that he had experienced year-to-year changes but acknowledged considerable day-to-day variations.

5. In his follow-up of Harvard graduates who had been studied intensively when they were students, Vaillant (1978) notes that a number had completely reversed their political and social attitudes without being aware that this was the case. See especially Chapter 10.

6. Might such differences have been negotiable? Perhaps. But both temperament and priorities in sources of satisfaction that had been thoroughly incorporated by their late 20s would almost inevitably lead to tensions and

annoyances. One cannot negotiate away one's temperament, though perhaps with some counseling or therapy the couple might have accommodated to each other with less tension. A large difference between marital partners in degree of gregariousness appeared to be a very frequent source of persistent complaints, even when the marriages lasted a lifetime.

7. Most of our study members were more conservative than their children, but professionals were more likely than other men to take liberal positions later in life.

8. Occasionally there were other reasons why husbands or wives of study members declined to participate (and fewer husbands than wives did participate) but tension in the family was a major reason for the failure of wives to do so.

Chapter 9

Competence in Men's Lives and Careers

1. The correlation coefficient between adolescent competence and competence at ages 30 or 37 was .64 and at ages 54 or 62 was .56. Since the measure of competence is subject to error (estimated reliability, .7 to .75), this suggests that early rankings tended to persist over a period of forty to forty-five years.

2. Because he entered the study at age 10, we cannot be sure what his early years in the family were like, nor do we know just when his life ended.

3. See Elder (1974, p. 156).

4. This is in accord with other research, though it directly contradicts the theories of some clinically oriented writers. See Clausen (1985, p. 104).

5. Elder (1986, p. 234).

6. The coding and summarization of the life history sample data was done by Dr. Harold Gelb and Dr. John Wilson after careful review of all materials available. Each case was coded twice and discrepancies resolved in consultation with me.

7. A thoughtful book on the topic is *Forty: The Age and the Symbol* (1987) by Stanley Brandes.

8. For a more detailed analysis of the occupational careers of the men as of 1972, see Clausen (1981).

9. There are several widely used indexes of occupational prestige, based on national studies, of which the most detailed is the North-Hatt scale. We have used the scale devised by Hollingshead (first described in Hollingshead and Redlich, 1958), which was applied to the follow-up data in 1960.

10. The substantive complexity of thousands of occupations is rated along these three dimensions in the *Dictionary of Occupational Titles,* which we have relied upon in our coding of the complexity of the jobs of our study members in 1981–1982.

11. In our study group, for example, a composite index of the complexity of work with people and with data correlated at .81 with the Hollingshead index of occupational prestige and at .53 with income from all sources as reported in 1982 after some of the men had retired.

12. The proportion of professionals in the labor force more than doubled in the two decades following World War II, and the proportion of managerial and clerical workers increased sharply, while unskilled and semiskilled blue-collar workers constituted a much smaller proportion. For a general discussion, see Wolfbein (1971, chap. 4).
13. See Sewell, Hauser, and Wolf (1980).
14. Ibid.
15. Much depends, of course, on the kinds of technical skills that are entailed. If one insists on complete equivalence, orderly careers are much less frequent than if one merely looks for a high degree of continuity. For a discussion of the concept by its originator, see Wilensky (1961b).
16. *The New Columbia Encyclopedia* (1975, p. 460).
17. For the defining statement of the adolescent psychosocial moratorium, see Erikson (1959).
18. Had we asked this question when the men were in their 40s, we might have found occupation winning out by a larger margin.
19. The scale utilized is described in Quinn and Staines (1979).
20. See Staw, Bell, and Clausen (1986).
21. See Osherson (1980).
22. For its dramatic presentation of the concept of the midlife crisis, Gail Sheehy's *Passages* became a best-seller. Her book was based in large part on Levinson's data, subsequently published in his *The Seasons of a Man's Life*, and together the two works claimed a high prevalence of personal crises at around age 40. Neither our interviews with study members at 37 (Oakland group) nor those at 40 (Guidance group) nor the retrospective reports of the men at 48, 53, or 62 suggest that there was a buildup of life crises around age 40. Nor do the life histories of the sixty persons whose lives were studied most closely.
23. See, for example, Howard and Bray (1988).
24. See Dubin (1956).

Chapter 10

Men's Lives: Beyond the Job

1. This formulation by Bernard (1973) has received support from almost all studies that have secured separate reports from husbands and wives.
2. Until the advent of the women's movement, it was generally the husband's needs that were most fully met, with many women taking a subservient role. Indeed, many women had been taught that this was the only appropriate role for them. Even in this instance, however, there were inevitably tensions as the woman's own needs were neglected.
3. Several major studies of divorce have focused on the short and longer-term effects of divorce on children. See, for example, Wallerstein and Blakeslee (1989) and Hetherington (1989).

4. Some interviewers took extensive and others very meager notes, so details relating to marriages and occupational careers were not always available. The primary focus was on personality, and here many ratings were made. There was also a great deal of attention to the study members' reconstructions of their adolescence.

5. The age of the Berkeley Growth Study members when seen for their first adult follow-up was 36 or 37, so they were very close in age to the Oakland Growth Study group at initial follow-up.

6. The difference was not statistically significant, despite the group's being made up of "survivors" who were presumably more happily married.

7. Skolnick (1981, p. 287).

8. The judges' ratings were somewhat more influenced by the social status and personalities of the study members than were self-ratings, which may have introduced an element of bias.

9. Again there is reason to believe that part of this relationship is due to the judges' having been influenced by the social status of the study members.

10. Differences of the magnitude found would not be expected by chance once in a hundred comparisons. Those among the less planfully competent adolescents who did return questionnaires were in many respects more like the planfully competent than like those who failed to return the questionnaire.

11. Many study members do keep us informed when they move or when there has been a death in the family. Those who do were most often numbered among the planfully competent, though there are many dedicated participants who had not gotten so fortunate a start by adolescence.

12. In both 1982 and 1990 we used two scales developed by Pearlin and Schooler (1978), called "non-acceptance" and "non-reciprocity," which assess each partner's feelings about the other's ways of relating in the marriage. The scales are described in Appendix B.

13. See Elder (1974, p. 186) for a more detailed discussion.

14. See Wilensky (1961a).

15. Mussen and Haan (1981, pp. 398–401).

16. Levinson (1978, p. 335).

17. Because the Q-sort was designed to distinguish pathology, normal individuals randomly paired will tend to show an average correlation approaching .30. Thus, a resemblance score of .33 suggests very little real resemblance. The range of resemblance scores was from –.20 to .86.

18. Peskin and Livson (1981).

19. Ibid. (p. 154).

20. Military service, early marital experience and occupational success or lack of it produced changes in both directions, but opportunities for occupational success were good, and most men who had not been self-confident gained especially in that respect.

21. In the last chapter we noted that high planful competence tends to lead to high occupational attainment, entailing work of high substantive complexity. The research of Melvin Kohn and Carmi Schooler (1983) has shown how work of high substantive complexity enhances both intellectual flexibil-

ity and self-directiveness. Unfortunately, our relatively small sample and lack of the kind of highly detailed data on occupational experience secured by Kohn and Schooler precludes my following up this lead. Clearly a man's occupation is the realm in which he is most subject to both pressures for performance and opportunities for growth.

22.   The measure, developed by Livson and Peskin, was described in Chapter 2.

23.   Glen Elder has written extensively on the military experience of the men. See especially Elder and Clipp (1989).

Chapter 12

Against All Adversity: Beth Green

1.   Rhodes (1990, p. 218).

Chapter 13

Planful Competence in Women's Lives

1.   Elder (1974, pp. 71–82).

2.   One of the greatest differences between the generation of our study members and that of their offspring is the disappearance of this gender difference, as we shall see in Chapter 15.

3.   Most of the women study members who had been in the labor force during the war were delighted to return to the domestic life they had envisioned in adolescence.

4.   Skolnick (1992, p. 70).

5.   College graduates, especially those in the labor force or interested in entering the labor force, were most likely to be responsive to the women's movement.

6.   These histories have been altered in certain respects to protect the anonymity of the study members, but the data on families, personalities, and life sequences are basically correct.

7.   Because the life history sample was selected by random numbers, there were not the same number of men and women in the sample. Despite the very small size of the groups compared, the overall consistency of the differences makes it extremely unlikely that these are chance variations.

8.   Recall Table 6.1.

9.   At each follow-up, we asked some questions about women's labor force participation and were able to construct fairly complete occupational histories for most of the women study members, but our data on wives of male study members are less adequate. It was only in 1982 that we explored women's occupational involvements in any real depth, and by then a number of women in the older cohort had retired.

10.   A fuller account of women's careers is to be found in Clausen and Gilens (1990).

11.   The correlation between adolescent planful competence of the women and

the number of children they bore was .40. In the relatively homogeneous population involved and the historical era of the study, both high competence and high intelligence were associated with larger families, regardless of religious persuasion. See Clausen and Clausen (1973).

12. See Appendix B for a fuller specification.

Chapter 14

Women's Lives: Marriage and Changing Roles

1. We do not have systematic data on parental drinking or physical abuse in the parental families. Most parents of the Oakland members came to adulthood well before the Volstead Act that made alcoholic beverages illegal between 1918 and 1934, while parents of the Berkeley samples were likely to have been adolescents when prohibition came to be the law of the land. During the depression years, alcohol became an escape for many of the unemployed fathers of study members.

2. So far as we know, unlike their daughters, very few of the young women lived with a man for any appreciable period prior to their first marriage.

3. See, for example, Udry, Talbert, and Morris (1986).

4. College attendance, especially attendance at coeducational institutions, afforded contacts with men having good occupational prospects, but having a highly educated, competent wife was also an aid to the husband's subsequent attainment.

5. For another analysis of women's status attainment through marriage, see Elder (1969).

6. For the evidence from a study focused on the menopause, see Neugarten (1963). The topic also receives considerable attention in Rubin (1974).

7. See Gilligan (1982) and Tannen (1990).

8. These scales are described in Gough (1957).

9. Peskin and Livson (1981).

10. See Clausen and Gilens (1990). These findings are consonant with those of Helson, Mitchell, and Moane (1984) who classified a somewhat younger sample of women in terms of their degree of compliance with the "feminine social clock" of marriage and childbearing in their early to mid-20s.

11. Livson and Peskin (1967).

12. For a fuller analysis of the consequences of bereavement, see Osterweis, Solomon, and Green (1984).

Chapter 15

Family Relationships

1. This was also the most critical influence on frequency of contact in the intensive large-scale study of intergenerational relationships by Alice and Peter Rossi, reported in *Of Human Bonding* (1990).

2. As parents become elderly and more fragile, their sons and daughters tend

to show increasing concern and to feel a need to express more tenderness toward their parents.

3. Many of the parents had remained in the same home they had occupied since the birth of their children.

4. Men are more likely than women to die of an acute illness while still reasonably intact physically and mentally, as well as having a substantially lower life expectancy.

5. This is a common finding in large-scale studies of older persons and their caretakers. See Stone, Cafferata, and Sangl (1987).

6. We do not always learn of the deaths of study members, or spouses, especially if they have moved without providing their new addresses, but most participants have kept us informed over the years.

7. Eichorn, Hunt, and Honzik (1981, p. 106).

8. Clausen (1981, p. 338).

9. See Klein (1984).

10. Hochschild (1989).

11. Jones (1981).

12. Clausen (1968).

13. Their parents' educational attainment was higher than that of the average study member, since the highly competent were overrepresented. Sixty percent of the fathers and 38 percent of the mothers of 1991 offspring respondents had graduated from college.

Chapter 16

The Later Years: Looking Forward and Back

1. See, for example, Parnes (1981).

2. In general, women tend to retire somewhat earlier than men, though recent trends show a sharper increase in early retirement on the part of men. See Robinson, Coberly, and Paul (1985).

3. Residential stability in the later years is typical of older homeowners. See Lawton (1985).

4. If data were available regarding nonrespondents to the 1990 questionnaire, there would undoubtedly be a much larger proportion with incomes under $30,000.

5. Because of their superior economic status and good health care, our study member respondents were in better health in 1990 than a representative sample of Americans of the same age.

6. The life review has become a topic of considerable interest to gerontologists and other researchers on the later years. The concept was first delineated by Robert Butler (1963).

7. Erikson (1950, pp. 231–232).

Chapter 17

Epilogue

1. Wolfbein (1971).
2. Smith (1968).
3. Ibid. (p. 277).
4. Stevenson and Stigler (1992) offer an incisive analysis, based on first-hand study, of why there is such a vast "learning gap" between American students and students in China and Japan.
5. A recent study by Schulenberg and others (1992), using a number of measures relating to a successful adolescent-adult transition, finds that adolescent binge drinkers were substantially less competent than their peers who were not binge drinkers.

REFERENCES

Allison, P. D., & Furstenberg, F. F., Jr. (1989). How marital dissolution affects children: Variations by age and sex. *Developmental Psychology, 25,* 540–549.

Baldwin, A. L., Kalhorn, J., & Breese, F. H. (1949). The appraisal of parent behavior. *Psychological Monographs, 63*(2), Whole No. 299.

Bandura, A. (1977). Self-efficacy: Toward a unifying theory of behavior change. *Psychological Review, 84,* 191–215.

Bandura, A. (1982). The psychology of chance encounters and life paths. *American Psychologist, 37,* 747–755.

Baumrind, D. (1973). The development of instrumental competence through socialization. In A. Pick (Ed.), *Minnesota symposia on child psychology* (Vol. 7, pp. 3–46). Minneapolis: University of Minnesota Press.

Baumrind, D. (1991a). Effective parenting during the early adolescent transition. In P. E. Cowan & E. M. Hetherington (Eds.), *Advances in family research* (Vol. 2, pp. 111–163). Hillsdale, NJ: Erlbaum.

Baumrind, D. (1991b). Parenting styles and adolescent development. In R. Lerner, A. C. Petersen & J. Brooks-Gunn (Eds.), *The encyclopedia on adolescence* (pp. 746–758). New York: Garland.

Bayley, N. (1933). Mental growth during the first three years: A developmental study of sixty-one children by repeated tests. *Genetic Psychology Monographs, 14.*

Bellah, R. N., et al. (1985). *Habits of the heart: Individualism and commitment in American life.* Berkeley: University of California Press.

Bernard, J. (1973). *The future of marriage.* New York: Bantam Books.

Berscheid, E., & Walster, E. (1974). Physical attractiveness. In L. Berkowitz (Ed.), *Advances in experimental social psychology* (Vol. 7, pp. 158–215). New York: Academic Press.

Block, J. (1961). *The Q-sort method in personality assessment and psychiatric research.* Springfield, IL: Thomas.

Block, J., in collaboration with N. Haan (1971). *Lives through time.* Berkeley, CA: Bancroft.

Block, J. H. (1984). *Sex role identity and ego development.* San Francisco: Jossey-Bass.

Block, J. H., Block, J., & Gjerde, P. F. (1986). The personality of children prior to divorce: A prospective study. *Child Development, 57,* 827–840.

Bloom, B. (1964). *Stability and change in human characteristics.* New York: Wiley.

Brandes, S. (1987). *Forty: The age and the symbol.* Knoxville: University of Tennessee Press.

Bronfenbrenner, U. (1979). *The ecology of human development: Experiments by nature and by design.* Cambridge: Harvard University Press.

Bronfenbrenner, U. (1986). Ecology of the family as a context for human development: Research perspectives. *Developmental Psychology, 22,* 723–742.

Butler, R. (1963). The life review. *Psychiatry, 26,* 65–76.

California Task Force to Promote Self-Esteem and Personal and Social Responsibility (1990). *Toward a state of esteem.* Sacramento, CA: State of California.

Campbell, A. (1981). *The sense of well-being in America.* New York: McGraw-Hill.

Caspi, A., Elder, G. H., Jr., & Bem, D. (1988). Moving against the world: Life course patterns of explosive children. *Developmental Psychology, 24,* 824–831.

Clausen, J. A. (1968). Perspectives on childhood socialization. In J. A. Clausen (Ed.), *Socialization and society* (pp. 130–181). Boston: Little, Brown.

Clausen, J. A. (1975). The social meaning of differential physical and sexual maturation. In S. E. Dragastin & G. H. Elder, Jr. (Eds.), *Adolescence in the life cycle* (pp. 25–47). New York: Wiley.

Clausen, J. A. (1981). Men's occupational careers in the middle years. In D. H. Eichorn, J. A. Clausen, N. Haan, M. P. Honzik & P. H. Mussen (Eds.), *Present and past in middle life* (pp. 321–351). New York: Academic Press.

Clausen, J. A. (1985). *The life course: A sociological perspective.* Englewood Cliffs, NJ: Prentice-Hall.

Clausen, J. A. (1991). Adolescent competence and the shaping of the life course. *American Journal of Sociology, 96,* 805–842.

Clausen, J. A., & Clausen, S. R. (1973). The effects of family size on parents and children. In J. T. Fawcett (Ed.), *Psychological perspectives in population.* New York: Basic Books.

Clausen, J. A., & Gilens, M. (1990). Personality and labor force participation across the life span: A longitudinal study of women's careers. *Sociological Forum, 5,* 595–618.

Clausen, J. A., Mussen, P. H., & Kuypers, J. (1981). Involvement, warmth and parent-child resemblances in three generations. In D. H. Eichorn, J. A. Clausen, N. Haan, M. P. Honzik & P. H. Mussen (Eds.), *Present and past in middle life* (pp. 301–319). New York: Academic Press.

Cohler, B. J. (1982). Personal narrative and the life course. In P. B. Baltes & O. G. Brim, Jr. (Eds.), *Life span development and behavior* (Vol. 4). New York: Academic Press.

Coleman, J. S. (Ed.) (1974). *Youth, transition to adulthood.* Chicago: University of Chicago Press.

de Tocqueville, A. (1835). *Democracy in America.* New York: Vintage Books, 1954.

Digman, J. M. (1989). Five robust trait dimensions: Development, stability and utility. *Journal of Personality, 57*(2), 195–214.

Dornbusch, S. M., Carlsmith, J. M., Bushwall, S. J., Ritter, P. L., Leiderman, H., Hastorf, A. H., & Gross, R. T. (1985). Single parents, extended households, and the control of adolescents. *Child Development, 56,* 326–341.

Dubin, R. (1956). Industrial workers' worlds: A study of central life interests of industrial workers. *Social Problems, 3,* 131–143.

Eichorn, D. H. (1981). Samples and procedures. In D. H. Eichorn, J. A. Clausen, N. Haan, M. P. Honzik & P. H. Mussen (Eds.), *Present and past in middle life* (pp. 33–51). New York: Academic Press.

Eichorn, D. H., Hunt, J., & Honzik, M. P. (1981). Experience, personality and IQ: Adolescence to middle age. In D. H. Eichorn, J. A. Clausen, N. Haan, M. P. Honzik & P. H. Mussen (Eds.), *Present and past in middle life* (pp. 89–116). New York: Academic Press.

Elder, G. H., Jr. (1969). Appearance and education in marriage mobility. *American Sociological Review, 34,* 519–533.

Elder, G. H., Jr. (1974). *Children of the Great Depression.* Chicago: University of Chicago Press.

Elder, G. H., Jr. (1986). Military times and turning points in men's lives. *Developmental Psychology, 22,* 233–245.

Elder, G. H., Jr., Caspi, A., & Van Nguyen, T. (1986). Resourceful and vulnerable children: Family influence in hard times. In R. K. Silbereisen et al. (Eds.), *Development as action in context.* Berlin: Springer Verlag.

Elder, G. H., Jr., & Clipp, E. C. (1989). Combat experience and emotional health: Impairment and resilience in later life. *Journal of Personality, 57,* 311–341.

Elder, G. H., Jr., & Rockwell, R. W. (1979). Economic depression and postwar opportunity in men's lives. In R. G. Simmons (Ed.) *Research in Community and Mental Health.* Greenwich, CT: JAI Press.

Erikson, E. H. (1950). *Childhood and society.* New York: Norton.

Erikson, E. H. (1959). The problem of ego identity. *Psychological Issues, 1* (1), 101–164.

Featherman, D. L. (1980). Schooling and occupational careers: Constancy and change in worldly success. In O. G. Brim, Jr., & J. Kagan (Eds.), *Constancy and change in human development* (pp. 675–738). Cambridge, MA: Harvard University Press.

Field, D., & Minkler, M. (1988). Continuity and change in social support between young-old and old-old or very-old age. *Journal of Gerontology, 43,* 100–106.

Frenkel-Brunswik, E. (1942). Motivation and behavior. *Genetic Psychology Monographs, 26,* 121–265.

Furstenberg, F. F., Jr. (1990). Divorce and the American family. *Annual Review of Sociology, 16,* 373–403.

Garmezy, N. (1981). Children born under stress: Perspectives on the antecedents and correlates of vulnerability and resistance to psychopathology. In A. E. Rabin, J. Aronoff, A. M. Barclay & R. A. Zucker (Eds.), *Further explorations in personality.* New York: Wiley.

Gilligan, C. (1982). *In a different voice: Psychological theory and women's development.* Cambridge, MA: Harvard University Press.

Gough, H. G. (1957). *California Psychological Inventory: Manual.* Palo Alto, CA: Consulting Psychologists Press.

Gould, R. (1978). *Transformations: Growth and change in adult life.* New York: Simon and Schuster.

Graubard, S. (Ed.) (1976). *Adulthood.* Cambridge, MA: American Academy of Arts and Sciences.

Greenberg, E. F., & Nay, W. R. (1982). The intergenerational transmission of marital instability reconsidered. *Journal of Marriage and the Family, 44,* 335–347.

Grotevant, H. D., & Cooper, C. R. (1988). The role of family experience in career exploration: A life span perspective. In P. B. Baltes, D. L. Featherman & R. M. Lerner (Eds.), *Life span development and behavior* (Vol. 8, pp. 231–258). Hillsdale, NJ: Erlbaum.

Haan, N., Millsap, R., & Hartke, E. (1986). As time goes by: Change and stability in personality over fifty years. *Psychology and Aging, 1,* 220–232.

Harter, S. (1990). Causes, correlates and the functional role of global self-worth: A life span perspective. In R. J. Sternberg & J. Kolligian, Jr. (Eds.), *Competence considered* (pp. 67–97). New Haven: Yale University Press.

Hatfield, E. & Sprecher, S. (1986). *Mirror, mirror...The importance of looks in everyday life*. Albany, NY: State University of New York Press.

Held, T. (1986). Institutionalization and deinstitutionalization of the life course. *Human Development, 29,* 157–162.

Helson, R., Mitchell, V., & Moane, G. (1984). Personality and patterns of adherence and nonadherence to the social clock. *Journal of Personality and Social Psychology, 46,* 1079–1096.

Hetherington, E. M. (1989). Coping with family transitions: Winners, losers, and survivors. *Child Development, 60,* 1–14.

Hetherington, E. M., & Anderson, E. R. (1988). The effects of divorce and remarriage on early adolescents and their families. In M. D. Levine & E. R. McAnarney (Eds.), *Early adolescent transitions* (pp. 49–67). Lexington, MA: Lexington Books.

Hochschild, A. (1989). *The second shift*. New York: Viking Penguin.

Holliday, S. G., & Chandler, M. J. (1986). *Wisdom: Explorations in adult competence*. Basel: Karger.

Hollingshead, A. B., & Redlich, F. (1958). *Social class and mental illness*. New York: Wiley.

Howard, A., & Bray, D. W. (1988). *Managerial lives in transition: Advancing age and changing times*. New York: Guilford.

Hunt, H. J., & Chaffey, J. (1934). A guidance program in the Claremont Junior High School. *University High School Journal, 13,* 232–238.

Jahoda, M. (1958). *Current concepts of positive mental health*. New York: Basic Books.

Jones, H. E. (1938). The California adolescent growth study. *Journal of Educational Research, 31,* 561–567.

Jones, M. C. (1960). A comparison of the attitudes and interests of ninth-grade students over two decades. *Journal of Educational Psychology, 51,* 175–186.

Jones, M. C. (1981). Midlife drinking patterns: Correlates and antecedents. In D. H. Eichorn, J. A. Clausen, N. Haan, M. P. Honzik & P. H. Mussen (Eds.), *Present and past in middle life* (pp. 223–242). New York: Academic Press.

Jones, M. C., & Mussen, P. H. (1958). Self-conceptions, motivations, and interpersonal attitudes of early- and late-maturing girls. *Child Development, 29,* 491–501.

Kaufman, S. R. (1986). *The ageless self: Sources of meaning in later life*. Madison, WI: University of Wisconsin Press.

Klein, E. (1984). *Gender politics*. Cambridge: Harvard University Press.

Kohn, M. L., & Schooler, C. (1983). *Work and personality: An inquiry into the impact of social stratification*. Norwood, NJ: Ablex.

Langer, E. J. (1989). *Mindfulness*. Reading, MA: Addison-Wesley.

Lawton, M. P. (1985). Housing and living arrangements of older people. In R. H. Binstock & E. Shanas (Eds.), *Handbook of aging and the social sciences* (pp. 450–478). New York: Van Nostrand Reinhold.

Lerner, R., & Busch-Rossnagel, N. A. (Eds.). (1981). *Individuals as producers of their own development*. New York: Academic Press.

Levinson, D. J. (1978). *The seasons of a man's life*. New York: Knopf.

Lieberson, S. (1980). *A piece of the pie: Black and white immigrants since 1880*. Berkeley: University of California Press.

Livson, N., & McNeill, D. (1962). Physique and maturation rate in male adolescents. *Child Development, 33,* 145–152.

Livson, N., & Peskin, H. (1967). Prediction of adult psychological health in a longitudinal study. *Journal of Abnormal Psychology, 72,* 509–518.

Lynd, R. S., & Lynd, H. M. (1929). *Middletown: A study of modern American culture.* New York: Harcourt, Brace and World.

Maas, H. S., & Kuypers, J. A. (1974). *From thirty to seventy.* San Francisco: Jossey-Bass.

Macfarlane, J. W. (1938). Studies in child guidance, 1: Methodology of data collection and organization. *Monographs of the Society for Research in Child Development,* Serial No. 19(3).

Macfarlane, J. W., Allen, L. B., & Honzik, M. P. (1954). *A developmental study of the behavior problems of normal children between twenty-one months and fourteen years.* University of California Publications in Child Development, vol. 2. Berkeley: University of California Press.

Maccoby, E. E., & Jacklin, C. N. (1974). *The psychology of sex differences.* Stanford, CA: Stanford University Press.

McLanahan, S., & Bumpass, L. (1988). Intergenerational consequences of family disruption. *American Journal of Sociology, 94,* 130–152.

McNeill, D., & Livson, N. (1963). Maturation rate and body build in women. *Child Development, 34,* 25–32.

Mannheim, K. (1952). The problem of generations. In K. Mannheim, *Essays on the sociology of knowledge.* London: Routledge, Keagan & Paul.

Marcus, H., Cross, S., & Wurf, E. (1990). The role of the self-system in competence. In R. J. Sternberg & J. Kolligian, Jr. (Eds.), *Competence considered* (pp. 205–225). New Haven: Yale University Press.

Marini, M. (1984). Age and sequencing norms in the transition to adulthood. *Social Forces, 63,* 229–244.

Mayer, K. U. (1986). Structural constraints on the life course. *Human Development, 29,* 163–170.

Merriam, L. B., & Clark, M. C. (1991). *Lifeline: Patterns of work, love, and learning in adulthood.* San Francisco: Jossey-Bass.

Meyer, J. W. (1986). The self and the life course: Institutionalization and its effects. In A. B. Sorenson, F. E. Weinert & L. R. Sherrod (Eds.), *Human development and the life course.* Hillsdale, NJ: Erlbaum.

Millsap, R., & Meredith, W. (1988). Component analysis in cross-sectional and longitudinal data. *Psychometrika, 53,* 123–134.

Modell, J., Furstenberg, F., Jr., & Hershberg, T. (1976). Social change and transitions to adulthood in historical perspective. *Journal of Family History, 1,* 7–32.

Moen, P. (1985). Continuities and discontinuities in women's labor force participation. In G. H. Elder, Jr. (Ed.), *Life course dynamics: 1960s to 1980s* (pp. 113–155). Ithaca, NY: Cornell University Press.

Mussen, P. H., & Haan, N. (1981). A longitudinal study of patterns of personality and political ideologies. In D. H. Eichorn, J. A. Clausen, N. Haan, M. P. Honzik & P. H. Mussen (Eds.), *Present and past in middle life* (pp. 393–409). New York: Academic Press.

Mussen, P. H., & Jones, M. C. (1957). Self-conceptions, motivations, and interpersonal attitudes of late- and early-maturing boys. *Child Development, 28,* 243–256.

Neugarten, B. L. (1963). Women's attitudes toward the menopause. *Vita Humana,* 6: 140–151.

Neugarten, B. L., Moore, J. W., & Lowe, J. C. (1965). Age norms, age constraints, and adult socialization. *American Journal of Sociology, 70,* 710–717.

Oppenheimer, V. (1982). *Work and the family: A study in demography.* New York: Academic Press.

Osherson, S. D. (1980). *Holding on or letting go: Men and career change at mid-life.* New York: Free Press.

Osterweis, M., Solomon, F., & Green, M. (Eds.) (1984). *Bereavement: Reactions, consequences and care.* Washington, DC: National Academy Press.

Parnes, H. S. (1981). *Work and retirement: A longitudinal study.* Cambridge, MA: MIT Press.

Pearlin, L. (1982). Discontinuities in the study of aging. In T. K. Hareven & K. Adams (Eds.), *Aging and life course transitions: An interdisciplinary perspective* (pp. 55–74). New York: Guilford Press.

Pearlin, L. (1989). The sociological study of stress. *Journal of Health and Social Behavior, 30,* 241–256.

Pearlin, L. I., & Schooler, C. (1978). The structure of coping. *Journal of Health and Social Behavior, 19,* 2–21.

Pedhazur, E. J. (1982). Multiple regression in behavioral research: New York: Holt, Rinehart, Winston.

Peskin, H., & Livson, N. (1981). Uses of the past in adult psychological health. In D. H. Eichorn, J. A. Clausen, N. Haan, M. Honzik & P. H. Mussen (Eds.), *Present and past in middle life* (pp. 153–221). New York: Academic Press.

Plomin, R., & Bergeman, C. S. (1991). The nature of nurture: Genetic influences on "environmental" measures. *Behavioral and Brain Sciences, 14,* 373–427.

Plomin, R., & Thompson, L. (1988). Life-span developmental behavioral genetics. In P. B. Baltes, D. L. Featherman & R. M. Lerner (Eds.), *Life span development and behavior* (Vol. 8, pp. 2–32). Hillsdale, NJ: Erlbaum.

Quinn, R., & Staines, G. L. (1979). *The 1977 quality of employment survey.* Ann Arbor: University of Michigan Survey Research Center.

Quinton, D., & Rutter, M. (1988). *The making and breaking of intergenerational links.* Aldershot, England: Asbury Press.

Rhodes, R. (1990). *A Hole in the World.* New York: Simon & Schuster.

Riley, M. W., Johnson, M., & Foner, A. (1972). *Aging and society.* Vol. 3: *A sociology of age stratification.* New York: Russell Sage.

Robinson, P. K., Coberly, S., & Paul, C. E. (1985). Work and retirement. In R. H. Binstock & E. Shanas (Eds.), *Handbook of aging and the social sciences* (pp. 503–527). New York: Van Nostrand Reinhold.

Rodin, J. (1990). Control by any other name: Definitions, concepts, and processes. In J. Rodin, C. Schooler & K. W. Schaie, *Self-directedness: Cause and effects throughout the life course* (pp. 1–17). Hillsdale, NJ: Erlbaum.

Rosenberg, M. (1975). The dissonant context and the adolescent self-concept. In S. E. Dragastin & G. H. Elder, Jr. (Eds.), *Adolescence and the life cycle: Psychological change and social context* (pp. 97–116). New York: Wiley.

Rossi, A. S., & Rossi, P. H. (1990). *Of human bonding: Parent-child relations across the life course.* New York: Aldine.

Rubin, L. B. (1976). *Worlds of pain: Life in the working-class family.* New York: Basic Books.

Rubin, L. B. (1979). *Women of a certain age: The midlife search for self.* New York: Harper & Row.

Ryder, N. (1965). The cohort as a concept in the study of social change. *American Sociological Review, 30,* 843–861.

Sarbin, T. R., & Scheibe, K. E. (1983). A model of social identity. In T. R. Sarbin & K. E. Scheibe (Eds.), *Studies in social identity.* (pp. 5–28) New York: Praeger.

Scarr, S., & McCartney, K. (1983). How people make their own environments: A theory of genotype environment correlations. *Child Development, 54,* 424–435.

Schulenberg, J., O'Malley, P. M., Bachman, J. G., & Johnston, L. D. (1992). Getting drunk and becoming an adult: Trajectories of binge drinking and competence during the transition to young adulthood. Paper delivered in Symposium on Competence during the Transition from Adolescence to Adulthood at Biennial Meetings of the Society for Research on Adolescence.

Sewell, W. H., Hauser, R. M., & Wolf, W. C. (1980). Sex, schooling, and occupational status. *American Journal of Sociology, 86,* 551–583.

Sheehy, G. (1976). *Passages: Predictable crises of adult life.* New York: Dutton.

Sheldon, W. H. (1940). *The varieties of human physique.* New York: Harper.

Simmons, R. G., & Blyth, D. A. (1987). *Moving into adolescence: The impact of pubertal change and school context.* New York: Aldine.

Skolnick, A. (1981). Married lives: Longitudinal perspectives on marriage. In D. H. Eichorn, J. A. Clausen, N. Haan, M. Honzik & P. H. Mussen (Eds.), *Present and past in middle life* (pp. 270–300). New York: Academic Press.

Skolnick, A. (1992). *Embattled paradise.* New York: Basic Books.

Smith, M. B. (1968). Competence and socialization. In J. A. Clausen (Ed.), *Socialization and society* (pp. 270–320). Boston: Little, Brown.

Spitz, G. (1988). Women's employment and family relations: A review. *Journal of Marriage and the Family, 50,* 595–618.

Staw, B., Bell, N., & Clausen, J. A. (1986). The dispositional approach to job attitudes: A lifetime longitudinal study. *Administrative Science Quarterly, 31,* 56–77.

Steinberg, L. (1987). Single parents, stepparents, and the susceptibility of adolescents to antisocial peer pressure. *Child Development, 58,* 269–275.

Sternberg, R. J., & Kolligian, J., Jr. (Eds.) (1990). *Competence considered.* New Haven: Yale University Press.

Stevenson, H. W., & Stigler, J. W. (1992). *The learning gap.* New York: Summit Press.

Stone, R., Cafferata, G. L., & Sangl, J. (1987). Caregivers of the frail elderly. *Gerontologist, 19,* 169–174.

Swanson, G. E. (1974). Family structure and the reflective intelligence of children. *Sociometry, 37,* 459–490.

Tannen, D. (1990). *You just don't understand: Women and men in conversation.* New York: Ballantine Books.

Thomae, H., & Lehr, U. (1986). Stages, crises, conflicts and life-span development. In A. B. Sorenson, F. E. Weinert & L. R. Sherrod (Eds.), *Human development and the life course* (pp. 429–444). Hillsdale, NJ: Erlbaum.

Udry, J. R., Talbert, L. M., & Morris, N. M. (1986). Biosocial foundations for adolescent female sexuality. *Demography, 23,* 217–230.

Vaillant, G. E. (1977). *Adaptation to life.* Boston: Little, Brown.

Vaillant, G. E., & Vaillant, C. O. (1990). Natural history of male psychological health, XII: A 45-year study of predictors of successful aging at age 65. *American Journal of Psychiatry, 147,* 31–37.

Wallerstein, J., & Blakeslee, S. (1989). *Second chances: Men, women, and children a decade after divorce.* New York: Ticknor & Fields.

Warner, W. L., & Lunt, P. A. (1941). *The social life of a modern community.* New Haven, CT: Yale University Press.

Weitzman, L. J. (1985). *The divorce revolution: The unexpected social and economic consequences for women and children in America.* New York: Free Press.

Wilensky, H. (1961a). Life cycle, work situation and participation in formal organizations. In R. Kleimeier (Ed.), *Aging and leisure: Research perspectives and the meaningful use of time* (pp. 213–242). New York: Oxford Press.

Wilensky, H. (1961b). Orderly careers and social participation. *American Sociological Review, 26,* 521–539.

Wolfbein, S. (1971). *Work in American society.* Glenview, IL: Scott Foresman.

Yarrow, M. R., Campbell, J. D., & Burton, R. V. (1970). Recollections of childhood: A study of the retrospective method. *Monographs of the Society for Research in Child Development,* Serial No. 138(35).

INDEX OF NAMES

Allen, L. B., 566

Baldwin, A. L., 155, 566
Bandura, A., 567
Baumrind, D., 155–156, 566
Bayley, N., 30, 31, 34, 561
Bell, N., 570
Bellah, R. N., 12, 559
Bem, D., 153, 564
Bergeman, C. S., 562
Bernard, J., 570
Blakeslee, S., 560, 570
Block, J., 34, 53, 562, 563
Bloom, B., 566
Brandes, S., 569
Bray, D. W., 560, 570
Breese, F. H., 566
Bronfenbrenner, U., 560
Burton, R., 564
Butler, R., 574

Cafferata, G. L., 574
Campbell, A., 559
Campbell, J., 564
Carnegie, A., 268
Caspi, A., 153, 565, 566
Chaffey, J., 32, 38, 48, 395, 562
Clausen, J. A., 22, 67, 151–152,
    468, 475, 561, 564–567, 570,
    572–574
Clausen, S. R., 573

Clipp, E. C., 572
Coberly, S., 574
Cohler, B. J., 564
Coleman, J. S., 162, 567
Cronbach, L., 52, 562

de Tocqueville, A., 12, 560
Dewey, J., 48
Digman, J. M., 563–564
Dubin, R., 278, 570

Eichorn, D. H., 31, 35, 460, 562,
    572
Elder, G. H., Jr., 34, 45, 153,
    165–166, 253, 559, 562, 565,
    566, 571, 572
Erikson, E. H., 268, 507, 566, 568,
    570, 574

Featherman, D. L., 560
Foner, A., 559
Frank, L. K., 27, 561
Frenkel-Brunswik, E., 33–34, 561
Furstenberg, F. F., 567

Garmezy, N., 560
Gelb, H., 65, 565, 569
Gilens, M., 572, 573
Gilligan, C., 441, 573
Gough, H. G., 573
Graubard, S., 559
Green, M., 573

Haan, N., 34, 35, 53, 57, 562, 563
Hartke, E., 57, 563
Hauser, R. M., 570
Helson, R., 573
Hershberg, T., 567
Hetherington, E. M., 560, 570
Hochschild, A. R., 471, 574
Hollingshead, A. B., 569
Honzik, M. P., 29, 40, 562, 566, 574
Howard, A., 560, 570
Huffine, C. L., 35, 562
Hunt, H. J., 48, 562
Hunt, J., 572

Jahoda, M., 6, 559
Johnson, M., 559
Jones, H. E., 27, 30–34, 64, 561, 565
Jones, M. C., 32, 149, 170, 472, 561, 566, 567, 574

Kalhorn, J., 566
Klein, E., 574
Kohn, M.L., 571– 572
Kolligian, J., Jr., 564
Kuypers, J., 562

Langer, E. J., 19, 560, 564
Lawton, M. P., 574
Lehr, U., 561
Levinson, D. J., 19, 174, 277, 301, 560, 561, 568, 570, 571
Lieberson, S., 559
Livson, N., 59, 303, 448, 449, 564, 566, 571, 572, 573
Lynd, H. M., 8, 164, 559
Lynd, R. S., 8, 164, 559

Maas, H. S., 562
Macfarlane, J. W., 28–30, 33, 38,

152, 561, 566
Mannheim, K., 559
Mayer, K. U., 560
McCartney, K., 562
McNeill, D., 566
Meredith, W., 53, 54, 563
Mill, J. S., 5, 559
Millsap, R., 53, 54, 57, 563
Mitchell, V., 573
Moane, G., 573
Modell, J., 567
Moore, J. W., 567
Morris, N. M., 573
Mussen, P. H., 562, 566, 572

Neugarten, B. L., 567, 573

Oppenheimer, V., 559
Osherson, S. D., 275, 570
Osterweis, M., 573

Parnes, H. S., 574
Paul, C. E., 574
Pearlin, L., 560, 571
Pedhazur, E. J., 567
Peskin, H., 59, 303, 448, 449, 564, 571, 572, 573
Plomin, R., 560, 562

Quinn, J. B., 277–278
Quinn, R., 570

Rhodes, R., 385–386, 572
Riley, M. W., 559
Robinson, P. K., 574
Rockwell, R. C., 567
Rodin, J., 567
Rossi, A. S., 573
Rossi, P. H., 573
Rubin, L. B., 573
Ryder, N., 559

Sangl, J., 574
Scarr, S., 562
Schooler, C., 571–572
Schulenberg, J., 575
Sewell, W. H., 570
Sheehy, G., 277, 570
Sheldon, W. H., 148, 566
Skolnick, A., 9, 23, 287–291, 388, 559, 561, 571, 572
Smith, M. B., 521, 575
Solomon, F., 573
Staines, G. L., 570
Staw, B., 570
Sternberg, R.J., 564
Stevenson, H. W., 575
Stigler, J. W., 575
Stolz, H. R., 27, 31–32, 310, 574
Stone, R., 574

Talbert, L. M., 573
Tannen, D., 441, 573
Thomae, H., 561
Thompson, L., 560

Udry, J. R., 573

Vaillant, G. E., 6, 66, 559, 568
Van Nguyen, T., 565

Wallerstein, J., 560, 570
Warner, W. L., 164
Webster, B., 65, 565
Wilensky, H., 297, 570, 571
Wilson, J., 569
Wolf, W. C., 570
Wolfbein, S., 570, 575

Yarrow, M. R., 564

INDEX OF SUBJECTS

Abortion, 43, 285
Adolescence
    as challenge to parents, 289,
        430–431, 478–479
    developmental tasks of, 48,
        162–166
    as preparation for adulthood,
        17–18
    transition to adulthood, 172–
        174, 252–254
    viewed from later maturity,
        503–505
Adolescent interests in 1930s,
    170–171
Adolescent society, features of,
    162
Aging
    concerns about, 495–497
    experience of, 493–495
Alcohol use
    and marital relationships, 292,
        425, 471–474
    and offsprings' drug use, 485
    and planful competence, 451,
        472
    Attractiveness, physical
    and husband's occupational sta-
        tus, 425–426
    as influence on development, 59
    and planful competence, 146–
        151

and women's labor force partic-
    ipation, 416–417

Berkeley Growth Study, 30–31

California Psychological Inven-
    tory, 447–448
California Q-set, 50–51
Children of study members
    as adults in 1991, 482–486
    relationships with, 477–482
    satisfaction with, 480–482
Choices
    if given another chance, 441–
        442
    importance of, 13, 17–18
Cohort, defined, 559
Competence (see also Planful
        competence)
    in adult years, 68
    continuity of, 306–308, 446–
        447
Concepts and measures, de-
    scribed, 49–60, 545–557
Confidants, 296, 476–477
Contexts of development
    cultural, 12, 44, 167, 527–528
    geographical setting, 44–45
    historical, 3, 9–11, 26–27, 47–
        48, 163–168, 170–171, 387–
        389, 517–519

Correlation coefficient, explained, 553

Criteria of exemplary life, 4–11

Data collection, 39–43

Deaths as source of crisis, 312, 451–452

Dependency of older children, 480–481

Depression, deprivation
effects on women's roles, 166, 387
impact of, 45, 165–166
long term effect, 504–505, 567

Divorce
in children's generation, 484
consequences for children, 15, 283, 421–422
consideration of, 289–292, 428–429, 432
of men, 286, 288, 290, 295
and planful competence, 432
of women, 436–438, 448

Education
and occupational attainment, 262–264
of offspring, 483
prediction of, 262–263

Effort or drive, 168–170, 525–526

Empty nest, 433–434

Follow-up studies, 33–36, 295, 482

Friendships
of men, 257, 300–301
of women, 440–441, 476–477

Gender differences
in early maturing, 149
in expectations, 167, 170, 173, 388
in meaning of planful competence, 313, 420, 519–521.
in social roles, 6, 10–11,

165–167, 173, 420, 517
in tobacco use, 475

Genetic influences, 14–15, 45, 144–146, 168–169

Guidance Study, 28–30

Happiness (see also life satisfaction) as criterion, 5

Health, physical
in later years, 494, 499–502
of parents, 458–460

Health, psychological
measurement of, 59
and personality resemblance, 305–306, 449–450

Heredity and environment, 14–15, 45, 560, 562

Identity
defined, 163–164
and occupational role, 270–272, 418–419
in old age, 490–491

Institute of Child Welfare
founding, 27
renamed, 33

Integrity vs. despair, 507–508

Intergenerational relationships, 14, 158–160, 454–460, 477–482

Interviewer effects, 40–41

IQ
and planful competence, 146–151
resemblance of spouses, 460
and social class, 164–165

Later years
activities in, 497–499
satisfaction in, 499–502

Leisure activities, 297, 438

Life course
crises in women's, 411–412, 450–453

Life course *(cont.)*
  crises in men's, 255–258, 269–
    270, 309–312
  criteria for assessing, 4–11
  expectable for historical period,
    171–172
  influences on, 14–18, 67–68,
    146–170
  as personal creation, 4, 168–
    170
  stages in, 174, 518
Life histories
  ideal evidence for, 61–62
  preparation of, 62–66
  strengths and dangers in use, 43
Life history interviews
  content, 63–64
  and life review, 502–516
Life history summary, 63
Life satisfaction
  charts, 90–92, 136–137, 202–
    203, 312, 344–345, 450–453
  in later years, 296, 514–516

Marital relationship, 286–296,
    426–438, 460–477
Marital satisfaction
  men's, 288–296
  and spouses' personality, 462–
    464
  women's, 432–435
Marriage
  age at, men's, 284–286
  age at, women's, 422–424.
  choice of partner, 284–285,
    421, 424–425
  men's, 282–296
  multiple marriages, 289, 397–
    398
  priorities in, 429
  women's, 420–438, 476
Menopause, 434
Mental health *(see also* psychologi-
    cal health)
  as criterion, 6

Mid-life crisis, 275–277, 453
Military service
  extent of, 253
  as turning point, 310–311
Moral character
  as criterion of exemplary life,
    6–8
Multiple regression, explained,
    159, 567

Oakland Growth Study, 31–33
Occupational careers (see also
    Women's labor force partici-
    pation)
  attainment, 261–266
  change at mid-life, 275–277
  and identity, 270–272, 280
  and income, 266–267
  mobility in, 265–266
  orderliness, 268–270
  preparation needed, 17
  satisfaction with, 272–274
Occupational choice, 259–261
Opportunities and obstacles,
    163–168

Parenting
  effects on planful compe-
    tence, 155–162, 169–170,
    525–526
  by female study members,
    427–428, 430–431
  by male study members, 255–
    258, 289, 293
  measurement of parenting,
    156–159
Parents
  marriages as models, 282–284,
    420–421
  relationships with, 454–460
  situation in old age, 458–460
Peer relationships, 162–163
Permissiveness, 156, 159
Personality
  defined, 50

influence of physical and intellectual attributes, 146–151
stability and change, 16, 19, 301–312, 445–449
and women's employment, 416–417, 448
Personality Q-sort
attributes incorporated, 50–52
as basis for assessing personality change, 58–59
components derived from, 53–58
Physique and personality, 146–151
Planful competence (*see also* competence)
characterized, 16, 19–22, 64–66, 243–244, 396–397, 523–527
and children's performance, 483–486
components of, 16
and cumulative advantage, 521–522
and educational attainment, 262–264, 413
hypothesized consequences of, 22–25, 313, 388, 527
importance of early attainment, 21
and life crises, 255–258, 410–412
low, examples of, men, 245–252
low, examples of, women, 397–405
and marital satisfaction, 294, 428, 432
measurement of, 54–58
and men's occupational careers, 264–268
opportunities and obstacles influencing, 163–168
and personality change, 302–306, 446–450

relevance for future generations, 484–486, 526–528
and rigidity, 308–309
Political orientations and involvement
of men, 297–299
of women, 440
Psychological health
assessment of, 59
and competence, 305–306, 449–450

Recreation, 297, 438
Reliability, explained, 563
Religious orientations and involvement
of men, 299–300
of women, 439
Representativeness of study group, 36–39, 44, 167, 561
Retirement
and activities, 497–502
contemplation of, 279–280.
and identity, 490–491
living arrangements in, 489–490
reasons for, 488–489
timing of, 488–489
Retrospective vs. current reports, 41–43
Roles, social
changes in women's, 10–11, 387–388, 517–519
performance priorities, 12–13, 18, 387–389, 518
sequences in life course, 174, 517–518
transitions and choices, 16–17

Schools, of study members, 47–49
Self-esteem, 2, 149, 158, 525, 528
Sexual relationships
in adolescence, 42–43, 289, 398, 422

Sexual relationships (*Cont.*)
  in adult years, 294–295, 429,
    432–433
Social change
  in employment experience, 11,
    387–388, 518
  in life patterns, 9–10, 518.
  in transition to adulthood, 172
Social class
  defined, 164
  and educational attainment,
    263, 413
  and meaning of physique, 149–
    150
  and occupational attainment,
    265–266, 417–418
  and opportunities, 164–165
Socialization
  in the family, 151–162
  in the peer group, 162–163
  tasks of early, 152–154
Social structuring of life course,
  17–18
Somatotypes, 147–149
Success as criterion, 5

Television viewing, 498–499
Tobacco use, 451, 474–475

Transitions, 16–17, 171–174
Turning points
  in men's lives, 309–312
  in women's lives, 442–445

Values and marital conflict, 461–
  462

Widowhood, 451–452, 492, 511
Wives' assistance to husbands' careers, 468–469
Women's labor force participation
  changing patterns, 10–11,
    387–389, 469
  correlates of, 414–419
  effect on children, 470
  husbands' attitudes, 256,
    469–471
  occupational attainment, 417–
    418
  work involvement, 415–417
Women's movement, 11, 388, 517
Work and family
  husbands' unavailability, 464–
    467
  spouses as coworkers, 468–469
  wives' employment, 469–471